Creating Games with Unreal Engine, Substance Painter, & Maya

Creating Games with Unreal Engine, Substance Painter, & Maya
Models, Textures, Animation, & Blueprint

Jingtian Li, Kassandra Arevalo, and Matthew Tovar

CRC Press
Taylor & Francis Group
Boca Raton London New York

CRC Press is an imprint of the
Taylor & Francis Group, an **informa** business

First edition published 2021
by CRC Press
6000 Broken Sound Parkway NW, Suite 300, Boca Raton, FL
33487-2742

and by CRC Press
2 Park Square, Milton Park, Abingdon, Oxon, OX14 4RN

© 2021 Taylor & Francis Group, LLC

CRC Press is an imprint of Taylor & Francis Group, LLC

ISBN: 978-0-367-51267-5 (hbk)
ISBN: 978-0-367-51263-7 (pbk)
ISBN: 978-1-003-05310-1 (ebk)

Typeset in Myriad Pro
by codeMantra

*To our amazing colleagues, supportive family,
and my beautiful fiancée Tong.*

– Jingtian Li

To my family and colleagues. Thank you for all the support.

– Kassandra Arevalo

Dedication to my parents, Alejandra & Manuel Tovar.

– Matthew Tovar

Contents

Acknowledgments

It takes the effort and support of many people to finish a book like this. We would like to say special thanks to everyone who contributed to this book.

First, many thanks to my most supportive mentor and colleague Adam Watkins. This book becomes much more organized, precise, and informative than it would be without his guidance.

Also, thanks to our Matthew Tovar and Kassandra Arevalo for writing the fantastic rigging and animation chapters; this book would not be complete without their effort.

Finally, special thanks to my amazing sister, Rui, and many other family members of our team. Your support has been of enormous help.

Authors

Jingtian Li is a graduate of China's Central Academy of Fine Arts and New York's School of Visual Arts, where he earned an MFA in Computer Art. He currently is an Assistant Professor of 3D Animation & Game Design at the University of the Incarnate Word in San Antonio, Texas.

Kassandra Arevalo is an instructor of 3D Animation & Game Design at the University of the Incarnate Word in San Antonio, Texas. She previously worked as an animator at Immersed Games.

Matthew Tovar is an industry veteran animator. He has worked at Naughty Dog, Infinity Ward, and Sony Interactive on such games as The Last of Us, Call of Duty: Modern Warfare, and, most recently, Marvel's Avengers with Crystal Dynamics. He is an Assistant Professor of 3D Animation at the University of the Incarnate Word in San Antonio, Texas.

Introduction

Making a game of their own is always the dream of many people since they are teenagers. As new technology emerges, that dream becomes more and more accessible each year. There is an exponential growth of game releases over the past decade. About 10,000 games were released on Steam in 2019, and around 1000 games per day were released on mobile devices.

One of the reasons that more games are coming out is because there are more and better tools to make them. With the release of free game engines like Unreal Engine and Unity, to name a few, start making games is within the reach of everyone. The competition between the game engine developers pushes them to implement new features every year, and we have seen a burst of improvements to the tools.

Outside of the game engines, new developments are happening in every corner of the game industry. Softwares like the Substance Suite solve the texturing process in innovative ways. Newer generations of hardware like Nvidia RTX and Playstation 5 push realtime rendering to new heights. And new categories of devices like Oculus Rift, Steam VR, and Microsoft Hololens are pioneering new user experiences. To add on top of that, services like Quixel Megascan and Adobe Mixamo are providing libraries of reusable assets that significantly improve productivity.

It is the best time than ever for anyone who wants to dip into a game development journey. However, making a game is never an easy task. It requires all kinds of talents to put together a working game that has amazing visuals, engaging gameplay, immersive audio, and an overall well-balanced system. There are many sources where you can learn different ingredients of game development, but only fewer sources explain the whole recipe. This book is dedicated to cover the entire process of making a game, from making assets to programming, and all the way to package a complete game.

Who's It For?

This book is designed for beginners who want to start their game development journey and are unsure where to start and which direction to go. As a reader, you are going to jump into a well-organized learning track that guides you through all aspects of game development. It also shields you from noises and focuses on the fundamentals, which gives you a solid foundation and is able to branch out to nitty-gritty details without losing the whole picture.

For any game enthusiasts or students, this book is a perfect fit to get started with game development. For teachers, this book offers a well-structured solution for your curriculum. For anyone who wants to utilize the game engine for interactive products, this book covers the skill you need extensively as well.

What Does this Book Cover?

This book covers all aspects of game development that includes but not limited to:

Environment Modeling

Environment modeling is the process of making 3D models for environments. We are going to cover what is a 3D model, how to make them, and how to optimize them for your game.

Character Modeling

Character modeling is the process of making 3D characters. We will cover how to approach organic shapes with additional modeling methods.

UV Mapping

We are going to learn how to create a 2D coordinate of a 3D model to map textures to the model. The process we call UV Mapping.

Texturing

Texturing is the process of defining the color and all other aspects of the appearance of the model.

Rigging

Rigging is a technical skill to add skeleton and controllers to animate the character.

Character Animation

We are going to cover the techniques and theories to animate characters.

Game Engine Lighting and Baking

We are going to practice workflows on lighting an environment, which includes how lights work in the game engine, and technical details of baking the lighting.

Game Programming

We are going to cover programming languages, theory, and practices to create gameplay.

We will also explore audio and VFX solutions and many other small details you need to know to create a game. At the end of this book, you should have everything you need under your belt to start making your next awesome game!

Final Notes

It is critical to point out that game development is time-consuming. Please dedicate your energy and time to the learning process, and don't easily give up on any obstacles. With the internet at your fingertip, you can find solutions for just about anything.

It is also important to acknowledge that tools change all the time, and you should always learn new stuff and explore new ideas. Please take away the theories we cover in this book, but don't be religious of the tools we use.

Alrighty, we know you are tired of reading introductions, and many people jump over it. It is time that we start this fantastic journey and start making some awesome games!

Jingtian Li
May 9, 2020
San Antonio, TX, USA

CHAPTER 1

Maya Modeling

We will jump into the production by discussing modeling. 3D models are the foundation of the graphics of modern games. They encompass the environment and characters you see on the screen. An eye-catching visual is one of the key components for a game to succeed. In this chapter, we will discuss in detail about how they are built.

Basics of Navigation

Autodesk Maya will be our tool of choice for modeling. It is not the best modeling tool on the market, but it is the most used over the entire production pipeline, especially

FIGURE 1.1 Maya's user interface. The origin is the area at the center of the grid.

for animation. So, let us get Maya up and running on your machine. The UI (user interface) will look like Figure 1.1. The large region in the middle of the UI is the viewport; this is where we see our models. It is currently empty, with just a grid in the middle to indicate the center of the world. The center of this grid is called the origin.

To Navigate around the viewport, hold down Alt key and drag the left-mouse button to look around the viewport. To zoom in and out, hold down the Alt key and drag the right-mouse button. To pan left and right, hold down the Alt key and drag the middle-mouse button.

A 3D space has width, height, and depth, each represented on three axes called the X, Y, and Z axes. The lower left corner of the viewport shows the directions of these axes.

Rendering

The shape is drawn by the Graphic API, but the lighting is calculated by the Fragment Shader written by the game engine programmer. It is a complicated process, and we do not have to understand the details and math behind it. It is enough to know that the *renderer* is the tool drawing whatever you see on screen. Maya's interactive renderer (that shows you what is currently in your scene) is called Viewport 2.0.

What is a 3D Model?

In the menus, go to Create->Polygon Primitives->Plane. This will create a shape in the middle of the viewport. On the right side of the UI, look for the Channel Box. This is a brief list of essential attributes we can tweak for the object. Under the INPUTS section, click on the polyPlane1 to open it and change the Subdivisions Width and Subdivisions Height to 1 to make the plane only one polygon (sometimes called a "face").

What we are seeing now is the building block of any model – a face with four corners that we typically call a rectangle in geometry classes; in 3D graphic terms, we call this a *quad.* Any complicated shape can be composed by assembling many quads together to create 3D forms.

Translation

On the right side of the UI, there is a column of manipulation tools. You can try and use the Q, W, E, and R buttons to switch between these tools: Q for the select tool, W for the move tool, E for the rotation tool, R for the scale tool.

To select the model, simply left-click on it or drag a selection box over it. To deselect the model, click in the empty space, or hold down Ctrl and click on the model, or drag a selection box over it.

To move the model, after selecting it, hit the W button. This will display new handles (called gizmos) that will allow you to move the object. Try dragging the various arrows to move it only along a particular axis. Look carefully at the gizmo, and you will see squares that can be dragged to move it along two axes at the same time; you can even drag the cyan square in the middle to move it freely along all axes in the 3D space.

To rotate the model, after selecting it, hit the E button, drag the circles on the gizmo to rotate it around different axes. You can also drag the yellow one on the outside to rotate it around a plane that is perpendicular to the angle of the viewport.

To scale the model, hit the R button, and drag the various boxes to scale it along their respective axes. You can also drag the various squares to scale it along two axes at the same time; you can even drag the yellow box in the middle to scale it up along all axes, essentially making it bigger.

There are more tricks about this sort of manipulation that we will cover later on when we jump into modeling.

Anatomy of a Model

Edge

Hold down the right mouse button on the model, and you will see a pop-up menu we call a *Marking Menu*. Here, we can see various parts of the form we can switch to. With the marking menu active, slide up and chose Edge; the four edges around the face now appear to be in a lighter blue color. You can click on any of the edges to select them. When an edge is selected, it will be highlighted with orange color. Once selected, you can change to the Move tool (hit W on the keyboard) and drag the three arrows to move the edge along the respective direction.

Vertex

You can also hold the right mouse button again and chose Vertex. Four purple points will show up on the corner of this face. These are the vertices where edges meet. You can click to select any of them and move them around just like how you can move an edge.

Face

Hold down the right mouse button again and chose Face; you can now select the face and move it around as well.

Edge, Vertex, and Face are the three important elements of any 3D form's polygons. We can add and tweak these elements to create any shape we want.

Object Mode

Hold down the right mouse button again. This time, we chose Object Mode. This will allow us to move the model altogether. Object, Vertex, Edge, and Face are the primary modes we keep switching between while making a model.

Normal

Use the alt-left, -middle, and/or -right mouse drag to rotate your camera to look at the bottom of the face. You can see it appears to be black. Any face in 3D has a front side and a back side. The front side will appear normal, while the back side will be black or invisible (depending on the rendering engine). Maya makes the back of the face black in the default setting. To view this, using the top menus find Display->Polygons->Face Normals.

Press the Q button to switch to the select mode to get rid of the Move tool handles. We can now see a green line sticking out from the front face of the model. In general, the front of the polygon should face outwards. It is possible though to render both sides of the face. Consider a situation like rendering a piece of paper. Here we would definitely want both sides of the polygons seen, but otherwise we want to avoid rendering both sides, if possible, to avoid performance overhead. Since games have to draw many frames each second, we want to always ensure that we aren't drawing anything we don't need to (Figure 1.2).

Modeling Rules

Before we start modeling anything, let's talk about a few important rules when modeling for games.

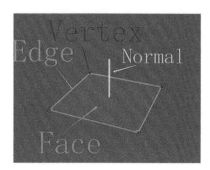

FIGURE 1.2 The elements and normal direction of the quad.

Polycount

Each of those four-sided faces we looked at earlier can be triangulated into two triangular polygons. We typically use the number of *triangles* of a model as the number for polycount, even we use quads to make a model. The reason we use the number of triangles instead of quads is because a triangle is guaranteed to be a flat surface, while this is not guaranteed for a geometric figure with more than three vertices. Thus, the rendering process uses triangles as the basic rendering unit. Fewer polygons means your game is easier to run (less data); so find the balance of including the needed number of polygons to describe a shape, but not extras.

Topology

Topology is how the faces are laid out on the model. Use quads if possible, because quads have a strong sense of directionality and are easy to represent shape evolution and deformation. We want the flow of the quads to represent the change of the surface. Figure 1.3 shows how topology is critical for deforming a face. The loops of faces around the orbicularis muscle, nasolabial fold, and orbicularis oris create an essential structure to support the facial expression. Long story short, topology is for the purpose of better representing the shape of the model and supporting the deformation for animation.

FIGURE 1.3 Effective topology (the flow of polygons) is critical to support the deformation that will come later in animation.

Size and Proportion

Size is a critical aspect in 3D modeling, no matter how detailed a model is. If the size or proportion is off, the model will never look right. In Maya, the default unit is a centimeter. This is the unit across many popular programs including Maya, Unreal Engine, Blender, etc. Other software, like Unity, use the meter as the default unit, but converting between the two scales is an easy math. One should always check sizes and dimensions to ensure things will work with physics simulation, rendering, and animation; for example, if you are modeling a staircase, then you have to know that the general height of a stair is around 18 cm and the depth is 28 cm. Converting to the right scale as you move assets from Maya to your game engine is trivial, but focus on building assets in Maya at the correct scale for its unit size (centimeters by default).

Basics of Modeling

We will jump into modeling right away and introduce various tools along the way. Keep in mind that the only way to improve is to practice; there is no shortcut to get better.

Tutorial 1.1: Modeling a Security Camera

> *Step 1: Basic Shape. Choose Create->Polygon Primitives->Cube. This will create a cube at the origin. This cube is also referred to as box by 3D artists. In fact, what we are doing now has a nickname called box modeling.*

Tips and Tricks

In Maya, with nothing selected, you can hold down the Shift+right mouse button to pull up a type of menu called a *marking menu*. If you do this in the Viewport where there is no other object, the marking menu that will show up allows for the creation of new object. You can use this to create a cube in the same way as Create->Polygon Primitives->Cube. Learning shortcuts like this will drastically improve your modeling speed.

> *Step 2: Dimension. With a bit of research, you will find that a common security camera is about 18 cm long, 10 cm high, and 10 cm wide. Make sure that the box is selected and look to the right side of the UI. In the Channel Box (Figure 1.4),*

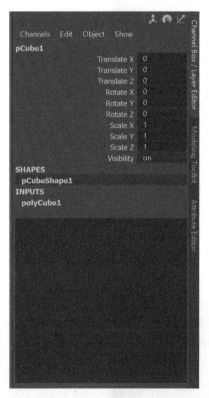

FIGURE 1.4 The Channel Box is at the top right of the Maya UI and allows you to change the position, rotation, and scale of a selected object.

change the Scale X and Scale Y to 10 and change the Scale Z to 18 (Figure 1.5).

Step 3: We are making a camera that looks like the one in Figure 1.6; one of the major differences between our box and the image is that the camera's corners are rounded.

Switch to edge mode (right-click and hold on the box, and choose Edge from the marking menu). Select the four edges across the length of the box (seen in Figure 1.7). Go to Edit Mesh->Bevel or press Ctrl + B to bevel these edges. This operation splits the edge you are selecting

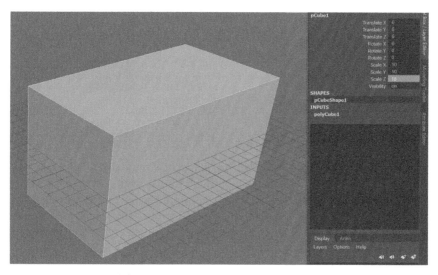

FIGURE 1.5 Adjusting the size of a cube (box) via the Channel Box.

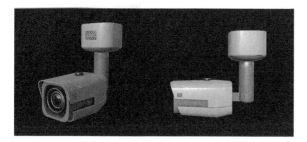

FIGURE 1.6 Our target camera.

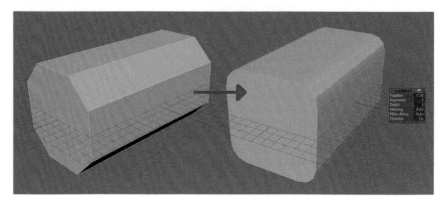

FIGURE 1.7 Using the bevel tool to round the edges of our cube.

to multiple ones. To round off these new edges, look for the pop-up menu (labeled polyBevel1) and change the Segments value to 3. Change the Fraction to 0.38 to shrink the distance between the newly beveled edges.

Tips and Tricks

To select the four edges, you can rotate the camera view to look at the side of the box, and then drag a section box over these four edges. Alternatively, you can select one of them, hold down the Shift button, and double-click the next one. Maya will select all edges that are between the same loop of faces; we call this selection of edges an edge ring.

Step 4: Soften edge. Swap out of Edge mode into Object mode by right-clicking (and hold) and choosing Object from the marking menu. Click in an empty space in the viewport to deselect the rounded cube. See a harsh line on the rounded-out corner? This is due to that edge being "hard." To soften it, swap to Edge mode and then select that edge and hold down the Shift button and double-click the next one to select the entire edge ring. Use Mesh Display->Soften Edge to make all the lines of this ring a soft edge (Figure 1.8).

Step 5: Frontal opening. Go to Face mode and select the front face of the camera. Go to Edit Mesh->

FIGURE 1.8 Softening the edges.

Extrude, or hold Ctrl + E to extrude the face. This creates another segment right at the faces we selected. Press the R button to switch to the Scale tool. Drag the yellow box in the middle of the Scale tool to scale the new face down to make the thickness of the shell. Take a closer look, and you can see the left and right contour of the opening is rounded. With the Scale tool, scale with just the red box handle (it will turn yellow when you are using it) to scale the face down across the X axis. Once done, we do not need this in the middle anymore, so press the delete button on the keyboard to delete it (Figure 1.9).

Step 6: Add Curvature to the side edges. To round the contour, we need more geometry. Go to Mesh Tools->Multi Cut. Hold down Ctrl, and hover the cursor on the side edge. Maya will give a preview of the edges that will be created if you click the mouse. Before clicking though, hold down the Shift button, to snap where the previewed ring will be created. This preview will snap every 10% across the length of this edge. Move the cursor until the preview lands at the middle of the edge, and click to finish adding the new subdivisions

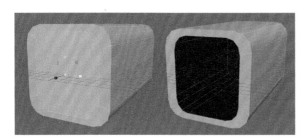

FIGURE 1.9 Using the Extrude tool to create an opening at the front of the camera.

(new edges). These edges have their tip and end connected. We call this kind of line an edge loop. Repeat and add the same edge loop on the other side (Figure 1.10).

Step 7: Turn on symmetry. Modeling is time-consuming, so we want to save time if possible. To do this, we can turn on symmetry, so we do not have to manually add the edge loop on the other side. The setting is located on the second row of buttons (Figure 1.11). By default, the setting is at Symmetry: Off. Click on the drop-down arrow on the right and choose Object X to toggle symmetry on across the X axis (Figure 1.11). After toggling symmetry on, selecting and performing commands on one side of the geometry will affect the other side.

Step 8: Add Curvature to the camera opening. Double-click on any edge of the edge loops we created in Step 6 to select the entire edge loop. Press Ctrl+B to bevel the edge loop and change the Segments to 2. Go to Vertex mode (right-click and hold on the shape, and choose Vertex from

FIGURE 1.10 Added edge loops on either side of the camera chassis.

FIGURE 1.11 Turning symmetry on to allow us to mirror our modeling work.

the marking menu) and select the vertex in the
middle on the edge of the hole. Use the Move
tool (W) to drag it away from the center a little.
Select the vertex above the middle vertex, hold
down shift, and click on the vertex below the
middle vertex to add it to the selection. Drag them
also away from the center. Work your way around
the opening and adjust the vertices until you get a
proper curvature for the side (Figure 1.12).

Step 9: Extrude the inner face. Double-click on any
edge of the hole to select the edge loop around
the hole. Hold down shift and left-mouse-
button and drag the loop inward a little; this
is a quick shortcut to extrude a new ring of
polygons. Select the edge ring along the newly
extruded edge and hold down the Shift + right
mouse button. In the resulting pop-up menu,
select Soften/Harden Edges->Soften Edge; this
will make the inner edges soft. This command
is the same command in the Mesh Display->
Soften Edge. Hit the R button to switch to the
Scale tool. Hold down Shift again and drag
the yellow box in the middle to extrude a new
small ring of polygons. Switch to Move tool,
hold down shift and drag the new edge ring
toward the back of the form to fill out the inside
(Figure 1.13).

FIGURE 1.12 Using Vertex mode and symmetry to adjust the opening to create a
round opening.

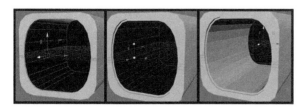

FIGURE 1.13 Using the Extrude tool (Shift-drag) to create polygons for the inside
of the form.

Tips and Tricks

Shift+right mouse button is a very common shortcut. Basically, it will pull up tools or commands to the current element you have selected. If nothing is selected, doing this will pull up a wide selection of primitive polygons. Almost all commands we need can be found in this pop-up marking menu.

Step 10: Camera lens. Click in some empty area of the Viewport to deselect the camera body. With nothing selected, hold down the Shift+right mouse button and chose Cylinder. Go to the Channel box and set the Rotate X to 90. This will rotate the cylinder 90 degrees in X and lay the cylinder down. Scale and move the cylinder so that it is roughly the size of the lens of the Camera.

Step 11: Lens frontal rims. Switch to Vertex mode. Select the vertex at the center of the front faces, hold down the Ctrl+right-mouse button, and in the resulting pop-up marking menu, chose To Faces->To Faces. This will select all faces that share this vertex. Turn off the symmetry (remember up in the second row of the interface). Press R to go to the Scale tool and hold down the Shift button and drag the yellow box to extrude the face in. Using the Move tool, hold down the Shift button and drag the face back in; keep on extruding with Scale and Move tools to create all the rims of the lens (Figure 1.14).

Step 12: Bevel the rim. Select the harsh edge loops on the rims of the lens (remember, you can do this by double-clicking on an edge while in Edge mode) and press Ctrl+B to bevel them. Select all the edges in the front of the lens, do a Soften edge command to soften the edge of the lens (Figure 1.15).

Step 13: Curvature of the lens. Select the vertex at the center of the lens. Hold down Ctrl+right mouse button and chose To Faces->To Faces. Switch to the Scale tool and hold down the Shift button while you drag the yellow box to extrude the faces down to about half of the original size. Use the Move tool to drag the faces forward a little. Grab the vertex at the center again and move it forward a bit more. Select the edge loop around the center vertex and press Ctrl+B to bevel it. This will give us the curvature we need for the

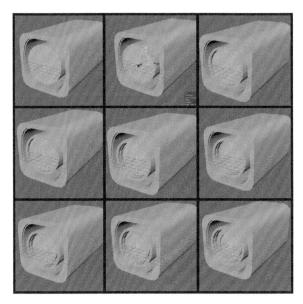

FIGURE 1.14 Using the Extrude, Move, and Scale tools to create the front rim of the lens.

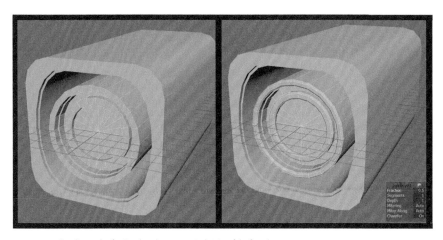

FIGURE 1.15 Beveling and softening the edges to create the rim of the front lens.

lens. Finally, soften the edge loops we created to make the lens feel smooth (Figure 1.16).
Step 14: Clean up history. Maya remembers everything we've done and stores this in the Input stack under the Channel Box (Figure 1.17).

15

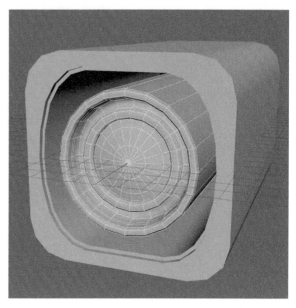

FIGURE 1.16 Finishing off the lens by adding curvature to the glass portion.

Go to Object mode and drag a big selection box to select both the shell and the lens of the camera. Go to Edit->Delete by Type->History to clean up the history. This will make all the construction history disappear (the shortcut for this operation is Alt+Shift+D). It is important to delete the history of the model regularly to ensure the model is stable and the scene is not getting heavier and heavier.

Step 15: Outer shell. Select the outer layer of faces of the lens that we made from a box. To do this, go to Face mode and grab one of the faces that goes across the depth of the model. Hold down Shift and double-click the next one to grab the whole loop across the depth of the model. Hold down Shift+right-mouse button and chose Duplicate Faces. Dragging the arrow that is facing away of the face that the arrows are sitting on, this Duplicate Faces command creates a new model from the faces selected. This allows you to shift the faces away so we can easily create a shell (Figure 1.18).

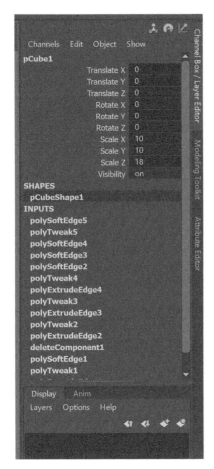

FIGURE 1.17 The Input stack of the Channel Box. This shows the History of steps created thus far.

FIGURE 1.18 Creating a shell by duplicating faces.

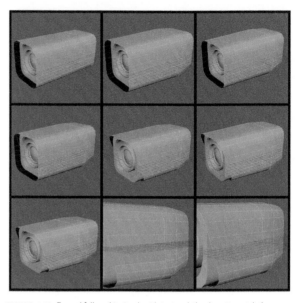

FIGURE 1.19 Try and follow this visual guide to tweak the shape to match the research.

Step 16: Tweak the shape. Figure 1.19 shows a sequence of steps using the techniques introduced in earlier steps. Try following the images to match the shape.

If you need help, the steps are: Grab the Outer shell we created in Step 15 and use the Scale tool to stretch it longer. Hold down Shift + right mouse button and chose Multi Cut. Hold down Ctrl and click to add an edge loop closer to the back end of the shell. Press Q to switch to selection tool and double-click on any edge of the newly created edge loop to select the whole loop. Scale this loop up and drag it slight down to create the wider portion of the shell. Add another loop closer to the front of the shell. With this loop still selected, press E to switch to the Rotate tool. Hold down Ctrl + Shift and rotate the loop to tilt it forward. (Note: you can see how the edge is constrained on the surface of the model when rotating, which is great to create the tilted frontal shape.) Select the front loop of faces and delete them. Toggle symmetry on and add edge loops to mark out the edge of

the opening in the middle of the shell. Select
the corresponding faces and delete them. Add
an edge loop really close to the edge where
the seam between the upper and lower shells
is. Finally, delete the face loop in-between to
open the seam.

Step 17: Upper shell hole. Add an edge loop at
the center of the model. Then select the new
loop, press Ctrl+B to bevel it and change the
fraction to 0.32. Switch to Move tool and use the
Ctrl+Shift trick to slide the edge in the center
forward to mark the front edge of the opening.
If you are not sure if the face is gone or not, you
can go to Object mode and grab the shell and
press Ctrl+1 to isolate it. You can press Ctrl+1 to
toggle the isolation (Figure 1.20).

Step 18: Add thickness. Grab all the faces of the
model (using Face mode and either double-
clicking on any polygon or marquee-selecting).
Press Ctrl+E and drag the arrow to extrude the
faces out to add the thickness.

Step 19: Back arm. Create a cube. Move and scale it
to create the basic shape of the back arm. Add
an edge loop in the middle and bevel it to give it
curvature. Don't forget to smooth the edges of
the rounded back (Figure 1.21).

Step 20: Connect back arm. Grab the back arm and
the inner shell of the camera. Go to Mesh->

FIGURE 1.20 Creating an upper shell hole, and finally isolating just the shell.

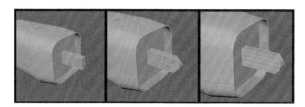

FIGURE 1.21 Creating the back arm by creating a simple cube, adding new edge loops, and tweaking those to create the desired shape.

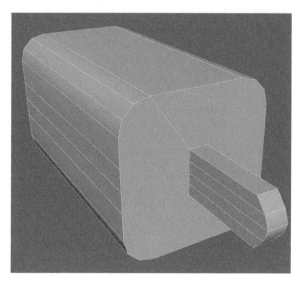

FIGURE 1.22 Using Booleans (Union) to merge two shapes together into one.

Booleans->Union. This will combine the selected meshes, blast out the overlapped part, and fuse the contact surface (Figure 1.22).

Step 21: Fix N-Gon. An N-Gon is any face with more than four edges. This can be a problem in 3D because it is unclear how the face should be divided into triangles for the rendering process. This can sometimes yield undesired output at the time of rendering. So it's best to rebuild N-Gons to either four-sided polygons (quads) or triangles. The big back face is a typical N-Gon. Switch to Multi Cut tool, and click and drag on one of the outer edges until it stops at one vertex. Click and drag on one of the inner edges until it hits another vertex. Maya will connect these two vertices with a new edge. Press the G button to commit the current operation and re-initiate the same tool again. Keep clicking and dragging to connect lines until there are no N-Gon anymore (Figure 1.23).

Why?

Notice that we had to end up with some triangles, and this is totally fine; otherwise, we need to add new edge loops

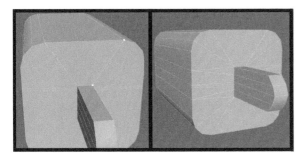

FIGURE 1.23 Using the Multi Cut tool to create new edges to rebuild the N-Gon into three- or four-sided polygons.

to the rest of the body, which takes more performance, and the render result will be the same.

Tips and Tricks

Click on the Modeling Toolkit button (Figure 1.24) on the right edge of the UI to switch to the Modeling Toolkit. Under the Tools section, you can also see Multi Cut. Click on it to toggle it on, and various settings of the tool will appear underneath. Scroll all the way down and open the Keyboard/Mouse Shortcuts section. You can see how versatile this tool is. Experiment with these different shortcuts to speed your workflow.

> *Step 22: Base. Create a cube, set the Scale X and Scale Z of the box to 13, and set the Scale Y to 8. Grab the vertical edge of the cubes and press Ctrl + B to bevel them. Change the Fraction to 0.62 and Segments to 3. Move it to the back of the camera body and drag it higher (Figure 1.25).*
>
> *Step 23: Base bottom shell. Select the bottom face and extrude it down. Scale the new faces down to match Figure 1.26. Next, go to Multi Cut tool, and in the Modeling Toolkit, toggle on Edge flow under the Cut/Insert Edge Loop Tool section. Add an edge loop to the middle of the newly extruded segment. In Figure 1.26, you can see how edge flow automatically added the curvature.*
>
> *Step 24: Base bottom arm. Grab the bottom face again. Hold down the Shift + right mouse button and choose Circularize Components. This will round the shape up to a perfect circle.*

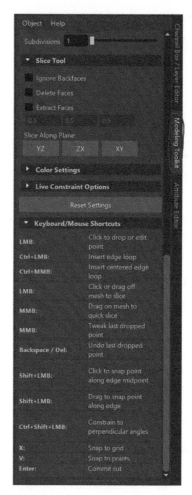

FIGURE 1.24 The Modeling Toolkit can provide faster ways to work with advanced modeling tools.

Unfortunately, it is tilted, but we can fix this by changing the Twist value to make it straight again. Extrude the face in the center down to create the length of the arm. Using the same technique used in Step 23, we can create a small rounded bottom for the arm. Finally, use the Multi Cut tool to fix the N-Gon (Figure 1.27).
Step 25: Create the arm bending socket edge. Select the edges across the bottom of the arm and press the R button to switch to Scale tool. This time,

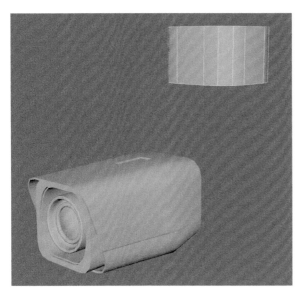

FIGURE 1.25 Using the same techniques covered above to create the base of the camera.

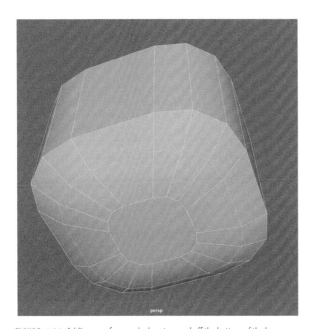

FIGURE 1.26 Adding new faces and edges to round off the bottom of the base.

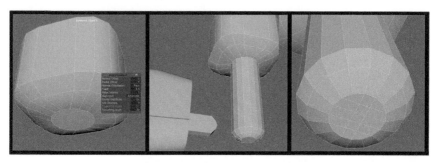

FIGURE 1.27 Creating the bottom arm and cleaning up the topology to eliminate N-Gons.

on the left side of the UI, look for the column of buttons we call the Toolbox. Try pressing Q, W, E, and R and you can see how to switch between these tools with the keyboard shortcuts. Double-click on the button that is highlighted when you press R to pull out the Scale tool settings. Check the Prevent Negative Scale option. Scale the lines on the X axis until they are flattened (they will not overshoot). Switch to Move tool and hold down the V button to turn on Vertex Snapping. While you are holding down the V button, drag the arrow of the move tool along the X axis (red-cone gizmo) and move your cursor to the point lying on the outer rim of the handle to snap the flattened line to that point only on the X axis. Do the same thing on the other side. Add another loop around the length of the handle to mark out the upper edge of the opening socket. What we are trying to achieve here is to mark the opening edge of the socket. The opening of the socket is highlighted in the last figure of Figure 1.28.

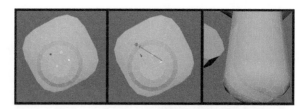

FIGURE 1.28 Building out the bottom of the arm using a few new tricks in each tool's options.

Tips and Tricks

Ctrl + Shift + right mouse button will also pull up the settings of the current tool. You can find the Prevent Negative Scale setting if you press R and then hold down the Ctrl + Shift + right mouse button. To quickly select part of a loop, select the beginning of the part of the loop and hold down Shift and double-click on the end of the part of the loop. This trick works on face loops, edge loops, and edge rings.

> *Step 26: Opening the socket. Delete the faces highlighted in the last figure of Figure 1.28. Grab the bottom edges and extrude them up. Scale them on the Y axis to flatten them. Switch to the Move tool and hold down V while dragging the edges up to snap the edges to the upper corner of the opening. Do not change the selection and hold down Shift + right mouse button and select the Bridge tool from the marking menu. This will bridge the two loops with faces. This command requires an equal number of polygons on the two loops (Figure 1.29).*
>
> *Step 27: Merge vertices. Select the edge on the upper corner of the opening and move it just a little bit in any direction. Notice that there are two vertices overlapping instead of one merged vertex (Figure 1.30); this creates a tear in the mesh.*
>
> *To fix it, we need to merge these vertices together. Press Ctrl + Z to undo the moving of the vertex. Then hold down Ctrl + Shift and drag over the two overlapping points to select both. Check to ensure that you are not*

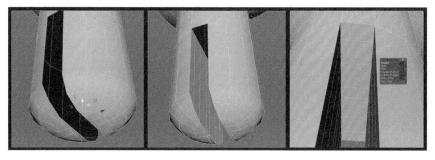

FIGURE 1.29 Creating the notch of the arm by deleting faces, extruding edges, and bridging.

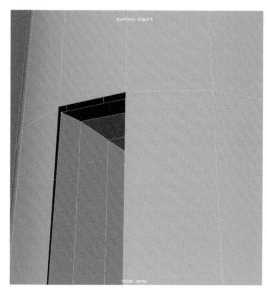

FIGURE 1.30 Our previous steps have created a form with holes in the mesh.

selecting anything else on the back of the form. You can choose Edit Mesh->Merge to merge these two vertices to one single vertex. Alternatively, you can hold down Shift+ right mouse button and select Merge Vertices, but this time, the Marking Menu will show a nested sub-menu. We just keep dragging up to select Merge Vertices to Center.

Step 28: Shrink and attach the camera to the base. Grab the faces of the back arm of the camera body and scale it up or down to make the size fit with the opening of the base. Move the base to attach the arm with the socket (Figure 1.31).

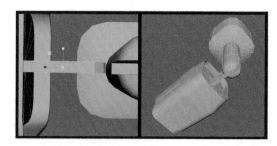

FIGURE 1.31 Scaling the faces of the back of the camera to fit the mounting base.

FIGURE 1.32 Roughing out the switch at the top using a cylinder.

> *Step 29: Top switch. Create a cylinder (Create->*
> *Polygon Primitives->Cylinder). Move and scale*
> *it to the opening of the top shell of the camera.*
> *In the input section of the Channel box, click on*
> *the polyCylinder1 and change the Subdivision*
> *Axis to 12 (Figure 1.32).*

Why?

We made the Subdivision Axis smaller to lower the polycount of the little top switch. It is such a small part that we do not need the same number of loops as the lens. In games, polycount is important, and trimming away those we don't need as we work will generate cumulative benefits in the long run.

> *Step 30: Reduce polycount. It is always possible to*
> *reduce polycount of a model to save a little bit of*
> *performance. Go to Display->Heads Up Display*
> *and check on Poly Count. You can see on the*
> *upper left corner of the viewport that we have*
> *1736 Tris in total. There are two ways we can*
> *reduce polycount:*
> 1. Delete edge loops that seems
>   unnecessary. Grab the outer shell of

the camera, select the edge loop in the middle, and hold down Shift+right mouse button and chose Delete Edge. Notice that there is no difference in the form after deleting it. Similar cleanups are shown in Figure 1.33.

2. If a loop cannot be completely deleted, triangulate parts of the loop. We clearly need no extra edge loop for the top flat surface of the outer shell, but we have two for the purpose of opening a hole on the top. To fix this, go to Object mode and hold down Shift+right mouse button and select Target Weld Tool. Click and drag the vertex in the middle area of the upper edge of the shell to the point next to it to weld it to that vertex. Using this technique, we can weld a lot of points without affecting the shape of the model. We may end up with some triangles, but it is totally fine for most non-deforming

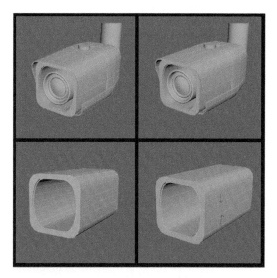

FIGURE 1.33 Strategically deleting unnecessary edges reduces our polycount without sacrificing form.

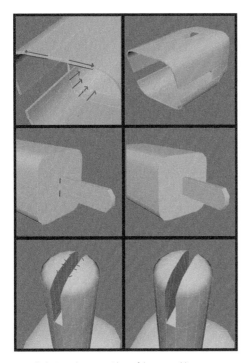

FIGURE 1.34 Reducing polycounts with careful vertex welding.

(not bending) forms, especially for a game model. Similar reducing results are shown in Figure 1.34.

Keep in mind that you still want to avoid too many triangles; triangles are harder to manage for the UV process (an important part of the texture process that we'll cover later), and they make it harder to do high-resolution sculpting (if you need to do so for complex forms including organic shapes). You can always consult the supervisors of your team to get their suggestions on the polycount if you do work for a studio. The final polycount after these optimizations is 1494 tris for our camera.

Tips and Tricks

The Delete Edge command should be what you use all the time to get rid of edges. The delete button on the keyboard does delete the edges but not delete the vertices on the edge, which means that when the renderer triangulates, it still produces the extra triangles from those left-over points.

> *Step 31: Clean up. On the top of the base, there is a big, flat N-Gon. Grab that top face and extrude it in. Hold down the Shift + right mouse button and select Merge Faces To Center. Select all models we created, press Alt + Shift + D to delete all the history. Finally, do a Modify->Freeze Transformation to clean up the transform.*

Why?

You may wonder what this Freezes Transformation does. Well, in Maya, a model has two primary components: transform and shape. Transform governs where the model is, how it is tilted, and how it is scaled; these are reflected in the translate, rotate, and scale values in the Channel Box. Shape governs the vertices, faces, and edges and how they are combined together to form the shape of the model; the final appearance of the model is the shape of the model moved, rotated, and scaled by the transform of the model. If you do recall, we have scaled the outer shell of the camera, and that scale value will appear in the Channel Box; freeze transform will clean that up and bake the scale we did to the transform of the model to the shape of the model. Many processes later (Rigging, UV Mapping) do require the transform of the model to be baked to the shape of the model through Freeze Transformation so that the final look of the model is the actual shape instead of a shape getting scaled, rotated, and moved by a transform.

> *Step 32: Naming and organization. On the left side of the UI, there is a pallet with a tab called Outliner; this is a list of the currently existing objects in the scene. Select anything in the*

viewport and you can also see it highlighted in the list of the Outliner. Alternatively, you can also select an object by clicking its name in the outliner. In the Outliner, you can hold down Shift to select multiple objects or hold down Ctrl to deselect.

Tips and Tricks

If you cannot see the Outliner, go to the column of buttons where we have the Move, Rotate, and Scale tools; the last button in that column is the toggle to show or hide the Outliner.

Select everything in the viewport in Object mode and press Ctrl+G to place them into a group. Something called group1 will appear in the outliner. This is a group (really a parent object). You can press the plus sign in front of it to open the group and see the children models inside of it. Double-click to rename any object there. For now, rename the group to security_cam_geo_grp. Spend some time renaming all other objects; the final naming is shown in Figure 1.35.

security_cam_switch_geo	
security_cam_outer_shell_geo	
security_cam_inner_shell_geo	
security_cam_len_geo	
security_cam_base_geo	

FIGURE 1.35 Names to use in naming the shapes build so far.

Tips and Tricks

Anything inside of a group will follow the group. You can now grab the group in the outliner and move the whole collection of shapes. You can put any object or objects under a group by grabbing the objects first and selecting the group last and pressing the P button on the keyboard. This is also something we call parenting. If you select something inside of a group and press Shift+P, this will get the object or objects out of the group (called unparenting). You can also parent one object to another object instead of a group. In the outliner, you can click the middle mouse button to drag anything around or drag one object to another to parent one object under another.

> Step 33: Clean up the outliner. We do not need any other objects in the scene; there could be other empty groups in the outliner due to some operations we did to the model. We can grab anything outside of security_cam_geo_grp and delete them. Alternatively, we can go to File-> Optimize Scene Size and let Maya clean these up for us.
>
> Step 34: Save the file. Go to File->Save Scene, in the pop-up Save window, change the File name to game_set_models, navigate to a folder that is safe and easy to find, and press the Save button to save it.

Other Useful Commands

We have introduced some of the most important commands for modeling. Let's start a new scene and go over a few more before we do some assignments.

Grow and Shrink Selection

Create a sphere (Create->Polygon Primitives->Sphere) and select the top vertex. Hold down Ctrl+right mouse button and choose To Faces->To Faces to select the top faces. Hold down Ctrl+right mouse button again and chose Grow Selection->Grow to select all the direct neighbor faces. Press the G button three times to redo Grow Selection three more times. You can also find Shrink Selection in the Ctrl + right mouse button marking menu.

Extract Faces

With the top four rows of faces selected, hold down Shift + right mouse button, and choose Extract Faces. Drag the blue arrow to shift the face away; you can now see how Maya separated the model into two objects. Notice that in the outliner, you can see the pSphere1 becomes a group, and there are two objects inside of it. That transform1 is the remaining construction history that you can use Delete History to get rid of.

Combine and Separate

Some commands, like Bridge, can only be used for component on the same object. So to bridge the upper shell with the lower shell (Figure 1.36), you have

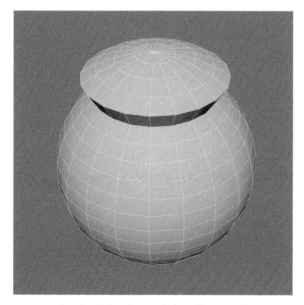

FIGURE 1.36 In order to bridge collections of polygons like this, you first must ensure that the polygons are parts of the same single object.

to combine the models together into one object. To combine models, grab all models you want to combine and use Mesh->Combine. By the way, you can also see the Separate command right below Combine. Separate will separate the model into multiple ones based on their connectivity.

Create Cables or Pipes

From time to time, we may want to create a cable or a pipe. Go to Create->Curve Tools->CV Curve Tool, and click and drag in the viewport to drop down a CV point. Click and drag again to add a new one; keep doing this and you will see a curve getting created. You can hit backspace to roll back and drag the middle mouse button to refine a placed CV point. When you are happy with the shape, hit Enter to finish the creation (Figure 1.37).

CV stands for Control Vertices. Maya will interpolate between the vertices to form a curve. This type of model is called NURBS, which uses mathematical interpolations between control vertices to create a form. These are fundamentally different from the camera model (polygon) we created earlier.

After creating the curve, you can still edit it by holding the right mouse button on it and choosing Control Vertex. Then you can move the CV to refine the shape as desired. The curve will be created on the grid by default. You can go to the front, top, or side view to create your curve

FIGURE 1.37 Using the CV Curve Tool to create a series of CVs that define a curve.

so that the curve snaps to the grid of that view. Go to Create->NURBS Primitives->Circle to create a circle. Grab the circle and the curve created previously, and go to Surfaces->Extrude☐ (be sure to click the square to pull up the Extrude Options window). There, change the Result position setting to "At path" and change the Pivot setting to "Component". Press the Extrude button, and you will see that a tube is created (Figure 1.38). This Extrude is not the same Extrude we did with polygons; it basically places the circle along the curve to create a frame and then interpolate a shape out of it.

You can scale the nurbsCricle1 to change the radius of the tube, and you can still tweak the shape of curve1 to change the shape of the tube (Figure 1.39).

However, this tube is not a polygon or polygon-based (which we will need for games). So to convert it into a polygon-based form, go to Modify->Convert->NURBS to Polygons☐. Change the tessellation method to "Control points". Press the Tessellate button to convert the tube to a polygon (Figure 1.40).

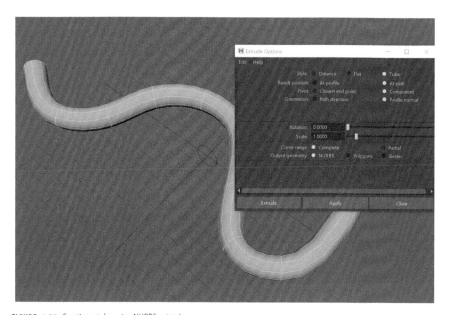

FIGURE 1.38 Creating a tube using NURBS extrude.

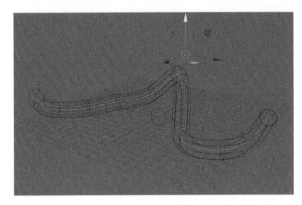

FIGURE 1.39 Once a NURBS form is created, the form can be adjusted by editing the curves used to create it.

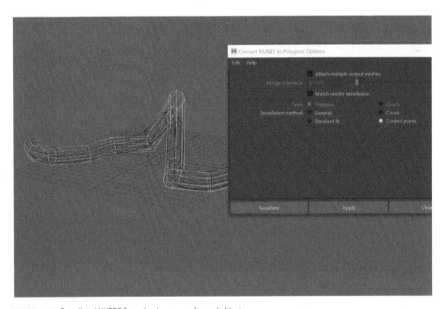

FIGURE 1.40 Tessellated NURBS form that is now a polygonal object.

Until now, you can still tweak the curves to change the radius and the shape of the curve. When you are happy with the form, select the polygonal shape and delete the history and delete all curves and the original NURBS surface as they're no longer needed.

Tips and Tricks

If, at any time, the tube model appears black, you can rotate the circle on the X axis until it flips back to normal. NURBS curves and surfaces are a different type of model that are mathematically interpolated between the control points we created. They are primarily used for architectural or industrial design. Most times, we don't use this type of model in game scenarios. However, they can be very useful to construct a form originally (that we then convert into polygons).

Extrude Along a Curve

Another variant of creating a tube is to create a curve in front of a face and then extrude that face along the curve. To do this, select both the face and the curve (Figure 1.41), and press Ctrl+E.

In the pop-up dialog boxes, increase the number of the Divisions setting to create a smooth extrusion along the curve (Figure 1.42). If the extrusion is backwards, you can grab the curve, do a Curves->Reverse Direction to fix it.

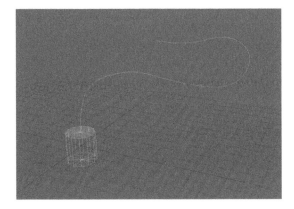

FIGURE 1.41 Extruding along a curve.

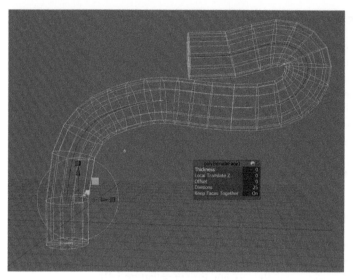

FIGURE 1.42 Tweaking the Extrude along curve options to get the resolution you desire.

Duplicate, Duplicate with Transform

You can grab any model and press Ctrl+D to duplicate it. The duplicated model will be at the same location as the original (although you'll see the name of the new form in the Outliner). Right after duplicating, you can use the Move tool to move the new duplicate away (Figure 1.43).

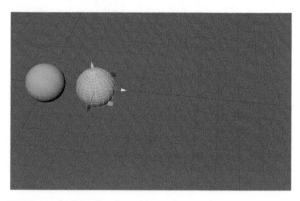

FIGURE 1.43 Duplicate allows for a quick copy of an original.

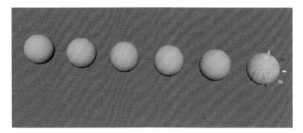

FIGURE 1.44 Duplicate with Transform (Shift + D) duplicates and transforms (moves) the object in the same command.

If you want to create another duplicate and have it move the same distance (or rotate the same amount), you can press Shift + D. You can keep pressing Shift + D to have multiple duplications, each offset the same amount as last time (Figure 1.44).

Duplicate Special

From time to time, we may want to create multiple duplications but as *instances*. An instance is a copy that keeps the link of the shapes between the original and the copy; we can adjust any one of the duplications to update the shape of all others (but not transform). Grab your model and go to Edit->Duplicate Special□. Change the Geometry type to "Instance". Change the first number of the Translate to 2 (the X axis), and the Number of copies to "10". Finally, press the Duplicate Special button, and you will see ten duplications of your model, each two units away from each other, and more importantly, editing any one of them will affect all others (Figure 1.45).

Mirror

Anytime you forget to have symmetry on and want to make the model symmetrical again, you can select the model in Object mode and do a Mesh->Mirror. Try different axes and directions to make sure you got the correct side mirrored. The merge threshold should be as low as 0.001 if you wish to only have the vertex in the center mirrored. You can also change the Border setting

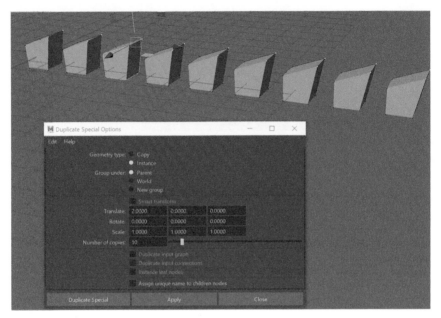

FIGURE 1.45 Using instances (as opposed to copies) to make copies of an object that will change when the original is manipulated.

to bridge or do not merge the geometry along the axis of symmetry to have a different result.

Center Pivot

You can grab any model in Object mode and do a Modify->Center Pivot; this will move the pivot of the model to the center of its bounding box. The Pivot is the location where the object is rotating around. It is needed whenever you want to be able to rotate or scale a model from its geometrical center.

Change Pivot

In any mode, you can hold down the D button on the keyboard and drag the gizmo to adjust the location or orientation of your pivot; you can also click on any elements on the model to snap your pivot to that element.

A good example that we want to do this is to change the pivot of the body of the camera to the hinge of the arm so that we can rotate it around the hinge.

Snapping

When moving an object or its various elements, you can hold down the X button to snap to the grid and V button to snap to vertices. The snapping toggles are on the Status line, which is the row of buttons under the main menu. The snap toggles are the six buttons with a magnet in their icon. Try these toggles and see what they do.

Hide Model

You can grab any model or its other elements and press Ctrl+H to hide them. To unhide, press Ctrl+Shift+H; this will only unhide the object you are selecting (probably in the Outliner) if you have something selected. It will unhide everything if you have nothing selected. After making a model, name it properly, freeze transformation, and hide it so you can move on to the next one without the other models blocking your view.

View Control

At any time, if your cursor is in the Viewport, you can press the spacebar to go to the Four View layout, and this will show you the Top, Perspective, Front, and Side views; you can then move the cursor to any view, and press the spacebar to maximize that view. However, we recommend to just hold down space and drag up, down, left, and right to go to these views.

Assignments

We have covered enough commands that you are now able to create models of your own; go ahead and start modeling some of your own models in Maya,

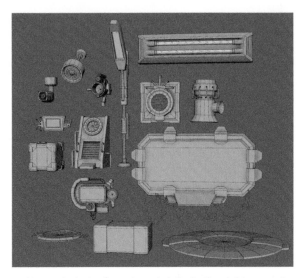

FIGURE 1.46 A selection of props that can be built using the techniques covered in this chapter.

and make sure you find references and get the correct measurement. Figure 1.46 shows a few examples of what we are looking for.

Geometry Errors

Sometimes in the modeling process, some errors can emerge. These errors might not even be readily visible in your model, but without fixing them, you can run into some serious problems later in a game engine. While these can be pretty technical, and the hard-core specifics are a bit outside the scope of this book, it's worthwhile to talk about them for a minute and – more importantly – evaluate how to fix them. Here are some typical geometry errors that we can now check on your model:

> **Non-Manifold Geometry.** *This geometry cannot be unfolded and flattened to a 2D surface. Typically, there is an edge shared by more than two faces or inconsistent normal directions. This type of model will confuse the renderer on which side is the outside of the geometry.*

Lamina Faces. *Two faces that share all of their edges. Typically, this is caused by duplicating and combining meshes that have the same faces.*
Zero Length Edge. *A self-descriptive situation in which an edge has no length.*
N-Gon. *We have covered N-Gon already; any face with more than four sides is a N-Gon.*

Luckily, even though the theory behind these errors is abstract, fixing them is usually pretty easy. To clean up the models, go to Mesh->Cleanup□. Under the Fix by Tessellation section, check on "Faces with more than 4 sides". Under Remove Geometry, check on "Lamina faces and Nonmanifold geometry". Press the Cleanup button; this will, in theory, clean up all the errors. Maya may choose to delete some of the faces because they are error geometries; make sure you check around the model and recreate any missing models.

Tutorial 1.2: Modular Set Pieces

Making a compelling and complex environment is a daunting task. To ease the pain, we are going to adapt to a modular workflow. This means we will make reusable pieces that are easy to combine with each other, like a system like Lego building blocks. The props we have made previously as assignments are already designed for that purpose, but to make the foundation of our game level, we need a more unified system. This means we need to have a chart of sizes that our models will have to exactly match, so they can be assembled seamlessly.

There are two size systems we can use: decimal and binary.

> For decimal, we will have sizes like 10, 20, 30, 50, 100…
> For binary, we will have sizes like 16, 32, 64, 128, 256, 512… (both in cm)

Both systems are popular, and we are going to follow the binary system. The author has found that it is easier to combine modules seamlessly and easier to match with textures sizes, which is also binary.

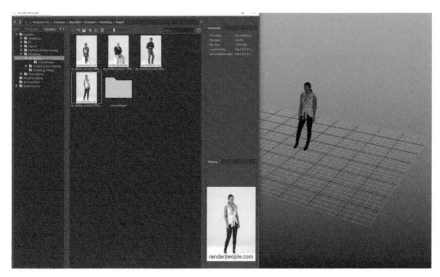

FIGURE 1.47 Setting up our grid to build modularly. The person acts as a size and scale reference.

Grid

Go to Display->Grid☐. Set the Length and width to 256, and set the Grid lines to 64 and Subdivisions to 4. Drag the slider of Grid lines and numbers to make it a blue color and press Apply and Close. This will create a grid that has its edge 256 cm away from the center and a blue grid line every 64 cm with four extra divisions in-between every blue grid line, which makes every grid 16 cm long.

To verify our sizes, go to Windows->General Editors-> Content Brower. Under the examples category on the left side of the window, choose Modeling->People. Drag a standing character to the viewport to import the human model; the height of the model should be slightly shorter than half of the grid length (Figure 1.47). If your character appears gray, hit 6 on your keyboard to have Maya show the materials as well.

Create a Base Floor

Step 1: Base floor dimension. Let's hide our other models, so we can start our new model with nothing else visible. Create a cube, set its

FIGURE 1.48 Creating and snapping the first-floor module to our grid.

Translate Y to −8, set its Scale X and Scale Z to 256, and set its Scale Y to 16. Switch to the Move tool and hold down both D and V buttons, and drag the pivot of the box to the upper corner on the negative X and Z quadrant. Release all the buttons. Now, hold down X button and drag the center of the gizmo to snap the model to the positive X and Z quadrant (Figure 1.48).

Why?

We want the model to be easily snapped together. Positioning the pivot to the corner of the box is extremely helpful for the snapping. We also want the pivot to be at the center of the world to avoid any offset.

Step 2: Floor edge trim. To help in adding trims to the side of the floor, grab the top face, and press Ctrl + E. Set the Offset setting to 16. This will give us a rim on the outside of the floor (Figure 1.49). Name this model floor_01 and hide it.

We are now done with this module. Every time we finish a module model, we can name it, hide it, and move on to the next one. This way, all of our models are created in one Maya file for easy access. This also allows us to maintain the scale of our game. We are not planning on making a whole lot of models for our environment, so keeping them all in one scene file is manageable. But if you'd rather, you are more than welcome to create new files for extra models instead. But be sure you

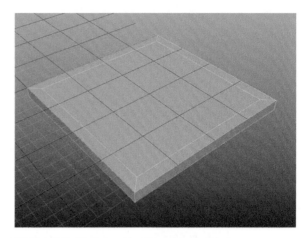

FIGURE 1.49 Creating the base trim of the module using Extrude.

maintain consistent Grid settings across the various scenes if you do so.

Step 3: Base wall dimension. Create a cube and set its Scale X to 256, Scale Y to 512, and Scale Z to 32. Snap its pivot to the lower back corner and then move it to the center of the grid (Figure 1.50).

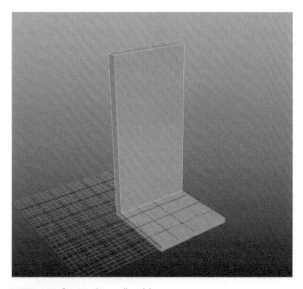

FIGURE 1.50 Creating a base wall module.

Step 4: Add bottom trim. Add an edge loop
toward the bottom of the wall module.
Extrude out the bottom face and move the
top edge of the extruded face down to create
a bottom trim (Figure 1.51); name this model
wall_01.

Step 5: Arch wall. Follow the steps of Figure 1.52.
Create a pipe (Create->Polygon Primitive->Pipe).
Under the Input section of the Channel Box, click
on polyPipe1 and set the Radius to 128, Height
to 512, and Thickness to 32. Set the Rotate Z of
the model to −90. Delete the frontal and bottom

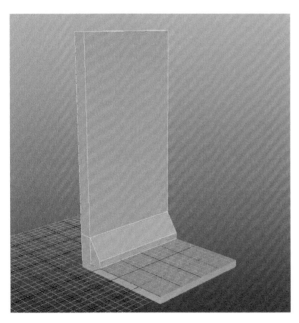

FIGURE 1.51 Creating trim for our wall_01.

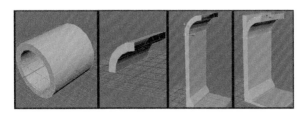

FIGURE 1.52 Creating the arched top of the wall by combining a pipe segment.

quarters of the pipe. Next, hold down D and V, and snap the pivot of the pipe to its back side corner. Hold down V and snap the pipe to the top of the wall we created in the previous two steps. Duplicate the wall and delete its top face. Combine it with the pipe by selecting both the wall and pipe and choosing Mesh->Combine. Grab the vertices of the pipe and the top of the wall and while holding down X drag them down until the top of the pipe is the same height as the height of the original wall. You can go to the side view to check out the alignment. Grab all the vertices and hold down Shift + right mouse button, go up and up again (or choose Edit Mesh->Merge). This will merge the vertices between the top of the wall and the bottom of the pipe. Double-click on one of the edges of the hole in front of the pipe and hold down Shift + right mouse button. Choose "Fill hole". Name this model wall_02.

Tips and Tricks

Step 5 has many steps, but the idea is simple. We want an arch on the top of the wall. Whenever we need something complex, we can break it up to smaller primitives. When we create these primitives, we can snap them together, combine them, and merge the vertices.

Step 6: Wall frame. Copy the arch wall we created and move its pivot to the origin. Change its Scale X to 0.25. Grab the front faces and press Ctrl + E. Change the Local Translate Z of the extrude to 16. Extrude the same amount again, but this time, scale the faces in on the X axis to create a little taper. Use scale or snapping to flatten the top front faces (Figure 1.53).

Step 7: Wall frame detail. Grab the faces in the front middle part of the model and hold down Shift + right mouse button and chose Duplicate Faces. Set the Local Translate Z to 16. Grab the bottom vertices and drag them up. Bridge the bottom edges and bevel the primary turning edges. This will give us extra volume; you can create additional ones to make the model more complex (Figure 1.54). Name this model wall_frame_01.

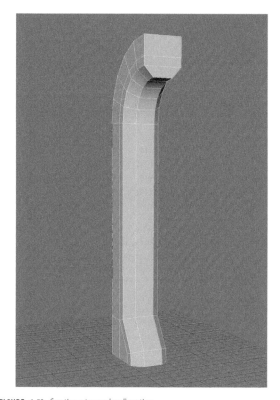

FIGURE 1.53 Creating a tapered wall section.

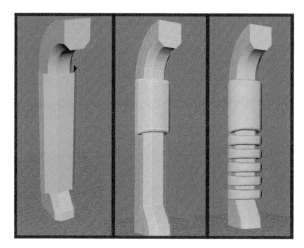

FIGURE 1.54 Extra detail on the walls.

Tips and Tricks

Always name and clean up your models when you have finished them. Your future self will thank you for making everything clean and tidy.

Step 8: Wall corner. We can create rounded corners for our rounded walls for when walls meet as we assemble them. Duplicate and snap our modules like the first figure in Figure 1.55. You can hold down the J button while rotating to snap your rotation for every 5 degrees. It is important that the modules are snapped to each other exactly. Have one blue (64 units) grid gap between the two hallways or corridors and the turning portion of the floor. This is to ensure that there is space for the rounded transition part.

Moving on to the second figure of Figure 1.55, select these two walls of the turning point, duplicate (Ctrl+D) them, and combine (Mesh->Combine) them. Grab the two columns of the faces that will connect to the turning portion. Hold down Shift+right mouse button and chose Bridge Faces. The result may look messy, so change the division to 7, and Curve type to Blend. The resulting middle part is going to be our turning module; delete the extra ones on the side and bridge the holes on the side to finish it. The outer corner is done the same way.

Step 9: Floor variations. Create a few varying sizes for the floor, like the gap we need to fill for

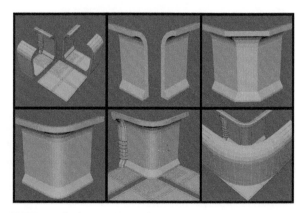

FIGURE 1.55 Creating a transition part for an outer corner.

the turning of the corridor we did for Step 4 (Figure 1.56). The sizes we choose to use are: 256×256×32, 256×128×32, 256×64×32.

Step 10: Stair frame. Create a cube and set the Scale X, Y and Z to 256. Snap its pivot to the back lower left corner and snap the cube to sit at the positive quadrant. Move (and snap) its bottom and top row of vertices to make a tilted frame for the stairs. Its bounding box length is 6×64 units (six blue grids). The footing of the shaft is 64 units, and the thickness of the shaft is 16 units (one gray grid). The results look like Figure 1.57.

Step 11: Stairs. Duplicate the stair frame to create the other side. Snap the duplication so that their whole width together is 256 units. Create a box, make its Scale X 32, Scale Y 8, and Scale Z 200. Move it to the first stairs location. It should be around 18 units high. Bevel all the edges of the box, and extrude from the two side faces to make the connection to the frame. Bevel the bottom edge of the frame to add a little detail. Fix the N-Gon after the bevel. Finally, bevel the edges of the frame (Figure 1.58).

Step 12: Stair handrail. Go to Create->Curve Tools-> CV Curve Tool; we have covered this tool

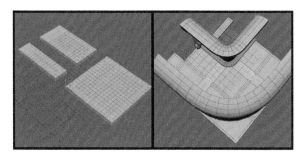

FIGURE 1.56 Creating other modular parts for floors.

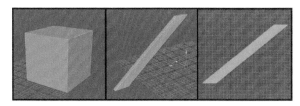

FIGURE 1.57 Building the stairs. Note that for modularity to work, the exact positions of the snapped vertices are important.

FIGURE 1.58 Creating the stair steps.

previously in the part about extruding along a curve. Use the Curve tool to create the profile of the handrail. Take care to make sure you have enough points on the arcing part; the amount of points you place will determine how many segments you will have on the final polygon shape. Use Extrude along curve techniques to create the handrail. Addition columns can be created using cylinders (Figure 1.59). Remember: be sure to covert the NURBS form into polygons.

Step 13: Other modular pieces. Other modular pieces are made with the same techniques covered previously; here is a list of all the pieces modeled:

Walls – *There are three walls, five wall frames, and some random small blocks. The size of the tall ones is 256×512 with a thickness of 32 (Figure 1.60).*

Arcs – *These arcs are having a radius of 256 units and a thickness of 32; an outside arc,*

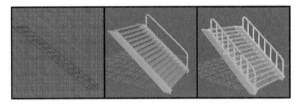

FIGURE 1.59 Creating the handrail using NURBS techniques.

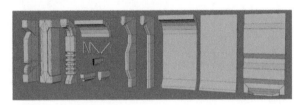

FIGURE 1.60 Completed wall modules.

a wall, and a wall bottom trim are also built (Figure 1.61).

Floor – *Floors with 256×256×32, 256×128×32, 256×64×32 are built to create hallways with different sizes. Two grid modules are also built (Figure 1.62).*

Pipes – *Pipes came with three sizes, each with a radius of 16, 8, and 4. Be sure to build some turning structures to support complicated combination (Figure 1.63).*

Stairs – *We have two stairs, a higher one with a 256 units elevation and a lower one with a 64 units elevation. Handrails were also built to support variations (Figure 1.64).*

Windows – *Window came in four sizes: 256×128×32, 128×128×32, 512×512×256, 96×64×160 (Figure 1.65).*

There are 57 modular pieces. It is hard to determine how many are needed, so it is wise to build less and try creating a hallway or a room and see if more modules are needed.

FIGURE 1.61 Completed arc modules.

FIGURE 1.62 Completed floor modules.

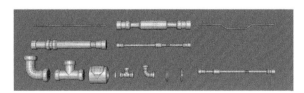

FIGURE 1.63 Collection of completed pipe modules.

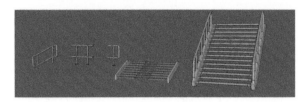

FIGURE 1.64 Stair modules.

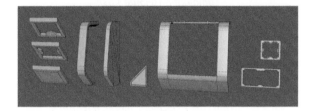

FIGURE 1.65 A variety of finished window modules.

Step 14: Hero assets. Hero assets are the assets that we only use a few times and so might need a bit of extra care and detail. We will create two hero assets for the final scene; the creation process of these hero assets is tedious, expect to spend a lot of time on them and have a higher polycount on these assets. But even though the fidelity might be higher for these assets, the tools and commands used to create them are no more than what we have covered (Figure 1.66).

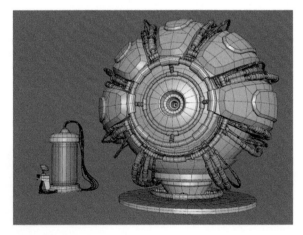

FIGURE 1.66 Hero assets.

Conclusion

We have finished the environment modeling part of our games. Well, of course, we've only created the individualized separated pieces; currently they aren't a level...yet. However, we will move them to the game engine and assemble them into our awesome level later. However, before we do that, we still need to go through UV mapping and Texturing so that our models are not white ghosts.

If you are able to complete these forms in this chapter, you're in good shape. If it is overwhelming and you'd rather move onto other stages, these completed models are available on the support website.

We will move on to the UV Mapping of our assets in the next chapter.

CHAPTER 2

Maya Set UV

UV Mapping is a pretty tricky concept for beginners but quite straightforward after you grasp the essence. It is a 2D coordinate to map a 2D image to the surface of the 3D model. Let us start with creating UVs for our first and simplest modular asset, the 256 × 256 floor piece (Figure 2.1).

The UV Editor

Go to the Workspace at the top right corner of the UI, and in the drop-down list, choose UV Editing; the viewport now splits into two windows. The UV Editor on the right is

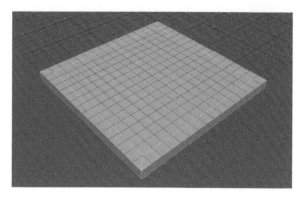

FIGURE 2.1 The 256 by 256 floor piece.

the place we edit our UVs. You can hold down Alt+middle mouse button to pan the view and Alt+right mouse button to zoom in or out. On the right of that window, we can also see a UV Toolkit panel, which contains many useful tools and commands to edit UV.

Select our floor piece; inside the UV Editor, you can see a blue shell that looks like an inverted T, this is the default UV of a cube. If you do recall, we started with a cube (if it is not blue, move the cursor to the UV Editor and press the number 5 button). Click on the checker icon at the row of buttons on top of the UI in the UV Editor. You can now see a checker texture getting displayed in both the UV Editor and on our model in the viewport (Figure 2.2).

Select the top face of the floor, and you can see how a face in the UV Editor is also highlighted. That face in the UV Editor is the UV of the top face of our 3D model. Go to the UV editor, press W to switch to move tool, and move this face in the UV editor to the U letter on the checker texture. You should also see the U letter appearing on the 3D model (Figure 2.3).

This face-to-face match is how UV works. UV is a 2D representation of the 3D model; it defines how an image can be mapped to the surface of the model. UV is also like a flattened shell of the 3D model if you will. This checker is a convenient way to preview how our UV maps texture on our model.

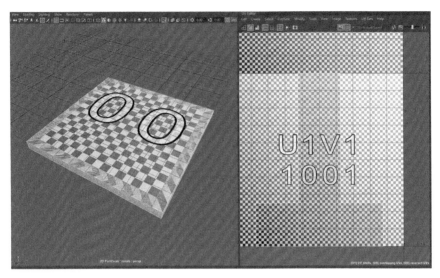

FIGURE 2.2 Check the UVs with the checker texture.

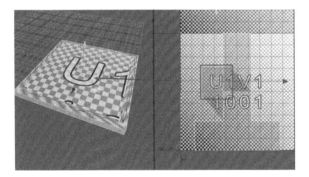

FIGURE 2.3 Make the letter U appear on the model by moving the UV.

UV Points

Other than edge, face, and vertex, there is a fourth
element called UV points. These UV points are a reference
to a vertex in 3D in the UV space, and they are the building
blocks of the UV of the model. Go to the UV Editor, hold
down the right mouse button, and chose UV. You can
now select UV points, and you can move, scale, and
rotate them around just like vertices in the UV Editor.

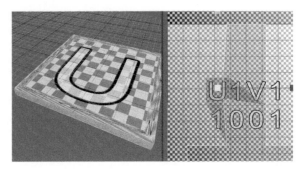

FIGURE 2.4 Scale the UV down to make the letter U look bigger than before.

Moving UV points affects the shape of the UV and affects the mapping of the textures. Figure 2.4 shows how scaling down the UVs of the top face down makes the letter U appear bigger than before.

UV Tiles

The checker texture has U1V1 1001 written on it, and this is the UV tile name. Pan the UV editor up, and you can see U1V2 1011 above U1V1 1001. This U1V2 1011 square area is just another UV tile. Hold down the right mouse button in the UV Editor and chose UV; drag a big selection box to select all the UV points. Press the W button to switch to the Move tool, and drag the UVs to the positive, X direction. You can see now Maya places more checker textures to the tiles your UV is overlapping with (Figure 2.5).

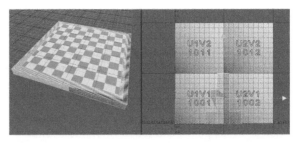

FIGURE 2.5 Maya places more checker textures to the tiles your UV is overlapping.

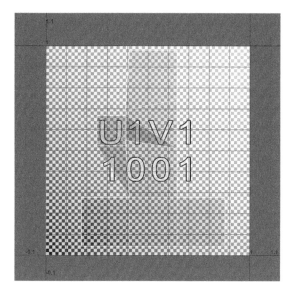

FIGURE 2.6 Maya shows only U1V1 1001 if all UVs are inside of the U1V1 tile.

In many modern renderers like Redshift, Octane, Arnold, or V-Ray, UV tiles can be used to apply multiple textures to one model. Every tile can receive a unique texture, but for our game engines, this feature is not supported. We have to ensure that all of our UVs are placed inside the U1V1 tile. You can grab all the UVs again and move them back and scale them down. You know they are all inside of U1V1 when Maya only shows one checker with U1V1 1001 on it (Figure 2.6).

Tips and Tricks

You are probably wondering what "U1V1, U2V2…" and "1001, 1002…" mean; they are essentially different UV tile naming conventions that different texturing software adapt. U1V1 is a system ZBrush uses. ZBrush is a sculpting software that allows artists to sculpt more detail on the surface of the model. 1001 is first used by Mari, a super-high-end texture software designed to create textures for movies. The texturing software we are going to use later is Substance Painter, which also adapts the 1001 system.

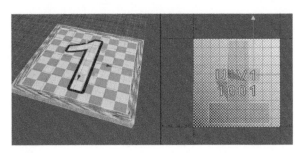

FIGURE 2.7 Cutting edges of the UV detach the face from the rest of the UV.

Cut UV

Select all the edges of the top face and go to the UV Editor. Hold down Shift + right mouse button (Remember that in the previous chapter, we talked about how this short cut will bring up the commands suited for the elements we are selecting), and chose Cut. You can now see these edges appearing thicker; switch to face mode and select the top face. Move the face around in the UV Editor. You can see how it is detached from the rest of the UV. You can now move it freely without affecting the UVs of other faces (Figure 2.7).

Try to select one of the edges of the detached UV and move it in the UV Editor; you can see how another edge also moves. This is because they are the same edge on the actual 3D model. In other words, they are two references of the same edge. UV points are also references of vertices, and sometimes they reference the same vertex.

The Problem

Looking at the checker texture mapped to our model, you can immediately see the outer frame of our model has a super-stretched texture. This stretching effect is due to the UV of these faces not being laid out correctly. We want all UVs of all faces to be flattened with the correct proportion and not overlapping with each other. We often don't rely on the default UV. Now, let's start creating the UV of our floor from scratch.

UV the Floor

Step 1: Project the UV. Select the floor piece in object mode, and freeze its transformation. Navigate the viewport so we are looking at the model at a non-straight angle. Go to UV->Planar☐. In the pop-up Planar Mapping Options window, go to the Project from section, and chose Camera. Check on keep image width/height ratio and hit the Project button. You can now see a projected figure of our model in the UV Editor. This planar projection projects our model form our viewing angle in 3D to UVs in the UV Editor, or to the UV space (Figure 2.8).

Step 2: Cut the UV Open. The projection will only project the model but will not be making a cut. Imagine you got a box package delivered to you. Without cutting the plastic tape open, there is no way you can flatten it to a 2D surface without faces overlapping each other. Let's check off the checker texture, so it is easier to see the edges.

Select all the edges of the bottom face, go to the UV Editor, hold down Shift + right mouse button, and chose Cut to cut them

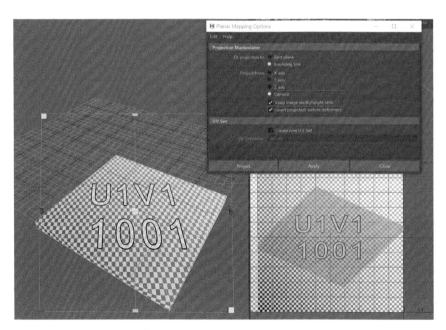

FIGURE 2.8 Project the UV to the UV editor.

open. *Hold down the right mouse button in the UV Editor and chose UV Shell. UV shell is a shell of UV that all faces of it are connected. Click on the top face of the model in the UV Editor; all UVs that are connected to the top face (or not cut out from it) should all be selected. Use the Move tool to move it away. Grab the four edges of the top part and four vertical edges of the floor and cut them also. The edges we cut should appear thicker (Figure 2.9).*

Step 3: Unfold. Select all the UVs in the UV Editor, hold down Shift + right mouse button, chose Unfold->Unfold. Maya automatically tries its best to unfold the UVs to the same 3D shape and with the same proportion for each face (Figure 2.10).

Step 4: Orient UV. Currently, all the UVs are tilted. To fix the orientation, go to the menus of the UV Editor, chose Modify->Orient Shells. Maya tries its best to make them straight. You can now grab any UV shell and rotate them while holding down the J button to adjust their rotation (Figure 2.11).

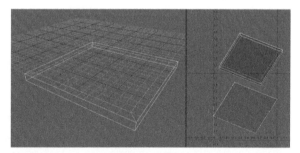

FIGURE 2.9 Cut the UVs of the floor.

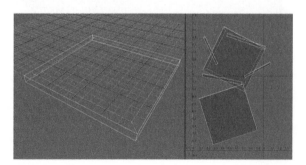

FIGURE 2.10 Unfold the UVs.

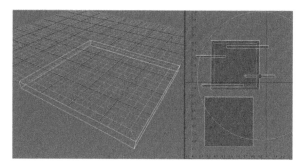

FIGURE 2.11 Orient the UVs.

Tips and Tricks

There is no telling how a UV should be oriented, and sometimes it doesn't make a huge difference, but we want similar UV shells oriented the same way most of the time.

> *Step 5: Layout the UV. Grab all the UVs, hold down the Shift and right mouse button, and chose Layout->Layout UV. The UV shells are now automatically rearranged into the U1V1 space. There is a small problem with this default behavior: there is no gap between the UV shells; there is also no gap between the edge of the U1V1 tile and the UV shells.*
>
> > *Many texture software bleed the color out of the UV shell a little to avoid the seam reading the background. Go to the Layout command again, but this time, click on the box icon of the command to pull out the Layout UVs Options window. Under the Layout Settings, change the Shell Padding and Tile padding to 10. This setting ensures that all UV shells are at least 10 pixels away from each other, and it also ensures they are 10 units away from the edge of the UV tile. Press the Layout UVs button, and you can see the difference this time in Figure 2.12.*

Tips and Tricks

Pixels are the smallest unit of a picture. If you zoom in close enough to any picture on a computer, you can see small, square, solid colors arranged in rows and columns.

FIGURE 2.12 Add shell padding and tile padding in the layout settings.

All digital pictures are put together this way. When we are talking about the resolution of a computer screen, like a 4K monitor, the 4K means there are around 4000 pixels across its width. The exact number of pixels a 4K screen has is 3840 pixels on its width and 2160 pixels on its height.

Steps 1 to −5 can be used for almost all UVs, even for a complicated character model. Do a planar projection to project our model to UV space, cut the seams we think are needed to flatten it, and then Unfold, Orient, and Layout.

There is no universal rule on how UV should be cut and arranged. However, it is essential to know that if you don't cut enough, your UV is destined to be stretched. If you cut too much, it's hard to arrange. For every cut you do, there is a potential to see discontinued texture patterns on that edge, and we call this a seam artifact. Seam artifacts become less of a problem with modern texturing software. One last important note: you want to cut any edge that is a hard edge. We are going to explain why later.

Let's do the UV of our security camera.

We have updated the security camera and separated the vertical arm from the base (Figure 2.13).

We need the separation to rotate the camera on the Y-axis. Changes like this happen all the time, especially when the

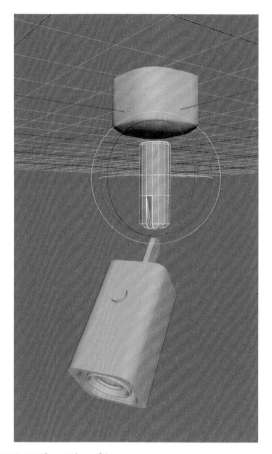

FIGURE 2.13 Separated arm of the camera.

mechanic of the object (arm rotation in this
case) was not taken into consideration.

Step 6: Project the UV. Select all the models of the
security camera, do a planar projection the same
way we did in Step 1 (Figure 2.14).

Step 7: Cut the outer shell. Select the outer shell of
the security camera, press Ctrl + 1 to isolate it
(Ctrl + 1 is the toggle for isolating the current
selection). Set symmetry to Object X (This could
be easily Object Z if your model is rotated
differently). Go to UV->3D Cut and Sew UV tool, in
our 3D viewport, click and drag on the outer and
inner edge loops of the thickness of the shells to
cut them open. You can also double-click to cut
an entire edge loop. Holding down Ctrl while

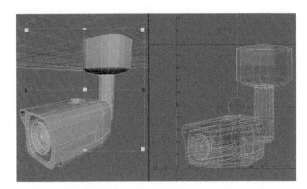

FIGURE 2.14 Project the UV of the camera.

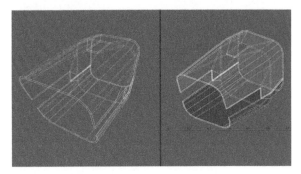

FIGURE 2.15 Cut the edges using 3D Cut and Sew UV tool.

dragging or double-clicking sews the edges back together. Go ahead and cut edges at the primary turnings of the faces along the thickness of the model (Figure 2.15). The 3D Cut and Sew UV tool adds color codding to shells once they are cut off.

Tips and Tricks

Cutting using the 3D Cut and Sew UV tool is no different than selecting the edges and cutting them in the UV Editor. Sometimes one method is easier than the other, and there are always multiple ways to achieve the same thing. Experience can help you to decide which way is faster.

Step 8: Unfold. Grab all UVs in the UV Editor, go to the UV Toolkit, under the Unfold section, click the Unfold button. This one is also no different than using the unfold command in the Shift + right mouse button marking menu. The author prefers the marking menu because one fast drag invokes the Unfold command right away (Figure 2.16).

Step 9: Optimize. With all the UV selected, go to the Modify menu under the UV Editor. Click on the square icon on the right side of the Optimize command to pull up the Optimize UVs Options window. Set the Iterations under the Optimize Options section to 100; to repeat it 100 times, click Apply and Close. You can see the UV has slightly changed; what Maya does here is to move UV points around to reduce stretching. In case you haven't tried, you can also find the Optimize command in the Shift + right mouse button marking menu and the UV Toolkit.

Step 10: Orient and Layout. Do an orient shell and layout exactly like in Steps 4 and 5 (Figure 2.17).

Step 11: Do the UV of the inner shell. Go ahead and create the UV of the inner shell the same way; the cut and result are shown in Figure 2.18.

Step 12: Do the other UVs. You can also create the other UVs the same way. Figure 2.19 shows all the cutting choices of the rest of the pieces.

Step 13: Combine UVs. Select all the models of the security camera, go to the UV Editor, grab all the UVs, do a Layout UV command (Figure 2.20).

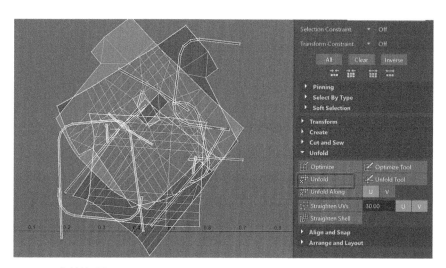

FIGURE 2.16 Unfold the UVs.

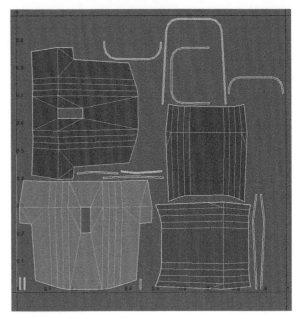

FIGURE 2.17 UVs of the outer shell.

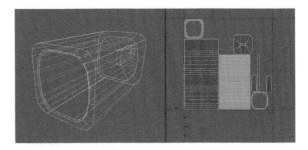

FIGURE 2.18 UVs of the inner shell.

Why?

We put all the UVs of all security camera models in one UV tile. By doing so, we can create one texture for the entire camera and save performance for our game. It is essential to pack UVs together in a uniform and organized way.

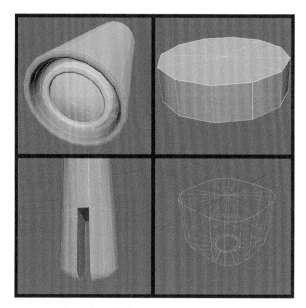

FIGURE 2.19 Cutting choices for the rest of the pieces.

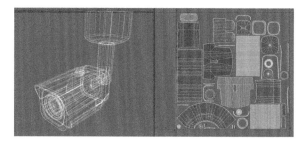

FIGURE 2.20 Layout the UVs of the entire camera.

Texel Density

Now we have two models UV mapped, so let's talk about texel density. Grab all your UVs of the camera, and go to the UV Toolkit. At the bottom of the Transform section, you will see a Texel Density (px/unit) part. Click on the Get button and you can see a value calculated; in our particular case, it is 3.1016. This value means there are 3.1 pixels per unit (cm) if you are using a texture of 512×512 resolution, which is defined in the Map Size section. Select the floor and press the Get button, and the value we get is 0.97. These two values indicate that the Camera is having 3×3 times, which is nine times the resolution of the floor. You can also visualize the difference in the viewport with the checker texture turned on. You can see how the edge length of the square on the camera is roughly three times smaller than the floor.

You may wonder what is so important about this. Through the experience we have gathered while developing games, consistency of the texel density helps a great deal in maintaining assets, saving performance, and having a consistent graphic. Ideally, 1 pixel of the texture on your model gets rendered as 1 pixel on your screen. A texture that has a higher resolution than that wastes performance. A texture that has a much lower resolution causes a pixelated or blurry result. If your texel density is not the same on different models, then some of the texture may feel more detailed than others, which causes inconsistency.

Chose the Right Texel Density

How high the texel density is depends on the camera view of your game. For third-person or first-person games, we can get to an object closer, and so we need more texel density. A top–down viewing angle requires lesser texel density. Strictly speaking, we also want the models closer to our player to have higher texel density, while things further away can have lower texel density.

Some games have two or three levels of texel densities. The assets to which the players can get as close as they want (characters, walls, weapons) have the highest texel density. Assets that are farther away that the player cannot reach but not very far (high ceiling, building, or trees outside of the window) have medium-level texel densities. Background assets (mountains, sky, the bird in the sky) have the lowest texel density.

Luckily for us, we are making an interior in which the player can pretty much get close to anything; so we are going for one consistent texel density. There are plenty of guidelines on exactly what the texel density is for various games. In our case, we aim for a medium- to high-quality texel density, like Uncharted 4. Our textures are going to range from 512×512 pixels to 4k (4096×4096 pixels), and the texel density is going to be around 5.12 pixels per centimeter or 512 per meter.

It is worth noting that we are not aiming for a fixed number for every asset. The texel density is allowed to vary a little; the only way to judge if something is too far off is by actually looking at it in the game engine.

> Step 14: Assign material and mark resolution. Go to our security camera, set the Map Size of the Texel Density section in the UV Toolkit to 1024, and press the Get button. We can see we are getting a texel density of 6.2, and we will settle with this for our camera. Select our camera models, hold down the right mouse button, chose assign new material, and select Blinn as the material. Hold down the right mouse button again on any of the models and chose Material Attribute to pull out the attribute editor on the right side of the UI. In the first text field of the settings, change the name of the material to SecurityCamera_1k. Naming the materials like this helps us remember the texture resolution we intend to use for our models.
>
> Step 15: Packing Floor. Go ahead and UV map all of our floor modules: there are five of them. Grab all of them, go to the UV Editor and select all the UVs. Go to the Layout UV option, Change the Packing Resolution under the Pack Settings section to 4096. Set the Texture Map Size under Layout Settings to 4096, set Shell Padding and Tile Padding to 10, and press the Layout UVs button. Maya should now pack all the UVs in to the U1V1 space.
>
> Go to the Texel Density section under the Transform section of the UV Toolkit and set the Map Size to 4096. Press the Get button; we get a resulting value of 4.2146, which is close enough to our goal of 5.12 pixels per unit (Figure 2.21).

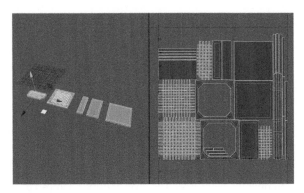

FIGURE 2.21 Packing the floor.

Why?

We packed all of our floors into one UV shell and used a 4k (4096×4096) texture for them with a resulting texel density of 4.2146 pixels per unit. Packing similar assets is a common practice; we pack models together to have a big texture for all of them, and this kind of texture is called an atlas. By using atlases, we are reducing draw calls from the game engine. 4K, of course, is a bigger texture and takes longer to load and needs more space in the memory. However, in many cases, the bottleneck is not how much memory is used, but rather how often you are reading and freeing memories. The standard may also vary from studio to studio; consult with your technical guides to determine the best practice for your platform and engine.

UV the Pod

One of the props we did for the environment was the pod (Figure 2.22).

The pod is the place where genetically engineered soldiers are created. It has a console, a tank, cables, and keyboards. Notice that we have two models for the pod, the glass and the rest of the pod. We do this because the glass is fundamentally different material wise. It is safe to separate these special types of materials, which makes it easier to work with later on in the game engines.

FIGURE 2.22 The pod model.

The glasses of the windows of our modular pieces are also separated the same way. Let's move on to the UV of the pod and introduce some more tricks of UV Mapping.

> *Step 16: Grab all the models of the pod, do a planar project like before.*
>
> *Step 17: Cut the cylindrical tank glass of the pod. Got to the back of the pod, select the vertical edge loop at the center of the glass of the tank, go to the UV Editor, and do a Cut command. Select all the UVs of the glass of the tank and do an Unfold, and an Optimize command (Figure 2.23).*
>
> *Step 18: Console monitor. Select the faces that belong to the display of the console. In the UV Editor, switch to face mode, hold down Shift+right mouse button, chose Create UV Shell. Switch to the Move tool and move the shell away from its original position. You can see how the outer edges are now cut; use Create UV Shell is a different way to separate UVs. Do an Unfold and Optimize command on the UVs of the display (Figure 2.24).*
>
> *Step 19: Keyboard UV Mapping. Select all the faces of the keyboard, and press Ctrl+1 to isolate them. Select the back faces and do a Create UV Shell.*

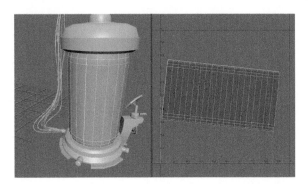

FIGURE 2.23 Cutting the tank of the pod.

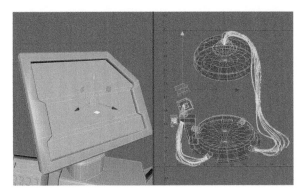

FIGURE 2.24 UV the monitor of the console by using the Created UV shell command.

Apply an Unfold and Optimize command, and move the shells out. Notice that the Create UV Shell command also switches the selection mode to Shell. We can use this to select all the keyboard buttons quickly, move them out, unfold, and optimize them (Figure 2.25).

Tips and Tricks

At the stage of cutting and unfolding UVs, we just do not worry about their arrangement. That's why we are moving them around freely. We can easily pack them back to the U1V1 space with the Layout UV command.

FIGURE 2.25 Create the UVs for the keys.

Step 20: Separate other parts of the keyboard. Select the face loop across the thickness of the keyboard, and select the face loop that represents the depth of the small monitor at the top of the console. Add select the loop that represents the depth of the depression of the area of the keys as well. Do a Create UV Shell command and move the separated shell out (Figure 2.26); you can see how easily we can separate UVs with this create UV shell trick.

Step 21: Cut and unfold other parts of the keyboard. Select the edges highlighted in Figure 2.27 and cut them, grab all the UVs of the keyboard, unfold, and optimize them.

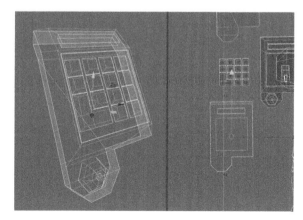

FIGURE 2.26 Separate other parts of the keyboard.

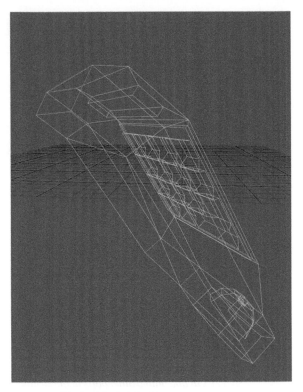

FIGURE 2.27 Edges to cut for the keyboard.

Step 22: UV Mapping the Cables. We have meticulously placed the cables for this model to give the model a sense of complexity and functionality. As complicated as they appear, the UV part is not as hard as you think. All we have to do is select an edge loop across the length of every individual cable, do a Cut, and then unfold and optimize (Figure 2.28).

Step 23: Other parts of the console. Other parts of the console should be straightforward; go ahead, and cut and unfold the rest of the console part.

Step 24: Packing. Grab all UVs of the pod, do a Modify->Orient Shells. Grab them again and do a Layout UV command, and make sure you have shell and tile padding set to 10 units in the Layout UV Options. Figure 2.29 shows the UV of our pod after layout. Notice that both UV sets have empty spaces. Maya sometimes does not do a good job using all the UV spaces.

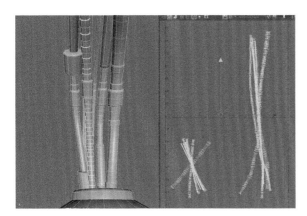

FIGURE 2.28 Create UV for the cables.

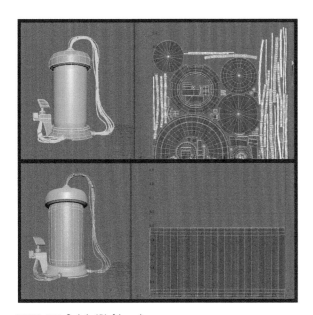

FIGURE 2.29 Pack the UV of the pod.

Step 25: Manual Packing. Other than relying on Maya to layout the UVs for us, we can also manually pack our UVs. Grab all UVs of the pod, switch to Scale tool, hold down D and X, and drag the pivot of the scale tool to the lower left corner of the U1V1 tile. Release the buttons and scale the UVs up. Our UVs now exceed the

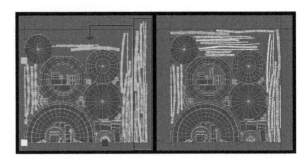

FIGURE 2.30 Manually pack the UVs.

U1V1 range. You want to control how much you are scaling, and the goal is to move the UVs exceeding the U1V1 range back to the remaining empty UV space inside of the U1V1 space (Figure 2.30).

Tips and Tricks

The texel density of our manually tweaked UV layout is 4.7617; the texel density before our tweak is 4.295, that is about 11% increase in resolution. We can always improve our texel density by manually adjusting the UV layout. However, it is going to be a time-consuming process. We need to keep popping out assets to meet the deadline, and sometimes this kind of optimization is not possible with the agenda of the production.

Step 26: Finish all other UVs. Now it is your turn to finish all other UVs. Please ensure that you have similar texel density and give every group of packed UVs a new material. Also, remember to name the materials with the resolution intended for these assets.

Figures 2.31–2.56 are the UVs and texel densities for the rest of the models

Step 27: Organization. Check your outliners and see if there is anything not named. Delete any empty groups; make sure all materials are assigned and appropriately named. When everything is checked, do a File->Optimized Scene Size to clean up redundant history and materials.

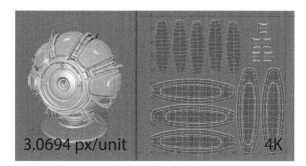

FIGURE 2.31 All the UVs and texel densities for the rest of the models.

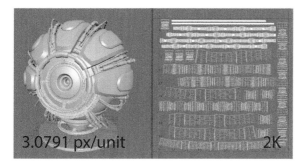

FIGURE 2.32 All the UVs and texel densities for the rest of the models.

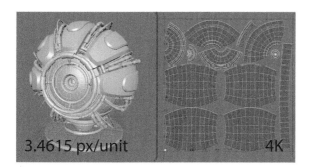

FIGURE 2.33 All the UVs and texel densities for the rest of the models.

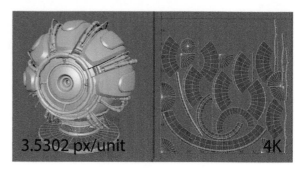

FIGURE 2.34 All the UVs and texel densities for the rest of the models.

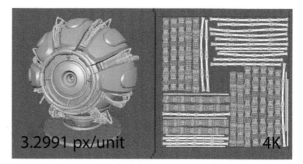

FIGURE 2.35 All the UVs and texel densities for the rest of the models.

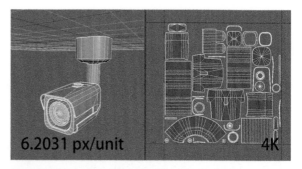

FIGURE 2.36 All the UVs and texel densities for the rest of the models.

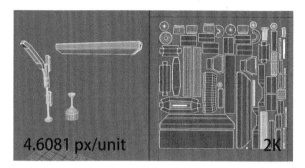

FIGURE 2.37 All the UVs and texel densities for the rest of the models.

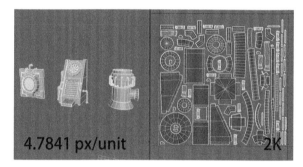

FIGURE 2.38 All the UVs and texel densities for the rest of the models.

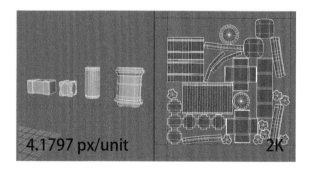

FIGURE 2.39 All the UVs and texel densities for the rest of the models.

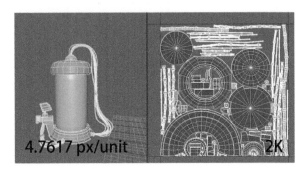

FIGURE 2.40 All the UVs and texel densities for the rest of the models.

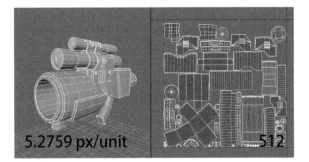

FIGURE 2.41 All the UVs and texel densities for the rest of the models.

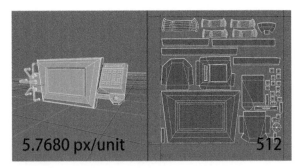

FIGURE 2.42 All the UVs and texel densities for the rest of the models.

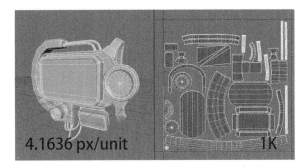

FIGURE 2.43 All the UVs and texel densities for the rest of the models.

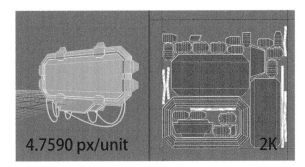

FIGURE 2.44 All the UVs and texel densities for the rest of the models.

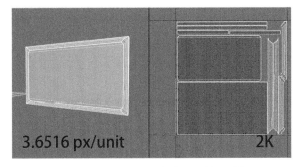

FIGURE 2.45 All the UVs and texel densities for the rest of the models.

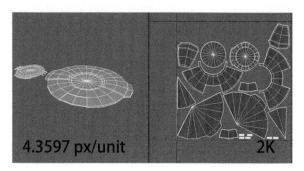

FIGURE 2.46 All the UVs and texel densities for the rest of the models.

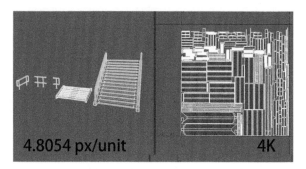

FIGURE 2.47 All the UVs and texel densities for the rest of the models.

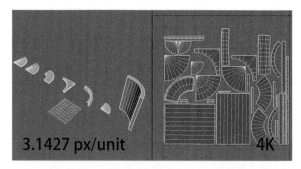

FIGURE 2.48 All the UVs and texel densities for the rest of the models.

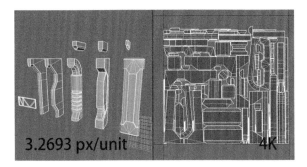

FIGURE 2.49 All the UVs and texel densities for the rest of the models.

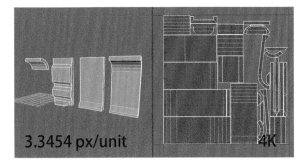

FIGURE 2.50 All the UVs and texel densities for the rest of the models.

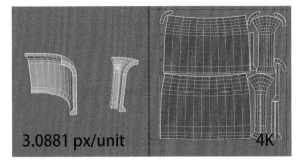

FIGURE 2.51 All the UVs and texel densities for the rest of the models.

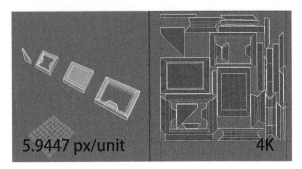

FIGURE 2.52 All the UVs and texel densities for the rest of the models.

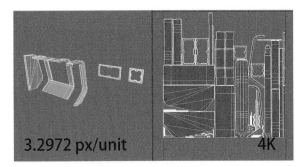

FIGURE 2.53 All the UVs and texel densities for the rest of the models.

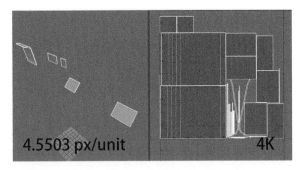

FIGURE 2.54 All the UVs and texel densities for the rest of the models.

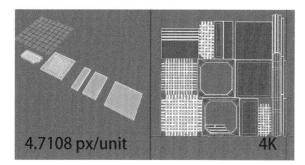

FIGURE 2.55 All the UVs and texel densities for the rest of the models.

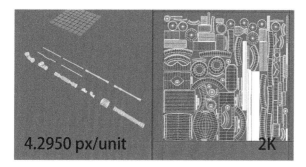

FIGURE 2.56 All the UVs and texel densities for the rest of the models.

Conclusion

The UV part of the model may not appear on the surface of the artwork. However, it is the foundation of the texture of the model and cannot be overlooked. There is an automatic UV command under UV->Automatic; it is wishful thinking that automatic UV can get you to a decent stage. Please don't use it unless you have a good reason. Based on the previous experience of teaching UV, the author already regrets mentioning this command. The students always think automatic UVs are fine – they are not.

Once UVs are done, the fun task of texturing starts. Let's jump into that in the next chapter.

CHAPTER 3

Set Texturing

UV Mapping is generally the painful part or at least an annoying part of making 3D art. However, once we are done with it, we can now jump into texturing, which is a real joy with modern texturing tools.

Texturing is the process in which we define the color, roughness, metalness, height information, and other aspects of the surface of the model. All those aspects are images that can be mapped to the surface of the model with the UV we created. Textures are applied to a material. The material will use the information on the texture to determine the lighting and shading behavior of the model. What is the color of the surface? Is the surface shiny? Is it a metal? All those play a significant role in how the model looks.

Texturing is considered as important as the modeling part. There are many ways to do texturing. You can paint the texture in 2D with a UV snapshot or in 3D with some dedicated software. We primarily use a 3D painting software called Substance Painter.

PBR

In the modern workflow, texturing has to define all aspects of a material, like the color, roughness, and metalness. In the game industry, we use a standard called PBR to define a material. PBR stands for Physically Based Rendering. It enforces the result of the rendering to be physically correct by limiting the number of inputs allowed to be adjusted. Other related material properties are calculated internally to ensure that the energy from the light is reflected, refracted, and absorbed by the surface of the model based on the laws of physics. For example, if you know the color and roughness of a metal surface, you can already calculate the brightness and color of the reflection using physics laws. There are variants of this standard, but the most popular one is called PBR-Metallic Roughness; it is composed of five surface attributes:

> *Base Color*
> *Height*
> *Roughness*
> *Metallic*
> *Normal*

Height and Normal attributes are surface shape details. Strictly speaking, you don't need any information in them to describe a material. However, some renderers still want to have them even they are only a flat color for consistency.

Baking

Texturing often requires another process called baking. Baking is a process that generates textures that contain different information about the geometry as follows:

Normal	Extract high-definition detail in tangent space; the rendering process will use this map to calculate the lighting and make the high-definition detail appear on the low-definition model as an illusion.
World Space Normal	Extract normal coordinates relative to a fixed frame in the object space.
ID	Identification map to quickly isolate areas on the model.
Ambient Occlusion	Becomes darker when the surface area is closer to other surfaces. Used to enhance detail.
Curvature	Extract a map that contains convexity/concavity information of the mesh.
Position	Extract the x, y, z world coordinates of all points at the surface of the mesh.
Thickness	Extract the thickness of the different parts of the model.

The effect of the maps can be more evident if we have a high-definition mesh with some sculpted detail on it. You can add sculpting details to a model using sculpting software. Currently, the best sculpting software is ZBrush. Although ZBrush is a powerful piece of software, it's beyond the scope of this book, so we won't be covering it. However, in the long term, if you plan to work in the game industry as a modeler, be sure you start working with this powerful piece of software.

For now, let's jump into texturing with Substance Painter where we will cover more essential aspects of texturing in the process.

Tutorial 3.1: Texturing Modular Pieces

> *Step 1: Set up a Maya project. Open our model file in Maya, go to File → Project Window, in the pop-up Project Window, click on the new button*

at the top row, and type in Game_Maya_Project. Click on the Folder icon in the second row to define a place to save our project, leave the rest as default, and click on Accept. Press Ctrl + Shift + S to save our file again, click on the scenes folder on the bottom left column of folders, and save our file there.

Why?

So far, we have been modeling with Maya with one single file. It is because model files are relatively small, and managing them in one file is tidy and straightforward. Another reason to have our models in one file is due to the scale of our game being small enough. At some point, we have to have more files for different models, characters, and rigs. When we are creating more and more assets and files, it is going to be harder and harder to trace stuff, so we need to have a way to manage our files. Step 1 creates a folder structure that contains subfolders for us to manage our files; we wouldn't need most of them. However, since we are doing textures, the sourceimages folder it creates is where we put our texturing file.

> *Step 2: Arrange our models. We are going to texture multiple assets in one file to help ensure consistency. However, to do that, we have to move them away to avoid overlapping models. Select all the modular pieces of our models, and press Ctrl + 1 to isolate them. Use the Move tool to arrange them so that similar pieces are put together but not overlapping each other (Figure 3.1).*
>
> *Step 3: Export models. Grab all the modular pieces, and go to File → Export Selection. In the pop-up Export Selection window, choose the sourceimages folder. Click on the yellow folder button at the top left corner of the window to create a new folder, and rename it to set_texturing. Go to the bottom of the window, type in modular_pieces in the file name, click the drop-down menu of the Files of type settings, and choose FBX export. Go to the right side of the window, and under the Options, check on the Smoothing Groups under the File Type Specific Options → Include → Geometry section.*

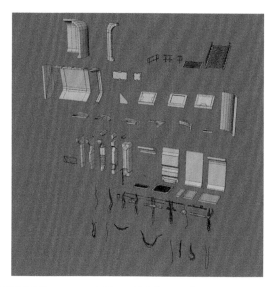

FIGURE 3.1 The arrangement of the models before exporting.

Click on the Export Selection at the lower right corner of the window to export the file.

Why?

What about the other models you may ask. Well, texturing files are, unfortunately, super big, and the performance is slow when there are so many models. We need to break our models into multiple texturing files.

Step 4: Import to Substance Painter. Open Substance Painter, and go to File → New. In the pop-up New Project window, set the Template to Unreal Engine 4. You can change this later upon output. Click on the Select button, find and select the modular_pieces file we export in Step 3, and press the Open button. Change the Document resolution to 2048, and press the OK button.

Why?

You may think, wait a minute, don't we require some of the models to have 4096×4096 (4k) textures? The answer is yes, but 4k is a heavy texture resolution for computers to handle. One of the superpowers of Substance Painter is the ability to upscale the resolution at any stage without losing any detail. It achieves that by remembering every stroke you did while painting your texture and upgrade them to 4k.

The Substance Painter UI

Substance Painter's UI is somewhat like Maya. As shown in Figure 3.2, the area in the red box is the menu where we load and change our models. The area in the yellow box is the Status Bar, which has generic controls like brush size, pressure sensitivity, symmetry, and perspective. The column of buttons in the purple box is the Tools bar. This bar has essential painting tools like paint, erase, project, and polygon fill. The viewport is in the middle area inside the blue box. It has a 3D viewport and a 2D viewport almost identical to our Maya UV Editing layout. The shelf is below the viewport in the cyan box. It contains brushes, alphas, grunge maps, materials, and other useful assets to help with texturing. Move to the right side. The brighter green box is the Texture Set List. You can see the names of the materials we created in Maya are listed here. Every material you created for the models in Maya ends up as a Texture set in the Texture Set List. You can

FIGURE 3.2 The UI of Substance Painter.

think of the Texture Set List as Maya's outliner. Substance Painter only cares about different materials and treat their associated models as different objects. The darker green box is the Layers. This is the area we go to a lot to stack multiple layers of textures together to get a final look. In the orange box is the PROPERTIES panel, which contains brush or layer-specific settings; things like tiling, channel toggles, alphas can be defined here. Finally, on the far right in the white box, we have the UI Panel. The UI panel lists all the panels that are not showing in the main UI. Click on the various buttons to pull out other hidden panels like Display Settings and Shader Settings.

Navigation

The navigation of the 3D viewport is the same as Maya; the navigation of the 2D viewport is the same as Maya's UV editor. You can press F2 to show only the 3D viewport, press F3 to show only the 2D viewport, or press F1 to show both.

Light Direction

To change the direction of the light, hold down Shift, and click and drag the right mouse button.

Step 5: Baking. Click on the TEXTURE SET SETTING tab on the left of the LAYERS tab. Find and click the Bake Mesh Maps button. In the Pop-up Baking window, set the Output Size under the Common parameters section to 4096, check on Use Low Poly Mesh as High Poly Mesh, and set the Antialiasing to Subsampling 8×8. Click on the Bake all texture sets button. Substance Painter now starts baking, and it may take a while. We set the output size of the texture to 4096 because it is the highest resolution we are after. The User Low Poly Mesh as High Poly Mesh setting makes the baker bake all mesh data from the mesh we imported to the mesh itself; this way, relevant mesh data like Curvature and Ambient Occlusion (AO) are generated. Antialiasing is crucial because it is going to reduce artifacts. It is also going to increase the

97

baking time. After baking, the model looks slightly different; its cavities or concave areas appear to be darker. The darker color is the result of the baked AO map, and it enhances the detail of the model.

Ambient Occlusion

Ambient Occlusion is a natural phenomenon. It is caused by the concaved surface or faces close to each other sucking the lights in. Lesser light rays can bounce out from these areas, which causes these areas to be darker. This phenomenon is almost like an acoustic Sound-absorption Panel will do to sound.

PBR Material Channels

Go to the TEXTURE SET LIST and click on floor_4k; this switches to the material of the floors, and notice that the 2D viewport switches to the UVs of the floors. You can also hold down Alt+Shift together and click on any model of the floor to switch to the floor. Press Alt+Q to toggle on isolation (press Alt+Q again to toggle off). Go to the LAYERS panel, click on the button with a tilted bucket icon, and you can see a new layer called Fill layer 1 got created above Layer 1. A fill layer is a layer that allows you to assign solid colors or textures to the model. Go to the PROPERTIES panel, and scroll down to the MATERIAL section. There are five buttons right under the MATERIAL section: color, height, rough, metal, and nrm. These five buttons are the toggle of the channels we mentioned in the PBR section of this chapter. For every layer, you can click on the buttons to toggle the channels on or off, which adds or removes that channel's effect from the layer.

The Base color defines the color of the model. You can change it to any color you want to test it.

The Height is how far the surface elevates. Height map is an illusion and is invisible unless there are some variations. Click on the Height uniform color button, in the search bar, and type in Metallic Grate wide; this should filter out others and only giving you the texture named Metallic Grate Wide. Click on Metallic Grate Wide to use it as our heightmap, and the patterns are now showing up on the surface of the model. We can assign textures like this to any channel we want. Change the direction of the light, and you can see how the height map reacts to the direction of the light, almost like there are actual height variations on the surface. If you zoom in and look at the model from a side angle, you can see that it is still a flat surface.

Roughness defines how rough the surface is: a higher value makes it rougher, while a lower value makes it smoother. Go ahead and drag the roughness slider to see the differences.

Metallic defines the metalness of the surface. In the natural world, surfaces are either full metal or not metallic at all. However, sometimes when a metal surface is covered with dust, we can use a middle value. Go ahead and drag the Metallic attribute to see the difference.

Normal map is like a height map but with more information about the directionality of the surface shape variation.

Right above the MATERIAL section, you can drag the Scale, Rotation, and Offset values to tweak the repetition, rotation, and offset of the applied textures.

> Step 6: Floor base material. Double click the name of the Fill layer 1 and type in Metal; this renames the layer to Metal. Set the base color of the layer to a dark grey. Click on the Roughness uniform color, in the pop-up menu, type Leak Dirty in the search bar on top, and choose the first one called Grunge Leak Dirty. Set the Metallic value to 1. We have just created a dark metal material with some variations on the roughness (Figure 3.3).

Why?

Notice that we only had variations on the roughness, and it can create fine details already. It is always worth noting

FIGURE 3.3 Basic dark metal material.

that roughness should never be overlooked. It is, in some sense, as important as the color, if not more important.

> *Step 7: Floor scratches. Create another fill layer, name it Scratches, and set the Roughness value to 0.25 and Metallic to 1. Because this layer is above the Metal layer, it is blocking the Metal layer. We want this layer to only appear on the sharp edges. Right click on the layer and choose Add black mask (this adds a mask to the layer). A mask with black color means completely see-through or transparent; that is why we are now seeing the Metal layer again. Right click on the black mask, and choose Add generator. Go to the PROPERTIES panel, click the Generator button, and choose Mask Editor. We can now see how the edges of the model are showing our scratches layer (Figure 3.4).*

Generators

Generators are an essential feature of Substance Painter. Generators generate colors based on the information and setting you give it. The most common usage of generators is to generate masks based on the baked mesh data to create things like edgewear or dust. We are going to cover more details of generators down the way.

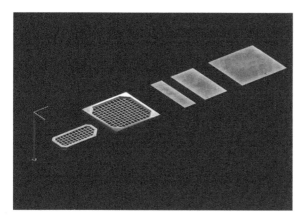

FIGURE 3.4 A new scratches layer.

Step 8: Tweak scratches. The Mask Editor is the essence of the procedural texturing workflow in Substance Painter; it is also the most commonly used generator. Click on the Mask Editor under the mask of the Scratch layer, and the PROPERTIES panel is now showing up all the settings it has. The settings may appear to be intimidating at first, but notice that there are just two sliders that are not 0: Global Balance and Curvature Opacity. Global balance is used to tune up or down the amount of opacity of the generated mask. Curvature is currently the only information used to generate the mask. Set the Global Balance to 0.6 and the Global Contrast to 0.2 to make the edge wear look stronger and slightly tighter.

Step 9: Add variation to the mask. Right click on the mask of the Scratches layer and select Add fill. Go to the PROPERTIES panel, click on the grayscale button on the bottom, search and choose Grunge Scratches Fine. Click on the Norm button on the right side of the Grunge Scratches Fine and choose Multiply. This setting is called the blending mode. Blending mode defines how to blend the current layer to the layers below it. The default blending mode is Normal, which blocks everything underneath. The Multiply blending mode multiplies the value of the current layer with the layer underneath as the result. This new layer adds subtle scratches to the mask, which makes it more detailed (Figure 3.5).

FIGURE 3.5 Add extra scratches to the scratches layer.

Tip and Tricks

We have created a decent dark metal material without drawing a stroke; this is called procedural texturing. Procedural texturing has two main drivers: layering and masks. With procedural texturing, not only can we get faster and cleaner results but also able to tweak any step of the process without having to redo other parts. Procedural workflow is also non-destructive because of that.

> Step 10: Create a Smart material. Hold down Shift, click on the metal layer and then the scratches layer, press Ctrl + G to group them into a folder, and rename the folder Dark Metal Scratched. You can click on the folder icon to expand or collapse the folder. Right click on the folder and select Create smart material. A smart material is now added to the shelf with the same name as the folder. You can see many other smart materials shipped with Substance Painter over there. A smart material is fundamentally a group or folder of layers. After creating our smart material, we can drag it from the shelf and add it anywhere we want. Delete our Dark Metal Scratched group in the LAYERS panel. Drag our Dark Metal Scratched smart material from the shelf above Layer 1 again. You can see that it just created the same thing.

Step 11: Top panels. Go to the SHELF, under the Smart materials section, look for Steel Painted Scraped Dirty, and drag it to the top of our layer stack in the LAYERS panel. Open the Steel Painted Scraped Dirty folder, and click on the layer named Paint to select it. In the PROPERTIES panel, click on the color bar under the Base Color, and a color pane pops out. Click and drag the three vertical sliders on the right to change the hue, saturation, and value (brightness) of the color. You can also click and drag anywhere in the color-gradient box on the right to pick a color there. Change its color to an orange color. This new material now covers almost all areas of our model.

Step 12: Paint height map. Create a new fill layer above the layer named Base Metal. Rename the new layer to OuterPanel. In the PROPERTIES panel, toggle off all channels except the height channel. Drag the slider of the Height setting up to 1. Give this layer a black mask. Right click on the black mask, and select Add paint. Go to SHELF. Click on the Brushes section, and click Basic Hard to use the Basic Hard brush. In the PROPERTIES panel, scroll down to the bottom and change the grayscale of the brush to white. Hold down Ctrl+right mouse button, and drag left and right to change the size of the brush. You can now try click and drag on the model to paint extra height (Figure 3.6).

Why?

We created a fill layer, make the value of its height 1, and use a mask to define where the height is. By doing so, we are now able to go back to the fill layer and change its height value to anything else. We could choose to create a new paint layer and define the height we want to paint in the brush settings, but then, it is harder to change the height value later.

Tips and Tricks

There are some basic shortcuts to tweak the brush. Hold down Ctrl+right mouse button, and go left and right to change the size of the brush. Hold down Ctrl+right mouse button, and go up and down to change the softness of

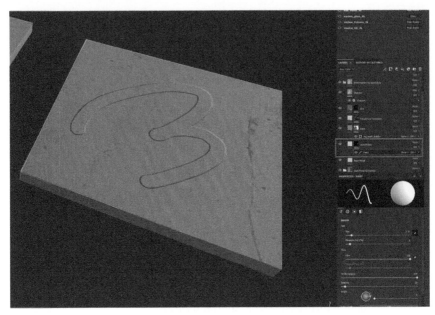

FIGURE 3.6 Test paint some height information on the model.

the brush. Hold down Shift+left mouse button, and go up and down to rotate the brush. Hold down Shift+left mouse button, and go left and right to change the opacity of the brush.

Step 13: Use the height as the mask of the outer panel. Right click on the mask of the OuterPanel layer, and select Add anchor point. Scroll up and find the group called Steel Painted Scraped Dirty (this is the group of the smart material we dragged in). Give the group a black mask. Right click on the mask, and select Add fill. In the PROPERTIES panel, click on the grayscale button, and under the ANCHOR POINTS tab, select OuterPanel Mask. What we should see now is that the orange outer panel should only appear in the area we painted the height (Figure 3.7).

Why?

Anchor points are references of a texture. Our Outer Panel Mask anchor point is a reference of the result of the layers

FIGURE 3.7 Using anchor point to share masks.

under it and inside the mask of the OuterPanel layer. The fill layer we added to the mask of the Steel Painted Scraped Dirty folder is using that anchor point. So, it is referencing the same mask we painted for the OuterPanel layer. That is why where we paint white for the mask of the OuterPanel, we also see the Steel Painted Scraped Dirty appear.

> Step 14: Set up symmetry. Press the L button to toggle on symmetry (you can also find it in the Status Bar, see what's toggled on after you press the L button). A Red plane shows up somewhere in the scene (you may have to zoom out to see it). Whatever you drew is going to be mirrored over to the other side of the plane. We want to draw the patterns symmetrically for the square floor piece on the right side. Press the Q button to toggle on the gizmo (blue handles to move the plane). Drag the blue arrows to the right to position the plane to the middle of the square floor piece (Figure 3.8).
>
> Step 15: Paint Panels. Press F6 to switch to the Orthographic view (you can also find the switch at the right side of the Status bar). The orthographic view has no perspective distortion,

FIGURE 3.8 Toggle symmetry and place it for the square floor piece.

which makes it perfect for painting precise shapes. Press the number 2 button to switch to the Eraser (it is also at the Tools bar). Click and drag to erase the painting we did earlier. Hold down Shift while changing the viewing angle to snape the viewing angle to a straight top view. Move the brush outside and below the shape of the Square floor piece and left click. Hold down Ctrl + Shift and move the brush up. A dashed line shows up from where we clicked to the current position of the brush; it also snaps every 5 degrees when you move the brush. Make sure that the dashed line is vertical and covers the entire floor piece and click again. A straight line is now drawn across the dashed line. Keep doing this until we have covered a good portion of the floor with a square panel (Figure 3.9).

FIGURE 3.9 Draw a square panel with precision.

Tips and Tricks

You may have to go up and down twice to draw a line all the way across. There are many ways we can fill a square. We use the Ctrl+Shift combination to help us draw straight lines. Once we have marked out the edge, how you fill in the middle is all up to you. You can switch to a bigger brush to free draw it to fill the gap.

> *Step 16: Paint extra panel Detail. Using Ctrl+Shift combination, we can quickly draw some extra detail to the panel (Figure 3.10).*

Tips and Tricks

There is no way you can position the mirror plane at the center of the floor accurately, but we can get close enough. We have to texture individual pieces in different substance files to have a perfect symmetry. However, it is hard to manage that way for our one-man-army approach, but if you have a team, then it is better to have them work on their files.

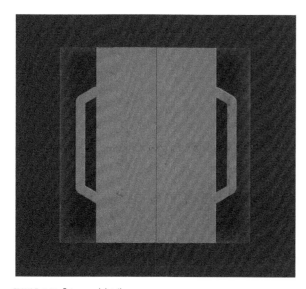

FIGURE 3.10 Extra panel detail.

Step 17: Anchor as micro detail. Our panel looks fine except that there is no edgewear (the scratches or other imperfections on the model). In the Default settings, only baked height and normal maps are used for finding edgewear. To include our painted height, go to the layer named Paint and click on its mask. Select mg_mask_builder. This mg_mask_build generates a mask that makes the edgeware appear on the edge of the model. It achieves that by using the baked normal and curvature maps. At the bottom of the PROPERTIES panel, click Micro Height and choose the anchor point we created for OuterPanel. The edgewear effect should now appear on the panel we painted (Figure 3.11).

Step 18: Use alphas. Go back to the Paint layer of the mask of the OuterPanel by clicking on it. Go to

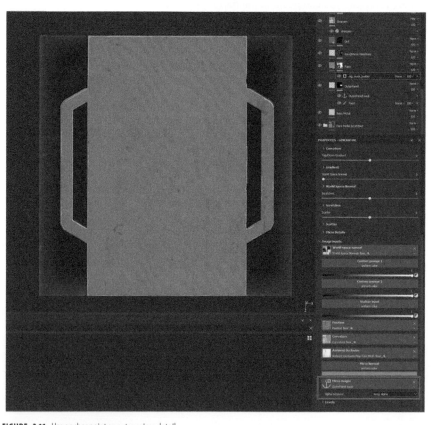

FIGURE 3.11 Use anchor point as extra micro detail.

SHELF and click on the Alphas section. Type in Shape Gradient in the search bar, and choose the first one in the search result. The shape of the brush is now the shape of the Shape Gradient alpha. Press the X button to invert the color of our brush. In our case, it changes from white to black. Hold down the Ctrl + left mouse button to go up or down to change the orientation of our brush. Hold down Ctrl + right mouse button to go left and right to change the size of the brush. To get accurate orientation, go to the Angle setting of the brush in the PROPERTIES panel, and hold down Shift while dragging the pin of the circular-shaped dial to snap to a certain angle. With an angle of 180 and black color, we can paint a cool ramp on the side of the panel (Figure 3.12).

Step 19: Try other alphas. There are many other alphas; try them out and see if you can create more breakups. Figure 3.13 shows the result of some new shapes added using alphas.

Step 20: Normal Detailing. Click on the button on the left of the button that we use to create fill layers to add a paint layer. While a fill layer only allows us to use a solid color or a texture, a paint layer is

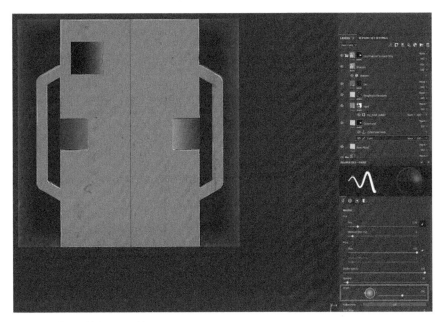

FIGURE 3.12 Ramp added using an alpha.

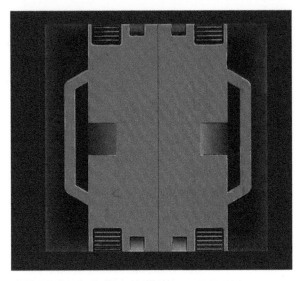

FIGURE 3.13 Extra details added with alphas.

a layer we can paint anything on. Name the new paint layer NormalDetail. In the PROPERTIES panel, turn off all channels but the nrm (normal) channel. Go to the Hard Surfaces section in the SHELF. Find Niche Rectangle Top Wide Rounded (you can search to find it or use other shapes if you don't like this one). Drag it from SHELF to the normal in the PROPERTIES panel. Click the X button on the Alpha of the brush to get rid of the alpha of the brush. We should now see that the normal shape appears on the brush fully. You can now click on the model to stamp that shape (Figure 3.14).

Tips and Tricks

Through height map and normal maps, we can add a whole lot of surface detail to the model; that is why we do not have to model too complicated shapes in Chapter 1. It is crucial to design your workflow with the tools at hand to determine the best way and best place to do certain things.

Step 21: Edgewear for the normal map detail. Right click on the NormalDetail layer, and choose Add anchor point. Go to the mg_mask_builder under the mask of the layer named Paint. In the

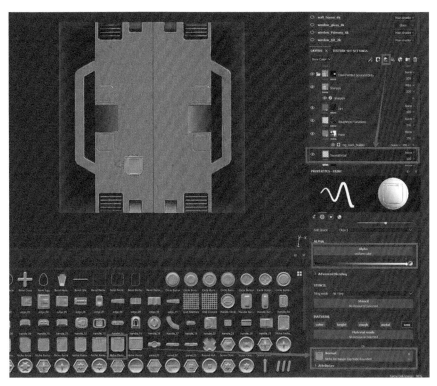

FIGURE 3.14 Stamp normal details to the model.

PROPERTIES panel, click on the Micro Normal, and in the ANCHOR POINTS tab, choose our NormalDetail anchor point. Set the Referenced channel to Normal, and this ensures that we are getting the normal information instead of the base color. The edgewear should now appear on the panels we painted with normal map. Scroll up to the Micro Details section in the PROPERTIES panel. Set the curvature Intensity down to 0.15 and Height Details Intensity to 10 to tighten up and sharpen our edgewear effect (Figure 3.15).

Step 22: Add more normal panel details. Please go ahead and try to use other normal maps in the Hard Surfaces section in the SHELF to add more detail to the model (Figure 3.16).

Step 23: Add cables. Create a new fill layer, drag it down to reposition it right above our Dark Metal Scratched group, and below our Steel Painted Scraped Dirty group. Rename the new fill layer

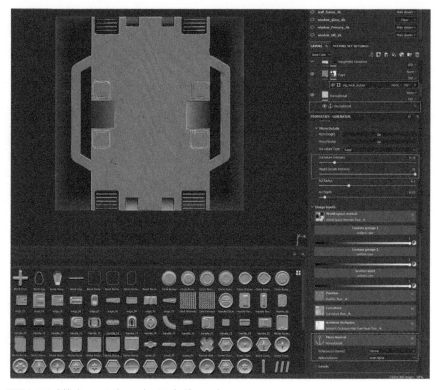

FIGURE 3.15 Add edgewear to the panels painted with normal.

Cables. Set the Base Color of the layer to a darker gray, and set the Roughness to 0.2 and Metallic to 1, set the Height value to 1. Give the layer a black mask and add a paint layer to the mask. Go to the Brushes section of the SHELF and choose Basic soft. You can now use the Ctrl + Shift button combination to draw straight lines to lay down some cables (Figure 3.17).

Step 24: Fix height blend mode. There is a problem of our blend mode of the height, and the height map of the cable we painted out is showing on the orange panel. To fix that, select Steel Painted Scraped Dirty, click on the drop-down list right below the label of the LAYERS panel, and change it to Height. We are now viewing and tweaking the height channel. Click the drop-down list on the right side of the Steel Painted Scraped Dirty layer, and change the setting to Normal. The blending mode of the height channel of

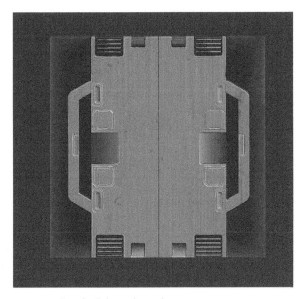

FIGURE 3.16 Extra details done with normal map.

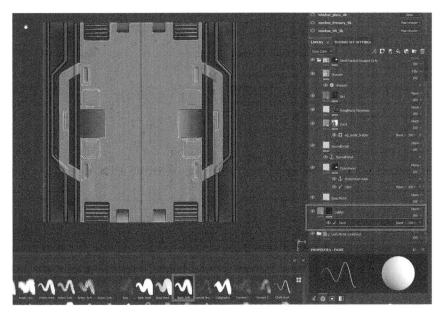

FIGURE 3.17 Paint out some cables.

this group is now normal, which blocks what is happening under it, and our orange panel should now block the cables (Figure 3.18).

Step 25: Extra layer of cables. Click on the number 100 on the right side of the paint layer of the mask of the Cables layer. Drag the slider down to 30; this makes it only 30% visible, or in other words, makes it weaker. Add another paint to the mask of Cables, and start drawing out new cables. The new cables should now be above the previous cables (Figure 3.19).

Step 26: Cable holders. Select Cables and press Ctrl+D to duplicate it. Rename the duplication CableHolders and make its Base Color slightly brighter and crank up the Roughness to 0.65. Right click on the mask of CableHolders and choose Clear mask, and this operation deletes the paint layers or other things in the mask. Add a new paint layer to the mask. Use the Basic Hard

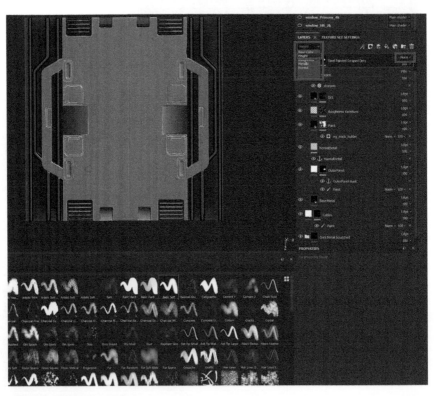

FIGURE 3.18 Height blend mode fixed.

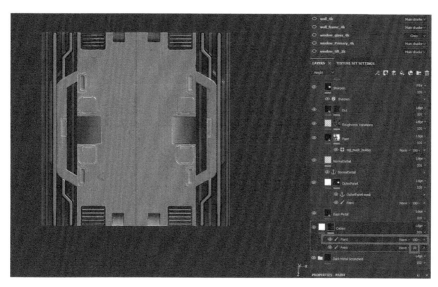

FIGURE 3.19 Extra layer of cable added.

> brush and paint some horizontal bands to mimic
> the holder for these cables. Press the X button to
> switch to black color, and click on the two sides of
> the cable holders to add two holes (Figure 3.20).

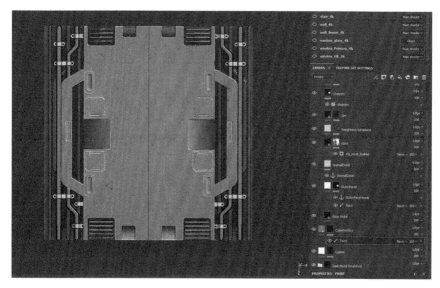

FIGURE 3.20 Added cable holders.

Tips and Tricks

We used a painted approach to get the cables, and it is fast and clean, but may not have the best shape. We could choose to model some cables instead, but it is going to be more cumbersome for the engine to handle. A different way to achieve this is to bake a normal map from a model that has cables modeled. To save time and reduce the volume of this book, we choose to omit that workflow.

Step 27: Paint other panels. Using the same technique, we can create many details already. Go back to the various layers we added and painted, and paint panel and cable details for our other two floor pieces. You do not need additional layers to do this. Figure 3.21 shows the result of the final design; the color of the panel was slightly changed.

Step 28: Limit the details to the top of the floors. Select all the layers except the Dark Metal Scratched and press Ctrl + G to group them. Name the new group Detailing. Give the group a black mask and add a paint layer to the mask. Press the number 4 button to switch to the Polygon Fill tool. The Polygon Fill tool allows us to select elements of the model to fill in colors. In the PROPERTIES panel, toggle on the square button of the Fill mode and set the color to 1. We can now click on any face of the model to fill that face to white color, and keep clicking until the details we painted all reappear on the top faces of the floor pieces. By doing this step, we have limited our painted details to the top faces.

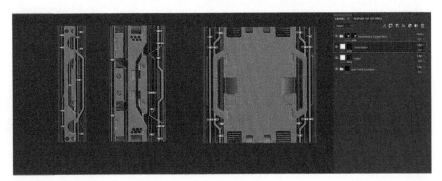

FIGURE 3.21 Paint the other two floor pieces.

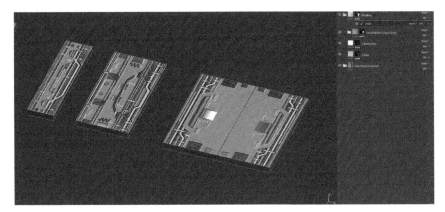

FIGURE 3.22 Limit the details to the top faces of the floors.

> *We have also got rid of the overshoot artifacts. Now, we have a clean edge cut right at the edge of the top faces (Figure 3.22).*

Tips and Tricks

The Polygon Fill tool is a clean way to define masks. There are four fill modes: Triangles, Quads, Objects, and UV shells, each represented by a triangle, a square, a cube, and a checker button. Switching to these modes allows you to click to fill these different elements with the color defined by the Color setting. For example, if you choose UV shell mode, change the color to black, click on any part of the model, and it is going to fill the UV shell that contains that part of the model to black color.

> Step 29: Create a smart material. Select all the layers and press Ctrl + G to group them and call it GameScifiPanels. Right click on the new group and select Create Smart Material.
>
> Step 30: Use the same material on the walls. Hold down Alt + Shift and click on any model of the walls to switch to the wall_4k texture set. Press Alt + Q to isolate it. Go to the Smart materials section of the SHELF, and search for our GameScifiPanel. Drag GameScifiPanels to the layers. We should now see the dark metal appears on the walls (Figure 3.23).

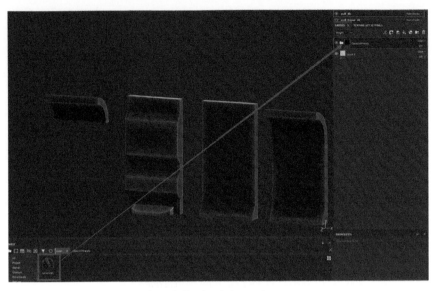

FIGURE 3.23 Drag the new smart material GameScifiPanels to the layer stack.

Why?

So, where are the orange panels? The answer is that they have no proper mask yet, neither do the cables. All Substance Painter remembers is that we painted something in the area of the floors, not on the walls; they are physically not at the same spot in the scene. Even if they were, the painting we did for the floor would not work for the walls. We have to repaint them for our wall models.

> Step 31: Paint wall Panels. Go to the various layers and paint the panels for our wall model, and don't forget that you can press the X button to switch to black color to cut the panels out. Make sure that you also try different alphas. We choose not to have cables on the walls, so we hid the layers of the cable. You can click on the eye-shaped icon in front of the layers to toggle their visibility (Figure 3.24).
>
> Step 32: Add extra panels to the walls. Add another fill layer on top of the OuterPanel. Name it ExtraPanel. Toggle off all the channels except the height channel, and set the height value

FIGURE 3.24 Paint the panels for the walls.

to 1. Add a black mask to the layer, and add a
paint layer to the mask. Switch to the Basic Hard
brush. Hold down Ctrl + right mouse button, and
drag down a little to make the brush softer. Start
painting some extra panels on top of the current
panels (Figure 3.25).

Step 33: Create edgewear for the extra panels. Right
click on the mask of the ExtraPanel layer and
select Add Anchor point. Go to the layer named
Paint, right click on it, and add a generator. Click
on the Generator button in the PROPERTIES
panel, and choose Curvature. Click the off button
after the Use Micro Details setting to toggle it
to On. Click the Micro Height button, and under
the ANCHOR POINTS tab, choose ExtraPanel
mask. We should now see orange colors appear

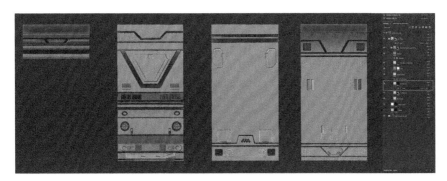

FIGURE 3.25 Add extra panels for the walls.

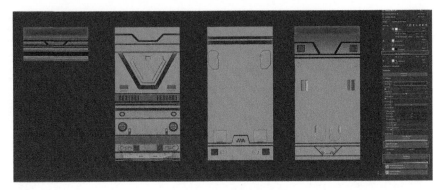

FIGURE 3.26 Extra Curvature generator to create edgewear for the extra panels.

only on the sharp ridges of the model and the height of the extra panels we painted. Toggle the Global Invert setting On. Go to the bottom of the PROPERTIES panel. Click on the X button of the Curvature map to unload it, and then drag the slider under it down to 0. Now the edgewear should appear only on the extra panels we painted (Figure 3.26).

Why?

We unloaded the curvature map because we do not want the baked curvature to affect the mask. We only want the painted height of the extra panel to have edgewear. Given the proper Micro Height, the Curvature generator is perfect for generating edgewear.

Step 34: Fix the blending mode of the Curvature layer. Notice that the only place we see edgewear is on the extra panel we created earlier. The effect of the new Curvature layer is blocking the Mask Builder layer under it. To get the edgewear, we set up earlier back. Simply change the blending mode of the Curvature layer to Multiply (Figure 3.27).

Step 35: Cables base material. Switch to the cables. Go to the Materials section of the SHELF, find, and drag the Iron Diamond Armor to the layers. In the PROPERTIES panel, drag the slider of the Scale setting all the way up to 128 to repeat the pattern more. In the LAYERS panel, set the channel to Height and set the opacity of the

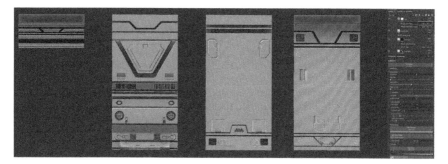

FIGURE 3.27 The result that shows all the edgewear for the panels.

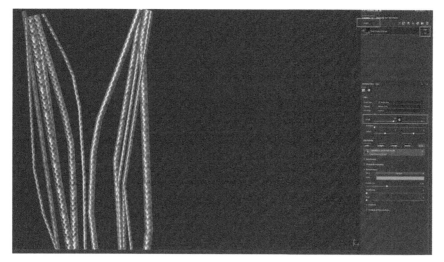

FIGURE 3.28 Base material for the cables.

height channel of the Iron Diamond Armor layer to 30 (Figure 3.28).

Why?

You may argue that using an existing material shipped with Substance Painter is not a good idea. After all, other people may use it too. We are not using it as it is, and we can combine multiple materials and get something unique enough.

121

Step 36: Add another variant. Add another fill layer to the layers, and name it straps. Change the blend mode of its height channel to Normal. Make the Base Color darker, lower down the Roughness to 0.2, and crank up the Metallic up to 0.7. Go to the Procedurals section of the SHELF. Find and drag Strips to the Height input of the fill layer in the PROPERTIES panel. Set the Scale to 16. It is too strong, but trying to lower down the opacity not only makes it weaker but also reviews the Iron Diamond Armor below it. Instead, right click on the Straps layer, and select Add levels. In the PROPERTIES panel, set the Affected channel to Height. Drag the black pin at the bottom of the graph to the right; the more you drag it to the right, the weaker the height becomes. Drag the black pin really close to the right side, so the height is weak enough (Figure 3.29).

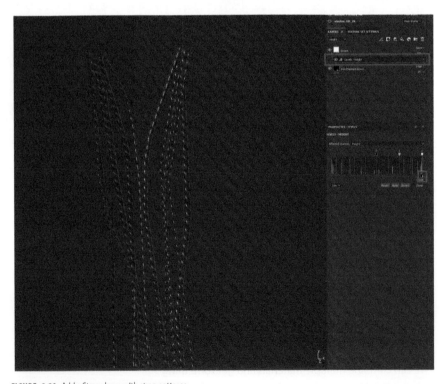

FIGURE 3.29 Add a Straps layer with strap patterns.

Levels

Levels is a typical color-adjusting tool. The graph of the levels shows the color distribution of the color from black (left side) to white (right side). There are three Pins on top of the graph. The black pin represents the total black color of the spectrum. The gray pin represents the mid-tone, and the white pin represents the total white color. Dragging them around clamps and shifts the color of the image. For example, drag the black pin to the middle, and any color darker than the mid-tone before becomes total black. Drag the gray pin anywhere, and the color of that point before becomes mid-tone. The two pins at the bottom of the graph remap the color again. The color that the black pin is pointing at become black. The color that the white pin is pointing at becomes white. The color outside the two pins becomes pure black and white, and the rest of the color is interpolated between these two pins.

> Step 37: Create random mask for the Straps layer. Give the Straps layer a black mask. Right click on the mask, and add a Generator; click on the Generator button under the PROPERTIES panel, and select UV Random color. Add a level above the UV Random Color, and drag the black and white pins at the top of the level to the middle. This setup makes half of the cables show our Straps, and the other half shows our Iron Diamond Armor. If you don't like the result, click on the UV Random Color and click the Random button of the Seed setting in the PROPERTIES panel to have a different result (Figure 3.30).

Why?

First of all, the UV Random Color generates a random color for each UV island. The Levels then tighten the colors up to either black or white. This way, half of the cables have a mask of white, and the other half have black.

> Step 38: Add carbon fiber band layer. Drag the Carbon Fiber material from the Materials section of the shelf to the top of the layers, and change

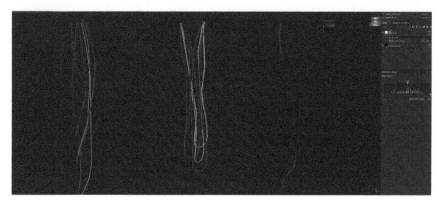

FIGURE 3.30 Create a random mask for the Straps layer.

its Scale setting to 128 to repeat the pattern more. Notice that the Carbon fiber has no height channel. We want to make it higher than the rest of the cables. Add another fill layer above it, toggle off all channels except the height channel of this new layer, name it CarbonFiberHeight, and set its height value to 1. Select both CarbonFiberHeight and Carbon Fiber. Press Ctrl + G to group them and name the group CarbonFiberWithHeight. Change the blending mode of CarbonFiberWithHeight to Normal. Give CarbonFiberWithHeight a black mask and add a paint layer to the mask.

Step 39: Paint the mask of the carbon fiber. Press F3 to go to the 2D view. Switch to the Basic Hard brush. In the PROPERTIES panel, set the Alignment setting to UV. Use the Ctrl + Shift button combination to draw a few straight lines across all the cables. Press F1 to see both the 3D and 2D views. We should now see bands get randomly placed on the cables. To make them more visible, click on the Carbon Fiber layer and set Color 1 and Color 2 to darker colors (Figure 3.31).

Step 40: Create material for the cable base and cable wrapper. For the cylindrical cable warper and the base, we can throw a Steel Gun Material at the top of the layer stack. Give the Steel Gun Matte group a black mask, and add a paint layer to it. Switch to the Poly Fill tool. Don't forget to change the color to white and change the fill mode to Objects this time (the button with the cube icon). Click on the two models to make the material show up on them (Figure 3.32).

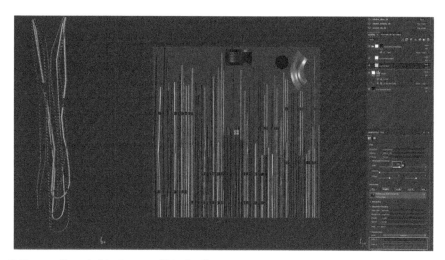

FIGURE 3.31 The result of the placements of the carbon fibers.

FIGURE 3.32 The material created for the cable base of the cable wrapper.

> *Step 41: Pipe Material. We can use the Steel Gun*
> *Painted also as the material of the pipes.*
> *Just switch to the pipes and drag the Steel*
> *Gun Painted smart material to the layers*
> *(Figure 3.33).*
> *Step 42: Glass Materials. Hold down Alt + Shift*
> *and click on one of the glass models to switch*
> *to the classes. Press Alt + Q to isolate them.*

FIGURE 3.33 Use Steel Gun Painted as the material for the pipes.

In the TEXTURE SET LIST panel, click on the Main shader drop-down list on the right side of the window_glass_4k texture set. Select Mew shader instance. The setting now shows as Main shader (Copy). Main shader (Copy) is a new shader. A shader is a collection of algorithms that calculate all the shading aspects of the 3D model. We need a new shader because the glass is fundamentally different— it has transparency. Click on the Sphere icon on the UI Panel to pull out the Shader Settings panel. Click on the PBR-metal-rough button, and change it to PBR-metal-rough-with-alpha-blending; this shader supports transparency. Change the Instance name to TransparentShader (Figure 3.34).

Step 43: Add Opacity channel. Go to the TEXTURE SET SETTINGS panel (on the right side of the LAYERS panel). Click on the + button on the right of the Channels setting, and choose Opacity (Figure 3.35). An opacity channel

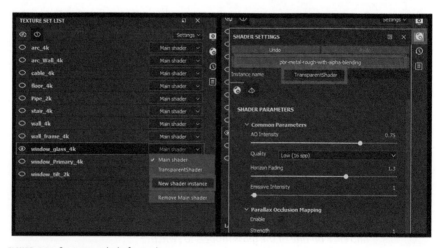

FIGURE 3.34 Create a new shader for our glasses.

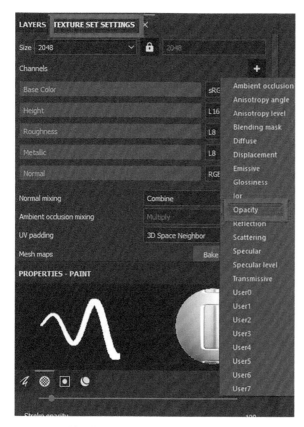

FIGURE 3.35 Add the Opacity channel.

is needed to feed opacity value to our TransparentShader.

Step 44: Create Glass Material. Go to the LAYERS panel and add a new fill layer. Name the new layer Glass. Under the MATERIAL section of the PROPERTIES panel, you can now see an extra channel called op. The op channel is the Opacity channel we added in Step 43. Set the Base Color of the fill layer to a mid-gray. Click on the Roughness button, search, and use Grunge Fingerprints Smeared as the Roughness input. Set the Opacity setting to 0.1 to make it more transparent. Glasses are generally no-metallic, so keep the Metallic setting 0 (Figure 3.36).

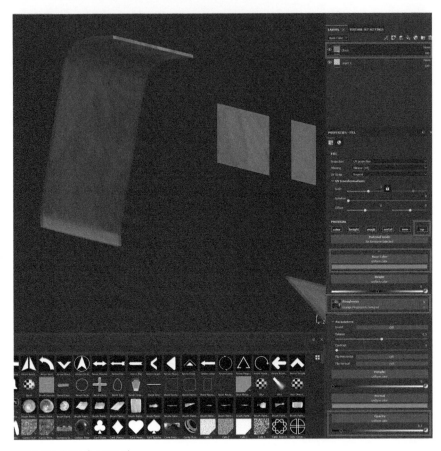

FIGURE 3.36 A new glass material.

Why?

We don't have too much stuff happening on this glass material. The shader of the game engine is going to be very different on stuff like transparency. We are going to define these attributes in the game engine when we create these materials.

> *Step 45: Create materials for all other modular pieces. We have covered enough techniques. It is now time for you to finish all the other materials. Figure 3.37 shows our result for the modular pieces, and Figure 3.38 shows a close-up shot of the textures of the stairs.*

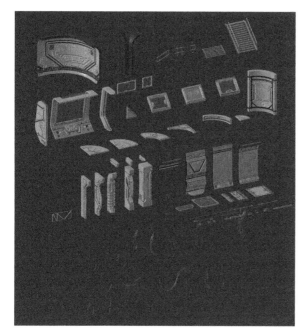

FIGURE 3.37 The texture result for the modular pieces.

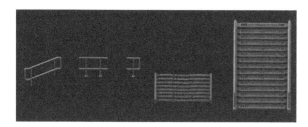

FIGURE 3.38 The close-up view of the stairs.

Assignment: Texturing the Rest of the Models

The way we texture the props and the hero asset is the same way we texture our modular piece. Figures 3.39–3.44 show the result of the textures we did. The only new thing here is that for the screens, we added an Emissive channel to the shader to allow emissive input

FIGURE 3.39 Screen capture of the textured screen assets.

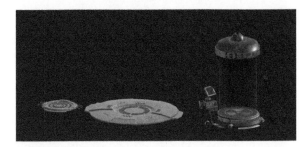

FIGURE 3.40 Screen capture of the textured pod.

FIGURE 3.41 Screen capture of the textured vents.

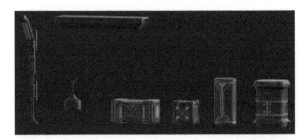

FIGURE 3.42 Screen capture of the crates and lights.

FIGURE 3.43 Screen capture of the textured grenade launcher and security camera.

FIGURE 3.44 Screen capture of the texture door and hero asset.

to make the screen a bright blue color. We end up with five substance files:

> *Modular_pieces_texturing.spp (Contains all of our modular pieces.)*
> *Props_texturing.spp. (Contains all the prop meshes that are not supposed to move in the game.)*
> *Security_camera_texturing.spp (Contains only the security camera.)*
> *Door_texturing.spp (Contains only the door.)*
> *Hero_asset_texturing (Contains only the hero asset.)*

There is no particular reason why we separate the camera, the door, and the hero asset other than some organization flaws we had during the production. You can have a completely different distribution. Please go ahead and have some fun texturing the rest of the models.

Conclusion

Texturing takes time, but it is more fun to do. However, it is not satisfying until we have our scene constructed.

We are now eager to move ahead and put our models to the game engine, set up the materials, and assemble our model to our impressive level.

In the next chapter, we are going to focus on importing and assembling our level in the game engine.

CHAPTER 4

Level Asset Creation

In this chapter, we are going to study the basics of Unreal Engine, create our game project, as well as importing assets, and create our materials. You may think that importing is just a click and drag operation, and it could be true in some scenarios. However, the nature of our modular workflow does need us to pay more attention to organization and consistency.

Keep in mind, though, whatever you do in this chapter cannot compensate for the flaws in your model. Please make sure that you check your models before moving on. We also have the files ready for you if you wish to move on with the models and textures we created. Also, it is not rare that we sometimes create new asset down the way if we think we need more. Making a game is not linear by nature. A professional team is going to have the modelers doing the models, while the animators are creating animations and the programmers implementing game mechanics. There are always discussions and decisions going on between teams or departments and files going back and forth.

Game Engines

Game engines are software built to make games. They have already built frameworks or modules for rendering Inputs, physics, AI, Networking, UI, VFX, and Audio. Game engines usually have an editor to build level and other content. They often support a set of programming languages for programmers to create game logic.

Unreal Engine

Unreal Engine 4 is going to be our engine of choice; it is among one of the first and best game engines. It is behind many of your favorite game titles: Fortnite, the Gears of War series, the Bioshock series, Player Unknown's Battlegrounds, Final Fantasy 7 remake, and the list goes on. As a game studio that keeps producing games of their own games, Epic Games always push the professionalism of Unreal Engine to the extreme. Unreal has a framework with feature-rich modules on all aspects of game production. Unreal offers an artist-friendly experience for content creators and gives professional programmers full access to its C++ source code.

Tutorial 4.1: Get Unreal Engine 4 and Visual Studio Up and Running

Step 1: Download and Install Epic Game Launcher. It takes minimal effort to get Unreal Engine downloaded. Open your web browser and visit https://www.unrealengine.com/.

Click on the blue DOWNLOAD button on the upper right corner. Click the Select button under Publishing License to get the installer downloaded (you may have to register for an account to get to the download). The web page may have changed by the time you read this book, so please find your own way to the download link if it is not the same as we described. After downloading, open the downloaded EpicInstaller to install Epic Game Launcher.

Step 2: Install the Unreal Engine. Open Epic Game Launcher and log in. Click the Unreal Engine on the list of sections on the left side column of the UI. Click on the Library tab up top. Press the yellow + sign after the ENGINE VERSIONS to add a new version. At the time we write this book, the engine version is 4.24.3. The version of Unreal Engine evolves super fast, so expect to see a much higher version on yours. Click on the Install button to install the engine. It is going to take a long time to install, so be patient (Figure 4.2).

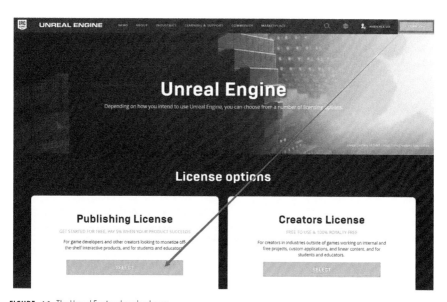

FIGURE 4.1 The Unreal Engine download page.

FIGURE 4.2 Install Unreal Engine using Epic Game Launcher.

Visual Studio

Visual Studio is an Integrated Development Environment (IDE) for programming, or in plain text, it is a fancy text editor in which we write our code. IDE has extra features like debugging and Intellisense. We are going to need Visual Studio at some point when we are building the game. It is better to have it ready when we start our Unreal Engine project.

Step 3: Install Visual Studio. Visit https://visualstudio. microsoft.com/vs/community/ and click on the purple Download Visual Studio button to download the installer. Run the installer and follow the steps until you got to a dialog box like Figure 4.3.

All you have to do here is to check on Game development with C++. And press the Install button at the bottom right corner. The installation is also going to take a long time. Please do not move on until Unreal Engine and Visual Studio are both installed.

Step 4: Create your Unreal game project. Click the yellow Launch button at the top right corner of the Epic Game Launcher to launch Unreal Engine. After loading, in the floating Unreal Project Brower, choose Games under the New Project Categories section and press the green next button. Select the First Person template because we are doing an FPS game. For anyone who wants to do a third person, please choose the Third Person Template. The coding later should be mostly the same. Press the Next button. Click on the With Starter Content and change it to No Starter Content. At the bottom,

FIGURE 4.3 Visual Studio Installation Workloads settings.

FIGURE 4.4 The Settings for creating your Unreal project.

click the button with the ellipsis and choose a folder to create our project. Type the name you want for the project. TheEscaper is the chosen name for our game, but you can go for anything else you like. Click the Create Project button to finish (Figure 4.4).

UI of the Unreal Editor

Unreal now start to create the project for us; when it finished the setup, the Unreal Editor will show up. The UI of the Unreal Editor is similar to that of Substance Painter. On the very top row, we have the Menu, where you can

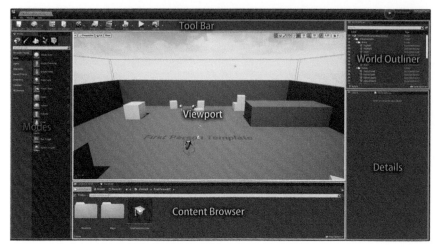

FIGURE 4.5 The Unreal Editor.

find common commands like save the level, showing UI elements, and preferences. As marked in Figure 4.5, the panel in the red box is the Modes panel. The Modes panel contains universal engine assets like lights, player start, primitive models, terrain, and various volumes. You can also find tools for editing terrain, vertex painting in the Modes panel. The Yellow box is the viewport; it shows our current level. The panel in the cyan box is the Content Browser; all assets we created or imported for our game are in here. The panel in the blue box is the World Outliner; this one is the same as the Outliner of Maya; all objects we put in the level are in this list. The panel in the orange box is the Details panel. The Details panel shows the settings for any objects we are selecting. Notice that there is another tab on the right side of the Details panel called World Settings. The World Settings panel shows settings associated with the current opening level.

Navigation

To Navigate the viewport, hold down the right mouse button and then use the W, A, S, D buttons to move around. Hold down the right mouse button and move the mouse to look around. Alternatively, you can also hold the Alt key down and Left, Middle, and Right-mouse drag similar to Maya (although the middle mouse drag is inverted to Maya's).

> Step 5: Test run the game. To Test run our game in the editor, just press the Play button in the Toolbar. The template has an FPS character in the level holding a gun. We are now possessing (or controlling) this character. You can use the typical W, A, S, D buttons to move around the level, left click to shoot and space button to jump.
>
> Step 6: Test build the game. Press the Esc button to get out of play mode. Go click on File → Package Project → Windows → Windows (64 bit). In the pop-up Package project window, navigate to the folder you choose for the project. Create a new folder there and name it Publish. Double click the Publish folder and click the Select Folder button. UE4 makes a high-pitch sci-fi sound, and a packaging notification appears at the bottom right corner. Give it a few moments until it says: Packaging complete. Open the publish folder, and you can see a folder with the name WindowsNoEditor; this is the game we have packaged. Open this folder and double click TheEscaper.exe to run our game.

So far, the game has no UI at all. We are just a robot holding a gun and shooting yellow balls. However, it is pretty exciting to have something built and working. Press the ` button (the button below the Esc button) to pull out the console and type in exit to quit the game.

Let's move on to get our asset into Unreal Engine.

Tutorial 4.2: Export Our Assets to Unreal and Build Our Material

> Step 1: Prepare our models. Open our Maya file that contains all our models. If you are using the file we provided, it is called Set_Model.mb. This file is also the file we used to export our model to Substance Painter. It has all our models. Figure 4.6 shows the Outliner of this file.
>> We have also moved our models away from each other for texturing. It is now the time to move them back to the origin.

FIGURE 4.6 The Outliner of our model file.

Select the All group in the Outliner. Go to the main menu and do a Select → Hierarchy command. All models are now in our selection, go to the Chanel Box, and set the Translate and Rotate values to 0 and Scale values to 1. All the models should now back to the origin (Figure 4.7). If some of them are still not back to the origin, select them, and do a Modify → Bake Pivot. Zero out their translation and Rotation again.

Step 2: Export our models. We are going to try to organize our files systematically. Instead of exporting all the models together as one file, we are going to export every group separately. We plan to create a folder in Unreal Engine for each group we have in Maya. Select the floors group. Go to File → Export Selection. In the pop-up Export Selection window, navigate to the folder that we created for our game project. Create a new folder called Assets and create a floors folder

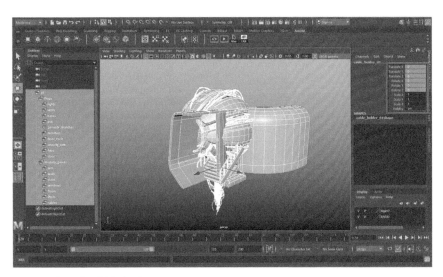

FIGURE 4.7 Move all models back to the origin.

inside of it. Set the Files of type to FBX export. Under the Options listed on the right side of the window, Open the Geometry section. Make sure that the Smoothing Groups and Triangulate are on and others are off. If the Animation is on, check if it is off too. Type in floors for the file name and hit the Export Selection button (Figure 4.8).

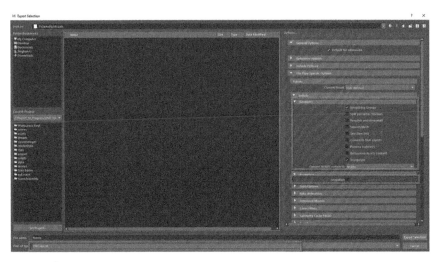

FIGURE 4.8 Export settings.

Step 3: Export all other models. Using the same method in Step 2, we can export all other models (Figure 4.9). Notice that we do not separate the Props and modular_pieces.

Step 4: Export Textures. Open our modular_pieces_texturing.spp file with Substance Painter. Hold down Alt + Shift and click on any part of the floor model to select the floor texture set. Go to File → Export Textures. In the pop-up Export document window, click on the long button that shows a directory right below the label of the Export tab. A file explorer pops out for you to choose a place to export the textures. Navigate to the floors folder we created for exporting our floor model. Set the texture format from png to targa. Set the Config to Unreal Engine 4 (Packed). In the Texture sets list, check off everything but floor_4k. Because we demand it to use a 4k texture, set the resolution on the right side of the foor_4k texture to 4096 × 4096. Uncheck the Export shaders parameters at the lower right corner. Press the export button to export the textures (Figure 4.10).

Step 5: Export the textures for the rest of the models. Please spend some time to export all other

FIGURE 4.9 Folders that have all groups in Maya exported separately.

FIGURE 4.10 Export settings for the floor textures.

> textures. Be aware that some of the models may
> have multiple texture sets, like the model of the
> hero asset. Put these textures to the hero folder
> altogether.

Why?

We spend a lot of time trying to organize our files. It
may seem redundant to do all these folders and naming
everything, but it is going to make our life much easier
later on. Imagine that you need to tweak the model of the
floors. You do not want to have to re-export everything
again. It is also easier to delete the floors by just deleting
the floor folder.

> Step 6: Import the floor to Unreal Engine. Go to our
> Unreal Editor. Right click on the Content folder
> in the content browser and select New Folder.
> Type StaticMeshes to rename the new folder
> to StaticMeshes. Double click to go inside the
> folder. Open a windows file browser and find our
> Assets folder that has all our folders of meshes
> and textures. Drag the floor folder from our file

browser to the content browser of Unreal Engine (Figure 4.11).

Unreal pulls out the FBX import Options. We just need to use the default settings for our static meshes and press the Import All button to import all the assets. We now got our floor models with a material called floor_4k and three textures imported. Notice that unreal also created a floor folder for us because we dragged in a folder (Figure 4.12). Press Ctrl+A to select them all and press Ctrl+S to save them.

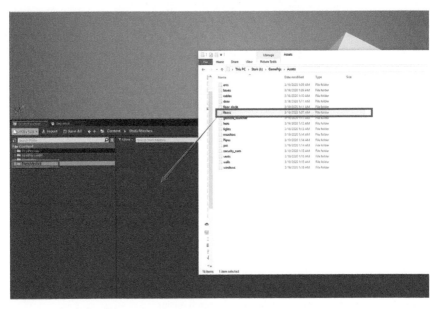

FIGURE 4.11 Drag the floor folder into the content browser.

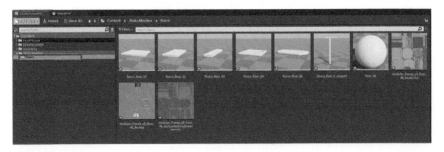

FIGURE 4.12 Imported floor assets.

Tips and Tricks

When an asset is imported to Unreal Engine, they are categorized into different types. The narrow color bar at the bottom of each asset shows their type. The assets with cyan color are static meshes. A mesh is the same as a polygon in our context. Static meshes are meshes without the ability to deform (or change shape). If you go to the Content → Character → Mesh folder, you can see a file with a pink bar called SK_Mannequin_Arms, and this asset is a skeletal mesh. A skeletal mesh has a skeleton under it that can control its movement, almost like how real-life creatures have bones. The process of setting up skeletons for a mesh is called rigging. We are going to cover rigging later when we are making our own player and NPC characters. Back to the floor folder, the one with the green bar named floor_4k is the Material of the floors. The other three are textures. Textures have a red bar.

The Material Editor

Double click the floor_4k Material to pull out the Material Editor. The Material Editor is where we can construct our materials. Hold down the right mouse button and drag to move around the graph. There are two Squares in the graph, and they might be overlapping each other; you can use the left mouse button to drag them away from each other. Each node contains either some data or do some operations.

The floor_4k node is the final output of the Material; it has similar attributes we see in Substance Painter like Base Color, Metallic, Roughness, and Normal. The Param node is a color node, and it contains a solid color. The dots on the left side of a node are its input pins, and the dots on the right side of a node are its output pins. There is a line connecting from the white output pin of the Param node to the Base color input pin of the floor_4k node. Lines like this are called connections. This particular connection means that the color of the Param node is passing to the Base Color of the Material. There is a Details panel at the lower-left corner of the Material Editor. Select the Param

FIGURE 4.13 Change the color of the Material in the Material Editor.

node, and the settings of this node appear in the Details panel (Don't confuse this Details panel with the Details panel of the main UI). Double click the gray bar of the Default Value setting in the Details panel to pull out the color wheel. Click and drag on the color wheel to select any color and press ok. The Material now should appear to be in the color we have picked (Figure 4.13).

Color R, G, B, A Channels

There are more output pins on the left side of the Param node. The red, green, and blue pins are the red, blue, and green channels of the node. Any color on a screen is a specific combination of red, green, and blue colors; combine them in different proportions, and you get a different color. The red pin outputs how much red color is used to create this color. The white pin at the very bottom is the alpha channel, a fancy name for a channel that represents the transparency of the color. These four

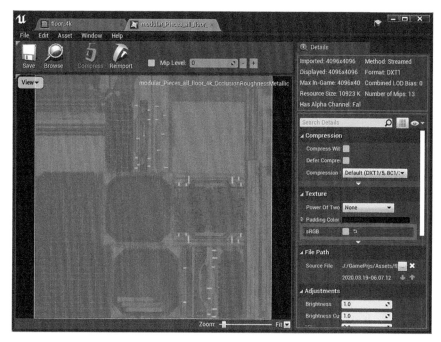

FIGURE 4.14 Uncheck the sRGB for the OcculsionRoughnessMetallic texture.

channels are known as R, G, B, A channels of color. You can also adjust them numerically below the Default Value in the Details panel. These values are ranging from 0 to 1. The value of the A channel is 0, which means that it is not transparent at all.

> *Step 7: Set up the OcclusionRoughnessMetallic textures. Double click on the texture with OcclusionRoughnessMetallic at the end of its name to open the Texture Editor. Un-check the sRGB under the Texture section in the Details panel and press Ctrl+S to save it (Figure 4.14).*

Why?

The sRGB setting is on for all textures that represent a color. What sRGB does is remapping the color to make it more suitable for our monitor; however, it does alter the original information. The reason we checked off the sRGB of the OcclusionRoughnessMetallic texture is that it does not represent a color. The R channel represents the Ambient Occlusion, G channel represents Roughness, and the B channel represents Metallic. Applying sRGB to these channels alters the Ambient Occlusion, Roughness, and Metallic values, which is not what we want.

> *Step 8: Set up the Material. Go back to the floor_4k. Hold down Shift and select all three textures we imported in the Content Browser and drag them to the Material Editor. The Material Editor creates three Texture Sample nodes to read the three textures. Drag them away from each other, so they are not overlapping. Click and drag the RGB output pin of the Texture Sample that reads our base color texture to the Base Color input pin of the floor_4k node. The color should appear on the ball inside of the viewport at the upper left corner of the Material Editor. The Texture Sample node that reads the blue texture reads our normal map, drag its RGB output pin, and connect it to the Normal input pin of the floor_4k node. The last Texture Sample node is reading the OcclusionRoughnessMetallic texture. Drag its R, G, B, output pins to the Ambient Occlusion, Roughness, and Metallic input pin of the 4k node (Figure 4.15). Press the Save button on the upper left corner of the Material Editor to save our changes.*

Close the Material Editor. We can see all of our models now updated with textures. If they are not showing the correct textures, select them all and right click on them to force an update. Drag the floors_floor_01 to the viewport. Press the F button to focus on it. Press the W button to invoke the Move Tool and drag it up so we can see it (Figure 4.16).

Tips and Tricks

The Move, Rotate, and Scale tools have the same shortcut as Maya. They work the same way as Maya also.

> *Step 9: Create the master material instance. Right click on the StaticMeshes folder and select New Folder. Name the new folder Shared. Go back*

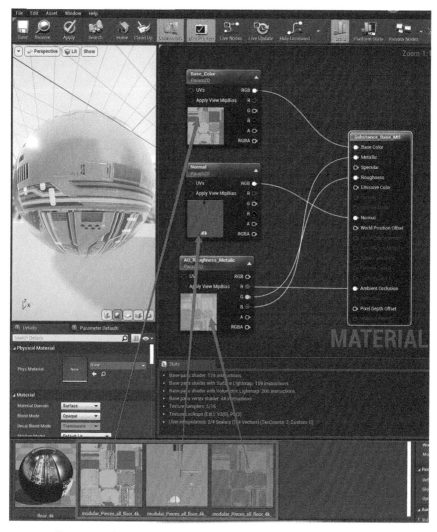

FIGURE 4.15 The connections for our Material.

to the floors folder, select floor_4k, and press F2
to rename it to Substance_Base_Mtl. Drag the
Substance_Base_Mtl to the Shared folder and
select Move Here. Double click on the Shared
folder and you can see our Substance_Base_Mtl
located in it. Right click on Substance_Base_Mtl,
select Create Material Instance, and press the
Enter button to commit the default name. You

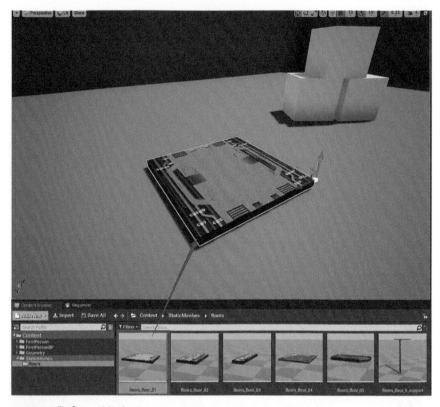

FIGURE 4.16 The floor model in the viewport.

FIGURE 4.17 Create a Shared folder and make a material instance out of the Substance Base Material.

are probably wondering what we are doing here. Keep following the steps, and you will see the reasons later (Figure 4.17).

Material Instance

Material Instances can be used just like materials. Material Instance does not need recompilation when you make changes. Material Instance has only settings you exposed through parameters in the parent material (we are going to cover how to do this part later).

> Step 10: Create a material instance for the floors. Right click on the Substance_Base_Mtl_Inst and select Create Material Instance. Name the new material instance floor_4k, drag it to the floor folder, and select Move Here. Open all the floor models and set their Element 0 material under the Material Slots section in the Details panel to our new floor_4k. You can drag the floor_4k Material from the content browser to the Element 0 slot of the model's asset editor to assign it (Figure 4.18).

FIGURE 4.18 Assign floor_4k material instance to the models.

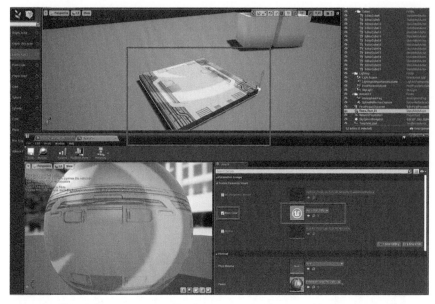

FIGURE 4.19 Change the Base_Color parameter of the floor.material changes the texture of the floor model right away.

Step 11: Convert texture samples to parameters. Go back to the shared folder and double click to open the Substance_Base_Mtl. Right click on the Texture Sample for our base color and select Convert to Parameter. Change the Parameter Name under the General section of the Details panel to Base_Color. Do the same thing for the other two Texture Samples, and name the one that reads our normal map Normal and the other one AO_Roughness_Metallic. Open our floor_4k material instance again. The three parameters have now appeared as grayed out texture slots. You can click on the checker box in front of these texture parameters to toggle them on. You can now change the base color to something else and see it update to the models right away (Figure 4.19).

Why?

The reason we chose to use material instances is to avoid having to set up the same thing again and again for different models. Because they all use three textures, we can easily create new material instances for all other models and only change the three texture parameters.

> Step 12: Import other models. Press Ctrl+Z a few times until the Base_Color of the floor_4k material instance is checked off. Double click on the StaticMeshes folder in the Content Browser to get inside of it. Open a Windows file explorer and go to our Assets folder again. This time, select all the folders except our floor folder (we got them imported already). Drag all these folders to the content browser with one go. In the pop-up FBX Import Options, set the Material Import Method under the Materials Section to Create New Instanced Materials. Click on the drop-down of the Base Material Name setting and select Substance_Base_Mtl_Inst. Press Import all to import the rest of the models and textures (Figure 4.20). Unreal gives us the same folder structure.
>
> Step 13: Fix sRGB settings for the OcclusionRoughnessMetallic textures. Click on the StaticMeshes folder, under the filters of the Content Browser, and search for OcclusionRoughnessMetallic. All textures that have OcclusionRoughnessMetallic in their name are now listed. Hold down Shift and click on the first one, and then the last one to select them all. Right click on any one of them and select Asset Actions → Bulk Edit via Property Matrix. In the

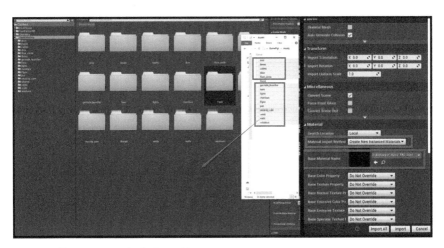

FIGURE 4.20 The import settings for all other models.

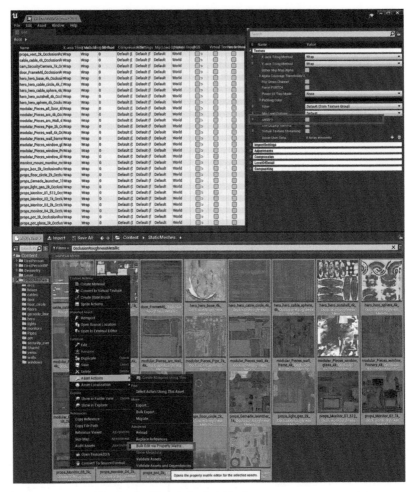

FIGURE 4.21 Check off the sRGB setting for all OcclusionRoughnessMetallic textures.

pop-up asset editor, hold down Shift and select everything in the list, and check off their sRGB setting (Figure 4.21).

Tips and Tricks

At any time, if you want to change settings of multiple assets, you can do it using the Bulk Edit via Property Matrix command.

FIGURE 4.22 Assign the corresponding textures to the material instances.

Step 14: Assign correct textures for other models. Go to any of the new folders added to the Content Browser. We can now see the models, textures, and material instances that have Substance_ Base_Mtl_Inst as their parent. Double click to open these material instances, check on all three texture parameters, and assign their corresponding textures (Figure 4.22). Go ahead and finish assigning all the textures to all the material instances. After assigning the textures, press the Save All button on the top row of the Content Browser to save out all of our models and drag a few models to the viewport to take a look (Figure 4.23).

Why?

You are probably trying to get your head around on this Material, material instance mix. First of all, it is not necessarily to be the only way. You could just create new materials for every model. But there are merits of doing it using instances. First of all, as you can already tell, material instances are faster. Second, this hierarchy can help us to make global changes. Figure 4.24 shows the hierarchy

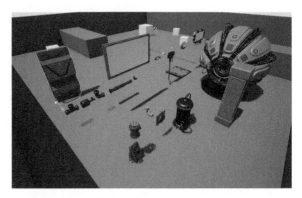

FIGURE 4.23 A few models dragged into the viewport.

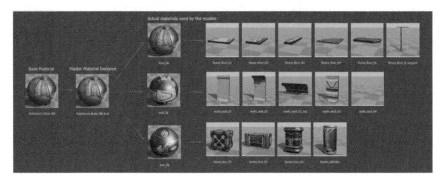

FIGURE 4.24 The hierarchy of the materials.

of the materials and material instances we have created. There is a base material called Substance_Base_Mtl. Substance_Base_Mtl defines how textures are connecting to the channel of the Material. We created a material instance of the Substance_Base_Mtl called Substance_Base_Mtl_Inst. Every other materials we use on the models are instances of this Substance_Base_Mtl_Inst. We need the Substance_Base_Mtl_Inst to help us to do global tweaks if needed. For example, if all the models appear to be too shiny, we could tweak the Substance_Base_Mtl_Inst to make them all rougher with one go. You are going to see how to set up controls for roughness and many other attributes of the material instances later.

Now we have all of our assets imported and materials created. We can move on to build our level already. But before we rush forward, let's build a testing hallway and see how our materials behave with lighting and tweak them if needed.

Tutorial 4.3: Set up a Test Hallway

Step 1: Create a new Level. Create a new folder under the Content folder of the Content Browser and name it Level. Go to File → New Level. In the pop-up New Level window, select Default. We do not need to save the current template level, so press Don't save. Once the new level is loaded, press Ctrl + S and save it in our Level folder and name it Test_Level.

Step 2: Set up snapping. Go to Edit → Editor Preferences. Click on the viewports section on the list on the left side of the Editor Preferences window. Under the Grid Snapping section in the right side of the window, check on Use Power of Two Snap Size (Figure 4.25).

Why?

We have built the entire sizes of our assets based on the binary system. Their sizes are all power of two sizes. We switch on Use Power of Two Snap Size so our model can snap together nicely.

FIGURE 4.25 Check on Use Power of Two Snap Size.

Step 3: Set snap sizes. On the top right corner of the viewport, there is a row of viewport quick settings. Click on the number 4 on the right side of the grid icon and choose 16. The number 16 means we are snapping every 16 unity when we are moving things around. We chose 16 because this number is the smallest size of our modular models (Figure 4.26).

Step 4: Build a simple hallway floor segment. Delete the floor model in the level. Go to the floors folder in the Content Browser. Drag floors_floor_01 to the level. In the Details panel, set the Locations X, Y, and Z to 0 to move it to the origin. Press W to go to the Move tool. Hold down Alt and drag the floor model on the X direction (the red arrow). A copy of the floor got created and moved out. Keep dragging until its edge aligns with the original one (Figure 4.27).

Step 5: Add two more half floors on the side. Drag the floors_floor_02 to the viewport and move the cursor close to the already existing floor pieces

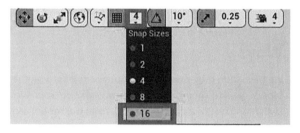

FIGURE 4.26 Set the Snap size to 16.

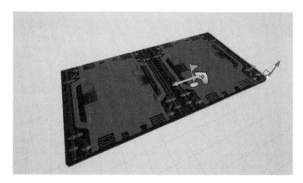

FIGURE 4.27 Create two aligned floor pieces.

so it can be placed close to them. Move the new half-sized floor piece until it snaps to the side of one of the square floor pieces. Hold down Alt and drag it to the other side. Rotate it 180 degrees (the rotating tool has a 10-degree snapping default setup) and move it again until it snaps (Figure 4.28).

Step 6: Build the walls. Go to the walls folder and drag walls_wall_03 on top of the floors on the side. Rotate and move it, so it snaps to the side of the floor. Hold down Alt and drag to have a copy and snap it to the other side (Figure 4.29).

FIGURE 4.28 Add two more half floors on the side.

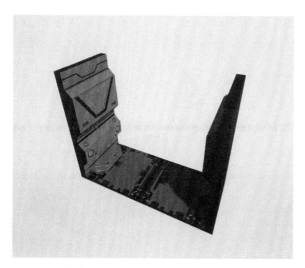

FIGURE 4.29 Add the walls.

Step 7: Duplicate the floors and walls. Hold down Shift and select all the models we dragged in. Hold down Alt and drag to have a copy of them and snap them until we got another section snapped perfectly to the original one (Figure 4.30).

Step 8: Add wall frames. Drag the walls_wall_frame_02 to the level. Snap it so it is aligned to the outer edge of the width of the hallway and half embedded in the wall. Drag a copy and align it to the other side (Figure 4.31).

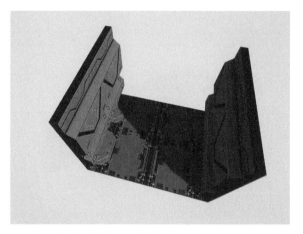

FIGURE 4.30 Duplicate the floors and walls.

FIGURE 4.31 Place the wall frames.

Why?

Why do we embed the wall frame only halfway? Well, when we duplicated it, the other half is going to be embedded in the duplicated walls.

> *Step 9: Add a few pipes. Drag a few pipes and pipe parts to the concave areas of the walls. This part is flexible, and you can create something completely different (Figure 4.32).*
>
> *Step 10: Add ceiling. Select all the floor pieces. Hold down Alt and drag them up until the copies snap to the top of the walls. We did not create ceiling pieces, so these floors also have to be our ceilings. Fortunately, their bottom is using a different material so that they do look different (Figure 4.33).*
>
> *Step 11: Select all pieces and Group them. Go to the World Outliner, and click on the Type button to sort the assets in the level by type. All the meshes should now be listed together. Click on the first model, hold down Shift, and click on the last one to select them all. Press Ctrl + G to group them into a group.*

Tips and Tricks

Grouping in Unreal Engine is not the same as Maya, and it does not put them into a folder, but rather just remembers that they are now "glued" together. The advantage here

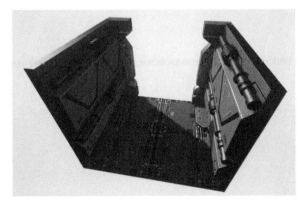

FIGURE 4.32 Add a few pipes.

FIGURE 4.33 Copy the floors to create the ceiling.

is that you can quickly click to select them all. But if you want to move one of the models in the group, you have to ungroup them (Shift+G).

> *Step 12: Duplicate the groups. Hold down Alt and drag the group to have a copy. Drag the copy away until it snaps to the original group. Drag out three more copies to create a hallway (Figure 4.34).*

FIGURE 4.34 Create the hall way by copying the group.

Step 13: Drag in the door. Go to the door folder.
Select all the static meshes and drag them into
the level. Position the door at the center of the
end of the hallway (Figure 4.35).

Step 14: Drag in more walls to block the side of the
doors (Figure 4.36).

Step 15: Drag two sets of windows above the
door. Go to the windows folder. Select
both the windows_window_01 and

FIGURE 4.35 Put a door at the end of the hallway.

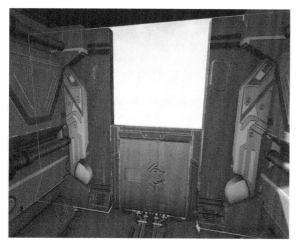

FIGURE 4.36 More walls to block the side of the door.

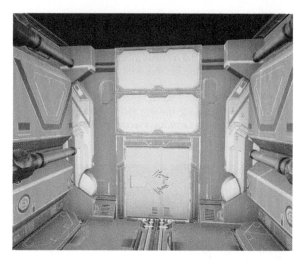

FIGURE 4.37 Use two windows to fill the gap above the door.

windows_window_01_glass, drag them to the level, and position them above the door. Hold down Alt and drag up to have another copy of the window. The two windows should be able to fill in the gap above the door (Figure 4.37).

Now we have built our hallway. We can immediately see that the lighting is flat. If there is no light in the hallway, it should appear to be much darker than it looks. You can also see a warning says: LIGHTING NEEDS TO BE REBUILT (199 unbuilt objects) on the upper left corner of the viewport. Go to the Toolbar, click on the drop-down arrow on the right of the Build button, and click Build Lighting Only. The shortcut of it is Ctrl + Shift +; (Figure 4.38).

Unreal now starts to build the lighting for the level. The building progress is displayed at the lower right of the window. Once Unreal finishes building the lights, it applies the results to the models, and our hallway is now looking extremely dark (Figure 4.39).

Why?

So what does Build Lighting do? Well, calculating lights in realtime is too heavy for current hardware. So, the lighting

FIGURE 4.38 Click the Build Lighting Only button.

FIGURE 4.39 THE DARK RESULT AFTER BUILDING THE LIGHT.

for anything that is not moving during gameplay is pre-rendered and applied to the model. This pre-rendering process is called light building.

Let's drag in some lights.

Step 16: Create some point lights. Go to the Mode panel. Click on the Lights section, drag a point light to the hallway, and place it slightly below the ceiling. This point light should do a good job lighting the dark hallway, press Ctrl + Shift +; to build the lighting again. After building the lighting, our hallway now feels more realistic (Figure 4.40).

Our models seem to be working so far. But there are two major flaws. First of all, by the look of the composition, we think that there is just too much orange. It would be better if we can make the floors white. Second, everything looks a bit shinier than what they look like in Substance Painter. We have two options here. One option is to go back to Substance Painter and make the color of the floor white and make everything rougher. But it may require us to go back and forth many times to get the right color and roughness we want. The second option is to set up some controls in the material so that we can make changes here.

Let's take a look at how we can set up the second method in Unreal Engine.

Tutorial 4.4: Create Parameters for Our Materials

Step 1: Set up a desaturation parameter. Go to the shared folder and double click on the Substance_Base_Mtl to open it in the Material Editor. There is still a Param node in there; select

FIGURE 4.40 A new point light added to the hallway.

it and press the delete button to delete it. Right click in any empty area of the graph and type in Desaturation. Hit the Enter button to create a Desaturation node. Connect the RGB output pin of the Base_Color node to the first input pin of the Desaturation node. Connect the output pin of the Desaturation node to the Base Color input of the Substance_Base_Mtl. Right click the empty area again and type in scalar, and in the search result, click on the ScalarParameter to create a ScalarParameter node. Connect the output pin of this ScalarParameter node to the Fraction input of the Desaturation node. Finally, in the Details panel, set the Parameter Name to Desaturation, and press the Save button to save the material (Figure 4.41).

Step 2: Test the desaturation parameter. Go to the floors folder, double click the floor_4k material instance to open it in the Asset Editor, under the Parameters Groups in the Details panel, check on Desaturation. Drag the desaturation value up to 1 to desaturate it completely. Our floors are now all white (Figure 4.42).

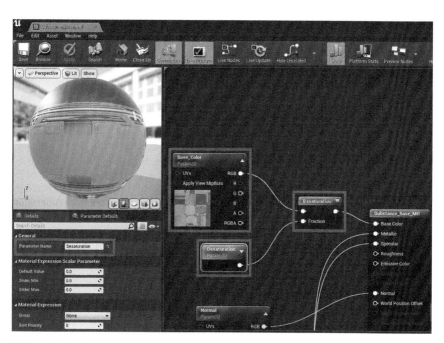

FIGURE 4.41 Add a Desaturation parameter.

FIGURE 4.42 Desaturate the floor.

Step 3: Create a hue shifting parameter. Go back to the Substance_Base_Mtl, and create a HueShift node in the same way we created the Desaturation node. Connect the RGB output pin of the Base_Color to the Texture (V3) input pin of the HueShift node. Connect the Result output pin of the HueShift node to the first input pin of the Desaturation node. Hold down the S button and click anywhere to add a ScalarParamater (this is a shortcut to create a ScalarParamater node). Name the new ScalarParamater node Hue_Shift and connect it to the Hue Shift Percentage (S) input of the HueShift node. Press the Save button again to save the change (Figure 4.43).

Step 4: Test the Hue_Shift parameter. In the shared folder, double click Substance_Base_Mtl_Inst to open it in the Asset Editor. Check on the Desaturation and Hue_Shift. Set the Desaturation value to 0.1 to make the color lesser saturated. Set the value of the Hue_Shift

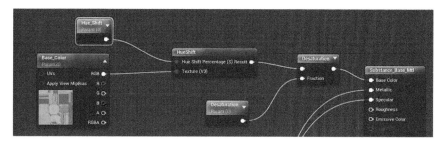

FIGURE 4.43 Added the Hue_Shift parameter.

to 0.015 to make it a bit yellower (you can use a different value if you want to have a completely different color). All the changes we have made here affect all models because it is the parent material of all other models; this is why we have this Substance_Base_Mtl_Inst. However, the floor remains white because the floors_4k has its own Desaturation checked, which overwrites what is happening to its parent (Substance_ Base_Mtl_Inst) (Figure 4.44).

Step 5: Add roughness contrast and shifting controls. Go back to the Substance_Base_Mtl again. Add a CheapContrast node (right click and search to find and create any node). Connect the G output pin of the AO_Roughness_Metallic texture parameter node to the In input pin of

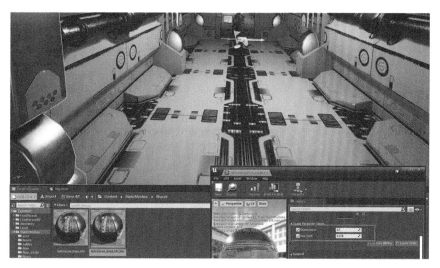

FIGURE 4.44 Make some subtle changes to the saturation and hue of the Substance_Base_Mtl_Inst.

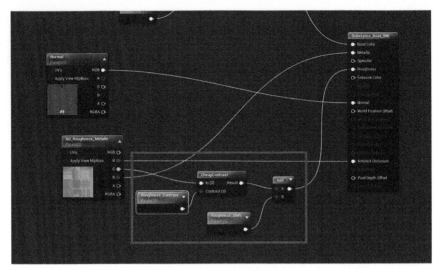

FIGURE 4.45 Add roughness contrast and shifting controls.

the CheapContrast node. Hold down S and click anywhere to create a ScalarParamater. Name the ScalarParamater Roughness_Contrast and connect it to the Contrast input pin of the CheapContrast node. Hold down A button and click to create an Add node. An Add node adds its input A and input B together as the output. Connect the Result output pin of the CheapContrast to the A input pin of the Add node. Hold down S and click to create another ScalarParamater and name it Roughness_Shift and connect it to the B input pin of the Add node. Connect the output pin of the Add node to the Roughness input pin of the Substance_Base_Mtl node. Press the Save button to save our material (Figure 4.45).

Tip and Tricks

What we have been doing in the Material Editor is called node-based scripting. In case you didn't notice, you are already doing some programming here. We have coded a shader that allows us to control many aspects of the material already. The programming we do later on is going to be very similar to this.

FIGURE 4.46 Tweak the Roughness_Contrast and Roughness_Shift parameters to get a more accurate roughness variation.

> *Step 6: Test the Roughness_Contrast and Roughness_Shift parameter. Double click Substance_Base_Mtl_Inst to open it. Check on the Roughness_Contrast and Roughness_Shift parameter. Set the Roughness_Contrast value to 0.15 and the Roughness_Shift value to 0.25 to get a much better roughness value and contrast (Figure 4.46).*

Why?

We cranked up the contrast of the roughness by setting the Roughness_Contrast bigger than 0, this is to enhance the variation we created for the roughness. Take a look at the highlights on the walls and floors. Notice that there are visible variations, which makes them feel very detailed.

> *Step 7: Create Glass Material. The material of the glass is fundamentally different because it has transparency. Select the Substance_Base_Mtl. Press Ctrl + W to create a copy of it and name the copy Substance_Base_Transparent_Mtl. Double click to open it in the Material Editor. Select the Substance_Base_Transparent_Mtl node. In the Details panel of the Material Editor, change the Blend Mode under the Material section from*

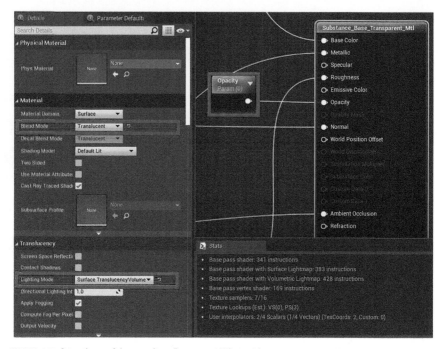

FIGURE 4.47 Set up the new Substance_Base_Transparent_Mtl material.

Opaque to Translucent. After the change, the Metallic, Normal, and Roughness input of the material become grayed out. To fix that, scroll down to the Translucency section. Set the Light Mode to Surface TranslucencyVolume. Hold down the S button, click to create a ScalarParameter node, and name it Opacity. Connect the Opacity ScalarParameter node to the Opacity input pin of the Substance_Base_Transparent_Mtl. Press the Save button to save the material (Figure 4.47).

Tips and Tricks

There are many settings under the lighting Mode in the Translucency section of the material. Luckily, if you hover your cursor on any of the options, a hint pops up to show you exactly what this option means. By reading through all the options, it is clear that the Surface TranslucencyVolume is the best setting for glass and water that is balanced for quality and performance.

Step 8: Apply the Substance_Base_Transparent_Mtl
to the glasses. Right click on the Substance_
Base_Transparent_Mtl and select Create
Material Instance and press enter to commit
the name. Go to the windows folder, double
click on the window_glass_4k to open it. Under
the General section of the Details panel in the
Asset editor, set the Parent to Substance_Base_
Transparent_Mtl_Inst. Go to the pot folder
and set the parent of pot_glass_2k also to
Substance_Base_Transparent_Mtl_Inst. Drag
both pot_pot_body and pot_pot_glass to the
level. Go back to the Shared folder and double
click Substance_Base_Transparent_Mtl_Inst to
open it. Check Opacity on and set its value to
0.3 to make it 70% transparent, which gives it a
glass-like feel (Figure 4.48).

Step 9: Set up refraction. Go back to Substance_Base_
Transparent_Mtl. Hold down L and click to create
a Lerp node. Lerp stands for linear interpolation. A
Lerp node interpolates between its A and B input
base on the Alpha input. If the alpha is 1, the value
of input B becomes the output; if alpha is 0, the
value of A becomes the output. If the alpha value

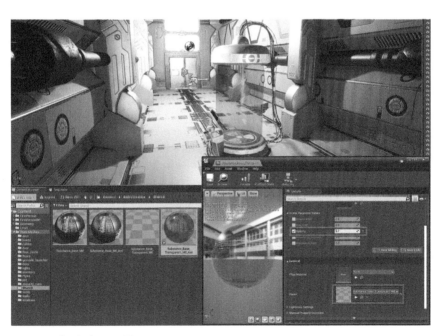

FIGURE 4.48 Test the glass material.

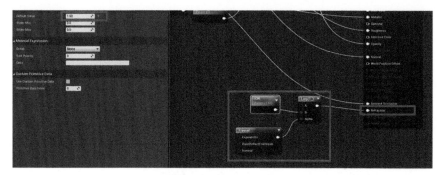

FIGURE 4.49 Set up the Refraction input of the material.

is a random value n (between 0 and 1), then the output is A×(1−n)+B×n. Select the Lerp node and set the Const A value to 1 in the Details panel. Create a ScalarParamater node and name it IOR. In the Details panel, set the Default Value to 1.52. Connect IOR to the B input pin of the Lerp node. Create a Fresnel node, and connect its output pin to the Alpha input pin of the Lerp node. Connect the output pin of the Lerp node to the Refraction input of the Substance_Base_Transparent_Mtl node (Figure 4.49). Press the Save button to save the material.

Why?

When lights hit the surface of a different medium, the direction of the light got changed (refracted). The refraction setup of our materials allows us to mimic that effect. IOR stands for index of refraction, and it represents how much light got refracted. The index of refraction of glass is 1.52. Fresnel node generates a grayscale gradient that is brighter at the edge of the model and darker at the center of the model. In our material setup, we use Fresnel as the alpha of the lerp to interpolate an value of 1 with the value of our IOR (1.52) and use the result as the Refraction input of the material. This setup means that the IOR at the edge of the model is 1.52, and the IOR at the center of the model is 1 (no refraction). We do this because lights refract more when it hit the surface at a bigger angle and do not refract (or change direction) at all when hitting direct on. Figure 4.50 shows the IOR value

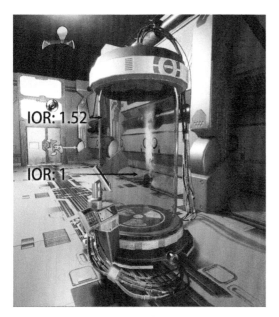

FIGURE 4.50 The IOR value across the glass of the pot and the result of our setup.

across the glass of the pot and the result of our setup. Notice how the edge of the glass is refracting the lights, which distorts the things we see behind it.

> *Step 10: Light emissive material: Go to the Shared folder. Right click in the empty area and select Material. Name it Emissive_Base_Mtl. Double click to open Emissive_Base_Mtl. Change the Shading Model to Unlit in the Materials section of the Details panel. The material now only has Emissive Color input available. Hold down V and click any empty area to create a VectorParameter (color parameter) node and name it EmissiveColor. Hold down the M button and click to create a Multiply node. Hold down the S button and click to create a Scalar Parameter node and name it EmissionIntensity. Connect the first output pin of the EmissiveColor node to the A input pin of the Multiply node, and connect the EmissionIntensity to the B input pin of the Multiply node. Connect the output pin of the Multiply node to the Emissive Color input pin of the Emissive_Base_Mtl. Press the Save button to save the material (Figure 4.51).*

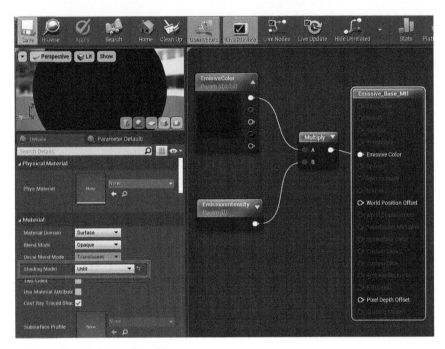

FIGURE 4.51 Set up the Emissive_Base_Mtl.

Step 11: Assign material to the lights. Right click on the Emissive_Base_Mtl, select Create Material Instance, and hit Enter to commit the default name. Double click to open it. Check on EmissiveColor and set the color to white. Check on EmissionIntensity and give it a value of 2. Right click on the Emissive_Base_Mtl_Inst and select Create Material Instance. Name the new material Instance Ceiling_light_01_light_mtl. Create another two material instances and name them Ceiling_light_02_light_mtl and Floor_light_light_ mtl. Drag the three new Materials Instances to the lights folder and select Move Here. Double click the lights_ceiling_light_01 model to open it in the Asset Editor. Drag Ceiling_light_01_light_mtl to the Element 1 slot to assign it to the light bulb part of the model. Drag lights_ceiling_light_01 to the ceiling of our hallway to check the result (Figure 4.52). Assign Ceiling_light_02_light_mtl to the lights_ceiling_light_02 and Floor_light_light_ mtl to the lights_floor_light the same way.

You are probably already noticing that the lights we modeled are just models.

FIGURE 4.52 Assign emissive materials to the lights.

They do not behave like a light when you drag them in even with emissive materials, not like the point lights we have in our test level, that is. To create a light that can lit the environment with the lights models as their shapes, we need to compose lights and our model into something we call an Actor.

Actors

Anything we can drag into our level is an actor. The model we dragged in is a type of actor called StaticMeshActor. The light we dragged in is a PointLight actor. If we hit the

Play button, the first-person character we are controlling is a type of actor called Character. We can make any custom actors and give them different functionalities. Let's make our light actors.

> *Step 12: Create a light Actor. Go to the lights folder in the StaticMeshes folder. Right click in the empty space and click on Blueprint Class. In the pop-up Pick Parent Class window, click on the Actor button. A new asset with the default name NewBlueprint got created in the Content Browser, and let's type in BP_ceiling_light_01 to name it.*

Why?

You are probably wondering what blueprint class is? What does Parent Class mean? These are programming terms that we will explain later. For now, all you need to know is we are creating a light actor that we can drag into the level to light the scene.

> *Step 13: Add Static Mesh components. Double click the BP_ceiling_light_01 to open it in the Asset Editor. You can see a viewport in the middle of the editor and a Components panel on the upper left corner. Click on the Add Component button in the Components panel and select StaticMesh. Go to the Details panel on the right side of the editor. Click on the drop-down list of the Static Mesh setting of the Static Mesh section. All static meshes (models) are listed here. Type in lights_ceiling_light_01 to find our lights_ceiling_light_01 model and click on it. Our lights_ceiling_light_01 now appears in the viewport in the middle (Figure 4.53).*

Tips and Tricks

Anytime we have a long list in a drop-down menu, we can type in keywords to filter out irrelevant items and find the one we are looking for. Sometimes you don't have to type in the full name.

> *Step 14: Add Spot Light component. Click on the Add Component button. Type Spot Light and hit Enter to add a Spot Light component. It also appears in*

FIGURE 4.53 Add lights_ceiling_light_01 as a Static Mesh component to the BP_ceiling_light_01.

the viewport in the middle. Use Rotate and Move tools to place it under the light and facing down. Go to the Details panel, set the Mobility under the transform section to Stationary, and set the Mobility of the StaticMesh component we added in the previous step to Static. Press the Compile button and the Save button in the Toolbar above the viewport to commit our changes (Figure 4.54).

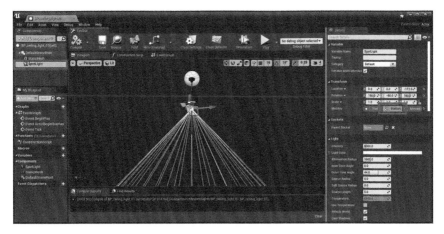

FIGURE 4.54 Add the Spot Light component.

Mobility

Mobility means the mobility of the object. Stationary and Static mobility both means that the object is not going to move. That is a requirement for anything you want to use for baked lighting. The Stationary option allows the lights to change color without rebaking the lighting. We are going to explain the details and differences of this option later in the lighting chapter.

> *Step 15: Test BP_ceiling_light_01. Delete all other lights and Drag BP_ceiling_light_01 to the ceiling of the hallway. Press Ctrl + Shift +; to build the lighting again. The BP_ceiling_light_01 is now lighting the hallway we created (Figure 4.55).*
>
> *Step 16: Create another two lights. Follow the same steps from Steps 12–15 to create BP_ceiling_light_02 and BP_lights_floor_light. The BP_ceiling_light_02 uses one-point light even there are two light pipes because using two lights means twice the cost, and we can get a similar result with one light. Set the Source Radius to 8 and the Source length to 195 to make the shape of the point light looks like a long pipe. One RectLight is used for the BP_lights_floor_light. Move the RectLight in front of the light of the model. To match the size of the RectLight to the model, set its Source Width to 20 (Figure 4.56). We are going to talk more details about lights in the lighting chapter.*

FIGURE 4.55 Test the BP_ceiling_light_01 in the hallway.

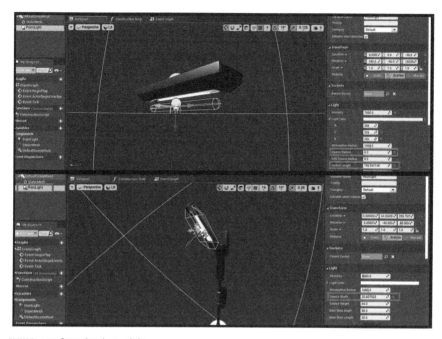

FIGURE 4.56 Set up the other two lights.

Step 17: Test all three lights in the hallway (Figure 4.57).

Step 18: Monitor material. The monitor material should be similar to the Emissive_Base_Mtl, but we want to give it a scanline effect, and we want the monitor to show something. Select Emissive_Base_Mtl and Press Ctrl+W to duplicate it, and name the duplication Screen_Base_Mtl.

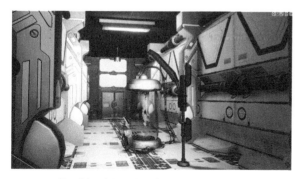

FIGURE 4.57 Test all three lights in the hallway.

Double click to open it. Delete the EmissiveColor parameter. Right click any empty area, type in TextureSampleParameter2D, and press enter to create a TextureSampleParameter2D (the same texture parameter we used to load our Base Color and other textures in the Substance_Base_Mtl). Name the new TextureSampleParameter2D node ScreenTexture. Connect THE RGB output pin of the ScreenTexture node to the A input pin of the Multiply node (Figure 4.58).

Step 19: Add Scanlines. Right click on any empty are and search for LinearSine. Press Enter to create it. Use the same method to create a LinearGradient node. Connect the VGradient to the Value (S) input pin of the LinearSine node. Create a Scalar Parameter, name it ScanLineSize, and set its Default value to 0.03. Connect ScanLineSize to the Period (S) input pin of the LinearSine node. Hold down the M button to create a Multiply node. Connect the Linear Sine output pin of the LinearSine node to the A input of the Multiply node. Connect the RGB output pin of

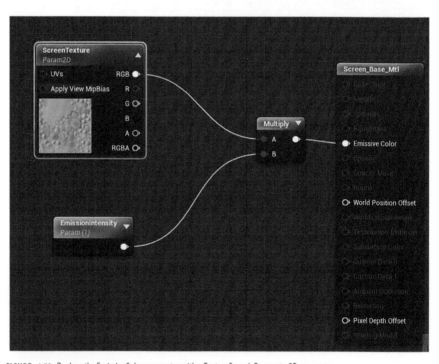

FIGURE 4.58 Replace the EmissiveColor parameter with a TextureSampleParameter2D parameter.

182

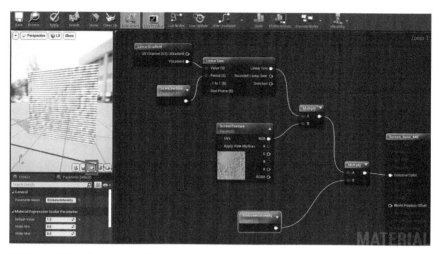

FIGURE 4.59 Add scanline to the material.

the ScreenTexture to the B input of the Multiply node. Finally, connect the output pin of this new Multiply node to the A input of the Multiply node that has EmissionIntensity connected to it. To visualize what we are having, change the Default Value of EmissionIntensity to 1. Go to the viewport at the upper left corner of the Material Editor. Click on the plane icon to switch the preview model to a plane. You may have to navigate the viewport to see the front of the plane (Figure 4.59).

Why?

Ok, for anyone who hates math, the LinearSine might already be making you scratch your head. However, math is the foundation of everything we do in computers. We do not have to learn the details of the Sine wave but you can imagine it as a repeating up and down (Black and White) wave. What we are building here is a wave across the V direction of the UV that has a wavelength of 0.03 (the value of the ScanLineSize parameter). The VGradient of the LinearGradient connects to the Value (S) input of the LinearSine ensures that it is a V direction wave. Try using the UGradient instead of the VGradient, and you can see the waves change to the U direction.

Step 20: Make the scanlines move. Create a Time node and a Multiply node. Connect the Time node to the A input of the Multiply node. Create another Scalar Parameter and name it ScanLineSpeed. Set the Default Value of ScanLineSpeed to 0.1. Connect ScanLineSpeed to the B input of the Multiply node. Hold down the A button and click to create an Add node. Connect the VGradient output pin of the LinearGradient to the A input of the Add node. Connect the Multiply node to the B input of the Add node. Finally, connect the Add node to the Value (S) input pin of the LinearSine node (where the LinearGradient was connecting to). We should now see scanlines moving (Figure 4.60).

Step 21: Fix shading group issues. Open the monitors folder. Double click to open monitors_Monitor_01. You can see that there is only one element in the Material Slots because we did not assign a different material for the screens of the monitor.

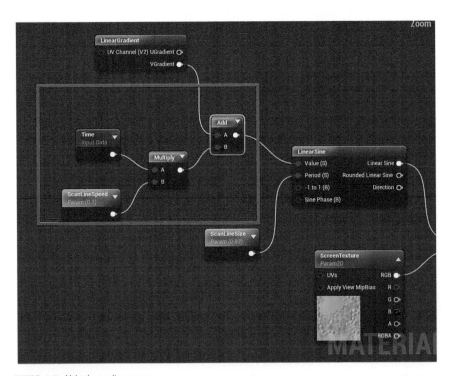

FIGURE 4.60 Make the scanlines move.

Open Maya again and load our Set_ Model.mb file. Go to the outliner and find Monitor_01. Press Ctrl+1 to isolate it. Select all the faces that belong to the monitor. Change the workspace to UV Editing. In the UV Editor, hold down Shift+Right mouse button and select Create UV Shell.

Hold down Shift+right mouse button again, and go to Modify → Layout □. In the pop-up Layout UVs Options, set the Scale Mode at the bottom to Non-Uniform and press Layout UVs. The UVs of the screen now fills the entire U1V1 Space. Make sure that the faces of the screen are still selected. Go back to the 3D viewport, hold down the right mouse button, and select Assign New Material. In the pop-up Assign New Material window, select Blinn. The Attribute Editor should pop up, if not, press Ctrl+A.

Hold down the right mouse button again and select Material Attributes. Set the name of the Blinn Monitor_01_Screen_01_Mtl. There is another small screen on the number pad on the side of the big screen. Make the same UV adjustments to that small screen and give it another Blinn material and name the material Monitor_01_Screen_02_Mtl. Do the same thing to all other Monitors Models. You need to rotate the UV shells after the UV layout command if the U1V1 checker texture is upside down or tilted and do a UV layout one more time. Figure 4.61 shows the result of the Monitor_02 model.

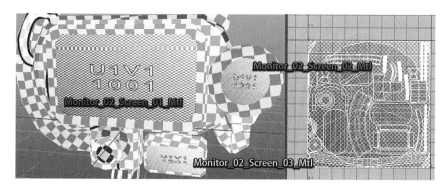

FIGURE 4.61 The new UV and Material Arrangement of one of the monitors.

Why?

We make the UVs of these screens fill the U1V1 space. This way, if we want to use a camera to capture the scene and show the captured scene on the monitor, it needs to read the full U1V1 space to read the full captured image. We also give every screen new material so we can assign our Monitor material to them.

> *Step 22: Reimport to UE4. Select the monitors group. Go to File → Export Selection. Navigate to the monitors.fbx file we exported earlier, click on that old file, and press the Export Selection button. A pop-up window shows up and asks if we want to replace it. Press Yes. Go back to Unreal Engine. Select all four monitors in the Content Browser, right click on any one of them, and choose reimport. A window pops up that asks about what to do to the new materials we assigned because they do not exist before. Just press the Done button to leave them empty. Double click monitors_Monitor_02 to open it, and now we can see that there are three more elements with the name Monitor_02_Screen_01_ Mtl, Monitor_02_Screen_02_Mtl, and Monitor_02_Screen_03_Mtl waiting to be assigned with new materials. They are now using worldGridMaterial, and this material is the default material for any slots that are not assigned (Figure 4.62).*

Tips and Tricks

Every time we need to update the model, we can just go back to Maya and make the changes. Export and replace the old fbx file, and right click on the model in the Content Browser and select Reimport.

> *Step 23: Create and Assign the screen material instances. Go back to the Shared folder. Right click on the Screen_Base_Mtl and select Create Material Instance. Press enter to commit the default name. Assign this material instance to all the screen material slots of all the monitors (Figure 4.63).*

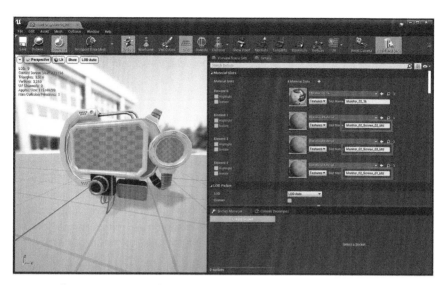

FIGURE 4.62 The new material elements of the monitor.

FIGURE 4.63 Create material instances for the screens.

187

We are going to replace the textures used for the monitors later when we are doing game programming. For now, they are just using a default texture that Unreal Engine supplies.

Conclusion

We have finished our asset import and material creation in our Unreal project. As you can see, transferring models and textures into the game engine is not as simple as we like it to be. Also, we have spent some time creating actors and materials to make light and monitors functioning. We have also covered changing and reimporting assets. All these steps are going to make our future steps easy.

We can now finally move on to build our game level. We are going to move upon that fun journey in the next chapter.

CHAPTER 5

Level Creation

In this chapter, we are going to use the assets we created in the previous chapters to build our level. We have built our LEGO pieces, and the time has come for us to use them In whatever way we see fit. After building the interior of the level, we are going to use the landscape feature of Unreal and other free assets to build a natural exterior.

To review the whole workflow. We have modeled our modular pieces and other props and created UVs for them in Maya. We created textures Using Substance Painter and relies heavily on it to add surface details. We Export all models in Unreal with careful organization and set up all the materials in Unreal Engine. It is crucial to remember that it has never been possible to create a game with one piece of software along. Understanding and learning software gives you informed ideas on how to tackle our goal efficiently and smoothly. Please keep learning new things and update your workflow if you find something worth trying.

Unreal Engine is designed to handle the best graphic possible with a crazy amount of models, shaders, and lights. As long as we create our model economically, we can throw a lot of them in the level before it is too much. So try to add and combine more models if you can when building the level.

When creating our level, keep in mind that other than the visual quality, the gameplay aspect of the level is also essential. We always want to think about how the player would go around our environment, will things get boring, is there any backtracking, and how to avoid that. After all, the game is an experience we created, and we want to make sure that the players feel what we want them to feel.

Let us jump right in to start building our level.

Tutorial 5.1: Create the Interior of Our Level

Step 1: A new Level. Press Ctrl + S to save our test level. Go to File → New Level and select the Default. A new level got opened with a floor, a generic sky, and a sun. Press Ctrl + S to pull out the Save Level window. Navigate to the Level folder and Type Level_01_Awaken in the Name text field. Press Save to save it. Go to Edit → Project Settings. In the pop-up Project Settings window, click on Maps and Modes in the list of categories on the left and set the Editor Startup Map and Game Default Map to Level_01_Awaken. The next time we open our project, Level_01_Awaken is going to be loaded (Figure 5.1).

Step 2: Building the floor plan for the starting room. Click the floor in the middle to select it and press Delete to delete it. Go to floors folder and

FIGURE 5.1 Set the Level_01_Awaken as Editor Startup Map and Game Default Map.

drag floors_floor_01_to the level. In the Details panel, set the Locations X, Y, and Z all to zero to bring it to the origin. We want to use the top faces of these floor pieces later on in the bigger rooms. Rotate it 180 degrees to flip it upside down. Make sure that the snapping of the grid is 16 units (upper right corner of the viewport). If the snapping options are somehow still by 10, go to Edit → Editor Preferences. In the Editor Preferences, type in power to filter the settings and check on Use Power of 2 Snap Size. After that, drag the floor down, so it is just under the grid (Figure 5.2).

Step 2: Create three floor pieces in a row. Hold down Alt and Drag the X (red) axis of the move tool to have a copy of the floor, and keep dragging until it aligns with the previous one. Drag out another duplication, so we have three floor pieces appropriately aligned (Figure 5.3).

FIGURE 5.2 Placing our first piece.

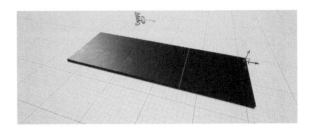

FIGURE 5.3 Create three floor pieces in a row.

Step 3: Fill the floor with nine pieces. Select all three pieces. Use the Alt and Drag method to copy two more rows of the floor pieces to create a 3×3 floor (Figure 5.4).

Step 4: Add variations. Select the floors_floor_04 piece in the Content Browser. Select the floor pieces at the four corners in the viewport. Right click on any of the selected pieces and choose Replace Selected Actor With Floors_floor_04 (the square piece has a frame and a metal grid inside). The four corners are now replaced with floors_floor_04 (Figure 5.5).

Step 5: Fill the bottom of the floors_floor_04 pieces. Drag floors_floor_03 to the level. Use the Alt and drag method to have three more copies, so the four of them together becomes a square piece. Press Ctrl+G to group them. Rotate the group 180 degrees. You can see that the back of them has pipe-like textures. Move the group under the grid piece. Copy the group using Alt and drag to all the other three corners (Figure 5.6).

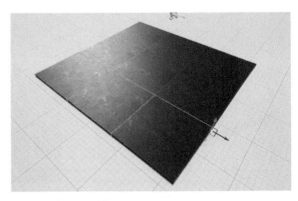

FIGURE 5.4 Create a 3×3 floor area.

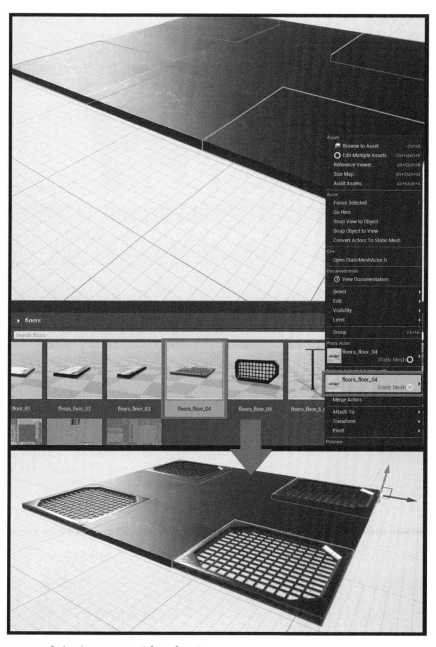

FIGURE 5.5 Replace the corner piece with floors_floor_04.

FIGURE 5.6 Add four floors_floor_03 pieces under the corner pieces.

Step 6: Add base to the wall pieces. Drag floors_floor_02 to the level. Move and duplicate it to make it surround two sides of the floor. Surround one side of the floor with floors_floor_03 (Figure 5.7). Notice that four floors_floor_03 pieces are used to cover the one side of the floor because of the extended length added by the floors_floor_02 pieces.

Step 7: Create wall pieces. Go to the walls folder. Drag walls_wall_01 to the level. Drag and duplicate the wall so that there is a wall above every one of the outer floor pieces. Align the walls with the floor pieces on the outside (Figure 5.8).

Step 8: Drag the walls_Turnning_wall_01 to the corners of the walls to block the opening (Figure 5.9).

FIGURE 5.7 Surround the floor with floors_floor_02 and floors_floor_03.

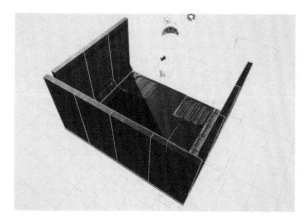

FIGURE 5.8 Place the wall pieces.

FIGURE 5.9 Block the opening of the walls with walls_Turnning_wall_01.

Tips and Tricks

When building our scene, there is no rule on how a piece should be used. The walls_Turnning_wall_01 is designed to be used for the turning of a hallway. It doesn't mean that we cannot use it for any other purposes like blocking the corner.

> *Step 9: Drag in the door. Go to the door folder. Select door_door_frame, door_door_l, and door_door_r. Drag them all to the level. Align the*

door to the edge of the middle floor piece of the opening side of the room (Figure 5.10).

Step 10: Add windows above the door. Go to the windows folder. Select both the windows_ window_01 and windows_window_01_glass. Drag them to the level and place them right above the door. Hold down Alt and drag up to stack another window on top (Figure 5.11).

Step 11: Add two extra door frames. Go to the walls folder. Drag the walls_door_frame_flat into the level and place it on one side of the door. Duplicate and place another one on the other side of the door (Figure 5.12).

Step 12: Fill the rest of the walls. Add two more walls_wall_01 on the side of the door. Fill the rest of the corners with walls_wall_corner_frame (Figure 5.13).

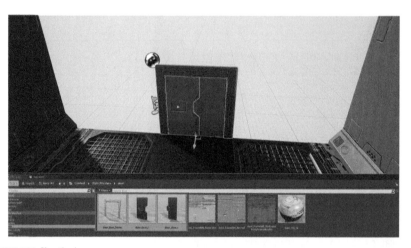

FIGURE 5.10 Place the door.

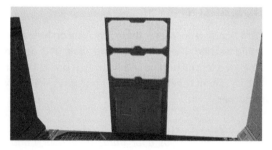

FIGURE 5.11 Place two windows above the door.

FIGURE 5.12 Add two extra door frames on the side of the door.

FIGURE 5.13 Fill the rest of the walls.

Tips and Tricks

It is up to you to fill in the walls and corners the way you see fit. Feel free to use different pieces.

> Step 13: Fill the room with some props. Go to the boxes folder. Drag a few boxes to the floor. Place them primarily in the corners. Drag a few more props you see fit in the level to fill the space but keep the middle empty. Our player's spawn point is in the middle (Figure 5.14). A copy of BP_lights_ floor_light is placed at one of the corners.

FIGURE 5.14 Fill the room with some props.

Step 14: Fill the ceiling. Fill the ceiling with the floor pieces. Make sure that their dark side is facing the inside (Figure 5.15).

Step 15: Decorate the Ceiling. Drag a BP_ceiling_ light_01 to the middle of the ceiling as the primary light. Drag a BP_ceiling_light_02 between the two door frames as the doorway guide lighting. Drag cables_Cables_10 behind the door light to give the illusion that cables are connecting to it. A ceiling vent is also added to decorate the ceiling better (Figure 5.16).

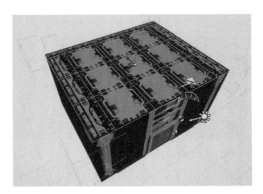

FIGURE 5.15 Fill the ceiling.

FIGURE 5.16 Add lights, cables, and a vent to the ceiling.

Tips and Tricks

We add a light to the door to help the player see it easily. The cables added behind the light help to make the door area more attractive and casting interesting shadows. The level designer should always think of ways to direct the eyes of the player.

> *Step 16: Add tilted windows. Go to the windows folder. Drag windows_Tilt_03 and windows_Tilt_window_03_glass to the level, and place them between the door frame and the column of the wall. These tilted windows add some break up to the 90-degree floor and wall transition (Figure 5.17).*
>
> *Step 17: Add pipes. Go to the Pipes folder. Drag a few pipes into the level, use the move, and rotate tool to assemble them. This part is all up to you; be creative on how they connect and turn. The snapping should allow you to match them nicely (Figure 5.18).*

FIGURE 5.17 Add two tilted windows to decorate the wall.

FIGURE 5.18 Add some pipes to the room.

Tips and Tricks

The pipes are one of our main assets to help make the level looks detailed. It can quickly make an area look complicated. It takes some time to build the pipe structures. However, they are just LEGO pieces waiting to be assembled; don't hesitate to use them a lot and try to experiment with variations.

Step 18: Create the floor of the tutorial hallway. Go to the outside of the door and place the floors_ floor_01 in front of it. Add two floors_floor_03 on each side of the floors_floor_01 piece. Rotate them to make them upside down, and re-align them with the floors_floor_01 piece (Figure 5.19). We name this hallway tutorial hallway. We are going to use this hallway to get the player familiar with the basics of the gameplay.

Step 19: Add detail to the floor. Just like how we add detail to the floor, move the four floors_floor_03 pieces down and place floors_floor_05 pieces above them (Figure 5.20).

FIGURE 5.19 Create the base of the hallway floor.

FIGURE 5.20 Add layering detail to the side of the floor.

Tips and Tricks

It is easy to feel repetitive with only one type of floor. Combining various pieces to make the floor different is crucial to avoid a boring scene.

> *Step 20: Group and duplicate the floor pieces. Select the floors_floor_01 and floors_floor_03 pieces we create for the hallway floor and press Ctrl+G to group them. You can now select them altogether by clicking on any one of them. The pivot is also centered on the bounding box of the whole piece. With the group selected, hold down Alt and drag the Y (green) axis to duplicate a few tiles (Figure 5.21).*
>
> *Step 21: Duplicate the grid. Select the two floors_floor_05 pieces. Because these grid pieces are shorter pieces than the others, we have to duplicate them differently. Press Ctrl+G to group the two floors_floor_05 pieces. Drag out a copy (hold down Alt and drag the Y-axis) of the group and align it to the original one. Go to the Details panel, and set the Scale X to −1 to flip them. Select both groups and drag out more copies to cover the rest of the side of the hallway. The last copy might extend too much out of the hallway. Press Shift+G to ungroup them, and delete the extra ones. Finally, move these grid pieces across the Y-axis to align the end of the grid pieces and the rest of the floor pieces (Figure 5.22).*

Tip and Trick

Grouping can be useful to organize the scene. Be aware that grouping in Unreal Engine does not create a folder

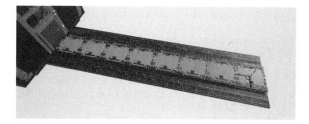

FIGURE 5.21 Group and duplicate the floor pieces

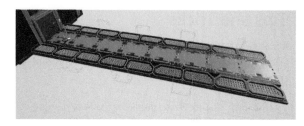

FIGURE 5.22 Duplicate the grid pieces.

to contain the pieces like Maya. Instead, Unreal creates an extra GroupActor in the World Outliner to represent the group. A different way to organize the scene is to create folders in the World Outliner. To create a folder, just click on the folder button on the right of the search bar at the top of the World Outliner. You can drag anything to the folder to put it under the folder. You can also drag anything out of the folder. If you have something selected and click on the folder button, it creates a folder with the selected objects placed inside the folder. Unfortunately, folders in Unreal Engine are not translations like Maya. You cannot move a folder to move all objects inside the folder. However, you can right click on any folder and select Select → All Descendants to select all the objects in the folder.

> *Step 22: Place the walls. Place the walls_wall_02 pieces for the wall of the hallway. You can group them before duplicating them for the other side (Figure 5.23).*
>
> *Step 23: Add ceiling to the hallway. Select the floors_floor_01 piece we created for the ceiling of the start room and drag out duplications as the ceiling of the hallway. Move them down 16 units (Unreal snaps every 16 units, so you just need to drag them down and stop dragging the first time it snaps.) (Figure 5.24).*
>
> *Step 24: Add lights, pipes, crates, and other props to add detail to the hallway. This step is mostly up to you to choose the combination of props you what to throw in the level. Keep in mind that you want to avoid blocking the way and experiment with variations (Figure 5.25).*
>
> *Step 25: Create the floor of the turning section of the hallway. The turning of the floor has*

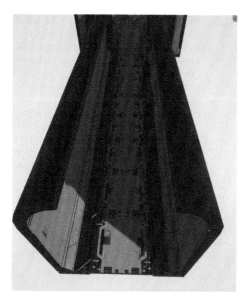

FIGURE 5.23 Add wall pieces.

FIGURE 5.24 Add ceilings to the hallway.

FIGURE 5.25 Add lights and details to the hallway.

four floors_floor_01 pieces in the middle and two floors_floor_02 pieces on each of the two sides that connect to the straight hallway segments. We had designed it this way when we were creating the models; Figure 1.56 in Chapter 1 shows the desired module layout (Figure 5.26).

Step 26: Add the walls of the turning section. Go to the walls folder. Drag the walls_Turnning_wall_01 and walls_Turnning_wall_02 to the level and place them, so they connect to the end of the walls of the hallway seamlessly (Figure 5.27).

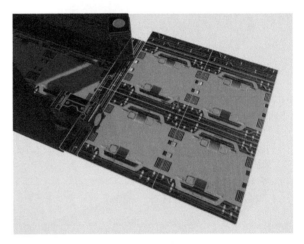

FIGURE 5.26 The floor of the turning section of the hallway.

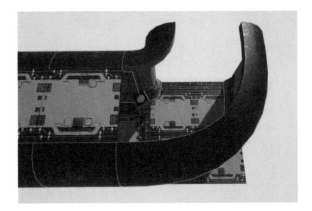

FIGURE 5.27 Add the turning walls.

FIGURE 5.28 Add ceiling to the turning of the hallway.

> Step 27: Create the ceiling of the turning section.
> For the ceiling of the turning section, we just
> need to drag a copy of the floor and move it up
> (Figure 5.28).

Why?

We could also model the floor of the turning section as
a different piece. However, it saves time to create only a
handful of pieces. We can get away with the extra surfaces
protruding out because the player can never see them.

> Step 28: Create the rest of the hallway. Go ahead
> and create the rest of the hallway that connects
> to the turning part. Use your imagination and
> creativity to LEGO it using any pieces you see fit
> (Figure 5.29).
> Step 29: Add wall frames. Go to the walls folder.
> There are some column models with "frame" in
> their naming. These frame models are intended
> to be protrusion shapes that work like the frame
> of the walls or supporting columns. For every
> two walls, add a frame model to break up the
> flatness of the walls (Figure 5.30). It is beneficial
> to place these frames right over the contacting

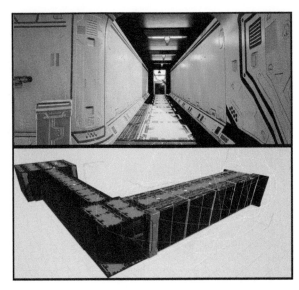

FIGURE 5.29 The rest of the hallway.

FIGURE 5.30 Placing wall frames (the red highlighted ones).

seam between two walls so that it is able to block baking artifacts that usually happens on seams. walls_door_frame_flat and walls_wall_corner_frame are the ones used here.

Step 30: Create the floor and wall for the camera room. Drag some floors, walls, and doors to block out the next room that connects to the end of our hallway. We call this new room camera room. This camera room contains a console that allows the player to check a security camera (Figure 5.31).

Step 31: Add extra height and break up to the walls. Add another 128 cm height to the walls to make it higher. The tilted windows are used to make it more interesting. Figure 5.32 shows the layout the book uses, but feel free to do it differently. Finally, drag a copy of the floors as the ceiling.

Step 32: Fix black reflections. You are probably wondering why the metal part of the pieces is so dark. Well, this is because they have no reflection data. In the default setting, reflection is not calculated in realtime but rather baked as a map to save performance. To get this baked reflection to work, we need to drag in reflection captures to capture the reflection map. Go to the Modes panel. Type Box Reflection Capture. Box Reflection Capture should now be the only option in the list below the search bar. Drag the Box Reflection Capture to the level. Move and scale it, so it's orange-bounding boxes covers the camera room. It is ok if the bounding boxes of the Reflection Capture is a little bigger than the room. Drag three more copies of the Box

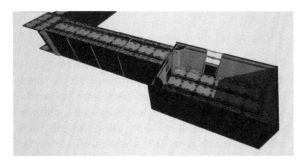

FIGURE 5.31 Create the floor and wall for the camera room.

FIGURE 5.32 Add extra height and ceiling to the camera room.

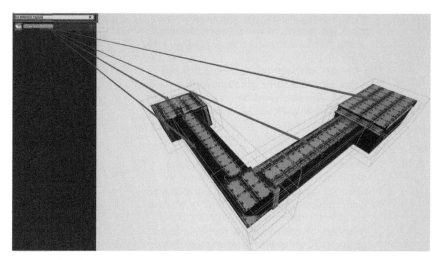

FIGURE 5.33 Add reflection capture.

Reflection Capture and use them to cover the two hallways and the start room; it is also fine to overlap them (Figure 5.33). We are now able to see the captured reflection on the metal part of the pieces.

Tips and Tricks

If your graphic card supports realtime raytracing, you can toggle it on, so you don't need to use reflection capture. It is, however, costly and is only suitable for high-end hardware. We are not going to use realtime raytracing at this point. But, by the time you are reading this book, realtime raytracing could already be cheap enough for your hardware, so don't hesitate to try.

Step 33: Add a grid platform. Drag a few grid floors, a staircase, and some handrails to the camera room to add variations to the height of the level (Figure 5.34). Again, the pieces and composition are up to you and do not have to be exactly like the figure. stairs_stair_low is used for the stairs here.
Step 34: Add a monitor. Go to the monitors folder. Drag monitors_Monitor_02 and monitors_ mointor_mounter to the ceiling to place and align them below the ceiling. Adjust the position

FIGURE 5.34 Place a grid platform.

so that the monitor is hanging in the middle of the room (Figure 5.35).

Step 35: Place other props. We have the gameplay-related assets placed. Now it is time for you to be creative and drop other assets in the scene. Figure 5.36 shows the finalized layout of the camera room.

FIGURE 5.35 Place the monitor.

FIGURE 5.36 The layout of the camera room.

Tip and Tricks

It is essential to consider good composition when you are building the level. Look at Figure 5.36, and you can see that two composition techniques are used:

1. Lighting. It is not apparent without building the lights. However, you can see the two ceiling lights emphasize the door and the monitor.
2. Guild lines. Cables, the direction of the handrails, and the crates are concentrating on the monitor.

Please take composition seriously throughout when you are building the level.

> Step 36: Build the floor of the security camera hallway. Use the same floor combination as the previous hallway to create another hallway outside of the other door of the camera room. Make this hallway longer than the tutorial hallway. This new hallway is our security camera hallway. We are going to challenge the player with more security cameras. Feel free to add more turns if you wish to make it more appealing or challenging (Figure 5.37).

Why?

The reason why we always start with the floor and work up from there is that the floor defines the playable area. We want to make sure that the playable area is defined first, and we can add walls, ceiling, and details later.

FIGURE 5.37 Build the floor of the security camera hallway.

Step 37: Create the base shape of the wall for the security camera hallway. Drag three walls_wall_03 pieces to the side of the floor and add three floors_floor_02 pieces at their bottom to block their bottom (Figure 5.38).

Step 38: Decorate the wall. Add some pipe structures and cables to the wall and add walls_wall_frame_02 at the edge of the wall (Figure 5.39).

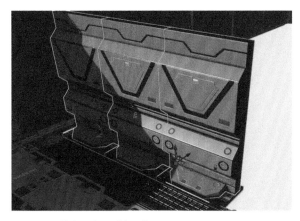

FIGURE 5.38 The base shape of the wall.

FIGURE 5.39 Decorate the wall with cables, pipes, and a wall frame.

Tip and Tricks

For the walls_wall_frame_02, we placed it the same way we placed the frames in Step 29. It is halfway aligned with the wall piece. This arrangement allows the next tile to match with it the same way nicely (Figure 5.40). The Frame is halfway aligned with the wall pieces.

> Step 39: Group and duplicate the wall. Select all pieces of the wall. Press Ctrl+G to create a group. Use the Alt and drag method to create more copies of the wall. Make sure that their edge snaps to each other nicely (Figure 5.41). Leave some space at the end of the hallway. We are going to make a stair and a door there before it leads to the next room.
>
> Step 40: For the other side of the hallway, we use the windows_arc_window as the wall so we can see some exterior. We also added a door leading to a side room at the beginning of the hallway. This side room is called the handgun room. The player is going to acquire a handgun in this

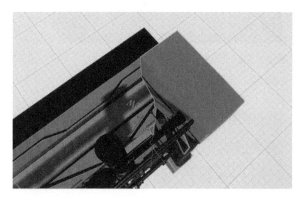

FIGURE 5.40 The Frame is halfway aligned with the wall pieces.

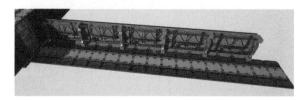

FIGURE 5.41 The duplicated walls.

handgun room after knocking down a guard in it. Also, two pieces of walls_wall_corner_frame are placed at the spot where the walls meet the camera room (Figure 5.42).

Step 41: Build the handgun room. The handgun room is relatively small. We used some arcs to make it feel different than the other rooms we have built. Some overlapping pieces are put together to add variations to the door area (Figure 5.43).

Step 42: Build the ceilings for the hallway and the handgun room. Use the floor and arc pieces to fill the ceiling of the security camera hallway and handgun room (Figure 5.44).

Step 43: Add a staircase at the end of the hallway. At the end of the hallway, place a stairs_stair_high to the middle of the hallway and add a few walls floors to help to block the surrounding (Figure 5.45).

Step 44: Finish the staircase area. It is no different than what we have been doing before. You place floors, walls, doors, windows, extra props, and decorations. Figure 5.46 shows the interior and

FIGURE 5.42 The other side of the hallway.

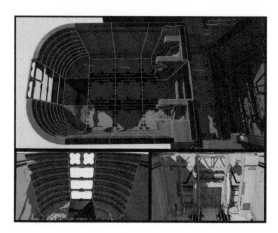

FIGURE 5.43 The layout of the handgun room.

FIGURE 5.44 The Ceilings of the hallway and handgun room.

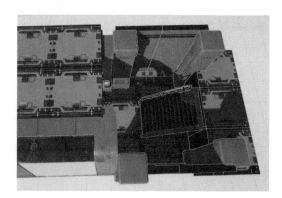

FIGURE 5.45 Add a staircase at the end of the hallway.

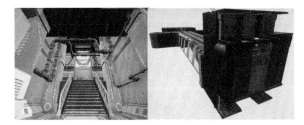

FIGURE 5.46 The finished staircase and the door at the end.

exterior of this section. There are protrusions at the top and bottom of the exterior, which are part of the pieces we use to block the interior of this area.

Step 45: *Add clusters of cables to the floor. Go to the cables folder. Drag cables_Cables_11 to the floor of the security camera hallway. The cables_Cables_11 is not long enough to cover the whole width of the floor. Have another copy of the cables_Cables_11 piece and try to align it with the previous one; it is ok if you cannot make it perfect (Figure 5.47).*

Step 46: *Fix the connection problems of the cable. Drag the cables_cable_holder_01 piece to the floor and use it as a strap to cover the connection between the two cables_Cables_11 pieces. We can use multiple copies of the cables_cable_holder_01 pieces to extend the end of the cables to the walls to make the whole cable piece complete (Figure 5.48).*

Tips and Tricks

The default gizmo is orient to the axes of the world. Go to the upper right corner of the viewport, and click on the button with a globe icon. The button's icon now changes

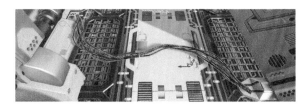

FIGURE 5.47 Add two copies of the cables_Cables_11 piece on the floor.

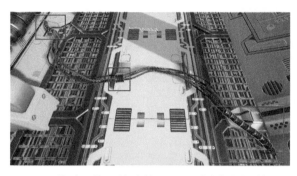

FIGURE 5.48 Use the cables_cable_holder_01 piece to help finish the cables.

to a cube. This button is the switch between world axes (globe icon) to local axes (box icon). The local axes is easier to work with when you are making copies of the cables_cable_holder_01 pieces.

> *Step 47: Add another branch to our cable cluster. Using the same method in Steps 45 and 46, we can add another branch of cables to the cluster (Figure 5.49). Go ahead and add more cables to the group to break up the repetitive wall and floor patterns.*
>
> *Step 48: Create the floor of the storage room. Let move on to something bigger—the storage room. This room is a place the player play stealth with a bunch of guards. This ground consists of 17 × 18 tiles of the floors_floor_01 pieces wrapped by grid pieces. A door is placed on the far side of the room (Figure 5.50).*
>
> *Step 49: Assemble the wall. Using the same method used in Steps 37 and 38, we can assemble the wall with walls_wall_03, walls_wall_04, and all the cable and pipe pieces. To add depth, we stuck more pipes in the depressions of the surface of the walls (Figure 5.51).*

FIGURE 5.49 Add another branch to our cable cluster.

FIGURE 5.50 The floor of the storage room.

FIGURE 5.51 The sidewall segment of the storage room.

Step 50: Duplicate the wall pieces. Group the wall we assembled in Step 49. Use the Alt and drag method to duplicate the walls until all three sides of the wall are covered. For the shorter side without a door, we chose to use windows_ arc_window to break up the repetition. windows_arc_window_sidewall is used to block the opening on the side of the windows_arc_ window piece. Walls_door_frame_zigzag is used for extra decoration and filling on the side of the doors (Figure 5.52).

FIGURE 5.52 The finished walls for the storage room.

Tip and Trick

At this point, selecting things by left-clicking might become difficult. You can hold down Ctrl + Alt and drag to marquee select. If you also hold down Shift, it does add select. Just be aware that you always select the Sky Sphere with marquee, make sure that you de-select it after you did your marquee select. Another useful tip here is right click on the selected models and go to Visibility → Show Only Selected; this command isolates your current selection. Ctrl + H make everything visible again.

Step 51: Add tilted windows. Add a row of titled windows on top of the long edges of the room. We have windows_Tilt_01, windows_Tilt_02, and windows_Tilt_03, be sure to use them all and have some variations (Figure 5.53).

Step 52: Add extra titled windows and ceilings. To make the whole ceiling more interesting, two-third of the room has two extra rows of tilted windows before getting a ceiling (Figure 5.54).

FIGURE 5.53 Add tilted windows on top of the walls.

FIGURE 5.54 The interior and exterior of the storage room after adding the ceiling.

Step 53: Fill the rest of the walls. For the remaining of the walls on the shorter sides of the room, we use windows_window_01, windows_window_02, and the windows_Tilt_04 piece. windows_Tilt_04 is used to block the triangle gap between the rectangular windows and the tilted windows (Figure 5.55).

Step 54: Stairs and platforms. Because this room is high, we can use the floors_floor_04, floors_floor_05, floors_floor_5_support, and the stairs_stair_high to create some higher platforms to add variation to the visual as well as the gameplay (Figure 5.56).

Step 55: Add crates. To make the stealth gameplay possible, we need to add covers or obstacles for the players to hide. We can use all the models in the boxes folder to build piles of crates in the room. After all, this room is called the storage room (Figure 5.57).

Step 56: Other decorations. Pipes, cables, lights, and vents are all added to the storage room to break it up and make it more visually appealing. This part might take a little time, but the process is no different to what we have done before (Figure 5.58).

FIGURE 5.55 Fill the rest of the walls.

FIGURE 5.56 Add Stairs and platforms to the storage room.

219

FIGURE 5.57 Add crates to the storage room.

FIGURE 5.58 Add other details to the storage room.

We have walked you through a whole lot of LEGO assembling already. At this point, you can already see the pattern of this level. It is shuffling rooms with hallways, and every room has a use for gameplay. By thinking of the progression of the game, we can direct the composition with confidence.

Now it is your turn to create one more hallway and the boss fighting room. Figure 5.59 shows the result we are going to use for the next chapter.

Assignment

Finish the last hallway and the boss room. The boss is the hero asset in the hero folder, and we also use the pot model only here in the boss room to make it more unique. This room is going to take you a good chunk of the day to finish. A lot of pipes and cables are used. Please finish the assignment before moving on.

After finishing our interior, look outside of the window, and we see the empty sky; it feels like we are just floating

FIGURE 5.59 The boss room and the hallway leading to it.

in the air. Also, we can see artifacts on the outside of the models. They are overlapping, clipping, and sometimes just do not make any sense. To fix that, we need exteriors to cover all these artifacts and give the player a sense of a complete, infinite environment. We are also going to take this opportunity to cover natural environment creation with landscape and how to use free assets from the Unreal ecosystem. Epic Games is one of the few companies that try hard to create an open, free-market. Their effort to offer all their users and partners free and professional tools are unprecedented.

Let's move on to create our landscape first.

Tutorial 5.2: Create the Landscape of Our Level

Step 1: Go to the Modes panel, and click on the button with an icon of a mountain. A green grid got created at the center of the world. This green grid is the coverage of the landscape. The size of the grid is too big so far, so set the Section Size to 15×15 to make it smaller. Drag the gizmo to move the landscape, and make sure that the bulk of the landscape is visible to the windows of the security camera hallway and the storage room (Figure 5.60).

Step 2: Sculpt the landscape. Press the Create button. The landscape now becomes a solid surface, and the Sculpt moded is toggled on. Simply click and drag on the landscape to raise the area under the brush. Press the left square bracket button ("[") to reduce the size of the brush and the right square bracket button ("]") to increase the size of the brush. Hold down the Shift button while sculpting lowers the landscape. There are three things to think about when sculpting:

1. Have enough variations and layers of distance when looked at from the windows.

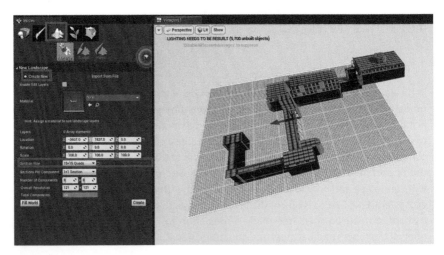

FIGURE 5.60 The grid of the landscape.

2. Use them to help block the player from seeing the outside walls of the buildings; we do not have to make sure that all walls are blocked, and we are going to use more natural assets to block the artifacts.
3. Make sure that they do not have abrupt up and downs.
4. Avoid the landscape clipping into the interior of the level.

If the shapes are getting too noisy, click on the Sculpt button, and in the drop-down list, choose Smooth. The sculpting tool now changes to Smooth. With the Smooth tool, sculpting on the landscape smoothes its surface.

Go ahead and sculpt some simple hills around the landscape (Figure 5.61).

Step 3: Erosion. *Change the tool from Sculpting or Smooth tool to Erosion. Make your brush bigger, click, and drag on the landscape to add some natural Erosion effect. The erosion effect sharpened the landscape and made it more realistic (Figure 5.62).*

Ok, now we have our terrain sculpted, let's set up its materials. We are going to leverage a service called Quixel Megascan to help us.

FIGURE 5.61 Sculpting the landscape.

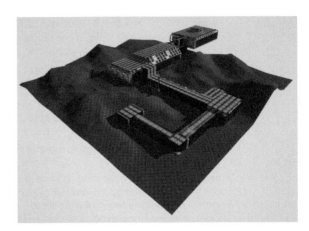

FIGURE 5.62 Apply erosion to the landscape.

The Quixel Megascan Ecosystem

Quixel Megascan is the biggest scan library. The Quixel team travels to every corner of the world; they capture the environment and convert them to textures and 3D models. With Quixel Megascan, everyone can have an access to a library where only big studios had in their hard drive before. Using Megascan, indie developers can create an excellent environment in a matter of hours.

Tutorial 5.3: Set Up Quixel Bridge

Step 1: Download and install Quixel Bridge. Go to https://quixel.com, and click the SIGN IN button at the upper right corner of the webpage. In the pop-up SIGN IN window, click on SIGN IN WITH EPIC GAMES. Log in with your Epic Games account. After logging in, scroll down, find BRIDGE, and click on it (Figure 5.63).

Click the DOWNLOAD FOR FREE button to download Quixel Bridge, install, and open it after downloading. Click on the SIGN IN button at the top right corner and sign in with your Epic Game account again.

Step 2: Download our first asset. Go back to Unreal Engine, Press the Save All button in the Content Browser, and Close Unreal Engine After saving. Go to Quixel Bridge, click on the button with a

FIGURE 5.63 The link to Quixel Bridge.

sphere icon on the left side of the UI, and choose Environment → Natural → Nordic Forest. The Nordic Forest is a collection of assets they scanned in the forests around Denmark, Norway, and Sweden. These forests have overgrown vegetation and complex and wet landscapes. There are many assets in the middle section of the UI. Scroll down until you find Mossy Ground, select it, and hit the DOWNLOAD button (Figure 5.64).

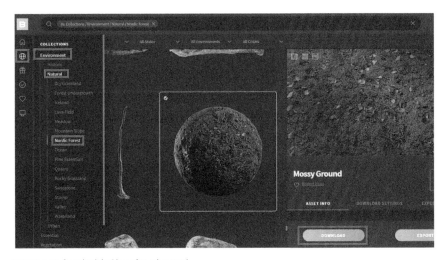

FIGURE 5.64 Download the Mossy Ground material.

Step 3: Export to Unreal. Go to the EXPORT SETTINGS tab, set the Texture Resolution to 2k, set the Texture Format to TGA, and set the Export To to Unreal Engine. Set the Engine Version to your Unreal Engine version. Click on the Installation Folder. In the pop-up Select Folder window, find your Unreal Engine Directory, and this is your engine installation path; in the default settings, it shoulde be in:
C:\Program Files\Epic Games\UE_4.2x\Engine\ Plugins
Once you set it up, the Quixel Megascan plug-in starts to get installed to Unreal Engine. Finally, set the project location to the path of your Unreal project. Just to give an example, the project path of our book is: J:\GamePrjs\ TheEscaper
Click on the EXPORT button to export the asset to your Unreal project (Figure 5.65).

Why?

We chose to use 2k instead of 8k because the landscape is outside, and the player will never reach there. Keeping it relatively low is going to save us performance.

Step 4: Download the Swamp Soil material. After finishing exporting, a notification pops up on the upper right corner that tells you it has succeeded. Go back to Unreal Engine, and you can see the material and its textures are now in the content browser. Find Swamp Soil in Quixel Bridge, download, and export it to our Unreal project the same way.
Now we have our Quixel assets in our project, let's move on to the landscape material setup.

Tutorial 5.4: Create the Landscape Material

Step 1: Set up a material function for our landscape layering. We want both Mossy Ground and Swamp Soil on our landscape as two layers. To set up the material, we can create a material function that can represent each one of them as

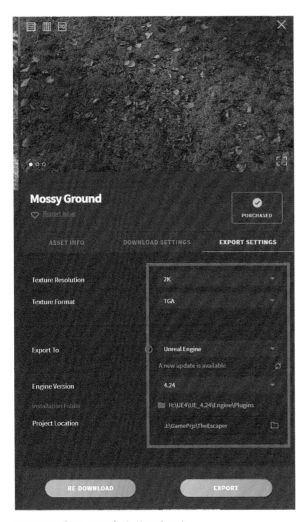

FIGURE 5.65 Export setting for the Mossy Ground.

a whole. Add a new folder to the Content folder in the Content Browser and name it Landscape. Go inside the Landscape folder, right click, and select Materials & Textures → Material Function. Name the new material function Landscape_ layer_MF (Figure 5.66).

227

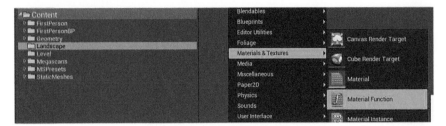

FIGURE 5.66 Create a material function.

Material Function

You can think of a material function as a custom node that we can build and use in the Material Editor. Just like the Multiply node and the Desaturate node we used earlier, a material function has certain functionalities, and it has inputs and outputs. In the next few steps, we are going to use the material function to help simplify the graph of the blending of the mossy ground and swamp soil material.

Step 2: Create a base color input for our material function. Double click to open Landscape_layer_MF. The Material Function Editor pops up. This Material Function Editor behaves just like the Material Editor. Right click in the Material Function Editor, search, and create a MakeMaterialAttributes node. Connect the output pin of the MakeMaterialAttributes node to the input of the Output Result node. Create a Function Input node by right clicking and search for it. In the Details panel, set the Input Name to BaseColor and connect the output of BaseColor to the BaseColor input of the MakeMaterialAttributes node (Figure 5.67).

Step 3: Create other color inputs. Go to the Megascans → Surfaces → Mossy_Ground_00 folder (created when exporting the materials from Quixel Bridge) in the Content Browser. You can see that there are six textures. The textures we do not need are thbjbhpr_2k_Displacement and thbjbhpr_2K_Bump. The displacement map is for displacing the shape of the surface out, and only super high-end hardware use this map. The bump map is a legacy way of representing surface details and is no longer needed. Create three more Function Input node for our material

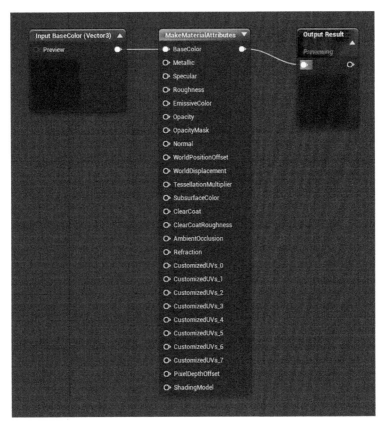

FIGURE 5.67 Add the BaseColor input for our material function.

function and name them according to the
textures we need to use: Normal, Roughness, and
AO. Connect them to the corresponding inputs of
the MakeMaterialAttributes node (Figure 5.68).
Press the Save button to save our material
function.

Step 4: Create the landscape material. Go back to the
Landscape folder. Right click and select Material,
name the new material Landscape_Base_Mtl,
and double click to open it. Drag our Landscape_
layer_MF from the Content Browser to the graph
of the Landscape_Base_Mtl in the Material
editor. You can see that our material function
does become a node that has four inputs. These
four inputs are the inputs we set up in Steps 6
and 7. Go back to the Mossy_Ground_00 folder

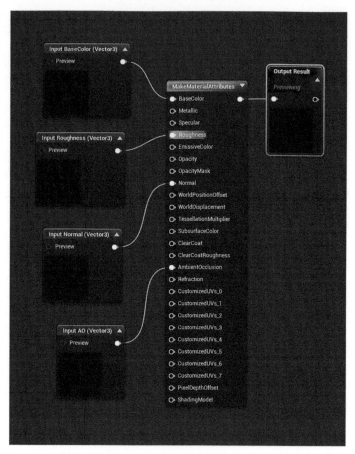

FIGURE 5.68 Finished material function graph.

and drag the corresponding four textures to the graph and connect them to the four inputs of the Landscape_layer_MF node (Albedo is for the BaseColor input). Select the Landscape_Base_Mtl node, and in the Details panel, check on the Use Material Attributes option in the Material section. The Landscape_Base_Mtl now collapsed to only having one input. Connect the output of the Landscape_layer_MF to the input of the Landscape_Base_Mtl. We should now see that the moss material appears in the material preview window at the upper left corner (Figure 5.69).

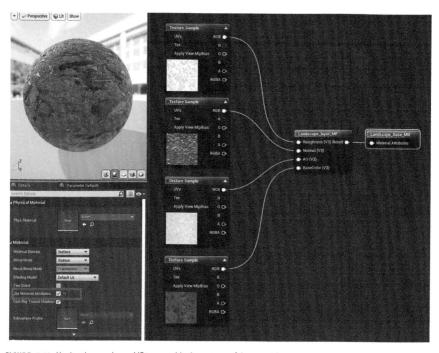

FIGURE 5.69 Use Landscape_layer_MF to assemble the textures of the material.

Step 5: Create the Swamp_Soil layer and set up
blending. Drag in another Landscape_layer_MF
to the graph. Go to the Swamp_Soild_00 folder,
drag the Albedo, AO, Normal, and Roughness
textures for the swamp soil material to the
*graph, and connect them to the new Landscape_*
layer_MF. Create a LandscapeLayerBlend node.
Go to the Details panel. Click the "+" button in
the Layers settings twice to create two layers.
Click on the triangle icon to open these two
layers, change the Layer Name of the first layer
to moss, and the second one to soil. Connect
the first Landscape_layer_MF to the Layer
Moss input pin of the Layer Blend node and
the second Landscape_layer_MF to the Layer
Soil input pin of the Layer Blend node. Finally,
connect the output of the Layer Blend node to
the Landscape_Base_Mtl (Figure 5.70). Press the
Save button to save the material.
Step 6: Set up the landscape. Go back to the
*Landscape folder. Right click on the Landscape_*
Base_Mtl and select Create Material Instance.

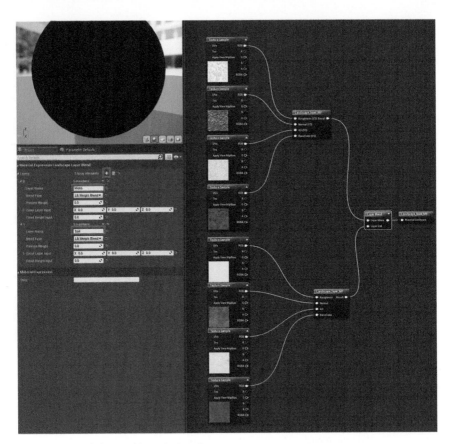

FIGURE 5.70 Set up the layering of the two landscape layers.

Select the landscape in the level and drag the new material instance to the Landscape Material slot In the Details panel to assign it to the landscape. A notification pops up with the text Compiling Shaders, and give it some time to finish the compilation. The landscape is now black. Press Shift+3 to switch to landscape mode, in the Mode panel, click on the Paint button to go to landscape painting mode. In the layers section, we should now see our Moss and Soil layer (the layer we defined in the LandscapeLayerBlend node). Click the "+" button of the Moss layer and select the Weight-Blended layer (normal). In the pop-up window, select the landscape folder and hit OK. Do the same thing to the Soil layer. The landscape now should show

the Moss material repeating on it (Figure 5.71).
Unreal Engine starts to compile shaders again,
and give it enough time to finish.

Step 7: Paint the layer distributions. We want most of
the area to be soil, right click on the Soil layer in
the Mode panel, and select Fill layer. Click on the
Moss layer, and start painting on the landscape
to add moss to the surface. The moss should
happen on some of the slopes. We are going
to throw many props and foliages to cover the
landscape, so we do not have to carefully paint it
(Figure 5.72).

Step 8: Set up tiling controls. One thing we can
notice here is both the soil and the moss are
visibly repeating. Go to the Landscape folder,
and double click Landscape_Base_Mtl to open
it. Create a LandscapeLayerCoords node. The
LandscapeLayerCoords gives the UV of the
landscape. The UV of the landscape maps to
individual small components of the landscape,

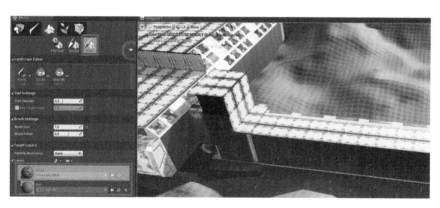

FIGURE 5.71 Set up the landscape material and layers.

FIGURE 5.72 Paint the layer distributions of the landscape.

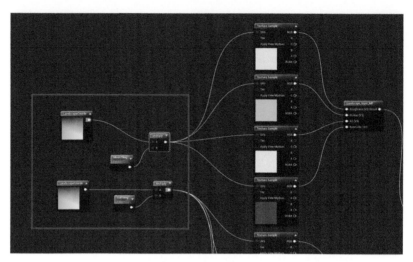

FIGURE 5.73 Set up tiling to the layers.

and we need to reference it first before making any additional adjustments. Add a Multiply node and a ScalarParamater node, and connect the LandscapeLayerCoords to the A input pin of the Multiply node. Rename the ScalarParamater node to MossTiling and connect it to the B input pin of the Multiply node. Set the default value of the MossTiling to 1. Connect the Multiply node to the UVs input pins of all four Texture Samples of the Moss layer. Do the same thing to the soil layer (Figure 5.73). Press the Save button to save it. Another round of shader compiling got triggered, and give it time to finish.

Step 9: Tweak the tiling of the layers. Open LandScape_ Base_Mtl_Inst. Toggle on MossTiling and SoilTiling, and set their values smaller than one to have lesser tiling. The value we set here is 0.3 for the MossTiling and 0.1 for the SoilTiling (Figure 5.74).

Once we are happy with our landscape model, we can move on to populate more assets.

Tutorial 5.5: Place 3D Assets on the Landscape

Step 1: Megascan assets. Go back to Quixel Bridge. In our NORDIC FOREST collection, find and download some 3D assets, export them to our

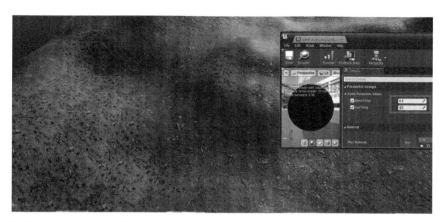

FIGURE 5.74 Reduce the tiling of the layers.

project. The process of downloading them is the same we did for the moss. We do not have to set up the EXPORT SETTINGS anymore. Figure 5.75 shows the selection of the assets we chose to use in our exterior scene.

Step 2: Filtering assets. Go to the 3D_Assets folder in the Megascans folder. Click on the Filters button on the side of the search bar and check on Static Mesh. All 3D models we downloaded now appear below. This filter option is a fast way to get a specific type of asset listed (Figure 5.76).

Step 3: Place Megascan assets. You can now drag and drop these assets into the level. You can move, rotate, and scale the assets as long as they make sense. The purpose of placing these assets to block any artifacts we have on the exterior of our building and add an illusion of infinite nature environment around the building. Feel free to place these assets in whatever way you see fit. Figure 5.77 shows the result.

Step 3: Create an asset transferer project. Before moving on to get more assets in, you are probably already noticing that you could have downloaded some asset that you end up not using. These not-used assets are only making your project bigger. Create a new Unreal Engine project using the same steps and setting we used while creating our current one, and give this new project a name: AssetTransferer. A new Unreal Editor opens and let's keep it open in the background. We are going to use this

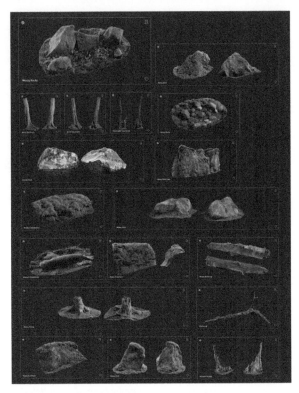

FIGURE 5.75 All assets used in our level.

FIGURE 5.76 Get all Megascan 3D assets listed in the Content Browser.

AssetTransferer as a receiver of new assets. After checking the assets out, we then decide if we transfer any of them to our TheEscaper project. Step 4: Get free assets in the marketplace. We still need some actual trees. Another way to get free asset is in the Unreal Marketplace. Open Epic

FIGURE 5.77 The Final Megascan placements.

Game Launcher, and click the Unreal Engine section and then the Marketplace section. Type in temperate Vegetation: Spruce Forest in the search bar at the upper right corner. Only one asset shows up in the search result, and this one is the free tree assets we are going to use. Click on the temperate Vegetation: Spruce Forest to go into the details of this asset, and click on the Free button at the lower right corner to get it for free. Once done, the Free button becomes an Add to Project button. Click on it. In the pop-up window, select our AssetTransferer project and click on the Add to Project button (Figure 5.78). Epic Game Launcher needs some time to download the assets; once finished downloading, it adds the assets to our AssetTransferer.

Why?

When downloading, you can see that the size of the temperate Vegetation: Spruce Forest asset is around 8 GB. The size of the package is way bigger than what we already have in our project. There are many trees and other foliages in this package, and we only need a fraction of them. Having it added to our AssetTransferer project allows us to pick only a few models in it and transfer only these models to our TheEscaper project.

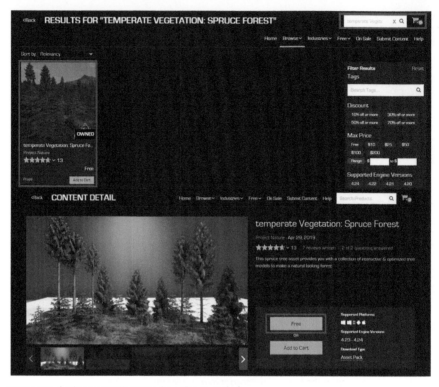

FIGURE 5.78 Get the temperate Vegetation: Spruce Forest asset for free.

Step 5: Transfer trees to our TheEscape project. Go to the new AssetTransferer project, and you can see a new folder called PN_interactiveSpruceForest that appears in the Content Browser. Go to PN_interactiveSpruceForest → Meshes → half → low, there are four trees in it. If the editor is busy compiling shaders, give it some time to do that. Select both the spruce_half_02_low and the spruce_half_03_low, right click on any one of them, and select Asset Actions → Migrate (Figure 5.79). A window pops up that shows all the dependencies of these two trees. Click the OK button, in the new pop-up file explorer window, navigate to the directory of the content browser folder of our TheEscaper project (Figure 5.80), and click the Select Folder button. The two trees are now getting transferred to our TheEscaper

FIGURE 5.79 Migrate the assets.

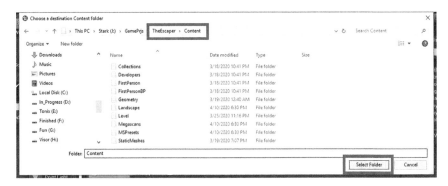

FIGURE 5.80 Locate the Content Browser folder.

project, and it only takes a few seconds. A notification at the lower right corner pops up once the engine finished the migration. Using the same method, go ahead and migrate the spruce_small_02 and spruce_small_05 in the PN_interactiveSpruceForest → Meshes → small folder to our TheEscaper project. A warning may pop up, saying that An asset already exists. Press the No All button to avoid copying them over again. These already existing assets are the shared materials that got imported already.

Step 6: Set up the foliages to paint. Go back to our TheEscaper project. Press Shift+4 to go to the foliage mode. You can also switch to this mode by going to the Modes Panel and click on the foliage button on the right of the landscape button. In the Content Browser, click on the PN_interactiveSpruceForest folder and toggle on the Static Mesh filter. Drag the four tree assets we migrated over to the empty space under the green Add Foliage Type button. The four trees are now added to the list of foliages we can paint over any surface (Figure 5.81).

239

FIGURE 5.81 Add trees to the paint list.

Step 7: Adjust foliage settings. Click and drag on the terrain or any other model to place trees there as foliage. The default result is too much. Click on the first tree in the paint list. Go to the settings below the list and set the Density/iKuu to 1 instead of 100 to reduce its paint density. Check off the Align to Normal setting. We also want to paint one type of tree every time. Hover the cursor on all other three trees and click on the checker box on the upper left corner of their icon to deactivate them. The icons of the deactivated foliages are darkened. Start painting again on the terrain to place only one tree at a time (Figure 5.82).

FIGURE 5.82 Adjust foliage settings.

Why?

Checking off the Align to Normal setting makes all the trees completely vertical, and for tall trees with straight trunks, it would be strange if they are titled.

> Step 8: Placing more trees. Once you are happy with the first tree, you can deactivate it and toggle on the second tree. Set the density of the second tree and start placing it. Do the same to all other trees until you have a decent amount of trees placed (Figure 5.83).
>
> Step 9: Adjust the trees. If you don't like one of the trees painted, click on the select button in the Model panel and click on any tree to select it. Once a tree is selected, you can move, rotate, scale, or delete it. Adjust the trees with the select to have more variations on size and delete the ones you don't want (Figure 5.84).
>
> We have now finished our entire scene assembly.

FIGURE 5.83 Paint more trees.

FIGURE 5.84 Adjust the trees.

Conclusion

Environment creation is always considered the most time-consuming process of game production. No matter how big your team is, or it is just yourself, you are going to have to work on the environment for the longest time. Luckily, there are many free assets like Quixel Megascan and the Unreal Marketplace. Leverage these free assets can save a tremendous amount of time. Doing environment creation is both challenging and exciting. There are many possibilities, variations in the creation of an environment, and you can always feel fresh while working as an environment artist.

Let's move on to the next chapter, where we start lighting, baking, and tweak the graphic of the level.

CHAPTER 6

Lighting and Baking

Lighting is a powerful tool; it drastically changes the appeal and perception of the scene. When done right, it enhances the mood, experience, and clarity of the game. When done poorly, the game becomes misleading, inconsistent, and distracting. In this chapter, we are going to tackle the lighting and baking of our games. We already have sunlight in the scene, and we have built some light actors, but we haven't tweak them in any way.

Baking

Baking is the process of rendering and storing lighting information. The stored lighting information is used

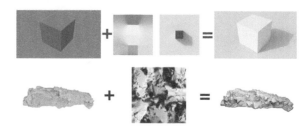

FIGURE 6.1 How baked lighting is used to get high-quality rendering results.

instead of calculating all aspects of lighting in realtime. The most common one is to render the lighting information as a grayscale map, multiplied on top of the model's base color texture. As shown in Figure 6.1, rendering a cube sitting on a plane takes around 10 seconds with medium-quality settings in Arnold Renderer (a professional renderer for movie production). Rendering a high-quality rock with lots of polygons and multiple textures take 2 minutes in the same renderer. Rendering 10 seconds or 2 minutes for one frame is fine for rendering an animation, but not practical for games. To reach the same quality, we bake the lighting information as grayscale textures and multiply these grayscale colors on top of their base color. By using baked lighting, we do not have to calculate the lighting in realtime. However, baked lighting does not support movable objects.

Lightmaps

The baked lighting information is called lightmap. The maps in the middle of Figure 6.1 are all lightmaps.

Lightmap UV

Lightmap may use a different set of UVs for optimization. Consider that all the floor pieces of our level share the same UV set, the UVs of the floors_floor_01 only take a small part of the UV space, and the other parts are empty. Using this kind of UV is wasting all the empty areas of the UV space. Go to the Content browser, find floors_floor_01, and double click to open it. In the Asset Editor, click on the

FIGURE 6.2 Checking different UV Channels.

UV button and select UV Channel 0. The UVs of the model now appear at the lower left corner of the Editor. This UV is the first UV channel that all the textures are using in the material. However, there is also a UV Channel 1 option. Click on the UV icon again and choose UV Channel 1 this time. A different UV layout shows up, and this one has bigger UV islands. This UV Channel 1 is used for baking and applying lightmaps. A model can have multiple UV Channels; UV Channel 0 is almost always for textures. Other UV Channels can be used for any other purposes like baking and mapping lightmaps (Figure 6.2).

Lightmap Resolution

In the Details panel of the Asset Editor, go to LOD 0 and open the Build Settings section. Set the Min Lightmap Resolution from 64 to 128 and press the Apply Changes. This setting tells Unreal Engine that the lowest lightmap resolution we are going to build for this asset is 128×128 pixels. 128×128 may seem low, but there is very little information in lighting compared to a color map. After changing it, the UV Channel 1 also changes, leaving smaller gaps between shells. Since the texture becomes bigger than before, the smaller gaps still contain the same number of pixels. To change the resolution for the actual lightmap, scroll down to the General Settings section and set the Light Map Resolution value to 128 as well (Figure 6.3).

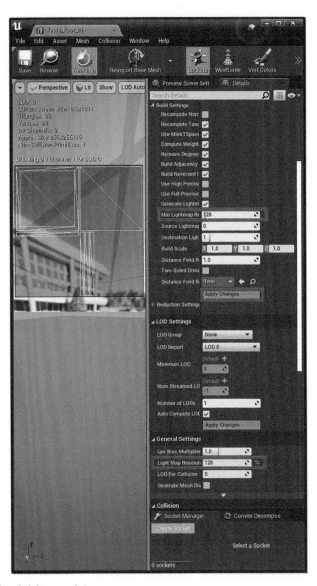

FIGURE 6.3 Adjust the lightmap resolution.

Lightmap Density

Press the Alt+0 button to switch to lightmap density viewing mode. The models are now color-coded with gride textures applied to them. This viewing mode shows the resolution of the lightmaps. Green color means ideal texel density, blue means the resolution is too low, and red means it's too high. This is not your texel density for the textures, but the baked lightmap that uses UV channel 1. It is not always necessary to make them all green. But we can spend some time to fix some extreme ones before we start baking. Press Alt+4 to go back to the Lit viewing mode, which is the normal viewing mode. These toggles can also be found in the drop-down menu on the upper left corner of the viewport.

Volumetric Lightmaps

Other than the 2D lightmaps we talked about earlier, there is also Volumetric Lightmap. Volumetric Lightmap is a matrix of sample points in the 3D space. Every point has baked information about the lighting of where that point is. It is the light probs of Unity if you are familiar with that. Figure 6.4 visualizes the Volumetric Lightmap. Every sphere in Figure 6.4 is a point we have talked about. Notice how some of the spheres have red tint at their lower corners, and the red color is from the bouncing red light of the point light. Go to the Show menu at the upper left corner of the viewport, find Visualize → Volumetric Lightmap, and check it on to visualize the Volumetric Lightmap just like Figure 6.4.

FIGURE 6.4 Volumetric Lightmap.

Mobility

Some actors are static, and their lighting can be all baked. Some other actors are moving during gameplay, like the player character or sliding doors. Baked lightmap does not work for them. Actors and lights have mobility settings that allow us to define how their lighting is calculated.

Select any model and go to the mobility section in the Details panel, and you can see that there are three options:

Static—The actor cannot move or update in any way. All lighting aspects from static and stationary lights are baked. All lighting aspects from movable lights are calculated in realtime.

Movable—The actor can move freely. Lighting from static lights only queries the baked Volumetric Lightmap, and no shadow is cast. Direct lighting and shadow from stationary lights are all calculated in realtime, indirect lighting from stationary lights queries the baked Volumetric Lightmap. All lighting aspects from movable lights are calculated in realtime.

Stationary—Same as Moveable, but cannot move in gameplay (can be moved when editing the level in the editor without rebaking). The shadow from movable lights is using the shadow of the previous frame if the light is not changed.

Lights also have the same mobility settings:

Static—The light is not changing in any way. It contributes to lightmap baking. Its lighting is baked as lightmaps for static meshes. Movable and Stationary meshes only query its baked Volumetric Lightmap and do not cast shadows from it.

Movable—Light can change freely and does not contribute to lightmap baking. Its lighting is calculated in realtime for all meshes. They are performance-intensive if they cast shadows.

Stationary—Light cannot be moved, but other aspects can be changed, like color, intensity, but not softness. Stationary lights contribute to lightmap baking.

For Movable and Stationary Actors, direct lighting and shadow are calculated in realtime and indirect lighting queries baked Volumetric Light Map. All lighting aspects from stationary lights are baked for static meshes.

It is in the author's opinion that all these lighting complexities are destined to disappear when computer hardware is getting better in the future. For now, all of the lights we have created in Chapter 4 are stationary. Stationary lights have the perfect balance between performance and quality. They are also suitable for meshes with any mobility settings.

Now we have explained the foundations of lighting in Unreal Engine, let's move on to optimize the lightmap resolutions of the models.

Tutorial 6.1: Optimize the Lightmap Resolution

Step 1: Optimize interior lightmap texel density. Open our Level_01_Awaken level. Press Alt+0 to toggle on Lightmap Density view mode. Select any interior model that is blue and press Ctrl+E to open it in the Asset Editor. Open the Build Setting section under the LOD 0 section, set the Min Lightmap Resolution setting to double the current value, and press the Apply Changes button. Under the General Settings, set the Light Map Resolution to the same value as the Min Lightmap Resolution. Press the Save button.

Go back to the viewport and check if the model now becomes green (just has to be close enough), if not, repeat the same process. Do not crank the resolution values higher than 512. For anything red, instead of doubling Min Lightmap Resolution and the Light Map Resolution, lower down the values by half. Keep doing this until all models in the interior are green (does not have to be exact).

There are models scaled differently (pipes, boxes). Stick with one value in the Asset Editor. Select the ones that need tweaking in the level, go to the Details panel, open the Lighting section, check on Overridden Light Map Res, and adjust it here. The Overridden

FIGURE 6.5 The optimized lightmap resolution for the interior.

Light Map Res overrides the settings in the Asset Editor for the instances you are selecting in the level (Figure 6.5).

Tips and Tricks

The best approach to lightmap resolution is not making everything green. We can break up the scene to three levels of resolutions:

1. **Playable Area**—the area that the player can reach as close as possible, make all models green. You can also make complicated models or models that may receive more complicated shadows redder.
2. **Middle Ground**—the area that the player cannot reach, but reasonably close, make these models lesser green or blue.
3. **Background**—the area that is too far, make them all blue.
   Step 2: Optimize landscape lightmap texel density. Select the landscape. Go to the Details panel. Set the Static Lighting Resolution to 16 under the Lighting section (Figure 6.6).

Why?

The landscape may still appear to be blue. However, it is a vast area and will take a long time to bake if we make it green; also, the player cannot reach it, so it is considered middle ground.

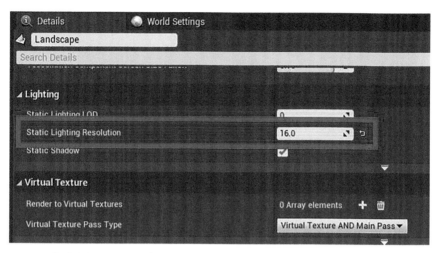

FIGURE 6.6 Set the lightmap resolution of the landscape.

Step 3: Fix the trees. The two tall trees (spruce_ half_02_low, spruce_half_03_low) we are using have five LODs. LOD stands for level of details, a model with multiple LODs means that there are multiple versions of this model, each with different level of details (different polycounts). Unreal Engine loads different models based on how close the camera (player) is to the model. This way, Unreal can load a lower version of the model when it is far away to save performance.

The first four LODs of the trees all have three UV channels, and the UV Channel 2 is for the lightmap. However, the last LODs of these two trees have no UV Chanel 2, which causes inconsistency and lightmap baking failure. Because we do not have the original models, the easiest way to make it work is to delete the last LODs of the two trees.

Open spruce_half_02_low in the Asset Editor. In the Details channel, find the LOD Setting section, change the Number of LODs from 5 to 4, and hit the Apply Changes button; this deletes the last LOD. Go to the General Settings section and set the Light Map Coordinate Index to 2. Do the same thing to spruce_half_03_low. The two tall trees should have grids appear now on their surface in the Lightmap Density viewing mode after our fix (Figure 6.7).

251

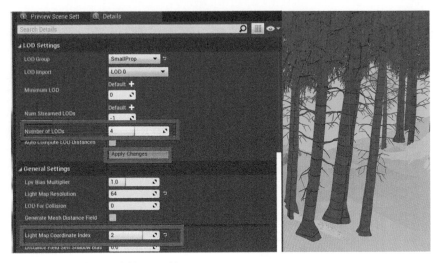

FIGURE 6.7 Fix the lightmap and LOD setting of the trees.

Step 4: Adjust exterior lightmap resolution. Because the trees are not directly reachable, we can make them a bit more bluish. For the other two foliages spruce_small_02 and spruce_small_05, because they are more close to the windows, we have made them more green. The lightmap resolution we used for all of these foliages is 256. For all other rocks, we also make them more bluish. Figure 6.8 shows how the exterior looks like in the Lightmap Density viewing mode.

After optimizing the lightmap resolution, we can now move on to place lightmass importance volumes.

FIGURE 6.8 Exterior lightmap resolution.

FIGURE 6.9 All the Lightmass Importance Volumes added to the level.

Lightmass Importance Volumes

Lightmass Importance Volumes are box volumes. When building lightmaps, Unreal Engine pays more attention inside these box volumes and creates more samples to bake these areas more accurately. Go to the Mode panel, and search for Lightmass Importance Volume; there should be only one result in the list. Drag the Lightmass Importance Volume to the level, move, and scale it to make it cover the starting room and the hallway connected to it. Drag out a few more copies of the Lightmass Importance Volume until the volumes cover all the playable area. It is ok to overlap the boxes (Figure 6.9).

We have a few lights added in when building our level, and there is a BP_ceiling_light_02 above every door, some of the hallways and rooms have ceiling lights also. We do not know how they feel like until we build the lighting, but we can expect them to work fine since we have tested them in our Test_Level while making them (Figure 4.57).

Lower Down Baking Quality for Quick Iteration

To test our lighting fast, we can globally lower down the lightmap resolution. Go to Build → Lighting info → LightMap Resolution Adjustment, check on Static Meshes and BSP Surfaces, and set Ratio to 20. Our baking now only bakes one-fifth of the lightmap resolution we have defined, which makes the render time faster (Figure 6.10).

253

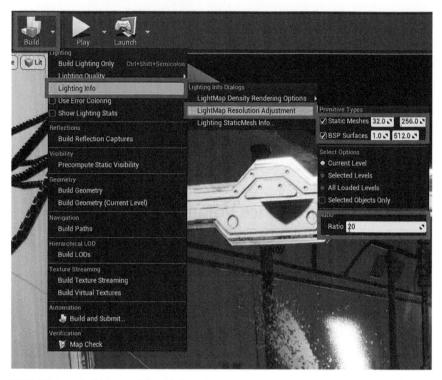

FIGURE 6.10 Lower the lightmap resolution globally.

We can also lower down the baking quality. Go to the Details panel, and click on the World Settings tab on the right side of the Details tab to switch to the World Setting panel. Open the Lightmass settings, and set the Static Lighting Level Scale to 2 and Indirect Lighting Quality to 0.5.

The Static Lighting Level Scale determines how many Unreal units equal 1 cm when baking. A value of 2 means 2 Unreal units is 1 cm, which makes our scene smaller and the baking time faster.

We also lower the Indirect Lighting Quality to 0.5 to make the baking faster (Figure 6.11).

Press Ctrl+Shift +; to build the lighting.

FIGURE 6.11 Tweak the World Settings.

FIGURE 6.12 Baking result after the quality adjustments.

The baking takes 10 minutes with our setting with an Intel(R) Core(TM) i7-6700K. This CPU is four generations behind the current core i7. Figure 6.12 shows the baking result.

Let's move on to adjusting and adding new lights to make the level look better than now.

Tips and Tricks

The more iterations we can make, the better our result could be. Reducing baking time is crucial to allow us to experiment with different lighting setups.

Tutorial 6.2: Adjust Lighting

Step 1: Adjust light intensity and color globally. We can all agree that the environment is a little dark. Select the BP_ceiling_light_01 in the starting room and press Ctrl + E to open it in the Blueprint editor. Select the SpotLight in the Components panel, go to the Details panel, and set the Intensity to 10,000. To make it look unique, set the Light Color to a bluish color. To keep the light color and the color of the light bulbs consistent, we can set the Emissive color of the Ceiling_light_01_light_mtl to a blue color also. For the other two lights, the light intensity of the BP_ceiling_light_02 is cranked up to 3000, and the light color is slightly warmer. The light intensity of the BP_lights_floor_light is now 2048, and the color is also a bit bluish. All the adjustments we did here should affect all the lights in the level (Figure 6.13). Feel free to adjust your lights differently to fit your needs and taste.

Step 2: Place more lights. The camera room and the security camera hallway are too dark, so place more lights to help some of the darker areas. Figure 6.14 shows some of the new lights added. Feel free to add more light in other areas that you think need more lighting.

Step 3: Tweak the materials. The crates appear to be too dark. To adjust the brightness of the color, we have to make some changes to our base material. Open the Substance_Base_Mtl, hold down the M button on the keyboard, and click to add a Multiply node. Hold down the V button and click to add a Vector parameter, name this Vector parameter ColorMult, and set its Default Value to white in the Details panel. Connect the Desaturation node to the A input

FIGURE 6.13 The changes made to BP_ceiling_light_01.

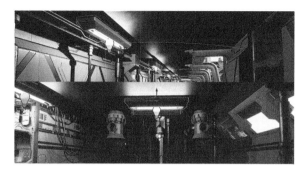

FIGURE 6.14 Add more lights to help brighten the level.

*pin of the Multiply node. Connect the Color
output pin of the ColorMult node to the B input
of the Multiply node, and connect the output
pin of the Multiply node to the Base Color of
the Substance_Base_Mtl node. Press the Save
button to save the change. We now have a new
ColorMult parameter that we can use to multiply
the color of the material. Open the Box_2K
material instance in the boxes folder. Check on
the ColorMult, click on the black color band to
pull out the Color Picker, and set the V value to 4
to brighten the color of the boxes (Figure 6.15).*

*The saturation of the walls is also too
intrusive. To fix it, we can set the Desaturation
parameter of the Substance_Base_Mtl_Inst to 0.3.*

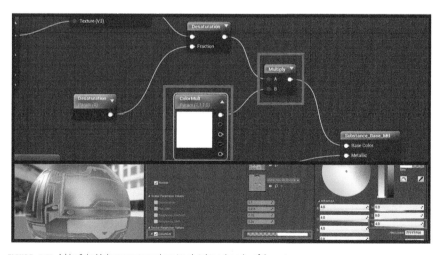

FIGURE 6.15 Add a ColorMult parameter and use it to brighten the color of the crates.

FIGURE 6.16 Some the lights shows a red cross to indicate that they are overlapping with too many other lights.

> *Step 4: Fix overlapping light limits. If you check every individual light, you can see that some of them are having a red cross on them (Figure 6.16).*
> *The red cross means that the light has more than two lights overlapping with it, and this is the technical limitation of lights with stationary mobility. We have two solutions here:*

1. All of our lights are set to stationary to suit both static meshes and our movable character later. However, we do not need all the lights to be stationary. Select any light that has a red cross, select its light component in the Details panel, and set the Mobility to static. Because static light does not cast shadows for movable objects, this option is suitable for areas that this light is not a primary light for moveable actors. The lights in the hallways are fixed this way (Figure 6.17).

2. Reduce the reach of the lights, so they are not overlapping each other. For all the lights in Unreal Engine, there is an Attenuation Radius setting. Attenuation Radius artificially limits the reach of the light. In Figure 6.18, the Attenuation Radius of the PointLight is reduced to 500 to avoid overlapping with too many other lights. The bright spherical wireframe indicates the furthest reach of the light. This option is preferred if you need this light to contribute detailed lighting and shadow to moveable actors. In this case, we want the light to help lit the hero asset, which is going to be moving in the future.

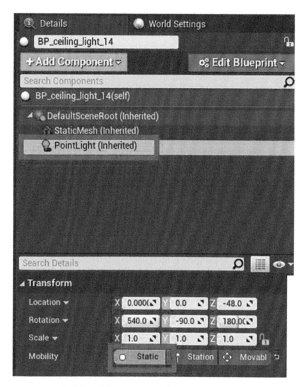

FIGURE 6.17 Set light mobility to static to fix the overlapping limit.

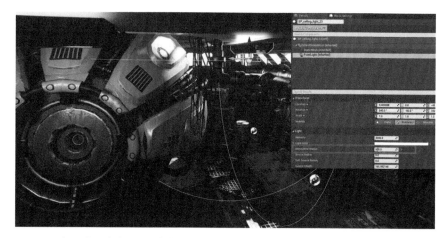

FIGURE 6.18 Lower down the Attenuation Radius to avoid the overlapping limit.

Only change the light to movable if none of the two options works.

Step 5: Setup mobility for the moveable objects. The doors and the hero asset are going to move in the future. Select the models of the doors and the hero asset, go to the Details panel, and set their Mobility to Moveable.

Step 6: Adjust Reflection captures. We have covered reflection captures already. Make sure that there are enough reflection captures to cover different areas. Figure 6.19 shows how every pot in the boss room has a reflection capture to help get better reflections. The security camera hallway is too long, and multiple reflection captures are used there.

Step 7: Build another test lighting. We have made enough changes here, press Ctrl + Shift +; to build lighting again to see the difference. Figure 6.20 shows the screenshots of the test result.

Step 8: More refinement. Please spend more time refining the lighting until you are happy with everything.

FIGURE 6.19 Place more reflection capture to get better reflections.

FIGURE 6.20 Another test lightings.

FIGURE 6.21 Final baking quality settings.

FIGURE 6.22 The high-quality baking results.

Step 9: Final baking. Once you are happy with the lighting test, click the drop-down arrow on the right of the Build button and select Lighting Quality → Production. In the same drop-down menu, select Lighting Info → LightMap Resolution Adjustment. Set the Ratio back to 100, make sure that the Static Meshes and BSP Surfaces are checked, and select Options to Current Level. Finally, go to the World Setting panel, and set the Static Lighting Level Scale to 0.25, Num Indirect Lighting Bounces to 4, Num Sky Lighting Bounces to 3, and Indirect Lighting Quality to 3 (Figure 6.21). Press Ctrl + Shift +; one more time to start baking. This baking is going to take a long time (12 hours with our 6-Gen Intel core i7).

The final baking result is shown in Figure 6.22.

Our lighting and baking are done, but there are more steps we can take to enhance the graphics further. Let's explore these extra steps.

Tutorial 6.3: Add Post Processing and Other Effects

Step 1: Add exponential height fog. For our forest environment, some haze or fog would exist. Go to the Mode panel and search for fog and drag Exponential Height Fog to the level. This Exponential Height Fog becomes thinner when it's higher. The fog appears to be too strong; so, go to the Details panel and set the Fog Density to 0.005 to make it thinner.

Step 2: Add Post Process Volume. Go to the Mode panel and search for Post Process Volume. Drag the Post Process Volume to the hallway. In the Details panel, go to the Post Process Volume Settings section and check on Infinite Extent (Unbound). This allows it to affect the whole world.

Post Process Volume

The Post Process Volume allows us to adjust many aspects of the final image, which gives the artists more control over the graphics. We can adjust the Lens effect, Color Grading, and add other rendering features like Screen Space Ambient Occlusion. Keep in mind though, Post Process Volume is not supposed to be used to fix any lighting problems. If the environment is too dark, you crank up the intensity of the lights.

Step 3: Add Vignette. Vignette is an effect that darkens the edge of the image. Compositionally, it helps to guide the eye to look at the center of the image. With the Post Process Volume selected, go to the Lens section, open the Image Effects, and check on Vignette Intensity. Set the value of the Vignette Intensity to 0.5 to create a very subtle vignette effect.

Step 4: Adjust Contrast and Saturation. Go to the Color Grading section. Under the global section, check on Saturation and Contrast. To make the image sharper, open the Contrast section and set the slider value to 1.1 under the color wheel. Higher contrast makes the colors more saturated; so, open the Saturation section and set the slider value under the color wheel to 0.8 to fix the saturation (Figure 6.23).

Step 5: Add Ambient Occlusion. Go to the Rendering Features section, open the Ambient Occlusion section, and check on Intensity and Radius. Drag the Intensity value up to 1. We have talked about Ambient Occlusion (AO) already in Chapter 3. AO means the same thing here. Adding AO enhances the detail of the models and adds weight to them.

FIGURE 6.23 Adjust the contrast and saturation using the post process volume.

Assignment

Now you have learned the different aspects of lighting, it is now up to you to fine-tune the lighting on our own. Please spend some time to tweak the number of lights you are having, adjust their intensity, and tweak their color. The Light Source directional light determines the sunlight. You can search for it in the world outliner, and you can rotate it to change the direction of the sun. Don't forget to experiment with post process volume also. The result we got is shown in Figure 6.24.

FIGURE 6.24 The lighting result.

Conclusion

Lighting the environment is truly fun, and if you enjoy experimenting, there is an infinite amount of possibilities. One thing to always keep in mind is to save performance, and we need to reduce the number of lights if possible. In terms of current generation computer graphics, it is not the polycount that slows down the performance, but the complicity of lighting and shaders. It is also super helpful to learn composition and lighting techniques, so you have good art guidance when trying different lighting ideas.

We are still dealing with cold metals or dead stuff; let's move on to the next chapter where we start making our character.

CHAPTER 7

Character Modeling

Hello, and welcome to the character modeling chapter! Character is always one of the critical aspects of a game. It may not take a lot of screen space, but it is what the player looks at for a long time; it is also what the players imagine as themselves. Therefore, developing a compelling character is an essential task of production.

Making characters requires dedication and patience so that every little detail is thought through and perfect. To keep the scope of this book suitable for all types of games, we will develop a full-body character that can fit into any camera placement. We will also ensure that it can be rigged and animated fully.

Concept Art

Concept art is one of the most critical steps of character development and should never be overlooked. The back story, environment, occupation, and all other parts of a character are thought through before the visual is touched. Visual appearance also takes many iterations to achieve the desired result. Our concept here is Ellen Mara. She is one of the genetic clones of a mindless killing army but somehow becomes self-aware and want to escape from fate. The design we settled on is shown in Figure 7.1.

Style Sheets

It is critical to have a clean style sheet that lays out the full character, and it is more practical to avoid fancy shading and use clear lines to represent the shapes. It is also essential to have different views of the character to match each other accurately. For example, the bottom of the chin should be in the same location in both the front and side view. There are two different poses we can model our character in: T pose and A pose. T pose has the arms straight, while A pose has the arms down naturally. We choose A pose for a better definition of the shape of the shoulder. Otherwise, the shoulder of the character in a natural pose has to be defined by rigging.

FIGURE 7.1 The design of Ellen Mara.

Workflow

Through the years of development, the workflow to make a character has changed a lot. The modern workflow mostly has a sculpting software called ZBrush involved. However, to limit the amount of software and the cost to follow this book, we are going for a more traditional approach – box modeling. Box modeling may not be the state-of-the-art workflow, but it is the best practice to teach topology, which is technically critical for rigging and animation. On the other hand, it is also going to force the artist to think about big shapes and proportions first.

Polycount

Polycount is one of the first things to think about before start making the model. It is drastically different based on the targeted platform, engine, and how many characters are going to appear on the screen. Polycount becomes lesser of a performance hit compared to the amount of lighting, shadowing, and textures, and we can safely assume an amount of 30k tris acceptable. This is not to say that we should reach 30k tris, finding the right balance between quality and performance is always needed.

Setting Up Image Plane in Maya

Step 1: Open a new Maya scene and save it as Ellen_Mara.mb.

Step 2: Go to the front view, choose View->Image Plane->Import Image, and load Ellen_Style_Sheet_Front.jpg.

Step 3: Switch to the right view, choose View->Image Plane->Import Image and load Ellen_Style_Sheet_Side.jpg.

Step 4: Create a cube, scale it up to 160 units, and move it up 80 units. The size of the cube is roughly the size of our character.

Step 5: Go to perspective view, select the two image planes, and scale and move them up so that the size of the character is roughly the size of the box.

Step 6: Go back to the front view and select ImagePlane1 in the outliner. Move it so that

FIGURE 7.2 Import and arrange the image planes.

the front view of the character is aligned to the center of the grid.

Step 7: Switch to the right view and select ImagePlane2 in the outliner. Move it so that the side view of the character is aligned to the center of the grid.

Step 8: Go to the perspective view and delete the cube. Move ImagePlane1 away from the center on the Z-axis and move ImagePlane2 away from the center on the X-axis (Figure 7.2).

Why?

The two image planes are references we need to get an accurate result. We are moving them away from the center to avoid clipping between our geometry and image planes.

Step 9: Select imagePlane1, press ctrl+a to open the attribute editor. In the Image Plane Attributes section, change the Display attribute to look through the camera. Do the same thing for imagePlane2.

Why?

This step is to keep the perspective view clean, but it is optional. Some modelers may think having image planes visible in the perspective view is more helpful.

Eyeball

> *Step 10: Create a polygon sphere and rename it*
> *Ellen_l_eye_geo. This sphere is going to be the*
> *eyeball (Create->Polygon Primitives->Sphere).*
> *Step 11: Reduce eyeball polycount. Select Ellen_l_*
> *eye_geo, go to the channel box, under the*
> *INPUTS section, click polySphere1, and change*
> *the subdivision Axis and Subdivision Height*
> *to 16.*

Why?

Although eyeball is important, our gamer is very unlikely to see it terribly close; reducing its polycount can help increase the frame rate in the game. Note that based on the type of the game, the subdivision level can very.

> *Step 12: Fix eye topology. Select the top center vertex*
> *of the eyeball (this is the front of the eye), holding*
> *down Ctrl, and then hit the delete button on the*
> *keyboard. We are now rid of all the triangles*
> *in the center. Switch to the Multi-Cut tool and*
> *connect the points to a grid-like topology*
> *(Figure 7.3).*

Why?

Any vertex that has more than four edges connected is called a pole. Pole is notoriously bad for smooth shading, especially when it has a lot of lines connected to it. Because the eye is one of the most important parts of a character, we choose to recreate the topology of the front.

> *Step 13: Fix curvature. Go to the front view, select the*
> *vertices of the top row, and holding down shift +*
> *right mouse button, in the marking menu, select*
> *Average Vertices. The Average Vertices command*

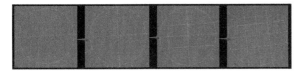

FIGURE 7.3 Recreate the topology of the front of the eye.

FIGURE 7.4 Change the shape back to spherical.

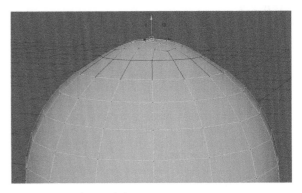

FIGURE 7.5 Create the cornea bulge.

averages the position of the selected vertices and give you some curvature. They are also collapsed down; use the move tool to move them back up. Repeat the Average Vertices and move operation until the eyeball is back to a spherical shape (Figure 7.4).

Step 14: Add cornea bulge. Switch back to the perspective view. Select the vertex at the top center, holding down the B button to enable soft selection. Drag the left mouse button to make the falloff range roughly the size of the cornea. Use the move tool to move up just a little bit to create the form of the cornea bulge (Figure 7.5).

Why?

The shape of the eyeball is not exactly a ball. The corneal area is bulging out a little bit more, mimicking the same shape that will help the refraction and highlight of the eyeball.

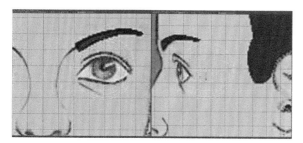

FIGURE 7.6 Match the eyeball model with the reference images.

Step 15: Rotate the eyeball 90 degrees on the X-axis.
Move and scale the eyeball until it matches the
left eyeball in both the front and side image
planes (Figure 7.6).

Step 16: Duplicate the eyeball, name the new one
Ellen_r_eye_geo, change its translate x from
positive to negative (mine went from 3.938 to
−3.938).

Create the Eyelids

Step 17: Make eyeball live. Select Ellen_l_eye_geo,
go to the Status-Line and click on the last
Magnetic Icon. Our eyeball model is now
live; when the geometry is live, any creation
or movement will be snapped to its surface.
Making the eyeball live helps us to get the correct
curvature of the eyelid.

Step 18: Draw eyelid geometry. Press the number
5 button on the keyboard to go to the solid
shading mode, in the viewport menu, select
Shading->X-Ray to turn on X-Ray. With nothing
selected, hold down the Shift button and the
right mouse button, select the Quad Draw Tool.
Go to the front view, click on the eyeball to the
drop-down points; create four points and then
holding down Shift and click in the middle
of the four points to fill in a quad geometry
(Figure 7.7).

Step 19: Finish the eyelid loop. Create two more
points and fill another quad that connects to
the first quad. Keep doing the same thing until
you get a loop wrapping around the contour of
the eyelid (Figure 7.8). You can drag any point or
edge to move them, hold down Ctrl+Shift, and
click on any point or edge to delete them.

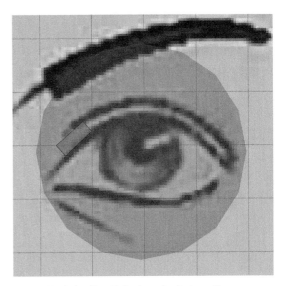

FIGURE 7.7 Use the Quad Draw Tool to draw a face for the eyelid.

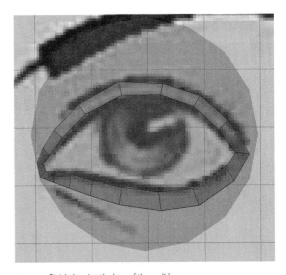

FIGURE 7.8 Finish drawing the loop of the eyelid.

Why?

Quad Draw Tool is a re-topologizing tool that allows us to create the topology for any geometry. We use it to get the correct curvature of the eye. One important usage of this

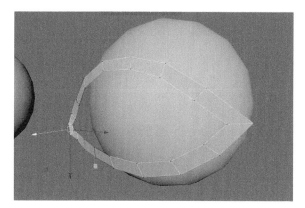

FIGURE 7.9 Drag the inner corner of the eyelid forward.

tool is to re-topologize a high-resolution model sculpted from a sculpting software like ZBrush, and we call that high to low workflow.

> *Step 20: Refine the eyelid shape. Turn off the live object, switch to the Selection tool, and go to object mode. Move the eyelid model forward a little, so there is a gap for the thickness of the eyelid. Go to side view and drag individual points to match the shape to the contour of the eyelid in the side view.*
>
> *Step 21: Refine the inner corner. Select the two endpoints of the inner corner; use Move, and soft selection to drag the inner corner area forward (Figure 7.9).*

Why?

Although the outer corner of the eyelid rests on the side of the eyeball, the inner corner does not. Underneath the inner corner of the eyelid, there are structures like caruncle and Papilla lacrimalis, which displace the inner eye corner forwards. That's why we drag it forward.

> *Step 22: Extrude the thickness of the eyelid. Go to edge mode, and double click to select the inner edge loop of the eyelid. Extrude the loop towards the eyeball, do another extrude to extend the inner surface to warp around the eyeball (Figure 7.10).*

273

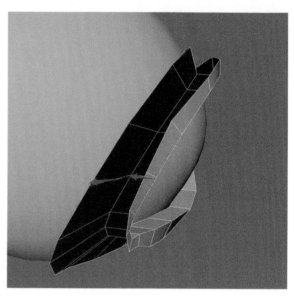

FIGURE 7.10 Extrude the thickness of the eyelid.

Step 23: Create the caruncle. Follow the steps shown in Figure 7.11 to create the caruncle.

Here, we first add an edge loop in the middle of the eyelid thickness face loop. We then select the top and bottom second faces from the inner corner and do a bridge face. After that, we select the loop of the hole between the inner corner and the new bridged face and delete it. We then double click the resulting hole and do a fill hole command, don't forget to fill the hole on the back as well. Finally, we add a horizontal edge loop to the new structure created, and move the vertices to make it looks like a flat oval shape.

FIGURE 7.11 Create the caruncle.

Why?

> *Step 23 seems to be a lot of work, but this part is a must-have to make the eyes look good. We are trying to achieve high-level results here; feel free to skip this if you are not trying to make a very detailed eye.*
>
> *Step 24: Round up the ridge of the eyelid. Select the loop at the turning edge of the upper eyelid that transitions from its front to its thickness, drag it up a little bit. Select the same loop of the lower eyelid and drag it down. This is to make the correct curvature of the transition of the eyelids; see Figure 7.12 for detailed illustration.*
>
> *Step 25: Soften the normal. Go to object mode, make sure Ellen_body_geo is selected, hold down Shift+right mouse button, and then choose Soften/Harden Edges->Soften Edge.*

Why?

We tend to limit our polycount, but we do not want to see hard polygon edges. Soften Edge command helps smooth out the shading between edges of the faces.

Create the Eye Socket

> *Step 26: Mark the edge of the eye socket. Select the outer edge loop of the eyelid, extrude out*

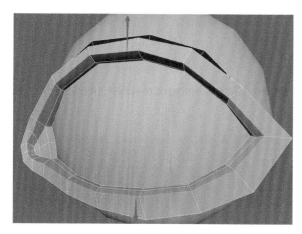

FIGURE 7.12 Drag the edges to round up the ridge of the eyelid.

another loop of faces, and move the vertices so that the new outer edge loop is at the edge of the eye socket (Figure 7.13).

Step 27: Eye socket Inter Detail. Add an edge loop in the middle of the face loop extruded in the previous step, and tweak the vertices to give it a correct curvature (Figure 7.14).

Step 28: Refine the inner structure. You can add more loops to any part around the eye to support more detail. In our case, three more loops around the eyelid were added and tweaked to support the bottom edge of the lower eyelid and the fold above the upper eyelid (Figure 7.15).

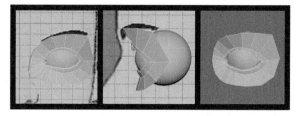

FIGURE 7.13 Create an edge loop that extends to the edge of the eye socket.

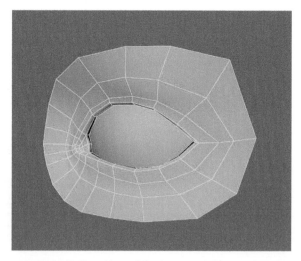

FIGURE 7.14 Add additional loop to define the inter detail of the eye socket.

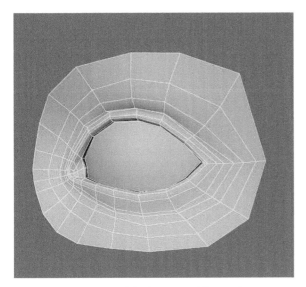

FIGURE 7.15 Add more loops to define the curvature of the eye socket.

Why?

From Step 26 to Step 28, we used a workflow of mark
the edge first and then added detail in the middle. This
workflow ensures that we can get the bigger shape first
and never lose control.

> *Step 29: Mirror. Select Ellen_body_geo, go to
> Modify->Freeze Transformations. Go to the front
> view, holding down D and X and use the Move
> tool to move the pivot to the center of the grid.
> Go to Edit->Duplicate Special☐. Change the
> geometry type to Instance, and change the scale
> to −1,1,1. This setting creates an instance of the
> model so we can see the full face while modeling
> on one side.*

Tips and Tricks

After modeling a while, your model might become heavy
due to all the construction histories. Make sure you press
Alt+Shift+D to delete history from time to time to avoid
performance issues, strange behavior, or crashes.

Forehead and Nose

Step 30: Root of the Nose. Select a few edges on the center side of the model, and extrude out these edges towards the center of the grid. Scale them down on the X-axis to flatten them, use Move, and grid snapping to snap them to the center. Go to the side view and drag them forward, move individual vertices to align them to the bridge of the nose (Figure 7.16).

Step 31: Add curvature to the root of the nose. Add a vertical loop to the root of the nose, and move it forward to distinguish the front and side plane of the nose. Keep adding new loops and tweak the vertices until it can represent the curvature of the nose. Two more loops were added, as shown in Figure 7.17.

Step 32: Connect nose to the eyebrow. Extrude the top loop of the eye socket twice and merge them

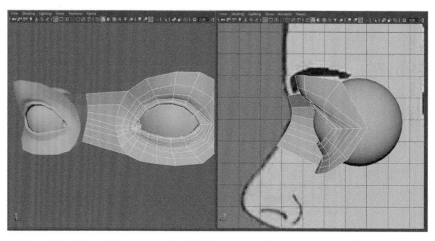

FIGURE 7.16 Create the root of the nose.

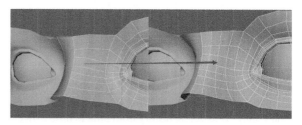

FIGURE 7.17 Add curvature to the root of the nose.

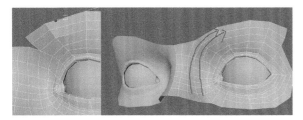

FIGURE 7.18 Connect the nose to the eyebrow.

> with the side loop of the root of the nose. We now
> have a geometry flow that went through the side
> of the nose to the brow ridge (Figure 7.18).

Why?

The edge flow is the only tool to represent turns of any
structure. We built the loop in Step 32 to accurately
represent the structural change of the nose and eyebrow,
almost like how you would place the bricks on an arch.

> *Step 33: Forehead. Extrude the top loops upwards to
> the edge of the forehead. Add more horizontal
> edge loops to support the curvature, just like
> what we did for the root of the nose (Figure 7.19).*

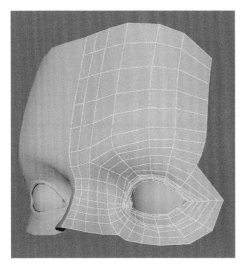

FIGURE 7.19 Create the forehead.

Step 34: Nose bridge. Extrude the bottom edges of the root of the nose downward and forward. Adjust the vertices to match it with the shape of the nose bridge (Figure 7.20).

Step 35: Mark the loop of the nasolabial fold. Extrude an edge downwards from the bottom of the nose bridge. Select the side edge of the new face, and extrude sideways around the side of the nose. Don't forget to rotate it after extrusion, so the loop's edge flows naturally as the direction of the face changes. Keep extruding until the entire nasolabial fold is created and extended around the mouth area (Figure 7.21).

Step 36: Tweak the loop of the nasolabial fold. Go to the right view. Drag the vertices of the nasolabial fold loop to adjust its shape, so it lays around the mouth nicely (Figure 7.22).

Step 37: Mark other essential loops. Extrude a few loops to represent the contour of the side of the nose, nostrils, and bottom of the nose. These loops help us define the primary areas of the nose (Figure 7.23).

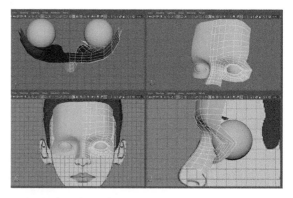

FIGURE 7.20 Create the nose bridge.

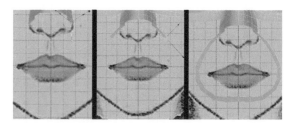

FIGURE 7.21 Mark the loop of the nasolabial fold.

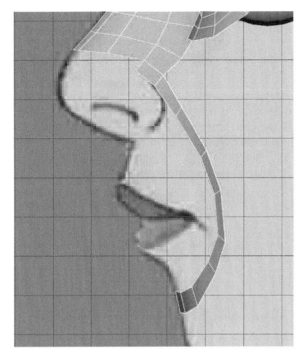

FIGURE 7.22 Adjust the loop of the nasolabial fold.

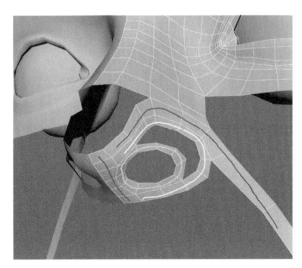

FIGURE 7.23 Essential loops of the nose.

Note that this is not a trivial task, and it takes careful moving of the vertices in all different views to ensure the shape is good at all angles. Some of the loops are touching, so their edges are fused.

Why?

Making the contour of different parts gives us the framework of the shape. Once finished, all we need to do is to fill in the gaps. Topology is basically edge loops like what we did in Step 36 with grid-like internal fills.

Step 38: Fill the side of the nose. Select the hole of the side of the nose, hold Shift+right mouse button, and choose Fill Hole. Use the Multi-Cut tool to fill in the geometry. In Figure 7.24, highlighted lines are the newly added lines to get a clean topology. Drag the vertices around to refine the shape of the side of the nose.

Step 39: Fill the tip of the nose the same way we did in Step 38 (Figure 7.25).

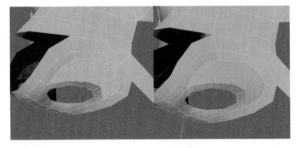

FIGURE 7.24 Fill the side of the nose.

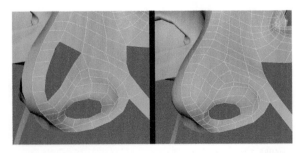

FIGURE 7.25 Fill the tip of the nose.

Mouth

Step 40: Mouth. Extrude from the bottom of the nose to create the philtrum. From the bottom of the philtrum, extrude out the loops for the lip. Add extra loops to help define the shape better. Be careful about the curvature of the model from different angles. It is very easy to end up with a flat result, so make sure that the arc of the contour is always managed (Figure 7.26).

Step 41: Fill in the gaps between the mouth and the nasolabial fold. Bridge the outer edge of the lips to the inner edge of the nasolabial fold; if there is a mismatch on polycount, just add more loops. A pole is needed to sort out the upper right corner mesh flows (Figure 7.27).

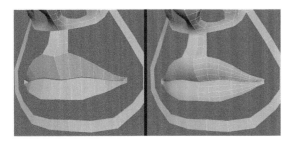

FIGURE 7.26 Create the topology of the mouth.

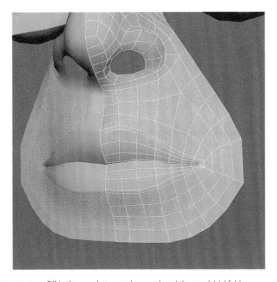

FIGURE 7.27 Fill in the gaps between the mouth and the nasolabial fold.

Rest of the Head

Step 42: Frame the rest of the head. Create more loops around the head to mark the edge of the side of the face, ear, top, and back of the head. Create loops for the neck and the jawlines as well (Figure 7.28).

Step 43: Fill in the front of the face. Start bridging faces of the front of the face using the Bridge, Extrude, Fill Hole, and the Multi-Cut command. Find the crucial loop that needs to be established first, and then fill in the gaps. Make sure that everything you added must be tweaked on some level to have the correct shape (Figure 7.29).

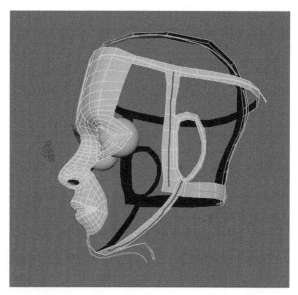

FIGURE 7.28 Frame the rest of the head.

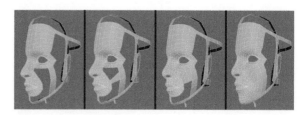

FIGURE 7.29 Fill the front faces.

Tips and Tricks

After filling in the gaps, the face might not look smooth at all. Select the model with object mode, hold down Shift+right mouse button and choose Sculpt Tool, hold down Shift+right mouse button again, and choose Grab. You can now drag any part of the model like you are sculpting it. Hold down B button, and then drag to change the brush size; be aware that the size of the brush might be too big, so you need to zoom out a lot to see it changing. You can also hold down Shift and then drag on the surface of the model to smooth it. Remember that shape is always more important, don't drown yourself in topology. You will get better and better at topology, but if you don't pay enough attention to shapes, you may not get better at it.

Step 44: Fill in the side of the face. We can fill the side of the face using the same method as in previous steps (Figure 7.30). The outer corner of the eye does not have enough polycount to connect to the other side, so two more loops were added to compensate that. They are marked in Figure 7.30.

Step 45: Fill in the top of the head. The topology of the top is basically a cube smoothed twice. The important thing is to find the two corner points, and they are indicated in Figure 7.31. It is these two points that redirect the flows of the polygons. After these two points, geometries either go from front to the back or from side to middle. Note that Grab and Smooth sculpting were used to achieve a smooth result after getting the topology working.

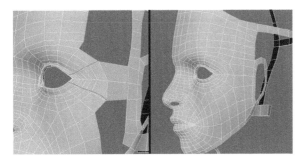

FIGURE 7.30 Fill the side of the face.

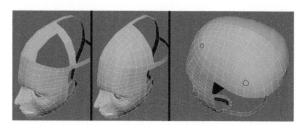

FIGURE 7.31 Fill in the top of the head.

Step 46: Fill in the back of the head.

Ear

The ear might be not as important as the eyes and nose, but it is something that if you do not do well, it jumps out and ruins your model. We will address the ear carefully in detail.

Step 47: Create the main loop of the ear. Just as how we did the nose, the ear can also be modeled by first laying out the primary structures using poly loops. Extrude from the back of the ear, and then start building the loops from there. There is a color-coded version of the ear loops in Figure 7.32.

Step 48: Fill the ear. We can use the bridge and extrude command to fill in the gaps between the loops; don't forget to leave a hole open to extrude out the ear hole (Figure 7.33).

Step 49: Connect the ear. Keep bridging and extruding faces to connect the ear to the face

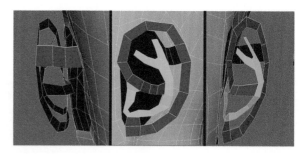

FIGURE 7.32 Create the main loop of the ear.

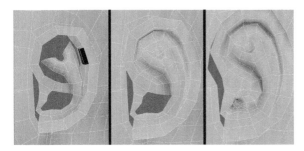

FIGURE 7.33 Fill the ear.

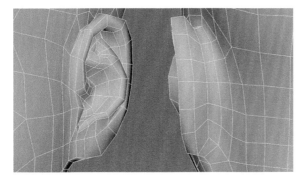

FIGURE 7.34 Connect the ear.

(Figure 7.34); the polycount might not match exactly, and you will need to choose to add or delete edge loops.

Neck

Step 50: Fill the bottom of the head. There are many lines coming down from the head. However, we do not want that much happening on the neck. Redirecting these edge flows to turn to the center and meet on the other side is a good way of getting rid of them altogether (Figure 7.35).

Step 51: Extrude the neck. We chose to make the neck as simple as possible because the turtleneck collar is covering it. All we do is to extrude from the bottom of the neck hole to the base of the neck, and add extra loops in the middle to match the shape of the concept (Figure 7.36).

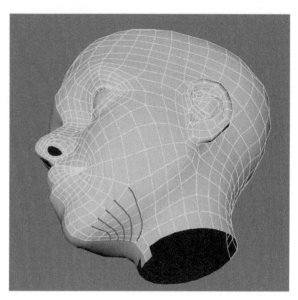

FIGURE 7.35 Redirect the line of the face loop to the center and fill the bottom of the head.

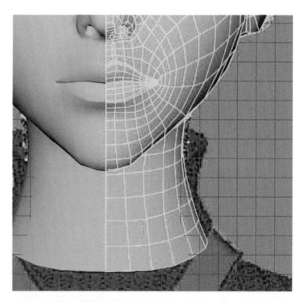

FIGURE 7.36 Extrude the neck.

Internal Structures

Step 52: Nostrils internals. Select the loop of the hole of the nostrils and extrude up and inwards a little bit; do it two more times so that the hole looks extended all the way, and make sure the end is not visible (Figure 7.37).

Step 53: Mouth internals. The mouth Internal is the same topology as the nostrils but needs more loops and inflation of the space inside. Select Ellen_body_geo, press Ctrl + 1 to isolate it. Then select the edge loop of the seam between the lips, extrude inwards, and then expand out. Make sure that there is space for the teeth. Keep Extruding more until the oval mouth internal cavity is constructed (Figure 7.38).

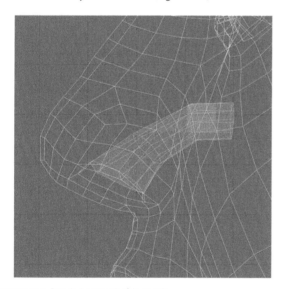

FIGURE 7.37 Extrude the internals of the nostrils.

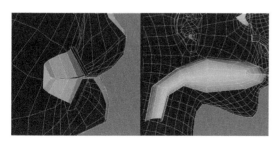

FIGURE 7.38 Extrude the internals of the mouth.

Body

Step 54: Create the center loop of the torso. Extrude from the front bottom of the neck; keep extruding until the geometry wraps around the contour of the right view. Merge to the back of the neck (Figure 7.39).

Step 55: Chest. Create loops around the chest and the armhole, then bridge a loop from the neck to the armhole to mark the range of the chest. Fill the hole of the chest; use the Multi-Cut tool to fill in the missing topology; add extra lines if the polycount does not work. Use the sculpting tool to smooth and refine the shape after getting the topology done (Figure 7.40).

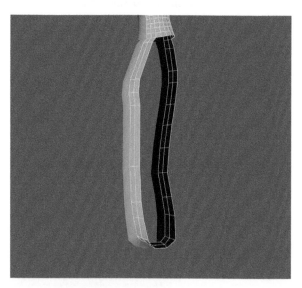

FIGURE 7.39 Create the center loop of the torso.

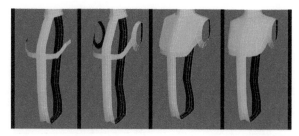

FIGURE 7.40 Create the chest.

Step 56: Fill the back. Using the same method of Step 55, we can fill the back of the body (Figure 7.41).
Step 57: Fill the torso. Using the same method of Step 55. We can fill the waist (Figure 7.42).
Step 58: Tweak the flow of the pelvis. Extrude out a loop from the bottom hole of the torso, and tweak the shape so that there is a loop around to represent the upper edge of the pelvis (Figure 7.43).

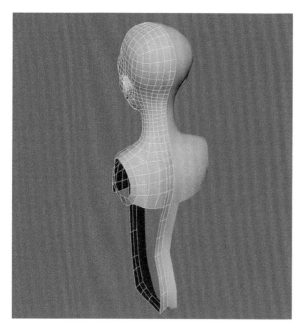

FIGURE 7.41 Fill the back.

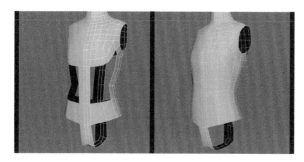

FIGURE 7.42 Fill the torso.

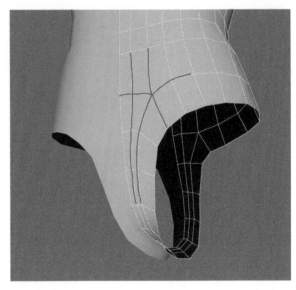

FIGURE 7.43 The tweaked topology of the pelvis.

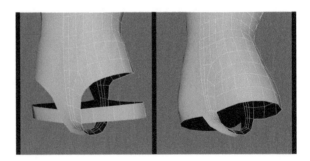

FIGURE 7.44 Create the loop of the leg hole.

Step 59: Loop of the leg hole. Create a loop of the leg and fill the gap between the pelvis loop to the leg loop (Figure 7.44).

Step 60: Create the leg. Extrude from the leg hole to make the leg. We can use a very simple cylinder-like topology to represent it; keep in mind that at least three loops are needed to bend the knee and ankle properly (Figure 7.45).

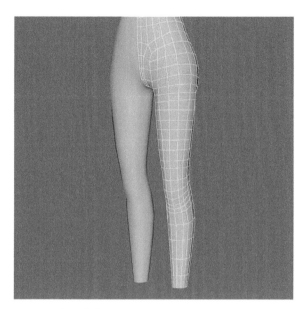

FIGURE 7.45 Create the leg.

Tips and Tricks

After we create the loops that outline different structures, it is critical to define its profile properly so that further extrusion or fills have the perfect shape already.

> *Step 61: Ankle. Extrude down from the leg, make an angle shape at the bottom. The bottom vertex will be the primary turning point of the edge loops – the pole (Figure 7.46).*

Tips and Tricks

One thing to always keep in mind is to have the same polycount on the two sides you know that will merge. In Step 61, you need to make sure that the front and back of the bottom point have the same polycount. Otherwise, you are going to have to add extra lines or delete lines later.

> *Step 62: Create the feet. We use the same technique we have been using to create the framework of the feet first and then fill in the gaps after (Figure 7.47).*

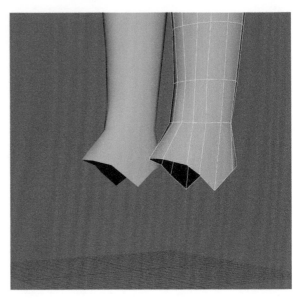

FIGURE 7.46 Create the ankle.

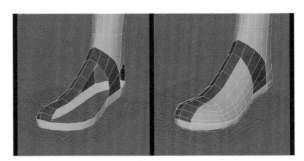

FIGURE 7.47 Create the feet.

Step 63: Create the deltoid. Go to edge mode, select the top half of the armhole. Extrude out two loops, bridge the side of the second loop to the edge right below the previously selected edges. Tweak the shape so that the contour matches the image plane and has a tilted armhole (Figure 7.48).

Step 64: Create the arm. Extrude from the armhole to create the arm. The process is exactly like how we did the leg (Figure 7.49).

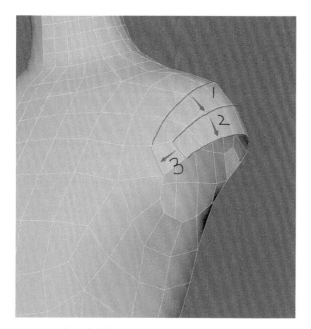

FIGURE 7.48 Create the deltoid.

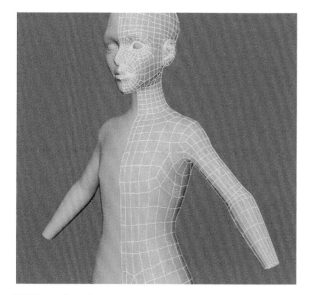

FIGURE 7.49 Create the arm.

Hands

Step 65: Palm. Extrude from the wrist to create the palm; add a few loops to define the size change of the palm (Figure 7.50).

Step 66: Thumb. Add one more loop to mark out the base of the thumb and then extrude the faces out to create the first segment of the thumb. Go to Edit->Circularize to make the extruded face more rounded, keep extruding, adding edge loop, and tweaking to finish the thumb (Figure 7.51).

Step 67: Thumb Tip Topology. Delete all the lines the tip of the thumb has, and use the Multi-Cut tool to create a new topology like Figure 7.52. Make sure that you tweak the shape afterward.

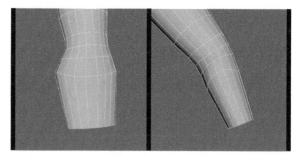

FIGURE 7.50 The base of the palm.

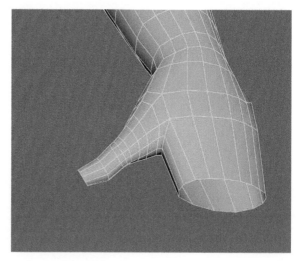

FIGURE 7.51 Extrude out the thumb.

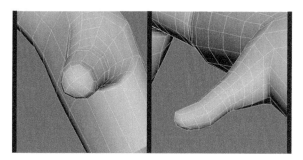

FIGURE 7.52 The topology of the tip of the thumb.

> *Step 68: Create the index finger. Start with a cube, move it to the base of the index finger, and extrude the tip out twice to mark the three segments of the finger. Tweak the size of the different segments (Figure 7.53).*
>
> *Step 69: Add finger detail. Delete the face at the root of the finger. We need it to open to connect to the palm. Switch to Insert Edge Loop tool; hold down Shift, and add two more edge loops to round up the finger (Figure 7.54).*

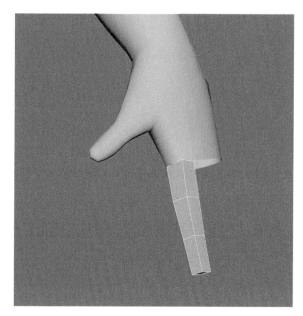

FIGURE 7.53 Create the base of the index finger.

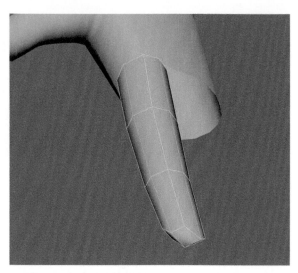

FIGURE 7.54 Add details to the finger.

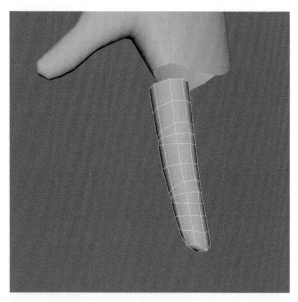

FIGURE 7.55 Add the finger loops to support bending.

Step 70: Add the finger loops. Add more loops to the finger; at least three loops are needed for the bending of each segment. Tweak the shape after adding new loops (Figure 7.55).

Step 71: Duplicate the fingers. Duplicate the index finger, move, and scale the duplication to the position of the middle finger. Keep in mind that the base of the four fingers is not a flat plane but rather a convex arc (Figure 7.56).

Step 72: Combine fingers. With all fingers selected, select Mesh->Combine. Select the inside two edges of the two adjacent fingers and bridge them. Add one vertical edge loop to the bridged faces and drag it inwards to mimic the gap between the fingers (Figure 7.57).

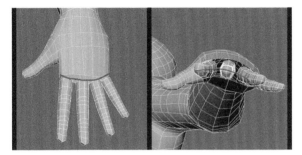

FIGURE 7.56 Duplicate the index finger for the other three fingers and arrange them properly.

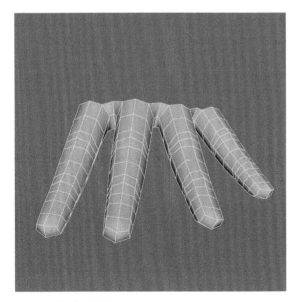

FIGURE 7.57 Combine the fingers.

299

Step 73: Attach fingers to the hand. Select both the body and the fingers; select Mesh->Combine. Press Alt+Shift+D to clean up the history. After combining, some redundant groups may remain. Delete all empty groups and name the combined model Ellen_body_geo. Bridge the faces of the two ends of the finger geometry and closest faces of the palm and fill the two holes left (Figure 7.58).

Step 74: Refine hand topology. Use Multi-Cut to connect the lines from the finger to the palm. It is obviously going to have different polycount; just cut through the edge of the palm for now. Make sure you spend some time evening out the vertices (Figure 7.59).

Step 75: Reduce polycount. Merge the two adjacent points to the point that belongs to the line that goes across the gap between the fingers (Figure 7.60).

Step 76: Clean up the triangles. Please reference the result of Figure 7.61. What we do is to delete the middle line of the resulting triangle shape in the previous step and drag the bottom point down. Use the Multi-Cut tool to add an extra loop that goes across the middle of the previous triangle shape and has a line connected to the middle line between the fingers.

Step 77: Fix N-gons. Use the Multi-Cut tool to redirect the extra lines that do not meet with the bottom structure sideways. These lines can meet and cancel each other out without having to add extra lines to the arm. One more edge loop is also added to the big gap between the fingers and palm. Figure 7.62 highlights all the new lines added.

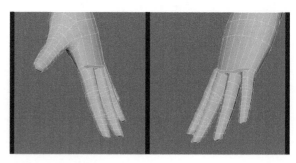

FIGURE 7.58 Attach the fingers to the palm.

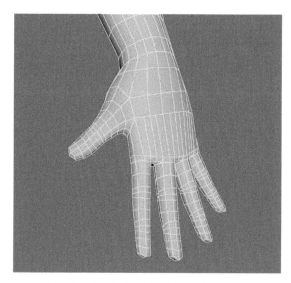

FIGURE 7.59 Use the Muti-Cut tool to fill the missing topology.

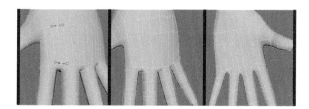

FIGURE 7.60 Reduce the polycount on the palm.

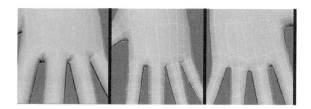

FIGURE 7.61 Clean up the triangles.

Step 78: Mirror. Select all the edges in the middle of the body, scale them along the X-axis to flatten them. Hold down X and drag them along the X-axis to snap to the center of the grid. Switch to object mode, hold Shift + right mouse button, and choose Mirror. In the floating setting menu, set the Merge Threshold to 0.01 (Figure 7.63).

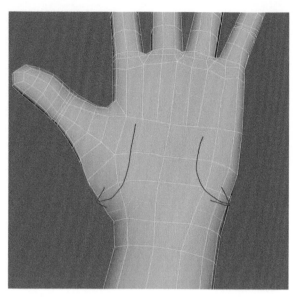

FIGURE 7.62 Fix the N-gon of the palm.

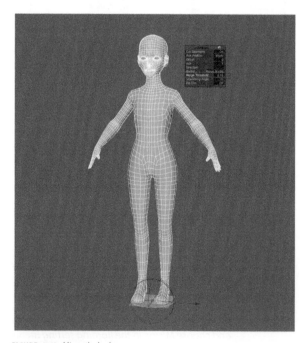

FIGURE 7.63 Mirror the body.

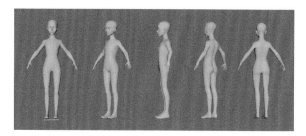

FIGURE 7.64 Tweak the body of the character.

> *Step 79: Tweak the overall shape. After the body is all done, it is a good time to tweak the global shape and proportion. Hold down W and drag the left button up and up again; this should turn on the symmetry and allow you to tweak the model symmetrically. Start tweaking the body with whatever tool you feel comfortable with (Figure 7.64).*

Hairs

> *Step 80: Hair Sculpt. Create a cube, move, and scale it to roughly the location and size of the hair. Smooth it four times (Mesh->Smooth), so we get many polygons to work with. It may shrink after smoothing, so scale it up again. Go to the Sculpting shelf, pick the grab tool to sculpt the shape of the hair. We only care about the shape of the hair for now. We can give it proper topology later (Figure 7.65).*
>
> *Step 81: Auto re-topologize the hair. Select the hair, choose Mesh->Retopologize. Maya now automatically creates a topology for us. After the retopology is done, more tweaks can be applied to make the shape of the hair better.*
>
> *Step 82: Add hair detail. Smooth the hair twice, and now you can use all the sculpting tools to tweak*

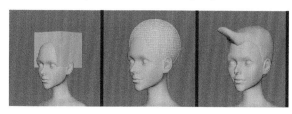

FIGURE 7.65 Sculpt the hair shape.

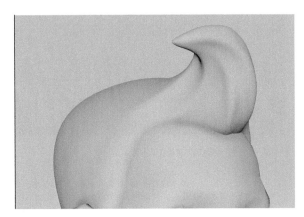

FIGURE 7.66 The sculpted hair shape.

and add more detail to the hair. In Figure 7.66, sculpt brush was used to add some basic clumping details to the hair.

Tips and Tricks

Maya is not the best tool to sculpt; if you want to create detailed hair, ZBrush is going to be the tool you use.

> *Step 83: Final Hair topology. Select the hair model. Go to Status-Line, click on the last magnetic icon to make it live. With nothing selected, hold down the Shift + right mouse button, and choose the Quad Draw tool. Click and drag on the hair to create new points, and hold down Shift to fill a quad between any points. Start re-topologizing the hair and make sure the loops flow with the direction of the clumps (Figure 7.67).*
>
> *Step 84: Finish hair topology. Keep re-topologizing the hair; keep in mind that the flow of the loop should follow the shape (Figure 7.68).*

Tips and Tricks

When doing topology for games, it is acceptable to end up with some triangles to save polycount. It is always possible, though, to avoid having triangles. After all, the cause of having a triangle is mismatched polycount.

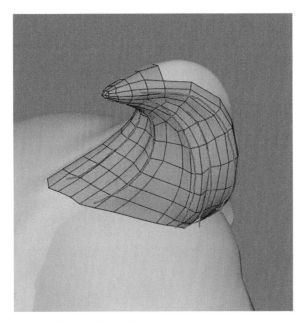

FIGURE 7.67 Start retopologizing the hair.

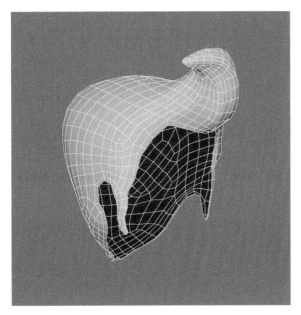

FIGURE 7.68 Finished hair topology.

Step 85: Eyebrow. Select the model and make it live. Use the Quad-Draw tool again to layout the geometry of the eyebrow. Extrude the eyebrow faces to give it thickness. Add a few edge loops across the eyebrow and drag the vertices to round it up; give the hair and the eyebrow a darker material (Figure 7.69).

Step 86: Eyelashes. Eyelashes can be done the same way we did the eyebrow, but more dragging is needed to make the shape stick out (Figure 7.70).

Step 87: Sweater base. Duplicate the model, and name it Ellen_sweater_geo. Delete the faces that are not part of the sweater. Do an extra tweak of the topology and the shape to give the sweater a clean edge on the chest. Select all vertices of the sweater model, hold down W+right mouse

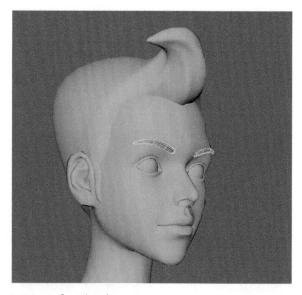

FIGURE 7.69 Create the eyebrow.

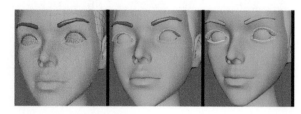

FIGURE 7.70 Create the eyelashes.

button, and choose Axis->Normal. Drag the N
axis just a little to inflate the sweater (Figure 7.71).
Don't forget to switch the moving axis back to
the object.

Step 88: Sweater collar and rolling sleeves. Extrude
from the top edge of the collar inwards and
then downwards to mimic the thickness of the
turtleneck. Add extra edge loops in the middle;
drag the face of the collar out to give it the
correct volume. Make extra adjustments to add
variations and crevices. It should appear to be
thicker on the top and bottom, and narrower in
the middle. The rolling sleeves can be done the
same way (Figure 7.72).

Step 89: Outer garment base. Duplicate the Ellen_
body_geo, name it Ellen_outfit_geo. Delete the
faces above the chest. Make the Ellen_body_geo
live again, select Ellen_outfit_geo, hold down
Shift+right mouse button, and choose the
Quad Draw Tool. Use retopology to create the
missing upper part of the outfit and refine the
already existing shapes. Tweak the shape so that
it is above the sweater, and add thickness by
extruding the edge of the outfit inwards twice
(Figure 7.73).

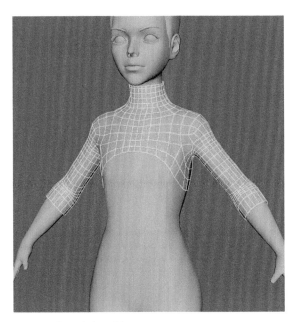

FIGURE 7.71 Create the base of the sweater.

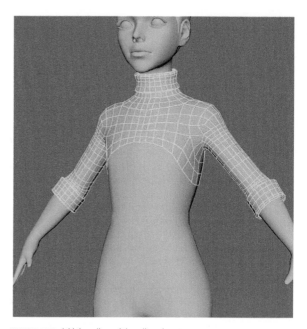

FIGURE 7.72 Add the collar and the rolling sleeves.

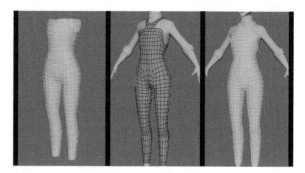

FIGURE 7.73 Create the base of the outer garment.

Step 90: Preview materials. Hold down the right mouse button on different models and choose Assign New Material; click on Lambert on the pop-up window. Go to the Attribute Editor and change the color of the material based on the reference. Assigning different colors can help us spot clipping geometry and better visualize our model (Figure 7.74).

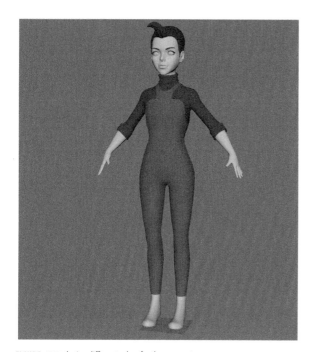

FIGURE **7.74** Assign different colors for the garments.

Step 91: Belt. Duplicate the Ellen_outfit_geo; delete everything but the loop around the belt. Extrude it out to make the belt. Extrude the middle two loops of the belt to mimic the buckle. Give it a new lambert material, make it darker, and name the belt Ellen_belt_geo. Select all the faces below the belt, assign a new lambert material to them, and change the color to the color of the pants (Figure 7.75).

Step 92: Create the patterns of the boots. Select Ellen_body_geo and make it live; use the Quad Draw tool to draw out the patterns of the shoes. Turn off the live object, adjust the shape of the boots to match the concept, and name the model Ellen_boots_geo (Figure 7.76).

Step 93: Boots bottom. Duplicate Ellen_body_geo one more time, and delete everything but the bottom of the foot. Adjust its edge so that it matches the shape of the bottom of the boot. Extrude all the faces down to give it thickness; select the faces on the back and extrude again to create the heel.

FIGURE 7.75 Create the belt.

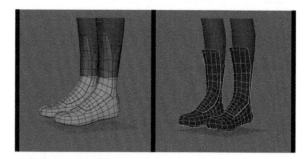

FIGURE 7.76 Create the patterns of the boots.

Select the edges of the upper and lower rim of the model, hold down the Shift+right mouse button, and choose Bevel Edge. In the pop-up menu, reduce the Fraction attribute to make the bevel smaller. Fix the N-gon generated by the bevel command (Figure 7.77).

Step 94: Add thickness to the patterns. Select the outline edges of the patterns of the boots, and extrude out the thickness. Bridge the edges of

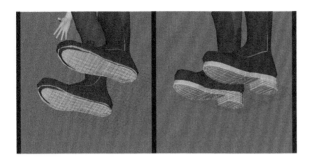

FIGURE 7.77 Create the bottom of the boots.

> the seam lines, select the rest of the outline, and
> extrude in again for extra thickness (Figure 7.78).
>
> Step 95: Boot Belts. Select Ellen_body_geo and
> make it live; use the Quad Draw tool to draw
> the upper belt out and extrude the thickness,
> duplicate, and move it down for the bottom one
> (Figure 7.79).
>
> Step 96: Create the base shape of the gloves.
> Duplicate Ellen_body_geo, select all faces that
> you wish to be the glove, press Ctrl + Shift + I to
> reverse the selection, and press delete button to
> remove all other faces. Select all points on the
> hand, hold down W + right mouse button, choose

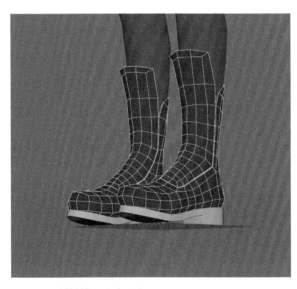

FIGURE 7.78 Add thickness to the patterns.

FIGURE 7.79 Add the belts of the boots.

Axis->Normal, and drag the N axis to move the points out (Figure 7.80).

Step 97: Add details to the glove. Add more loops at the wrist part of the glove; scale them up and down to mimic a layering effect. At the opening of the glove, extrude more loops, and scale them to create a ridge. Eventually, add thickness to the glove by extruding the edge loops on all the openings to add thickness (Figure 7.81).

Step 98: Glove belt. Create the belt of the glove using the same method as in Step 97 (Figure 7.82).

Step 99: Watch. Follow the steps shown in Figure 7.83 to create the watch.

Start with a cube, add edge loops in the middle, and expand the loop in the center. Bevel the four corner loops to create the base shape of the watch. Extrude the top face in and down to create the area of the watch panel. Don't forget to use the Multi-Cut tool to fix the N-gon in the center. Extrude from the side of the watch to add the connections for the watchband. Select the primary turning edges of the watch and bevel it; move it to the right hand when it's all done.

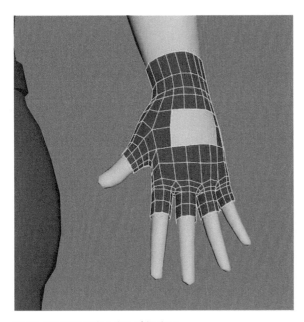

FIGURE 7.80 Create the base shape of the gloves.

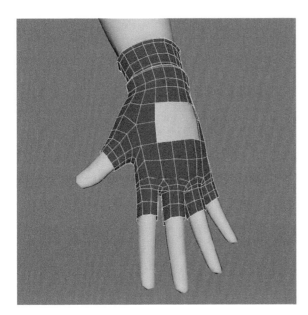

FIGURE 7.81 Add details to the glove.

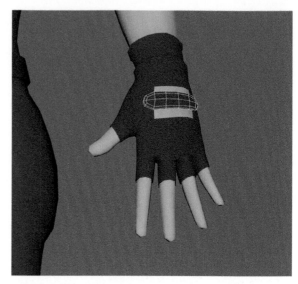

FIGURE 7.82 Create the belt of the glove.

FIGURE 7.83 Steps to create the watch.

Step 100: Watchband. The wrist band can be easily done the same way we created the boot belts in Step 97 (Figure 7.84).

Step 101: Final body adjustment. Spend some time to adjust the whole body; if you have a team, it is also an excellent chance to talk with them. The adjusted result of the character looks like that seen in Figure 7.85. A few pockets were added to the belt.

Weapon

Step 102: Create the base shape of the gun. Create a cube, name it Ellen_gun_geo, scale it down on its X-axis to make it narrower, and extrude from its front, back, and bottom faces to create the slide and handle. Keep adding loops and extruding to

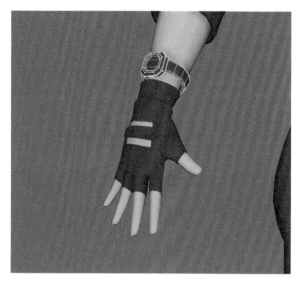

FIGURE 7.84 Create the watchband.

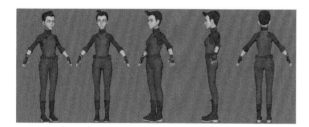

FIGURE 7.85 The finalized model.

FIGURE 7.86 The process to create the base shape of the gun.

*add extra detail. Figure 7.86 shows the process of
the shape evolving.*
*Step 103: Add extra detail to the gun. Duplicate
the gun, select the faces that could be the extra*

FIGURE 7.87 Add extra detail to the gun.

FIGURE 7.88 Create the gun holster.

panels on the gun, press Ctrl + Shift + I to reverse the selection, and press delete to get rid of other faces. Extrude out the thickness of the panels, drag the vertices around to make the shape more interesting, add new edge loops, and extrude out extra detail (Figure 7.87). Combine the body and the panels together, delete the history, and name it Ellen_gun_geo.

Step 104: Gun holster. Follow Figure 7.88, move the gun to the side of the right leg, and make the Ellen_outfit_geo live. Use the Quad Draw tool to layout the shape of the base of the gun holster, and move it outwards a little afterward to separate it from the leg. Using the same method, we can get the profile of the outer layer of the holster. We need to move points out to wrap it around the body of the gun. A few loops were added to support the curling shape. Two straps were created around the leg afterward.

Tips and Tricks

When making weapons, it is crucial to make sure that the size of the weapon is suitable to the character. The handle of the gun was extended to make sure it fits in the hands of the character.

Final Clean Up

> *Step 105: Delete hidden geometry. Duplicate the Ellen_body_geo, name it Ellen_full_body_ref, and press Ctrl + H to hide it. Select Ellen_body_geo, select the faces that are hidden under the garments, and delete them (Figure 7.89).*

Why?

We have a copy of the full body and hid it as a backup in case something needs to be changed or added. We rely on the body to add all the garments and props. For rigging, it is easier to bind the joints with a full-body, do the skin weighting, and copy the weight over to the garments.

> *Step 107: Separate and rename. Select Ellen_body_geo and Click on Mesh->Separate. The model now separates to multiple ones based on connectivity. Combine the hands and arms, and name the new model Ellen_hands_geo. Select the head and name it Ellend_head_geo. Press*

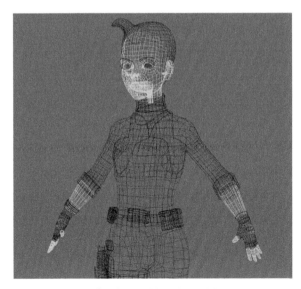

FIGURE 7.89 Delete the faces that are hidden under the clothing.

FIGURE 7.90 The outline of the finished model.

Alt + Shift + D to delete the history. Select the resulting group Ellen_body_geo, and click Edit->Ungroup to ungroup it. The outliner ends up as shown in Figure 7.90.

Tips and Tricks

Facial Expression rig requires something called Blendshape. It is much cheaper to do Blendshape on a simpler model; that is why, if possible, separate the head from the body.

Conclusion

We made it! We have a character that is ready to go for UV texturing, rigging, and animation; the polycount is 29,250 Tris, a little lesser than our prediction. The whole character is designed and modeled in a week. We have used many techniques. However, there are far more areas of character modeling we have not touched, like ZBrush sculpting and Marvelous Designer, to name a few. If you ever want to have more advanced knowledge on character modeling, ZBrush is the next to jump in, and it is a super fun software. Feel free to stay here and do more tweaking of the shape of the character before moving on. It is critical to have a good-looking character with proper topology for rigging and animation. The final model is shown in Figure 7.91.

In the next chapter, we will go over the UV Mapping of the character. UV is the foundation of texturing and is of great importance to bring life to our solid colored character.

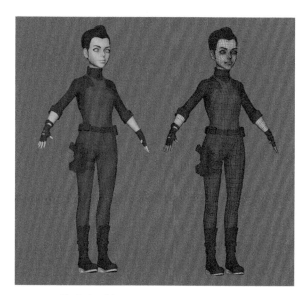

FIGURE 7.91 The final model.

CHAPTER 8

UV Mapping

UV for characters is particularly important. It is the foundation of good texture mapping, which is the primary way we add color and detail to our character. With a proper texture set, we can make a 30k tris polygon looks like a million tris.

It is, however, safe to say, modeling is more critical now than it was 10 years ago. This is the last time we are asking you to check your model before moving on. Make sure that you and your team are 100% happy with the shape of the character. Once we move further on, changing of the shape will need you to change the UV to avoid stretched textures.

UV Mapping

UV mapping algorithm has been improved through the years; so, all artists need to do is to define the seam properly and lay out the UV the efficient way. There are other tools like Unfold 3D that are dedicated for UV Mapping, but Maya's UV tools are already amazingly good. So, we will stick with Maya for the ease of not having to move to a different package.

Tutorial 8.1: Character UV Mapping

In this tutorial, we will jump into UV mapping of the character. We are going to do a basic error checking of the model, define seams of the UV shell, unfold them, layout and organize the UV, and assign shading groups. Along the way, we could discover more modeling problems, and we will address it right away.

Mesh Inspection and Cleanup

Based on how experienced you are at modeling, there could be many problems in your model. Let's review some of the common problems in case you have them on your model.

Step 1: Flipped faces. In the viewport menu, go to Lighting and check off Two-Sided Lighting; if any faces of the model appear to be black, select these faces and do Mesh Display->Reverse.

Step 2: Check N-gon. Select the model you want to check, go to Mesh->Clean Up□. Change the Operation to Select matching polygons and check on Faces with more than four sides in the Fix by Tessellation section. Press the apply button. If there is any face that is selected, they are N-gons.

Step 3: Fix N-gons. N-gon is basically caused by polycounts that are not matching; to fix N-gon, you either add more loops on one side or delete loops on the other side. Figure 8.1 shows two options to fix a pentagon; unless there is a particular reason to add a new loop, deleting one is a better choice. Another option is to use

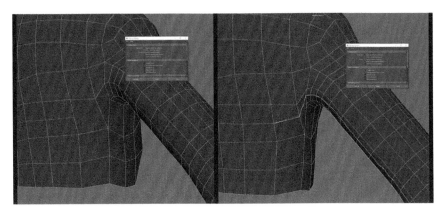

FIGURE 8.1 Two ways to fix an N-gon.

the Multi-Cut tool to cut the N-gon to triangles
and quads.

Step 4: Overlapping faces. There could be a chance
that you have two faces stacked right on top of
each other and sharing the same edges. Select
the model and hit 3 to smooth preview the model
and check the flow of the wireframe. If you find
something irregular (Figure 8.2), you know that
something must be wrong. It is recommended to
delete these faces and redo them to ensure it is
bug-free.

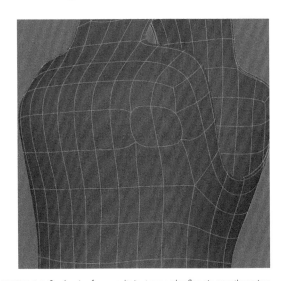

FIGURE 8.2 Overlapping faces results in strange edge flows in smooth preview.

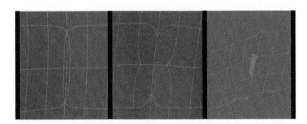

FIGURE 8.3 Potential topology errors that could happen to the middle of the model.

> *Step 5: Middle line problem. Select the model you want to check, go to edge mode, double-click to select the vertical loop in the center. If the selection is not all the way to the other side, go check the breaking point and fix it. The problem could be that the points there are not merged; an extra face is extruded, or more lines are overlapping in there (Figure 8.3). It is also recommended to delete the problematic area if it is unclear what is wrong.*
>
> *Step 6: Clean up the history and freeze transformation. Select all models and press Alt + Shift + D to delete their history. Go to Modify->Freeze Transformations to clean up their transformation.*

Why?

Topology error occurs all the time, even for industry veterans. It's important to fix them before moving on to the next steps to avoid having to redo things like rigging, UV, and more.

We have done UV mapping with the environment already, and the techniques we will be using here are not that different. In the author's opinion, it is sometimes easier to do UV for organic shapes because there are no clear hard edges. Most of the times, we think of only three things: hide the seam, avoid stretching, and texel density.

Body UV

> *Step 7: Setup workspace. Go to the upper right corner of the UI, and under workspace, select UV Editing. Move the cursor to the UV editor, press*

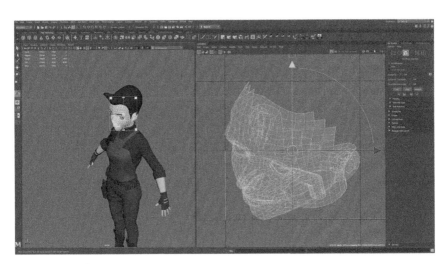

FIGURE 8.4 Project the UVs.

> the number 5 button to toggle on the Shaded
> viewing mode. This view mode gives every
> different UV shell a different solid color.
> Step 8: Projection. Select Ellen_head_geo; navigate
>   the view to a 3-quarter view, go to UV->Planar☐.
>   Under the Project from section, choose Camera.
>   Click on apply to project the UV from the
>   perspective camera that we are currently looking
>   through (Figure 8.4).
> Step 9: Cutting the ear. Go to object mode, hold
>   down W, and drag the left mouse button up and
>   up again to turn on symmetry. Choose UV->3D
>   Cut and Sew UV Tool. Click and drag the lines
>   around the ear until it is cut off. You know it's
>   completely cut off when it turns a different color.
>   Double-click the loop of the earhole to cut it out
>   to avoid stretching. Don't forget to double-click
>   on one of the inner loops of the ear hole to cut it
>   open like a cylinder (Figure 8.5).

Tips and Tricks

When using 3D Cut and Sew UV Tool, click and drag cuts
the lines under the cursor. A double-click cuts an entire
edge loop. Holding down Ctrl while doing the previous
operations sews the lines back together.

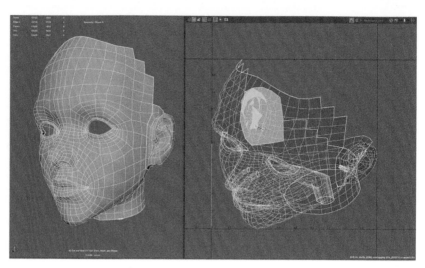

FIGURE 8.5 Cut the UVs of the ears.

Step 10: Cut the mouth and the nostrils. Double-click to cut the edge loop that is the touching edge loop on the inner side between the upper and lower lip; this will cut off the mouth cavity. Double-click to cut the center loop of the upper part of the mouth cavity. Using the same method, we can cut the inner part of the nostrils out (Figure 8.6).

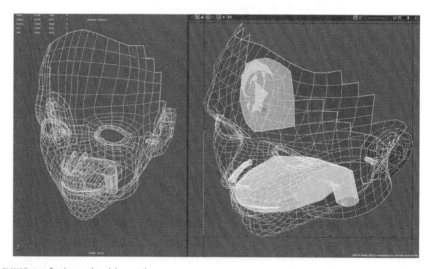

FIGURE 8.6 Cut the mouth and the nostrils.

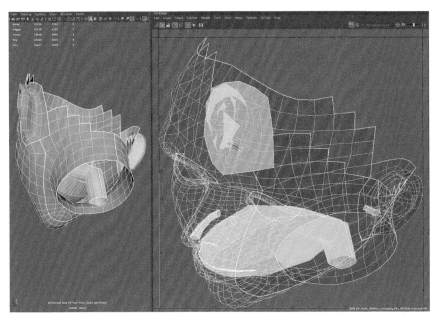

FIGURE 8.7 Cut the jaw and the neck.

Step 11: Cut the jaw and neck. Cut the loops under the jawline and the back of the neck (Figure 8.7).

Step 12: Cut arms and hands. Project the UV of Ellen_ hands_geo the same way using UV->Planar. The arm is basically a cylinder. Go to UV->3D Cut and Sew UV Tool and double-click the bottom loop of the arm to cut it open. Cut the middle line on the side of the fingers to separate them into up and bottom shells (Figure 8.8).

Step 13: Unfold and optimized the UVs. Turn off symmetry, go to object mode, and select both Ellen_hands_geo and Ellen_head_geo. In the UV Editor, hold down the right mouse button and choose UV, and drag-select all the UV points. Hold down the Shift + right mouse button, go to unfold->unfold□, and set the Method to Unfold 3D; press the Apply and Close buttons. The shells should now be unfolded nicely.

Hold down the Shift + right mouse button, go to Optimize□. Under the Optimize Options section, set the Iterations setting to 30, press Apply and Close (Figure 8.9). You can do optimize many times to reduce stretching further.

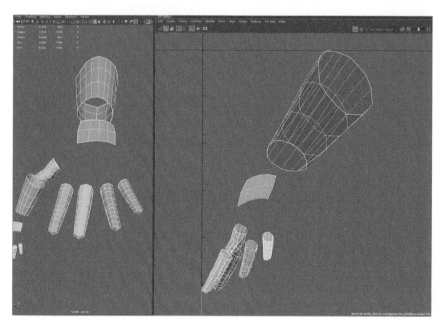

FIGURE 8.8 Cut the arms and the hands.

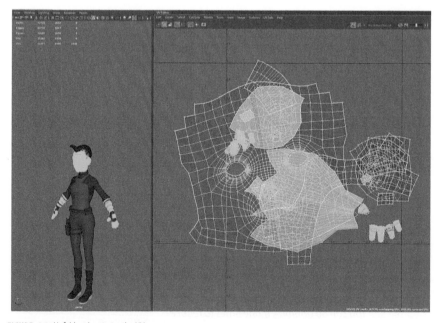

FIGURE 8.9 Unfold and optimize the UVs.

Tips and Tricks

When using Optimize to help reduce stretching, it may cause some UV to overlap each other. Make sure that you check for overlapping UV after using the Optimize command.

> *Step 14: Layout UV. With all the UVs selected in the UV Editor, hold down the Shift + right mouse button, go Layout->Layout□. Under the Pack Settings section, change Packing Resolution to 4096; under Layout Settings section, set Texture Map Size to 4096, Shell Padding to 30, and Tile Padding to 30. Click on Apply. The UVs are now arranged for us automatically (Figure 8.10).*
>
> *Step 15: Manually adjust the UV layout. The UV laid out is technically fine but could be enhanced. We can see some unutilized space and some tilted shells that could be more straight. Double-click any UV point of a UV shell to select the entire shell; in the UV editor menu, select Modify-> Orient shells to make it straight. Rotate the shell*

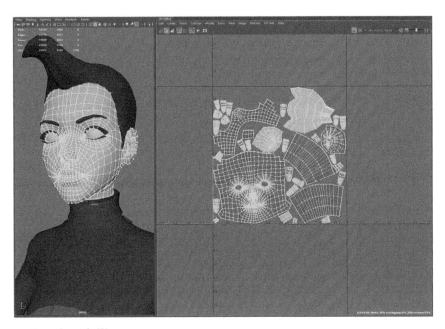

FIGURE 8.10 Layout the UVs.

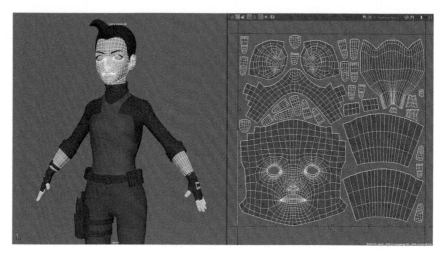

FIGURE 8.11 Manually adjust the UV layout of the character.

while holding down the J button on the keyboard to snap it to the correct orientation. Scale all UV up a little bit, and move and rotate the shells around to get maximum UV space utilization. Avoid overlapping of the shells and keep all shells inside of the UV space (Figure 8.11).

Why?

We want to squeeze all the possible performance and quality out. That means even a little better UV space utilization is a win; that's why manually adjusting the UV is necessary.

Eye UV

Step 16: Eyeball UV Mapping. Select Ellen_l_eye_ geo, go to UV->Planar to project it to the UV Space. Go to UV->3D Cut and Sew UV Tool, and double-click to cut the vertical loop in the middle of the eyeball. Select all the UV vertices, hold the Shift + right mouse button; go Unfold->Unfold. Double-click any UV point of the front shell to select the entire shell, hold the Shift + right mouse button, go Layout->Layout. Scale the shell down just a little bit to avoid it touching the edge. Select the back shell, scale it down, and move it to any corner (Figure 8.12).

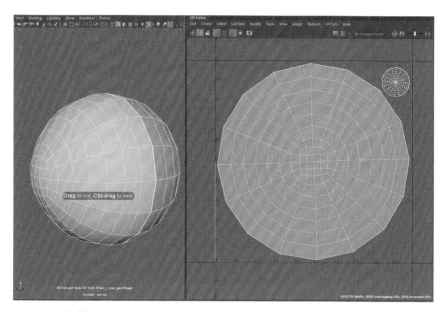

FIGURE 8.12 UVs of the eyeball.

Why?

We will never see the back of the eyeball, so there is no point in wasting UV space; that's why we scaled it down and moved it to a corner.

> Step 17: Copy UV to the other eyeball. Select Ellen_l_
> eye_geo, add select Ellen_r_eye_geo. In the main
> menu, go to Mesh->Transfer Attributes☐. Under
> the Attribute Settings section, set the Sample
> space to Component, and press the Transfer
> button. Press Alt + Shift + D to delete the history.
> After the operation, both eyeballs should have
> identical UV Layout.

Hair UV

> Step 18: Hair UV. Project the hair UV to the UV Editor
> the same way we did for the body and eyeball.
> Go to 3D Cut and Sew UV Tool, find a relatively
> hidden loop to cut the frontal hair clump open;
> it is also helpful to cut the back half of the hair
> open. With all UV vertices of the hair selected, do

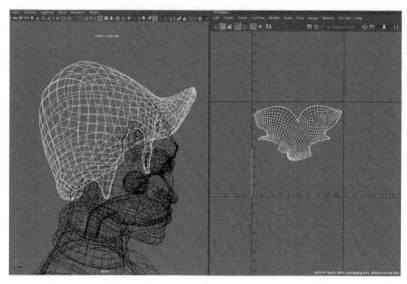

FIGURE 8.13 Create UVs for the hair.

an Unfold command and an Optimize command to unfold it. Move it, so it fits in the UV space nicely (Figure 8.13).

Step 19: Eyebrow UV. Select Ellen_eyebrow_geo, and do a planner projection. Go to 3D Cut and Sew UV Tool, cut the backside and bottom edges to open it. Select all the UV vertices of the eyebrow, do an Unfold, Optimize, and Layout command (Figure 8.14).

Step 20: Eyelash UV. Do the eyelash UV the same way we did in Step 19 (Figure 8.15).

Step 21: Combine the UVs of the eyebrows, eyelashes, and the hair. Select Ellen_hair_geo, Ellen_eyebrow_geo, and Ellen_eyelashes_geo. In the UV Editor, select all UV vertices. Do a layout command. Select all the eyebrow and eyelash UVs. Scale, rotate, and move them to take over all the UV space (Figure 8.16).

Why?

We have scaled the eyebrow and eyelashes up, and this will result in uneven UV distribution. However, it gives us more resolution for the eyebrow and eyelashes. It is going to help us to add more detail to them if necessary.

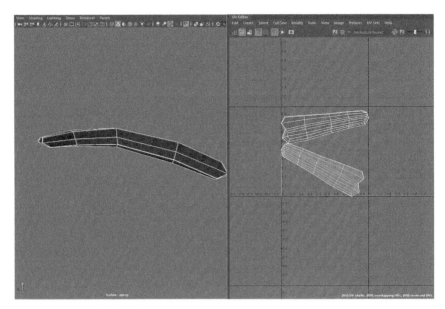

FIGURE 8.14 Create the UV of the eyebrows.

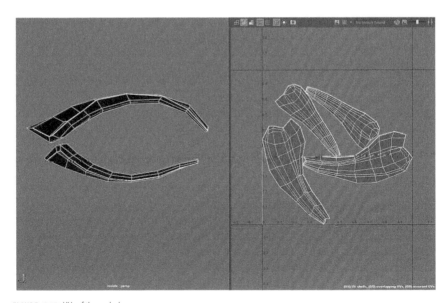

FIGURE 8.15 UVs of the eyelashes.

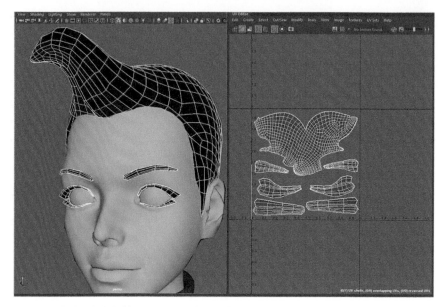

FIGURE 8.16 Combine the UVs of the eyebrows, eyelashes, and the hair.

Garment UV

Step 22: Project the rest. Select the rest of the models together, go to UV->Planner to project them all at once (Figure 8.17).

Step 23: Cut the sweater. Select Ellen_sweater_geo; use the 3D Cut and Sew UV Tool to cut the sweater. Cut the two arms, two rolled back sleeves, and the collar out; these parts are basically cylinders. Just find a relatively hidden loop to cut them open. Cut the rest of the body to front and back pieces in the middle (Figure 8.18).

Step 24: Cut the outfit. Select Ellen_outfit_geo, Cut the model to front and back pieces through the middle on the outside and between the legs. Cut through the loop of the waist where we have the separation of the color of the pants and the upper part (Figure 8.19).

Step 25: Cut the UVs of the belt. Select Ellen_belt_geo, cut the loop on the inner side of the bottom of the belt, cut the center vertical loop on the back, and cut the buckle out (Figure 8.20).

Step 26: Cut the pockets. The pockets are basically a cube; if you look at the default UV of a cube, that is going to be exactly how we cut the pockets,

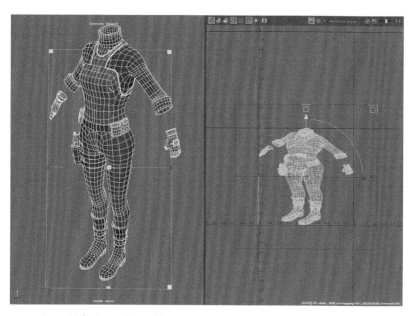

FIGURE 8.17 Project UVs for the rest of the model.

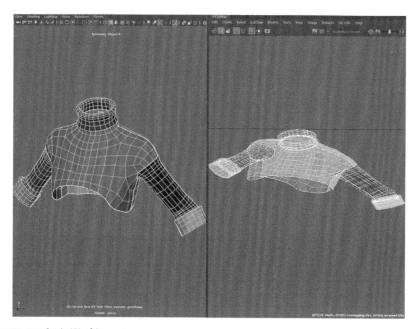

FIGURE 8.18 Cut the UVs of the sweater.

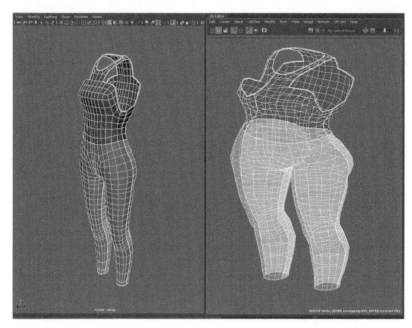

FIGURE 8.19 Cut the UVs of the outfit.

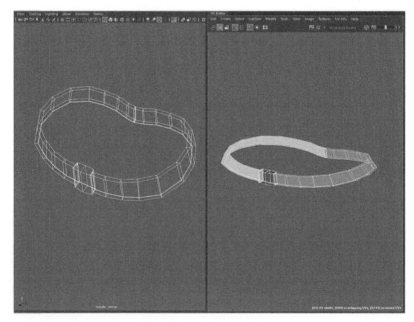

FIGURE 8.20 Cut the UVs of the belt.

almost exactly how a pizza box is opened
(Figure 8.21).

Step 27: Cut the gun. The gun is a bit complicated,
but just like any hard surface UV we have done,
we can deal with individual pieces one by one;
the cutting choices we've made are shown in
Figure 8.22.

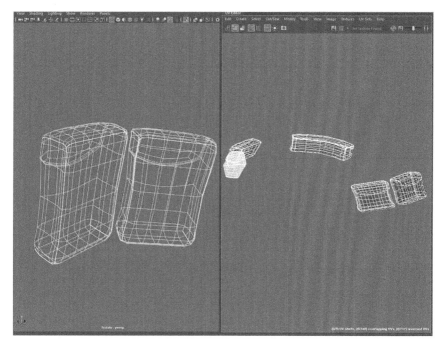

FIGURE 8.21 Cut the UVs of the pockets.

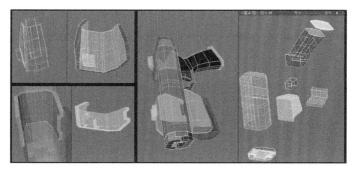

FIGURE 8.22 Cut the UVs of the gun.

337

Tips and Tricks

When we are trying to figure out where to cut the UV, there are three things to think of:

1. **Stretching** – Find the primary turning part of the shape and cut there. If not, stretching is most likely to happen.
2. **Hide the Seams** – Cut places that are hard to see if possible. Try to cut less if possible.
3. **Texel Density** – Make sure there is a consistency of the resolution of the textures on the 3D model.

It is also up to the texturing habit of the artist and the nature of the tools to determine some of the cutting rules. Texturing with photoshop will require lesser seams while texturing in Substance Painter is pretty much free from seam problems, or the seam is at least easily fixable.

Step 28: Cut the rest of the model. Using a similar method as before, we can cut the rest of the models. Figure 8.23 shows all the cutting choices we've made.

Step 29: Unfold, optimize, and layout. Grab all the garment models we projected and cut. Select all UV vertices, do an Unfold, Optimize, and Layout command (Figure 8.24).

Step 30: Separate the UVs. We can Separate the UVs of all the garment into four UV sets:

1. *the upper body.*
2. *the pants, shoes, and belts.*
3. *the gloves and watch.*
4. *the gun.*

First, move all the UVs away from the U1V1 space. Start with selecting the upper body parts, and this includes the sweater and the upper part of the outfit. After selecting, do a Layout command to lay out the UVs selected to the U1V1 space. Don't forget to do some manual arrangements afterward.

Go to the UV Toolkit on the right side of the UV Editor. In the Transform section, change the value of the Move setting to 1. Click on the right-angle arrow to move the UV

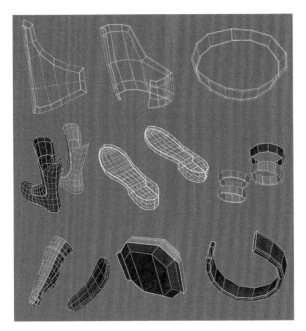

FIGURE 8.23 All the cutting choices of the rest of the models.

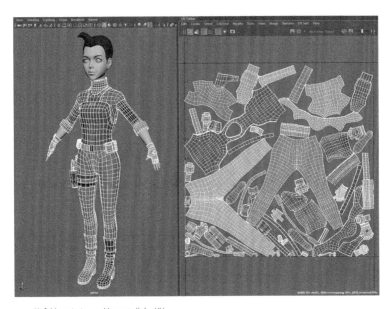

FIGURE 8.24 Unfold, optimize, and lay out all the UVs.

FIGURE 8.25 Separate the UVs and put them into different UV tiles.

set to the next UV space on the right; click six more times to move it to the seventh UV tile on the right. Keep doing this until all four tiles are created (Figure 8.25).

Why?

We have purposely arranged the UV to the four tiles to get more resolution. The gloves, the watch, and the gun also have higher resolution because they are close to the viewer in the game. We can check the relative resolution by checking on the Checker Map option in the Textures menu in the UV Editor. The smaller the checker pattern is, the higher the resolution.

Tips and Tricks

When it comes to arranging the UV sets, it is helpful to arrange them based on material type. Fabric, metal, and leather should be put into their separate UV sets.

Step 31: Assign garment materials. We will give each UV set we created a different material. Starting by selecting all the faces of the gun in the UV Editor, hold down the right mouse button in the perspective view, and choose Assign New Material. In the pop-up window, select Lambert. In the attribute Editor, name the material Gun_mtl, and drag the slider of the Color attribute of the material down to make it darker to differentiate it from others. Do the same thing for the other three tiles. Then, name them as Lower_body_mtl, Glove_and_watch_mtl, Upper_body_mtl, and Gun_ mtl. After assigning the materials, grab the UVs of each UV set and use the Move button in the Transform section of the UV Tool Kit editor to move these all back to U1V1 space.

Step 32: Assign all other materials. Grab Ellen_ hands_geo and Ellen_head_geo, give them a

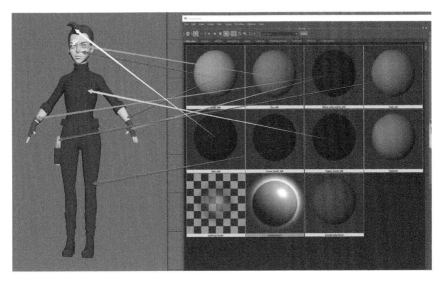

FIGURE 8.26 Final Material distribution of the character.

Lambert material and name the material Body_mtl. Grab the two eyeballs, give them a Lambert material and name the material Eye_mtl. Finally, grab the hair, eyebrow, and eyelash models, give them a Lamber material and name the material Hair_mtl. The final material distribution is shown in Figure 8.26.

Why?

There are seven materials created for the character; it is a little heavy to use, but we are going to get good quality. How many materials are used is based on the engine and the target platform. For our desktop game, we can spoil ourselves a little.

Conclusion

We have now finished the UV Mapping process. It takes some time but is often not considered difficult to do. All we did here is to project, cut the seams open, unfold, and layout. However, the arrangement and the packing of these UV pieces require some serious thinking. UV

Mapping is the foundation of the texturing process and cannot be overlooked. Please double and triple check your UVs and material assignments to ensure that there are no overlapping UVs and all materials are named properly. We are going to move on to the next exciting chapter – Character Texturing.

CHAPTER 9

Character Texture Painting

Character texturing is very similar to the set texturing we did in Chapter 3. However, a more complicated process might be needed to get a good-looking skin and enough detail on the clothing. It is also a fun part of doing 3D art. Since we have talked about the tools before, we will jump into the texturing process right away.

> *Step 1: Export. Select all models except the hidden full-body, and go to File->Export Selection. In the pop-up widow, change the Files of type setting to FBX export, and set the File Name to Ellen_ Texturing_to_ SP.fbx. Click on the sourceimages*

under the Current Project list, click on the yellow folder shaped button on the top row of the window to create a new folder, and name it ellen_texturing. Double-click the newly created ellen_texturing folder, then click on the Export Selection button to export the model.

Step 2: Import the model to Substance Painter. Open Substance Painter; here, we import our model with the same setting we used when we import our environment assets.

Step 3: Baking. On the right side of the UI of Substance Painter, find TEXTRUE SET SETTINGS panel; click on the Bake Mesh Maps Button. Change the Output Size to 4096. Check on Use Low Poly Mesh as High Poly Mesh, and change the Antialiasing to Subsampling 8×8. Click on the Bake All Texture Sets button to start baking. We set the best quality, give it a few minutes to finish the baking task (Figure 9.1).

Step 4: Check baking error. Look around the model to check if there are any baking errors. It is very unlikely to see errors if we bake the model using the Use Low Poly Mesh as High Poly Mesh option. Zoom in to the head, the eyeballs may appear to have some baking artifacts. The artifacts on the eyeballs are due to overlapping UVs – both eyeballs are using the same UV mapping. Hold down Ctrl + Alt and right-click on one of the eyeballs to select the Eye_mtl. Go to TEXTURE SET SETTING, and under the Mesh maps section, click on the X button on all the maps in the list to get rid of the baked maps.

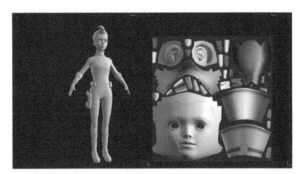

FIGURE 9.1 The baking result of the character.

Why?

The eyeballs can look around, baking an ambient occlusion map and other maps would not make much sense. There are other moving parts like the mouth that we should, in theory, open when baking so that no dark ambient occlusion is baked on the part where the upper and lower lips meet.

Skin Texturing

Step 5: Basic skin color. Hold down Ctrl + Alt and right-click on the face to switch to Body_Mtl. Go to the LAYERS panel. Click on the bucket icon to add a fill layer. Double-click on the name of the Fill layer 1 to rename it as Skin_Base. Go the PROPERTIES panel, change the base color to a basic skin color, and drag the Roughness slider higher to make it less shiny (Figure 9.2).

Step 6: Skin red tint base. Create another fill layer, rename it to Red_Tint, change the color to a pure red color. Under the MATERIAL section, click on height, rough, metal, and nrm to turn off these channels. Right-click on the Red_Tint layer and select Add black mask. Right-click on the black mask and select add fill. On the right side of the fill, set the visibility percentage to 80. In the PROPERTIES panel, click on the grayscale, type in clouds in the search bar and click Clouds 1, set the Projection to Tri-planar projection, and set the Scale setting to 16 (Figure 9.3).

Why?

It may appear to be crazy after Step 6. However, we are going to layer multiple textures together to get a proper final skin result. And we can get very rich color variation by doing it this way. Tri-planar projection projects the texture from the front, side, and top views of the model; this enables the avoidance of any seams.

Step 7: Paint red color distribution. Right-click on the mask of Red_Tint, and select add paint. Press 1 button to switch to the paint brush. Go to SHELF,

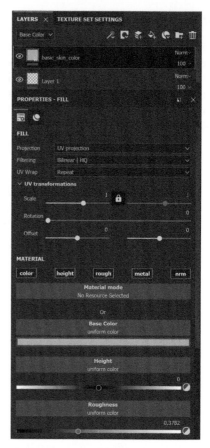

FIGURE 9.2 Add a basic skin color with a fill layer.

under Brushes, find and click on the Dirt 1 brush. Turn on symmetry, and start painting on the redder areas. These areas are the cheek, tip of the nose, lips, ear, and anywhere with more blood, typically the muscles and higher areas of the face (Figure 9.4).

Step 8: Paint blue color distribution. Select Red_Tint, and press Ctrl+C and then Ctrl+V to duplicate the layer. Name the new layer Blue_Tint, and change the color of the layer to a pure blue color. Click on the mask of the layer, and select Clouds 1. In the PROPERTIES panel, click on the grayscale Clouds 1 button, switch it to Clouds 3 so that the blue color uses a different noise.

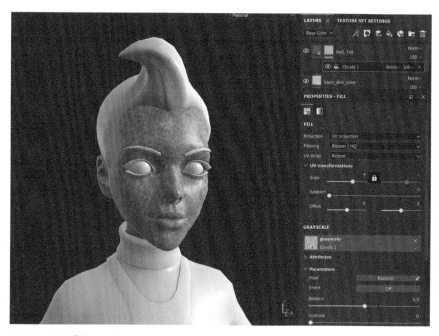

FIGURE 9.3 Add a fill layer with red noises.

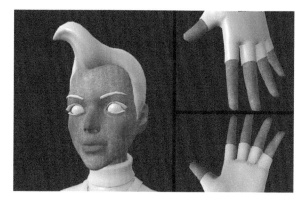

FIGURE 9.4 Paint the redder area.

Click on the X button on the right side of the Paint mask layer to delete it. Create a new Paint layer and start paint the variation of the blue color. The areas on the face that have more blue tint are the eye socket, jaw, and typically low areas or cavities. Some of

347

the areas of the face like the cheek and nose may need lesser blue tint; hit the X button to change the color of the brush to black and erase blue off these areas (Figure 9.5).

Step 9: Paint yellow color distribution. Copy paste the Blue Tint layer, and name the new layer Yellow_Tint. Change the color to a slightly greyed out warm yellow color. The color should be close to the color of the bone but more saturated. Click on the mask of the layer, select Clouds 3, and set its visibility to 30; under the PROPERTIES panel, change the Scale setting to 3. Delete and recreate the paint layer and paint the variation of the yellow color. Yellow color mostly appears on the bony area (Figure 9.6).

FIGURE 9.5 Paint the blue area.

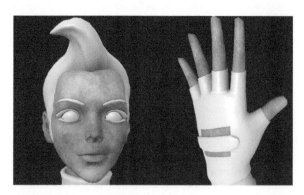

FIGURE 9.6 Paint the yellow color distribution.

Tips and Tricks

The color variation of a human face is complicated. However, you can follow this rule of having the high areas red, low areas blue, and bony areas yellow.

Step 10: Add a white color overlay. Copy and paste the Yellow_Tint layer, name it White_Cover, change the Cloud 3 to Fractal Sum 1, and reduce the opacity to 50. We do this to add an overall white coverage to even out the color variation (Figure 9.7).

Step 11: Balance skin variation. Select Red_Tint layer, hold down Shift, and click on White_Cover layer to select all the color layers. Press Ctrl+G button to create a group. Name the group Color_Variation. Add a black mask to this group and add a fill layer to the mask. In the PROPERTIES panel, change the GRAYSCALE value to 0.15. Add a paint layer to the mask; use the paint brush to make the color tint more visible on the cheek, nose, and eye socket (Figure 9.8).

Step 12: Overall adjustments. Add a new paint layer on top of the Color_Variation folder. Change the name to Overall_Adjust. On the upper right corner of the layer, change the blending mode

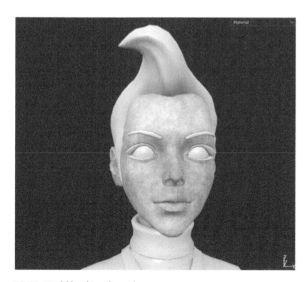

FIGURE 9.7 Add a white color overlay.

FIGURE 9.8 Balance the skin variations.

from Norm to Passthrough. Any adjustment we apply to this layer should affect all layers below with the Passthrough blend mode.

Right-click on the Overall_Adjust layer, and select Add Filter to add a filter to it. Select the Filter layer added to it; under PROPERTIES panel, turn off height, rough, metal, and nrm. Click on the Filter button, and chose HSL Perceptive. We can now use the setting in the PROPERTIES panel to tweak the hue, saturation, and lightness of the texture. The Hue, Saturation, and Lightness are set to 0.51, 0.53, and 0.51, respectively. Add another adjustment layer, and chose Blur as the filter; set the Blur Intensity to 2. The visibility of the Blue_Tint layer is also reduced to 80 (Figure 9.9).

Why?

It seems a huge waste of time doing all the blending and eventually blurring it. However, it can make a substantial difference with all the noisy blendings. It is also because of the stylized art style that we blurred our texture quite a bit to make it look clean.

FIGURE 9.9 Skin appearance after adding the adjustment.

> *Step 13: Lips. Create a new fill layer, and name it Lip, set its color to a darker red color, and set its roughness to 0.2. Give the layer a black mask, and add a paint layer to the mask. Go to the Brushes shelf, chose the Basic Soft brush, and paint on the lips to make them red.*
>
> *Reduce the visibility of the Lip layer to 50 to have better blending. Add another filter to the mask; in the PROPERTIES panel, change the Filter to Blur, and set the Blur Intensity setting to 1.5 (Figure 9.10).*

Tips and Tricks

Instead of trying to figure out the color of the lip, it is easier to control by adding a pure red color first and then reducing the visibility to determine the color. After all, the reason the lip is redder is because it has more blood vessels.

> *Step 14: Fingernails. Create a new fill layer, and name it Fingernails. Set the color of the layer to white, and set its roughness to 0.3. Give the layer a black mask and add a paint layer to the mask. Go to the Brushes shelf, chose the Basic Hard brush, and paint on the fingernails. Finally, reduce the visibility of the Fingernails layer to 40 to have better blending (Figure 9.11).*

FIGURE 9.10 Add color to the lips.

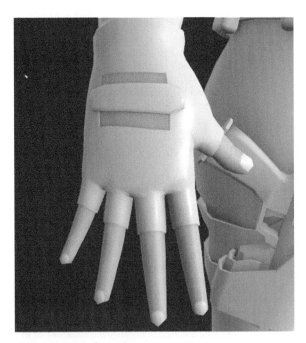

FIGURE 9.11 Paint the fingernails.

FIGURE 9.12 Draw lines to mimic the edge of the various clumps of the hair.

Hair

Step 15: Hair base color. Hold down Ctrl + right mouse button on the hair to switch to the Hair_ mtl. Add a new fill layer, and name the new layer Hair_Base. Set the Base Color of Hair_Base to a dark red and set the roughness to 0.45.

Step 16: Hair dark color. Copy and paste Hair_Base and name the duplicate as Hair_bottom. Make the color darker and change its Height to −0.5. Right-click on the layer and give it a black mask. Add a paint layer to the mask. Press the D button to toggle the steady stroke; steady stroke makes your stroke more fluid. Start drawing lines to mimic the edge of the various clumps on the hair (Figure 9.12).

Tips and Tricks

When drawing the hair clumps, make sure that the lines are fluid and flow with each other. When a line meets another, make sure its direction is gradually aligned with the other line when they meet instead of cutting into the other line directly.

Step 17: Blur the hair clumps. Right-click on the mask of Hair_Bottom, and chose Add filter. Click the Filter layer, go to the PROPERTIES panel, change the Filter to Blur, and set the Blur value to 1.5 (Figure 9.13).

Copy and paste the Hair_Bottom layer; name the duplicate as Hair_Bottom_Sharp. Change its Blur value of the Blur filter of its mask to 0.5. Make another duplication

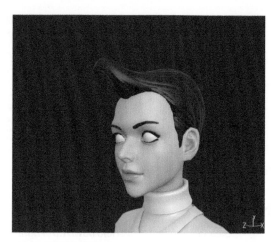

FIGURE 9.13 Blurred hair clumps.

FIGURE 9.14 Add more layers to refine the curvature of the hair clumps.

and name it Hair_Bottom_Soft, change its Blur value of the Blur filter of its mask to 3 (Figure 9.14).

Why?

We used three layers to add the height information and utilized different blur values to achieve good control

FIGURE 9.15 Add bright tint to the high ground of the hair clumps.

of the slope of the hair clumps. It would be difficult to achieve both defined and soft results at the same time with only one layer.

> *Step 18: Hair bright color. Copy and paste the Hair_bottom layer, name the duplicate Hair_Top, change the color to a brighter color, and change the Height to 1. Right-click on the Paint layer in the mask, select Add filter, change the new filter layer to Bevel, and change the Distance setting of the Bevel to 1. Add another filter layer on top of the Bevel layer and change the Filter to Invert. Set the visibility of the Hair_Top layer to 10. The hair should now have a subtle bright tint on the high ground of the hair clumps (Figure 9.15).*
> *Step 19: Eyebrow and eyelashes. Create another paint layer on top of the mask stack of the mask of the Hair_Top layer; paint black color over the eyebrow and eyelashes to make them dark.*

Eye

> *Step 20: Eye white. Switch to the Eye_mtl, create a new fill layer, and name it Eye_White. Change the color of the layer to a red color, give it a black*

mask, and add a fill layer to the mask. In the PROPERTIES panel, click on the grayscale button. In the search bar, type in polygon 2, and select polygon 2. Toggle the Invert option on, and set the Histogram position to 0.65. Under the Pattern section in the PROPERTIES panel, change the Sides setting to 32. The eye white should now have some red tint on the corner.

Step 21: Iris group. Click the folder icon under the LAYERS panel to create a new folder, and name it Iris. Create a new fill layer, drag it into the Iris folder, and rename it as Iris_Base and change the color of Iris_Base to a dark brown color. Right-click on the Iris folder and add a black mask; give the black mask a fill layer, and make it polygon 2. This time, set the Histogram position to 0.28, Histogram contrast to 0.96, and Sides to 32. The mask now constraints everything under the Iris group in the circle area defined by polygon 2 (Figure 9.16).

Why?

We chose polygon 2 as the mask instead of painting it ourselves with a brush. Using polygon 2 makes it more flexible and cleaner; this is also something we call procedural texturing.

Step 22: Iris contour. Copy and paste Iris_Base and name the new layer Iris_Contour. Make the color darker, and give it a black mask. Right-click on the mask of Iris folder, chose Copy mask, right-click on the Iris_Contour, and chose Paste into mask. The polygon 2 from Iris group is now copied to Iris_Contour. Add another fill to the mask of Iris_Contour, chose polygon 2 again, and change the fill layer blend type to Subtract. In the PROPERTIES panel, set the Histogram position to 0.23, Histogram contrast to 0.9, and Sides to 32 (Figure 9.17). Again, we have procedurally made the dark rim of the iris with the polygon 2 texture.

Step 23: Pupil. Copy and paste Iris_Base, name the new layer Pupil, make the color darker, give it a black mask, and add a fill layer to the mask with polygon 2. In the PROPERTIES panel, set the Histogram position to 0.1, Histogram contrast to 0.85, and Sides to 32 (Figure 9.18).

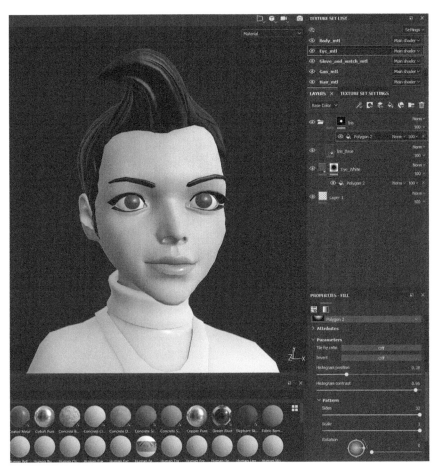

FIGURE 9.16 Create a folder for the iris and add a mask to it.

Step 24: Iris top shading. Copy and paste Iris_Base, name the new layer Iris_Dark and make the color darker. Give the new layer a black mask, and add a fill layer to the mask. In the PROPERTIES panel, click on the grayscale, search, and choose Gradient Linear 1. Under the Parameters section in the PROPERTIES panel, set the Balance to 0.475, and the Contrast to 0.9 (Figure 9.19).

Step 25: Iris bottom light. Copy and paste Iris_Base; name the new layer Iris_Bright. Make the color brighter, click and drag it to move it above Iris_Dark. Give Iris_Bright a black mask and add a paint layer to it. This time, we use the Basic

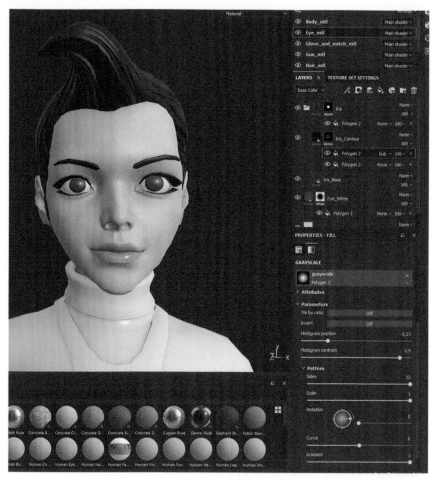

FIGURE 9.17 Add the contour of the iris.

Soft brush to paint around the bottom portion of the Iris to mimic lights traveling out of the Iris (Figure 9.20).

Add another filter to the mask of Iris_ Bright and change the filter to Blur to blur the mask (Figure 9.21).

Why?

In theory, the darkness of the upper portion of the iris is caused by shading. The brighter color on the bottom part

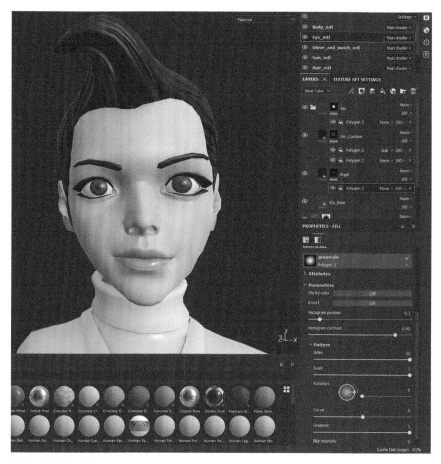

FIGURE 9.18 Add pupils to the eye.

of the iris is lighting traveling out. Our model is too simple to support such accurate shading, so we faked it using textures.

> *Step 26: Iris fiber. Create a new fill layer above Iris_Bright, name it Iris_Fiber, change its color to a dark brown, and set the height value to −0.3. Give the layer a black mask and add a fill layer to the black mask. In the PROPERTIES panel, click on the grayscale, search and select Circular Stick. In the Parameters section, set the Number to 64, Offset to 0, Bar Length to 1, and Bar Width to 0.005. We now have a dense fiber covering the*

FIGURE 9.19 Add top shading to the iris.

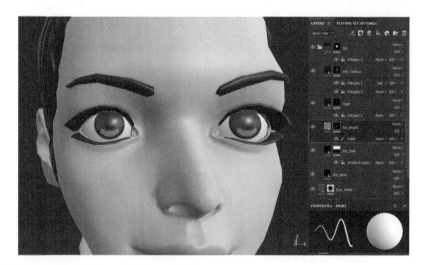

FIGURE 9.20 Add a brighter layer at the bottom of the iris.

FIGURE 9.21 Blur the brighter color at the bottom of the iris.

iris. Add a blur filter to the mask to make it softer (Figure 9.22).

Step 27: Fix height error. Select the Iris_Contour layer, under the LAYERS panel, right beneath the LAYERS label, and change the Base Color to Height. Change the blending mode of the Iris_Contour to Normal to make the dark contour block the height information below it.

Select the bottom Polygon 2 in the mask of the Iris_Contour layer, set the Histogram Position to 0.3 and Histogram contrast to 1 to cover the outer edge of the Iris (Figure 9.23).

Step 28: Eye roughness. Create a new fill layer at the top of the layer stack and name it Roughness. In the PROPERTIES panel, turn off the color, height,

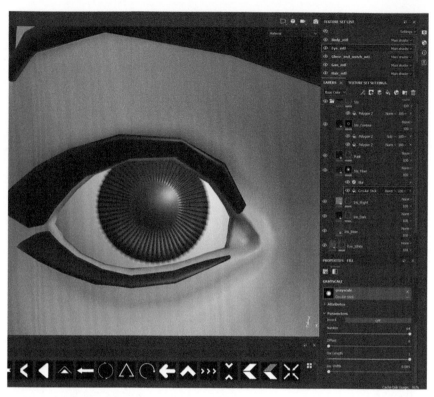

FIGURE 9.22 Add fibers to the iris.

metal, and nrm channels. Set the roughness to 0.25 to tighten up the highlight (Figure 9.24).

Upper Body

Step 29: Sweater base. Switch to the Upper_body_ mtl, add a new fill layer and name it Sweater_ Base, change its color to a dark gray, and roughness to 0.8. Press Ctrl+G to group it under a folder; name the folder Sweater. Add a black mask to the folder and give the mask a paint layer. Hit the number 4 button on the keyboard to toggle the polygon fill tool; in the PROPERTIES panel, click on the checker box button to switch to UV shell selection mode. Change the Color to 1, go to the 2D view, and click on the UVs of the sweater (Figure 9.25). The mask should now be white on the sweater.

FIGURE 9.23 Make the contour of the iris block the height of the fibers.

Step 30: Sweater pattern. Go to Materials, find Scarf wool, drag it above Sweater_Base, and rename it as Sweater_Pattern. In the PROPERTIES panel, change the color to a dark gray; under the Technical Parameter, change the Height Range to 0.25 (Figure 9.26).

Step 31: Fix the pattern direction of the left sleeve. Add a white mask to the Sweater_Pattern and add a paint layer to the mask of Sweater_Pattern. Hit the number 4 button to switch to polygon fill tool, change the color to black, and click on the sleeves and the collar. The pattern should now be removed from these parts.

Duplicate the Sweater Pattern, name the new layer Sweater_Pattern_Sleeve_L, delete the paint layer of the mask of the new

FIGURE 9.24 Tweak the roughness of the iris.

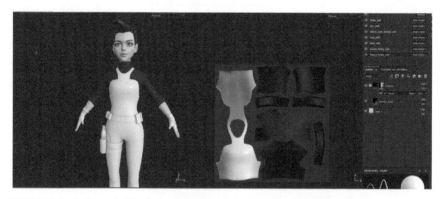

FIGURE 9.25 Create a layer and a folder for the sweater.

layer, and add a new paint layer. Hit the 4 button, change the color to black, and click on the UV shells that are not the left sleeve to mask them out. Go click on the icon of the new layer and change the rotation in the PROPERTIES panel so that its direction is aligned with the left sleeve. Create two more duplications of the layer to fix the pattern direction of the right sleeve and the collar (Figure 9.27).

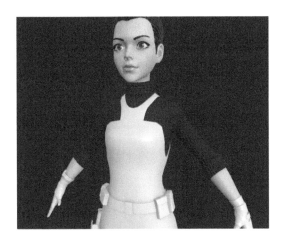

FIGURE 9.26 Add the Scarf wool material to the sweater.

FIGURE 9.27 Fix the direction of the patterns with new layers.

Step 32: Add smart material to the outfit. Go to the SHELF, select Smart materials in the left column, and find Fabric UCP. Drag it to LAYERS and move it below Sweater. Open the folder added called Fabric UCP, find Fabric UCP layer, go to PROPERTIES, and change Color 01, Color 02, Color 03 to three different blue colors (Figure 9.28).

365

FIGURE 9.28 Add Fabric UCP as the material of the outfit.

Step 33: Edge variation. Duplicate Fabric UCP and name the duplicate as Fabric UCP_Edge. Right-click on the layer and click add levels. Select the newly added Levels – Base Color, drag the middle pin of the top row of the level graph to the left just a little to make the color brighter.

Create a new black mask to Fabric UCP_Edge, go to the Smart Masks in the SHELF, and drag Fabric Edge Damage to the mask of Fabric UCP_Edge. The edge of the garment should now become brighter, which mimics real-life scratches (Figure 9.29).

Step 34: Top strap height. Create a new fill layer below Fabric UCP_Edge, name it Top_Strap_Height. Turn off the color, rough, metal, nrm channel of the layer, and change its height value to 0.75.

Create a black mask for Strap_Height and give the mask a paint layer. Use the Basic Hard brush and white color to paint on the areas that belong to the top strap layer (Figure 9.30).

FIGURE 9.29 Add subtle edge wear to the outfit.

Tips and Tricks

Don't worry about painting over the sweater, we can change the height blend mode of the Sweater folder to normal to override it.

> *Step 35: Sewing seam. Duplicate Top_Strap_Height, name it Sewing_Seams, set its height to 1, delete, and recreate the paint layer in the mask. Hold down Shift while clicking to create the sewing seams (Figure 9.31).*

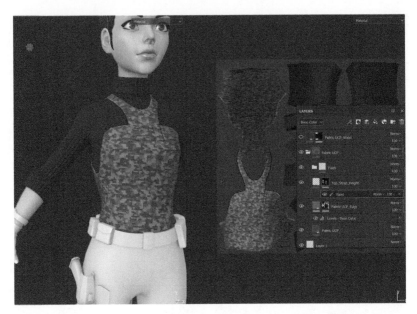

FIGURE 9.30 Add height to the top strap.

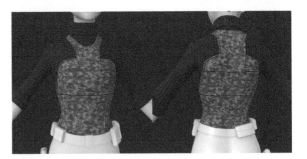

FIGURE 9.31 Add Sewing seams to the outfit.

Why?

It is difficult to paint clean lines, so we use the Shift-click trick to draw straight lines instead of trying to create a fluid arc line.

> *Step 36: Waist patch color variation. Duplicate Fabrick UCP and name the duplication Fabrick UCP_Waist. Make the color of the new layer*

FIGURE 9.32 Add color variation to the waist patch.

> darker and more saturated. Gave the new layer
> a black mask and add a paint layer to the mask.
> Use Brush Hard to paint over the area on and
> below the horizontal seam in the middle painted
> in Step 34 (Figure 9.32).
>
> Step 37: Waist side patch. Create a new fill layer
> above Fabric UCP_Edge, name it Waist_Side_
> Patch. Go to the PROPERTIES panel, set the
> Scale value to 25, click on the height uniform
> color button, in the search bar, type in Circles
> to find the Circles mask, and click on it to
> use it as our height. Set the height blending
> mode of Waist_Side_Patch to Normal, give
> it a black mask and add a paint layer to the
> mask, and use the Basic Hard brush with white
> color to paint over the side patch of the outfit
> (Figure 9.33).

Tips and Tricks

Whenever we need to paint something clean, we can hold
down the Shift button and do left mouse clicks to draw
straight lines to mark out the contour of the area and then
fill in the middle.

FIGURE 9.33 Add circular patterns to the side patch of the outfit.

Pants

Step 38: Pants base color. Switch to the Lower_body_mtl, go to SHELF, click on the Materials section, search for Fabric Baseball Hat, and drag it to the layers. Name the new layer Pants_Base, change the Scale of the layer to 3, and tweak the rotation value so that the direction of the lines in the pattern becomes vertical. Finally, change the color to a darker grayed out blue color (Figure 9.34).

Step 39: Pants gradient. Duplicate Pants_Base, name the duplication Pants_Darker, and make the color of Pants_Darker darker and bluer. Give the layer a black mask, add a generator to the mask, in the PROPERTIES panel, and change the generator to Mask Editor. In the PORPERTIES panel, set the Curvature Opacity to 0 and the Position Gradient Opacity to 1. Open the Position Gradient section, turn on the Invert, and set the contrast to 0.7. Tweak the Balance value so that the transition of the brightness of the color starts around the knee (Figure 9.35).

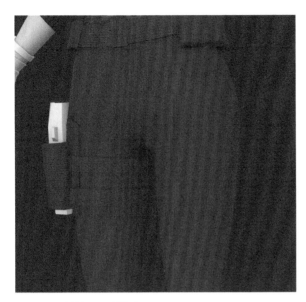

FIGURE 9.34 Add the material for the pants.

FIGURE 9.35 Add a gradient to the color of the pants.

Tips and Tricks

Gradients are happening all of the places in nature, they are great for add detail.

>*Step 40: Pants front flipper. Create a new fill layer above Pants_Darker, name it Pants_Height_ High. Toggle off the color, rough, metal, nrm channel of the layer, and change the Height to 1 to make it a high ground. Add a black mask as well as a paint layer to the mask.*
>
>>*Draw a long square at the front of the hip to mimic the shape of the flipper. Create a new fill layer above Pants_Height_High, name it Pants_Height_Low, change its height to −1, and give it a black mask and add a paint layer; make the brush smaller and draw a vertical line on the side of the flipper (Figure 9.36).*
>
>*Step 41: Pockets. Add a new paint layer to the mask of Pants_Height_High and name it Pocket_ Height. Drag it beneath the previous paint layer, turn on symmetry, and use the Basic Hard brush to paint over the area of the pockets. Make sure the brush size is big and covers much more area around the pocket.*
>
>>*Add a Blur filter above Pocket_Height and below the Paint layer; set the Blur Intensity to 7.*
>
>>*Add another paint layer to the mask, call it Pocket_Opening. Make the brush smaller, press the X button to flip the color from white to black. Paint across the opening of the pocket to cut the seam open, and paint off all the high areas behind the opening of the pocket (Figure 9.37).*

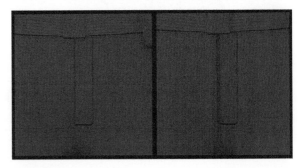

FIGURE 9.36 Create the high ground and the seam of the flipper of the pants.

FIGURE 9.37 Add the shape of the pockets.

Tips and Tricks

Whenever we need to paint something more complicated, we can break it down to multiple steps, just like we did in Step 40. We create the soft bump with the combination of a harsh brush stroke and a blur filter. We then paint half of it out to mimic the opening of the pocket.

> Step 42: Seams. Go to the paint layer of the mask of Pants_Height_Low, use a small brush to cut the seams on the side of the pants (Figure 9.38).
>
> Step 43: Back Pocket. Use similar techniques we used for the pockets and flipper; we can create the back pockets with ease. Don't afraid to paint over to other parts because we will cover these with materials on top (Figure 9.39).
>
> Step 44: Stitches. Create a new layer on the very top and name it Stitches. In the PROPERTIES

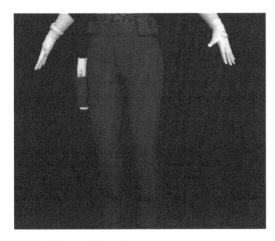

FIGURE 9.38 Add seams to the pants.

373

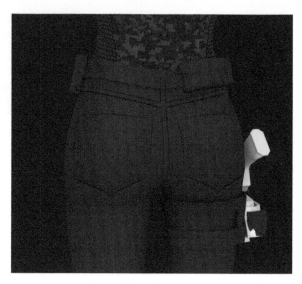

FIGURE 9.39 Create the back pocket.

panel, toggle off metal and nrm, set Base Color to white, set the Height, and the Roughness to 1. Give it a black mask with a paint layer. In the Brushes section of the SHELF, find and click on Stitches 1. Reduce the size of the brush to 0.9, use the Shift-clicking techniques to draw stitches out on the sewing lines of the pants (Figure 9.40).

Step 45: Organization. Select all layers we created so far, press Ctrl+G to group them in a folder, and name the folder Pants.

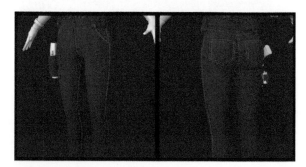

FIGURE 9.40 Add stitches to the pants.

Belts, Straps, Pockets, Holster, and Boots

Step 46: Leather material. Go to the Smart materials section in the SHELF. Find Leather Stylized, drag it above the Pants folder, and give Leather Stylized a black mask with a paint layer. Press the number 4 button to switch to Polygon Fill tool. In the PROPERTIES, click on the checker box button to switch to UV shell mode. Set the color to white, click on the Belts, Straps, Pockets, Holster, and Boots to make the leather show up on these parts. Open the Leather Stylized folder, select Base Color, change its color to a darker brown color (Figure 9.41).

Step 47: Refine curvature. Add a paint layer to the mask of the Curvature layer inside Leather Stylized. Select the Basic Soft brush in the Brushes section of the shelf. Change the color of the brush to black and paint out the overgrown edge wear on the pockets and gun holster (Figure 9.42).

Step 48: Boots bottom. Go to the Smart materials under the SHELF. Drag Rubber Dry to the top of the layer stack and name the group Boots_ Bottom. Give it a black mask with a paint layer.

FIGURE 9.41 Add leather material to the leather parts.

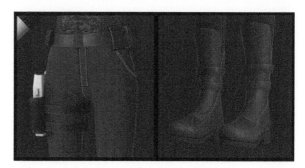

FIGURE 9.42 Refine the edge wear of the leather materials.

FIGURE 9.43 Add the Rubber Dry material to the bottom of the boots.

Use polygon fill tool with UV shell selection mode to assign the rubber material to the bottom of the shoe (Figure 9.43).

Gloves

Step 49: Glove Base. Switch to the Glove_and_watch_ mtl and drag Leather Stylized into the layer stack. The result should look like Figure 9.44.

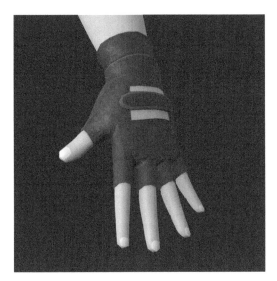

FIGURE 9.44 Glove material artifacts.

We can see many bad triangular artifacts. These artifacts are due to us baking using the low-resolution geometry as the high-resolution one. It is all fine if our texture does not rely heavily on the curvature map. Pull out the baked curvature map, and you can see the artifacts already existing on the baked map (Figure 9.45).

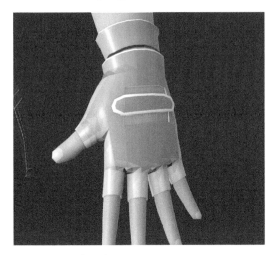

FIGURE 9.45 Baked artifacts of the glove.

We have two solutions:

1. Go to TEXTURE SET SETTINGS, under the Mesh maps column, click on curvature, set the Algorithm to Per Vertex, this will give us a much clean curvature map (Figure 9.46).

2. Go back to Maya, select the glove models, go to Mesh->Smooth, smooth the glove model twice (Figure 9.47).

We can use this smoothed model as the high-resolution model. Grab both the gloves and the watch, export them out as an fbx file. Back to Substance Painter; go to TEXTURE SET SETTINGS and click on Bake Mesh Maps. In the common settings, check off Use Low Poly Mesh as High Poly Mesh. On the side of the High-Definition Meshes list, click on the file icon to load the file exported from Maya, then bake again (Figure 9.48).

Solution 2 was used to get a better curvature map, and the result is that the leather material on the glove looks like Figure 9.49.

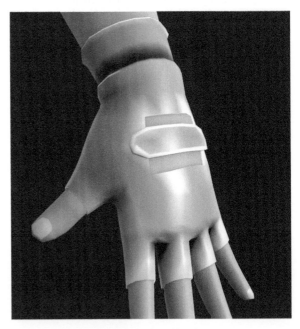

FIGURE 9.46 Baking result with the Per Vertex Algorithm.

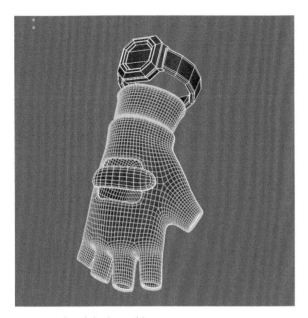

FIGURE 9.47 Smooth the glove model.

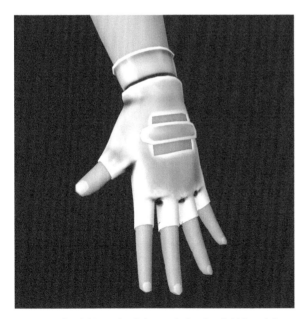

FIGURE 9.48 New baking result with the smoothed mesh as the high-resolution model.

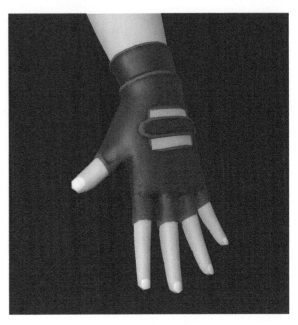

FIGURE 9.49 New leather material appearance with the new curvature map.

Step 50: Refine the amount of edge wear. Open the Leather Stylized folder and select the Mask Editor of the Curvature layer. In the PROPERTIES panel, change the Global Balance to 0.35 and the Global Contrast to 0.83. Go to the mask of the Darker Touch layer and select its Levels layer. In the PROPERTIES panel, drag the three pins on the top of the LEVELS graph to the right to minimize the amount of darker touch. Go to the Base color layer and change it to a darker color (Figure 9.50).

Step 51: Add extra height to the glove. Create a new fill layer above Base Color, name the new layer Glove_Extra_Height. In the PROPERTIES panel, toggle off color, rough, metal, nrm, and change the Height attribute to 1. Add a black mask with a paint layer, and use the Basic Hard brush to start painting in some extra layers around the finger and palm. Add a Blur filter above the paint layer to blur out the slope of the height (Figure 9.51).

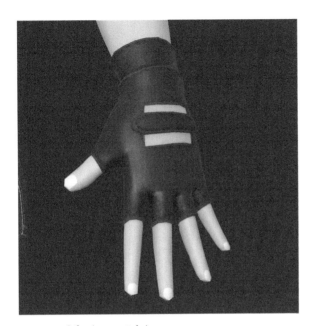

FIGURE 9.50 Refine the amount of edge wear.

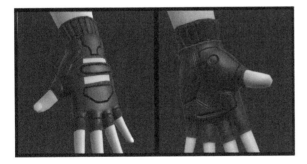

FIGURE 9.51 Add extra height detail to the glove.

Tips and Tricks

The Shift-click trick was used a lot to create clean straight lines. Now, hit the X button and erase to create valleys. We use the Hard brush first to lay out the patches, and then we blur it using a blur filter. This workflow gives us the flexibility to tweak how blurred we want it to be.

Step 52: Extra scratch to the new patches. Duplicate the Curvature layer, name the duplication Extra_Curvature, and toggle its height on and set the height value to −0.05. Delete the Mask Editor under its mask and add a new Generator to the mask. In the PROPERTIES panel, add a Curvature as the Generator; under the PROPERTIES, set the global balance to 0.7 and global contrast to 0.45 to get a basic color variation on the edge and high grounds.

Right-click on the mask of Glove_Extra_Height, select Add Anchor Point (we have covered anchor point before). Back to the Curvature mask of Extra_Curvature, in the PROPERTIES panel, toggle on Use Micro Detail. Under the Image inputs, click Micro Height, go to the ANCHOR POINTS tab, and select Glove_Extra_Height mask. Go to the Micro Detail section, drag Curvature Intensity up to 5, and set the Height Detail Intensity to 1.8 (Figure 9.52).

Step 53: Refine the edge wear. Add a paint layer on top of the Curvature under the Extra_Curvature. Use Dirt1 brush to paint extra edge scratch and imperfections (Figure 9.53).

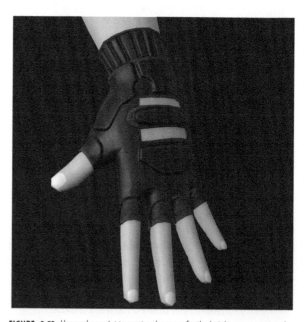

FIGURE 9.52 Use anchor point to create edge wear for the heightmap we painted.

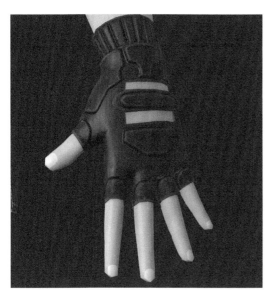

FIGURE 9.53 Hand paint more details to the edge wear of the glove.

Watch

Step 54: Add a basic material to the watch. Go to the shelf, drag the Plastic Fake Leather material on top of the Leather Stylized. Give it a black mask with a paint layer, press the number 4 button to use Poly Fill tool, and change the mode of the Poly Fill tool to UV shell mode. Set the color to white, and click on the watch to assign the material to the watch (Figure 9.54).

Step 55: Add material to the screen of the watch. Create a new fill layer and name it Watch_ Monitor. Change the Base Color of the layer to a dark gray, height to −0.35, roughness to 0.01, and the blend mode of the Height channel to normal. Give it a black mask and use the Poly Fill tool to make it appear only on the screen of the watch (Figure 9.55).

Step 56: Add extra height to the watch. Create a new fill layer, name it Watch_Extra_Height, and drag the Height down to −1. Add a black mask with a paint layer and start to paint extra detail on the watch. After painting, drag both Watch_Monitor and Watch_Extra_Height to Plastic Fake Leather and rename the folder Watch (Figure 9.56).

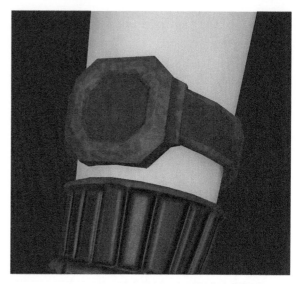

FIGURE 9.54 Use the Plastic Fake Leather material as the base material for the watch.

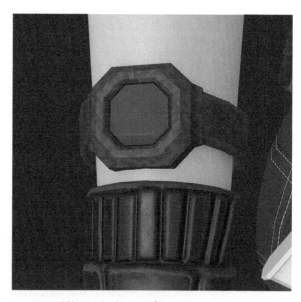

FIGURE 9.55 Add material to the screen of the watch.

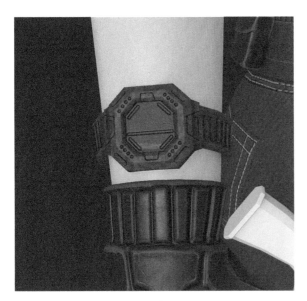

FIGURE 9.56 Paint extra height to the watch.

Gun

> *Step 57: Gun rebake. Switch to the Gun model and press Alt + Q to isolate the gun. The portion inside of the holster is darker due to the baked Ambient Occlusion. Open Maya and load the model in there, grab the Ellen_gun_geo, go to File->Export Selection, use the FBX format, and export with the name Gun_High. Back to Substance Painter, go to TEXTURE SET SETTINGS, and click Base Mesh Maps. Check off Use Low Poly Mesh as High Poly Mesh, load Gun_High in the High-Definition Meshes, and click on Bake Gun_mtl Mesh Maps to bake the mesh maps for the gun again.*
>
> *Step 58: Texture the Gun. The Method we use to texture the gun is the same we used to texture our environment modules. Go ahead and finish texturing it; Figure 9.57 shows our result.*

Other Details

> *Step 59: Chest Logo. Switch back to Upper_body_mtl and create a new fill layer above Fabric UCP. Name the new layer Chest_Logo, change its*

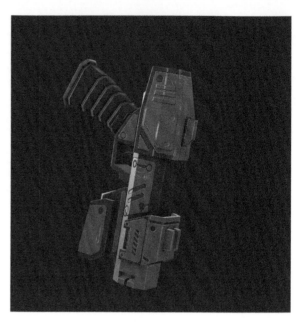

FIGURE 9.57 The finished texture of the gun.

color to a darker gray, height to 1, and give it a black mask with a paint layer. Use the Basic Hard brush to paint out the circle of the logo, shrink the brush size, and hit the X button to reverse the color. Paint out the middle to create the outer ring of the logo.

Change the Stroke opacity slider above the viewport to 50 and hit the X button to reverse the color back to white. Make the brush a little smaller and paint over the middle of the circle to add a half-transparent and half-height circular pattern. Change the Stroke opacity back to 100 and use the Shift + Left click combinate to draw a letter "A". Finally, hit X again to switch back to black; make the brush small and paint the dots across the outer circle (Figure 9.58).

Step 60: Metal bolts. Switch to the Lower_body_mtl, go to the Materials of the shelf, find and drag

FIGURE 9.58 Paint a chest logo.

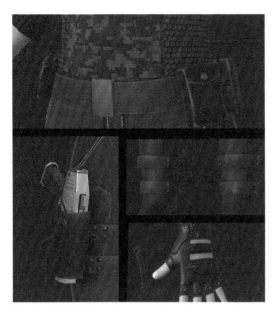

FIGURE 9.59 Add metal bolts.

Nickel Pure to the top of the layer stack, and name it Bolts. Change the height blending mode of this new layer to replace. Toggle on the height channel and set the Height value to 0.5. Change the color to a darker brown and increase roughness to 0.3.

Give Bolts a black mask with a paint layer, and press the number 1 button to switch to the paint brush. Use Basic Soft as the brush, hold down Ctrl and drag right mouse button up to make the brush sharp. You can now left-click to add bolts or paint any areas that are supposed to be metal. Do the same thing to the gloves (Figure 9.59).

Export Textures

Step 61: Export Textures. Go to File->Export Textures. In the pop-up Export Document settings window, go to CONFIGURATION and choose the same configuration we did in Chapter 4. Go back to EXPORT, change the format from png to targa, click on the directory, and change it to the sourceimages folder of the Maya project. Add a new folder there and name the folder

Ellen_Textures. Select Ellen_Textures, and press Select Folder. Change the resolution of the Eye_mtl and Hair_mtl to 1024×1024 to save some performance; press Export to export all maps.

Step 62: Test the textures in Maya. Open our character scene in Maya, select Ellen_head_geo, and press Ctrl+A to open the attribute editor. Select the Body_mtl and click the checker box icon after the color to pull out the Create Render Node window. Select File in the list and click on the Folder button on the right side of the Image Name setting in the Attribute Editor; choose Ellend_Body_mtl_BaseColor.tga and press open to load it. Press the number 6 button on the keyboard to show the texture.

Hold down right mouse button on the model and select Material Attributes to go back to the material. In the Attribute Editor, click on the checker box to assign a file node to the bump mapping. Maya creates a bump2d node automatically. Change the Use As setting to Tangent Space Normal in the Attribute Editor. Click on the button with a square and an arrow on the left side edge to go to the file node. Load the Ellen_Body_mtl_Normal.tga; for a normal map, we need to change the Color Space setting to Raw.

Do the same to all other materials (Figure 9.60).

Step 63: Move the gun to the origin. We have placed the gun to ensure that the gun works with the proportion and color scheme, but for rigging and game mechanics, the gun should be placed at the origin. Select Ellen_gun_geo, and switch to the Move tool, hold down D button, and click on a side face of the barrel to move the pivot to that face. Go to Modify->Bake Pivot. Maya then generates transformation values based on the current location and orientation of the pivot.

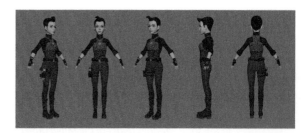

FIGURE 9.60 Test the textures in Maya.

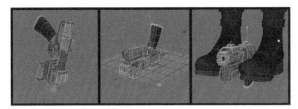

FIGURE 9.61 Move the gun to the origin.

> *Go to the Channel Box and zero out all the translate and rotate values; the gun should now no longer be tilted. Do a Modify->Center Pivot, hold down D and drag the Y and Z axes to move the pivot to the handle; do another Bake Pivot and zero out the translate and rotate values. Finally, rotate the gun back if it is flipped and do another Modify->Freeze transformation (Figure 9.61).*

Why?

Bake pivot calculates the location and rotation of the pivot relative to the origin and overrides the translation values with that. We can use it to get the rotation of a tilted model back, even if we have done a freeze transformation on it.

Conclusion

That's it, we have finished our character texturing! Overall, with Substance Painter, the texturing process should be a joyful one. With smart masks, generators, height map painting, and PBR workflow, we can get many things done. Be aware that we have seven texture sets, or materials, each with 2k images to achieve this crisp, high-resolution result. It is a pretty ambitious setup and would not be recommended for low-performance platforms. However, we could spoil ourselves on a PC game like what we are doing.

Moving on from here, we will jump into a pretty technical process – Rigging.

CHAPTER 10

Rigging

Now that we have the 3D model created and UV mapped and textured, we can now begin the rigging process. Rigging is essentially placing joints inside the character so that the animator can then animate those joints and bring the character to life. Each joint will influence a nearby polygon vertice and cause the deformation of that polygon. Once there's enough joints influencing enough vertices, the character will appear to be in motion. This will make more sense as we go on. Let's first take a quick look at how joints behave in Maya.

Joint Behavior

Create a new Maya file and go to the side view. In the rigging module, click Skeleton and create joints. Click in the side view once, then move your cursor to a new area above and click again. Do this one final time and press Enter. We now have a three-joint chain created (Figure 10.1).

Take a peek in the outliner and notice that the joints are created in the hierarchy when clicks. The top joint is the first joint you created. Look at the first joint and notice the orientation is pointed in the direction of the next joint. As joints are created, they automatically orient to the direction of the next joint. There are ways to add or

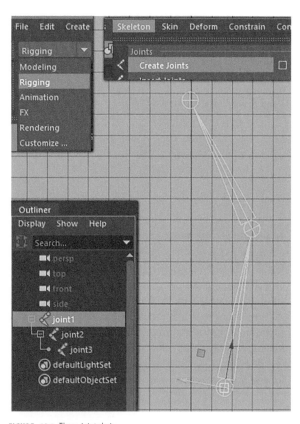

FIGURE 10.1 Three-joint chain.

remove joints to your joint structure, but for now, the main thing to know is to press Enter to finalize your joint chain.

Few things to note:

1. The best views to create joints are in the top, side, or front views.
2. If you hold down the shift button while creating joints, the joints will be created in a straight line.
3. You can easily change the hierarchy of joints in the outliner. For example, select joint 3 and press Shift + P. You have now unparented joint 3, and it now stands alone, as seen in the viewport. To add it back to the hierarchy of joint 1, select joint 3 in the outliner and middle mouse drag it under joint 2. As you can see, we are now back to our original joint hierarchy.
4. You can translate joints in the viewport to get them in the position you want, but generally, you do not want to rotate the joints. We'll discuss this more as the tutorial progresses, but ideally, you want your joint rotations to be at 0, 0, 0. This will make the animation process go much more smoothly.

To get comfortable with the joint creation process, create a few new joint chains and alter their structure in the outliner. Once you're comfortable with creating joints and moving them into positions, we should be ready to create a skeletal joint structure for our game character.

Joint Placement—Hip, Spine, Neck, and Head

Let's start this chapter by creating joints for the root, spinal cord, neck, and head. We will use the create joints tool.

Tutorial 10.1: Create the Joint Chain for Our Character

Step 1: Reference in the model. Create a new Maya file. Then go to File → Create Reference and point toward the 3D character Maya file we created in the previous chapters.

Why?

Referencing is an industry-standard process. We reference in characters, environment, rigs, into scenes so that should the characters, environments, or rigs be updated, and the file that we are working on automatically grabs those updates. This allows us to make sure that we are working on the most up to date models and rigs.

Step 2: Go to your side view.

Why?

By creating our joints in the side view, the joints will be created directly in the center of the character. This is especially important because we'll be mirroring our left arm and left leg joint to the right side to save some time.

Step 3: Create a spine joint chain. Go to the menu of the viewport and check on Shading → X-Ray Joints to see the joints through the models. Create the root joint by clicking in the middle of the hip area. Once that's done, while holding down the shift button, add three more joints going straight up and press Enter. You should now have a four-joint chain (Figure 10.2).

Step 4: Rename the joints. Let's name our joints before we move on, starting with joint 1. Double click joint 1 in the outline and type in hip. For the rest of the joints, label them spine_01, spine_02, and chest.

Step 5: Make the joints evenly apart. Let's make it so that spine_01, spine_02, and the chest joint are equally apart from each other. We can do this by using the translation attribute in the right-side channel box. Select spine_01, spine_02, and chest, go to the Channel Box, and type in a value of 8 in Translate X. The value may vary depending on the size of your character. The goal here is to get the chest joint to end up a little below the chest area of your 3D character. This is where the chest will rotate from.

Once that's done, we can now move onto the neck and head area. We'll do this by creating a new joint chain.

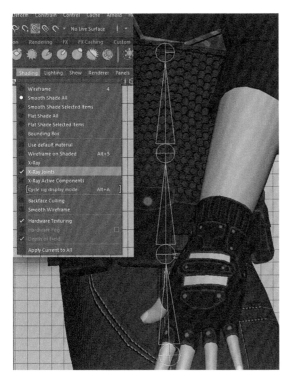

FIGURE 10.2 Root and spine joints.

Step 6: Create the joint chain of the neck. Hit Create joints again and start with the base of the neck. Place the next joint right below the w line and then while holding shift, make the last joint be at the top of the head. See Figure 10.3.

Step 7: Name the joints. Let's name these joints to neck, head, and head_end.

Step 8: Parent neck joints to the spine. We have now created the joint chain we'll use to animate the neck and head of our character. The next thing we need to do with this chain is to add it to our existing hip joint hierarchy. To do this, we are going to go in the outliner and middle mouse drag it onto the chest joint. Your joint system hierarchy should now look like this (Figure 10.4).

Before we move on, there's a couple of things to note. So far, we've only been translating our joints. Double check that all your joints have no values in the rotation channels

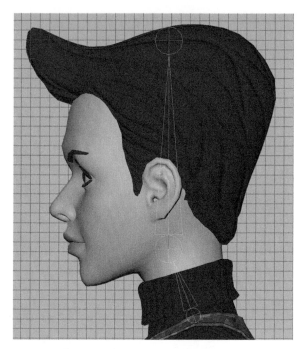

FIGURE 10.3 The joint chain for the neck.

Why?

This is the cleanest way of setting up a rig for animation. By keeping the rotation values at zero, animators can easily reset the joints to their original position by entering values of zero in the rotation rather than some odd number.

World Joint

One joint that we need to add is the 'parent' of the root joint. It is a world joint that goes at the origin.

Let's go ahead and create that.

> Step 9: In the front view, add a new joint at the base origin and rename to root_motion. If there are values in the translation, go ahead and zero all of those out. Parent the hip joint to root_motion (Figure 10.5).

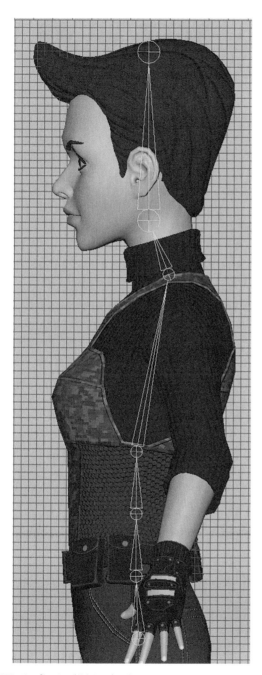

FIGURE 10.4 Parent neck joints to the spine.

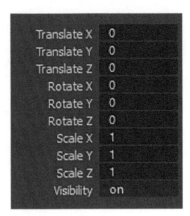

Translate X	0
Translate Y	0
Translate Z	0
Rotate X	0
Rotate Y	0
Rotate Z	0
Scale X	1
Scale Y	1
Scale Z	1
Visibility	on

FIGURE 10.5 World joint created at the origin.

Joint Placement—Left Arm

Let's now move onto creating the left arm joint structure. The goal here is to create a left arm structure along with a simple finger joint setup and then mirror that same setup to the other side for the right arm.

> *Step 10: Create the clavicle joint. Switch to the Create Joint tool, and in the front view, click in the area where the clavicle would be between the shoulder and neck area.*
>
> *Step 11: Create the arm joints. While holding down the shift button, add the shoulder, elbow, and wrist joint, they should form a horizontal joint chain at the moment (Figure 10.6).*
>
> *Step 12: Rename the joints. Let's relabel those: left_clavicle, left_shoulder, left_elbow, and left_wrist. We now need to rotate the joints to be in their correct direction. However, we do not*

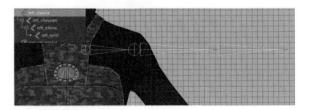

FIGURE 10.6 Create the arm joints.

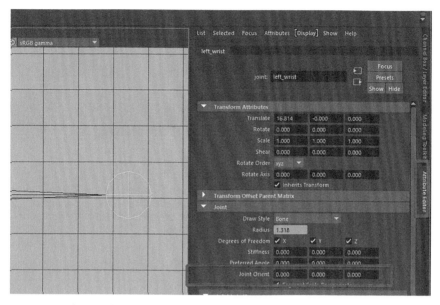

FIGURE 10.7 Attribute editor for the left_wrist joint.

want to rotate using the regular joint rotation.
We want to use what's called joint orient, which
can be found in the attribute editor once you
select a joint (Figure 10.7).

Why?

Using joint orient allows us to rotate the joints while
keeping the original joint orientation clean.

Step 13: Position the arm joints to the right spot.
First, move the clavicle if it is too far in the front
or in the back. Next, select the left_shoulder joint,
and go to the attribute editor. While holding
down the Ctrl key, middle mouse drag the values
in the joint orient box that corresponds with the
direction you need to rotate the joint. In our case,
we need to rotate both the joint orient Z and Y to
get the direction of the shoulder to properly line
up with the arm. Once the direction of the joint
is correct, you can change the translate X of the
child joint (left_elbow) to change the length of
the shoulder joint (Figure 10.8).

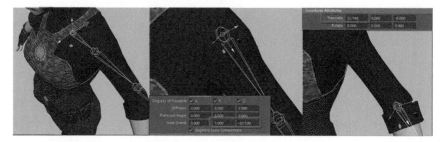

FIGURE 10.8 Position the clavicle and shoulder joint.

Step 14: Repeat the process we did for the shoulder joint to the elbow and wrist joint until the arm joints are all positioned to the right spot (Figure 10.9).

FIGURE 10.9 Finish the arm joints.

Tips and Tricks

Through the instruction experience we have, more than half of the students don't follow this rule. So we are going to write this down three times with all capitals:

DON'T ROTATE THE JOINT, CHANGE JOINT ORIENT!

DON'T ROTATE THE JOINT, CHANGE JOINT ORIENT!

DON'T ROTATE THE JOINT, CHANGE JOINT ORIENT!

> *Step 15: Parent the left_clavicle underneath the chest joint (Figure 10.10).*
> *Now it's time to create the finger joints. We'll just use a basic setup for the fingers that consists of three animate-able joints for each finger.*
> *Step 16: Turn on the Snap to Projected Center option. Let's turn on 'Snap to Projected Center' option, which can be found in the top menu among the buttons with icons of magnetics. This allows us to create joints in the 'perspective' viewport and automatically place the joints inside the hand mesh (Figure 10.11).*

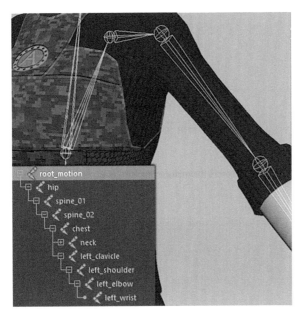

FIGURE 10.10 Parent the left_clavicle to the chest joint.

FIGURE 10.11 Turn on the Snap to Projected Center option.

Step 17: Create the index finger joints. Create the first joint at the base of the knuckle, and add three more joints down the finger, with the last one being at the tip of the finger.

Step 18: Name the finger joints. Let's now label these joints, left_hand_index_01, left_hand_index_02, left_hand_index_03, and left_hand_index_04 (Figure 10.12).

It's possible that our joint orientations from each other are a little skewed after creation. Let's go and zero out the values of the joint orient of left_hand_index_02, left_hand_index03, and left_hand_index_04.

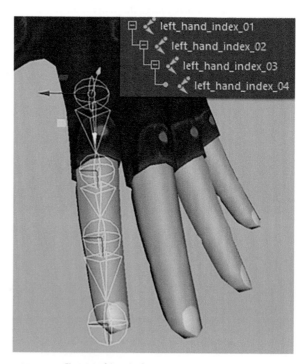

FIGURE 10.12 The joints of the index finger.

Why?

Upon doing this, we now have a clean structure of which the fingers are all straight. Now we can get the orientation correct by changing the joint orientation values in the attribute editor the same way we did for the arm joints.

Now that we got that all cleared up and ready to go, let's duplicate and use that same joint setup for the rest of the fingers.

> Step 19: Duplicate the index finger for the rest of the fingers. Select the left_hand_index_01 and press Ctrl + D. This makes a duplicate copy of that joint system. Move that new system onto the middle finger and adjust the joint orient accordingly. Remember only to translate the joints and use the joint orient to rotate the joints into place. It's your choice to either create the thumb from scratch or duplicate from the index finger.
> Repeat the same process for the rest of the fingers and name them accordingly (Figure 10.13).

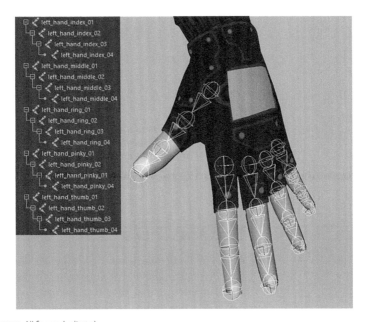

FIGURE **10.13** All fingers duplicated.

403

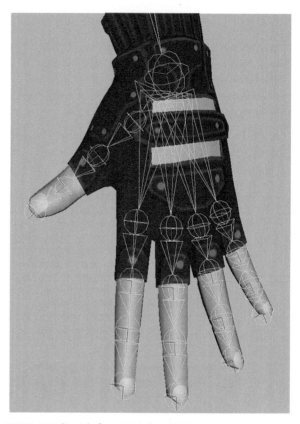

FIGURE 10.14 Parent the finger joints to the wrist joint.

Step 20: Parent the fingers to the wrist. The last step is to grab all the first finger joints in the outliner and middle mouse drag them underneath the left_wrist joint. This will connect all the fingers to the wrist (Figure 10.14).

Tips and Tricks

As you're doing this, be sure to keep your orientations cohesive. Make sure that all your fingers rotate the same direction so that as you are animating, you can grab all the fingers and animate them all at once in one axis.

Joint Setup—Right Arm

To get the right arm created, we could run through the whole process again, but we're going to take a shortcut for this one. We're going to do a process that's called Mirror Joints. This will essentially duplicate one side of the joints to the opposite side and save us much time.

> *Step 21: Mirror the joints. Select the left_clavicle, in the Rigging menu, select Skeleton → Mirror joints□. Here, set the Mirror across to YZ, so the joints are getting mirrored across the Y and Z plane. The other thing we want to do is relabel all of our new joints to start with right, instead of left. In the Search for text field, type in left. In the Replace with text field, type in right. If you labeled all of your left joints correctly, all of your new mirrored joints should be properly labeled for the right side (Figure 10.15).*
>
> *Hit the Apply button. And we've finished the right arm.*

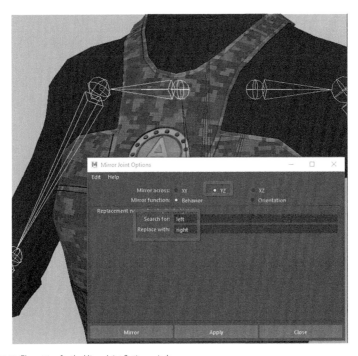

FIGURE 10.15 The setting for the Mirror Joint Options window.

Joint Setup—Legs

The legs will be most likely animated using a method called Inverse Kinematics or IK. However, for now, we need to create a basic joint structure. Few things to note, we'll be creating this in the side view, and we need to be sure not to create the joint structure straight down. We need to create a slight bend from the thigh, to knee, to the ankle.

> *Step 22: Create the leg joints. In the side view, create a new joint at the center of the hip area and name it left_thigh. Create another joint at the knee and then the ankle, and name them accordingly (Figure 10.16).*

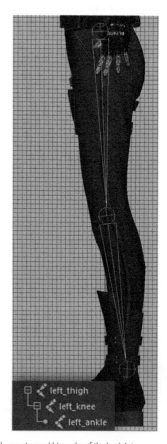

FIGURE **10.16** The naming and hierarchy of the leg joints.

Step 23: Create the foot joints. Add two more joints for the ball of the foot and the toe, name them, and parent the ball joint to the ankle joint after creation (Figure 10.17).

Once our structure is created, we need to go to the front view of the character, move left_ thigh to match the leg joints to the left leg and parent it to the hip joint (Figure 10.18).

Step 24: Mirror the leg joints. The next step would be to mirror this leg the same way we mirrored the clavicle.

Step 25: Parent the hip (thigh) joints underneath the hip joint.

Once that's done, we now have the left leg joint structure complete. We can now create

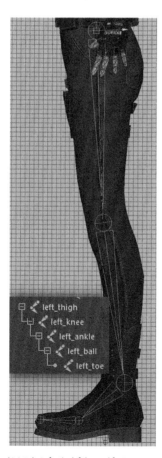

FIGURE 10.17 Final joint chain for the left leg and foot.

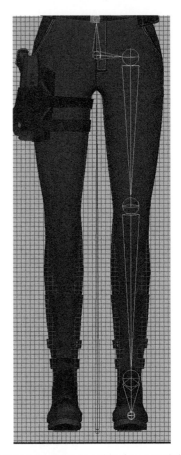

FIGURE 10.18 Match the leg joint to the model and parent it to the hip.

what's called an Inverse Kinematic chain for the leg. Inverse Kinematics works a little differently than the Forward kinematics that we've been using so far. Inverse Kinematics allows us to move a point or a target and have the connected joints automatically rotate the joint to point to that target. This will make much more sense as we create one, so let's do that for the left leg.

Step 26: Go to Skeleton → IK handle☐ and click on the Reset Tool button. We will only need the default setting of this tool.

Step 27: Apply the IK handle to the leg. Click the center of the left hip joint and then at the left ankle joint. The IK handle has now been created.

*To see how this works, grab the ikHandle1 in the
outliner, and translate it around. The leg is now
animating with inverse kinematics instead of
forward kinematics. Go ahead and name this IK
handle, left_leg_ankle_IK.*

*Step 28: Create IK chains for the foot joints. Create
another IK handle from the ankle to the ball.
Label the new IK handle, left_leg_ball_IK. Create
a final IK handle from the ball to the toe and
label it left_leg_toe_IK. We should now have
three IK chains. If you cannot see them, go to the
menu of the viewport and check on Shading →
X-Ray (Figure 10.19).*

*Step 29: Make the IK handles sticky. The last step
for these IK chains is to make them sticky. To
achieve this, go to the outliner and select the IK
handles, then in the attribute editor under the IK
handle Attributes section, turn on Sticky under
Stickiness. Do this for each of the IK handles
(Figure 10.20).*

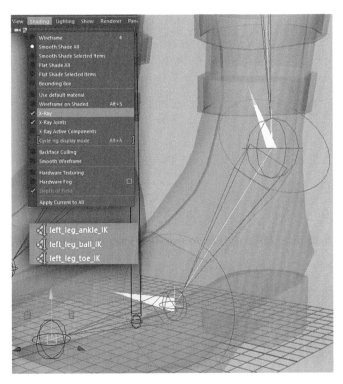

FIGURE 10.19 The new joint chain.

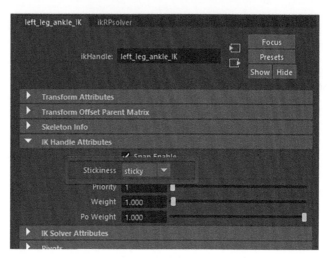

FIGURE 10.20 Make the IK handles sticky.

Foot Roll Rig

The next thing we need to do is create controllers for the foot. We'll be animating these later instead of trying to grab the IK chains in the outliner.

> *Step 30: Create the controller for the left toe. Go to Create → NURBS primitives → Circle. This will create a NURBS circle at the origin. Let's label this one left_toe_ctrl. NURBS models are mathematically constructed, and they are lightweight and perfect for creating controllers.*
> *Step 31: Group the controller. After labeling the curve, we need to group it by selecting the NURBS curve and then pressing Ctrl+G. Name the group, left_toe_ctrl_group. The group is what we'll use to position the curve where we need it to go, leaving the NURBS curve attributes clean.*

Why?

We'll be animating with the NURBS curves later on, and we need those to not have any values on them to make the life easier on the animators. By keeping the values empty, we can easily reset the controller back to default by entering 0 in the values.

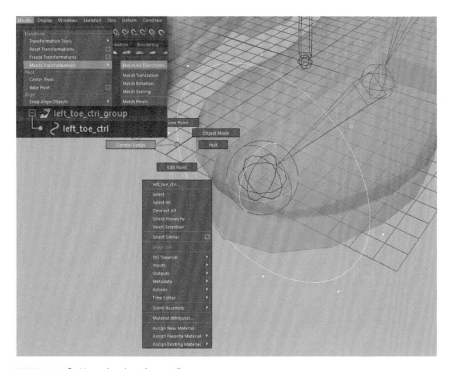

FIGURE 10.21 Position and re-shape the controller.

> Step 32: Position the group to the toe joint. Select
> the left_toe_ctrl_group and then add select the
> left_toe joint. In the top menu, select Modify →
> Match Transformations → Match All Transforms.
> The left_toe_ctrl_group should now be moved to
> the left_toe joint.
>> If you don't see the controller, press Ctrl + 1 to
> isolate the group, and you can see that it is just
> too small. To make it bigger, hold down the right
> mouse button on the curve and select Control
> Vertex. Marquee select, scale, and rotate all the
> vertices shown in Figure 10.21.

Why?

We could easily scale the controller up, but that
introduces scale values in the Channel Box, which will
cause problems for animation and rigging later on.
Always remember that the Translate X, Y, Z and Rotate

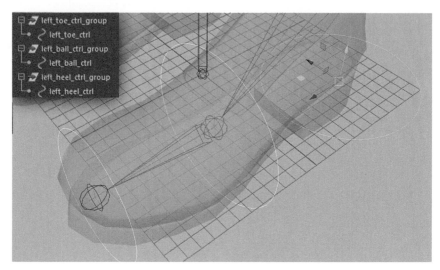

FIGURE 10.22 The left foot controller setup.

X, Y, Z values of your controller should remain 0, and the Scale X, Y, and Z values should remain 1.

You can press Ctrl+1 again to toggle isolation.

> *Step 33: Create the controller for the left ball joint. Repeat the same process from Step 29 to Step 31 for the left_ball joint.*
> *Step 34: Create the heel controller. Create another controller and group pair, and name them left_heel_ctrl and left_heel_ctrl_group. This time, instead of match transformation, place the left_heel_ctrl_group to the base of the heel (Figure 10.22).*

Setting Up the Foot Hierarchy

The next part of the process is putting the controllers into the correct hierarchy so they can control the joints.

> *Step 35: Parent IK to the controllers. Make Left_leg_ankle_ IK a child of left_ball_ctrl. We can achieve this by middle mouse dragging left_leg_ankle_ IK onto left_ball_ctrl. Follow the same trend, do the following parenting operations:*
> *Make left_leg_ball_IK a child of left_toe_ctrl*

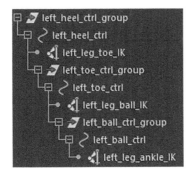

FIGURE 10.23 Left foot rig setup hierarchy.

Make left_ball_ctrl_group a child of left_toe_ctrl
Make left_leg_toe_IK a child of left_heel_ctrl
Make left_toe_ctrl_group a child of left_heel_ctrl
Your hierarchy should now look like Figure 10.23.

Step 36: Create a main foot controller. Create another controller and group pair. Name the controller left_foot_ctrl and name the group left_foot_ctrl_group. Place left_foot_ctrl_group directly underneath the foot. Hold down the right mouse button on the curve and select Control Vertex. Marquee selects all the vertices and scales them to match their size to the bottom of the foot. Finally, parent left_heel_ctrl_group to left_foot_ctrl.

Step 37: Repeat Steps 25–35 on the right leg.
Currently, the joints are not influencing any of the geometry. The next thing we need to do is have it so that the joints are now influencing the character vertices or polygons. To do this, we'll be using a method called Bind skin.

Tutorial 10.2: Bind and Paint Skin Weighting

Step 1: Select all the joints and the models. In the outliner, select the root_motion joint and then on the top menu, go to Select → Hierarchy; this will select all the joints. Now, while holding down the Ctrl button, add all the character meshes except the gun to the selection.

Step 2: Bind the models to the joints. In the Rigging menu, go to skin → bind skin□. In the pop-up Bind Skin Options window, click on Edit →

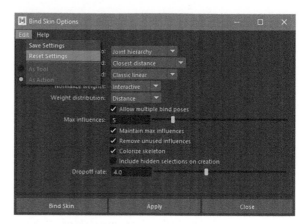

FIGURE 10.24 Bind skin options.

Reset Settings to use default skinning options (Figure 10.24).

Press the Bind skinbutton. (Binding skin will bind the vertices to the closest joints so that when you rotate or translate the joints, the corresponding geometry deforms accordingly.)

Now that our geometry is bound to the joints, we need to refine the skin weights. The process is known as painting skin weights, which is the process of adjusting the intensity values on each vertice to the corresponding joint. This part of the rigging process is one of the most important as it allows us to make sure each joint is deforming the corresponding geometry properly and smoothly.

Painting Skin Weights

The goal here is to make sure only the specified geometry bends with the corresponding bind joint. Another thing we're going to do is copy the skin weights from one side of the body to the other. So we'll pain the skin weights for the character's left side and copy them to the right side.

To make things easier, we'll paint the skin weights on the Ellen_full_body_ref geometry and then transfer the skin weights to the main character geometry.

Step 3: Hide all the geometry except for the Ellen_full_body_ref. Select the geometry pieces in the outliner and press Ctrl+H. Next, be sure to unhide the Ellen_full_body_ref if it's hidden. Select the geometry in the outliner and press Shift+H.

Step 4: Open the Paint Skin Weight Tool. Select the Ellen_full_body_ref in the viewport, hold down the right mouse button, and select the Paint Skin Weights tool. This now activates the skin weighting process for the geometry and joints.

There are a few things to take note of in the Tool Settings that pop up. The first is that you'll see a list of all the joints. Select one of the joints in the list, and you'll see which part of the geometry that joint is affecting. The controlled geometry area is displayed in white, as shown in Figure 10.25. We will be mainly using the Add and the Smooth options under paint operation.

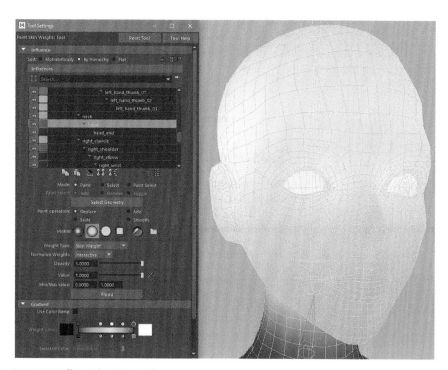

FIGURE 10.25 Skin weight painting window.

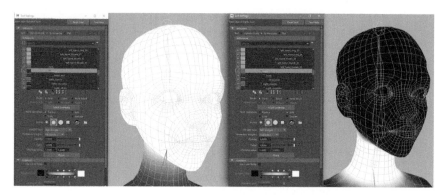

FIGURE 10.26 Paint the weighting for the head and the neck.

Step 5: Paint the weighting for the head. Let's start with the head joint. Select the head joint in the influences list on the paint weight tool settings box that popped open. Once selected, make sure that the paint operation is set to Add and the opacity is at 1.0000. We'll also put the Value at 1.0000. The goal here is to paint the head geometry to have a value of 1 so that when the head joint is animated, the head geometry rotates accordingly.

Paint the whole area of the head to white to make the head joint take full control of the head. Moving down to the neck joint and paint the neck area to white to make the neck joint control the neck (Figure 10.26).

Tips and Tricks

When painting, completely white means that vertice has a weight value of 1.

Step 6: Smooth the weighting between the head and the neck. Now that we've got the head and the neck completely painted with an influence of 1 (white), what we'll want to do is smooth the weighting between the two joints. To do this, select the head joint in the list and switch to the Smooth operation option in the tool settings. Once that's selected, press the Flood button (located under the opacity option) a few times. You'll now see that the blend is much smoother to the neck joint. This will allow for a smooth deformation when bending the joint.

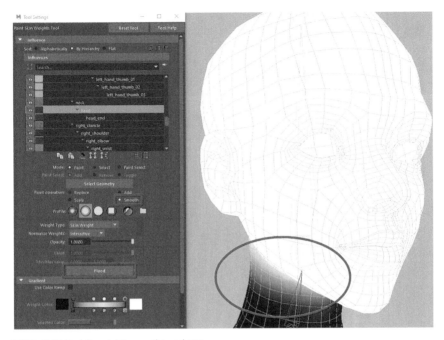

FIGURE 10.27 Head skin weighting smooth to neck joint.

Tips and Tricks

You can also hold down Shift and paint to smooth out any area. To verify your skin, weights are looking nice and clean, grab the head joint, and rotate it. You'll see how the geometry is deforming. Once you're done testing it out, be sure to set the joint back to 0, 0, 0 (Figure 10.27).

> Step 7: Paint the weight down the chain. The next step would be to work our way down the chain. The chests would be the next joints to paint. Do the same process as before and use Add and paint the influence of the chest joint. Once done with that area, you can smooth out the transitions (Figure 10.28).

Tips and Tricks

Sometimes, as you're going through your paint-weighting process, you'll see a vertice with influences from an

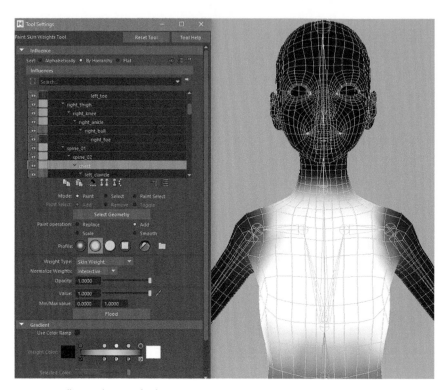

FIGURE 10.28 Chest weighting completed.

unwanted joint. In these cases, select the vertice and go to the Windows → General editors → Component Editor. Once there, you'll see a Smooth Skins tab that shows which joints are influencing that vertice. If there's a joint that is influencing and you do not want it to, you can enter 0 in the box associated to that joint (Figure 10.29).

Step 8: Repeat the weight-painting process for the rest of the spine. You will repeat this process down the spine. Below is an image showing the cutoff points for each joint (Figure 10.30).

 Once you're done with the spine, it's time to do the arms and legs. Remember, we're only doing one side, and then we'll copy the weighting to the other side. So, let's do the character's left side.

Step 9: Paint the weighting for the left clavicle. Starting with the left clavicle, repeating the

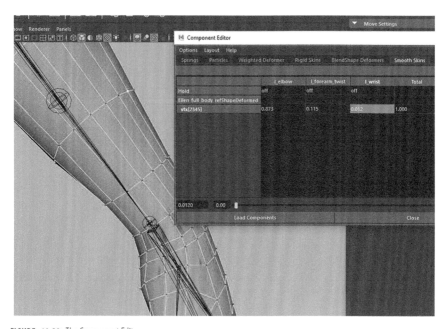

FIGURE 10.29 The Component Editor.

> *process of painting in Add mode, and then smoothing out (Figure 10.31).*
>
> *Step 10: Finish the weighting of the rest of the body. The next joint would be the shoulder and then the elbow, wrist, and finger joints. Once the arm is done, the next thing to do would be the left leg, starting from the hips.*

Mirroring the Skin Weights

Instead of painting the right side of the body, we're going to mirror the skin weights from the left side.

> *Step 11: Mirror the skin weights. Select the geometry and go to Skin → Mirror Skin Weights☐. In the Mirror Skin Weights Options window, make sure that the Mirror across option is set to YZ, and the Direction Positive to negative (−X to X) is checked so that it's mirroring from Positive to Negative (+x to −x) (Figure 10.32).*
>
> > *Hit Mirror. The skin weights have now been mirrored to the right side of the body. Be sure to*

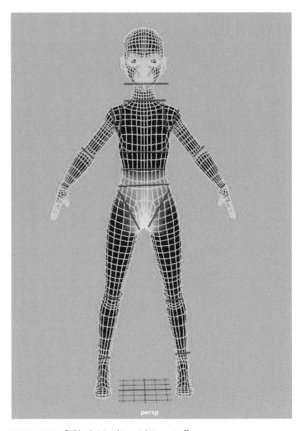

FIGURE 10.30 Full body joint skin weighting cut-off areas.

double-check this is in fact the case. Test it by animating or rotating the joints. Be sure to set them back to 0, 0, 0 afterward.

Copying the Skin Weights

Now that we've got the Ellen_full_body_ref painted, we're going to transfer the skin weights from this model to the rest of the models. This is a simple process that'll only take a few minutes.

Step 12: Unhide the models. Unhide the geometry that we hid before. Select all of the geometry in the outliner and press Shift + H.

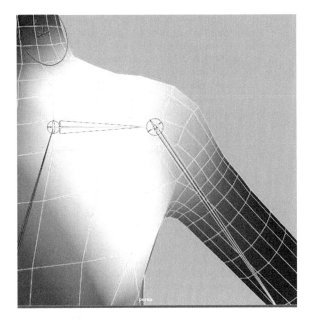

FIGURE 10.31 Left clavicle skin weighting.

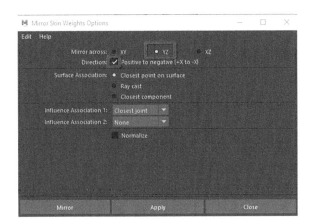

FIGURE 10.32 The mirror skin weights settings.

> *Step 13: Copy skin weight to the sweater. Select*
> *Ellen_full_body_ref and then shift select*
> *Ellen_sweater_geo. Go to Skin → Copy Skin*
> *Weights. The order of selection is important,*
> *you must select the source first, and then the*
> *destination. Once you've hit copy skin weights,*

the skin weighting should now be applied to the Ellen_sweater_geo. Test it out again by animating the joints.

Step 14: *Repeat the same process for all of Ellens geo.*
   Once you've copied all of the skin weights over, test out the deformations. While copying the skin weights over does a great job, it's never 100%, so be sure to test out and adjust accordingly using the paint skin weights process that we did before.
   Now that the skin weighting is out of the way, let's start creating controllers for the arm.

Tutorial 10.3: Set Up Arm Controls

Step 1: *Duplicate the left arm joints. Select the left_shoulder joint and press Ctrl+D to duplicate it. You should now have a new chain called left_shoulder1, left_elbow, left_wrist. The fingers were also probably duplicated, but we don't need those. In the outliner, delete the duplicated finger joints.*

Step 2: *Unparent the new joint chain. Grab left_shoulder and press Shift+P. This will unparent the new joint chain that we created since we want it to function separately from the deformation joint system.*

Step 3: *Rename the new joints. Rename the duplicated joints to left_drv_shoulder, left_drv_elbow, and left_drv_wrist. As a final step on this joint chain, place it under a group and name the group left_drv_arm_group (Figure 10.33).*
   This new joint chain we created is often called a driver joint chain. It receives the controller's input and drive the original joints. We also call the original joints the binding joints.
   What we want to do now is create controllers to control this driver joint chain.

Step 4: *Create the controller. Go to the top menu and select Create → Nurbs Primitives → Circle.*

FIGURE 10.33 New arm joint setup.

This will create a NURBS circle at the origin. If you do not see it, be sure to go to the perspective view.

Step 5: Delete history. With the circle selected, go to Edit → Delete by Type → History.

Step 6: Rename the controller to left_fk_shoulder_ctrl.

Step 7: Group the controller. With the controller selected, press Ctrl+G. This creates a group on top of the controller. Rename that group, left_fk_shoulder_ctrl_grp.

Step 8: Match the group to the shoulder joint. Select the group and then shift select the left shoulder joint. Go to the top menu, Modify → Match Transformations → Match all Transformations. This will place the group and controller in the exact place and orientation of the selected object.

Step 9: Tweek the shape of the controller. You'll want to resize the controller if it is not looking right. Manipulate the control vertices to change its size and shape (Figure 10.34).

Step 10: Duplicate the controller group. Select the left_fk_shoulder_ctrl_grp and duplicate it by pressing Ctrl+D. This creates another group; rename the group to left_fk_elbow_ctrl_grp. Open the group and rename the controller under it to left_fk_elbow_ctrl.

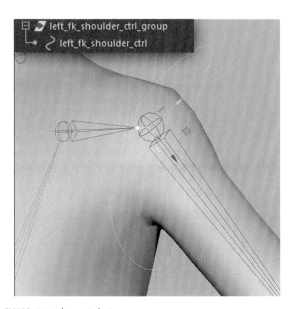

FIGURE 10.34 Arm control setup.

Tips and Tricks

It's important to keep the actual controls clean with zero values on them. That's why we're using the groups to move them into position and adjusting the control vertices to rotate or scale them into your desired size and shape.

> Step 11: Match the left_fk_elbow_ctrl_grp to the elbow joint. Grab the left_fk_elbow_ctrl_grp, add select the elbow joint, and do a match all transformations. Then, resize the controller to your liking by manipulating the control vertices.
>
> Step 12: Repeat Steps 10 and 11 for the wrist.
>
> Step 13: Put the controller into their correct hierarchy. The last step for the controller set up is the hierarchy of the groups and their controls. It's important that after we do this, we are moving the groups on top of the controls in the outliner. The hierarchy should be from the shoulder down. So, first, grab the elbow group and drag it underneath the shoulder controller (not the group, the controller under the group). Then, grab the wrist group and drag it under the elbow controller (Figure 10.35).
>
> Step 14: Use the controllers to control the driver joints. Select left_fk_shoulder_ctrl, then shift select the left_drv_shoulder joint, and select Constrain → Orient. (Be sure that the maintain offset option is checked in the settings.) Do the same thing for the elbow and wrist. In the end, you should have three orient constraints, one on each joint. If you did things correctly, you should be able to rotate the controllers and see the joints rotate with it. These will be the FK arm setup.

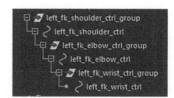

FIGURE 10.35 Arm controller hierarchy.

Constrains

After you apply constrain to objects, the second one in the selection starts to follow the first one in the selection. Orient constraint makes the object follow the rotation only. Go to the constrain menu and you can also see Parent and Point. Parent constraint makes the object follow both the translation and the rotation. Point constraint makes the object follow the translation only.

IK Arm Setup

Now let's set up the IK arm controls.

> *Step 15: Create the IK controller for the wrist. Duplicate the left_fk_wrist_ctrl_grp and unparent the new duplicate. Replace the "fk" in the names of the new group and the controller under it with "IK."*
> *Step 16: Re-shape the new IK controller. Re-shape the new controller by right clicking and going into the Control vertex mode. All you have to do is make it look different than the left_fk_wrist_ctrl (Figure 10.36).*
> *Step 17: Create the IK controller for the elbow. Duplicate the left_ IK _wrist_ctrl_grp and replace the "wrist" in the name to "elbow." Select the new group and match it to the elbow joint with*

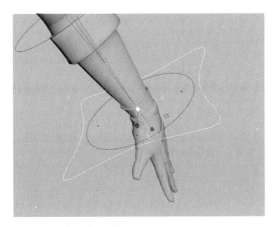

FIGURE 10.36 Re-shape the new IK controller.

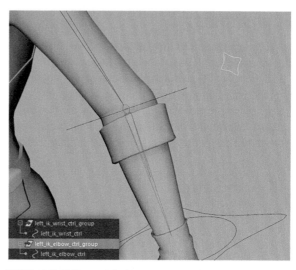

FIGURE 10.37 IK elbow control setup.

Modify → Match Transformations → Match all Transformations. Select the group and translate it back so it sits behind the elbow. Change the shape of the controller as shown in Figure 10.37.
  Next, let's set up the IK control system for the arm.

Step 18: Create the IK Handle. Go to the rigging module, and then Skeleton → Create IK handle. Use the default settings. Click on the left_drv_shoulder, and then left_drv_wrist (isolate them so you can easily click on them). This will create an IK handle. Rename it to left_wrist_IK.

Step 19: Parent the IK handle to the IK wrist controller. Select the left_wrist_IK in the outliner and middle mouse drag it onto the left_ IK_wrist_ctrl. Now left_ IK_wrist_ctrl should be driving the IK system.

Step 20: Set up the IK elbow control. Select the left_ IK_elbow_ctrl you created in the outline. Hold down Ctrl and select the left_wrist_IK, and go to Constraint → Pole Vector. This pole vector control should now be able to control the IK elbows position.

Step 21: Apply wrist rotation control. The last thing we need to do is add an orient constraint between the left_ IK_wrist_ctrl and the left_ drv_wrist joint. Select the left_ IK_wrist_ctrl, *and then shift select the left_drv_wrist joint and select Constrain → orient constraint.*

Now that we have the IK created, one of the last things we need to do is constrain the new duplicate arm driver joints to the original binding joints. What we'll be doing is parent constraining our binding joints to the new driver joints.

Step 22: Parent Constraint the binding joints to the driver joints. Select the new left_drv_shoulder joint and shift select the left_shoulder binding joint. Select Constrain → Parent Constraint to apply a parent constraint to the binding joint, go ahead, and do the same thing for the elbow and the wrist joints.

Now that we have our arm rigs done, we need to clean up the groups in the outliner.

Step 23: Group all the controllers. Select left_fk_shoulder_ctrl_group, left_ IK _wrist_ ctrl_group, and left_ IK _elbow_ctrl_group. Group them and name the new group left_arm_ctrl_group.

Step 24:Group the controllers and the driver joints. Select left_arm_ctrl_group and left_drv_arm_ group. Group them and name the new group left_arm_rig_group (Figure 10.38).

You will need to repeat the entire Tutorial 10.3 for the right arm.

Tutorial 10.4: Finger Controls

Now that we have the arm completed, we need to create controls for each finger joint.

Step 1: Create the fk controllers. Create the fk controllers for the fingers the same way we create the controllers for the arm. You can think

FIGURE 10.38 The final hierarchy of the left arm.

of the fingers as mini arms. Don't forget to parent the controllers to their correct hierarchy the same way we did for the arm controllers (do not create the IK ones).

Step 2: Parent constraint the joints. Once you're done with all of the fingers' controls, you'll need to parent constraint the joint to each corresponding finger controller. This is the same process that we've been doing for the other controls. The finger joints should now rotate as you rotate the controls.

Step 3: Group the controllers. Next, let's group all finger groups under one group and call it left_hand_group. This group should hold all your finger controls and their group (Figure 10.39).

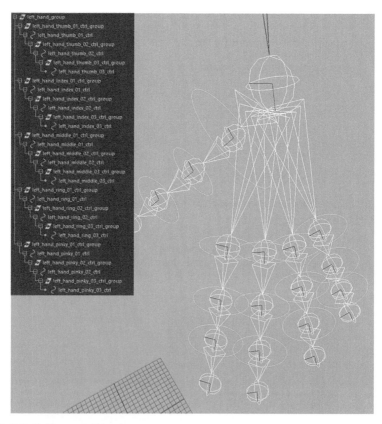

FIGURE 10.39 Final finger control hierarchy.

Step 4: Make the hand follow the wrist. The last step of this process is to parent constrain the left_hand_grp to the left_drv_wrist joint. This will make sure that the group follows along with the arm motion.

Tutorial 10.5: Clavicle and Body Controls

Since we have the driver joints and the binding joints for the arm, we need to do a similar setup for the clavicles.

Step 1: Create the driver joint. To start things off, we need to duplicate the left_clavicle joint. This will duplicate the joints underneath. We only need the clavicle and shoulder, and go ahead and delete everything else. Once those are deleted, rename the joints to left_drv_clavicle and left_drv_shoulder. Group left_drv_clavicle and rename the group to left_drv_clavicle_group. Finally, unparent the group (Figure 10.40).

Step 2: Creating Clavicle controls. Now we need to create controls for the clavicles using the same method as before. Create a NURBS circle, and group it. Move the group to the position of the clavicle joint by matching all transformations. Name the controller, and the group following the safe convention we've been using. Finally, group the top group of the controller and the driver joint to a new group called left_clavicle_rig_group (Figure 10.41).

Step 3: Create an IK handle. Next, we are going to create an IK handle to animate the clavicles when the arm is in IK mode. Go to Skeleton → Create IK handle☐. In the Tool Setting window, change the Current Solver setting to Single-Chain Solver. Click on left_drv_clavicle, then left_drv_shoulder to create an IK handle and name it left_clavicle_IK (Figure 10.42).

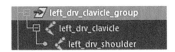

FIGURE 10.40 Left clavicle and shoulder joint setup and hierarchy.

429

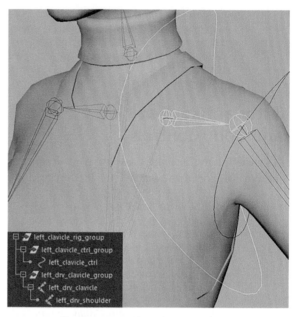

FIGURE 10.41 Clavicle rig groups and hierarchy.

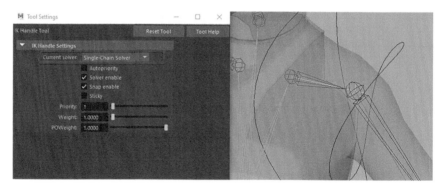

FIGURE 10.42 Clavicle IK and joint setup.

Step 4: Parent left_clavicle_IK to the left_clavicle controller (Figure 10.43).

Step 5: Constraint the original joints. Next, we need to have these driver joints drive the binding joints. Select the left_drv_clavicle joint and then shift select the left_clavicle joint. Do a Constrain → Parent Constraint.

Step 6: Constraint the shoulder driver joints. Next, we need to select the left_drv_shoulder of the

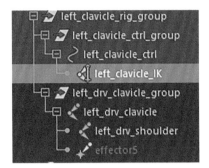

FIGURE 10.43 Left clavicle IK and controller hierarchy.

clavicle driver joints and then add select the left_drv_arm_group and do another parent constraint. This will allow the driver joints from the arm to follow the clavicle.

Step 7: Constraint the shoulder FK controllers. Select the left_drv_shoulder of the clavicle driver joints and then add select the left_fk_shoulder_ctrl_group, and do one more parent constraint.

Step 8: Make the clavicle follow the chest. Now, we need to make the clavicle group follow the chest control. Select the chest joint, and then shift select the left_clavicle_rig_group, and do one last Constrain → Parent Constraint.

> *Now you have done the left clavicle, do the same thing for the right clavicle.*

> *Now it's time to create the root and spine controllers. Remember, the controls will all need groups.*

Step 9: Create the hip controller (NURBS circle), name it, group it, and rename the group as well.

Step 10: Grab the group and match all transformations to the hip joint.

Step 11: Parent constrain the hip joint to the hip controller.

Step 12: Repeat this same process for the joints that lead all the way up to the head (Figure 10.44). Figure 10.44 Body controller setup.

Gun Joint

We now need to add one last joint that will be used for the weapon in the game.

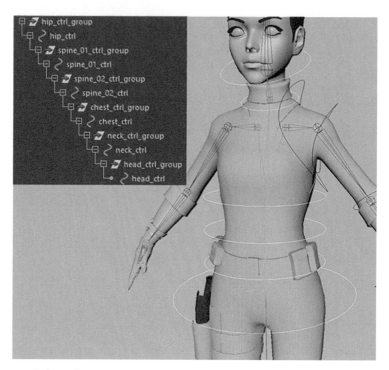

FIGURE 10.44 Body controller setup.

Step 13: Select Skeleton → Create joints. Create a joint at the origin and then translate it inside the gun and rename the joint to gun_joint.

Step 14: Bind the geometry of the gun to gun_joint. Select the gun geometry, add select the gun_joint, and do a Skin → Bind Skin.

Step 15: Paint the weight of the gun so that the gun_joint has complete control of the gun.

Final Hierarchy

Now that we have all the controls created, we just need to clean them up in the outliner and make sure that they're placed in the correct order and under the proper groups.

Step 16: Create the world controller. Create a new controller at the origin and rename it to world_ctrl. Group the world controller and rename it to Ellen_rig_grp.

*Step 17: Parent other controllers and driver joints
under the world controller. The world controller
should be the root of the hierarchy. Parent all
the controllers and driver joints under the world
controller (Figure 10.45).*

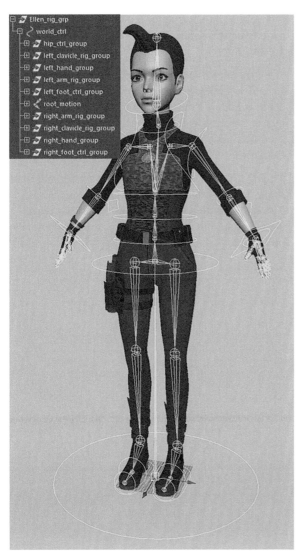

FIGURE 10.45 Final hierarchy of the whole rig.

Conclusion

We have finished our rig, but bear in mind that this setup is the bare minimum of rigging. We ripped off everything we could to keep rigging simple for you. However, if you want to have more advanced rigs, there are plenty of auto rigs out there. Plug-ins like Advanced Skeleton, Rapid Rigs, can make all the controls for you in a matter of minutes. Maya has its own auto rig as well located at Control → Create Control Rig.

There are more things to explore in the world of rigging. To name a few, we did not do any facial expression controls, and we cannot even move the eyes or open the mouth. We also did not set up any stretching. However, we should always avoid overdoing the rig. If we don't need facial expressions, it makes total sense not to rig the face.

Rigging can be super confusing, so if you don't understand some of the steps, try to read through them again. Also, if you don't feel like rigging at all, we have a finished rig file for you, and you can work the animations with it in the next chapter.

See you there!

CHAPTER 11

FPS Animation in Maya

FPS Animation Overview

First-person shooter (FPS) animations are utilized in games where player immersion is significant. It is as if the player were stepping into the character's shoes and becoming that character. The player will usually only see their character's hands and weapon if the gameplay calls for one. Since we only see a fraction of the character, creating FPS animations is usually simpler than animating characters we will see in full view, such as non-player characters. In the animation phase, our job is to create believable character movement. There are a few technical considerations to think about before starting the FPS animations, but once those are set up, breathing life into our character should be straightforward. Before moving on, if you feel like speeding up the workflow, you can jump to the next chapter where the second half shows how to use motion captured data as our animation instead of doing it manually.

Referencing the Character Rig

Instead of opening Ellen_rig as usual, you have the option of referencing the character rig in a new Maya file. Referencing in the rig will allow you to animate an instance of the character while leaving the original file untouched.

> *Step 1: Start with a clean Maya file, and go to File>Create Reference. Navigate to Ellen_rig and click on Reference to bring in the instanced version of the Ellen rig. This is the file you will begin your animations in.*

Why?

When you start animating and maybe realize that you need to make model or rigging adjustments, you can jump into the original rig file, Ellen_rig, and make those changes. When you return to your animation file with the referenced rig, those adjustments will be reflected on the model and/or rig, and your animation should still be intact. If you do not see those changes immediately, go to File>Reference Editor, right click on the rig name in the newly appeared window, and choose Reload Reference to bring in those changes into your animation file.

Besides the ease of updating the model and rig separately from the animation data, referencing makes it such that altering the rig while you are animating is impossible. You will not be able to delete any controls or any parts of the model by accident.

Tips and Tricks

Referencing character rigs is optional and not required to animate. You can always just animate straight on the original rig file. Be sure to incrementally save your files regardless of which method you decide to go with. For example, let us say you have been working in a Maya scene named AnimationFile_1. After an allotted time, such as 10 minutes, I would recommend creating a new iteration named AnimationFile_2. Sometimes animation files can crash, so if AnimationFile_2 becomes corrupted in an unexpected crash, you will still have AnimationFile_1 as a backup.

Save Files

All the animations for each weapon set will be housed in their own Maya file. When you save this Maya file, name it Ellen_gun_animations to distinguish it from other files.

Display Layers

Seeing your character without any obstructions is important while you animate. Display layers can be used to hide certain aspects of the model or rig when they are not needed, while also removing the need to dig through the Outliner every single time you want to hide those character parts.

> Step 2: Shift-select all the parts of the geometry that we do not need to see for FPS animation creation. Navigate to the Display Layer Editor in the lower right-hand side of the screen, and go to Layers>Create Layer from Selected. A new display layer named layer1 will appear right below the area you just clicked. Let's rename the new layer to something more specific by double clicking on the name layer1. In the Fdit I ayer window, type RestOfBodyMesh in the Name input box and click on Save to exit the window.
>   The columns of boxes to the right of the display layer name will allow us to quickly control the display layers. The first column containing the letter "V" controls the visibility of the object. To turn off the RestOfBodyMesh display layer, click on the letter "V" so that the box becomes empty. Ellen's upper body and arms should be the only visible parts of the geometry in your viewport.

437

Step 3: Repeat this process with the controls that are not needed for FPS animations and name the layer NotNeededControls.

Step 4: Let's also create a display layer for the visible parts of Ellen's mesh and instead utilize a different feature of display layers. When you click on the blank third column box, the letter "R", meaning referenced, will eventually be revealed. Turning on the letter "R" will cause the geometry to not be selectable.

Why?

During the animation process, you will want to only move the controls created during the rigging process, not the character geometry. By putting Ellen's upper body, arms, and weapon geometry on their own display layers with the referenced option active, you will not have to worry about setting stray keyframes beyond the controls. Figure 11.1 shows an example of the various display layers created so far.

Tips and Tricks

As you animate, you will need to quickly preview your animation without the controls, which is how we will ultimately see the character in the game. In the Viewport menu bar, click on Show, which will bring up a long list of components that you can hide and unhide, as seen in Figure 11.2. Click on NURBS Curves or use the keyboard shortcut Alt + 1.

FIGURE 11.1 List of display layers.

FIGURE 11.2 Show>NURBS Curves to hide the controls.

This will cause both the checkmark next to NURBs Curves and all the controls in the scene to disappear temporarily, which is like turning off the visibility of a display layer. I recommend using the display layer visibility toggle if you want to hide a part of the character for a long period of time. Use the Show>NURBS Curves hotkey shortcut while you are in the middle of animating to do quick checks on movement clarity.

Camera Configuration

Step 5: Select the Front/Persp quick layout button, located right above the Outliner button, to bring up two viewports on your screen. We will create a dedicated FPS camera in the left-hand viewport by going to Panels>Perspective>New. Name it FPS_Cam. In that same viewport, turn on the resolution gate by clicking on the icon seen in Figure 11.3. Also click on the gate mask icon, which is to the right of the resolution gate icon, so that a light grey, shaded area will appear around the gate.

FIGURE 11.3 Resolution gate icon.

Step 6: On the right-hand-side viewport, we will move FPS_Cam so that it mimics the player character's line of sight. If you do not see a floating green camera, check if camera visibility is on by going to Show>Cameras in the Viewport menu bar. Grab FPS_Cam and move it so that is near Ellen's eyes (Figure 11.4). You may turn on the visibility of the RestofBodyMesh display layer temporarily so you can position the camera with Ellen's head geometry on.

Why?

This viewport setup will allow you to see the FPS camera view and your working area at the same time. Since the resolution gate and gate masks are visible on the left-hand side, you will be able to focus on what the player will see in the game. Grabbing controls will be easier in the right-hand-side viewport since you can move freely around the scene.

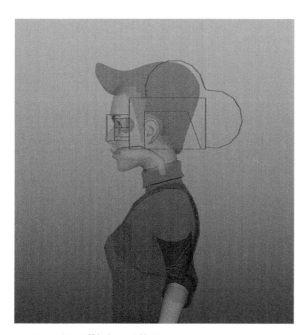

FIGURE 11.4 Line up FPS_Cam with Ellen's eyes.

*Step 7: Now that we have a dedicated FPS
camera, we will create our own reticle based
off this camera's location. In the main menu,
create a locator by going to Create>Locator.
Locators have a variety of uses, such as acting
as a middleman when connecting different
parts of a rig. We will be using the locator as
our reticle in Maya. Select the locator, shift-
select FPS_Cam, and go to Modify>Match
Transformations>Match Translation. The locator
will snap to FPS_Cam's location. Translate the
locator along the z-axis so that it is directly
in front of the camera. You should be able to
see the locator in the middle of the left-hand-
side viewport, as seen in Figure 11.5. Make the
locator unselectable by putting it in a referenced
display layer. You can also lock its movement
by going to the Channel Editor, click-dragging
all the channel attributes, right clicking the
blue highlighted selection, and clicking on Lock
Selected (Figure 11.6).*

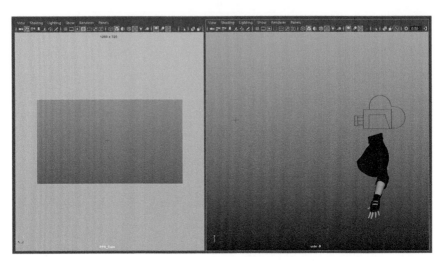

FIGURE 11.5 Creating the reticle.

Why?

In FPS games, a reticle is a small icon, like a crosshair or dot, in the center of the screen that is used to assist the player with aiming. There will be a different reticle created in the game engine, but our locator reticle will still be useful. We can reference it while posing our character and make sure that the weapon is pointed towards the reticle.

Game Animations

We are close to being able to animate full speed ahead. At this point, we can start crafting our first pose. Game characters have a set of animations that will play in the game depending on the circumstances. One of the most important animations will be the idle. An idle animation will be playing when the player has not input any commands. It is meant to keep the character alive even though they are not performing any specific movements. The idle is the first to be created in a set because it will serve as the returning point for most animations. When Ellen is done walking or has finished firing her gun, she will return to the idle animation.

FIGURE 11.6 Right clicking channel attributes to lock the locator's movement.

The only time Ellen will not return to idle is after she is caught by the security cameras and the game is over. The other animations that Ellen will need are attack, walk, "got caught", and reload.

Creating a Pose

Animation is a time-based art form, and the illusion of movement is created when a series of poses are played one after another. When we create a pose, we will need to tell Maya that we want it to be played at a specific time. The Time Slider at the bottom of the screen will be where we define those times. The grey highlight is the current time indicator and can be changed by click-dragging left and right on the Time Slider. The length of your animation can be adjusted by entering values in the entry fields on either side of the Time Slider.

You can create the pose by translating or rotating the character controls that were set up in the rigging stage. When you are ready to save the pose, select all the controls and press "S" to set a keyframe. A red tick will appear at the selected frame number on the Time Slider. The key tick's timing can be adjusted by shift-selecting it and click-dragging it to a new time. If you do not like a pose, you can remove it by selecting all the character controls, right clicking on the unwanted keyframe and pressing Delete. When there are multiple key ticks you would like to adjust, click-drag across those ticks while holding down Shift. This will create a red highlighted selection that can be moved or deleted.

Once you place your first keyframe, do not be afraid to tinker with its original timing later. Getting a feel for the correct timing is an essential part of the animation process.

Weapon Movement Simplified

One thing to consider is how our character will hold her weapons: will Ellen carry her weapons with one hand or both hands? Before attaching the weapon to the character, it is good to begin creating the idle pose first. If she will hold them with one hand, follow Step 8 and skip to Step 12. If she will hold the weapons with two hands, head straight to Step 9 and continue through Steps 10 and 11.

> Step 8: Move Ellen's right arm to an upright pose. The rigging file we provide has one more feature we did not go over in the rigging chapter. It has an IK FK blend slider, located on the outside of the arm (looks like a lollipop). If you are using your rig done in chapter 10, your arm will not move with the FK controllers. You need to do 2 things to make the FK work.

The first thing is to find left_ik_wrist_ctrl and select the left_wrist_IK parented under it. In the Channel Box, set the Ik Blend attribute to 0 to switch to FK(set it back to 1 to switch back to IK). The second thing is about the wrist, select left_drv_wrist; in the Channel Box, find the last 2 attributes: Left Fk Wrist Ctrl W0 and Left Ik Wrist Ctrl W1. Set the Fk one to 1 and Ik one to 0 to switch to FK(flip the values to switch back). The lollipop slider we provided in the rig does these 2 things automatically if you drag it up and down. The names of the controllers might be different in the rig we provided. Because of the length restrictions, we removed this lollipop controller in the rigging chapter. However, this animation chapter was developed parallel with the rigging chapter when we have this lollipop controller. Select the shoulder control ac_r_fk_shoulder, use "E" on your keyboard to turn on the Rotate Tool and rotate the arm so that it is almost parallel to the ground. Rotate the elbow and wrist controls, ac_r_fk_shoulder and ac_r_fk_wrist, to help the arm pose look more natural. Translate the gun model group, Gun_grp, so that the gun is resting in Ellen's right palm. Rotate the finger controls so that the fingers are wrapped around the gun handle (Figure 11.7).

Once you have solidified the finger posing, select ac_r_fk_wrist and shift-select Gun_grp in the Outliner. With the Rigging menu set to active, create a parent constraint connection between the wrist control and the gun group by using Constrain>Parent. Now, whenever the right arm moves, the gun will also move.

FIGURE 11.7 Creating the single-handed gun idle pose.

Select all the arm controls and press "S" to save this pose on frame 0. Head straight to Step 12.
Step 9: *For Ellen to hold the weapon with two hands, we will have to switch the arm movement method from forward kinematics (FK) to inverse kinematics (IK). Drag the lollipop sliders on both side of the arms down to switch to IK. (or use the method mentioned at the beginning of step 8 if you are using your rig file).*

Use the ac_r_ik_wrist and ac_l_ik_wrist controls to move Ellen's hands upward so that she can aim the gun in front of her. When you select one of the controls, use "W" to turn on the Translate Tool. When the arms are in IK mode, they can be moved via translation and rotation. Keep in mind that the elbow controls, ac_r_ik_drv_elbow and ac_l_ik_drv_elbow, could be used to help the pose feel more natural. Once you have the arms roughly positioned in the lower right-hand section of the FPS_Cam viewport, translate the gun group, Gun_grp, so that the handle is resting in between Ellen's hands. We will not permanently attach it just yet. Use the gun model as a frame of reference for adjusting both hands and moving Ellen's fingers. Rotate the finger controls so that the fingers are wrapped around the gun handle. The left-hand fingers should be wrapped around the right-hand fingers (Figure 11.8).

Select all the controls that were moved and press "S" to save the pose on frame 0. Continue to Step 10.

Tips and Tricks

Be sure to be check the FPS_Cam viewport as you pose the character in the perspective viewport. The gun and hand should end up in the lower right-hand side of the screen and not be blocking the reticle.

Two-Handed Weapon Setup

If you decided to go the two-handed weapon route, we will need to create a way to move both hands and the weapon all at once. Trying to move the hands and weapon in sync will be hard without tying them together using

FIGURE 11.8 Left hand wrapped around the right hand.

locators and parent constraints. Our goal is to create a single NURBs curve that will move the hands and weapon all together. In this chapter, we will cover this setup with the handgun, but this system can be applied to both the pipe and grenade launcher.

> *Step 10: Create a new NURBs circle named gun_CTRL and translate it so that it is positioned around the center of the gun and scale the circle up so that is slightly larger than the gun mesh (Figure 11.9). This NURBs curve will drive the primary movement of the hands and gun, so make sure it is easy to grab in the viewport. While holding down "D", translate gun_CTRL's manipulator so that the pivot point is at the gun handle, as seen in Figure 11.10.*
>
> > *Now we need to attach the gun to the new control. Navigate to the Outliner, select gun_CTRL first and then shift-select Gun_grp. With the Rigging menu set active, create a parent constraint connection between the two objects by using Constrain>Parent. Whenever gun_CTRL is moved, the gun will now follow.*
>
> *Step 11: To wrap up the two-handed weapon setup, we will now attach the hands to gun_CTRL.*

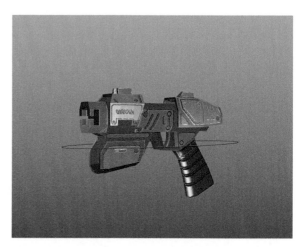

FIGURE 11.9 Creating a control for the gun.

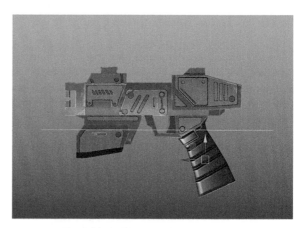

FIGURE 11.10 Changing gun_CTRL's pivot point.

Create a locator named rightHand_locator, shift-select ac_r_ik_wrist and match the IK control's position by going to Modify>Match Transformations>Match Translation and Match Rotation. Shift-select rightHand_locator, select ac_r_ik_wrist_grp in the Outliner and create a parent constraint so that the locator moves the right hand while still giving you the freedom to move ac_r_ik_wrist. Select gun_CTRL, shift-select rightHand_locator, and then create one more parent constraint. Now the right hand will follow gun_CTRL. The rightHand_locator can now be hidden for the time being. Repeat this process for the left hand. You will primarily use gun_CTRL in your animation workflow.

Frame Rate

Animations created for film and television are generally created at 24 frames per second. Standard playback rates for video games are 30 and 60 fps. Always double check the frame rate in Maya before starting an animation.

Step 12: Change the frame rate from 24 frames per second to 30 frames per second using the drop-down menu below the right-hand side of the Time Slider (Figure 11.11). Go to Windows>Settings/Preferences>Preferences and click on Time Slider in the left-hand column. Under Playback, change the Playback speed to 30 fps×1 (Figure 11.12).

FIGURE 11.11 Standard game animation frame rate is 30 frames per second.

Idle Animation

We will create a breathing idle animation for Ellen. It is possible to create idle breakers that are animations that still play when the player has not input any commands, and they generally show a bit more personality. Our main idle animation will be a simple inhale and exhale with a touch of weight shifting.

Step 13: Since most game animations loop continuously, they need to have the same start and end pose. Select all controls, right click on frame 0 on the Time Slider, which should contain

FIGURE 11.12 Switching Playback speed to 30 fps×1.

449

FIGURE 11.13 Time Slider with the idle key poses.

the pose that was created when we attached the gun to the hand(s), and click on Copy. Drag the current time indicator to frame 60, right click on the Time Slider, and press Paste>Paste. The pose from frame 0 should now be on frame 60. Paste this same pose one last time on frame 120. Frames 0, 60, and 120 will be the inhale moment of the idle. Have the gun move downward on frame 30, set a keyframe for all the controls by pressing "S", and do the same on frame 90. Your Time Slider should look like the one in Figure 11.13.

The shortcut to play and pause an animation is Alt+ "V". Play through your animation to make sure that the poses flow together and the overall movement makes sense.

Tips and Tricks

In the beginning stages of an animation, it is smart to set a key on all the controls each time you create a main pose. Adjusting the timing will be easier since you will know that all controls have been accounted for in each of the main poses.

Step 14: Add a simple weight shift to add more variation to the breathing. On frame 60, have the hands and gun move towards our right a tiny bit. From frames 0 to 60, Ellen will weigh shift to our right, and from frames 60 to 120, she will return to the idle pose by weight shifting to our left.

Cleaning Up Odd Jitters

You might start to notice weird glitches in the animation, even if you did not set any specific keys to define that movement. Right clicking on the timeline and pressing Tangents>Auto should remove those hitches.

Ease-In's and Ease-Out's

The main poses have been set for the idle animation, but the movement might feel floaty. There is no sense of weight in the animation yet. We can insert additional keyframes to help show ease-in's and ease-out's. This is important to utilize in your animations because most movements take time to start up and come to a natural stop. Ease-in's and ease-out's can also be used to add a moment of hold. If you take a deep breath in real life, your upper body will hold still for a few seconds before exhaling. That stillness is like an ease-in. When you exhale, you are gradually easing out of the inhale "pose."

Graph Editor

Animators must become acquainted with the Graph Editor to finetune their work. All keyframes are represented on a graph as plotted points that can be adjusted, and the interpolation between each keyframe is represented as curves. With a basic understanding of curves, the Graph Editor can be used to create quick ease-in's and ease-out's.

Tips and Tricks

Try opening the Graph Editor by going to Windows>Animation Editors>Graph Editor. If you have a second monitor available, I suggest having the Graph Editor maximized on one screen. If you have one monitor, you can have it open on one of the viewports by going to Panels>Panel>Graph Editor.

> *Step 15: Select ac_r_fk_shoulder if you are animating just one arm or select gun_CTRL if you are animating both hands holding the weapon. Open the Graph Editor. On the left-hand side, select the primary channel that is responsible for the upward and downward movements. For the one-handed weapon setup, select Rotate Y, and for the two-handed weapon setup, select Translate Y. That specific channel is the only one that is visible (Figure 11.14). If you cannot see the*

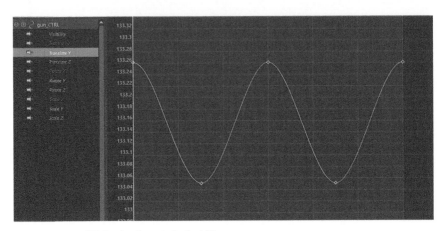

FIGURE 11.14 gun_CTRL's Translate Y curve in the Graph Editor.

green curve clearly, press "F" to quickly zoom in towards the curve.

Similar to scrubbing through the Time Slider, you can adjust the time by click-dragging the yellow Current Time Marker left and right within the Graph Editor. Select the Insert Keys tool in the upper right-hand corner of the Graph Editor and click on the curve to insert keys on frames 13, 25, 35, 46, 73, 85, 95, and 106. Press "W", click on frame 13, and middle-mouse-click-drag it upwards closer to frame 0. Grab frames 25 and 35 and middle-mouse-click-drag those keys towards frame 30. Continue this for the remaining keys that we just added. Refer to Figure 11.15 for a general idea of how your curve should look. Do not worry if it is not an exact replica. The animation should have a slight moving hold each time the character inhales.

Why?

Understanding what the curve shapes represent is more important than just simply copying. The curve shape from frames 0 to 13 is an ease-out. The gentle slope represents small movement over a long period of time. We know that frames 13–25 will be faster due to the steep slope that showcases a large value change over a short period of time. Frames 25–35 is another ease-in. Ease-in's and

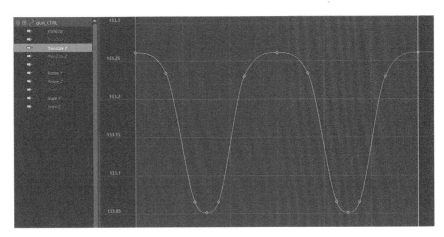

FIGURE 11.15 Added keyframes to create ease-in's and ease-out's.

ease-out's help vary the spacing between each main pose and helps add more weight to the movement.

Keywords Aside

Timing is the object's *speed*, while *spacing* is how the object will move from point A to point B. Spacing will help determine moments of acceleration and moments of hold.

Tips and Tricks

When you are adding ease-in's and ease-out's, you do not necessarily have to select all the controls and press "S". At this stage of the animation, you can be more selective with keyframe placement.

Attack Animation

The attack animation is up next. The gun firing should be rapid and impactful. As soon as the player presses the button to attack an enemy, we want the player to see and feel an immediate response in the gun. A combination of fast timing and careful spacing consideration help us achieve this goal.

> Step 16: Select all the controls, copy the first frame of the idle animation, and paste it on frames 200 and 212. Frame 200 will be the start of the attack animation, and 212 will be the end. On frame 204, create the recoil pose by moving the gun back closer to Ellen and rotate the gun so that it is pointing upward. Maya should now show the initial movement between frames 200 and 204, but it is still too slow. To help show snappy gunfire, move the gun backwards towards Ellen on frame 201.
>
> Step 17: Let's add some final touches to the attack animation. Set a keyframe on frame 208 for the main movement control. Open the Graph Editor and create an ease-in using the newly added keyframe. Go through all the Translate and Rotate channels on the left-hand-side bar to check if there is a moving curve to add an ease-in. Figures 11.16 and 11.17 are two examples of how this ease-in could be implemented on frame 208. If there is a horizontal line instead of a trending curve, this means that there is

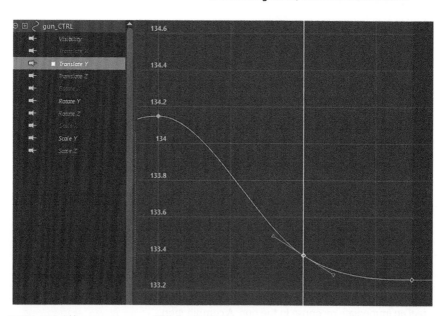

FIGURE 11.16 Adding an ease-in on gun_CTRL's Translate Y curve.

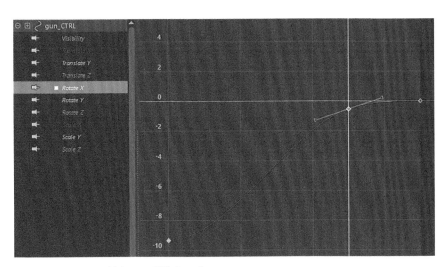

FIGURE 11.17 An ease-in added to gun_CTRL's Rotate X curve.

no movement, so you will not need to add the
ease-in for those specific channels. Once you
have finished this step, the animation should
come to a more natural stop.

Walk Animation

A basic walk animation consists of the following main
poses: contact, down, passing, up, and back to contact
pose to repeat the cycle. This animation will be simpler
to create as first-person shooter animation in contrast
to a full-body piece, but we can still move the arms and
weapon in accordance with the main poses.

Step 18: Begin the walk cycle by setting down the
contact poses. Select all controls, copy the idle
pose from frame 0, and paste a key on frames
300 and 331. Slightly rotate the gun so that it
points to our left on frame 315. On contact pose,
the upper body will twist the most side to side.

Step 19: The next pose to block is in the passing pose,
which is the halfway point between each contact
pose. On frame 307, translate the character to
our left, and on frame 323, translate her to our
right. The character has shifted their weight the
most to the left or right on passing pose.

455

Step 20: We will finish blocking in the walk with the down and up poses. The character should translate down on frames 303 and 318, and she should translate upward on frames 312 and 327. The gun should also rotate down and up, but we can add an offset in the rotation's timing so that movement feels looser and more broken up. Rotate the gun down on frames 308 and 324 and add in an upward rotation on frame 316.

Step 21: As a final touch, add ease-in's and ease-out's to make the animation feel less even. Figures 11.18 and 11.19 showcase how the ease-in's and ease-out's could be applied to the contact and passing main keys in the Graph Editor.

"Got Caught" Animation

When Ellen is caught by one of the security cameras, she will raise her hands up in shock. If you are animating her with both hands on the weapon, we will need to detach one of the hands from the gun handle. This animation will be "game over" for the player, so we do not necessarily have to loop the animation.

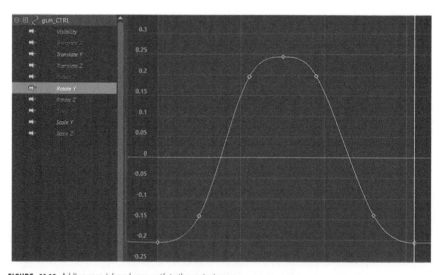

FIGURE 11.18 Adding ease-in's and ease-out's to the contact poses.

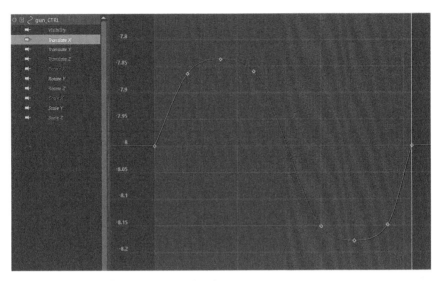

FIGURE 11.19 Additional keyframes to give more weight to the passing poses.

> *Step 22: Select all the controls, copy the idle pose, and paste it on frame 400. If you are animating with the two-handed weapon setup, select leftHand_locator and make sure that it also has a keyframe at 400. If the locator did not have any keyframes placed beforehand, you should notice a new attribute in the Channel Box called Blend Locatorleftparent 1. On frame 400, Blend Locatorleftparent 1 should be set to 1. To detach the left hand from the gun handle, change Blend Locatorleftparent 1 to 0 on frame 401. Hide leftHand_locator while you create the "Got Caught" animation. You can now move ac_l_ik_ drv_wrist independently of gun_CTRL.*

Tips and Tricks

Remember to select leftHand_locator and change Locatorleftparent 1 back to 1 when you want the left hand to be attached to the gun handle again.

> *Step 23: Create the last pose of the animation on frame 426. The right hand still holding the gun will move back and move towards the right of*

the screen. Move the left hand towards the left edge of the screen and spread the fingers out (Figure 11.19).

Keywords Aside

Depending on the speed of an action, we might need to add an *overshoot* pose to give more time to the audience to take in what just happened. The overshoot will move past the last pose we just created and will settle into the last pose more slowly.

Step 24: Let's add in an overshoot to both hands on frame 413. Select all controls, copy frame 426, and paste it on frame 413. This will be our starting point for the overshoot pose. The left hand's last pose ends up close to the left side of the screen, so the overshoot will be a tiny continuation of that movement. Translate and rotate the left hand ever so slightly to the left, and do the same for the right hand, except towards the right-hand side of the screen. The left-hand fingers can also be a part of the overshoot. Rotate the fingers to the left just a tad bit (Figure 11.20).

Step 25: We can create a more fluid motion in both hands by examining their motion trail. Select the left-hand control, and with the Animation menu set active, go to Visualize>Create Editable Motion Trail. A curve representing the left hand's path of action has now appeared (Figure 11.21). When you add a keyframe to that control, the motion trail should update. Move the hand downward on frame 402 so that it will dip before traveling

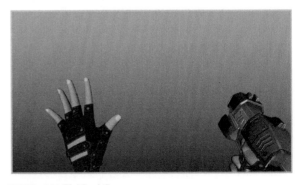

FIGURE 11.20 "Got Caught" pose.

to the main pose on 406. In your perspective viewport, zoom in close to the motion trail at frames 413–426. Add additional keyframes to create a more rounded shape in the motion trail (Figure 11.22). Compare Figures 11.21–11.23. The motion trail has more apparent arcs. Go ahead and delete motionTrail1Handle in the Outliner. Repeat this entire step for the other hand.

FIGURE 11.21 Motion trail representing the left hand's path of action.

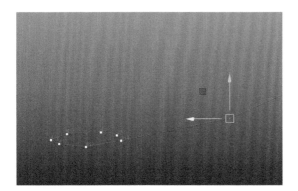

FIGURE 11.22 Adding more keyframes to round out the motion trail.

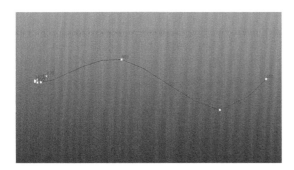

FIGURE 11.23 Final motion trail for the left-hand control.

Why?

Most living beings move in arcs, while machinery tend to move in a linear fashion. Exaggerating the arcs of an object's motion trail can be a quick way to add a layer of fluidity to the animation.

> *Step 26: Use the Graph Editor to assist in creating a natural settle for the ending of the animation. Add an ease-in at frame 416.*

Reload Animation

The reload animation will be a culmination of everything that we have covered, as well as adding one more object for Ellen to interact with. If the two-handed setup is in use, the left hand will need to leave the gun handle once more. The added challenge is that we must get the character to return to the idle pose, in contrast to the "Got Caught" animation that did not have to loop. In this animation, Ellen will first shake the empty magazine out of the gun. Her left hand will temporarily leave the screen to grab the new magazine. Once the left hand returns to the player's view, Ellen will reload the gun, and the left hand should return to its original idle pose.

> *Step 27: We will create a system in which the magazine can be attached to either the gun or left hand. Create an empty group named gunClip_CTRL_group. Match the group's transforms to Gun_clip_grp. Create a locator named gunClip_Locator, match its transforms to Gun_clip_grp, and make it a child of gunClip_CTRL_group. Select gun_CTRL, shift-select gunClip_CTRL_group, then create a parent constraint so that the magazine will now follow the main gun control. Select the left-hand control, shift-select gunClip_Locator, and create a parent constraint so that we can tell the magazine to follow the left hand.*
> *At the start of the reload animation, we will want the magazine to be following the gun control. Let's turn off the gunClip_Locator's constraint for the time being.*

With the locator selected, change Blend Parent 1's value to 0.

Step 28: Start off the animation by copying the idle pose and pasting it on frame 500. At frame 510, have the left hand completely leave the screen and raise the right hand up in anticipation for the shake. Create the right hand's lowest point in the shake at frame 515, and have it rise just a little to settle into the main pose at frame 526. Use gunClip_Locator to translate the magazine out of the gun from frames 512 to 522. Select gunClip_Locator, set a key on frame 500 and 512, and ensure that Blend Parent 1 is 0 on those two keys. Change Blend Parent 1 to 1 on frame 529 so that it will be attached to the left hand.

On frame 538, rotate the right hand towards the camera. Bring the left hand back up into view with the magazine resting against the bottom of the gun grip. You can also rotate the fingers so that they have a better grip on the magazine (Figure 11.24).

Step 29: Let's continue the second half of the reload animation. On frame 545, move the left hand up and to our right so that the magazine can be reloaded into the gun. The right hand should also slightly move in reaction to the left hand's movement. The magazine will need to switch parents from the left hand to the gun control. Make sure that gunClip_Locator's Blend Parent 1 is set to 1 on frame 538. Change Blend Parent 1 to 0 on frame 541. If the magazine rotates oddly on frames 539 and 540, go ahead and fix it by rotating the magazine to align with the grip. Paste the idle pose on frame 564.

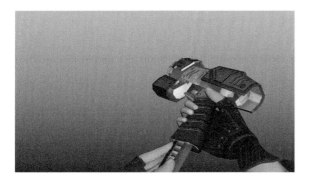

FIGURE 11.24 Pose before the gun is reloaded.

461

Step 30: Add final touches to the animation. Track each hand's motion trails and see if you can round out any arcs. Use ease-in's and ease-out's to create a moving hold for the key poses on frames 526 and 538. Finally, have the gun come to natural settle at the end with a gradual ease-in to the last pose.

Considerations and Conclusion

Once you have created your first animation set, animating the grenade launcher and pipe will both be a familiar and new process. While the other weapons' movement will not be the same as the handgun, most of the main poses should remain the same. There are some differences in the story that is told through each weapon. The grenade launcher and pipe might have slower timing since they are heavier than a handgun. The pipe will not have its own reload animation because it is a melee weapon. The grenade launcher will only be able to hold one grenade at a time, so you will not need to animate Ellen shaking away an empty cartridge.

Animation can be easy to pick up, but there are still obstacles to consider from both a technical and artistic standpoint. Have fun and challenge yourself to create believable, responsive movement.

CHAPTER 12

Unreal Character Asset Creation

In the previous chapters, we have our character modeled, textured, rigged, and animated. It's a lot of effort to make a working character, but now it's all behind us. In this chapter, let's move back to our Unreal Engine project and start importing our character assets.

We are going to get the model into our Unreal Engine project, create the materials, and import the animations. After getting our own assets in, we are also going to cover how to get motion captured data to our character. With motion capture, we don't have to do all the animations from scratch.

If you want to use the character we did for this book, it's in the support files. However, we highly encourage you to use the one you did. The best way to know if you did a good job or not is to put the work you did into the next step of the production and test it.

Tutorial 12.1: Character Asset Import

> *Step 1: Unparent the models and the joint. Open the rig file (Ellen_rig.mb) with Maya. Find the root joint of the rig and press Shift + P to unparent it. Select All the models of the Character (not including the gun) and also unparent them.*

Why?

Why do we unparent the model and the joints? Well, if we don't, Maya may still export their parent groups and the world_ctrl controller. These extra nodes are not helpful and only make the asset heavier. We also ignore the gun because it is considered as another object; we are going to attach it to the hand in the game engine.

> *Step 2: Export Skeletal Mesh. Select the models and the joint we unparented in Step 1. Go to File →‍ Game Exporter. In the pop-up Game Exporter window, change the Export All to Export Selection. Click on the folder icon in the Path settings, choose the assets folder, and click the Choose button. Type in Ellen_Skeletal_Mesh as the file name in the Enter a filename text field. Press the Export button to finish exporting (Figure 12.1).*
>
> *Step 3: Prepare a base material instance. Go back to our game project. Create a new folder called Blueprints, and add a new folder called Characters in it. Open the Characters folder and create a new folder called Ellen. Create a material instance based on the Substance_Base_Mtl and put it into the Ellen folder; name the new material instance Ellen_Base_Mtl_Int.*
> *This Blueprints folder will be the master folder for our character and many other*

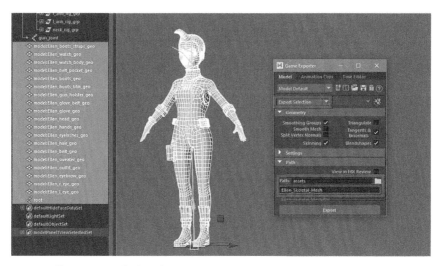

FIGURE 12.1 The export settings for the mesh.

things, and we are going to explain what
blueprint is in the following chapters.

Step 4: Import Ellen to Unreal Engine. Click the
Import button in the Content Browser, find the
Ellen_Skeletal_Mesh we exported in Step 2,
and double click it to import it. In the pop-up
FBX Import Options window, click the Reset
to Default button. Make sure that the Import
Animations checker box is off, scroll down to
the material section, and set Material Import
Method to Create New Instanced Materials. Set
the Base Material Name to Ellen_Base_Mtl_Inst.
There is a list of attributes we can override.
Knowing that all textures and material setup
from Maya is not compatible with Unreal Engine,
we just override all properties with a random
pick. If we do not override, Unreal is going to
create materials instead of material instances.
Press the Import All button (Figure 12.2).

Step 5: Export and assign textures. Select all the
textures imported from Ellen_Skeletal_Mesh
and simply delete them. Go to our Substance
Painter file and export the textures there with
the same setting we did for our environment
models. Import these textures to our game
project and attach them to the various material
instances.

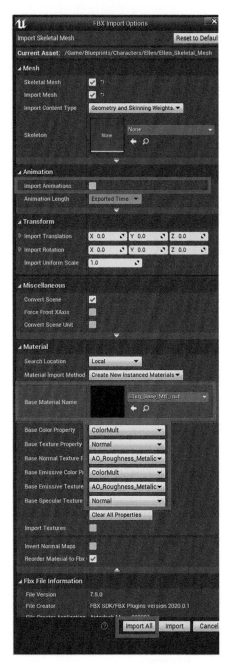

FIGURE 12.2 Import options for Ellen_Skeletal_mesh.

Step 6: Organize the assets. There are currently many assets in the Ellen folder. Create a folder called Material and move all textures and material instances to that folder. Now we have only a Material folder and three more assets in the Ellen folder. Let's explain these three assets:

Skeletal Mesh, Skeleton, and Physics Asset

A skeletal mesh is a mesh with joints. The one with the purple bar is our skeletal mesh. Double click to open it, and you can see all the materials assigned to it in the Asset Details panel. Click on the Skeleton Tree table on the right of the Asset Details tab, and you can see all the joints listed in it (Figure 12.3). We can import animations for these joints or animate them here. There are two more assets created with our Ellen_Skeletal_Mesh. Ellen_Skeletal_Mesh_PhysicsAsset is the asset that defines the collision and physical material of the model. Ellen_Skeletal_Mesh_Skeleton is the skeleton structure of Ellen.

FIGURE 12.3 All skeletons of the Character listed in the Skeleton Tree panel.

Because multiple assets can share the same skeleton, Unreal de-couples the skeletons and the meshes.

Step 7: Skin Material. Unreal offers a dedicated skin-shading model. Go to the shared folder that we have our Substance_Base_Mtl. Select Substance_Base_Mtl and press Ctrl + W to duplicate it. Name the duplicated material Substance_Skin_Base_Mtl, and double click to open it. In the Material Editor, go to the Details Panel. Under the Material section, set the Shading model to Subsurface Profile. Create a new ScalerParameter and call it SubsurfaceScattering. Connect SubsurfaceScattering to the Opacity input pin of the Substance_Skin_Base_Mtl node (Figure 12.4). Press the Save button to save the changes.

Step 8: Set up the skin material with a profile. Open the Body_Mtl of Ellen, and set its parent to Substance_Skin_Base_Mtl. Check on the SubsurfaceScattering parameter and set its value to 1. Under the Material Properties Overrides section, check on Subsurface Profile. Click on the drop-down list, and select Subsurface Profile under the Create New Asset section. In the pop-up Save Asset As window, navigate to Content/Blueprints/Characters/Ellen/Material. Type in EllenSkinSubsurfaceProfile as the Name, and press Save (Figure 12.5).

Drag an instance of Ellen_Skeletal_Mesh to the scene and take a look, and you can see how the skin of the Character feels fleshy (Figure 12.6).

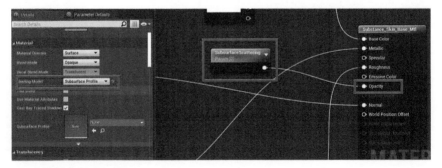

FIGURE 12.4 Create a skin material.

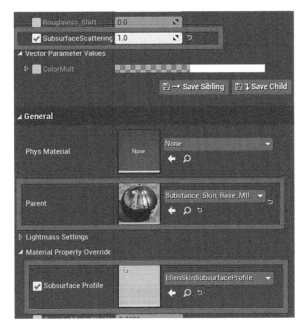

FIGURE 12.5 Set up the skin material with a profile.

FIGURE 12.6 The skin appearance of Ellen in the level.

Subsurface Scattering

When light rays hit surfaces like skin, wax, leaf, or plastic, a small number of the rays penetrate through the surface and scatter inside. Some of the scattering light rays may travel back out of the surface, which makes the surface of the object looks blurred. This phenomenon is called subsurface scattering. How much the light is scattering and the color is defined in the subsurface profile.

> *Step 9: Tweak the subsurface profile. Double click to open EllenSkinSubsurfaceProfile. There are two types of subsurface: Burley Normalized and USubsurface Profile. Burley Normalized is more accurate than USubsurface Profile; check on Enable Burley to enable it. The Mean Free Path Distance controls how far the lights scatter inside; adjust it, so it is not too blurry. Other settings should be good for normal human skin; feel free to hover the cursor on these settings to see what they do (Figure 12.7).*

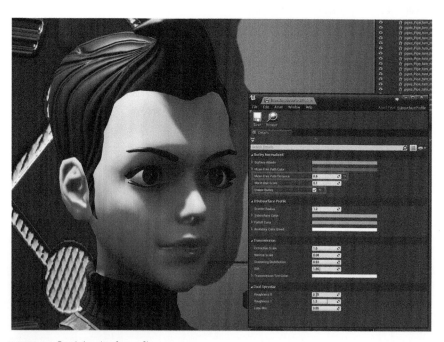

FIGURE 12.7 Tweak the subsurface profile.

*Step 10: Export the FPS skeletal mesh. The FPS
skeletal mesh is the same model without the
head and bottom part of the body. We could
do some trick in the game engine to hide these
parts (like scaling the head joint down to zero
to hide the head), but commonly this should be
a different model. Go ahead and export the FPS
skeletal mesh the same way we exported the
full-body one. The only difference here is that we
do not select the models we do not wish to see.
Figure 12.8 shows the models selected.*

*Name the FPS skeletal mesh
Ellen_FPS_Skeletal_Mesh.*

*Step 11: Import the FPS Skeletal mesh. Click the
Import button in the Content Browser and
select Ellen_FPS_ Skeletal_Mesh. In the pop-up
FBX Import Options window, make sure that
the Skeleton setting is Ellen_Skeletal_Mesh_
Skeleton. Check off Import Animations, and
set the Material Import Method to Do Not
Create Material. Press the Import All button
(Figure 12.9).*

*There should be only two assets
imported: Ellen_FPS_Skeletal_Mesh and
Ellen_FPS_Skeletal_Mesh_PhysicsAsset. The
materials should be automatically connected,
and they share the same skeleton as well.
However, if you made a completely different
model for your FPS character, you should
import it as a new one. Figure 12.10 shows
what's in the Ellen folder after importing the
skeletal meshes.*

*Now we have the visuals done, let's get
the animations out.*

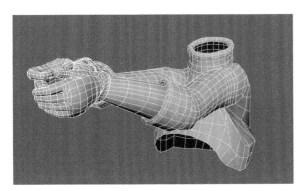

FIGURE 12.8 Model selection for the FPS skeletal mesh.

471

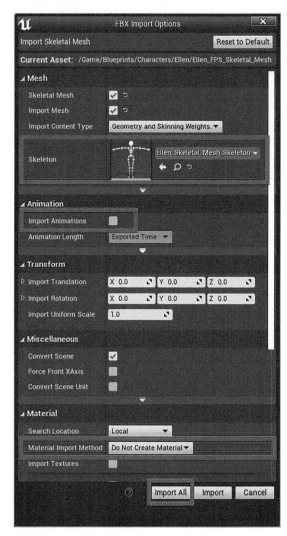

FIGURE 12.9 Import settings for Ellen__FPS__Skeletal__Mesh.

FIGURE 12.10 The assets in the Ellen folder after importing the skeletal meshes.

Tutorial 12.2: Export FPS Animations

> *Step 1: Bake Animations. Open the gun animation file (Ellen_gun_animations.ma) in Maya. Select the root joint, go to select → Hierarchy to select all the joints underneath, and go to Edit → Keys → Bake Simulation □. In the pop-up Bake Simulation Options window, make sure that the Time range is the range of the Animation you want to export. In our case, the time range should be the range that appears on the Time Slider, so the default setting is good for us. If yours is not the same as the Time Slider, set the Time range setting to Start/End and specify your Start and End Time to bake. Press the Bake button to bake the Animation.*

Bake Animation

Game engines understand joint skinning, but not the iks, controllers, and constraints. We need to bake our Animation to the joints so that the Engine can understand it.

> *Step 2: Export Animations. Unparent the models in the viewport and the root joint (again not including the gun). With the models and the joint selected, go to File → Game Exporter. In the pop-up window, click on the Animation Clips tab. Set the Export All to Export Selection. Click on the "+" sign under the Animation Clips section to add a new clip. Type Idle in the Clip Name field. Set the start value to 0, and the End value to 120. 0–120 is our frame range for the idle Animation. Add another clip and call it Attack, and set its time range to 200–211. Add one more clip and call it Walk; for this one, the time range is set to 300–330. Following the same trend, add two more clips for the Caught and Reload Animation (all these time ranges are based on the Animation you did). Click on the folder button of the Path setting, navigate to your assets folder of our Maya project, and click the Choose button. Finally, type in Ellen_FPS_Gun_ as the Clip File Prefix and press the Export button (Figure 12.11). Go ahead and export all other*

FIGURE 12.11 Export settings.

Animations the same way, including both the pipe and the grenade launcher.

Step 3: Import animations to our Unreal Engine project. Go back to our Unreal Engine project. Go to the asset folder of our Maya project, and drag the animations we exported there to the Ellen folder. In the pop-up FBX Import Options, make sure that the Skeleton setting is Ellen_Skeletal_Mesh_Skeleton. Because we have the meshes already, check off Import Mesh. Press the Import All button to import all the animations (Figure 12.12).

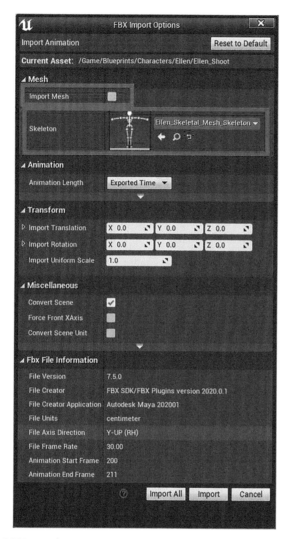

FIGURE 12.12 Import settings.

Tips and Tricks

Because our FPS mesh and the full-body mesh are using the same skeleton and the same materials, we do not want to create new materials and skeletons. If you could share the same skeleton across multiple assets, you can also share the same skeletal Animation.

> *Step 4: Organize the files into folders. The animations have a dark green bar at the bottom of their icon. Create a new folder called Animations and move all the animations to that folder. For the rest of the assets, move them to a new folder called MeshAssets.*

Tips and Tricks

Organizing the folders is critical to avoid confusion and mistakes. Remember, people got fired because they didn't organize their folders.

Now we have the FPS animations in, let's talk about motion captured data and Animation retargeting. We are going to leverage a free online motion capture library called Adobe Mixamo. They have a decent collection of animations we can use.

Tutorial 12.3: Motion Captured Data

> *Step 1: Prepare our model. Open the rig file in Maya again. Select all the body models (not including the gun). Press Ctrl+D to duplicate them, then Ctrl+G to group the duplication, and finally, press Shift+P to un-parent the group; name the group Model_to_Mocap. With the group selected, go to File → Export Selection. Set the File name to Ellen_NPC and change the File of type to FBX. In the Options panel, check off the Embed Media (optional, but texture files take too long to upload). Export it to the assets folder.*
>
> *Step 2: Upload it to Mixamo. Open your web browser and search for Adobe Mixamo. The first one pops up with the link www.mixamo.com should be the one we need to go, but it might be different by the time you read this book. Please try to find the most relevant one. Open the website, log in if you have an adobe account, sign up for free if you don't. After logging in, go to the upper*

right corner of the page and click on Upload
Character. In the pop-up UPLOAD A CHARACTER
window, click on Select character file. Locate and
open the Ellen_NPC.fbx we exported in Step 1.
It may take a while for the character to upload;
once the uploading is finished, you should
see the character appear in the window. Press
Next, and follow the instructions to place the
landmarks of the body to our character. Press
next, wait for it to finish rigging, and next again
to finish the setup (Figure 12.13).

Step 3: Search and preview animations. Click on
the Animations tab at the top left corner of
the webpage. Search for pistol in the search
bar. In the search result, find and click on the
one named the Pistol Walk. Our character in
the viewport on the right should already be
previewing it. We don't want the character
to move forward in this case. Check on the
In Place checker box to lock it at the origion
(Figure 12.14).

FIGURE 12.13 Important steps to upload Ellen to Mixamo.

FIGURE 12.14 Search and preview the animations.

477

Why?

So why do we want the character to be fixed in place? Well, the motion of the character should be taken care of by the game programming and not driven by the Animation. You don't want the Animation to tell you how fast your character should be moving.

Step 4: Download animations. Press the orange download button. In the pop-up DOWNLOAD SETTINGS, set the Frames per Second to 60. Press the DOWNLOAD button to download the Animation. Go ahead and download the Shooting, Pistol Idle, and Death From The Back the same way. Create a new folder called MixamoAnimations in the assets folder and put all four downloaded animations there (Figure 12.15).

Step 5: Import skeletal mesh. Go back to our Unreal project. Create a folder named Mixamo under the Animations folder. Import the downloaded Pistol Walk with the setting shown in Figure 12.16.

Step 6: Import the rest of the mixamo animations. Import the rest of the animations, but this time, check off Import Mesh (Figure 12.17).

Why?

Unreal Engine requires a skeletal mesh to import animations, so we have to create one in Step 5. However, for the rest of the animations, they can use the same skeletal mesh. That's why we checked off the Import Mesh settings in Step 6.

We are going to use these animations for our NPC, but there is a problem. These animations are for the skeleton done by Mixamo; double click to open Pistol_Walk_ Skeleton, and you can see the skeleton tree is not the

FIGURE 12.15 Download the Animation.

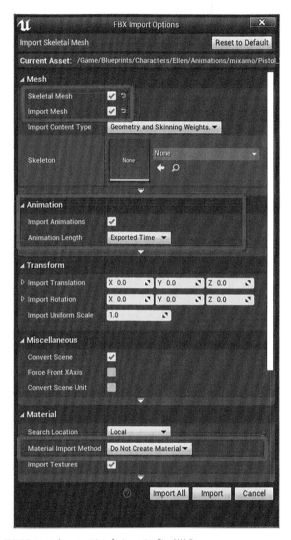

FIGURE 12.16 Import settings for importing Pistol Walk.

same as our Ellen_Skeletal_Mesh_Skeleton (Figure 12.3). Because of the difference, they cannot use each other's animations. It's bad practice to have the same model using different skeletons with different animations unless you have a good reason. Let's use Unreal Engine's Animation retargeting feature to transfer these animations to Ellen_Skeletal_Mesh_Skeleton.

479

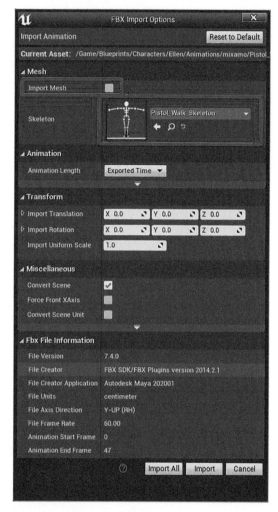

FIGURE 12.17 Import setting for importing the rest.

Tutorial 12.4: Animation Retargeting

Step 1: Set up a Rig. Open Pistol_Walk_Skeleton. Click on the Retarget Manager button in the toolbar. The Retarget Manager now appears on the left side of the window. Under the Set up Rig section, click on the drop-down list of Select Rig *and select the Humanoid Rig. A whole list of bone names appears at the bottom of the UI. Go to the viewport, go to Character → Bones, check on the Bone Names, and set the Bone Drawing to All Hierarchy. We can now see all the bones (joints) of the skeleton. Follow the assignment shown in Figure 12.18 to set up all the targets on the list. What we are trying to do here is to set the targets to be the equivalent ones of the sources.*

Step 2: Set up the advanced ones. Click on the Show Advanced button to switch to the advanced targeting. This area includes small things like fingers and ball joints. Figure 12.19 shows the assignments, and you only have to set up the selected ones.

Step 3: Set up preview mesh. Go to the toolbar again and click on the Preview Mesh button. Select Pistol_Walk as the preview mesh. Look at the lower right corner of your screen and you can see a notification. Press the Apply To Asset button on it to set the preview mesh permanently

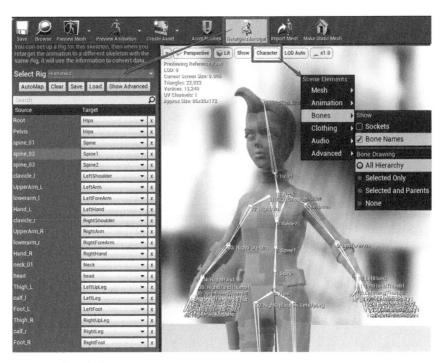

FIGURE 12.18 Set up the Targets.

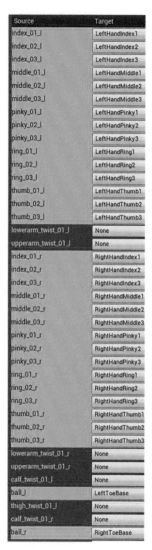

Source	Target
index_01_l	LeftHandIndex1
index_02_l	LeftHandIndex2
index_03_l	LeftHandIndex3
middle_01_l	LeftHandMiddle1
middle_02_l	LeftHandMiddle2
middle_03_l	LeftHandMiddle3
pinky_01_l	LeftHandPinky1
pinky_02_l	LeftHandPinky2
pinky_03_l	LeftHandPinky3
ring_01_l	LeftHandRing1
ring_02_l	LeftHandRing2
ring_03_l	LeftHandRing3
thumb_01_l	LeftHandThumb1
thumb_02_l	LeftHandThumb2
thumb_03_l	LeftHandThumb3
lowerarm_twist_01_l	None
upperarm_twist_01_l	None
index_01_r	RightHandIndex1
index_02_r	RightHandIndex2
index_03_r	RightHandIndex3
middle_01_r	RightHandMiddle1
middle_02_r	RightHandMiddle2
middle_03_r	RightHandMiddle3
pinky_01_r	RightHandPinky1
pinky_02_r	RightHandPinky2
pinky_03_r	RightHandPinky3
ring_01_r	RightHandRing1
ring_02_r	RightHandRing2
ring_03_r	RightHandRing3
thumb_01_r	RightHandThumb1
thumb_02_r	RightHandThumb2
thumb_03_r	RightHandThumb3
lowerarm_twist_01_r	None
upperarm_twist_01_r	None
calf_twist_01_l	None
ball_l	LeftToeBase
thigh_twist_01_l	None
calf_twist_01_r	None
ball_r	RightToeBase

FIGURE 12.19 Advance target assignments.

(Figure 12.20). This preview mesh needs to be set for our retargeting to work.

Step 4: Set up Ellen_Skeletal_Mesh_Skeleton. Go to Blueprints/Characters/Ellen/MeshAsset, find our Ellen_Skeletal_Mesh_Skeleton, and repeat Steps 1–3 on it. The target assignment is shown in Figure 12.21.

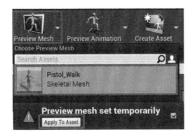

FIGURE 12.20 Set up the preview mesh.

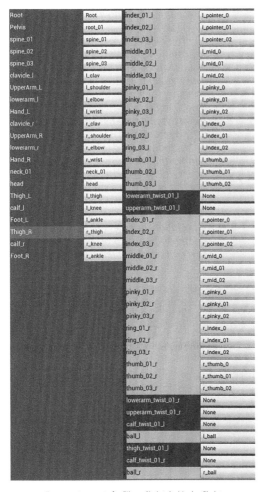

FIGURE 12.21 Target assignments for Ellen_Skeletal_Mesh_Skeleton.

Now we have our two skeletons all targeted to the same source hierarchy, and they can now copy animations from each other through the target—source mapping.

Step 5: Transferring Animation. Go back to our mixamo folder, right click on Pistol_Idle, and select Retarget Anim Assets → Duplicate Anim Assets and Retarget. In the pop-up Select Skeleton window, select Ellen_Skeletal_Mesh_Skeleton and hit Retarget (Figure 12.22). A new animation with the same name as Pistol_Idle got created in the root directory of the content browser. This new Animation is now working with our Ellen_Skeletal_Mesh_Skeleton.

You may have to go back and check the assignment of the targets if you see bad results. It is easy to select the wrong joints.

Step 6: Retarget the rest of the animations. Select the other three animations together and repeat Step 5. Select all the retargeted animations and move them to the Animations folder.

Step 7: Fix retargeting issues. Open Pistol_Walk_Anim, zoom in, and take a closer look. You can see that the arms and the legs are too far apart. This is because the two skeletons are not positioned the same. Go to the Skeleton Tree, click on Options and check on Show Retargeting Options. A new column called Translation Retargeting appears. Right click on the Animation drop-down list of the first row and select Recursively Set Translation

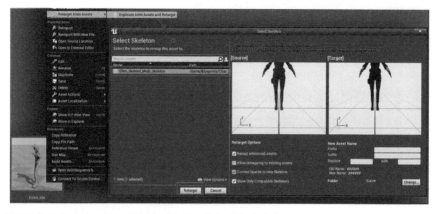

FIGURE 12.22 Duplicate and retarget Pistol_Idle to Ellen_Skeletal_Mesh_Skeleton.

*Retargeting Skeleton. What this does is basically
saying, the translation of the joint remains
the same as the skeleton, not following the
Animation (the rotation still does). Set the Root
and Root_01 back to Animation afterward
(Figure 12.23).*

*Alrighty, now we have all the animations
we need. Figure 12.24 shows our animation
library.*

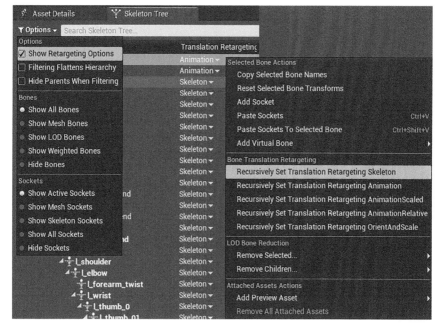

FIGURE 12.23 Fix the retargeting issue with retargeting options.

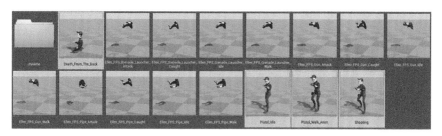

FIGURE 12.24 All the animations.

485

Conclusion

We now have all of our character assets set up and ready to go. We are also finally done with the character creation process. Character modeling is one of the most challenging jobs in the game and animation industry. Modeling, texturing, material, rigging, animation, and all these things have to work together beautifully to bring a character alive. It will go through many hands during the process, and if any of the processes messed up, it takes quite a lot of rework to fix it.

We have also hit a significant milestone as we have officially done with making assets. We are ready to jump into a completely different task—programming. Buckle up because the real bumpy road is about to begin!

CHAPTER 13

Basics of Programming

Game is no fun without interactions, and programming is the tool to achieve that. Programming is a difficult task, not because the languages are hard, but the logic and algorithms you have to implement. There was a joke about what programming is:

> *Programming is to teach the stupidest thing in the world to do stuff.*

The stupidest thing referred to in this joke is the computer. It is stupidly fast, but also blindly stupid. Computers follow instructions to the letters, and they only do whatever you told them to do. If you ask a computer to self-destruct, it is going to self-destruct without hesitation or any sense of self-preservation. There is no intelligence when computers execute their programs nor does it understand your real intension.

With that being said, you, the programmer, take full responsibility for what happened. We, as humans, can make mistakes. We could forget things, and we could misunderstand a problem. It is not uncommon that a programmer, even professional ones, would have to write and rewrite a piece of code several times to understand the task thoroughly. It takes even more time to know how to do takes efficiently, and worst of all, how errors should be handled properly.

Relevant Programming Languages (From Hard to Easy)

C++

For game engines like Unreal Engine or Unity, and all the software we have been using, the foundation or low-level programming is done with C++ (pronounced as C Plus Plus). C++ or CPP is the foundation of many modern languages, it runs on every hardware, and it can squeeze every bit of performance out of the computers. C++ is also the most difficult language to master. Scott Meyers, the world's foremost authorities on C++, describes C++ as a party of five languages or programming styles in his famous book *Effective C++: 55 Specific Ways to Improve Your Programs and Designs* (Addison-Wesley, 2005). Because of its complexity, programmers came up with this famous joke:

> *No one really knows C++*

C++ has direct access to the hardware, which, in theory, when used properly, can produce the most performant software. C++ is often the answer to software that needs excellent performance.

C#

C#, pronounced as C Sharp, is a high-level programming language. C# simplifies most of the complex aspects of C++ and provides a much faster development speed. You can also think of the "#" letter as 4 "+" stack together, which is C++++. Although Unity is developed with C++, Unity users adapt C# as the programming language for game development.

Python

Python is a superstar in modern programming languages. Python focuses on the programming experience of the developers and lowers the bar of programming for everyone. Python has a clean and elegant coding syntax, and is more flexible in many details. There are many Game Engines that are developed with C++ and designed to be used with python.

Blueprint

Blueprint is a visual scripting language developed by Epic Games to help with faster development. Blueprint uses nodes, and lines connect to them to program game logic. It is bound with C++ under the hood and can communicate with C++ seamlessly. Unreal Engine supports both C++ and Blueprint; in most of the cases, Blueprint can be converted into C++ to improve performance. The best practice to use Unreal Engine is to use both C++ and Blueprint. However, to ease the learning curve, we are not going to touch a lot of C++ and focus on Blueprint.

Let's learn some basics of Blueprints through some UI work.

Tutorial 13.1: Create an UI

Step 1: Create the UI Widget. Go to the Level folder in the Content Browser. Right click and select Level. Name this new level StartMenuLevel, and

489

double click on it to open it. The level should be pitch-black. Go to the Blueprints folder, and create a new folder called WBP. WBP means widget Blueprint. A widget is a UI or a UI element we can put on the screen. Right click in the WBP folder, and select User Interface → Widget Blueprint. Name the new Widget Blueprint to WBP_StartMenu.

Step 2: Add a button. Double click the WBP_StartMenu to open it with the Widget Editor. Go to the Palette panel at the upper left corner, and you can see some prebuilt UI elements we can use. Drag a button to the canvas at the center of the window (Figure 13.1).

Step 3: Drag a text to the button. In the Palette panel, find and drag Text to the button we created to add a text to the button. You should see the text snaps to the button, and under the Hierarchy panel, you can also see that the text is inside the button. This Hierarchy is the same as the Maya Outliner we are familiar with. Currently, the text is parented under our button (Figure 13.2).

Step 4: Name the button and the text. Right click on the Button_141 (yours could be a different number) in the Hierarchy and select rename; rename this button to StartButton. Click and drag the edge or corner of the button on the canvas to make it bigger. Make sure that the

FIGURE 13.1 Add a button to the UI.

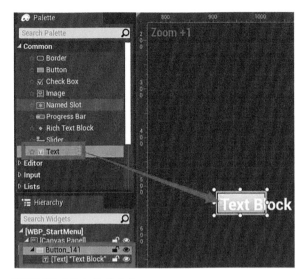

FIGURE 13.2 Add a text to the button.

> text is not clipping out of the edge of the button.
> Click on the [Text] "Text Block" in the Hierarchy to
> select it. Go to the Details panel, and under the
> Content section, set the Text to Start Game. Press
> the Save button to save the changes.
>
> Step 5: Bind the button click. Select our StartButton
> in the Hierarchy. Go to the Details panel, scroll
> down to the bottom, and find the Events
> section. Click on the plus button on the right
> side of the On Clicked text. The UI changes
> to the Event Graph, with a node named On
> Clicked (StartButton) highlighted in the middle
> (Figure 13.3).

Event Graph

The Event Graph is where we create our Blueprint code.
Many assets have Event Graph that allows us to write code
to that asset, and the navigation of the Event Graph is the
same as the Material Editor.

> Step 6: Our first code. Right click anywhere in the
> Event Graph, search for Print String, and hit Enter
> to create a Print String node. Click and drag
> the triangle pin of the On Clicked (StartButton)

FIGURE 13.3 Create an event for the button click.

node to the triangle pin on the left of the Print String node (Figure 13.4). Press the Compile (we will explain what compile means soon) and Save button on the upper left corner to save the changes.

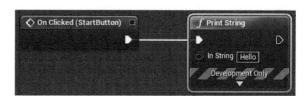

FIGURE 13.4 Create a Print String node.

Execution Pin and the Order of Execution

The triangle pins we connect in Step 6 are called execution pins, and these pins show the flow of the program. When we are programming, we write down a sequence of instructions to tell the computer what to do. The direction of the triangles and the lines connected to them shows the order of the instructions to execute, or we call the order of execution. In this case, the program flows left to right. It can be read as:

The button is clicked, then do Print String.

The execution pin on the left side of the node is called in execution pin, and the execution pin on the right side of the node is called out execution pin.

> Step 7: Create level GameMode. Create a new folder called GameModes in the Blueprints folder. Go to the World Settings panel, and under the Game Mode section, click on the "+" sign on the right of the GameMode Override setting. In the pop-up Create New GameMode window, navigate to the GameModes folder, type in GM_StartMenuLevel in the Name setting, and press OK (Figure 13.5).

FIGURE 13.5 Add GameMode override to the level with a new GameMode.

493

GameMode

GameMode is part of the framework Unreal Engine adapts in the default setting. GameMode controls the major components of the game, like the number of players in the game, character the player is controlling, and the heads-up display (HUD). GameMode also controls the rules of the game, like the win–lose conditions, level transitioning. Unreal Engine has a complete and mature framework that is battle-tested by many games. We are going to stick with the Unreal Framework. However, you can program everything from scratch if you wish to.

> *Step 8: Add our UI to the viewport using GameMode. Go to the GameModes folder and double click to open GM_StartMenuLevel. Click the Event Graph tab above the viewport in the middle to switch to the Event Graph. Create a Create Widget node by right clicking and searching. Click on the drop-down menu of the Class settings of the Create Widget node and set it to our WBP_StartMenu. Connect the execution pin from the Event BeginPlay to the input execution pin of the Create Widget node.*

Create a Get Player Controller node (again, just right click and search). Connect the Return Value output pin of the Get Player Controller node to the Owning Player input pin of the Create Widget node. Create an Add to Viewport node and connect the out execution pin of the Create Widget node to the input execution pin of the Add to Viewport node. Connect the Return Value output pin of the Create Widget node to the Target input pin of the Add to Viewport node (Figure 13.6).

Play the game now, and the Start Game button should appear in the viewport. Click on the button, and a hello get printed at the upper left corner of the screen.

Tips and Tricks

When we are trying to create a node, right click in an empty area and start typing in the keywords to start

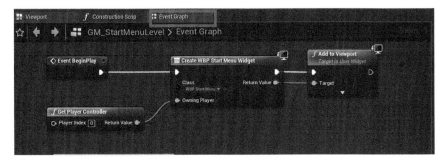

FIGURE 13.6 Code to create UI and add it to the player's screen using GameMode.

searching. The node may appear in the search before you type the full name, and you can use the up and down arrows to move in the list and pick the one you want. Press the Enter button to create it.

Functions

The Create Widget, Add to Viewport, and Get Player Controller nodes are all functions. Functions perform certain tasks and sometimes take inputs and spit out outputs. Functions can also be considered as reusable pieces of code that we can use multiple times. The inputs are called arguments of the function, and the outputs are called return values. In the realm of Blueprint, arguments are also called parameters. No matter what they are being called, they are information the function needs to perform its task. We call a function by connecting to the in execution pin of a function. Functions do not run if there is nothing connected to their in execution pins. Most of the time, we call a sequence of functions to achieve a certain game logic, and the order of the execution is based on the flow of the connections of the execution pins.

The Create Widget is a typical function, and its function is to create an instance of a widget. The Create Widget function has two inputs: Class and Owning Player. The Class input determines what kind of widget to create, and the Onwing Player input determines which player owns the new widget. The Create Widget needs those

495

two inputs to know what to create and who takes the ownership. The Return value output is the new widget created.

The Add to Viewport is also a function that adds a widget to the viewport. The Target input of this node determines which widget to add to the viewport.

The Get Player Controller is a pure blueprint function. Pure Blueprint functions have no execution pins and will be run when some other function is taking their return values. Get Player Controller gives us the PlayerController, which is the representation of the player. The Player Index input is set to 0, which means that we are getting player1's PlayerController.

Event BeginPlay is an event, and under the hood, an event is a simplified function. Events do not spit out outputs and support some other blueprint features that we are going to explore later. This Event BeginPlay will automatically run when the game starts. In the world of Unreal Engine, functions and events are interchangeable in most of the cases, and under the hood, they are the same thing in C++.

To translate this piece of code in English:

When the game starts, create a WBP_StartMenu for player1 and add it to player1's viewport.

Machine Code, Source Code, and Compiling

Computers are binary machines; internally, all instructions boil down to a sequence of 0s and 1s. These 0 and 1 sequences are what we call machine code. The computer can understand and execute machine code, but it is not very easy to read by humans. It is even more painful to write machine code. Code written by programmers like the Blueprint code we are writing is called source code. Source code is the source of generating machine code. Source code is readable by humans, but the computer cannot understand it.

The process of converting source code to machine code so the computer can understand it is compiling, and the tools to make the conversion are called compilers. When we are done with our coding, pressing the Compile button converts our Blueprint Code to machine code so it can run in our computer.

> Step 9: Make the button load our Level_01_ Awaken: open the WBP_StartMenu and go to the Event Graph by clicking the Graph button at the upper right corner of the window. Delete the Print String node, create an Open Level node, and type in Level_01_Awaken in the Level Name. Connect the output execution pin of the On Click(StartButton) node to the input execution pin of the Open Level node (Figure 13.7). Run the game and press the button, then the Level_01_Awaken is now open, and we can start playing.
>
> So far, everything works fine, but there are two design flaws in our coding style.
>
> Problem 1: The UI should only be in charge of taking input from the player and not deal with direct tasks like opening a level. What if we have some conditions or rules that prevent the loading of another level? Like the player is not finished with all the tasks needed? Is UI going to handle all these? If we make the UI handle all these, what if we want to create a new UI? Do we have to rewrite all these in the new UI? What we are doing now is like asking the receptionist of a company to do the manager's job.
>
> Problem 2: We typed in Level_01_Awaken in the Level Name of the Open Level function, so it is going to open Level_01_Awaken. There is nothing wrong here, but imagine that you have to load Level_01_Awaken in other places also, then you need another Open Level with

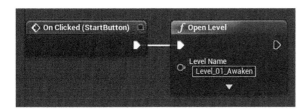

FIGURE 13.7 Set the button click event to open our first level.

Level_01_Awaken in its Level Name. Then maybe you decided to rename Level_01_Awaken to Level_01_Escape. Then you have to find all the Open Level functions and change their Level Name to Level_01_Escape. It would be nice if we can change it in one place only.

Questions like Problems 1 and 2 are related to what we call design patterns. You can code anything anywhere, but it is better to keep things organized, easy to understand, easy to make changes, and easy to communicate with other code. The process of adjusting and organizing the code is called refactoring.

Let's refactor our structure here and learn some new concepts of Blueprint and programming in general.

Tutorial 13.2: Refactoring Our Load Level Mechanic

Step 1: Move Open Level function to the GameMode. Open our GM_StartMenuLevel and go to the Even Graph. Right click and search for custom event, and choose the Add Custom Event to add a new custom event. A custom event is like a function that we can call somewhere else. Name this custom event to LoadTheFirstLevel (you can select it and press F2 to rename it). Create an Open Level Node, and connect the output execution pin from the LoadTheFirstLevel custom event to the input execution pin of the Open Level node (Figure 13.8).

Step 2: Use a variable to represent the name of the first level. Go to the Variables section under the My Blueprint panel located at the bottom left corner of the window. Click on the "+" sign at the right of the Variable label. A new item called NewVar_0 got added to the list under the variable section. This NewVar_0 is a variable.

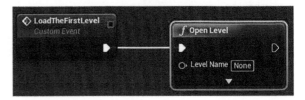

FIGURE 13.8 Create a custom function to load our level.

Variable

Variables are containers that store data in them, and the data they store can be changed or used somewhere else. A variable has three essential aspects:

1. The name of the variable.
2. Variable type. It can be a number, a letter, or a custom type.
3. The value of the variable.

Variables can be passed around, and any other part of the code can use the values of the variables.

Variable Types

Variable types are strict in Blueprint and many other programming languages. One type of variable should not be used as other types. Figure 13.9 shows the basic variable types Blueprint has. Every type of these variables has a color associated with them. You know that the two variables are the same type if they have the same color.

Let's explain some of the essential variable types:

FIGURE 13.9 The variable types.

Boolean	Boolean has two possible values: true or false. It is primarily used for conditions to determine what to do.
Integer	Integer represents a whole number, a number that is not a fraction.
Float	Float represents a number with a decimal point. Or has fractions.
String	A sequence of letters. Can represent things like names, sentences, or passwords.
Name	Represents a name. Compared to string, name is a specialized type that only represents names.
Vector	Represent a collection of numbers. A translate of an object has three numbers: translateX, translateY, and translateZ. A vector can represent a translate but not limited to that.

We will explain other types in detail when we use them.

For this NewVar_0 variable, we want to give it a name called FirstLevelName. With the NewVar_0 selected, go to the Details panel and set the Variable Name to FirstLevelName.

The variable type of the variable should be Name because we are going to use it as the input of the Open Level function. The Level Name input of the Open Level function is of the type Name. In the Details panel, click the drop-down menu of the Variable Type setting and select Name.

The value of this variable should be Level_01_Awaken. To change the value, we have to press the Compile button first to commit the changes we have made. After clicking the Compile button, go back to the Details panel and set the First Level Name under the Default Value section to Level_01_Awaken (Figure 13.10).

> Step 3: Use our variable as the Open Level input. Drag the FirstLevelName variable from the Variables to the Level Name input pin of the Open Level node (Figure 13.11). Press Compile and save to commit the changes.
> Step 4: Make the UI call the LoadTheFirstLevel event. Go back to the WBP_StartMenu and delete the Open Level node. Create a Get Game Mode node and a Cast to GM_StartMenuLevel node. Connect the Return Value of the Get Game Mode node to the Object input of the Cast to GM_StartMenuLevel node. Drag the As

FIGURE 13.10 The steps to set up our FirstLevelName variable.

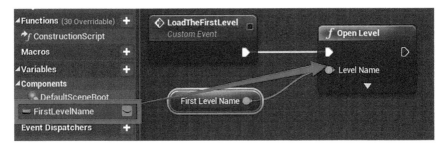

FIGURE 13.11 Use the FirstLevelName variable as the Level Name input of the Open Level function.

FIGURE 13.12 Make the UI call the LoadTheFirstLevel event.

GM Start Menu Level output pin of the Cast to
GM_StartMenuLevel node to an empty area. In
the pop-up menu, search for Load the First Level
and press the Enter button to create a call to
the LoadTheFirstLevel event. The execution pins
between the Cast To GM_StartMenuLevel and
the Load the First Level node gets automatically
connected. The As GM Start Menu Level now
feeds in the Target input of the Load the First
Level node. Finally, don't forget to connect the
On Clicked(StartButton) to the Cast to GM_
StartMenuLevel node (Figure 13.12).

The code here in plain English is: Get
the GameMode this level is using and call
its LoadTheFirstLevel event. Play the game
again, and you can see the game now
behaves the same as before. The Get Game
Mode function and Get Player Controller
function are both pure blueprint functions.

Tips and Tricks

You may wonder what this Cast to GM_StartMenuLevel is.
It does take much other knowledge about programming

501

to explain this function. We will cover it after we dip into a new concept called class in just a bit.

The functionality is not changed after our adjustment. However, this change is essential to make our code clean and manageable. With our FirstLevelName variable, we can use it anywhere we want. If the level name changes, we just need to change the variable. If there are other criteria to load the first level, we can add them to the LoadTheFirstLevel event. Anytime we need a new UI, or need to load the first level somewhere else, we can get the game mode and call its LoadTheFirstLevel event. What happens now with our receptionist and manager analogy earlier is:

The receptionist is now asking the manager to do the job requested.

The steps we have gone through is a sneak peek of what a programming job is done. We first started with a simple approach to make the button load Level_01_Awaken. Then, we did some adjusting to make it better, a process we call refactoring. Often, it takes at least these two steps to finish a program and sometimes many iterations of these two steps to bring the code to perfection.

All the functions and events we have been calling are built-in functions of the Unreal Engine framework except the LoadTheFirstLevel event we implemented ourselves.

Let's learn some more important concepts before moving on.

There are two different variable categories: built-in variable types and custom variable types. Both categories are used in the same way. Built-in variable types are what the programming language already have, and custom variable types are the types the programmers created for their particular project:

Built-In Variable Types

Boolean, Integer, and Float are examples of built-in variables types, and they are the essential data types that everyone needs to start programming. Most programming languages have them.

Custom Variable Types

The Name variable type is not a built-in variable type of the low-level language Unreal uses (C++). It is a custom variable type that Unreal developers created for Unreal Engine only. There are more custom variable types than built-in types. In fact, the BP_ceiling_light_01, BP_ceiling_light_02, and BP_lights_floor_light we created in Chapter 4 are all custom variable types we have created. You can even find them in the drop-down menu of the Variable Type settings (the setting we were tweaking when we create the FirstLevelName variable). Our new WBP_StartMenu and GM_StartMenuLevel are also custom variable types.

Custom variable type also has an official name called class.

Class

Class is a feature designed to describe real-world objects, and they are also called custom variable types, as described above. In real life, there are many different types of things, like animals, human beings, cars, and companies. It is possible to store data about these different types of things in various variables of built-in variable types, consider these two essential aspects of a human being:

Name
Age

Name can be represented with a variable of type string. Age can be represented with a variable type of integer. If there are two human beings in our game, one is the player and the other is the enemy, then we can create four variables to represent them:

A string called PlayerName with a value "Ellen."
An integer called PlayerAge with a value 26.

A string called EnemyName with a value "EvilEllen."
An integer called EnemyAge with a value 26.

This looks manageable. However, what if we have more things that we need to represent. It makes total sense to have hit points, move speed, skills, equipment, and other things we could need to describe our player and enemy or enemies. Let's say we have 1 player and 20 enemies, we need to keep records of their names, ages, hit points, speeds, skills, and equipment. There are six variables for each one of them, and there are 21 of them. So, we need 21 times 6, which are 126 variables to represent all of them! It is a disaster to represent them with 126 variables for the reasons listed below:

1. What if you forget to create one of the variables?
2. What happens if one of the enemies got eliminated? Do you still keep these variables around?
3. If the player used some skills to restore hit points, how do you prevent it from getting over the maximum allowed? You probably need a function to help with that just like the LoadTheFirstLevel function we create in the GM_StartMenuLevel.

The list goes on and on, and it is just too messy to manage all the aspects of one object as separated variables of built-in variable types and also potentially functions. It would be nice if we can package all the variables and functions needed to represent the player or an enemy in one package.

For the reasons listed above, class is invented to package variables and functions together to describe a new custom variable type. A class is essentially a collection of variables and functions that describes a new variable type that the program needs. We have created five classes already we created three lights in Chapter 4 (BP_ceiling_light_01, BP_ceiling_light_02, BP_lights_floor_light), the GM_StartMenuLevel, and the WBP_StartMenu. These are all classes. We can examine their composition as variables and functions:

For the three lights, every one of them consists of a static mesh and a certain type of light. The static mesh and the light are the variables of the light classes. The variable of a class is also called a member variable of that class. In this case, the variable type of the static mesh and the light are custom variable types that only Blueprint has. You can also consider static mesh, and lights are built-in types of Blueprint, but not built-in types of C++; after all, they exist in Blueprint already.

For the GM_StartMenuLevel, we have a variable called FirstLevelName and an event called LoadTheFirstLevel. An event or function of the class is called a member function (again, you can think of events and functions are the same thing in Blueprint, they are the same in the C++ level).

For our WBP_StarMenu, the button and the text are member variables, and the On Clicked(StartButton) is a member function.

One thing that we need to be clear here is that classes represent variable types and not actual variables. They are the blueprints of different types of variables. Just like in the real world, the word "human" is describing all human beings as a type of animal, but not one human. An actual human being is an instance of the human class. Similarly, a variable of a class is called an instance of that class. For example, the FirstLevelName variable we create for our game mode is an instance of the Name class. The variables of classes can also be called objects.

With the basic concept of classes in mind, let's make another set of classes to future explore other features of classes. Play the game and click the start game button. The player should land in the start room. However, we cannot get out of the room because the door is locked. Let's make a class that can describe an automatic sliding door.

Tutorial 13.3: Make a Sliding Door Class

Step 1: Create a Triggerable class. Go back to the Level_01_Awaken level, and create a new folder called Triggerables in the Blueprints folder. Right click in the Triggerables folder, and select Blueprint Class; any class we create

FIGURE 13.13 Create a new blueprint class called BP_Triggerable.

in the editor is a blueprint class. In the Pick Parent Class pop-up window, click Actor. A new blueprint is now added to the folder, rename it BP_Triggerable (Figure 13.13).

Parent Class

When creating a class, we can choose to give it a parent class (or not to). A class with a parent class automatically has all the variables and functions of its parent, or in other words, they can do whatever their parent can do.

A child class can be passed around and used as if it was its parent class, but not the other way around. For example, suppose we have a Human class and we created a child class of Human class called Programmer. A Programmer is a human, but a human is not necessarily a programmer.

All classes we have created have their parent class, and a lot of the heavy lifting is done with their parent classes under the hood. Objects of the Actor class can be placed in the level, and our triggerable class needs that functionality; that is why we chose Actor as its parent class. Give a class a parent class is called inheriting, a class is the child class of its parent class.

Step 2: Add a trigger to the BP_Triggerable. Double click to open the BP_Triggerable blueprint class. If you got a window like Figure 13.14, just click the Open Full Blueprint Editor to open it with the full editor. Click on the Add Component button at the upper left corner of the window. Type in box collision and press Enter to add a box collision component. Select the new component and press F2 to rename it Trigger.

Step 3: Add an on component begin overlap event. Select the Trigger, go to the Details panel, scroll down to the bottom, and find the Events section. Click on the green plus button on the right of the On Component Begin Overlap label. A new event called On Component Begin Overlap (Trigger) is created in the event graph (Figure 13.15).

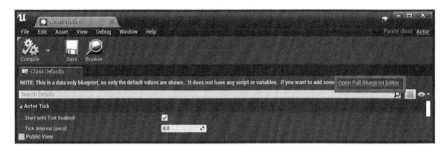

FIGURE 13.14 Click the Open Full Blueprint Editor text to open a blueprint class fully.

FIGURE 13.15 Add an on component begin overlap event.

Step 4: Add an on component end overlap event. Select the Trigger again and go to the Details panel; this time, click on the green plus button of On Component End Overlap. This creates another function called On Component End Overlap (Trigger).

The On Component Begin Overlap (Trigger) event will be called when some other actors start overlapping with it. The On Component End Overlap (Trigger) event will be called if other actors stop overlapping with it.

Step 5: Create custom events. Right click in the empty place and type in custom event, press Enter to create a custom event, and name this new custom event Overlapped. With this custom event selected, go to the Details panel. Hover the cursor on the "+" sign on the right of the label of the Inputs section, and click to add a new parameter. Under the Inputs section, type in Other Actor as the name of the new parameter. Click on the Boolean to open the drop-down list, search for Actor, and select Actor → Object Reference. This parameter is now an input pin of this new Overlapped event, and it is of the Actor class. Create a Print String node, and connect the out execution pin of the Overlapped event to the in execution pin of the Print String node. Drag the Other Actor output of the Overlapped event to the In String input pin of the Print String node. Unreal creates a Get Display Name node automatically in between to get the name of the Other Actor input and pass that to the In String of the Print String node. Create another custom event and call it UnOverlapped. Set the UnOverlapped event the same way we did for the Overlapped event (Figure 13.16).

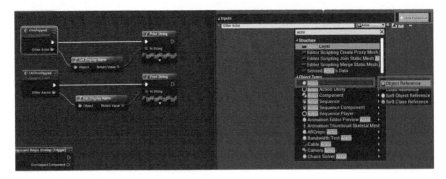

FIGURE 13.16 Create the Overlapped and UnOverlapped custom event.

Step 6: Add call to the custom events. Right click in the empty space, search, and create an Overlapped node and an UnOverlapped node. These two new nodes are function calls to the Overlapped and UnOverlapped events we create in Step 5. Connect the out execution pin of the On Component Begin Overlap (Trigger) to the in execution pin of the Overlapped node. Connect the Other Actor output pin of the On Component Begin Overlap (Trigger) to the Other Actor input pin of the Overlapped node. Connect the On Component End Overlap (Trigger) and the UnOverlapped node in the same way we connect the On Component Begin Overlap (Trigger) node and the Overlapped node (Figure 13.17).

Go back to the Content Browser, and drag the BP_Triggerable to the level to create an instance of BP_Triggerable. Remember where it is, play the game, and walk over it. You can now see that the name of the FirstPersonCharacter got printed out at the upper left corner of the UI. The code we did translate into plain English is:

When an actor overlaps and stops overlapping the trigger, print the name of that actor.

Read the sentence carefully and you can see a potential problem here. Any actor can trigger it. However, we only want the player and the enemy to be able to trigger this.

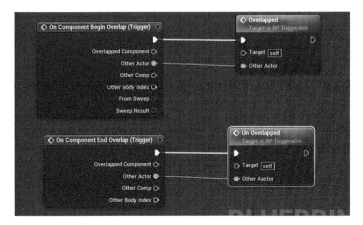

FIGURE 13.17 Add calls to the two new custom events.

FIGURE 13.18 Check the parent class of the FirstPersonCharacter class.

Let's solve this problem by checking the class type of the actor that triggered it.

Step 7: Add checking to the class of the actor. Go to the FirstPersonBP/Blueprints folder, and double click to open the FirstPersonCharacter class. Click on the Class Settings button, and you can find that the Parent Class of this FirstPersonCharacter is Character (Figure 13.18).

Character

A character can move around the level and can be possessed by the player or AI. For most of the time, we would use Character as the parent class for a player character or AI-controlled enemy. In this case, if we want to make sure that only the player or the enemy can trigger it, we just need to check if the overlapped actor's parent class is Character.

Go back to the Event Graph of the BP_Triggerable class, and drag the Other Actor output pin of the On Component Begin Overlap (Trigger) node out to an empty area. Release the mouse, and a list of actions we can do to this actor appears. Search for GetClass and hit Enter to create a GetClass function call. This function returns the class of the Other Actor. Drag out the Return value output pin and search for Class Is Child Of and hit Enter to create a Class Is Child Of function call. Set the parent class argument of the Class Is Child Of to Character.

The pin of the Return Value of this Class Is Child Of function is red. A variable of red color is of type Boolean. A Boolean variable has two possible values: true or false. In this case, if the Test Class is the Child of the Parent Class, the return value is true; otherwise, the return value is false.

Hold down the B button and click anywhere to create a Branch node. Connect the Return Value of the Class Is Child Of to the Condition input pin of the Branch node. Connect the out execution pin of the On Component Begin Overlap (Trigger) to the in execution pin of the Branch node. This Branch node is not a function. It is a flow control statement. If the Condition input is true, the execution flow continues after the True out execution pin. Otherwise, the flow goes toward the False execution pin.

Connect the True out execution pin of the Branch node to the in execution pin of the Overlapped node.

This part of the code can now translate in plain English as:

If the class of the Other Actor is the child of the Character class, then call the Overlapped function.

Set up the same parent class checking in the On Component End Overlap (Trigger) (Figure 13.19).

Play the game, and the behavior of the trigger should still work as expected. However, we now have the peace of

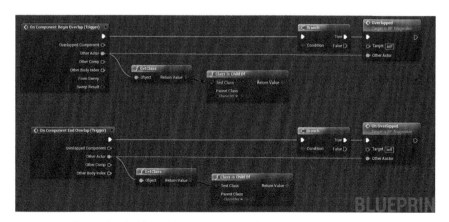

FIGURE 13.19 Add parent class check for the Other Actor to determine if the trigger should activate.

511

mind that only an object of the Character class or its child class can trigger it.

Step 8: Create a sliding door class that inherits the BP_Triggerable. Go back to the Triggerables folder, right click on the BP_Triggerable class, and select Create Child Blueprint Class. Name the new class BP_SlidingDoor. Double click to open it. Under the Components panel, you can see that there is already a Trigger component, and it is Inherited from the BP_Triggerable class. Components are the same as member variables, and they are called components just to conceptually make more sense. Like what we have mentioned before, the child class automatically got (inherits) all the member variables and functions the parent class has.

Step 9: Add the door meshes to the class as static meshes. Go to the StaticMeshes/door folder in the Content Browser. Select the door_door_frame, door_door_l, and door_door_r meshes in the folder and drag them to the component list of the BP_SlidingDoor to add all three meshes as static mesh components to the BP_SlidingDoor class. You can now see the doors in the viewport of the class (Figure 13.20).

Step 10: Add variables to store the door open position. Left click to select the left door in the viewport. Hit W to switch to Move and move it to slide it open. Go to the Details panel, right click on the Location label under the transform section, and select Copy. Add a variable by pressing the "+" sign in the Variables section and name the new variable l_door_open_pos. Go back to the Details panel, and change the Variable Type to Vector. Press the Compile and Save button to commit all the changes. Go back the Details panel. Right click on the L Door Open Pos label under the Default Value section and select Paste. This l_door_open_pos variable now stores the open position of the left door. Create another vector variable called r_door_open_pos to store the open position of the right door (Figure 13.21). Don't forget to move the doors back afterward.

Step 11: Create function overrides. A child class inherits all functions its parent has. So our BP_SlidingDoor has the Overlapped and UnOverlapped functions the BP_Triggerable

FIGURE 13.20 Add the door meshes to the BP_SlidingDoor class as components.

FIGURE 13.21 Add variables to store the open positions of the doors.

class has. However, we want different behavior when we triggered the door. A child class can override a parent function to redefine what the function does in the child class. Go to the My Blueprint panel, hover the cursor above the Functions label, and click on the Override button. Select Overlapped in the drop-down list to create an override of the Overlapped function. An Event Overlapped node got created in the Event Graph. This Event Overlapped event looks like a regular custom event, but it is an override of the Overlapped event of the parent class. Go ahead and create an override to the UnOverlapped function as well (Figure 13.22).

Step 12: Test our override events. Add two Print String nodes, call one of them with the Event Overlapped, and change the In String to door overlapped. Call the other one with the Event UnOverlapped and change the In String to door unoverlapped (Figure 13.23). Go to the Content Browser and drag the BP_SlidingDoor to the level and place it side to side with the BP_Triggerable we placed earlier. Play the game, and you can see "door overlapped" got printed when you approach the door, and "FirstPersonCharacter" got printed when you approach the BP_Triggerable.

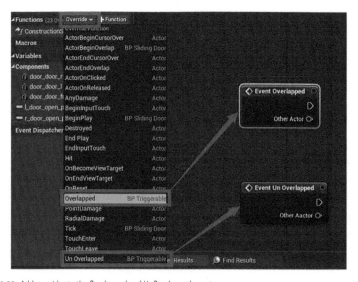

FIGURE 13.22 Add overrides to the Overlapped and UnOverlapped event.

FIGURE 13.23 Add a Print String to both the events.

Tips and Tricks

Print String may not be very useful for creating gameplay. However, it is a fantastic testing tool; use it to print out information to verify if the code behaves as expected.

As you can see, overriding a function inherited from the parent class completely redefines what the function does in the child class.

Why?

So why do we go through the trouble of making a parent class and a child class? Well, there could be other stuff in the game that can be triggered. Let's say we need to create an automatic light that can be triggered if the player gets close. If we don't have a parent class, we have to create everything from scratch, including the box collision component and the overlapping events. With the BP_Triggerable parent class, we can just inherit from it and overwrite the Overlapped and UnOverlapped functions.

> Step 13: Create a timeline. Delete the two Print String nodes. Right click and search for Add timeline and press Enter to create a timeline. Name the timeline DoorOpenAmount and double click to open it. There is currently nothing in the timeline; click the first button with a lowercase "f" and a "+" sign as its icon to add a float track. This float

FIGURE 13.24 Add a new float track to the timeline and name it DoorOpenAmount.

track is the same as the Graph Editor we have covered in our animation chapters, and we are now creating an animation curve. You can now type in DoorOpenAmount to rename this float track and hit Enter to commit (Figure 13.24).

Step 14: Add keys to the animation. Right click anywhere in the coordinates and select Add Key to CurveFloat_1 to add a key to the animation curve. A diamond-shaped point got added to the animation curve, and this point is a new key. With the new key selected, set the time and value at the top of the graph to 0 and 0. This new key now moves to the (0, 0) coordinate. Add another key and set its time and value to 1 and 1, respectively. Also, set the Length attribute of the float track to 1 at the top of the graph (Figure 13.25). You can use the same way we navigate the Event Graph to navigate the graph of the timeline.

Step 15: Use the timeline to drive the door movement. Go back to the Event Graph, and create a Lerp (Vector) node by right clicking and searching. Connect the DoorOpenAmount output pin of the DoorOpenAmount timeline node to the Alpha input pin of the Lerp (Vector) node. Drag the l_door_open_position from the Variables section in the My Blueprint panel to the B input pin of the Lerp (Vector) node. Keep the A input pin values as it is.

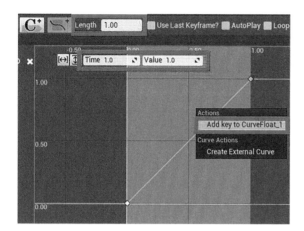

FIGURE 13.25 Add keys to the animation and set its length to 1 second.

Drag the door_door_l static mesh component from the Components panel to the graph to create a reference for it. Drag out the Door Door L output pin and type SetRelativeLocation and hit Enter to create a SetRelativeLocation node. Connect the Return Value of the Lerp (Vector) node to the New Location input pin of the SetRelativeLocation node.

Finally, connect the out execution pin of the Event Overlapped node to the Play execution pin of the DoorOpenAmount timeline node. Connect the out execution pin of the Event UnOverlapped node to the Reverse execution pin of the DoorOpenAmount timeline node. Connect the Update out execution pin to the in execution pin of the SetRelativeLocation node (Figure 13.26).

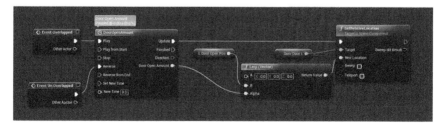

FIGURE 13.26 Set up the timeline to drive the movement of the left door.

What we did here can translate to plain English as:
When overlapped, play the animations in the timeline and update the relative location of the left door. The relative location of the door is (0, 0, 0) at the beginning of the animation and becomes l_door_open_ position at the end of the animation. When someone stops overlapping, reserve the current animation.

Why?

Based on the animation curve we set up in the timeline, when started, the Door Open Amount output value of the timeline changes from 0 to 1 gradually in 1 second.

The value of the Door Open Amount feeds into the Alpha of the Lerp (Vector) node. For any type of lerp node, input A, input B, Alpha, and the Return Value fulfill the following equation:

$$\text{Return Value} = A \times (1 - \text{Alpha}) + B \times \text{Alpha}.$$

Or in other words, the Return Value of the Lerp node is the blend of the A and B input based on the Alpha input. Alpha is ranging from 0 to 1. The closer the alpha value is to 1, the closer the Return Value is to the input B.

Step 16: Set up the right door. Set up the right door the same way we set up the left door. The difference this time is the SetRelativeLocation node of the right door is after the SetRelativeLocation node of the left door. They are also sharing the same timeline node (Figure 13.27).

Play the game, and when you walk toward the door, the door automatically opens.

Step 17: Scale the trigger box. The trigger box is too small for our sliding door. Go to the viewport of the BP_SlidingDoor Blueprint, select the trigger, and scale it up like in Figure 13.28. Go back to the level, and you should see the BP_SlidingDoor we placed in the level is also updated with the bigger trigger box.

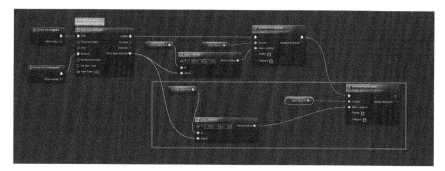

FIGURE 13.27 Set up the right door the same way we set up the left door.

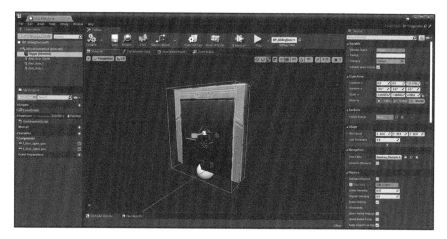

FIGURE 13.28 Scale the trigger box.

Play the game again, and you will notice that we still cannot go through the door event it opens as expected. This is due to the collision setup of the door frame.

Step 18: Check door frame collision. Go to the StaticMeshes/door folder and double click to open the door_door_frame static mesh. Click on the Collision button at the top of the Asset Editor and select Simple Collision. You can now see a green box shows up in the viewport. This green box is the collision shape of this model (Figure 13.29).

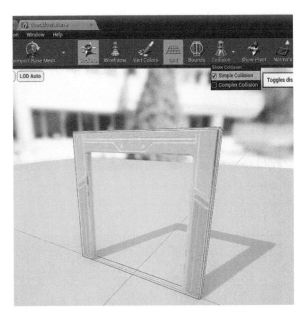

FIGURE 13.29 Check the collision of the door_door_frame static mesh asset.

Collision

To simplify the calculation of the collision, Unreal Engine does not use the actual model to calculate collisions. When an asset is imported, Unreal Engine generates a convex primitive based on the shape of the model and uses it as the shape to calculate collisions. The green box we see is the generated collision shape of the door frame.

> *Step 19: Fix the door frame collision. Click on any edge of the green collision primitive of the door frame to select it. Use the translation tools to scale and move it, so it covers one side of the column. Hold down Alt and drag to create a copy of the primitive and drag it to cover the other side of the column. Drag out another copy and tweak it to make it cover the upper beam of the door (Figure 13.30).*
>
> *Save the asset and play the game again. This time, we should be able to go through the door.*
>
> *Many beginner programmers may think that their job of creating a sliding door is done here, and it might be true in some situations.*

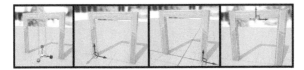

FIGURE 13.30 Steps to fix the door frame collision.

However, remember the general process of programming we have talked about? What is missing here?

The answer here is refactoring.

Let's open BP_Triggerable and go to the Event Graph. The code seems all good and pretty clean as well. But there is an import part of the code that has its purpose untold. What does the GetClass and Class Is Child Of function do for our game? As the creator of the code, we can say with great certainty that this piece of code ensures only the player and the enemy can trigger it. And the odds are high for another programmer to assume the purpose of this piece of code correctly. This is too simple.

However, even the simplest thing in the code could cause bugs that we cannot detect, and making the purpose of any piece of code clear is essential. Let's enhance it by wrapping it with a function to make the purpose clear.

Step 20: *Create a function to check if the other actor should activate the trigger. Hover the cursor over the label of the Functions section under the My Blueprint panel. Click on the Function button to create a new function. Type in ShouldTriggerReactToActor as the name of the new function. A new tag got added to the right of the EventGraph tab, and it is now highlighted. We are now in the body of the function (Figure 13.31).*

Step 21: *Add input and output. Just like how we add input to our Overlapped and UnOverlapped event, we can add input to our function. Again, functions and events are the same. Go to the Inputs section of the details panel, press the "+" sign to add a new input, and set its name to ActorToCheck and its type to Actor. Add an output and name it ShouldReact, and change its type to Boolean (Figure 13.32).*

If we add outputs to a function, a Return Node is added with the outputs as its input pins for us to specify the value of the outputs.

521

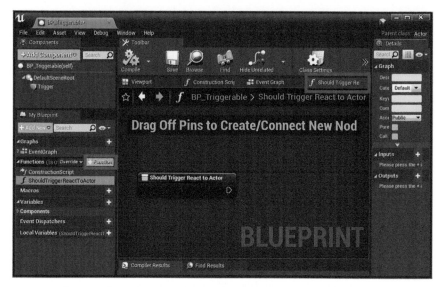

FIGURE 13.31 Create a new function.

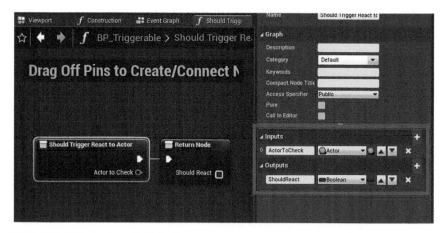

FIGURE 13.32 Add input and output to the function.

We now have two nodes in the Function. The Should Trigger React to Actor node is the beginning of the function, and the Return Node is the end of the function. Whatever we put in between these two nodes are the body of the function and will be run based on the order of execution.

Step 22: Implement our function. Create a GetClass node and a Class Is Child Of node. Connect the Actor to Check output pin of the Should Trigger React to Actor to the Object input pin of the GetClass node. Connect the Return Value of the GetClass node to the Test Class input of the Class Is Child Of node. Connect the Return Value of the Class Is Child Of to the Should React input of the Return Node. Set the Parent Class parameter of the Class Is Child Of node to Character (Figure 13.33).

Step 23: Use the Function. Click on the Event Graph tab to go back to the Event Graph. For the On Component Begin Overlap (Trigger), delete the GetClass and Class Is Child Of nodes and create a Should Trigger React to Actor node by right clicking and searching. Connect the out execution pin of the On Component Begin Overlap (Trigger) to the in execution pin of the Should Trigger React to Actor node. Connect the Other Actor output pin of the On Component Begin Overlap (Trigger) to the Actor to Check input pin of the Should Trigger React To Actor node. Connect the out execution pin of the Should Trigger React to Actor node to the in execution pin of the Branch node. Finally, connect the Should React output pin of the Should Trigger React to Actor node to the Condition of the Branch node. Do the same thing to the On Component End Overlap (Trigger). Figure 13.34 shows the result.

Play the game again, and the behavior of the door should remain the same. There are two major improvements here:

1. The Should Trigger React to Actor is self-explanatory. The purpose is very clear.

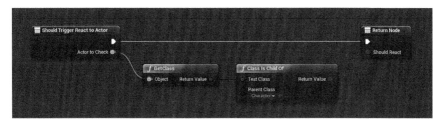

FIGURE 13.33 Implement the function.

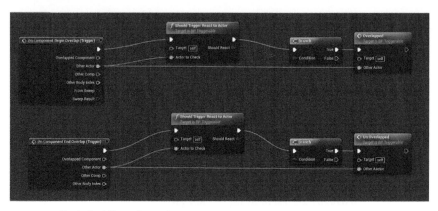

FIGURE 13.34 Use the Should Trigger React to Actor.

2. If we need to change the criteria, we just need to change the body of the function. And both events should work right away.

Tips and Tricks

Functions are our friends. Whenever you need to write down the same kind of code multiple times, you should create a function for it.

> *Step 24: Replace all other doors. We have successfully created a working sliding door. Go ahead and replace all the doors in the level, and now you can enjoy walking around the whole environment.*
>
> *Let's try to give you a glimpse of one more important concept before moving on to the next chapter.*

Casting

Remember the Cast To GM_StartMenuLevel function we used earlier in the UI but did not explain? Let's try to make sense of it now. First of all, our GM_StartMenuLevel is a child class of another class called GameModeBase Class, and this class is the default game mode used if we do not override one. The GetGameMode function only returns an instance of the type GameModeBase. The engine has no idea what child class of GameModeBase you will create to be your game mode to use in the level, so the GetGameMode only returns a GameModeBase.

Remember we have talked about a child class can be used and passed around as if it was its parent? Here is exactly what's happening. The Return value is actually a GM_StartMenuLevel, but it is taking a form of its parent type. However, we need to cast it to GM_StartMenuLevel to use its LoadFirstLevel function. The Cast To GM_StartMenuLevel does precisely that.

Casting is very flexible, you can try to cast anything to anything. As long as the data structure matches the type you are trying to cast to, but it may fail if the data structure is not compatible. Casting a string to an integer could fail, for example. You do not want to cast unrelated types because the result might be unpredicted.

Conclusion

We have covered functions, events, variables, and classes to some extent. We have used some useful blueprint classes like GameMode, Character, Actor, and Widget. However, we have barely touched the surface. Keep in mind that learning programming is a daunting process. To understand one concept, you may have to understand many others. Consider this:

A function object is any object for which the function call operator is defined.

This description is from the cppreference.com, one of the online documentation of C++. To understand what this function object is, you have to understand what a function is. You also have to understand what are operators and what is a function operator. Worst of all, what does "the operator is defined" even mean. You could almost feel like you are reading an alien language.

It is ubiquitous for beginners to encounter this kind of description, which renders them frustrated. Our suggestion is to have the mindset of accepting your ignorance and carry on with the learning.

Try to understand as much as you can and don't get too carried away by one or two tricky concepts. You will understand more in the future if you don't give up learning.

Remember, the best way to improve your programming is to practice with it.

We are going to explore the Unreal Engine framework and set up our player character in the next chapter.

CHAPTER 14

Player Character

The player character is one of the essential parts of the game. So far, we are using a first-person shooter template so we can explore our scene while building it, but now, it is time to create a player character of our own. After all, we spent much time making our Character.

Unreal Engine provides a set of classes to help create player characters fast. The Engine provides a robust framework that allows us to organize classes and data. We are going to cover many aspects of this framework and built our system on top of it. Although it is possible to build everything from scratch, it is going to be time-consuming. There is little to none merit to reinvent the wheel unless you want to practice; with the length budget of this book, we will opt to use the prebuilt systems whenever it is possible.

Tutorial 14.1: Create the First-Person Shooter Character

Step 1: Create a base class for all characters. Go to the Characters folder, right click, and select Blueprint Class. In the pop-up Pick Parent Class window, select Character. Name the new Character BP_Character_Base. Double click to open BP_Character_Base. Select the Mesh component in the Components panel. Go to the Details panel, and set the Skeletal Mesh to Ellen_Skeletal_Mesh. The body of Ellen now appears in the viewport. Move her down, so the feet are on the ground and rotate her −90 degrees to make her face the direction of the blue arrow (Figure 14.1). Press the Compile and the Save button to commit the changes.

Step 2: Create the FPS character. Right click on BP_Character_Base, select Create Child Blueprint Class, name the new child class BP_Ellen_FPS, and open it. Change the Skeletal Mesh of the Mesh component to Ellen_FPS_Skeletal_Mesh. Press Compile and Save to commit the change.

Step 3: Make the game mode. Go to Blueprints/Gamemodes. Right click in the empty area of the folder, and select Blueprint Class. In the pop-up Pick Parent Class window, select Game

FIGURE 14.1 Set the character Base.

FIGURE 14.2 A new game mode that uses our BP_Ellen_FPS as the default pawn class.

Mode Base. Rename the Game Mode Base to GM_Ellen_FPS, and double click to open it. Set the Default Pawn Class to BP_Ellen_FPS (Figure 14.2).

Pawn and Character

Pawn is the parent class of Character.

We have mentioned the Character class in Chapter 13. A character can be possessed (controlled) by the player or AI. It has a skeletal mesh component to represent it visually and can move like a human. Character is the parent class of the FirstPersonCharacter—the mechanic arm holding a gun that we possess when we hit the play button.

Just like characters, pawns can also be possessed, but a pawn does not have a mesh component, and it cannot move out of the box. We use the pawn class when we want something simpler than a human. The Default Pawn Class of the game mode determines the class of the Pawn the players are going to possess when the game starts. In our case, we want it to be our BP_Ellen_FPS.

We can use our BP_Ellen_FPS as the Default Pawn Class because it is a child class or Character, and Character is a child class of Pawn. Any child class can be used as if it was its parent class.

529

FIGURE 14.3 Set the default game mode used to GM_Ellen_FPS.

Step 4: Set the default game mode. Go to Edit →
Project Settings. Click on the Maps & Modes
section in the list on the left side of the pop-up
Project Settings window. Change the Default
GameMode to GM_Ellen_FPS (Figure 14.3).

Play the game and we can see that we are
no longer controlling the mechanic arms that
hold a gun. Instead, we cannot see our body and
cannot move.

You can press the F8 button on the keyboard
to unpossess our Character. F8 triggers a
debugging feature of Unreal Engine that allows
you to unpossess your current Character and
navigate the world the same way you do when
editing the level. Move away and look back, and
we can see the FPS body of Ellen, which means
that we have successfully switched out the player
character.

Any level that does not override its game
mode is going to use the default game mode
defined in the Project Settings window. If you
recall, we have overridden the game mode of
StartMenuLevel by going to the World Settings
and set the GameMode Override to GM_
StartMenuLevel. The StartMenuLevel still uses the
GM_StartMenuLevel as its game mode.

Step 5: Set up a camera. We can add a camera as
the eye of the player to the Character. Open
BP_Ellen_FPS, click the Add Component button,

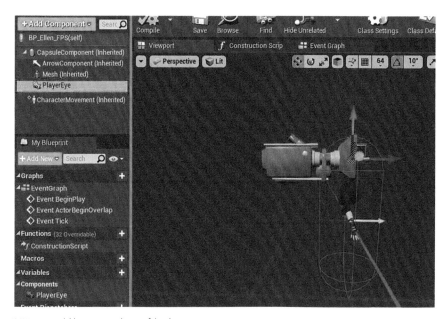

FIGURE 14.4 Add a camera as the eye of the player.

search for camera, and press Enter to create a camera. Rename the camera PlayerEye. Go to the Viewport of the Blueprint Editor and you can see a camera got added. Select the camera and move it up, so it sits above the neck (Figure 14.4).

Play the game, and now we see through the PlayerEye camera. You can verify that by moving the camera back a little so it can see the body. Play the game again, and you should see the body. Don't forget to move the camera back after testing.

Unreal finds a camera component as the viewpoint of the player if the Auto Active checker box of the camera in the Details panel is on, which is the default setting for a new camera. If there is no camera component, Unreal sets the viewpoint at the height defined by the Base Eye Height member variable of the Pawn.

Step 6: Check the input settings. Go to Edit → Project Settings. In the Project Settings window, click the Input section. Under the Bind section of the Input section, you can see two categories of input binding: Action Mappings and Axis Mappings. Click the small triangle buttons on the left of the labels of the categories to open them.

We can see that some inputs are already defined. Open the first one called Jump, and you can see a list of keys and controllers that are bond with it (Figure 14.5). These key bindings are from the template.

For the Jump key binding, you can see not only Space Bar in the list but also Gamepad, Vive, Daydream, Oculus Go, and many other devices in the list. This Jump key binding receives inputs from all these different devices. Whenever the spacebar is pressed, or any triggers of these various devices in the list are used, a global event called InputAction Jump will be triggered. Notice that you can change the name of this Jump key

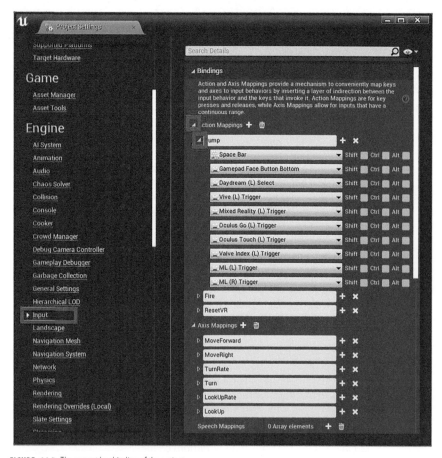

FIGURE 14.5 The current key binding of the project.

binding, which means that the name of the event is all arbitrary.

Step 7: Implement the jump event. Go back to BP_ Ellen_FPS and switch to the Event Graph. Right click in an empty area and type in input jump, and press Enter to create an InputAction Jump event. Drag out from the Pressed out execution pin of the InputAction Jump event, search, and create a Jump function call. Press Compile and Save to commit the change (Figure 14.6).

Play the game again and press the spacebar, and you can already jump.

Because jumping is such a standard action in an ordinary game, Unreal Engine has implemented it for us already. The Jump function is a function of the Character class that makes the character jump. When the spacebar is pressed, it triggers this InputAction Jump event, which calls the Jump function in our setup.

There is a MoveForward key binding in the Axis Mappings category, open it, and you can see even more keys are bond with it. W and S are among the keys, and pressing them triggers the InputAxis MoveForward event.

Step 8: Implement the MoveForward event. Go to the Event Graph of BP_Ellen_FPS. Create an InputAxis MoveForward event and an Add Movement Input function call. Connect the out execution pin of the InputAxis MoveForward event to the in execution pin of the Add Movement Input node. Connect the Axis Value of the InputAxis MoveForward event to the Scale Value of the Add Movement Input node. Because we are trying to move forward, the World Direction input should be the forward direction of the Character. Search and create a Get Actor Forward Vector node. Connect the Return Value of the Get Actor Forward Vector node to the World Direction of the Add Movement Input node (Figure 14.7).

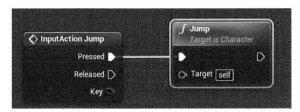

FIGURE 14.6 Implement the InputAction Jump event.

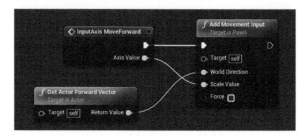

FIGURE 14.7 Implement the MoveForward event.

> *Press Compile and Save. Play the game and press the W button to move forward and S to move backward. The Add Movement Input function is a function of the Character class Unreal already implemented for us that moves the Character in the World Direction you specified. The Get Actor Forward Vector gives us the forward direction of the Character. Character is a child class of Pawn, and Pawn is a child class of Actor; this Get Actor Forward Vector function is a member function of the Actor class.*

Why?

Why the S button allows us to move backward? Look closer to the MoveForward key binding in the Project Settings, and you can see that the S button has a Scale value of –1. This Scale value is the Axis Value output of the InputAxis MoveForward event. When you press the W button, the Axis Value is 1; when you press the S button, the Axis Value is –1. When you hold down the S button, a value of –1 one is passed to the Scale Value of the Add Movement Input function, which causes the Character to move forward by –1 (move backward).

You can try the up and down arrows on the keyboard to move forward and backward because they are also in the list of the keys that bond with the InputAxis MoveForward event. You can add new keys to the list by pressing the "+" button on the right of the MoveForward text field, or you can press the "X" button to delete a key binding in the list or the entire key binding. To add a new keybinding to the

Mappings, just click on the "+" button on the right of the Mappings label.

The Action Mapping is triggered once per button press or release. Axis Mappings are always in action or being triggered, or they are triggered every time the game updates. When no button is down, the Axis value is 0. When a button is down, the Axis value is the Scale value of that button. Notice that the Gamepad Thumbstick can give you a Scale value anywhere from –1 to 1 because you can push or pull the stick to the extreme or halfway through.

Step 9: Implement the MoveRight event. Using a similar setup, we can quickly implement the InputAxis MoveRight event. The difference here is that we are using the Get Actor Right Vector instead of the Get Actor Forward Vector (Figure 14.8).

Step 10: Implement the Turn event. There is a Turn binding in the Axis Mappings list. Open it, and you can see that the Mouse X is bond with it. Mouse X is the left and right movement of the mouse (Y is up and down). Go to the Event Graph of BP_Ellen_FPS and create an InputAxis Turn event and an Add Controller Yaw Input node. Connect the out execution pin of the InputAxis Turn event to the Add Controller Yaw Input node. Connect the Axis Value of the InputAxis Turn event to the Val input of the Add Controller Yaw Input node (Figure 14.9).

Play the game again, and now you can look left and right by moving the mouse left and right.

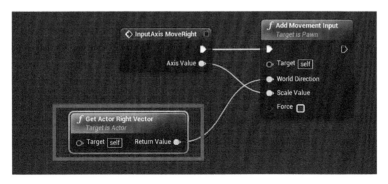

FIGURE 14.8 Implement the Move Right event.

535

FIGURE 14.9 Implement the Turn event.

Roll, Yaw, Pitch

You can think of Roll, Yaw, Pitch as different names for local rotation x, y, and z. Roll means rotating around the forward axis of an object, Yaw means rotating around the Up axis of an object, and pitch is rotating around the right axis of an object. Or in other words, doing roll is to tilt your head left and right, doing yaw is to swing your head like you are saying no, and doing pitch is nodding your head up and down like you are saying yes.

Controller

You may not notice this, but the naming of this Add Controller Yaw Input function is a bit strange, why is it called Add Controller Yaw Input instead of Add Yaw Input? Well, because it adds input to the controller of the Character instead of the Character itself. Controller is a class, and a controller can possess a character. There are two child classes of Controller in Unreal Engine:

PlayerController

When a player joins the game, the game mode creates an instance of the controller class specified in the Player Controller Class member variable in the game mode. This PlayerContoller is the representation of the player. As long as the player stays in the game, the PlayerController remains in the game as well. On the other hand, the Character the player possesses through the PlayerController might die, or the player might need to switch to a different Character. In all these two cases, the PlayerController does not change, and the only thing changed here is the Character being possessed.

AIController

AIControllers can possess any character, just like PlayerControllers can. The difference here is that the AIController does not represent a human player, and it is an AI or a bot if you will.

> *Step 11: Implement the LookUp event. Use an Add Controller Pitch Input to implement the InputAxis LookUp event (Figure 14.10).*
>
> *Play the game again; but this time, you cannot look up or down as you would expect. In the default settings, the Character uses the controller's yaw input, but not the pitch input. Click on the Class Defaults button and go to the Details panel. You can see that the Use Controller Rotation Yaw is checked, but the Use Controller Rotation Pitch is not (Figure 14.11).*
>
> *It makes sense to turn the whole body left and right, but not tilt it up or down, when is the last time you tilt your whole body like Michael Jackson's incredible 45-degree lean?*
>
> *If we want to look up or down, it's better to pitch the camera instead of the whole Character.*
> *Step 12: Make the PlayerEye camera following the controller's pitch input. Select PlayerEye in the Components panel. Go to the Details panel, and under the Camera Options section, check on the Use Pawn Control Rotation option (Figure 14.12).*

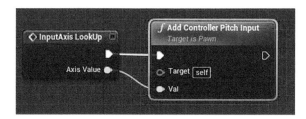

FIGURE 14.10 Implement the LookUp event.

537

FIGURE 14.11 Check the Class Defaults on the Roll, Yaw, Pitch usage.

FIGURE 14.12 Check on the Use Pawn Control Rotation for the PlayerEye.

Play the game again, and now we can look up and down by moving the mouse. If you look down, you can even see the body.

Because we are doing an FPS game, we do not want to see the body of the Character. The simplest approach here is to make the Mesh follow the camera.

Step 13: Make the mesh of the body follow PlayerEye. In the Event Graph of BP_Ellen_FPS, you can also find the Event BeginPlay event. It is already calling another event named Parent: BeginPlay. This Event BeginPlay is an override of the Event BeginPlay of the parent class (BP_Character_Base). The Parent: BeginPlay is a function call to the Event BeginPlay of the parent. What is happening here can be translated in plain English as:

When the game starts, do whatever the parent class does in its Event BeginPlay first.

By adding this Parent: BeginPlay, we are saying that we do not want to ignore what's happening entirely in the parent class. We do whatever the parent does first, and then we can add new stuff afterward. You can add a function call to the overridden function of the parent class in any function you override in the child class.

Drag out from the out execution pin of the Parent: BeginPlay node; search for AttachToComponent; and in the search result, select AttachToComponent (Mesh). An AttachToComponent node got created with the Mesh component automatically connected as the Target. Drag PlayerEye from the Components panel directly to the Parent input pin of the AttachToComponent node. Set the Location, Rotation, and Scale Rule to Keep World so that when attaching, the body does not snap to the camera's location, but it still follows with the offset they have.

What we added here can be translated to plain English as:
When the game starts, attach the mesh of the body to the camera.
Play the game again, look down, and you can no longer see the body because it is now following the camera. However, if you walk below some light and look down, you can still see the shadow of the body, and we do not wish to see the shadow because it is not a full body after all. Select Mesh in the Components panel, and go to the Details panel. Check off the Cast Shadow option under the Lighting section to disable the shadow of the mesh of the body.

We have now successfully created the essential movement control of BP_Ellen_FPS. But there is no animation yet. Let's move on to set up the animations.

Tutorial 14.2: Set Up the Animation

Step 1: Create the Animation Blueprint. Go to the Content Browser, and navigate to Blueprints/Characters/Ellen/Animations folder. Right click and select Animation → Animation Blueprint. In the pop-up Create Animation Blueprint window,

539

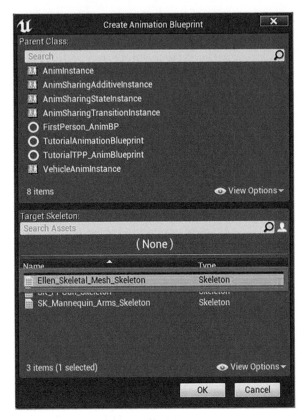

FIGURE 14.13 Create a new Animation Blueprint.

select Ellen_Skeletal_Mesh_Skeleton as the Target Skeleton and click OK. Name the new asset AnimBP_Ellen (Figure 14.13).

Animation Blueprint

Animation Blueprint is a special type of class that controls the animations of a pawn. It has two major components:

Event Graph

The event graph of an Animation Blueprint is the same as other blueprint, and you can program anything here.

Animation Graph

The Animation Graph controls what kind of animation is playing.

Let's set up a basic idle–walk animation.

> Step 2: Gather the moving information in the Event
> Graph. Double click to open AnimBP_Ellen and
> go to the Event Graph. You can see that two
> nodes are already in there. The Event Blueprint
> Update Animation is called every time the game
> updates. The Return Value of the Try Get Pawn
> Owner is the Pawn that uses this blueprint. Drag
> out from the Return Value, search, and create a
> Get Velocity node. The Get Velocity returns a data
> type of vector.

Vector

We have been using vectors for a while now, and the Location, Rotation, and Scale value of an object are all vector data types. A vector is a collection of float values. It can represent a location, a rotation, a scale, or anything that needs multiple float numbers to represent it. In this case, it represents the velocity which is the speed on the X, Y, and Z-directions of the Pawn that uses this Animation Blueprint.

The Vector class in blueprint has three float member variables: X, Y, and Z. Vector can also be viewed as an arrow that has a direction and a length. If we put the start of the arrow at the origin, the tip of the arrow sits at the coordinates of X, Y, and Z. The length of the arrow is the distance from the origin to coordinates X, Y, and Z (Figure 14.14).

We want to check if the player is moving or not. When it comes to velocity, the length of the vector determines the speed. Drag out from the Return Value of the Get Velocity node, search, and create a Vector Length node. Drag out from the Return Value of the Vector Length node and type in ">", and select the float > float option in the list to create a new comparison node. This comparison node returns true if the first input is bigger than the second input.

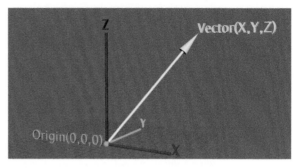

FIGURE 14.14 A vector viewed as an arrow.

What we are checking here is if the length (the speed) of the velocity of the Pawn is bigger than 0.

Drag out from the output pin of the comparison node, and click the promote to variable option right below the search bar. Unreal automatically added a variable to the Blueprint class with the data type of the pin you dragged out (bool in this case) and created a set node to set the value of the new variable. Go to the Details panel and change the Variable name to isMoving.

Connect the out execution pin of the Event Blueprint Update Animation to the input execution pin of the Set node (Figure 14.15).

> *Step 3: Set up idle and walk variables. Go to the lower left corner of the window and you can find the isMoving variable added in the variables section. Add two more variables there (by clicking the "+" button), and change the variable type to Anim Sequence Object Reference in the Details panel. Compile and save the blueprint. Select the IdleAnim in the Variables section, go to the Details panel, and set the Default Value*

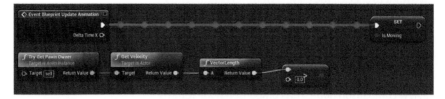

FIGURE 14.15 Gather the moving information in the Event Graph.

FIGURE 14.16 Set up the IdleAnim and WalkAnim variable.

to Ellen_FPS_Gun_Idle. Set the WalkAnim to
Ellen_FPS_Gun_Walk (Figure 14.16).

Step 4: Test animation in the AnimGraph. Go to the
MyBlueprint panel at the lower left corner and
find the Animation Graphs section. Double click
the AnimGraph to open it. This AnimGraph is the
place we define what animation to play for the
Character who uses this animation blueprint.
For now, there is only an Output Pose node.
Whatever that is connected to the Result of this
Output Pose node becomes the final animation.

The Result input pin with a small human
figure is an animation pose pin. We are going to
call this kind of pin pose pin.

Right click in the empty place and type play,
and scroll up to the top of the search list. You can
see all our animations here, and choose any one
of them to create a Play Animation Sequence
node. Its name may say play some animation.
Select this new node and go to the Details panel.
Check on the checker box after the Sequence
label to expose the sequence being played as an
input pin. Drag our IdleAnim from the Variables
to the Sequence input pin of the Play node. Drag
the out pose pin of the Play Animation Sequence
node to the Result in pose pin of the Output
Pose node. Press the Compile and Save button,
and now you can see that the Character in the
viewport at the upper right corner is now playing
the Idle animation (Figure 14.17).

The figure may appear to be the full body
or our FPS body, and it really does not matter
because they share the same skeleton. You can
change it by clicking the Preview Mesh button
in the toolbar above the viewport and select the
other one (Figure 14.17 also shows where this
button is).

Step 5: Set up a state machine for the idle and walk
animation. Delete the two nodes we create in
Step 4. Right click in the space and type Add

543

FIGURE 14.17 Set the IdleAnim as the animation played.

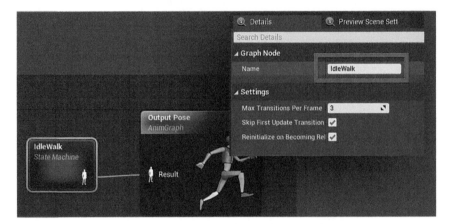

FIGURE 14.18 Create a new state machine and name it IdleWalk and use it as the final pose.

New State Machine to create a state machine node. Select this New State Machine node in the Details panel, and change the Name to IdleWalk. Connect the out pose pin of the IdleWalk to the Result of the Output Pose node (Figure 14.18).

State Machine

When playing a game, your Character is going to enter different states like idling, walking, and shooting. A state machine allows you to define different states and the rules to transition between different states. Let's see how it works for our animation right away.

Double click to open the IdleWalk state machine. Drag out from the pin of the Entry node and select Add State…. This creates a new state. Select it and press F2 to rename it. Let's call it Idle. There is a gray outer rim on every state node. Drag out from the rim of the Idle state and select Add State… again to add another state. Name the new state Walk. Drag from the Walk state and drop the arrow to the rim of the Idle state to create another arrow back to the Idle state (Figure 14.19).

The arrows connected between the states are called transitions. The direction of the arrow defines the direction of the transition. For now, you can see a transition going from the Idle state to the Walk state and another transition going from the Walk state to the Idle state.

Every transition has a rule to decide if the transition should happen. Double click the circle icon with back and forth arrows of the transition from the Idle state to the Walk state to open its rule graph. You can see a Result

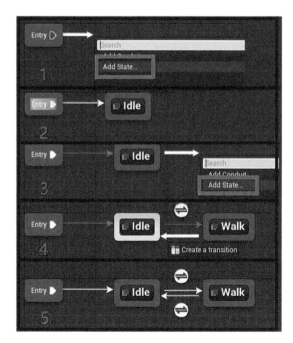

FIGURE 14.19 Steps to create the states and their transitions.

node with a Can Enter Transition input pin in the graph. The color of the input pin is red, which means that it is of the type bool. When the input becomes true, then the transition starts to happen. Drag the isMoving variable to the Can Enter Transition input pin of the Result node.

We want the transition from Idle to walk to happen when the player starts moving. Luckily, we have that information already. In Step 2, we have created a variable called isMoving, and it indicates if the player is moving. Drag the isMoving variable to the Can Enter Transition input pin to make a connection (Figure 14.20).

To translate what we have done here in English is:

> When the player starts to move, transition the state from the Idle state to the Walk state.

Right at the top of the graph, there is a navigation bar. It's like a folder structure that shows where you are in the hierarchy of the whole animation graph (Figure 14.21).

Click the IdleWalk to go back out to the IdleWalk state machine with our two states and the transitions. Let's go into the rule graph of the transition from Walk to Idle and set it up.

For the transition from the Walk state to the Idle state, we want the opposite rule. We can hold down Ctrl and drag the isMoving variable to the graph to create a reference for it. Drag out from the Is Moving node and create a

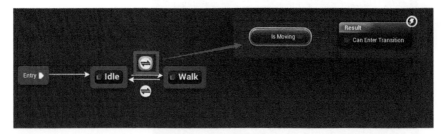

FIGURE 14.20 Use isMoving as the transition rule for the transition from Idle to Walk.

FIGURE 14.21 The navigation bar of the animation graph.

FIGURE 14.22 Set up the transition rule for the transition from Walk to Idle.

NOT Boolean node. Connect the NOT node to the Result (Figure 14.22).

The NOT node is self-explanatory, and it flips the value of the input as its output. What we did here can be translated to English as:

When the player is not moving, transition back to the Idle state.

> Step 6: Define the states. Double click to open the Idle state. You can see an Output Animation Pose node in the graph, whatever connects to it becomes the animation for this Idle state. Repeat what we did in Step 4 to use the IdleAnim variable as the animation for the Output Animation Pose. Go back out and set up the Walk state to use the WalkAnim (Figure 14.23). Compile and save the blueprint.
>
> Step 7: Use the animation blueprint in our player character. Open BP_Character_Base and select Mesh in the Components panel. In the Details panel, set the Anim Class to AnimBP_Ellen (Figure 14.24).

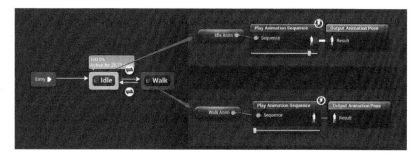

FIGURE 14.23 Set up the states.

547

FIGURE 14.24 Set up the animation class used for the Character.

Play the game now, and we can now see that the Ellen_FPS_Gun_Idle animation is playing. Start moving, and the animation transitions to Ellen_FPS_Gun_Walk smoothly, stop walking, and it also transitions back.

We have now finished some animation set up with the animation blueprint. As you can see, animation blueprint has two major components:

1. An event graph that allows us to communicate with the player character.
2. An animation graph to determine what animation to play.

These two components allow the animation blueprint to know what is going on with the player and play the animations accordingly.

Let's review the unreal engine framework we have covered. So far, we have talked about these major components:

Game Mode

Game mode determines the major classes and the rules of the game. It defines the player character class, the player controller class, HUD, and many other classes the framework has that we have yet to explore.

Player Controller/ Controller/AIController

We have only mentioned their existence. Whenever you start the game, a player controller got created to represent you. It then possesses the default pawn defined in the game mode, which you own through the player controller. Player controller is a child class of Controller. Controller already can possess a pawn, and it's tied up with the pawn and able to react to many things that happened to the pawn. Controller has a child class called AIController, which represents an AI instead of a human player.

Actor

Anything you can place in the level is an actor. It is the parent class of many other classes like Pawn and Character. It is also the parent class of classes that do not necessarily need a physical representation. Game mode is a child class of Actor as well.

Pawn

Pawn is the base class for anything that can be possessed by a controller. A pawn is the physical representation of a controller, and a controller is the soul of a pawn.

Character

Character is a child class of Pawn. It has many built-in features like movements, a mesh to represent the body, and a capsule to represent its collision.

Skeletal Mesh

Skeletal mesh is a class that represents a rigged model with joints that can use different animation assets.

Animation Blueprint

Animation blueprint is a class designed to communicate with a pawn and control the animation of a skeletal mesh through its animation graph.

549

Widget Blueprints

Widget Blueprint is the basic UI class that can be spawned, owned by a player controller, and can be added to the viewport.

As you can gradually see, each class defines a specific type of object and does its own thing. Classes can also talk with each other and tie together into a framework for a working game. How to design these classes is critical for the game and the game engine, and it takes a tremendous amount of experience and testing to polish up and create an optimal design.

One thing we can learn from Unreal Engine's framework here is that classes we define should have specific purposes and can be added, changed, and swapped out. Consider making a game from scratch. You are likely going to create a player character class that has many things built in it. You will probably not have a player controller class in mind. But then you are going to realize that assuming the player and the character the player is playing as one thing has a problem:

What if the character the player is controlling is dead? But the player stays in the games as an observer? What if you want to change the thing the player is controlling from a human character to a tank? Then it makes sense to make the player a different entity other than the character.

There is no best practice on how games should be structured because all games are different. However, the general rule of thumb is to make your system easy to work with and need minimum tweaks when you need to make changes or add new features. Separating different parts of the game into smaller, logically different modules is a great way to achieve that.

We are going to create our weapons in the next chapter, and we are going to design our weapons with the same ideal.

CHAPTER 15

Weapons

Walking around empty-handed is not a very good idea to survive in this highly guarded facility. Let's create some weapons in this chapter to give the player some power. Buckle up, because this chapter is considerably longer and harder than the previous ones—we have a lot to cover.

Before moving on, also be aware that this engine version we are using now is Unreal Engine 4.25. If yours is a different version, the UI layout could be slightly different. Also, we have provided the models for the three weapons we are going to create in the support file, and they are in the folder called weapons. Go ahead and import them to the project, and set up their materials as well.

In this chapter, we are going to implement three weapons:

1. A pipe that can knock down an enemy.
2. A gun that shoots bullets and deals Damage to an enemy.
3. A grenade launcher that shoots out grenades and deals Damage.

Let's analyze what parts of the three weapons can be generalized or, in other words, can be in a parent class.

1. Visual. They all need a physical representation or a model.
2. UI and icon. Most weapons need a UI and an icon. We can add an icon of each weapon to the lower right corner of the game to show the player what they have. For UI, we need crosshair for the gun and the grenade launcher.
3. They all attack in one way or another. It is an abstract idea that can be generalized.
4. Attack damage. Again, not all of them need it, but a general part that most weapons would have.
5. Reloading. Well, the pipe cannot reload, but an electric staff that shoots out lighting balls might need some sort of recharging. Reloading is also an abstract idea here. We assume that most weapons need to replenish at some point, and we choose to include this for the scalability of the game.
6. Animations. All animations needed for walking, idle, Attack, and Reloading need to be specified.
7. Attachment. We need to define how the player should hold these weapons.
8. Hotkey. We need a keyboard or gamepad short cut for each weapon.

As you can see, we need plenty of stuff already, and they can all be generalized into a base class, just like the BP_Triggerable we created for anything that can be triggered. You can come up with your own list of stuff you think that you want in all your weapons, and sometimes you just have to start working on it to know what is needed. You cannot predict everything you ever need. It is common to modify this list during development, so we are not married to any of these ideas yet.

Meanwhile, we also have to develop our player character while developing the weapons for picking up a weapon, reloading, attacking, and switch weapons.

Let's start with making a base weapon class that all other weapons will inherit from. We are going to use the pipe to set up a base class; the asset of the pipe is provided in the support files if you are using your project.

Tutorial 15.1: Create a Base Weapon Class

Step 1: Create a blueprint class. Create a new folder called Weapons in the Blueprints folder. Inside the folder, create a new blueprint class, pick Actor as its parent class, and name it BP_Weapon_Base.

Step 2: Add visual representation to the class. Open BP_Weapon_Base, add a StaticMesh component to it, and name the component Mesh. Set the Static Mesh to weapon_pipe (Figure 15.1).

We chose pipe just to be able to see something. The child classes will define their visuals differently by changing this static mesh.

To be able to hold it in the character's hand, we need to define where precisely in the hand of the player character to attach it. We can achieve that by defining a socket in the skeletal mesh of the player character.

FIGURE 15.1 Add visuals to the base class.

553

Step 3: Set up the socket for the pipe. Go to
Blueprints/Characters/Ellen/MeshAssets/ and
*double click to open Ellen_Skeletal_Mesh_*
Skeleton. Click on the Preview Animation in the
*toolbar at the top of the UI and choose FPS_*
Pipe_Idle. The mesh now plays the FPS_Pipe_Idle
animation. It doesn't matter if you see the
full-body mesh or the FPS mesh in the viewport
because you can change the Preview Mesh to the
other one if you wish. The animation is playing,
click on the pause button at the bottom of the
window to pause it.

In the Skeleton Tree list, find r_wrist,
right click on it, and select Add Socket. A
new socket called r_wristSocket got added
to the list, double click, and rename it to
PipeHandSocket.

Socket

There are plenty of times you need to attach something
to the character, and you can attach anything to any joint
of the skeletal mesh. However, it is improbable that you
want the attachment to be precisely where the joint is,
but preferably with an offset. You can add a socket as a
predefined location in the hierarchy of a skeleton for you
to attach anything to it. Any joint can behave like a socket
as well.

Right click on PipeHandSocket and select Add Preview
Asset, search, and select weapon_pipe. Go to the
viewport, move, and rotate it to make the pipe fit into the
hands nicely (Figure 15.2). Press the Save button to save
the changes.

Step 4: Add an attachment variable. Go back to
BP_Weapon_Base. Add a new variable and
name it EquipSocketName. Make the Variable
Type Name, compile it, and set the Default value
to PipeHandSocket. We add this variable, so the
weapon can always refer to it to find the correct
attachment (Figure 15.3).

Now the weapon knows where it should
attach to, let's make the character to hold it.
Step 5: Create a function for the character to acquire
a new weapon. Go back to BP_Character_Base.

FIGURE 15.2 Add a socket for the hands.

FIGURE 15.3 Add a variable to store the name of the socket the weapon should attach to.

> Add a new custom event (right click and
> search for add custom event), and name it
> AcquireNewWeapon. Go to the Details panel and
> add a new input parameter to it. Name the new
> parameter WeaponClass and change its type to
> BP_Weapon_Base; make sure that you choose
> Class Reference (Figure 15.4).

FIGURE 15.4 Add a new custom event to make the character acquire a new weapon.

FIGURE 15.5 Create Spawn Actor from Class node and call it with AcquireNewWeapon.

By choosing a class reference, we are taking in a class instead of an object of a class. We can now use this class to spawn a weapon:

Create a Spawn Actor from Class (right click and search) node. Connect the out execution pin of AcquireNewWeapon to the in execution pin of the Spawn Actor NONE node to call it with AcquireNewWeapon. Connect the Weapon Class pin of AcquireNewWeapon to the Class input pin of the Spawn Actor NONE node (Figure 15.5).

For the Spawn Transform, we can use the transform of the socket. Hold down Ctrl and drag the Mesh from the Components panel to the graph to create a reference for it. Drag out from the pin of the new Mesh node, search, and create a Get Socket Transform node. Connect the Return Value of the Get Socket Transform node to the Spawn Transform input pin of the SpawnActor node.

For the In Socket Name, drag out from the Weapon Class pin of the AcquireNewWeapon, search, and create a Get Class Defaults node. Drag the Equip Socket Name pin of the Get Class Defaults node to the In Socket Name of the Get Socket Transform node (Figure 15.6).

This piece of code spawns a BP_Weapon_Base at the socket of the weapon.

Click the expansion arrow at the bottom of the SpawnActor node, and you can see that we can specify an owner and an instigator for this new weapon.

FIGURE 15.6 Set the Spawn Transform as the transform of the equip socket of the weapon.

Owner

Owner is a handy member variable of the actor class, and it is used to store the logical Owner of the Actor.

Instigator

Instigator is another handy member variable of the actor class, and it should store the logical instigator of the damage or other events this Actor causes.

The Owner and instigator of an actor could be the same thing, and they usually are. However, consider a grenade of a grenade launcher; logically, the grenade launcher is the Owner of the grenade, but the instigator should be the player who is holding the grenade launcher. After all, it is the player who pulls the trigger. It is also common for an actor to have no owner or instigator. These are abstract concepts that are built-in in Unreal Engine, and other systems in the engine use them as part of the payload data. In our case, we want this BP_Character_Base as the Owner and instigator of the new weapon.

Right click in an empty area and search for "self", in the drop-down list, select Get a reference to self. Connect this new Self node to the Owner and Instigator input pin of the SpawnActor node (Figure 15.7).

Finally, create an AttachActorToComponent node, and call it with the SpawnActor node. Use the return value of the Spawn actor node as the Target, use the Mesh as the Parent, and use the Equip Socket Name of the Get Class Defaults node as the Socket name. Set the Location, Rotation, and Scale rules to Snap to Target.

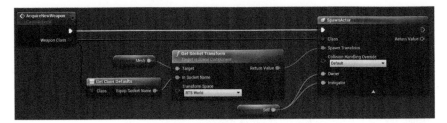

FIGURE 15.7 Use the character itself as the Owner and Instigator of the SpawnActor node.

Notice that the line connecting from the Equip Socket Name of the Get Class Defaults node to the Socket Name of the AttachActorToComponent node is too long. The line is also overlapping the nodes in the middle. Double click anywhere on the line to create a reroute node, and move the reroute node to make the line go around other nodes (Figure 15.8).

What we did with this AcquireNewWeapon can be translated to plain English as:

> *Create a new weapon and attach it to the corresponding slot of the mesh.*

The Get Class Default node is self-explanatory; it gives us the values of the variables we set up in the class. AttachActorToComponent attaches Target to Parent. If there is a specified socket name, the attachment is to the socket. Otherwise, the attachment attaches to the root of Parent.

Figure 15.8 shows all the things we did in Step 5. As you can see, node-based scripting or visual scripting can get complicated quickly, and good organization becomes very important.

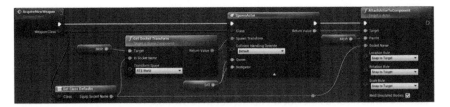

FIGURE 15.8 Attach the new weapon to the Mesh.

558

Why?

We implemented this function or event in BP_Character_Base class instead of the BP_Ellen_FPS. The reason is primarily for the scalability of the game. We can create AI characters based on BP_Character_Base as well, and the AI should have the ability to acquire a weapon right away.

As you have gotten familiar with blueprint scripting, from now on, let's omit trivial details of the creation and connect of the nodes to save your reading time. We are going to focus on mentioning the essential part of the node graph.

Step 6: Test our function. Zoom out of the graph, find the Event BeginPlay event, and call our AcquireNewWeapon function with Event BeginPlay. Play the game and you should see the character now holding the pipe (Figure 15.9).

There are two flaws here. First of all, try to move around, and you will have a hard time moving forward. This is because the pipe is colliding with you. Secondly, the animations are for the gun and not the pipe. Let's address these two issues.

Step 7: Fix the weapon collision. Open BP_Weapon_Base and select the Mesh in the Components panel. In the Details panel, find the Collision section and set Collision Presets to NoCollision. Play the game again and you should be able to move freely.

Step 8: Add animation variables to the weapon class. Add two more variables to BP_Weapon_Base, and set their variable type to Anim Sequence object reference. Name the first one IdleAnim,

FIGURE 15.9 Call AcquireNewWeapon with Event BeginPlay and do a playtest.

559

and set its default value to Ellen_FPS_Pipe_Idle. Name the second one WalkAnim and set its default value to Ellen_FPS_Pipe_Walk.

Adding these two variables does not do anything good for us, and we need to let the animation blueprint know and use them. Also, we will implement weapon switching and pick up functionalities. Every time we pick up a new weapon or switched to another weapon, the animations in the animation blueprint should update. Let's create a variable to store the current active weapon and implement a function that can spit out the idle and walk animation of that weapon.

Step 9: Create a current active weapon variable. Go back to BP_Character_Base and add a new variable. Name the new variable CurrentActiveWeapon and set the variable type to BP_Weapon_Base object reference. Go to the AcquireNewWeapons, break the connections between the SpawnActor node and the AttachActorToComponent node, and insert a Set Current Active Weapon Node in-between (Figure 15.10).

Step 10: Create a function to get the animations from the current active weapon. Add a new function to BP_Character_Base and call it GetActiveWeaponAnims. Implement it as Figure 15.11.

Be aware that this is a function added by clicking the "+" button in the Functions section under the My Blueprint panel. We had created a function before when we

FIGURE 15.10 Add a new CurrentActiveWeapon variable and set it in AcquireNewWeapon.

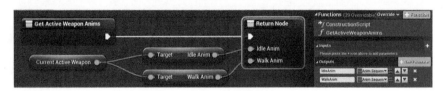

FIGURE 15.11 The implementation of the GetActiveWeaponAnims function.

were doing the BP_Triggerable. We created a function instead of a custom event because we need to have return values. Return values are added by selecting the entry node of the function and click the "+" sign in the Outputs section of the Details panel.

The body of the function is relatively simple. We get the CurrentActiveWeapon and get its idle and walk animation as the return values of the function.

Step 11: Call the function in the animation blueprint to update the animations. Go to Content/ Blueprints/Characters.Ellen/Animations and open AnimBP_Ellen. Go to the My Blueprint panel and double click the EventGraph under the Graphs section to go to its event graph. After the SET node, add the blueprint script shown in Figure 15.12.

By using the Try Get Pawn Owner function, we can get the pawn that this blueprint is attached to. In our case, the Owner is our BP_Character_Base, so we cast it to BP_Character_Base to get access to the GetActiveWeaponAnims function. We then call that function and use its return values to update our IdleAnim and WalkAnim variables.

Play the game again, and now you should see that the correct idle and walk animation are being used for the pipe. Just like how we get the IsMoving set up before for the animation blueprint, we have now set up the animations as well.

What is happening now is that the animation blueprint constantly updates its IdleAnim and WalkAnim by calling the GetActiveWeaponAnims function of BP_Character_Base and uses them as the animation in the state machine.

FIGURE 15.12 Call the GetActiveWeaponAnims function in the animation blueprint to update its animation.

However, when you press the escape button to stop playing, a Message Log window pops up and shows two errors. They all read as "Accessed None trying to read property CurrentActiveWeapon." The message also shows where the error occurs; in this case, the return node of the GetActiveWeaponAnims function.

At the very beginning of the game, the animation blueprint is already calling GetActiveWeapons. At that moment, the AcquireNewWeapon is not called or maybe not at the step of setting up the CurrentActiveWeapon variable yet. The value of the CurrentActiveWeapon variable is empty or None. We cannot pull data from an empty variable because there is no data, and this is why we got the errors. If you think about it now, there are two design flaws in our current set up:

1. What if the player hasn't picked any weapon yet? We do want the player to have no weapons at the beginning of the game and will pick up new weapons while exploring the level.
2. We do not need the animations to be updated every time the game updates; we only need to change them when the player picks up or switches to a different weapon.

Knowing what you want in your game is critical when it comes to design the structure of your game. In our case, the player will have no weapon at the beginning. And when they pick up a new weapon or switch to another one, we want to put the hands-down first. We then attach the new weapon to the hands off-screen and raise the hands with the correct animation associated with that attached weapon. Let's make that hands-down animation first and use that to drive the weapon pickup and switching mechanics.

> Step 12: Set up a weapon switch animation. Make sure that you save your blueprints. Close and reopen Ellen_Skeletal_Mesh_Skeleton so that no preview animation is used. Go to the toolbar at the top of the window, and click Create Asset → Create Animation → Current Pose. Select the Animations folder in the pop-up window, and

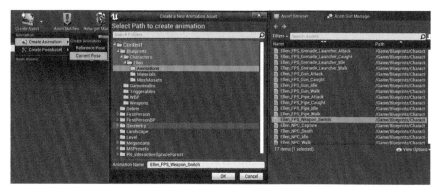

FIGURE 15.13 Create a new animation asset.

*set the Animation Name to Ellen_FPS_Weapon_
Switch. Unreal now creates a new animation,
and we can see it in the list of the Asset Browser
at the lower right corner of the window
(Figure 15.13). It is also currently selected.*

Persona

The window we see now is called Persona. It collects all
the essential parts of the skeletal mesh. At the top right
of the window, you can see five major parts: the skeleton,
the mesh, the animation, the animation blueprint, and the
physics assets. We can quickly switch to these assets by
clicking on them. Figure 15.14 shows the break down of
the UI.

FIGURE 15.14 The UI of the Sedona window.

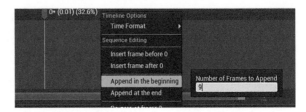

FIGURE 15.15 Append 9 frames at the beginning of the animation.

The buttons in the red box allow us to switch to other assets associated with the skeletal mesh quickly. The blue box is the Asset Browser, and it has a list of all the animations. The area in the yellow box is the timeline, where we can edit the animation and add other gameplay elements. We have talked about the other parts already.

So far, this new animation we added has one frame, as indicated at the bottom of the timeline. Right click anywhere on the timeline and select Append in the beginning. Type in 9 for the Number of Frames to Append and hit Enter. We now have ten frames in total. Click the Pause button at the bottom left corner of the timeline to pause the animation playback (Figure 15.15).

Why?

Ten frames for a switching animation seem to be too little, but we want the player to feel the game being super responsive. In many cases, it is not about how realistic the game is. It is about how good the user experience is.

In the Skeleton Tree panel, select spine_04. Rotate it to bend the body forward in the viewport (about 60 degrees) and press the S key on the keyboard to add a key. It doesn't matter on which frame we added the key because we only need a fixed bend-down pose. Click the Apply button in the toolbar to commit the changes.

Go to the Asset Details panel (it is shuffled with the Skeleton Tree panel). Under the Additive Settings section, set the Additive Anim Type to Local Space. This animation now becomes an animation that will be added on top of other animations when used. The Base Pose Type is

Skeleton Reference. This setting means that it calculates the difference between the poses in this animation with the default skeleton pose in local space and extracts the delta as the additive or offset information (Figure 15.16). Press the Save button to save the asset.

> Step 13: Create the weapon switch animation montage. Click the Create Asset again and select Anim Montage. Name it Ellen_FPS_Weapon_ Switch_Montage and hit ok. Unreal now has created an animation montage for us and opened it in Persona. Notice that it shows with a blue icon in the Asset Browser. Go to the Asset browser, find, and drag Ellen_FPS_Weapon_ Switch to the DefaultGroup.DefaultSlot row of the timeline (Figure 15.17). Press the Save button to save the asset.
> Go to the Asset Details panel. Open the Blend In and Blend Out sections in the Blend Options section. Set both Blend Time settings to 0.15. This makes the animation to blend in and out in 0.15 seconds.

FIGURE 15.16 Add a bend down key pose to the animation and set it to local space additive animation.

FIGURE 15.17 Drag Ellen_FPS_Weapon_Switch to the Ellen_FPS_Weapon_Switch_Montage.

Animation Montage

From time to time, we just want to quickly play an animation on top of the current state machine animations, and Animation Montage is designed for that purpose. Animation montage montages the animation in it on top of others. Animation montage has a slot assigned to it. The default slot for a new animation montage is DefaultGroup.DefaultSlot. When we ask the engine to play an animation montage, it finds its slot in the AnimGraph of the animation blueprint and plays its animation over there. Let's add the slot in the animation graph.

Step 14: Add the DefaultSlot. Click the Blueprint button at the top right corner of the window to switch to our animation blueprint. Double click the AnimGraph in the My Blueprint panel to open the animation graph. Create a Slot 'Default Slot' node and insert it in-between IdleWalk and the Output Pose (Figure 15.18). Compile and save the animation blueprint. Remember, you can Alt-click on any pin to delete the connections to it.

Step 15: Add a custom event to play the animation montage. Go back to BP_Character_Base. Create a new custom event called SwitchActiveWeaponTo and implement it as shown in Figure 15.19. The Montage to Play is set to Ellen_FPS_Weapon_Switch_Montage.

We will add more stuff to this function, so it does what the name says. For now, we are just testing the animation montage.

Step 16: Test the animation Montage with the fire button. Create an InputAction Fire node and call the SwitchActiveWeaponTo with InputActionFire (Figure 15.20).

Play the game again, try left clicking, and you can see the hands go down and back up again.

FIGURE 15.18 Add the DefaultSlot to the AnimGraph.

FIGURE 15.19 Create a SwitchActiveWeaponTo function.

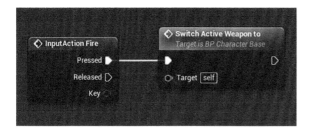

FIGURE 15.20 Add a call to the SwitchActiveWeaponTo event with InputAction Fire.

Ok, we have gone through many small things here to get to this stage. Let's explain what is going on when we left click before adding too much stuff.

When we press the left mouse button, the system triggers the fire event (defined in the input bindings). The fire event calls the SwitchActiveWeaponTo event, which asks the Mesh to play the Ellen_FPS_Weapon_ Switch_Montage animation montage. Ellen_ FPS_Weapon_Switch_Montage is assigned with the DefaultGroup.DefaultSlot, and the Mesh finds that slots in the AnimGraph of the animation blueprint and plays the animation montage there. The animation in the montage (Ellen_FPS_Weapon_Switch) is additive. So, the montage adds on top of the current Ellen_FPS_Pipe_Idle animation to bend the body down. The body then bends down smoothly in 0.15 seconds and bends back up after the animation is over (in 0.15 seconds as well).

As you can see, the whole system works in a somewhat complicated way. This is the nature of Unreal Engine. It is not an easy engine, like what we have covered before;

Unreal values professionalism and scalability more than simplicity. You will constantly see Unreal Engine enforces workflows like this that you don't grasp right away. However, once you finally understand it, you will realize that it is probably the best way (although strange sometimes) to do it.

Let's go back and think about what the weapon should do when it comes to acquiring or switching new weapons. Because we are doing an FPS game, we don't have to put the weapon somewhere else when we equip it or switch it out. Whenever we got a new weapon, it attaches and remains attached to the hands, but we make it invisible first. When we switch to one of the weapons, we play the animation montage to make the hands go down. When they are off-screen, we hide whatever is currently visible (or not if the hands are empty). We then unhide the weapon we want to switch to, update the animations, and then the hands go back up with the new weapon.

That means that the weapon has two states: in inventory and in hand. In inventory means that it is invisible; in hand means that it is visible. Let's create two functions in the BP_Weapon_Base class to change the weapon to these two states.

Step 17: Create a WeaponInInventory and a WeaponInHand custom event. Open BP_Weapon_Base and quickly implement a WeaponInInventory and a WeaponInHand custom event as shown in Figure 15.21.

The Set Visibility function sets the visibility of the Target input. Make sure that you drag the DefaultSceneRoot from the Components to the Target and check on Propagate to Children so everything will be toggled.

FIGURE 15.21 Implementation of the WeaponInInventory and a WeaponInHand custom event.

*Step 18: Use the WeaponInInventory function
in the AcquireNewWeapon functions. Go
back to the AcuqireNewWeapon function
of BP_Character_Base and delete the Set
node between SpawnActor and AttachActor
ToComponent. Drag out from the Return Value
of the SpawnActor node, search, and create
a call to Weapon in Inventory as shown in
Figure 15.22. Make sure that you still call the
AttchActorToComponent eventually.*

*What we have changed here is when we
get a new weapon, we put it in the inventory
first (which makes it invisible). After this step,
we then have to play the weapon switch
animation montage to put the hands down.
Then we make the weapon visible (by calling
WeaponInHand) and tell the animation
blueprint to update to the new animations,
and then the hands go back up. We can put
these parts in the SwichActiveWeaponTo
event.*

*Step 19: Refine SwitchActiveWeaponTo. Add a new
Input parameter to the SwichActiveWeaponTo,
name the parameter NewActiveWeapon, and
make the variable-type BP_Weapon_Base.
Drag out from the New Active Weapon of the
SwitchActiveWeaponTo and select Promote
to variable. A new variable got automatically
added, and a Set node got created as well. This
is a quick way to make a new variable and set
its value. We will not mention steps like this
anymore. When you see a Set node like this with
a variable name you haven't seen before please
assume that we created a new variable with the
Promote to variable command.*

*Name the new variable
PendingNextActiveWeapon, and the Set node
automatically changes. Connect the Set node
as Figure 15.23.*

FIGURE 15.22 Call WeaponInInventory after spawning the weapon.

569

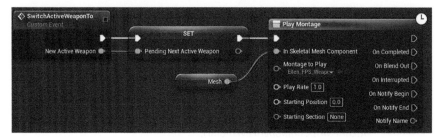

FIGURE 15.23 Modified SwitchActiveWeaponTo custom event.

While we are at it, let's also add a call to SwitchActiveWeaponTo at the End of the AcquireNewWeapon event (Figure 15.24).

Notice that we added two reroute nodes between the Return Value (the spawned new weapon) and the New Active Weapon input parameter of the SwitchActiveWeaponTo node. You can create a reroute node, just like how you create other nodes (right click and search). What we are doing here is after acquiring a new weapon, we want to switch to it right away.

However, the SwitchActiveWeaponTo does nothing more than set a PendingNextActiveWeapon variable and play the animation montage at the moment. Play the game now, and we no longer see the pipe or the hands. Quit the game and we even get more errors. Luckily, they are all complaining about one thing: the CurrentActiveWeapon is None. This makes sense because we never set it after we adjust the code. We want to set it when it is actually in hand and that should

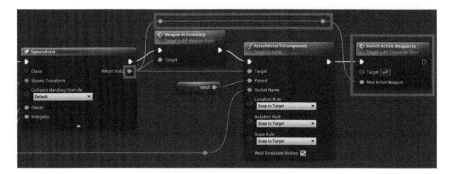

FIGURE 15.24 Add a call to SwitchActiveWeaponTo at the End of the AcquireNewWeapon event.

happen when the hands are down during the animation montage. To know when the hands are down, we can place an animation notify in the animation montage.

Step 20: Add an animation notify. Go to Blueprints/ Characters/Animations/ and find Ellen_FPS_ Weapon_Switch_Montage. Double click to open it, and press the space bar to pause the animation playback. There are multiple sections of the timeline listed at the left side column. The Montage section has our Ellen_FPS_Weapon_ Switch animation, and this is the part that you populate animation assets for the montage. The Notifies section underneath is where we can add animation notifies, and there is currently one track named "1" in it. Right click anywhere of that one track in the timeline and select Add Notify → New Notify. In the pop-up Notify Name, type in WeaponSwitchHandDown as its name and press Enter to add it. A diamond-shaped point with a WeaponSwitchHandDown sticker got place in the timeline; drag it to reposition it around frame 5 (Figure 15.25).

When the animation montage is playing, it fires an event called WeaponSwitchHandDown when the animation reaches frame 5, and this is the time the hands should be down at the lowest point. To listen to that event, we just need to add a call to it in the animation blueprint. Let's go ahead and do that.

Step 21: Add an AnimNotify event. Go to the event graph of the animation blueprint (you can switch to different graphs by double clicking them in the My Blueprint panel). Right click in the graph and search for WeaponSwitchHandDown, and there should be only one option called Event AnimNitofy_WeaponSwitchHandDown. Click on it to add it to the graph. This event runs when

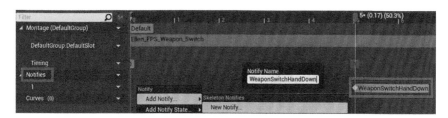

FIGURE 15.25 Add an animation notify.

571

the notify is hit in the timeline. Let's print out a "Hands are down" message with it using the print function (Figure 15.26).

Play the game now, and you can see that the message got printed, and every time you left click, the message will be printed after five frames because that is when the notify is hit in the timeline.

Step 22: Create a function to set up the active weapon. Go back to BP_Character_Base. Create a function called WeaponSwitchHandsDownNotify. Add a Sequence node, and press the Add pin label of the Sequence node to add another pin. Construct the rest of the function as Figure 15.27.

This WeaponSwitchHandsDownNotify event does two things:

First of all, it checks if there is a CurrentActiveWeapon by passing it through an Is Valid node, and then calls its WeaponInInventory event to hide it.

Second, it sets the CurrentActiveWeapon variable to be the PendingNextActiveWeapon we set up in the SwitchActiveWeaponTo event. This should set the value of the CurrentActiveWeapon to the new weapon we acquired. It then calls the WeaponInHand function to make the new weapon visible.

FIGURE 15.26 Add the AnimNotify and print out a message with it.

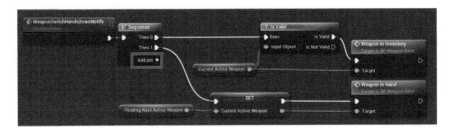

FIGURE 15.27 Implement a WeaponSwitchHandsDownNotify event.

The Sequence is a convenient way of saying do one thing first and then the next one. So, it will do Then 0 followed by Then 1, and you can add more pins to do more stuff in a sequence. We use it to make the graph easier to understand. The function can also be done like Figure 15.28, and you have to call the Set node after both the Weapon in Inventory and Is Not Valid execution pin.

We chose to use the sequence node because it looks clean.

Step 23: Call WeaponSwitchHandsDownNotify in the animation blueprint. Go back to the animation blueprint. Remove the print node and reconstruct the AnimNitofy_WeaponSwitchHandDown event as Figure 15.29. Delete all the nodes after the Set Is Moving node in the Event Blueprint Update Animation event.

What happens now is when the animation notify fires, we call the WeaponSwitchHandsDownNotify event of the BP_Character base, and the function does the show and hide of the weapons and updates the value of the CurrentActiveWeapon variable. After that, we then gather the new animations for the animation blueprint.

To be able to see the result, go to BP_Character_Base and insert a Delay node between Event BeginPlay and Acquire New Weapon. Set the Duration of the Delay node to 2.0 (Figure 15.30). This Delay node adds a 2-second delay before calling the Acquire New Weapon event.

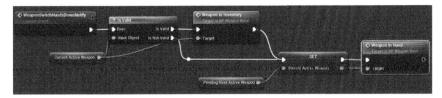

FIGURE 15.28 Alternative way to construct the function without a Sequence node.

FIGURE 15.29 New body of the AnimNitofy_WeaponSwitchHandDown event.

573

FIGURE 15.30 Add a 2-second delay before calling the Acquire New Weapon event.

Play the game again and now you can see that we start with the gun idle animation. After 2 seconds, the hands go down and come back again with the pipe. The animation is also switched correctly.

Step 24: Remove the gun animations. We should not be playing the animations of the gun at the beginning of the game. Go to the Animation blueprint, and select the IdleAnim variable in the Variables section. Go to the Details panel, click the drop-down of the default value of the IdleAnim, and select clear to make it empty. When it's empty, the default pose is used. You can also delete the InputAction Fire event. It is only created for testing.

Play the game one more time, and the player should now start with no animations. After 2 seconds, the player's character pulls out a pipe.

If you are having trouble keeping track of what is going on, you can create diagrams like Figure 15.31 to have an overview of the series of events. Diagrams like this can also be a tool for planning the program.

We are not entirely done with this part yet. We will revisit it after we have more than one weapon. Meanwhile, let's move on to add the attack animation.

Step 25: Create the Attack animation montage. Go to Blueprints/Characters/Ellen/Animations and find Ellen_FPS_Pipe_Attack. This animation is the Attack animation of the pipe. Right click on it and select Create → Create AnimMontage. An animation montage got created in the same folder; press Enter to use the default name Unreal gives it (Ellen_FPS_Pipe_Attack_Montage).

Open BP_Weapon_Base, select the WalkAnim variable, press Ctrl+W

AquireNewWeapon
1. Creat a new weapon
2. Hide it (Weapon in inventory)
3. Attach it to the hand

SwitchActiveWeaponTo
1. Store the new weapon as a variable(Pending\extActiveWeapon)
2. Play the Switch weapon animation montage

Montage plays
1. Aniamtion plays as additive and bends the body down
   The hands are down in the animation after 5 frames
2. Montage hits the notify in the timeline
3. Anim\otify_WeaponSwitchHandDown is triggered.

AnimNotify_WeaponSwitchHandDown
1. Finds the character and calls
   the WeaponSwitchHandsDown\otify event

WeaponSwitchHandsDownNotify
1. Make the current active weapon invisible(WeaponInInventory)
2. Set the current active weapon as the new weapon
   (Pending\extActiveWeapon)
3. Makes the new current active weapon visible(WeaponInHand)

2. Get the new animations from the character and
use them as the IdleAnim and WalkAnim

4. Montage keeps going and eventually blends back

FIGURE 15.31 A diagram to show the game logic of the acquire and switch weapons.

*to duplicate it, and name it AttackAM.
Change the variable type of AttackAM
to Anim Montage object reference.
Compile and save the blueprint and then
set the default value of AttackAM to
Ellen_FPS_Pipe_Attack_Montage.*

Step 26: *Create an event to play the attack
animation montage. Create a PlayAttackAM
event for BP_Weapon_Base as shown in
Figure 15.32.*

*This PlayAttackAM event does what
the name says: play the attack animation
montage. The Get Owner function returns*

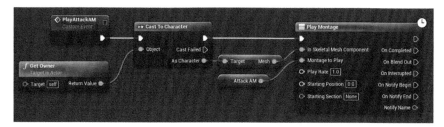

FIGURE 15.32 Create a PlayAttackAM custom event.

the Owner of this weapon; if you do recall, we set it to the BP_Character_Base that acquires this weapon in the AcquireNewWeapon function. The return value is an actor, and we cast it to a character so we can get access to its Mesh component. We then ask its Mesh component to play the AttackAM animation montage.

Step 27: Refactor the part to get the Mesh component into a function. We will need to get the Mesh component in other places of BP_Weapon_Base. Let's refactor this part of the code into a function to clean up our code. With the Get Owner, Cast To Character, and Target Mesh selected, right click on any one of them and select Collapse to Function. A new function got created that has all three nodes inside. Go to the My Blueprint panel, select the New_Funcntion_0, press F2, and rename it to GetPawnSkeletalMesh (Figure 15.33).

Step 28: Make the function blueprint pure. Select GetPawnSkeletalMesh in the My Blueprint panel. Go to the Details panel and check on the Pure checkbox. The function is now a pure function. Pure functions do not have execution pins; they are called when their return values are used (Figure 15.34).

Step 29: Make an empty CommitAttackAnimNotify event. We want to do the real attacking things like deal damage or launch a grenade at some

FIGURE 15.33 Refactor the part to get the skeletal mesh of the pawn into a function.

FIGURE 15.34 Convert GetPawnSkeletalMesh into a pure function.

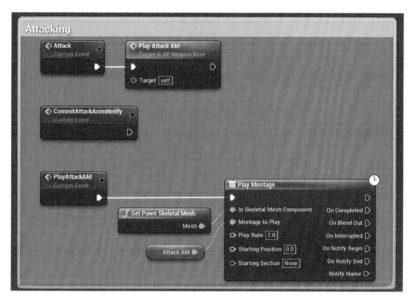

FIGURE 15.35 The Implementation of the Attacking part of the weapon.

*point in the animation. The event doesn't
necessarily happen at the beginning of the
animation. We can use animation notify to
inform the weapon at the time we really want
to do the attacking things. Create a new custom
event called CommitAttackAnimNotify and leave
it empty.*

*Step 30: Create the Attack event. Create a
new custom event and call it Attack. Call
PlayAttackAM with it. Drag a big marquee
selection box to select all the nodes of the
Attack, the CommitAttackAnimNotify, and
the PlayAttackAM event. Press the C button on
the keyboard to make a comment box. Type
in Attacking to rename the box to Attacking
(Figure 15.35).*

Comment Box

You can select any nodes and press the C button to warp
them around with a comment box. This comment box
does nothing to the programming, and it is a note for
organization purposes only. You can drag the title of the
box to move the entire box around.

Step 31: Set up the attack input. Go to BP_Ellen_FPS. Add the InputAction Fire event here, and implement it as shown in Figure 15.36. Play the game again, and you can now left click to attack after the player character gets the pipe.

Step 32: Fire the CommitAttackAnimNotify with an animation notify. Open Ellen_FPS_Pipe_Attack_Montage and add an animation notify at the time that the pipe attack animation seems to about to hit something. Call this new notify CommitAttack (Figure 15.37).

Go to the animation blueprint and implement the notify event as shown in Figure 15.38.

What is happening now is when we left click, the player character calls the attack

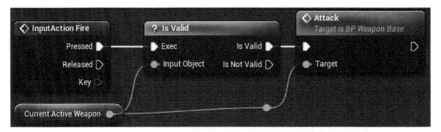

FIGURE 15.36 Set up the attack input.

FIGURE 15.37 Add a CommitAttack animation notify to the Ellen_FPS_Pipe_Attack_Montage.

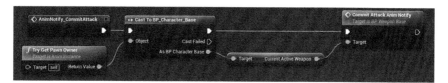

FIGURE 15.38 Implement the AnimNotify_CommitAttack event.

function of the active weapon, and it then
plays the animation montage. When the
montage hits the CommitAttack animation
notify, it calls the CommitAttackAnimNotify
event of the active weapon. This structure is
very similar to the structure of the acquired
new weapon part. You will see this structure
being used for the reload as well.

Why?

Alrighty, we have made a weapon class and able to attack
with it. Well, only with animation, that is. However, it is
pretty exciting already, and we have made a few things
that may make your head tile and frown. You could argue
that some of the things could be more straightforward.
The attacking part we just did, for example:

Why don't we just call Play montage with the Attack
event?
Why do we create an empty event called
CommitAttackAnimNotify?

Well, for the first question, attacking and play-attacking
animation are two different things, and attacking needs
to do the play-animation montage, but what if you are out
of ammo? We separate these two functions so that we can
insert more logic, and we combine these steps differently
for different child classes. This coding style is also called
abstraction. It helps with the scalability of the game. It is
abstract because it does apply to all weapons. It works for
the weapon we have now, and it is going to work for the
weapons we decided to add in anytime later on.

For the second question, yes, it is empty, and it is going to
remain empty. We call this kind of empty function virtual

functions. It is empty because there is nothing we can generalize here; the pipe and the gun attack in entirely different ways. In BP_Weapon_Base, we just set up the calling of this event, and the child classes will override the CommitAttackNotify with whatever things they need to do, things like apply Damage or launch a grenade.

Step 33: Make a BP_Pipe, a BP_Gun, and a BP_Grenade_Launcher class. Right click on BP_Weapon_Base and select create child class, and name the new class BP_Pipe. Create two more classes the same way, name one of them BP_Gun and another one BP_Grenade_Launcher.
Open BP_Gun and change the Static Mesh setting of the Mesh component to gun_Gun_body. We also have the gun_Gun_clip and the gun_bullets model for the gun. Drag these two assets from the Content Browser to the Components to add them, and don't forget to set their collision presets to NoCollison as well. Open BP_Grenade_Launcher and just change the Mesh to Grenade_launcher. Figure 15.39 shows the hierarchy of the classes and the setting of the gun and the grenade launcher.

Step 34: Set up the socket and Attack montage of the gun. Set up the socket of the gun the same way we set up the pipe and name it GunHandSocket. If the pipe is in the way, right click the PipeHandSocket and select Remove All Attached Assets (Figure 15.40).

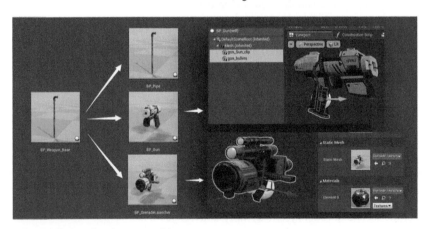

FIGURE 15.39 The hierarchy and appearance of the weapons.

FIGURE 15.40 Set up the socket of the gun.

FIGURE 15.41 Use the already existing CommitAttack notify in Ellen_FPS_Gun_Attack_Montage.

> *Create the attack animation montage of the gun the same way we created Ellen_FPS_Pipe_Attack_Montage. However, when you create the animation notify, instead of adding a new one, you can find the CommitAttack in Add Notify → Skeleton Notifies → CommitAttack (Figure 15.41).*
>
> *Step 35: Populate the variables of BP_Gun. Open BP_Gun. Select the BP_Gun(self) in the Components panel. In the Details panel, change the Equip Socket Name to GunHandSocket. Set the Idle Anim, Walk Anim, and Attack AM to the ones of the gun.*
>
> *Step 36: Set up BP_GrenadeLauncher. Add the socket and animation montage for the grenade launcher and set up BP_GrenadeLauncher the same way we set up BP_Gun.*
>
> *Step 37: Test the three weapons. Open BP_Character_Base and find Event BeginPlay. Change the Weapon Class of the Acquire New Weapon function call in the Event BeginPlay to BP_Pipe, BP_Gun, or BP_GrenadeLauncher. Play the game again and you can see all three of them work as expected. After creating the base class, we can quickly create child classes, and they should work with minimal setup. When we have a class that is inheriting a parent class, we can also say that the class is derived from the parent class. In this case, all three weapons are derived from BP_Weapon_Base. If we ever need another weapon, we create another child class of the BP_Weapon_Base.*

We have now laid out the foundation of the weapons and created all three weapon classes as well. Let's dip into more details of the weapon classes.

Play the game and let's spam the left mouse button and you can see the Attack animation just keep restarting. Let's set up a weapon cooldown mechanic.

Tutorial 15.2: Weapon Attack Cooldowns

Step 1: Create a weapon state enumeration. Go to the weapons folder, right click, and select Blueprints → Enumeration. A new enumeration asset got created; name it EWeaponState.

Enumeration

When programming, sometimes, we want to describe a list of possible selections or status that each one of them is unique. In the case of our weapons, all weapons could have three states: Idle, Attacking, and Reloading. Enumeration (or enum in short) is a built-in variable type that's designed precisely for situations like this.

Double click to open EWeaponState. Click on the New button at the upper right corner of the window three times to create three entries. Change their display name to Idle, Attacking, and Reloading (Figure 15.42).

Why?

So why do we name it EWeaponState instead of WeaponState? Well, the E means it's an enum, just like we add BP_ in front of the blueprints, we add E here, so it is

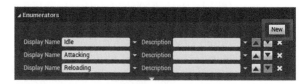

FIGURE 15.42 Create an enum called EWeaponState.

self-evident that it is an enum. It is a naming convention we try to stick with.

> Step 2: Add a EWeaponState variable to BP_Weapon_Base. Add a new variable called WeaponState to BP_Weapon_Base, and set the variable type to EWeaponSate. Compile and save the blueprint, and you can see that the default value is Idle. Click on the Idle, and we can see a drop-down list with three options: Idle, Attacking, and Reloading. You can only select one of the options in the drop-down list (Figure 15.43).
>
> Step 3: Create an animation notify state for the attack cooldown. Right click in the empty area of the Weapons folder and select Blueprint Class. In the pop-up Pick Parent Class window, type in AnimNotifyState in the search bar under the All Classes section. Select AnimNotifyState in the search results, and hit the Enter button to create an AnimNotifyState. This process is how we create a class inherit from any other existing classes. Next time when we do this, we will just say create a class derived from some thing.
> Name the new blueprint ANS_WeaponAttack.
>
> Step 4: Set up the animation notify state in the animation montages. Open Ellen_FPS_Pipe_Attack_Montage. Hover the cursor over the "1" label of the notify track under the Notifies section in the timeline. Click on it and wait for a second, and you can then rename this track. Let's name it Attacking. Right click on an empty area of the Attacking track and select Add Notify State → ANS_WeaponAttack. A new notify got added to the track, and this time, it has two diamond pins. Drag the left pin to the beginning of the track. Drag the other pin so that the range between the two pins covers the time that the weapon is on cooldown and cannot attack again. Figure 15.44 shows our intention here.

FIGURE 15.43 The drop-down list of the enum.

FIGURE 15.44 Use the ANS_WeaponAttacking to mark the time that the weapon is on cooldown.

Go ahead and add ANS_WeaponAttack to the attack animation montage of the gun and the grenade launcher as well.

Why?

You could argue that we can attack again only when the animation is finished. But in reality, the waiting time is too long, and the player will feel frustrated by the attacking rate. It's very common in many games to allow the player to attack again before the attack animation reaches the end.

Step 5: Implement ANS_WeaponAttack. Open ANS_WeaponAttack. Go to the My Blueprint panel, hover the cursor on the Functions section, and click Override → Received Notify Begin. A new function called Received_NotifyBegin got added to the Functions, and it is also opened for us (Figure 15.45).

This function is called when the animation hits the left pin of the animation notify state. Implement it as shown in Figure 15.46.

The Mesh Comp is the skeletal mesh that is currently playing the animation. The Get Owner gets the Owner of the Mesh Comp; in this case, it's BP_Character_Base; we cast

FIGURE 15.45 Override the Received_NotifyBegin function.

FIGURE 15.46 Implement the Received_NotifyBegin function.

it, get its CurrentActiveWeapon, and set the
WeaponState variable to Attacking. To create
the Set node, drag out from the Current Active
Weapon and search for set weapon state.

Go to the Functions section again,
override the Received Notify End function,
and implement it as shown in Figure 15.47.

This function is called when the
animation hits the right pin of the animation
notify state. What we do with this function
is to set the WeaponState variable back to
Idle. So long story short, when the attacking
animation starts (where the left pin of the
animation notify state is), the WeaponState
changes to Attacking. When the attacking
animation hits the right pin of the animation
notify state, the WeaponState changes back
to Idle. All we need to do now is to check if
the WeaponState is Idle or not; we can attack
again only when the WeaponState is Idle.

Step 6: Create a CanAttack function. Add a new
function to BP_Weapon_Base, and name
it CanAttack. Implement it as shown in
Figure 15.48.

The node that the WeaponState variable is
connected to is an Equal node; to create it, drag

FIGURE 15.47 Implement the Received_NotifyEnd function.

FIGURE 15.48 Implementation of the CanAttack function.

FIGURE 15.49 Modified Attack event.

out from WeaponSate and type in Equal and choose Equal (Enum). This node then returns true if WeaponState is Idle, it returns false if WeaponState is not Idle. This function returns true only when the WeaponState is Idle.

Step 7: Insert a CanAttack call in the Attack event. Double click the EventGraph under the My Blueprint panel to go back to the EventGraph. Modify the Attack event as shown in Figure 15.49.

What we did here is to check if we can attack and only attack if we can. Play the game again, and now we have proper weapon cooldowns. Again, all three weapons should work.

Let's move on to the attack damage.

Tutorial 15.3: Weapon Damage

Step 1: Pipe damage. Open BP_Pipe, go to Functions and override the Commit Attack Anim Notify function; if you do recall, this function is called when the animation hit the CommitAttack animation notify. Let's go step by step to implement this function as shown in Figure 15.50. There are a few new things in this graph.

Create a SphereOverlapActors function and call it using Event Commit Attack Anim Notify. Create a GetActorLocation for the

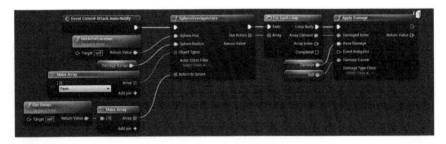

FIGURE 15.50 Implementation of the Commit Attack Anim Notify function.

Sphere Pos input of the SphereOverlapActors node. The GetActorLocation returns the location of the Target. Self means the actor of this blueprint, or in other words, the pipe.

Drag out from the Sphere Radius input pin of the SphereOverlapActors node and select Promote to variable. A new variable got added to the blueprint, name it DamageRange, compile, and set the default value to 100. Drag out from the Object types and search and create a Make Array node. This node makes an array(list) of items. And now, it has only one item: item 0. Set the Item 0 from WorldStatic to Pawn. We only want it to overlay with pawns and ignore other types.

Array

Imagine that there are three weapons in the game. When the player picks them all up, logically, we can have three variables to store them: weapon_1, weapon_2, and weapon_3. However, there is a problem with this approach. What if you don't know how many weapons you will need for your game? What if you have 2000 different weapons in a game? Do you create 2000 variables?

It makes much more sense to keep track of these weapons as a list of items or elements instead of separated individual variables. An array is a list of the same type of variables. Each item or element in an array has an index associated with it. The first item has an index of 0, and the second one has an index of 1. The next item has an index of the previous item's index plus one. Every item has a unique index, and the index is used to query that item. You can add or remove an item in an array, and you can merge two arrays if they hold the same type of variables.

This SphereOverlapActors needs an array of Object Types because it needs to know what kind of object types you want it to overlap with, and it can be multiple types. An array input or output pin has a grid-like shape instead of a circle. As you can see, both Object Types and Actors to Ignore are arrays.

Drag out from the Actors to ignore and create another Make Array node. Create a GetOwner node and connect it to the [0] input pin of the Make Array node. Again, the SphereOverlapActors needs to know an array of actors you want it to ignore. We only want to ignore the owner of the pipe, but you can add more if needed by clicking the Add pin button.

You know that the Out Actors return value of the SphereOverlapActors node is also an array because its icon is a grid. Drag out from the Out Actors and create a For Each Loop node.

Loop

Whenever you want to do something multiple times, you can use a loop. This For Each Loop loops through every element of its Array input. If the array has 100 items, the Loop Body out execution pin fire 100 times; each time it fires, the Array Element output pin is a different item. The Array Index output pin gives the index associated with that array element.

Connect the Loop Body with an Apply Damage node. Connect the Array Element to Damaged Actor, drag out from the Base Damage input pin, and promote a variable to connect to it. Name the variable Damage and set the value to 100. Finally, connect a Self node to the Damage Causer because the pipe itself is the causer of the damage.

What this function does is to draw an imaginary sphere at the location of the pipe. It then collects all the actors that overlap with this sphere and apply damage to every one of them. The Apply Damage function is part of a built-in damage feature of the game engine. Any actor can subscribe to this event and receive damage.

> *Step 2: Test the attack of the pipe. Open_BP_ Character_Base, search, and create an Event AnyDamage. Call Print String with Event AnyDamage, and connect the Damage output pin to the In String of the Print String (Figure 15.51). Set the Weapon Class of the AcquireNewWeapon function call in the Event BeginPlay to BP_Pipe. Drag a BP_Character_ Base to the level and play the game. After*

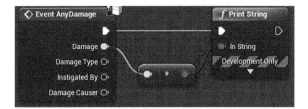

FIGURE 15.51 Set up a test of our pipe attack damage.

getting the pipe in hand, let's get close to the BP_Character_Base, press the left mouse button to attack, and we should see 100.0 got printed.

Step 3: Gun Attack Line Tracing. Open BP_Gun and create an override to Commit Attack Anim Notify. Implement it as shown in Figure 15.52.

The LineTraceByChannel traces a line between the Start and the End input. It returns an Out Hit, which contains the trace result. The owner here again is the BP_Character_Base that owns this gun. The Get Actor Eyes View Point is a handy function, and it gives you the location and rotation of the "eye" of the Target input. This eye is an abstraction. If a player possesses the target, it returns the location and rotation of the camera the player is looking through. If an AI possesses the target, it returns the logical location and rotation of the AI controller.

We use the Out Location (the location of the eye) as the Start input. The get-forward vector converts a rotation to a vector that points to the forward direction of the rotation; in Unreal Engine, it is the X-axis.

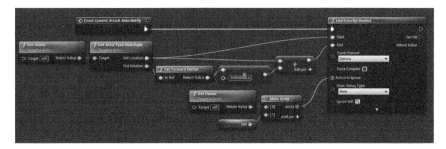

FIGURE 15.52 Implementation of the Commit Attack Anim Notify.

We then multiply it with a huge float number, which makes it almost like an infinitely long vector. You can create that multiply node by dragging out from the Return Value of the Get Forward Vector, type an "*" in the search bar, and choose vector * float. We add this infinitely long vector to the Out Location as the End input of the LineTraceByChannel to indicate that we want to trace forward from the eye as much as possible. Again, the + node can be created by dragging the Out Location out, type in "+" in the search bar, and choose vector + vector. The rest of the code should be straightforward.

One last thing you probably didn't notice here is that the Trace Channel is set to Camera. There are many prebuilt channels in Unreal Engine. An actor can choose to respond to any channel in three different ways: ignore, overlap, or block. The line trace only traces actors that block the channel it is tracing. Open BP_Character_Base and select the CapsuleComponent in the Components panel. Go to the Details panel and find the Collision section. Expand the Collision Presets to view the collision responses. You can see that it chose to ignore the Visibility channel (Figure 15.53).

We change the Trace Channel of the LineTraceByChannel to Camera so that the trace does not ignore BP_Character_Base.

Step 4: Apply Damage. On the other side of the LineTraceByChannel, we just simply do an Apply Damage. Drag out from the Out Hit of the LineTraceByChannel node, search, and create

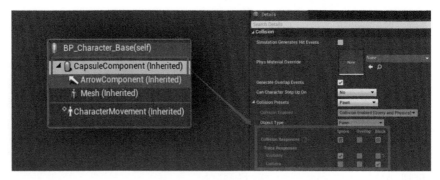

FIGURE 15.53 Check the collision responses of BP_Character_Base.

a Break Hit Result node. Click the downward arrow at the bottom of the Break Hit Result node to expand it. You can see that a whole lot of information is collected here. Use the Hit Actor as the Damaged Actor input of the Apply Damage node. The Damage and self node is created the same way as the pipe, but let's make the value of the Damage variable 10 instead of 100 (Figure 15.54).

Step 5: Add a sparkle VFX to the hit location. In the support files, find the VFX folder. Copy the VFX folder to the content folder in your game project. Go back to the editor, and you should see the VFX folder got added to the Content folder in the content browser as well. Open this VFX folder and you can see some VFX assets inside of it. These VFX assets were built with Unreal Engine's Niagra system. Due to the length limit of this book, we can't cover how to make them, but it takes little effort to find some tutorials about Niagra online.

Continue after Apply Damage, create a call to Spawn System at Location node, and set the System Template to Gun_Hit. The Location of the Break Hit Result goes to the Location input. Drag out from the Normal of the Break Hit Result and create a Make Rot from X. Connect the Return Value of the Make Rot from X node to the Rotation input (Figure 15.55).

Set the acquired weapon to BP_Gun, play the game, and test it. A sparkle gets generated at

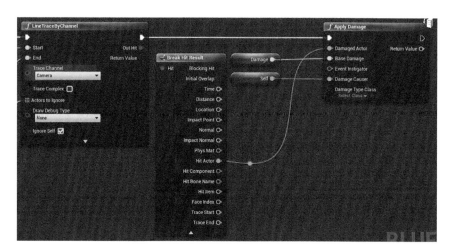

FIGURE 15.54 Apply damage to the hit actor.

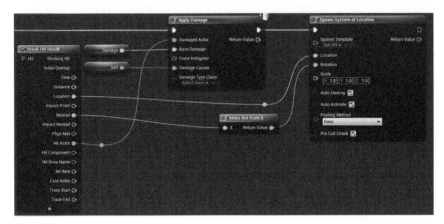

FIGURE 15.55 Spawn a gun-hit VFX.

the hit point of the gunshot every time you shoot. You can also shoot the BP_Ellen_Base and see the damage printed at the upper left corner of the screen. The X-direction of the normal is the normal direction of the hit point. Make Rot from X gives us the rotation of the normal; we then use it as the rotation for the VFX to make the sparkles splash outward from the surface.

Step 6: Grenade launcher grenade. For the grenade launcher, we need a different approach. It has to throw out an actual grenade. Create a Blueprint class derived from Actor and name it BP_Grenade. Add a StaticMesh component to it and set it to Grenade_launcher_grenade. Drag the StaticMesh up, overlap it with the DefaultSceneRoot, and release the mouse button to replace the scene root with the StaticMesh (Figure 15.56).

With the StaticMesh selected, go to the Details panel and set the Collision Presets under the Collision section to NoCollision (we don't want it to collide with the player when it is in the barrel).

FIGURE 15.56 Replace the DefaultSceneRoot with the StaticMesh.

Step 7: Implement an Ignite event. Go to the event graph and implement a custom event called Ignite as shown in Figure 15.57.

When we load a grenade, we attach (make it follow) it to the grenade launcher. When we fire, we want to call this Ignite function of the grenade. The function first detaches itself (the Target is self) from whatever it is attached to and add a projectile movement component to it. When a projectile movement component gets added to an actor, it makes the actor move like a projectile. There are a few other movement components built-in in Unreal Engine, and we will explore them later.

A projectile movement component has a velocity variable we can set. This velocity variable defines the direction and speed of the projectile in the form of a vector. We want to be able to set the direction of the velocity when calling the function, so we added a Fire Direction input to the Ignite event. We then multiply it with a promoted variable called Projectile Speed to specify the value of the velocity. Set the Projectile Speed variable to 2500.

The yellow Set Velocity node is created by dragging out the Return Value of the Add Projectile Movement Component and search for Set Velocity. After setting the velocity, we enable the Collision of the Static Mesh component.

Select the Add Projectile Movement Component node. Go to the Details panel and check on the Rotation Follows Velocity and Should Bounce. These two settings make the projectile face the direction of its velocity and also enable collision (Figure 15.58).

Step 8: Add an explosion when hit and deal damage. With the StaticMesh component selected, go to the Details panel, and scroll down to the

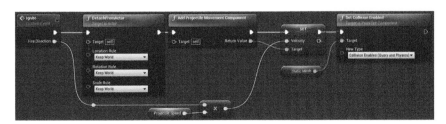

FIGURE 15.57 Implement an Ignite event.

593

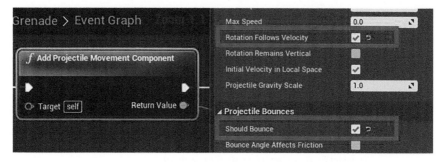

FIGURE 15.58 Settings of the Add Projectile Movement Component.

bottom to find the Events section. Click on the green button on the right of the On Component Hit label to create an On Component Hit (StaticMesh) event. This event fires when the StaticMesh hits anything. Implement this event as shown in Figure 15.59.

When this hit event fires, we first check if the Other Actor (the actor the mesh hit) is not the owner of the grenade. That != node is created by dragging out from the Other Actor output pin and search for !=, it returns true if the other actor is not the owner of the grenade. When the Other Actor is not the owner, we call a Spawn Emitter at Location function, and set the Emitter Template to P_Explosion and the Location to be the location of the grenade. This code spawns an explosion VFX at the location of the grenade. Next, we call the Apply Radial Damage with Falloff function. This function applies damage with a falloff, and we set the Damage Falloff to 1. It applies damage to all actors overlap with a sphere located at the Origin and has a radius of the Damage Outer Radius. The damage is the strongest at the origion and falls

FIGURE 15.59 Implementation of the On Component Hit (StaticMesh) event.

off to 0 at the edge of the sphere. Explosion
Damage and Damage Range are two promoted
variables, and their values are both 200. After
applying damage, we destroy the grenade by
calling the DestroyActor with self as the Target.
DestroyActor deletes the Target out of the game.

Step 9: Set up a grenade launch point socket.
Open the Grenade_launcher static mesh. Go
to the Socket Manager and click on the Create
Socket button to create a new socket; name it
GrenadeLaunchPoint. Set the Preview Static
Mesh to the grenade, move, and rotate it, so it fits
into the barrel nicely (Figure 15.60).

Step 10: Preload a grenade. Open BP_Grenade_
Launcher. Implement a function called
LoadGrenadeOnSpawn as shown in Figure 15.61.
And call it in the Event BeginPay.
The LoadGrenadeOnSpawn event is
very similar to the AcquireNewWeapon

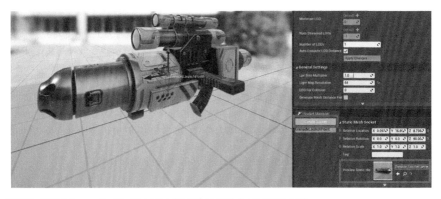

FIGURE 15.60 Set up a grenade launch point socket on the grenade launcher static mesh.

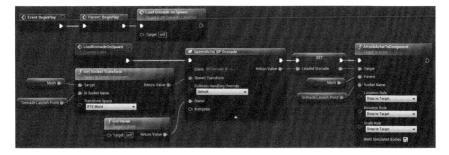

FIGURE 15.61 Implement LoadGrenadeOnSpawn and call it in BeginPlay.

(Figure 15.8). We spawn a BP_Grenade at the GrenadeLaunchPoint socket and notice that we set the Owner to be the owner of the grenade launcher, which should be the BP_Character_ Base that owns this grenade launcher (Why?). We then promote the spawned grenade as a new variable called Loaded Grenade and attach it to the GrenadeLaunchPoint socket of the mesh. The GrenadeLaunchPoint variable is a promoted variable, and its value is the same as its name. We call this event in the Event BeginPlay, so a grenade should be loaded already when we got the grenade launcher.

Switch the acquired weapon of BP_ Ellen_Base to BP_GrenadeLauncher, play the game, and you should see that the grenade is already in the barrel.

Step 11: Shoot the grenade. Go back to BP_ GrenadeLauncher and override the Event Commit Attack Anim Notify as shown in Figure 15.62.

In this event, we first check if the Loaded Grenade is valid (we set it in the LoadGrenadeOnSpawn event). If we have a loaded Grenade, we get the look direction of the owner by calling the Get Actor Eyes View Point (we have done this before). We then ignite the Loaded Grenade toward that direction. After that, we consider that the grenade launcher no longer has a loaded grenade. So, we set the Loaded Grenade to nothing (if we don't connect anything to the Set node, we set the value to null).

Play the game again and try to shoot with the grenade launcher. What is cool here is that the printed damage value is different depending on the distance. You can also hurt yourself, which isn't necessarily a bad thing when it comes to gameplay; we will keep it this way.

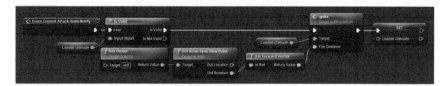

FIGURE 15.62 Implementation of Event Commit Attack Anim Notify.

There is one more thing left for the gun and the grenade launcher—Reloading. Let's implement that before wrapping up the weapons chapter.

When it comes to Reloading, we need to have an ammo system to keep track of how many ammo are in the clip and the inventory. Even though the grenade launcher only got one grenade after reloading, all the logic of realoading should apply to both the gun and the grenade launcher. So let's insert a BP_Ranged_Weapon class to generalize the Reloading for both the gun and the grenade launcher.

> *Step 1: Create a BP_Ranged_Weapon class. Create a new class called BP_Ranged_Weapon derived from BP_Weapon_Base. Open BP_Gun, click on the Class Settings button in the toolbar, go to the Details panel, and set the Parent Class to BP_Ranged_Weapon (Figure 15.63). Do the same thing to BP_Grenade_Launcher.*
>
> > *Our class hierarchy has changed a little bit as shown in Figure 15.64.*
> >
> > *It is common to have multiple layers of classes that the base classes take care of the standard stuff, and child classes implement their specific feature.*
>
> *Step 2: Add variables for the ammo. Add three variables to BBP_Ranged_Weapon. AmmoInInventory, AmmoInClip, and ClipCapacity. Make their variable-type integer.*
>
> *Step 3: Override Can Attack. In BP_Ranged_Weapon, go to the functions and override the Can Attack function. Unreal created a new function for us with the same name and already added a call to the parent function (Figure 15.65).*
>
> *Step 4: Implement the Can Attack function. Hold down Ctrl and drag the AmmoInClip to the graph, drag out from it, search for ">," and*

FIGURE 15.63 Re-parent BP_Gun to BP_Ranged_Weapon.

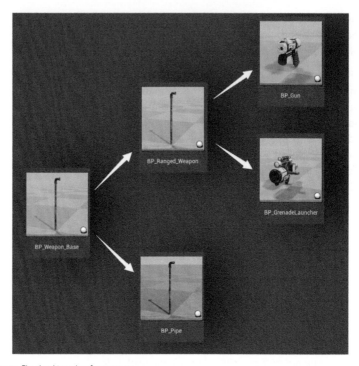

FIGURE 15.64 The class hierarchy of our weapons.

FIGURE 15.65 Override the Can Attack function.

select integer > integer. Drag out from the Result of the Parent: Can Attack function, create an AND Boolean, and connect the output pin of the integer > integer node to the second input of the AND Boolean node. Finally, the output pin of the AND Boolean goes to the Result of the Return Node (Figure 15.66).

What we did here is to ensure that two things have to be true to allow attack. First of all, AmmoInClip has to be bigger than 0, or in other words, there is ammo in clip; second,

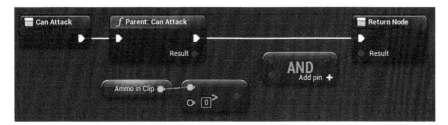

FIGURE 15.66 Implementation of the Can Attack function.

whatever the parent function has to ensure. You can double click to open the Parent: Can Attack function; it brings you to BP_Weapon_Base and shows you what's inside of that function; in our case, it checks the WeaponState.

The AND Boolean node only returns true if all inputs are true; it returns false if any one of the inputs is false or if they are all false. Long story short, what we are saying here is that the weapon has to be in Idle state and has ammo in the clip to attack.

Step 5: Implement DecreaseAmmoInClip. Create a new custom event, call it DecreaseAmmoInClip, and implement it as shown in Figure 15.67.

The logic here is straightforward. If there is ammo in the clip, remove one. The last node is called a decrement node, and you can create it by dragging out from Ammo in Clip and search with 2 "–" (minus) characters. What decrement does is set the value of the input to input – 1.

Step 6: Override CommitAttackAnimNotify. We should only decrease ammo when the attack is committed in the animation. Override CommitAttackAnimNotify and call DecreaseAmmoInClip with it (Figure 15.68).

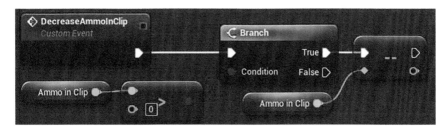

FIGURE 15.67 Implementation of the DecreaseAmmoInClip event.

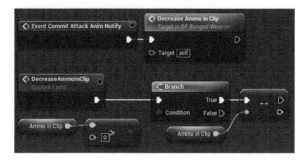

FIGURE 15.68 Override CommitAttackAnimNotify and call DecreaseAmmoInClip with it.

Why?

So you are probably wondering why don't we just move whatever in DecreaseAmmoInClip to CommitAttackAnimNotify? Well, Decrease Ammo may mean different things for other weapons, and putting it in a custom event allows the child class to override this part of the game logic. This coding style is called encapsulation. Other than being able to override it, another advantage of encapsulation is clear of intention. The name of DecreaseAmmoInClip explains what this part of the code does.

> *Step 7: Add parent call to CommitAttackAnimNotify in the child class. Open BP_Gun and find its CommitAttackAnimNotify. Right click on Event CommitAttackAnimNotify and select Add call to parent function. A Parent: Commit Attack Anim Notify got added, and insert it at the beginning of Event CommitAttackAnimNotify (Figure 15.69). Do the same thing to the BP_Grenade.*

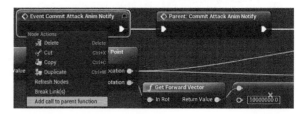

FIGURE 15.69 Add a call to the parent function of CommitAttackAnimNotify.

*Try to play again, and we cannot fire
anymore. This is because the ammo is 0 by default.*
Step 8: Create an UpdateUI event. We don't have a UI
yet, but it does not prevent us from creating one
and implement it properly later. Add an empty
custom event called UpdateUI to BP_Weapon_
Base (Why?). Go to BP_Ranged_Weapon and
override it. For now, let's make a call to Print
String. Drag out the In String of the Print String
node, search, and create an Append node. Add a
new pin to the Append node. Hold down Ctrl and
drag the AmmoInClip and the AmmoInInventory
to the graph. Connect AmmoInClip to the input A
of the Append node. Connect AmmoInInventory
to the Input C of the Append node. Type in "/"
for input B. This will print out AmmoInClip/
AmmoInInventory for us, so we can quickly check
the ammo count. Add a call to UpdateUI at the
end of DecreaseAmmoInClip (Figure 15.70).
Step 9: Set up the ammo variables. Open BP_Gun
and click the Class Defaults button in the
toolbar. Set the Ammo in Inventory, Ammo
in Clip, and Clip Capacity all to 5. For the BP_
GrenadeLauncher, set the Ammo in Inventory
to 3 and set both the Ammo in Clip and Clip
Capacity to 1.

*Play the game again, and try to shoot.
You can now see the ammo count got printed,*

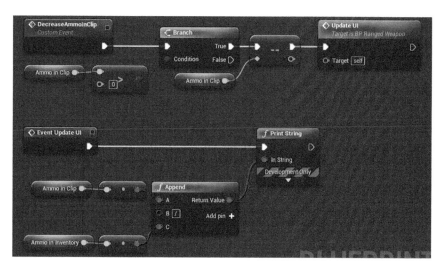

FIGURE 15.70 Implement UpdateUI and call it at the end of DecreaseAmmoInClip.

and you can no longer shoot if you have no ammo left in the clip.

Step 10: Create the Reload events and CanReload function. The Events and functions of the reloading part are similar to the attacking. We need a Reload event, a CanReload function, and a PlayReloadAM event. But we need more notify events. Open BP_Weapon Base and implement them as shown in Figure 15.71.

For the Can Reload function, we simply make it return a false in BP_Weapon_Base (some of the weapons do not need to reload). The ReloadAM is a new variable of the type Anim Montage, the same type as AttackAM.

For the notify events (the events we call with animation notifies), we have a ReloadStartNotify, and we set the weapon state to Reloading with it. We have a ReloadCompleteNotify and we set the weapon state to Idle with it. The others are weapon-specific; for the gun, we have ClipDropNotify, NewClipInHandNotify, and ClipAttachedNotify. For the grenade launcher, we have NewGrenadeInHandNotify and GrenadeAttachedNotify. They are all empty in BP_Weapon_Base.

Step 11: Create the reloading animation montage for the gun. Go to the animations folder, find Ellen_FPS_Gun_Reload, and create an AnimMontage with it. Open the new AnimMontage, make sure the preview mesh in hand is the gun, and add the following new notifies (Figure 15.72):

1. ReloadStart: Positioned at the beginning of the animation.

2. ClipDrop: Positioned at the time the empty clip drops out.

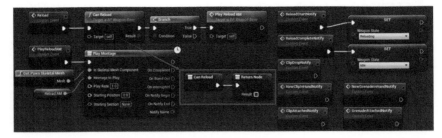

FIGURE 15.71 Implementation of the Reload Events and the CanReload function.

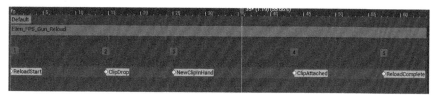

FIGURE 15.72 Animation notifies added to the gun reloading animation montage.

3. NewClipInHand: Positioned at the time that the animation has a new clip added to the left hand (in Maya).
4. ClipAttached: Positioned at the time when the clip is pushed into the gun.
5. ReloadComplete: At the time when the hands settle down, we think that the player can attack again.

We did not bring in the clip models in Maya done by the animators. That's why we need to recreate them all in here. Ideally, the weapons should be rigged as well with animations we can import. However, for the simplification of the rigging chapter and the animation set up here, we choose not to elaborate rigging the weapons.

Step 12: Add the sockets for the clip and the grenade. Go to the Skeleton tab to switch to the skeleton. Let's add two more sockets for the grenade and the clip of the gun and name them GrenadeHandSocket and ClipHandSocket. We need these two, so we can attach them when reloading. Don't forget to remove the attached assets and then attach the asset you need to see to better position the socket. And of course, switch to the corresponding reload animations as well (Figure 15.73).

Step 13: Create the reloading animation montage for the grenade launcher. Create the reloading

FIGURE 15.73 Add the GrenadeHandSocket and ClipHandSocket.

AnimMontage for the grenade launcher, and add the following notifies (Figure 15.74):

1. ReloadStart: This is the same as the gun.
2. NewGrenadeInHand: Positioned at the time when the new grenade pops into existence in the left hand when the left hand is off screen.
3. GrenadeAttached: Positioned at the time when the grenade is loaded in the barrel.
4. ReloadComplete: This is the same as the gun.

Step 14: Implement notifies in the animation blueprint. Go to the event graph of the animation blueprint, and implement all the notifies we added in the animation montage here. They are all implemented the same way as the AnimNotify_CommitAttack. Get the pawn owner, cast it to BP_Character_Base, get the active weapon, and call the corresponding event we added in Step 10 (Figure 15.75).

Now all our weapons can receive these notifies if they override these events. It's a bit of repetitive work, but we can indeed manage.

Step 15: Assign the corresponding reload Animation montage to the weapons. The ReloadAM variables are still empty in BP_Gun and BP_GrenadeLauncher. Assign the animation montages we just created to them in the Class Default settings.

Step 16: Set up the reload input and Implement then event in BP_Ellen_FPS. Go to the main UI and find Edit → Project Settings. Click on the Input section. In the Action mapping, let's add a new binding, call it Reload, and set the button under it to R. Go to the event graph of BP_Ellen_FPS, search and create an InputAction Reload. Implement the InputAction Reload as shown in Figure 15.76.

FIGURE 15.74 Animation notifies added to the grenade launcher reloading animation montage.

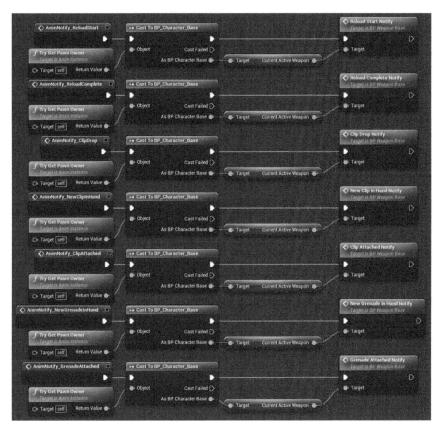

FIGURE 15.75 Implement notifies in the animation blueprint.

FIGURE 15.76 Set up the reload input and Implement then event in BP_Ellen_FPS.

Step 17: Implement CanReload. Open BP_Ranged_
Weapon and override the CanReload function as
shown in Figure 15.77.
We are checking three things here. First
of all, is there any ammo left in the inventory.
Second, AmmoInClip has to be smaller than
ClipCapacity (otherwise, the clip if full, no
need to reload). Finally, the weapon state

605

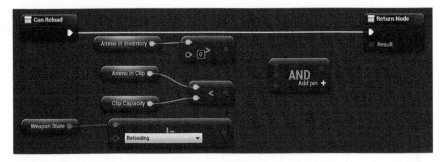

FIGURE 15.77 Implementation of the CanReload function.

should not be reloading (we don't want to reload again when we are already reloading). All three have to be true for the AND Boolean to return true.

Play the game again, and our reloading should be half-working. The ammo reduces as expected when we shoot, and we can reload by pressing R if the clip is not full. We cannot reload or even shoot during reloading (which is good, and why?). However, the most important thing is not done; the ammo in the clip should replenish. Let's implement this part of the functionality.

Step 18: Implement MoveAmmoToFillClip. Create a new custom event to BP_Ranged_Weapon and call it MoveAmmoToFillClip. Implement it as shown in Figure 15.78.

This function is the first function that we do some mathematics. Please try to understand it yourself before continue reading, and we will cover it in the next paragraph.

ClipCapacity – AmmoInClip gives us how many ammo is needed to fill the clip.

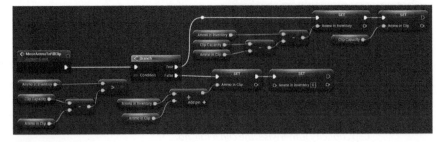

FIGURE 15.78 Implementation of MoveAmmoToFillClip.

AmmoInInventory > (ClipCapacity – AmmoInClip) returns if there is enough ammo in the inventory to fill the clip. Based on that, we branched out our calculation:

If there is enough in the inventory (True), we take out the number of ammo needed from AmmonInInventory by setting AmmonInInventory as AmmonInInventory – (ClipCapacity – AmmoInClip). And then, we set the AmmoInClip to the ClipCapacity to make the clip full.

If there is not enough, we add what's left in the AmmoInInventory to the AmmoInClip and set the AmmoInInventory to empty.

This algorithm is not the only way to achieve this, but it is logically easier to understand. Figure 15.79 shows an alternative to tackle this.

We choose the first one because it is logically not only easier to understand but also faster. It is faster because it does not create a new variable (Try Full Fill Ammo Left) and also it did not call a Clamp function, which internally costs much more. How much faster you ask? Twice, about twice as fast.

Although we are not trying to be software engineers, we are just regular programmers. But it is still worth noting that we should always be aware of the costs of different algorithms. It is always possible to find alternatives that could make your game run faster or slower if you are not careful.

Step 19: *Call MoveAmmoToFillClip in ReloadCompleteNotify. Create an override of ReloadCompleteNotify, add a call to its parent function first, then call MoveAmmoToFillClip, and then add a call to UpdateUI as well (Figure 15.80).*

Play the game now, and the gun should work already, you can try to reload, and it reloads

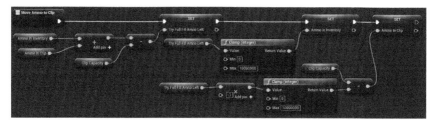

FIGURE 15.79 An alternative way to do the calculation.

FIGURE 15.80 Override Event Reload Complete Notify.

and prints out the numbers nicely. The grenade launcher reloads and does update the numbers. However, there is no new grenade to fire out after the first one goes out.

Step 20: Spawn new grenade. Open BP_GrenadeLauncher, override the GrenadeInHandNotify event, and implement it as shown in Figure 15.81.

What we do here is to spawn a new BP_Grenade the same way we did in LoadGrenadeOnSpawn. The only difference here is we want to attach it to the GrenadeHandSocket on the left hand of the skeletal mesh instead of the GrenadeLaunchPoint. We created a variable called GrenadeHandSocket, and the value is the same as its name.

Step 21: Attach the new grenade to the GrenadeLaunchPoint when notified. Override the GrenadeAttachedNotify event and implement it as shown in Figure 15.82.

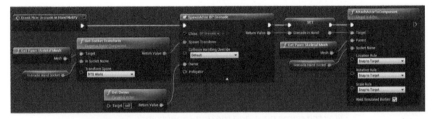

FIGURE 15.81 Override and implement the GrenadeInHandNotify event.

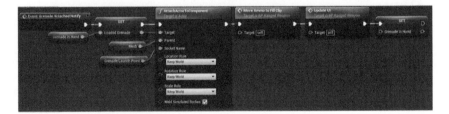

FIGURE 15.82 Override and implement the GrenadeAttachedNotify event.

GrenadeAttachedNotify is called when the reload montage hit the GrenadeAttached animation notify. This is the time the new grenade is attached to the barrel. So, we set the LoadedGrenade to GrenadeInHand to make it the newly loaded grenade. We then attach it to the GrenadeLaunchPoint. We then move the ammo to fill the clip, update the UI, and clear the value of the GrenadeInHand variable. Notice that the Location, Rotation, and Scale Rule of the AttachActorToComponent is Keep World; this way, we avoided the hustle of having to match the GrenadeLaunchPoint and GrenadeHandSocket exactly. If the settings are all Snap to Target, the grenade will pop when the attachment is changed.

Play the game now, and the grenade launcher should have a completely working reload functionality. However, if you do recall, we did call the MoveAmmoToClip in the parent class already. Although calling it again here doesn't hurt (why?), but let's go to BP_Ranged_Weapon and delete the override of the ReloadCompleteNotify.

Step 22: Create a clip actor that automatically drops. Create a new blueprint class derived from Actor. Name it BP_Gun_Clip_Drop and double click to open it. Add a static mesh component to it and set the mesh to gun_Gun_clip. Under the Physics section of the Details panel, check on Simulate Physics. Set the Collision Presets in the Collision section to Custom, expand it, and set all responses to Ignore. Go to its event graph, add a call to the Delay function in Event BeginPlay, and set the Duration to 2. Add a call to DestroyActor after the Delay node (Figure 15.83). This setup makes it self-destruct after 2 seconds.

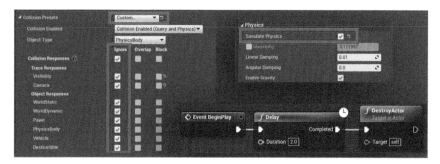

FIGURE 15.83 Create a BP_Gun_Clip_Drop class and make it self-destruct after 2 seconds.

Step 23: Override the ClipDropNotify event. Go to BP_Gun, and drag the gun_bullets in the Components panel over the gun_Gun_clip to parent it under gun_Gun_clip. Override the ClipDropNotify event and implement it as shown in Figure 15.84.

We parent the gun_bullets to gun_Gun_clip so we can hide them with one go. In the ClipDropNotify event, we hide the gun_Gun_clip first (make sure that the Propagate to Children is checked on for the Set Visibility node). We then spawn an instance of BP_Gun_Clip_Drop at the transform of the gun_Gun_Clip. The BP_Gun_Clip_Drop simulates physics, so it drops down right away as if it was the gun_Gun_Clip that we hid drops down. Because we set BP_Gun_Clip_Drop to self-destruct after 2 seconds, we don't have to do anything here.

Step 24: Create a BP_Gun_Clip_Full class. Create another blueprint class derived from Actor. Name it BP_Gun_Clip_Full, and open it. Add two static mesh components to it: make one of them the gun_bullets and another one the gun_Gun_clip. Set the collision presets of both components to NoCollision. We just need them to be the visual of the new clip during the animation.

Step 25: Override the NewClipInHandNotify. Override the NewClipInHandNotify event in BP_Gun as shown in Figure 15.85.

You should be pretty familiar with this pattern already. What we do here is to spawn a BP_Gun_Clip_Full and attach it to the ClipHandSocket. We also promoted it to a new variable called ClipInHand.

Step 26: Override the ClipAttachedNotify. Override the ClipAttachedNotify event in BP_Gun as shown in Figure 15.86.

Our intention here is when the new clip is attached, we un-hide our actual clip

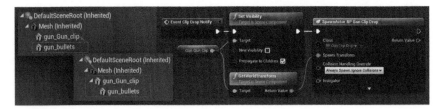

FIGURE 15.84 Parent the gun_bullets to gun_Gun_clip and override the ClipDropNotify event.

FIGURE 15.85 Override the NewClipInHandNotify event.

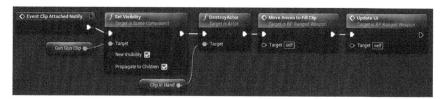

FIGURE 15.86 Override the ClipAttachedNotify.

model, and destroy the one attached to the ClipHandSocket. We then move the ammo to fill the clip and update UI.

Step 27: Refactor Reload and Attack to BP_ Character_Base. Go to BP_Character_Base and implement an Attack and a Reload custom event there; each of them just get the CurrentActiveWeapon, and check if it is valid and then do Attack and Reload. Go to BP_Ellen_FPS and modify InputAction Fire and InputAction Reload to call the Attack and Reload event we just created (Figure 15.87).

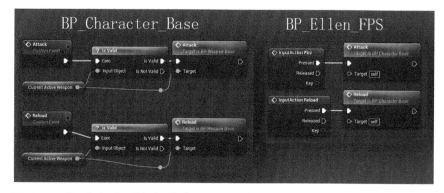

FIGURE 15.87 Move the Attack and Reload to BP_Character_Base and call them with the inputs in BP_Ellen_FPS.

FIGURE 15.88 Implementation of AutoReloadIfClipIsEmpty.

We do this to give our system more scalability. If we want the AI to attack, they can also call the Attack event. It is no longer only triggered by InputAction fire and can be called by other things (which we will do in the next step).

Step 28: Auto reload. It would be strange if the character does not automatically reload when there is no ammo in the clip anymore. Go to BP_Ranged_Weapon, and add a new custom event called AutoReloadIfClipIsEmpty. Implement it as shown in Figure 15.88.

It can be simply read as: if there is no ammo in the clip, ask the owner to reload.

Why?

Why don't we just call the reload function of the weapon? Instead, we are getting the owner to do the reload. Well, because logically, it should always be the owner to do the reloading. What if the owner is dead? What if the weapon is in inventory? There are situations we haven't implemented yet. Having two entries to do one thing is an ingredient for nasty bugs.

Step 29: Call AutoReloadIfClipIsEmpty in Event Commit Attack Anim Notify. Find the Event Commit Attack Anim Notify in BP_Ranged_Weapon, and add a call to AutoReloadIfClipIsEmpty at the end of the event (Figure 15.89).

FIGURE 15.89 Call AutoReloadIfClipIsEmpty in Event Commit Attack Anim Notify.

FIGURE 15.90 Modified Received_NotifyEnd.

We may want to call AutoReloadIfClipIsEmpty in some other places too, but for now, this is a logical place to call it.

Alrighty, at this point, things should be working on a practical level. There is, however, a little bug in our current setup. Try playing the game with the gun and keep spamming the R button and the left mouse button. And you will see that there is a change for the gun to fire after you started reloading. Try to fix it yourself and see if you can spot the problem. We'll cover the solution in the next paragraph.

There is a chance that the reloading is triggered just when the attack animation is about to reach Received_NotifyEnd. Because two animation montages are blending, animation notifies in both animation montages can all be triggered. The ReloadStart notify changes the weapon state to Reloading first, but because the animation is still blending, Received_NotifyEnd can still fire and changed it back to idle, which means that you can attack again based on our CanAttack function.

Step 30: Add state check to ANS_WeaponAttack. Open ANS_WeaponAttack. And go to the Received_NotifyEnd function. Modify it to the one shown in Figure 15.90.

What we added here are the nodes that are selected in Figure 15.90. We simply check if the weapon state is Reloading; if the state is not reloading, we can proceed to change it to idle, but if it is reloading, we don't change it to idle.

Play the game again, and the bug should disappear.

Conclusion

We have all three weapons built. They can attack, deal damage, reload, and auto-reload. We have carefully structured our classes and hierarchy so that many of the common behaviors of the weapons are generalized into base classes. We have also used animation montages and animation notifies to drive the weapon behaviors, visuals, and game logic. We have also covered reasons for many of our programming choices. In every corner of our structure, we try to make it flexible, scalable, short, and elegant.

At this point, if you want to add a new weapon to the game, it takes just a few steps to implement it based on the foundation we have built. A good design pattern values consistency, extensibility, and causes the smallest ripple in the system when you add new features or make changes. However, overdoing this would cause too much abstraction and hard to keep track of what is going on. One should always be clear on what the goal is and design the program based on that.

Let's move on to the next chapter and start building the health and damage system.

CHAPTER 16

Health and Damage

In this chapter, we are going to work on the health and damage system for our game. We have built a weapon system, but we cannot deal with damage yet. What is happening now on the weapon's end is calling an apply damage function. However, on the receiver's part, we are only printing out the number of the damage. The game is no fun if we cannot blast anything. The good news is that we already have an excellent interface for us to plug in any health and damage system.

Until now, we are working with an object-oriented paradigm with classes and inheritance. But to create our health system, it may not work like the weapons. Consider having a bunch of different things in the game that can be damaged: the player, a security camera, a patrolling AI, and a boss. These four things do not necessarily have to fit into a master base class just to be able to have a health functionality. They just share one thing in common: they all take damage.

Let's explore another way of doing OOP: Component and Interface.

Tutorial 16.1: Create a Health Component

> Step 1: Create a health component class. Add a new folder called Components in the Blueprints folder. Create a new blueprint class derived from Actor Component in the Components folder, and name the new blueprint class BP_HealthComp.

Actor Component

Actor components are components you can attach to an actor. They cannot be placed in the level by themselves and they die with their host actor.

> Step 2: Set up a few variables. Open BP_HealthComp and add two variables of the type float. Name the first one MaxHealth and the second one CurrentHealth. Set both of their values to 100.
>
> Step 3: Subscribe to the damage system. In the Event Graph, create a Get Owner node. Drag out from the Return Value of the Get Owner node, search for bind event to on take any damage, and press Enter to create a Bind Event to On Take Any Damage node. There is an Event input pin of this new node, drag out from it, search for add custom event, and hit Enter to create a custom event. Name the new custom event TakeDamage. This new event has some input added already. By binding it to the On Take Any Damage of the owner, it got called whenever the owner takes damage. Call the Bind Event to On Take Any Damage from the Event BeginPlay. In the TakeDamage custom event, we can try to print out the name of the damaged actor for now (Figure 16.1).

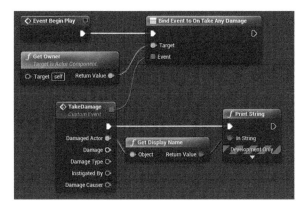

FIGURE 16.1 Bind an event to the owner's OnTakeAnyDamage.

Step 4: Test the binding. Open BP_Character_Base.
Click on the Add Component button under the
Components panel, search, and add our new BP_
HealthComp. Delete the Event AnyDamage event
we created in the previous chapter. We don't
need it anymore because the BP_HealthComp is
now binding with it. Play the game and shoot the
BP_Character_Base in the level, and we can see
the BP_Character_Base got printed.

Step 5: Calculate damage. Add a new event called
CalculateDamage. Implement it and call it with
TakeDamage as shown in Figure 16.2.

What we do here is to subtract damage
out of the CurrentHealth and clamp it
between 0 and MaxHealth. If the Value input
of the clamp node is bigger than the Max
input, the Return Value is the Max input. If
the Value input of the clamp is smaller than
the Min input, Return Value is the Min input.
Otherwise, the Return Value is the Value
input. This ensures that after the subtraction,
the CurrentHealth remains in its reasonable
range. We deleted the Print String and added

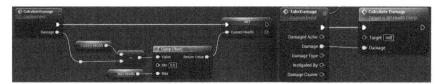

FIGURE 16.2 Implement and call CalculateDamage.

the CalculateDamage function call in the TakeDamage custom event.

Step 6: Add a health blueprint interface. We want to inform the owner when it is hurt, dead, or it needs to update its UI. But the problem here is we don't know who the owner is, and we want it to work for anyone. Let's use a new concept called blueprint interface to tackle this issue.

Right click in the empty place in the Content Brower and select Blueprints → Blueprint Interface. Rename the new interface BPI_HealthComp and double click to open it. Go to the My Blueprint panel, and rename the NewFunction_0 to HealthCompNotify_TookDamage. Go to the Inputs section of the Details panel and add an Actor object reference input called DamageCauser.

Add two new functions by pressing the "+" sign twice. Name one of them HealthCompNotify_Dead and the other one HealthCompNotify_UpdateUI. With the HealthCompNotify_UpdateUI selected, go to the Details panel and add a new float input called HealthPercentage (Figure 16.3).

Let's tie things up before explaining this.

Step 7: Add interface call. Go back to BP_HealthComp, create a RequestUpdateUI and a CheckDeath custom event, and implement them as shown in Figure 16.4.

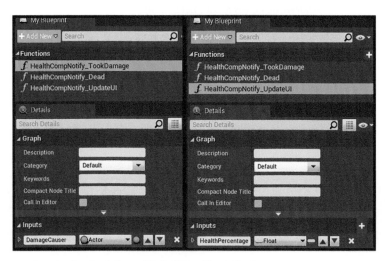

FIGURE 16.3 Create three functions in the new BPI_HealthComp blueprint interface.

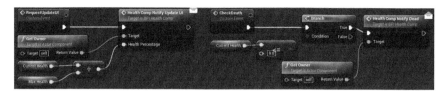

FIGURE 16.4 Implementation of the RequestUpdateUI and CheckDeath custom event.

For the RequestUpdateUI, we use the result of Current/MaxHealth to calculate the percentage of the health left. The ÷ node is created by right click and searches for /; the one we used here is float/float. To let the owner know it should update UI, we get the owner and called the HealthCompNotify_ UpdateUI interface function. You can call interface function on anything as if it has that function. CheckDeath is very similar. If the CurrentHealth is smaller or equal to 0 (search for <= to create it), we get the owner and call the HealthCompNotify_Dead interface function.

Step 8: *Call RequestUpdateUI and CheckDeath in TakeDamage. At the end of the TakeDamage function, add more stuff as shown in Figure 16.5.*

We first inform the owner that it took damage and then called RequestUpdateUI and CheckDeath. Whenever the owner took damage, we calculate it, tell the owner that it took damage, ask it to update UI, and tell it its death if the CurrentHealth is 0.

Step 9: *Add BPI_HealthComp interface to BP_ Character_Base. Open BP_Character_Base, and click on the Class Settings in the toolbar. Click on the Add button in the Interfaces section in the Details panel. Search and add BPI_HealthComp (Figure 16.6).*

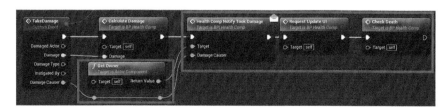

FIGURE 16.5 New stuff added to TakeDamage.

FIGURE 16.6 Add BPI_HealthComp interface to BP_Character_Base.

Step 10: Make BP_Character_Base receive interface call. After adding the interface, a new section called Interfaces got added in the My Blueprint panel. Open it and you can see all the functions we created in BPI_HealthComp. Right click on each one of them, and select implement function. Three new events got created; implement them as shown in Figure 16.7.

For the HealthCompNotify_UpdateUI, we print out the name of self and then the percentage followed by % health left. We time the Health Percentage by 100 because its value would be ranged from 0 to 1. For HealthCompNotify_TookDamage, we just print out Ouch! For the HealthCompNotify_Dead, we destroy the actor.

Play the game and shoot the BP_Ellen_Base we placed in the scene, and we can see all the correct information printed, keep shooting, and we can eventually kill that BP_Ellen_Base.

Switch the weapon in BP_Character base in the Acquire New Weapon function called in Event BeginPlay to BP_GrenadeLauncher. Try to shoot our own feet (shoot downward), and we should be able to kill ourselves with

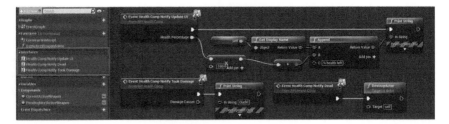

FIGURE 16.7 Implementation of the three interface functions.

620

the grenade. If we want anything to take damage, we simply add BP_HealthComp and BPI_HealthComp, and implement these functions. More importantly, if we want the whole health system to work differently, we modify BP_HealthComp, and everyone got the new update.

We still have many problems. The character does not react when hit, and when the character is killed, it just pops out of existence. Having some hit and death animation would be nice. Also, when the character is gone, the weapon stays. We have never told the weapon to die with its owner.

Tutorial 16.2: Character Hit and Death

Step 1: Create a hit react animation. Just like how we create the weapon switch animation, let's create a quick hit animation that does nothing more than a ten-frame body bend back. Make sure that it has only one key frame, and set it to additive. Call it Ellen_Hit, and make an animation montage out of it which can be called Ellen_Hit_Montage (Figure 16.8).

Step 2: Test the hit animation montage. Go back to Ellen_Character_Base, and change the implementation of Event HealthCompNotify_ TookDamage to Figure 16.9.

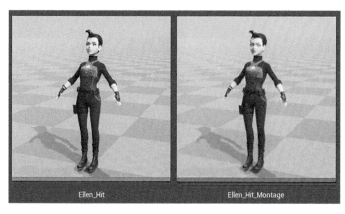

FIGURE 16.8 Create a quick hit animation.

621

FIGURE 16.9 New implementation of HealthCompNotify_TookDamage.

What we do here is asking the mesh to play an animation montage. A new parameter called HitAM set to our new hit animation montage is used for the Montage to Play input. Play the game again, hit the enemy with the gun, and you can see that the animation got played nicely.

Let's have some fun and make an AI that shoots forward blindly, so we can test the hit effect on the player.

Step 3: Create a dummy AI. Create a child blueprint class of BP_Character_Base and name it BP_Dummy_AI. Open it and find the Event Tick. This Tick function is called every time the game updates and call Attack with it, which makes this dummy AI shoot forward as fast as possible (Figure 16.10).

Replace the BP_Character_Base in the level to BP_Dummy_AI, and rotate it to make it face the player. Play the game and face that BP_Dummy_AI, and she starts to shoot you as fast as possible after getting the gun. She even reloads, which is pretty cool. But there is one thing strange here: if you hit her a few

FIGURE 16.10 Create a dummy AI and call Attack in its Tick event.

times, she stops shooting. You would think that she is out of ammo, but that can't be the case because you have the same amount of ammo, and you know it takes one round of reloading to run out of ammo. So what is going on here? Try to figure out the reason before moving on. You don't have to fix it yet.

Well, it's because of the hit montage. Any new montage fired overrides the previous one in the same group, and all of our montages use the default group. The hit animation montage overrides the shoot montage, which makes the shoot montage stop prematurely and that causes the ANS_WeaponAttack never reach to the end notify to change the WeaponState back to idle. We can fix this issue by assigning the hit montage to a different group and slot.

Step 4: Create and assign a new group and slot to the hit animation montage. Open Ellen_Hit_Montage, and go to the Anim Slot Manager on the lower right corner of the window (it might be shuffled behind the Asset Browser). Click on the Add Group button and type in Reaction as the new group name. A new group called Reaction gets added to the Slot Name list. With (Group) Reaction selected, click the Add Slot button to add a new slot to it and type in Hit as the slot name. Finally, go to the timeline, under the Montage section, click the tiny drop-down triangle button of the DefaultGroup. DefaultSlot, and select Slot Name → Reaction. Hit (Figure 16.11).

Step 5: Add the slot to the animation blueprint. Go to the AnimGraph of the animation blueprint. Add a new Slot 'DefaultSlot' and insert it between the old Slot 'DefaultSlot' and the Out Pose node. With this new slot selected, go to the Details panel and set the Slot Name to Reaction.Hit (Figure 16.12).

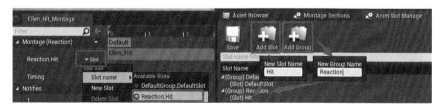

FIGURE 16.11 Create a new group and slot for Ellen_Hit_Montage.

FIGURE 16.12 Insert a Reaction.Hit slot to the AnimGraph.

Play the game again, and you can see that the hit animation montage does not override the other animations anymore. Animation montages that have different groups do not cancel each other.

Step 6: Create the death animation montage. Find the Dealth_From_The_Back animation, create an animation montage from it, and keep the default name. Open the new Dealth_From_The_Back_Montage in the Details panel and check off the Enable Auto Blend Out under the Blend Options section. We don't want it to blend back; that would make the character stand up again.

Step 7: Create a StartDeathSequence custom event. Go back to BP_Character_Base and create a function called StartDeathSequence. Implement the event as shown in Figure 16.13. And call it after Event HealthCompNotify_Dead.

First of all, we connect it to a Do Once node, and the Do Once node only allows the execution to go through it once. It makes sense because, well, you only die once. We then ask the Mesh to play the death animation montage, and the DeathAM is a new variable set to Dealth_From_The_Back_Montage. Then we get the length of the death animation montage, and wait for how long the length of the animation montage

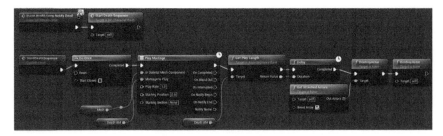

FIGURE 16.13 Implementation of StartDeathSequence and call it after Event HealthCompNotify_Dead.

is to wait for it to finish. Then it destroys all attached actors before destroying itself.

Play the game again and keep shooting the dummy character. However, when the character is dead, surprisingly, nothing happens, and the character will keep shooting and finally disappears. Well, it is because the character never stops attacking. And the attack animation montage again cancels the death animation montage. To fix it, we have to prevent attacking if the character is dead.

Step 8: Create a CanOperateWeapon function. Add a new function to BP_Character_Base, and name it CanOperateWeapon. Implement it as shown in Figure 16.14 and insert it with a branch at the beginning of the Attack and Reload event.

The function is relatively straightforward. We check the health and make sure that it is not 0 (not dead). Play the game again, and this time, when the character is out of health, it plays the death animation and disappears afterward. When the character is lying on the ground, if you hit it again, there is still hit reaction, and you can keep it this way if you want. Or, you can prevent it by stop sending TookDamage interface calls if the health is 0 in BP_HealthComp.

Step 9: A little refactoring. Think about what we have done so far, and there is one thing worth modifying. The Do once does its job nicely to prevent the death sequence from happening again. But should it be in BP_Character_Base or should it be in the BP_HealthComp? Well, if you want this dead only once behavior to happen to all your objects in the game, then putting it in BP_HealthComp makes more sense. Otherwise, you have to add Do Once to all the death functions. Let's remove it from

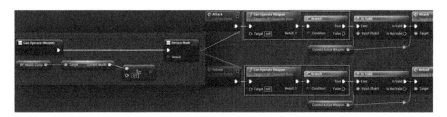

FIGURE 16.14 Implement and call CanOperateWeapon at the beginning of the Attack and Reload event.

FIGURE 16.15 Refactor Do Once to the CheckDeath event in BP_HealthComp.

StartDeathSequence and add it to CheckDeath as shown in Figure 16.15.

Refactoring like Step 9 is essential and often overlooked by beginners, what a function should be called, what should it include or not, takes much consideration to decide.

Let's move on to make the player's death sequence as well.

Step 10: Player character death pawn. For the player, we want to switch to a top-down view and see the full body of the character playing the death animation as well. Create a new class derived from Pawn and name it BP_Player_Death_Pawn. Add a Skeletal Mesh component to it. In the viewport, rotate the mesh to make it face the X-axis and move it down 150 units. Go to the Details panel and set the Skeletal Mesh to Ellen_Skeletal_Mesh. Under the Animation section, change the Animation Mode to Use Animation Asset, and set the Animation to Play to Death_From_The_Back. Check off the Looping under the Animation to Play as well (Figure 16.16).

Why?

Why do we move it down 150 units? Well, when the player character is dead, we want to spawn it. At that point, the only position we can use is the player controllers position, which is about that much above the ground.

Step 11: Set up a camera. Select the DefaultSceneRoot in the Components panel. Add a Spring Arm component and a Camera component. Make sure that the camera is parented under the spring arm. Rotate the spring arm up to −60 degrees on the Y axis, and move it up 50 units (Figure 16.17).

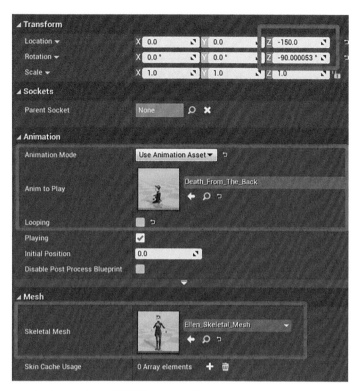

FIGURE 16.16 Settings for the skeletal mesh of BP_Player_Death_Pawn.

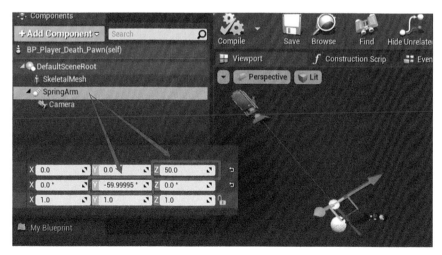

FIGURE 16.17 Set up a camera to look through.

The sprint arm component is a special type of component that moves the attached component in front of any collisions. The spring arm ensures that the camera does not end up on the other side of the walls. We move it up 50 units to prevent it from colliding with the ground.

Step 12: Set up a player controller. Create a new class derived from PlayerController and name it BP_Ellen_FPS_PlayerController. Click on the Class Defaults button in the toolbar, go to the Details panel, and check off the Auto Manage Active Camera Target option. In the Event Graph, right click, search, and create an Event On Possess and an Event On UnPossess. These two events are called when this player controller possesses and unpossesses a pawn. Implement them as shown in Figure 16.18.

We checked off the Auto Manage Active Camera Target to allow us to set the camera transitions in whatever way we want. When we possess a pawn, we want to set the view target to the Possessed Pawn. When the player character is dead, the player controller triggers the Event OnUnPossess; in there, we spawn a BP_Player_Death_Pawn at the location of the player controllers viewpoint (Get Actor Eyes View Point). However, the rotation is only the yaw rotation of the viewpoint (we don't want the spawned BP_Player_Death_Pawn to tilt or pitch in any way).

After creating the new BP_Player_Death_Pawn, we set the view target to the new pawn. However, this time, in that Set View Target with

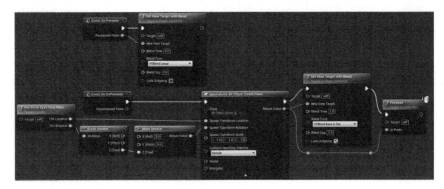

FIGURE 16.18 Implement the Event On Possess and Event On Unpossess.

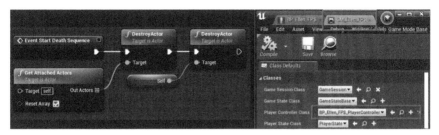

FIGURE 16.19 Override StartDeathSequence and set the PlayerControllerClass.

> Blend function, we set the Blend Time to 1, Blend
> Func to VTBlend Ease in Out, and the Blend Exp
> to 1 to have the camera blend to the target with
> ease in ease out effect. Finally, we possess the
> new BP_Player_Death_Pawn.

Step 13: Override StartDeathSequence and set
   the PlayerControllerClass in the game mode.
   Open BP_Ellen_FPS, and in the Event Graph,
   override the StartDeathSequence just to destroy
   all attached actors and the destroy self. Go to
   Blueprints/GameModes/, open GM_Ellen_FPS,
   and set the Player Controller Class Under the
   Classes section to BP_Ellen_FPS_PlayerController
   (Figure 16.19).
> Play the game again and let the dummy
> AI shoot you. When you die, you will see
> yourself playing the death animation and
> smoothly transitioned to a third-person view.
> The game would be too hard if there is no
> way to regenerate health; let's quickly create
> a health regeneration actor.

Tutorial 16.3: Health Regeneration

Step 1: Create BP_HealthRegen and set up its
   visual. Go to the Blueprints folder, and create
   a new folder called HealthRegen. Inside of
   HealthRegen, create a new blueprint class
   derived from BP_Triggerable. Name the new
   class BP_HealthRegen. Open BP_HealthRegen,
   add a static mesh component to it, and set the
   mesh to floor_circles_floor_circle_deco_01. Add
   two Cube Components to it, scale, and rotate
   them to create a 3D cross figure. Drag one of
   the cubes on to the other one to parent it to the
   other one, and rename the parent cube Cross.
   Set the Collision Presets to NoCollision on both

cubes. Go to StaticMeshes/Shared, create a new material instance of Emmisive_Base_Mtl, and name the instance HealthRegen_Cross_Mtl_Inst. Move this material instance to the HealthRegen folder. Make it green, and assign it to the cubes of BP_HealthRegen. Figure 16.20 shows the final visual of the setup.

Step 2: Make the Cross rotate. Go to Event Graph, find Event Tick, and add the code shown in Figure 16.21 at the end of Event Tick.

Event Tick is called on every frame, which is also every time the game updates. The Delta Seconds is the time it took between this frame and the previous frame. It usually is a very small number because the game has to update around 60 frames per second. We multiply it with 200, make a rotator out of it, and add that much rotation to our Cross. Rotator is a type that represents a rotation. Drag a BP_HealthRegen to the level, play the game, and you should see it spin nicely.

Step 3: Add regeneration functionality to the BP_HealthComp. Open BP_HealthComp, add

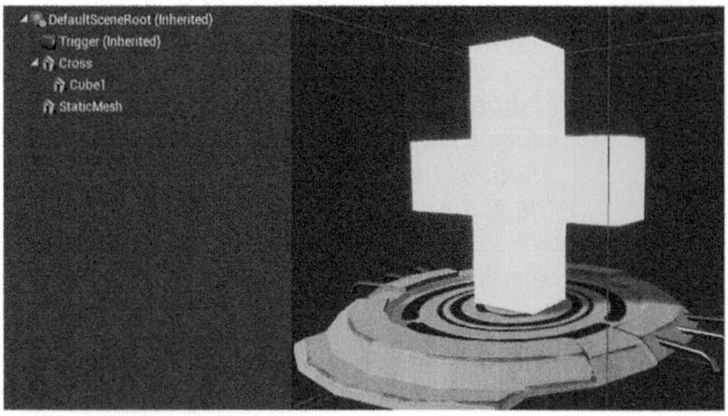

FIGURE 16.20 Create BP_HealthRegen and set up its visual.

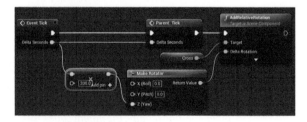

FIGURE 16.21 Make the Cross rotate.

a new function called RegenerateHealth, and implement it as shown in Figure 16.22.

This function takes a float input called Amount and returns a boolean called Regen Successful. We check if the health is full (CurrentHealth = MaxHealth). If the health is full, return false. If the health is not full, add the Amount input to CurrentHealth, clamp it, so it does not become bigger than MaxHealth, and set it. Don't forget to request to update UI, and return true.

Step 4: Implement a Consumed custom event.
Implement a new custom event called consumed in BP_HealthRegen and implement it as shown in Figure 16.23.

This event takes an Actor object reference as input called Consumed By. When consumed, we hide our Cross and set Trigger not to collide, which disables it. We then spawn an NS_Healed VFX attached to the root component of the consumer.

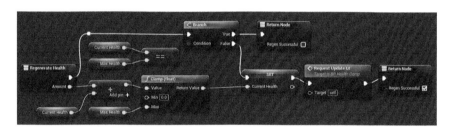

FIGURE 16.22 Implementation of RegenerateHealth.

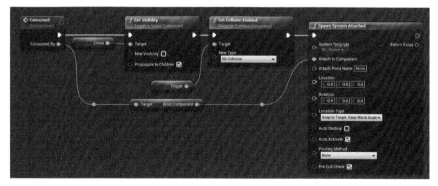

FIGURE 16.23 Implementation of Consumed.

631

Step 5: Override Overlapped event. Override the Overlapped event as shown in Figure 16.24.

What we do here is to get the actor's BP_HealthComp by calling Get Component by Class and set Component Class to BP_HealthComp. This function finds a BP_HealthComp (if there is any) and returns it. We then call the RegenerateHealth function of the BP_HealthComp. For the Amount input, we generate a random number from 10 to 50 to make the gameplay more unpredictable. If the regeneration is successful, we then call the Consumed event we implement earlier. Play the game again and take some damage. You should now be able to consume the BP_HealthRegen (Figure 16.25).

Step 6: Make it go back after 10 seconds. At the end of our Consumed event, add the code shown in Figure 16.26.

What we do here is Delay for 10 seconds and set our Cross and Trigger back to normal.

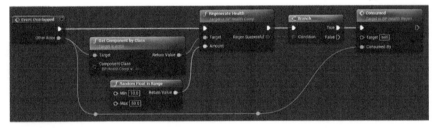

FIGURE 16.24 Override Event Overlapped.

FIGURE 16.25 Regenerate health.

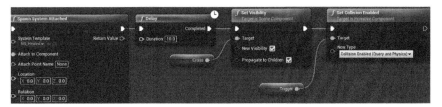

FIGURE 16.26 Reactivate the regeneration functionality after 10 seconds.

Give the game another go, and now you can consume it when you take damage, it will go back again after 10 seconds.

Conclusion

We have now finished the health, damage, health regeneration, and death of the characters. A critical takeaway from this chapter is the component and interface paradigm, which offers more flexibility than classic inheritance-based OOP. Things are getting more interesting as we go. However, we still have much to cover, one of the essential parts of the game is the inventory and the UI; let's move on to that in the next chapter.

CHAPTER 17

Inventory and UI

A game is hard to play if there is no UI to tell you the current status of your health, weapon, and ammo. And we finally have enough to start building an inventory system and a UI. In the meantime, we will also cover short cuts to switch weapons. A well-designed UI makes the player's experience more enjoyable. In contrast, a bad UI makes the player smash their controllers or keyboard. We are going to try to make the UI simple to understand and easy to read.

But before we dip into that, we need to have a weapon pick up and an inventory system. Let's jump into that right away.

Tutorial 17.1: Weapon Pickup

Step 1: Refactor the Mesh of the weapons into a variable. It is not possible to access the meshes of a weapon class in the Blueprint level, and it's an excellent opportunity to learn the construction script.

Open BP_Weapon_Base. Add a new variable called Visual and change its variable type to Static Mesh object reference. Go to the Variables section of the My Blueprint panel and click on the little closed eye icon to make it open. Go to the Functions section in the My Blueprint panel and double click to open the ConstructionScript. Implement the Construction Script as shown in Figure 17.1.

The construction script is called when the object is being created, but not spawned yet. What we did here is to set the Mesh of the weapon to the value of the Visual variable we added. This way, we can set and access the mesh used by the weapon through this Visual variable.

The little eye icon of the variables is their access specifiers. If the eye is closed, the child class cannot access it, and if they are not, then the child class can access them. When the eye is closed, we call this variable private; when it is open, we call it public.

Step 2: Set the Visual variables of the three weapons. Open BP_Gun, and you can see its model disappear. Go to its Class Defaults (by clicking the Class Defaults button on the Toolbar and go to the Details panel). Set Visual to gun_Gun_body. Set the other two weapons accordingly.

Step 3: Create a BP_Weapon_Pickup class. Create a new blueprint class called BP_Weapon_Pickup

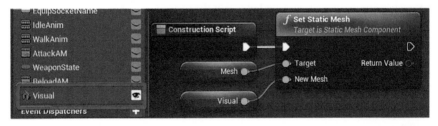

FIGURE 17.1 Construction Script of the BP_Weapon_Base.

derived from BP_Triggerable. Give it a StaticMesh component and a RotatingMovement component. Add another variable called WeaponClass, make this variable a BP_Weapon_Base class reference (not object reference), and make the WeaponClass variable public. Implement the construction script as shown in Figure 17.2.

What we do here is once we know the weapon class, it gets the Visual variable of the weapon class by calling Get Class Defaults, and use it as the StaticMesh. The RotatingMovment component makes it rotate.

Step 4: Test the visuals. Drag a copy of BP_Weapon_Pickup into the level in the Details panel and set the Weapon Class to BP_Gun, and you can see that it now shows the model of the gun. Hold down Alt and drag to have a copy of it; this time, set the weapon class to BP_GrenadeLauncher, drag out another copy, and set it to BP_Pipe. You can see how our setup allows us to change the visual of the pickup by changing the weapon class. Play the game, and you can see that they are rotating (Figure 17.3).

Step 5: Add a Weapons variable. Go to BP_Character_Base, and add a variable called Weapons. Set the type of Weapons to BP_Weapon_Base, click on the button on the right side of the Variable type to pull down a drop-down list, and select the one with an icon that has a 3×3 boxes. This Weapons variable is now an array of BP_Weapon_Bases (Figure 17.4).

Step 6: Add the new weapon acquired to the Weapons array. Find the AcquireNewWeapon function. At the end of the event, create an

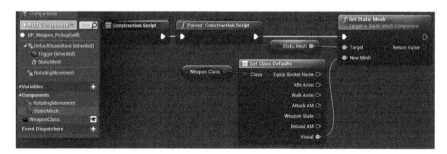

FIGURE 17.2 Components and implementation of the construction script of BP_Weapon_Pickup.

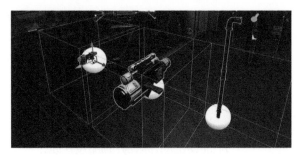

FIGURE 17.3 Test the visuals.

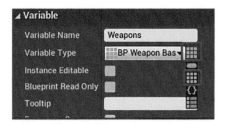

FIGURE 17.4 Add a weapon variable and set it to an array to BP_Weapon_Bases.

ADDUNIQUE (add unique) node. Drag the Weapons variable from the Variables to the first input of the ADDUNIQUE node. Drag out from the reroute node that goes to the New Active Weapon input of the Switch Active Weapon to node and and connect it to the second input of the ADDUNIQUE node. Finally, connect the out execution pin of the Switch Active Weapon to node to the in execution pin of the ADDUNIQUE node (Figure 17.5).

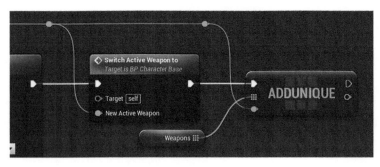

FIGURE 17.5 Add the new weapon acquired to the Weapons array.

The Weapons variable is an array of BP_Weapon_Bases, and the ADDUNIQUE node adds an item to it. What we are doing here is to add the new weapon spawned to the Weapons array.

Step 7: Create a check function to see if we have a weapon already. When we pick up weapons, we need to know if we have that weapon already; if we do, we don't want to acquire a new one. We may pick up the ammo, but not have a new weapon. Add a new function called HasWeaponType and implement it as shown in Figure 17.6.

What we are trying to check here is if we have a weapon that has the class type of the weapon class already. Or in other words, if we have this type of weapon already.

This function takes a BP_Weapon_Base class reference as an input and returns two outputs. The first output is a Boolean that shows if we already have the type of weapon or not. The second output returns the weapon that we already have.

We start by using a foreach loop to loop through all the elements Weapons have. Because we add every new weapon we acquired to this Weapons array in Step 7, we are looping through all the weapons we have. Then, in the Loop Body, we check the class of the element against the input; if they are the same, then we have this type of weapon already. We return with a Result of true along with the weapon that has the same class type. Any Return node causes the whole function to return, meaning that the first time we encounter a class-type match, we stop the function and return.

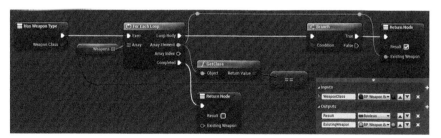

FIGURE 17.6 Implementation of HasWeaponType.

If all the elements (weapons we have) are compared without a match, then we don't have this type of weapon, and the execution reaches to the Completed execution pin. We return with a false Result and none for the Existing Weapon.

Step 8: Implement WeaponPickupOverlapped. Create a new function called WeaponPickupOverlapped. Implement it as shown in Figure 17.7.

This one is relatively simple, well, after the heavy lifting jobs done by HasWeaponType. The logic here is when we overlap a weapon pick up, we check if we have a weapon of the weapon class type already. If we don't have one, then we move on to the AcquireNewWeapon event. If we have one, we print out a message says: I have this already.

Step 9: Implement the overlap event in BP_Weapon_Pickup. Open BP_Weapon_Pickup and override the Overlapped event as shown in Figure 17.8.

What we do here is also simple; we cast the other actor to BP_Character_Base. We then call its WeaponPickupOverlapped and use the WeaponClass variable as the Weapon Class input. If the return value is true, then the weapon is picked up; we destroy this pickup.

We can now play the game, and you should be able to pick up the weapons. This is pretty exciting! However, if you start with a gun, then

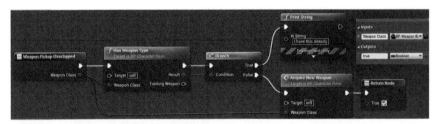

FIGURE 17.7 Implementation of WeaponPickupOverlapped.

FIGURE 17.8 Implementation of Event Overlapped.

you cannot pick up the gun again. Instead, it prints out: I have this weapon already. Also, the new weapon you picked up becomes your active weapon, and you cannot change it back (good luck if you pick up the pipe at last). There is another bug; if you are reloading and you pick up another weapon, the clip or the grenade in your hand might not get destroyed. Let's tackle these issues one by one.

Let's make the weapon replenish ammo when trying to pick an already existing weapon.

Step 10: Implement ReplenishAmmo functions. In BP_Weapon_Base, create a new function called ReplenishAmmo, make it return a boolean, and set the return value to false. Go to BP_Ranged_Weapon, and override it as shown in Figure 17.9.

In the base class, we implement it as an empty function that returns false, and this assumes that the default behavior of a weapon is not replenishable. But for the ranged weapon, we want to replenish ammo, so we override it.

In BP_Ranged_Weapon, we get the class of the weapon, get the default values of the AmmoInInventory and AmmoInClip variable, and add them to our current weapon's AmmoInInventory. We also call the AutoReloadIfClipIsEmpty and UpdateUI (they are all reasonable things to do after changing the ammo). Finally, we return true to indicate that the replenish is successful.

Step 11: Tweak the WeaponPickupOverlapped function. Go back to BP_Character_Base, and tweak the WeaponPickupOverlapped function as shown in Figure 17.10.

Here, we replaced the Print String node with calling the ReplenishAmmo function of the Existing Weapon returned by the HasWeaponType function. Let's examine our entire pickup logic here:

So whenever we overlap with a pickup, we check if we have the type of weapon the pickup offers.

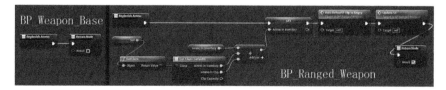

FIGURE 17.9 Implement ReplenishAmmo functions.

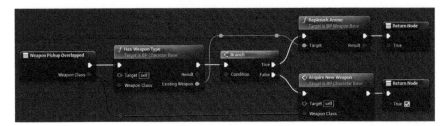

FIGURE 17.10 Tweaked WeaponPickupOverlapped function.

If we have one, we call ReplenishAmmo on that one; if it can replenish, return true; if not, return false.

If we don't have one, we acquire a new weapon.

Play the game again, and now we can replenish ammo when picking up an already existing weapon.

We have finished the weapon pickup class. Let's move on to our weapon switch.

Tutorial 17.2: Weapon Switching

All of our weapons are stored in the Weapons array. So our weapon switch should be working around that.

Step 1: Implement SwitchToNextWeapon. Go to BP_Character_Base. Create a new custom event called SwitchToNextWeapon. Implement it as shown in Figure 17.11.

We have covered array, its elements, and index. Let's revisit array one more time before explaining the function:

An array is a container that has a list of elements in it. Every element in an array has a unique index number associated with it. The first

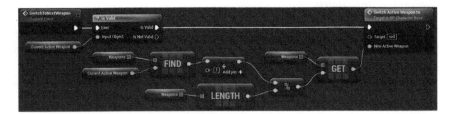

FIGURE 17.11 Implementation of SwitchToNextWeapon.

element in an array has an index number of 0, and the second has an index number of 2. The next one in the list has an index of the previous one's index + 1. You can ask for an element by providing the index through the GET function. You can add new element to an array by calling ADD, and the new element is added to the last in the list. You can find an element's index by calling the FIND function. Every array has a length. The length of an array equals the number of elements an array has. You can ask the length of an array by calling the LENGTH function. The index of the elements starts with 0 and keeps incrementing without skipping any numbers. The index of the last element is guaranteed to be the length of the array minus 1 (why?).

Back to our custom event. First of all, we check if we have a current active weapon; if we don't, well, we don't have a weapon at all (the system is set to equip a weapon as soon as you got it). Then we called a FIND function to find the index of the CurrentActiveWeapon in the Weapons array. We add one to the index, which in theory should be the index of the next one in the list. But consider this:

What if CurrentActiveWeapon is the last one, there is no next one! We want to go back to the first one on the list.

To circle back to the first one, we used a little mathematic trick here, the % (Modulo) operator.

The % operation returns the remainder of the division of the two inputs. If the length of the array is N, then the last index should be $N - 1$. We can try to imagine how each remainder of index/N is:

$$0 \div N = 0\,R\,0$$
$$1 \div N = 0\,R\,1$$
$$2 \div N = 0\,R\,2$$
$$\cdots$$
$$(N-1) \div N = 0\,R\,N-1$$
$$N \div N = 1\,R\,0$$

As you can see, the last one circles back to 0. This algorithm is what we are using in the code. So, after adding one to the index of the CurrentActiveWeapon, we create a % (right click and search %, chose integer). We Modulo it with

643

the length of the Weapons array to ensure that the number circles back to 0 after the last index is reached. After that, we use the GET function to get the element of the calculated index and call SwitchActiveWeaponTo to switch to that weapon.

Step 2: Implement SwitchToPreviousWeapon. Create another custom event called SwitchToPreviousWeapon and implement it as shown in Figure 17.12.

This one finds the index of the CurrentActiveWeapon, and subtract that by 1. After that, we check if the value is smaller than 0; if it is, then the current one is the first one, and we want to move to the last one. The Blueprint array has a convenient function to get the last index (LAST INDEX). We use that to get the last element and switch to it. If the subtraction is not smaller than 0, then we are still in the middle of the list; use the value of the subtraction as the index for the previous one.

Steps 1 and 2 are functions we do algorithms, and these are the harder things to do in programming. You want them to be accurate, but you also want to make them run fast. What we have seen are the simpler ones; much-complicated algorithms are used in the lower level of the game engine.

Step 3: Key binding. Go to Edit → Project Settings. Find the Input section. Under the Bindings, add two more Action Mappings. Name one of them NextWeapon, and use Mouse Wheel Up as the input; name the other one Previous Weapon, and use Mouse Wheel Down as the input. Open BP_Ellen_FPS, and implement two input actions as shown in Figure 17.13.

Play the game again, and now you can use the mouse wheel for cycling through your weapons.

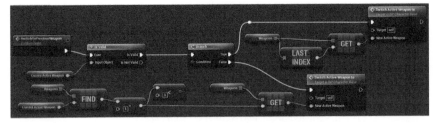

FIGURE 17.12 Implementation of SwitchToPreviousWeapon.

644

FIGURE 17.13 Set up the inputs and implement the input actions.

Step 4: Give weapon shortcuts. Open BP_Weapon_ Base and add a new variable called Shortcut. Set the type of the Variable to Key and make it public. Compile and save. Open BP_Pipe, go to the Class Defaults, and set the Short Cut to 1. For BP_Gun, we can set it to 2. For BP_GrenadeLauncher, we can set it to 3. These key settings are all arbitrary, and there are many keys in the drop-down list, and you can set it to any key.

Step 5: Implement ShortcutWeaponSwitch. Go back to BP_Character_Base. Implement a custom event called ShortcutWeaponSwitch (Figure 17.14).

This ShortcutWeaponSwitch event has an input of type Key. We loop through all the weapons and check if their Shortcut is the same as the Short Cut Key input. If we find a match, we switch to that weapon. This For Each Loop with Break works just like a For Each Loop. However, it has a Break in execution pin; when that pin is called, the loop stops immediately. What we did here is connect the out execution pin of the Switch Active Weapon to node to the Break in execution pin of the For Each Loop with Break node. Then we double click on the connected line to add two more reroute nodes, and drag them down to create a clear circle back loop. Our intention here is whenever we found a match, stop the loop.

FIGURE 17.14 Implementation of ShortcutWeaponSwitch.

645

Step 6: Set up the input. Go to BP_Ellen_ FPS, create an Any Key node, call ShortcutWeaponSwitch with it, and connect the Key output pin to the Short Cut Key input of the ShortcutWeaponSwitch node (Figure 17.15).

Play the game again, and now you can use the shortcut you set up to switch to different weapons.

Step 7: Weapon switch cooldown. We can keep doing the switch if you spam the keyboard, we want it to be fast, but not infinitely fast. Go BP_Character_Base and find the SwitchActiveWeaponTo custom event, let's modify it to the one shown in Figure 17.16.

First, before we even do anything, we check if this weapon we want to switch to is already the CurrentActiveWeapon. If it is, we do nothing. Second, we added a Do Once node to block the constant input. At the end of the function, we added a Delay node, and the Duration is taking the value of a new float variable called WeaponSwitchInterval. We set the WeaponSwitchInterval to 0.25, which means after 0.25 seconds, the Delay Completes and calls the Reset of the Do Once. When you Reset a Do Once, the Do Once resets and allows the execution to go through it one more time.

Give the game another run, and you can no longer switch weapons as fast as possible. The switch now has a 0.25 second cool down.

FIGURE 17.15 Bind Any Key to ShortcutWeaponSwitch.

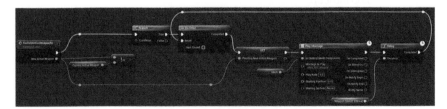

FIGURE 17.16 Modified SwitchActiveWeaponTo.

Tips and Tricks

Sometimes, the child class does not update the variable when you change the parent class. Make sure you check the variables like WeaponSwitchInterval in BP_Ellen_FPS if things do not seem to work.

Step 8: Disable weapon operation when switch. We can easily disable the other weapon activities by adding a limitation in the CanOperateWeapon function. Let's promote the weapon switching animation montage played in the SwitchActiveWeaponTo to a new variable, and call it WeaponSwitchAM. We can then go to the CanOperateWeapon, and add some changes as shown in Figure 17.17.

In CanOperateWeapon, we check what animation montage is playing by calling the Get Current Montage function, and we then check if it is the WeaponSwitchAM. If we are playing the WeaponSwitchAM, that means that we are switching weapons, and we don't want to operate the weapon. So we use!= to check against it and use AND to combine it with the previous criteria.

Step 9: Reset Weapon state. Every time we switch a weapon out, we are not sure what is its weapon state. When we switch a weapon back, we shall set the weapon state back to idle. Add a new custom event called Activated in the BP_Weapon_Base, and set the weapon state to Idle there. Call the Activated event after the On Completed execution pin of Play Montage node at the end of the SwitchActiveWeaponTo event (Figure 17.18).

The On Completed out execution pin of the Play Montage node is called when the animation montage reaches to the end. It is a

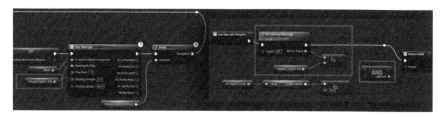

FIGURE 17.17 Promote the switching animation montage to a variable and check it in CanOperateWeapon.

647

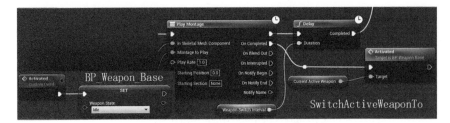

FIGURE 17.18 Create an Activated event to set the weapon state to idle and call it at the end of the weapon switch.

good time for us to set the weapon state back to idle by calling the Activated event.

Step 10: Auto-reload after weapon switch. We also want the auto-reload to happen when we switch weapons. Go to BP_Ranged_Weapon, override the Activated event we did in the previous step, and add a call to AutoReloadIfClipIsEmpty after calling the parent function (Figure 17.19).

Step 11: Clean up the visuals when switching. For the gun and the grenade, if we switch to another weapon during the reloading process, we want to clean up the attached clip and grenade in the left hand. Go to BP_Gun and BP_GrenadeLauncher, and override the WeaponInInventory event to destroy these attached actors if they exist (Figure 17.20).

FIGURE 17.19 Override the Activated to make it call AutoReloadIfClipIsEmpty in BP_Ranged_Weapon.

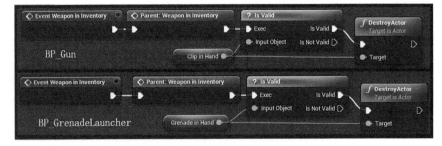

FIGURE 17.20 Clean up attached visuals in during reloading in the WeaponInInventory event.

We did almost the same thing in the two weapons. In BP_Gun, we destroy the Clip in Hand variable if it does exist. In BP_ GrenadeLauncher, we do that to the Grenade in Hand variable.

All right, we have reached a point that we have reasonably good inventory and weapon switching. There are things here and there that we could do more refactoring. But considering the length of this book, we decide to leave you to do more cleanup if you want.

Let's move on to the UI.

Tutorial 17.3: Create the In-Game Weapon UI

Step 1: Create a Master UI class. Go to our WBP folder, and create a new Widget Blueprint. Name the new blueprint WBP_Master.

Step 2: Add a widget switcher. Open WBP_Master. Go to the Palette panel, open the Panel section, drag a Widget Switcher to the Canvas Panel of the Hierarchy panel, and name the added widget switcher to UI_Switch (Figure 17.21).

Widget Switcher

Typically, when we play a game, there are two sets of UIs: a playing UI and a pause UI. If we put them under a widget switcher, we can quickly switch to one of them.

Step 3: Add two Canvas Panels: Drag two Canvas Panels to the UI_Switch; name one of them Playing and the other one Pause (Figure 17.22).

Canvas Panel

Canvas Panel is a regular canvas for you to place any UI elements in it. If you look close, the parent of the UI_ Switch (the default one added in there) is a canvas panel.

Step 4: Set the Anchors of the UI_Switch. You can see the two canvas panels of the UI_Switch located at the upper left corner of the 2D canvas in the

649

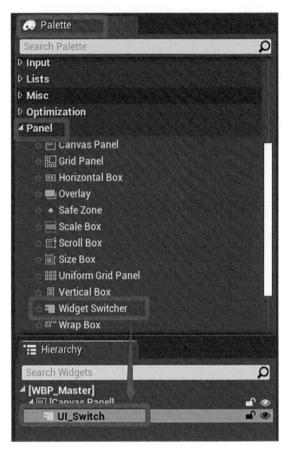

FIGURE 17.21 Add a new widget switcher.

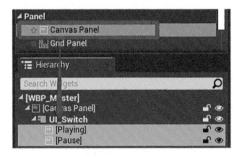

FIGURE 17.22 Add two canvas panels to the switch and name them.

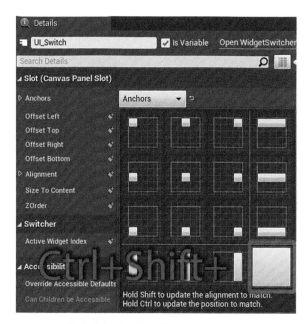

> *middle, and they look rather small. The parent of the canvas panel determines its size. Select the UI_Switch, and go to the Details panel. Click on the Anchors drop-down list, hold down Ctrl + Shift, and click on the big square at the lower right corner to set it to fill the entire canvas (Figure 17.23).*
>
> *Step 5: Add a tile view for the weapons. Go to the Lists section of the Palette panel, drag a Tile View to the Playing canvas panel in the Hierarchy, and name it WeaponsList. Go to the Anchors setting, hold down Ctrl and Shift, and click on the icon that has the small square positioned at the bottom right corner (Figure 17.24). The WeaponsList is now at the bottom right corner.*

Anchors

Anchors allow us to define how to place the UI element on the canvas. The white rectangle in these options shows how the UI is attached and filled into the whole canvas. For the UI_Switch, we chose the last one, which fills the

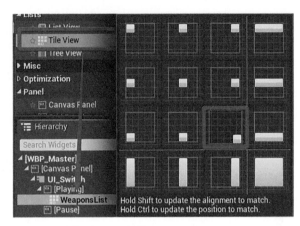

FIGURE 17.24 Add a tile view to the Playing canvas.

entire space. For the tiled view, we want to position it at the bottom right corner; that's why we chose the one that has the square placed at the bottom right corner.

Try to compile, and we got an error which says that the WeaponsList has no EntryWidgetClass (Figure 17.25).

For the Tile View to work, we have to specify an entry or what kind of widget is used for the list to show. Let's create one right now.

> Step 6: Create another widget blueprint for the entry. Create another widget blueprint and call it WBP_Weapon. Open WBP_Weapon, go to the top right corner of the 2D canvas, and change the Fill Screen to Desired. The Desired size make the canvas the size of its content, and because there is no content yet, it becomes super small. Go ahead and add drag an Image UI element from the Palette to the Canvas Panel of the Hierarchy, and name it WeaponIcon. Set its Anchors to be in the center, and check on Size To Content (Figure 17.26).
>
> Step 7: Import UI Assets. Go to our support files, and find the UI folder. Drag the UI folder to the

FIGURE 17.25 Error we got after compiling.

FIGURE 17.26 Create WBP_Weapon.

FIGURE 17.27 Set up the WeaponIcon and set the texture group of the image to UI.

Content Browser to import them. This UI folder has some premade images for the weapons (rendered in Unreal Engine), a button with different states, health bars, crosshairs, and a title.

Step 8: Set up the WeaponIcon. With the WeaponIcon selected, go to the Details panel. Under the Appearance section, set the Image to GrenadeLauncher_icon. And the Image Size to 100×100. This size is arbitrary, and we can adjust it later. Double click to open GrenadeLauncher_icon, and in the Details Panel, set its Texture Group Under the Level Of Detail section to UI (Figure 17.27).

Tips and Tricks

Unreal processes different textures based on their usage; for any UI textures, you need to set their Texture Group to UI. Make sure you change that for all other UI textures.

Step 9: Add some text to show weapon status and shortcut. Drag two Text from the Palette to the Canvas Panel of the Hierarchy.

653

For the first one, we want it to show the ammo count, and name it Status. Set the Anchors to the center, and check on the Size to Content option. In the Context, set the text to 10/10. Under Appearance, open the Font section and set the Size to 8. Adjust the Y value of the Alignment to 3.5 to position it at the top of the icon.

Alignment

The alignment setting defines the distance the upper left corner of the UI element is to the anchor proportionally. The text is anchored to the center. For the X and Y direction, a value of 0.5 means that the upper corner of the UI element is 50% away from the center. We set the Y of the text to 3.5 to move it up 3.5 times (of its size).

For the second text, name it Shortcut and anchor to the bottom-center. Check on Size to Content, set the Text to 1, and set the Size to 16. Figure 17.28 shows the settings for both text elements.

Step 10: Make WBP_Weapon inherit UserObjectListEntry. To use this WBP_Weapon as an entry of the WeaponsList we added to WBP_Master, we have to make it inherent an interface called UserObjectListEntry. Click the Graph button at the top right corner to go to the graphs for the widget. Click on the Class Settings

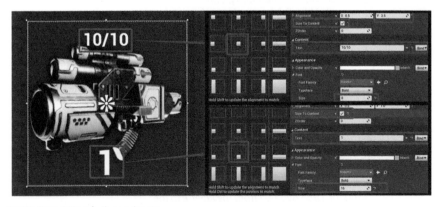

FIGURE 17.28 Settings for the text elements.

in the Toolbar, go to the Interfaces section of the Details panel, and click the Add button. Search and select the UserObjectListEntry. A list of events got added to the Interfaces, which we will implement later (Figure 17.29). This UserObjectListEntry works the same way as our BPI_HealthComp.

Step 11: *Use WBP_Weapon as the entry for the WeaponsList. Go to WBP_Master, and select WeaponsList in the Hierarchy. Go to the Details panel, and check on the Size To Content option. Under the List View section, change the Orientation to Horizontal. Finally, set the Entry Widget Class under the List Entries section to WBP_Weapon, and set both Entry Height and Entry Width to 150. We should now be able to compile and save the widget. After compiling, we can see a list of our WBP_Weapon got added to the bottom left corner (Figure 17.30).*

Step 12: *Implement UIAddNewWeapon to WBP_Master. Go to the Graph of WBP_Master, and implement a new custom event called UIAddNewWeapon as shown in Figure 17.31.*
    This UIAddNewWeapon takes a BP_Weapon_Base as an input; we check if it is valid, and we add it to the WeaponsList. The Add Item is created by holding down Ctrl and drag the WeaponsList from the Variables to the graph and then drag out from WeaponsList; search for Add Item. When we call Add Item on WeaponsList, we ask it to create a new entry of the entry widget class we set up. It then associates the new entry with the Item we connect to the Item input pin. This Item, on the other hand, can be anything.

FIGURE 17.29 Make WBP_Weapon inherit UserObjectListEntry.

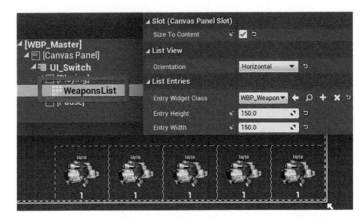

FIGURE 17.30 Set up WeaponsList and use WBP_Weapon as the entry.

FIGURE 17.31 Implement UIAddNewWeapon.

Step 13: Create and Add the UI to the viewport. Go to BP_Ellen_FPS, add a new variable called UI, and set its type to WBP_Master object reference. Go to BP_Ellen_FPS_PlayerController and add the same variable. Go back to BP_Ellen_FPS, implement a new function called CreateUI, and call it at the end of Event BeginPlay (Figure 17.32).

We start with getting the controller and cast it to BP_Ellen_FPS_PlayerController (the player controller we set in the game mode). We then created a widget of the class WBP_Master and set the owner player to BP_Ellen_FPS_PlayerController. We then use the new UI as the values of the UI variables we added

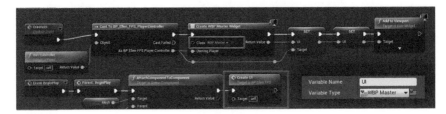

FIGURE 17.32 Implement CreateUI and call it at the end of Event BeginPlay.

to both the BP_Ellen_FPS_PlayerController and BP_Ellen_FPS. The first SET is created by dragging out from the AS BP_Ellen_FPS_PlayerController output pin of the Cast node and search for Set UI. And finally, we add it to the viewport. We call CreateUI at the end of Event BeginPlay, so we have the UI added when we start the game.

Give the game another run, but surprisingly, we don't see any UI. The five entries we saw in WeaponsList is just for previews; to add an actual one, we have to call the UIAddNewWeapon we have created.

Step 14: Call UIAddNewWeapon after AcquireNewWeapon. In BP_Ellen_FPS, create an override of AcqurieNewWeapon, and implement it as shown in Figure 17.33. Play again, and we got a new entry added every time we pick up a new weapon.

Here, we call the parent function first to ensure that we do all the things needed to be done in the parent class, we then get our Weapons array, and get the last one in it (the new weapon). Then, we get the UI and call its UIAddNewWeapon event with our new weapon as the New Weapon to Add input.

So why are all the entries show the grenade launcher? Well, like what we have covered, when we add a new thing to WeaponsList in WBP_Master, it creates an entry of the type WBP_Weapon for it. But none of the processes provide what the icon, the status, and the short cut should be in the new WBP_Weapon. We can provide that in the interface we added to WBP_Weapon earlier, but before we do that, let's add the UI information to BP_Weapon_Base.

Step 15: Add UI variables to BP_Weapon_Base and set them up in the weapons. Add three

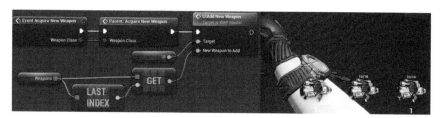

FIGURE 17.33 Override AcqurieNewWeapon in BP_Ellen_FPS.

Variables to BP_Weapon_Base. A UIWidget with the type of WBP_Weapon object reference, a WeaponIcon, and a WeaponCrosshair, both of the type Texture2D object references. Go ahead and set them up in BP_Gun, BP_Pipe, and BP_GrenadeLuancher accordingly (Figure 17.34).

Notice that the WeaponCrosshair for BP_Pipe is empty, because it is does not have a crosshair. For the other two, even it looks like a white box, if you double click to open them, you can see their actual shape.

Step 16: Create a GetWeaponUIInfo function. In BP_Weapon_Base, create a new function called GetWeaponUIInfo and make it a blueprint pure function. Implement it in BP_Weapon_Base and override it in BP_Ranged_Weapon as shown in Figure 17.35.

In BP_Weapon Base, we are just returning all the UI variables we created in Step 15, the shortcut key, and a status. One thing worth noting is that we returned the display name of the Shortcut key. If the shortcut is the 1 button on the keyboard, the Get Key Display Name is 1, and the type of it is Text. Also, we returned an empty Status Output of the type Text as well for the Status text widget we added to WBP_Weapon.

In BP_Ranged_Weapon, we override it. Here, we hold down Ctrl and drag the AmmoInClip variable to the graph, drag out from it, search, and created a ToString node to convert it from an integer to a string. We do the same for AmmoInInventory so we can Append these two with a "/" to create an ammo gauge that shows

FIGURE 17.34 Add UI variables to BP_Weapon_Base and set them up in the weapons.

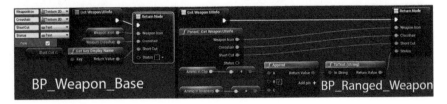

FIGURE 17.35 Implementation of GetWeaponUIInfo.

the ammo status. We then converted it to a text as the Status output.

Step 17: Create an UpdateUI function in WBP_ Weapon. Open WBP_Weapons and click on the Designer button at the top right corner to switch back to the Designer part of the widget. In the Hierarchy panel, select the Status text widget, go to the Details panel, and check on Is Variable. Do the same thing to the Shortcut text widget. We have to check Is Variable on to access these two text widgets in the Graph. Go to the Graph of WBP_Weapons, and create and implement a new custom event called UpdateUI (Figure 17.36).

Because we have done the information gathering and conversion in GetWeaponUIInfo, what we do here is pretty lightweight. We take an input of BP_Weapon_Base and set the Weapon Icon to use the WeaponIcon of the weapon. We then set the Shortcut and Status from the GetWeaponUIInfo. All three Set nodes are created by dragging from the three UI widgets and search.

Creating these functions doesn't do us any good unless we call them. An interface call of On List Item Object Set fires on the creation of any new entry in WeaponsList. Let's implement it now.

Step 18: Implement On List Item Object Set. Go to the Interfaces section under the My Blueprint panel. Right click on the On List Item Object Set in the list and select Implement Function. Implement it as shown in Figure 17.37.

Because you can add anything to WeaponsList as a new item, the List Item Object is of the type Object (parent class of Actor). This List Item Object is the weapon we passed into the Add Item function in the UIAddNewWeapon event. We first cast it to BP_Weapon_Base, and

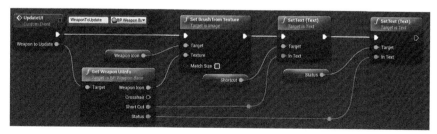

FIGURE 17.36 Implementation of UpdateUI.

FIGURE 17.37 Implementation of the On List Item Object Set event.

then we set the weapons UIWidget variable to this widget; by doing so, every weapon knows their associated WBP_Weapon widget. We then pass the weapon to the UpdateUI event to update the UI widgets.

Play the game again; when we pick up a new weapon, we now get a UI entry added with the correct information (Figure 17.38).

Let's review how everything is tied up here. First, we added a tile view widget called WeaponsList and specify an entry of type WBP_Weapon for it. Every time we acquire a new weapon, we add the weapon as a new item to WeaponsList. When we add a new item to WeaponsList, it creates a WBP_Weapon, and fire the On List Item Object Set event interface call to it. The On List Item Object Set takes the new weapon as the input parameter, and we use it along with the functions we created to modify the new WBP_Weapon.

Remember the BP_HealthComp and the BPI_HealthComp? What is happening here is similar to our health system. Coding using interface allows abstraction of the objects involved. The tile widget does not have to know the type of its entry and only requires the inheritance of the interface. Just like how our HealthComp knows nothing about its owner, all they have to communicate to is the interface.

Step 19: Update ammo. Go to BP_Ranged_Weapon and look for the UpdateUI event we created before. We are only printing out the ammo

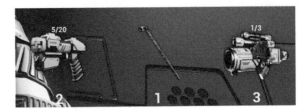

FIGURE 17.38 The correct UI entries.

now. Let's change it to update our actual UI (Figure 17.39).

> *We just call the UpateUI on the UIWidget this weapon is associated with. It was set up in the On List Item Object Set event.*

> *Play the game again and shoot out some ammo, you can see the ammo count on the weapons UI updates nicely.*

Step 20: Set up crosshair. Go to WBP_Master and drag an image widget to the Playing canvas panel. Anchor it to the center and check on its Size To Content. Under the Appearance section, open the brush subsection and set the Image to Gun_Crosshair. Set the Visibility to Hidden under the Behavior section (Figure 17.40).

> *We set it to hidden because we don't want to have it on if we don't have a ranged weapon.*

Step 21: Create UIWeaponSwtiched. Create and implement a new custom event called UIWeaponSwtiched to WBP_Master (Figure 17.41).

> *We make the event to take a BP_ Weapon_Base object reference input called NewActiveWeapon. We supply the new active*

FIGURE 17.39 Change the UpdateUI event.

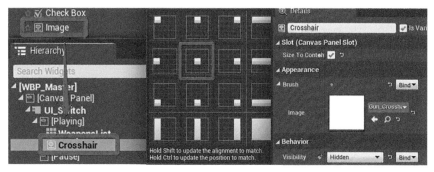

FIGURE 17.40 Set Add a crosshair image to the center of the UI.

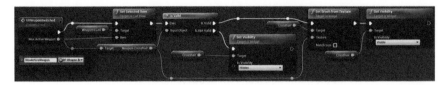

FIGURE 17.41 Implementation of UIWeaponSwitched.

weapon here when we call this event. In the
event, we get the WeaponsList and call Set
Selected Item with the new active weapon,
which triggers an interface call on the entry
(WBP_Weapon) that we can implement later. We
then get the WeaponCrosshair variable from the
new active weapon and check if it is valid (pipe
does not have a valid one). If it is valid, we set the
Crosshair widget to use it as the texture and set
the widget to be visible. If it is not valid, we simply
hide the widget.

Step 22: Call UIWeaponSwitched when we switch to
a new weapon. Open BP_Ellen_FPS and override
the WeaponSwitchHandsDownNotify. In here,
we just add a call to the UIWeaponSwitched
event on the UI with our currently active weapon
(Figure 17.42).

Give the game another go, and this
time, when you pick up or switch to a ranged
weapon, the crosshair appears; when you
switch back to the pipe, it goes away.

Step 23: Set up the selected and unselected effect. Go
to WBP_Weapon. Create two Vector2D variables:
name one of them DeselectedIconSize and the
other one SelectedIconSize. Create two Slate Font
Info variables: name one of them DeselectedFont
and the other one SelectedFont. Their values are
shown in the bottom left corner of Figure 17.43.
If you cannot see the Roboto font in the Font
Family drop-down list, click on the viewOptions
at the bottom right of the list, and check on Show
Engine Content.

FIGURE 17.42 Override the WeaponSwitchHandsDownNotify event.

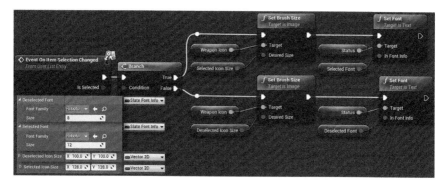

FIGURE 17.43 Add the new variables and implement the On Item Selection Changed interface.

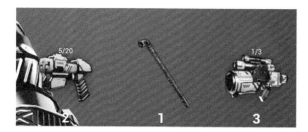

FIGURE 17.44 The selected weapon becomes bigger in the UI.

After setting up the variables, implement the On Item Selection Changed interface as shown in Figure 17.43.

We have mentioned in Step 21 that calling the Set Selected Item on WeaponsList triggers an interface call to the entry. This On Item Selection Changed event is that interface call. Whenever an entry is selected or deselected, its On Item Selection Changed is fired. What we do here is set the icon and font bigger when selected, and set them smaller when deselected.

Play the game again, and now you can clearly see which weapon is active (Figure 17.44).

Let's move on to the health bar.

Tutorial 17.4: Create the Health Bar

Step 1: Create a health bar material. Create a new material called HealthBar_Mtl. Open it, and in the Details panel, set the Material Domain to User Interface and the Blend Mode to

Translucent. Go to our UI folder, and drag the FPS_Health_bar to the Material Editor. If you do recall, the OcclusionRoughnessMetallic textures we exported from Substance Painter have three channels each representing a different attribute of a material. This FPS_Health_bar also has its channels represent different things. The green channel is the outline, and the red channel is the alpha of the whole figure. There is nothing in the blue channel.

Step 2: Set up basic connections. Connect the R output to the Opacity input of the HealthBar_Mtl node. Hold down L and click to create a Lerp node, and connect the G channel to the Alpha of the Lerp node. Hold down V and click to create a color parameter; name it OutlineColor. Set the color of the OutlineColor parameter to white and connect its first output pin to the B input of the Lerp node, connect the output pin of the Lerp node to the Final Color input pin of the material. You should now see the outline appears in the upper-left preview window. Create another color parameter and name it LifeColor; make it green.

Create a LinearGradient node (right click and search), and hold down M and click to create a Multiply node. Connect the VGradient of the LinearGradient node to the A input of the Multiply node, and connect the first output pin of the LifeColor node to the B input of the Multiply node. Finally, connect the output of the Multiply node to the A input of the Lerp node. You should now see a green gradient place in the outline (Figure 17.45).

Step 3: Set up health bar control. Hold down S and click to create a scalar parameter; name it HealthAmount. In the Details panel, set its Default Value to 0.5 and Slider Max to 1. Hold down O and click to create a 1 − x node; this one returns the result of 1 − input. Connect HealthAmount to the input of the 1 − x node. Create an If node by right click and search. Connect the 1 − x node to the A input of the If node. Connect the VGradient of the LinearGradient node we created in the previous step to the B input of the If node.

Hold down 1 and click to create a float number node, and in the Details panel, set its value to 0.1. Connect it to the A > B input of the If node. Create another float number node, set it to 1, and connect it to the A < B

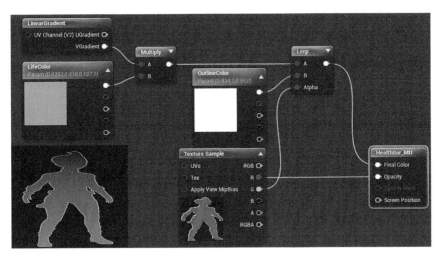

FIGURE 17.45 Basic connections of the Material.

input of the If node. Finally, connect the output pin of the If to the A input pin of the Multiply node we created in Step 2. You should now see a half-filled health bar. Changing the health amount from 0 to 1 changes the health bar from empty to full.

The logic here is to compare the HealthAmount with the VGradient. The VGradient is 1 at the bottom and 0 on the top. We use If to make the values bigger than HealthAmount becomes almost black (0.1), and the values smaller than HealthAmount becomes White (1). That then got multiplied to the green color (Figure 17.46).

Step 4: Make the color red if the health is low. Add another color parameter, name it LifeCriticalColor, and change its color to red. Create another If node. Connect the LifeColor to the A > B and A = B input of the new If node. Connect the LifeCriticalColor to the A < B input of the If node. Select the HealthAmount we created in Step 3 and press Ctrl + W to duplicate it. Connect the duplicated HealthAmount to the A input of the new If node. Create another scalar parameter node, name it CriticalThreshold, and set its default value to 0.3. Connect the CriticalThreshold node to the B input of the new If node. Finally, connect the new If node to the B input of the Multiply node (Figure 17.47).

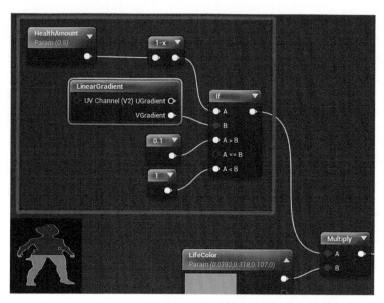

FIGURE 17.46 Set up the health bar control.

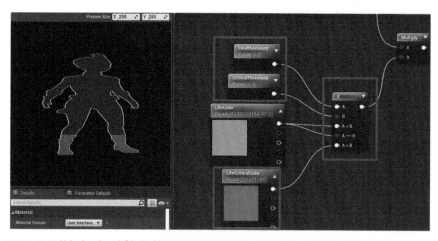

FIGURE 17.47 Make the color red if the health is low.

We used a similar logic here. If HealthAmount is smaller than CriticalThreshold, change the color to red. Apply, save the material, and close the Material Editor.

Step 5: Create a material instance. Create a material instance of the HealthBar_Mtl.

*Step 6: Create an enemy health bar material.
Duplicate the HealthBar_Mtl and name the
duplication EnemyHealthBar_Mtl. Open it,
replace the Texture Sample used to the Enemy_
Health_bar, and change the part we did in Step 3
to what is shown in Figure 17.48.*

*Because the enemy health bar is
horizontal, we use the UGradient instead of
the VGradient. Replace the 1 − x node with a
reroute node. Switch the connections of the
1 and 0.1 float numbers on the If node. These
changes are needed to make the bar have the
correct increase or decrease direction. Save
the material, and create a material instance
from it as well.*

*Step 7: Create a WBP_HealthBar Widget. Create a
new widget named WBP_HealthBar and open
it. Set its size to Desired at the top right corner.
Give it an Image widget anchored at the center
and set the name of the image HealthBar. In
the Details panel, check on the Size to Content.
Under the Appearance section, set the Image
to HealthBar_Mtl_Inst and the Image size to
128×256 (Figure 17.49).*

*Step 8: Implement an UpdateHealthBar event. Go
to the Graph of our WBP_HealthBar, and create
and implement a new custom event called
UpdateHealthBar (Figure 17.50).*

*This UpdateHealthBar event takes a float
number input called Health Amount. We*

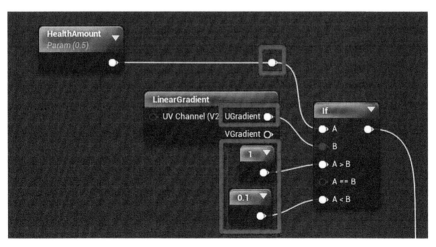

FIGURE 17.48 Adjustment done in EnemyHealthBar_Mtl.

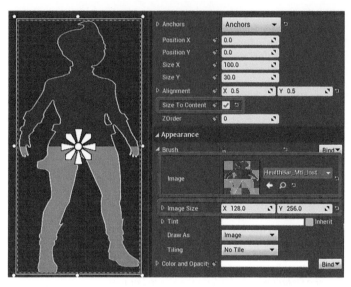

FIGURE 17.49 Settings for the HealthBar image widget.

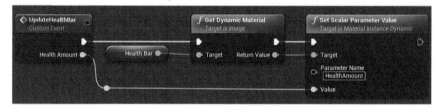

FIGURE 17.50 Implementation of UpdateHealthBar.

get the Dynamic Material of the HealthBar image widget and set the HealthAmount parameter of the material to the input. The Dynamic Material is the material used by HealthBar (HealthBar_Mtl_Inst). It is dynamic because it is a copy of the HealthBar_Mtl_Inst dynamically created in the game when the UI is created. Whenever a material is dynamic, it is unique, and changing it does not affect the original one. Whenever this event fires, the HealthAmount parameter of the material is changed, which increases or decreases the health bar based on the input value.

Step 9: Add WBP_HealthBar to WBP_Master. Open WBP_Master, and in the Palette panel, open the User Created section and drag the

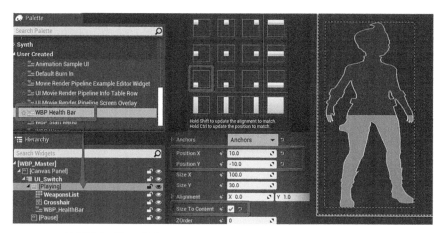

FIGURE 17.51 Add WBP_HealthBar to WBP_Master.

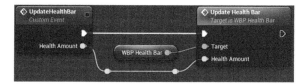

FIGURE 17.52 Create another UpdateHealthBar in WBP_Master.

WBP_HealthBar in there to the Playing canvas panel of the Hierarchy. Set the anchor to bottom left, set the Position X to 10, and Position Y to −10 to offset it away from the corner 10 pixels. Check on Size to Content (Figure 17.51).

Step 10: Create another UpdateHealthBar in WBP_Master. Go to the Graph of WBP_Master, create another UpdateHealthBar event that also takes a float input, and use it to call the UpdateHealthBar event of the WBP_HealthBar (Figure 17.52).

Why?

So why do we create a new widget instead of just adding an image to the WPB_Master? Well, it depends on if you want to use it in other places too. We want to use it on the enemy as well, so an already built widget will come in handy.

Step 11: Update the health bar when the player takes damage. Open BP_Ellen_FPS, and override the HealthCompNotify_UpdateUI interface as shown in Figure 17.53.

What we do here is pretty simple; when the health component asks us to update the UI, we get the UI and call the UpdateHealthBar event. We don't want to start with half health; open HealthBar_Mtl_Inst, and set the HealthAmount there to 1; do the same to EnemyHealthBar_Mtl_ Inst. Play the game again, take some damage from the BP_Dummy_AI, and you can see the health bar updates nicely.

Step 12: Add health bar to BP_Dummy_AI. We are going to change BP_Dummy_AI to our Patrolling AI, so it is an excellent time to set up the health bar for it as well. Open_BP_Dummy_AI and add a Widget component to it. With the new widget component selected, go to the Details panel and set the Widget Class under the User Interface section to WBP_HealthBar. We do not want to use the human figure as the health bar, but let's pretend that it is the enemy health bar, and use the transform tools to put it above the head (Figure 17.54).

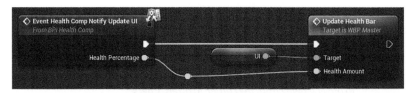

FIGURE 17.53 Override the HealthCompNotify_UpdateUI in BP_Ellen_FPS.

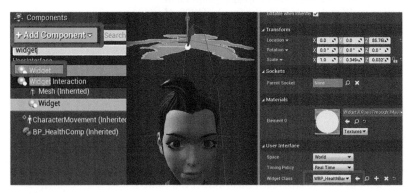

FIGURE 17.54 Add a health bar to BP_Dummy_AI.

Step 13: Change the health bar appearance. Go to the event graph. Add the code shown in Figure 17.55 to the Event BeginPlay node.

What we do here is to get the widget object from the Widget component first. We then cast it to WBP_HealthBar. We get its HealthBar image widget and set its material to EnemyHealthBar_ Mtl_Inst. Play the game again, and now you can see the health bar appear nicely on the head of the character. However, when you look at the character from the side, you can see that it is not facing you (Figure 17.56).

Step 14: Make the Health bar face the player. Add the code shown in Figure 17.57 to the Event Tick.

The Find Look at Rotation is a convenient function. It gives you the rotation needed for an object at the location of the start input to look at the location of the Target input. We supply the

FIGURE 17.55 Change the health bar appearance in Event BeginPlay.

FIGURE 17.56 The health bar does not face the player when looking from the side.

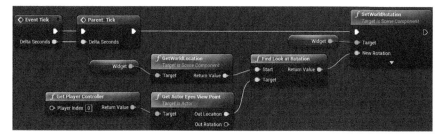

FIGURE 17.57 Make the Health bar face the player in Event Tick.

671

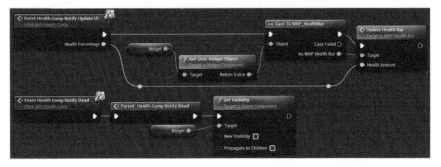

FIGURE 17.58 Receive the notifies from the HealthComp.

world location of the widget as the Start input, and the player's eye viewpoint location as the Target input. The Find Look at Rotation then returns the rotation needed for the widget to look at (face) the player. We then set that as the rotation of the widget on every tick to make the widget face the player constantly. Give the game another run, and the health bar is now always facing the player. We also removed the Attack function call. It was there just for testing.

Step 15: Receive the notifies from the HealthComp. Implement the HealthCompNotify_UpdateUI and the HealthCompNotify_Dead as shown in Figure 17.58.

When the HealthComp request UI update, we get the widget and call the UpdateHealthBar event; when the character is dead, we set it to invisible. We want this invisible behavior because we don't want it to be there while the death animation is playing. It will eventually get destroyed when the character is.

Play the game and shoot the enemy to test if the UI updates; it should also disappear when you kill the enemy (Figure 17.59).

Alrighty, one last UI to go before we wrap this up: the pause and game over UI.

Tutorial 17.5: Create the Pause and Game Over UI

Step 1: Add a button. Open WBP_Master, and drag a Button from the Palette panel to the Pause canvas panel. Name the button Restart, and anchor it to the center. Go the Details panel, and

FIGURE 17.59 Test the enemy health bar.

set the Size X and Size Y to 256×256 in the slot section to define the size of the button.

Open the Style subsection in the Appearance section. Set the Image of Normal to button_normal. Set the Image of Hovered to button_hover. Set the Image of Pressed to button_down and set the Image of Disabled to button_disabled. For all four of them, set their Draw as to Image.

Drag a Text from the Palette panel to the Restart button to attach a text to it. Change the text to Restart (Figure 17.60).

Step 2: Duplicate two more buttons. Select the Restart button and press Ctrl + W twice to create

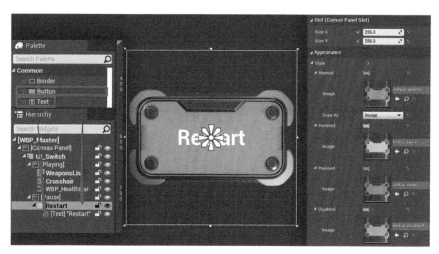

FIGURE 17.60 Add a button to the Pause canvas panel.

two copies. Set the Position X and Position Y of the two new buttons back to 0. Set the Alignment X of the first duplication to 1.8, and set the Alignment X of the second duplication to −0.8. The three buttons should now be aligned in a row. Change the text of the first button to Resume, and the text of the second button to Quit (Figure 17.61).

Play the game, and we don't see the buttons; this is because the UI_Switch widget switcher is by default switched to its first child, which is the Playing canvas panel. All the buttons are in the Pause canvas panel.

Step 3: Set up a switching enum. Create a new Blueprint Enumeration and call it EUISwitch. Give it three entries: Playing, Pause, and GameOver.

Step 4: Create a UISwitchTo event to switch UI. Go to the Designer of the WBP_Master, select the Playing canvas panel, and check on Is Variable in the Details panel. Do the same thing to the Pause canvas panel. Create and implement a new event called UISwitchTo in WBP_Master (Figure 17.62).

We check on the Is Variable setting for the Playing and Pause canvas panel to get access

FIGURE 17.61 The arrangement of the three buttons.

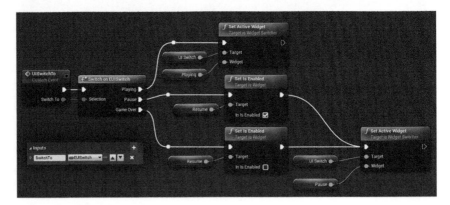

FIGURE 17.62 Implementation of UISwitchTo.

to them in the Graph. The function takes a EUISwitch input parameter named Switch To. Drag out from Switch To and search for Switch on EUISwitch to create that yellow Switch on EUISwitch node. For the three out execution pins of the Switch on EUISwitch node, only the one matches the value of the Switch To parameter is fired. For the Playing out execution pin, we simply ask the UISwitch to switch to the Playing canvas panel. For the Pause, we set the Resume button to Enabled first and then switch to the Pause canvas panel. For the Game Over, we set the Resume button to not Enabled so that the player cannot resume when the game is over. We then switch to the Pause canvas panel as well.

Step 5: Add UISwitch input. Add an Action Mapping to the Inputs in the Project Settings. Call it Menu, and assign the Escape and the Q button as the keys. We add the Q button because when we play in the editor, the Escape button is occupied by quitting the game. Implement the InputAction Menu in BP_Ellen_FPS as shown in Figure 17.63.

All we do here is to get the UI and make it switch to Pause. Give the game another run and hit the Q button, and we can indeed see the buttons pop up. However, we can't click on them, there is no cursor, and we can even keep playing the game.

Step 6: Set input mode and cursor visibility when switching UI, and add set pause. At the end of the Set Active Widget function calls of the UISwitchTo function in WBP_Master, add the extra code shown in Figure 17.64.

After the Set Active Widget for the Playing canvas panel, we get the owning player and set

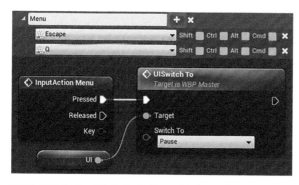

FIGURE 17.63 Add input binding for the Menu and implement the input action.

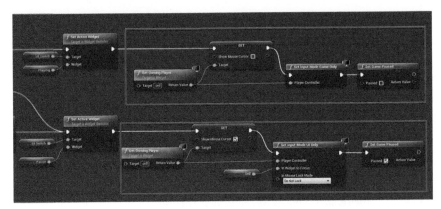

FIGURE 17.64 Set input mode and cursor visibility when switching UI and add Set Pause.

the mouse cursor not to show. And call Set Input Mode Game Only to evade all UI elements. We then called the Set Game Paused function and make it not pause. For the switching to the Pause canvas panel, we show the mouse cursor, call Set Input Mode UI Only, make this UI as the focused UI, and pause the game. Another crucial thing we have to do here is going to the Class Defaults, and check on the Is Focusable option. Focusing on a UI that is focusable is needed to cancel all gameplay movements. We can play the game again, hit the Q button to switch on the UI, and see the cursor pop up. The buttons are not doing anything yet.

Step 7: Create a GameOver and a Restart event in GM_Ellen_FPS. Open GM_Ellen_FPS. Go to its Event Graph and implement a Restart and a Quit event (Figure 17.65).

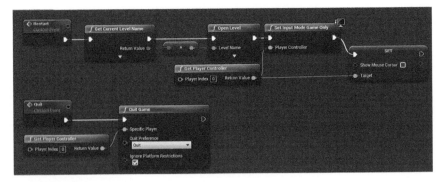

FIGURE 17.65 Implement a Restart and a Quit event in GM_Ellen_FPS.

676

For the Restart, we get the name of the current level, and open it by calling Open Level. The node between the Return value of the Get Current Level Name and the Level Name input pin of the Open Level node is automatically added when you connect these two. We then get the player controller and set the input mode back to game only and hide the mouse cursor (this does not happen automatically). The Quit event just calls the built-in Quit Game function.

Step 8: Implement the Button commands. Go back to WBP_Master, and select the Quit button in the Variables. Go to the Details panel, and click on the green button labeled with On Released in the Events section. An OnReleased (Quit) event got added to the Graph. This event fires when you click and release the Quit button. We chose to use the OnReleased because the On Clicked is too abrupt. We get the game mode, cast it to GM_Ellen_FPS, and call its Quit event with OnReleased (Quit). For the Restart button, we do the same thing except we call the Restart event of the game mode. For the Resume, we simply call UISwitchTo and set the Switch To input to Playing (Figure 17.66).

Test the game again, and all buttons should work as expected.

Step 9: Switch the UI to game over when the player is dead. Open BP_Ellen_FPS_PlayerController, and find the Event On UnPossess. At the end of the

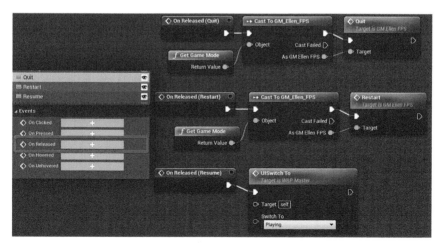

FIGURE 17.66 Implement the Button commands.

677

event, add a call to a Delay node with a 3-second duration. Then we get the UI and call UISwitch To and set the Switch To input to GameOver (Figure 17.67).

Play the game again, and shoot your feet with the grenade launcher to kill yourself. After 3 seconds, the UI should pop up automatically with the resume button disabled.

Step 10: Add a title to the screen. When we pause the game, we want to see a paused text on the screen; when we switch to game over, we want to see a game over text on the screen. Add a Text to the Pause canvas panel and name it MenuTitle. In the Details panel, check on Is Variable, and anchor it to the center.

Set the Alignment Y to 2two to offset it up, check on Size To Content, set the Text to Paused, go to the Appearance section, and set Font Size to 100.

In the UISwitchTo event, insert two SetText nodes after the two Set Is Enabled nodes to set the text of the MenuTitle text widget to Pause and Game Over (Figure 17.68).

FIGURE 17.67 Switch UI to game over after the player is dead.

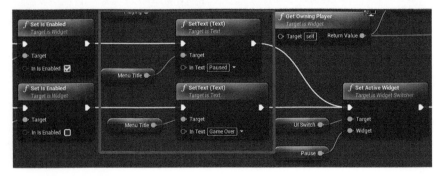

FIGURE 17.68 Add a title to the screen.

All right, that's about all the UI we want to cover in this book; however, feel free to add things and experiment. Just one more clean up to do: go to BP_Character_Base and delete the Delay and Acquire New Weapon function call in Event BeginPlay. These are only for testing. We said we want the player to start empty-handed.

Assignment

Now you have done the in-game UI, remember the start menu we created on Chapter 13? It is now time to refine it! There is a UI image called Title. Use it to your advantage. You also want to throw a few assets in the StartMenuLevel to spice it up (Figure 17.69)!

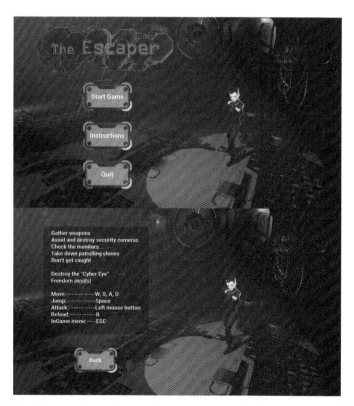

FIGURE 17.69 The main menu we have created eventually. It has a security camera in it that we are going to build later, but other than that, you can create the rest of the scene.

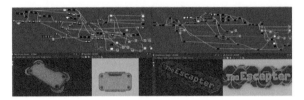

FIGURE 17.70 Sneak peek of the creation of the UI elements with Substance Designer.

Tips and Tricks

If you want to know how the buttons and the title are made so you can create your own, take a look at Substance Designer. It is a sister software of Substance Painter. Substance Designer uses a node-based approach to create textures instead of using layers (Figure 17.70).

Conclusion

We have finished the inventory, weapon pickup, weapon switch, health bar, and the main UI in this chapter. The player part of the game now feels fairly complete. Through the process, we keep following the rules of keeping the code clean and tidy. For the weapon inventory, we explored more ways to manipulate array and learned how to set up short cuts properly. For our UI, we try to communicate with it through custom-built functions.

Between the Weapon and the UI, we store icon, short cut, ammo count on the weapons, and we pass these data to the UI with well-built functions. It is essential to understand that there should be only one place to store these data. You don't want any information hardcoded to the UI, and it is only a receiver to show the data from relevant game objects.

There are still many aspects of the code that could be improved. But we are in a good spot to move on for building the enemies, and the real fun shall begin when we move on to that.

CHAPTER 18

Security Camera

In this chapter, we shall explore the perception system of Unreal Engine, along with other game mechanics. We are going to build a sight perception and use that on a security camera.

We are also going to explore how C++ and Blueprint tie together with just a little C++ programming with visual studio. Don't get too scared because you will soon learn how scripting with C++ is not that different compared to Blueprint.

With that being said, our focus is still Blueprint. We need to leverage just a little C++ to get access to some handy variables that Blueprint does not have access to. By giving you a little taste of C++, so you can also explore it yourself.

Let's implement an AI perception actor in C++.

Tutorial 18.1: Implement an AISeer in C++

Step 1: Create a C++ class derived from Actor. Right click anywhere in the content browser and select New C++ Class. A new Add C++ Class window pops up; select Actor in the list and click next. In the next page, set the name to AISeer, press Create Class, and let it run for the rest to the setup (Figure 18.1).

If you get errors, one thing you want to do is to close your project and update your Visual Studio to the latest version. If you get specific errors, check for the error online. It is usually

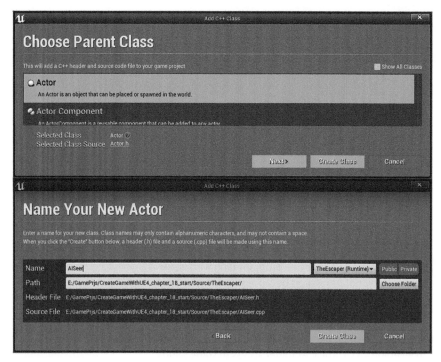

FIGURE 18.1 Create a C++ class called AISeer derived from Acotor.

FIGURE 18.2 Steps to build the project from source.

some missing components like not having the correct version of Microsoft.NET Framework. Please download and install any of these missing components.

Next (if you are getting errors), go to your project folder, right click on your unreal project file, and select Generate Visual Studio Files. A new visual studio solution file with the same name of your project got added after the generating process. Double click to open the visual studio solution with Visual Studio. Go to the menu, and select Debug → Start Without Debugging. Visual Studio then starts to build the project, and open it after completion (Figure 18.2).

Step 2: Open AISeer in Visual Studio. A file called AISeer.h should now be open in Visual Studio. If you don't see it, go to the Solution Explorer, open Games/TheEscaper/Source/TheEscaper/, and you should see AISeer.h in there. Double click to open it. You should also see another file called AISeer. cpp. Double click to open AISeer.cpp as well. You can switch two files by clicking on their tab above the text editor.

Tips and Tricks

The Solution Explorer is like your content browser, and all the classes you created are here. The editor we are using in this book is using the dark theme. You can switch to the dark theme by going to Tools → Options to open the Options window. Find the General section under Environment and set the Color Theme to Dark.

Step 3: Include the AI Module. Open the TheEscaper. Build.cs located at the same location as the AISeer. Find the line that says:

683

```
PublicDependencyModuleNames.
AddRange(new string[] { "Core",
"CoreUObject", "Engine", "InputCore"
});
```

Insert a comma and then "AIModule" after "InputCore." So, it becomes (Figure 18.3):

```
PublicDependencyModuleNames.
AddRange(new string[] { "Core",
"CoreUObject", "Engine", "InputCore",
"AIModule" });
```

Go back to your Unreal project and click on the Compile button in the toolbar and wait for it to finish. It should take a minute or two (adding a new module takes time). After completion, a notification should pop up and tells you Compile Complete. If you get errors, go back to Visual Studio and check if you have missed any comma, quotation marks, or have any miss spells. Keep in mind that case matters in C++. If you type an uppercase letter to a lowercase, it is not going to work. This AI module is needed for us to use the built-in AI perception system.

Step 4: Include necessary files into AISeer.h. Open AISeer.h, go to the top of the file, and insert the following three lines after the line that says #include "GameFramework/Actor.h:"

```
#include "Perception/AIPerceptionComponent.h"
#include "Perception/AISenseConfig_Sight.h"
#include "Components/SpotLightComponent.h"
```

What these three lines do is to include (copy and paste) these three files to the AISeer.h so AISeer.h can use whatever is in these three files. We need the AIPerceptionComponent, AISenseConfig_ Sight, and the SpotLightComponent located in these three files. After all the #include lines, you can see the AISeer class and many familiar faces like Actor, BeginPlay, and Tick. The name of the AISeer in C++ is AAISeer, where the

FIGURE 18.3 Add the AIModule.

extra A indicates that it is a child class of Actor (remember how we add an extra E in front of the enumerations we created before?).

We don't need to understand everything here, but Figure 18.4 shows a high-level view of the meaning of each line.

Step 5: Add an AIPerceptionComponent variable. Go to the line right after the AAISeer(); and let's add the following code:

```
UPROPERTY(EditAnywhere, BlueprintReadOnly,
Category = "AI")
UAIPerceptionComponent* PerceptionComp;
```

The first line here declares that what's next is an Unreal Engine variable. This variable can be edited anywhere. Blueprint can read it, but not assign it to a different thing, and it is also in the AI category. The second line is the actual variable, it is of the type UAIPerceptionComponent, and we name it PerceptionComp. That * means that this variable is a pointer. We don't have to understand what a pointer is for our purposes. The semicolumn at the end of the second line indicates that it is the end of this statement. Adding these two lines adds a variable called PerceptionComp that is of the

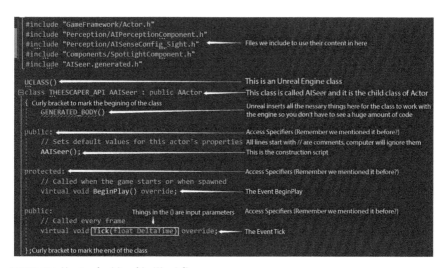

FIGURE 18.4 Meaning of each line of the AISeer.h file.

685

type UAIPerceptionComponent. The first line is needed if we want to get access to this variable in Blueprint.

This UAIPerceptionComponent is needed for any actor who wants to see, hear, or sense anything. Ideally, this should be added to an AI Controller as the documentation recommends, but add it to an actor works as well. We need to give it configurations to tell it what kind of sense we want to use. For our project, we want to give it a sight configuration.

Step 6: Add a UAISightConfig_Sight variable. After the lines added in Step 5, add the following code:

```
UAISenseConfig_Sight* SightConfig;
```

This one also adds a variable, but it does not have that UPROPERTY part; we don't need it because we don't want access to it in Blueprint. This UAISenseConfig_Sight is a sight configuration we need to add to the PerceptionComp to enable seeing capability.

Step 7: Add a USportLightComponent. Following the same trend, let's add one more variable:

```
UPROPERTY(EditAnywhere,
BlueprintReadWrite)
USpotLightComponent* SeerLight;
```

In this one, we added the UPROPERTY part because we wanted to access it in Blueprint. However, we did not give it a category—it is optional. The variable we add here is of the type USportlightComponent, and we give it a name SeerLight. As you can gradually see, to add a component, you write the type first followed by an *, add a space after that, and then write down the name of the variable.

Now we have created some variables for our AISeer actor. Let's see how we can create functions.

Step 8: Add a SetSightRadius function. Add the following code after the code we add in the previous step:

```
UFUNCTION(BlueprintCallable,
Category = "AIPerception")
void SetSightRadius(float newRadius);
```

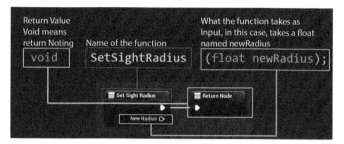

FIGURE **18.5** Breakdown of the function.

For the first line, we declare that what's next is an Unreal Function. It can be called by Blueprint, and its category is AIPerception. The second line is the actual function. We can break it down and compare it with a Blueprint function as shown in Figure 18.5.

As you can see, this is just a different way of describing a function. We want to use this function to set the radius of the sight, and we will cover how to implement it in just a bit.

Step 9: Add a SetSightPeripheralVisionDegrees function. Let's add another function right below SetSightRadius:

```
UFUNCTION(BlueprintCallable,
Category = "AIPerception")
void SetSightPeripheralVisionDegre
es(float Degree);
```

This one is almost the same as the previous one, except the name of the function and input is different. We want to use this one to set the peripheral vision of the sight.

Alrighty, we have created all the variables and functions we need for our new AISeer class. Figure 18.6 shows everything we add to the code.

The Header and the Source File

There are two files for every class in C++: the header file and the source file. The header file has a ".h" at the end and the source file has a ".cpp" at the end. So far, we have worked on the AISeer.h, which is the header file of AISeer.

```
public:
    // Sets default values for this actor's properties
    AAISeer();
    UPROPERTY(EditAnywhere, BlueprintReadOnly, Category = "AI")
    UAIPerceptionComponent* PerceptionComp;
    UAISenseConfig_Sight* SightConfig;
    UPROPERTY(EditAnywhere, BlueprintReadWrite)
    USpotLightComponent* SeerLight;
    UFUNCTION(BlueprintCallable, Category = "AIPerception")
    void SetSightRadius(float newRadius);
    UFUNCTION(BlueprintCallable, Category = "AIPerception")
    void SetSightPeripheralVisionDegrees(float Degree);
```

FIGURE 18.6 All the coded added to AISeer.h.

Go to the Solution Explorer and open AISeer.cpp and you can also see some familiar faces in here: the BeginPlay and the Tick event.

The header file shows the variables and functions a class has. The header file is like a list, but not showing any detail.

The source file shows the detailed implementation of the functions. As you can see in AISeer.cpp, there are curly brackets after every function which encapsulates the implementation of these functions. Figure 18.7 shows how this could be compared to a Blueprint class.

You can think of the header file as the Components and the My Blueprint panel, where you add new components, variables, and functions. You can think of the source file as the Event Graph, where you write code with the components, variables, and functions. In the source file, the body of the function is inside the two curly brackets. As shown in Figure 18.7, the body of the BeginPlay function is inside the two curly brackets underneath it.

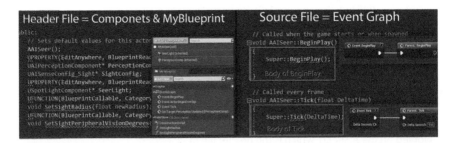

FIGURE 18.7 C++ files compared to Blueprints.

Let's write our code in AISeer.cpp.

> *Step 10: Construct the components. The first function in AISeer.cpp is the construction script equivalent, and it is called the constructor of the class. Its name has an AAISeer:: added in front of it, and this means that this function belongs to AAISeer. In the body of the constructor, add the following code:*

```
SeerLight = CreateDefaultSubobject<US
potLightComponent>("SeerLight");
PerceptionComp = CreateDefaultSubobje
ct<UAIPerceptionComponent>("Perceptio
nComp");
SightConfig = CreateDefaultSubobject<
UAISenseConfig_Sight>("sightConfig");
RootComponent = SeerLight;
```

> *These three lines are after the PrimaryActorTick. bCanEverTick=true; the first line creates an actual spotlight component and assigns it to SeerLight. This CreateDefaultSubobject is a function that creates a component. The USportLightComponent in the angle brackets indicates the type of the component, and the SeerLight in the quotation marks is the arbitrary name we supply. The next two lines create the PerceptionComp and SightConfig the same way.*

Why?

In the header file, we only created the variables but not assigning anything to them, so they were still empty. After these three lines, actual components are created and assigned (using "=") to the variables.

> *Step 11: Set up the root component. Add the following line after the lines added in the previous step:*

```
RootComponent = SeerLight;
```

> *This line set the root component of the actor to SeerLight, which means that this light is now the root of all other components.*

Step 12: Set up the SightConfig variable. Keep adding the following line:

```
if (SightConfig && PerceptionComp)
{
PerceptionComp ->
ConfigureSense(*SightConfig);
}
```

Here, we first did something called an if statement. If statement checks if the things in the parentheses are true. The code in the curly brackets only runs when the things in the parentheses are true. What we are checking in the parentheses is if both the SightConfig and PerceptionComp are all valid. The two "&" strings combined are the syntax for and.

If Both components are valid, which they should, we move on to the line in the curly bracket. Here, we call a function of PerceptionComp named ConfigureSense. The space in front of the line is added by hitting the Tab button. In C++, calling a function of an object is written as object -> function(inputs...). The -> is called the access operator (consists of a "-" and a ">"), and we use it to get something from an object. If we want to get a variable from an object instead of a function, we write it down as object -> variable.

This ConfigureSense takes a UAISenseConfig as the input, and it configures the PerceptionComp to use the UAISenseConfig as a sense. The SightConfig we passed in here is of the type UAISenseConfig_Sight, which is a child class of UAISenseConfig. We pass it in to give the PerceptionComp a sight configuration.

Log story short, we have now given the PerceptionComp (as well as the AISeer), the ability to see stuff. Figure 18.8 shows how the AAISeer::AAISeer() function looks like eventually.

Step 13: Set up the attributes of the SightConfig in BeginPlay. Now you have got the hang of how to implement new things in C++, and add the following code to the AAISeer::BeginPlay() function:

```
if (SeerLight && SightConfig &&
PerceptionComp)
{
```

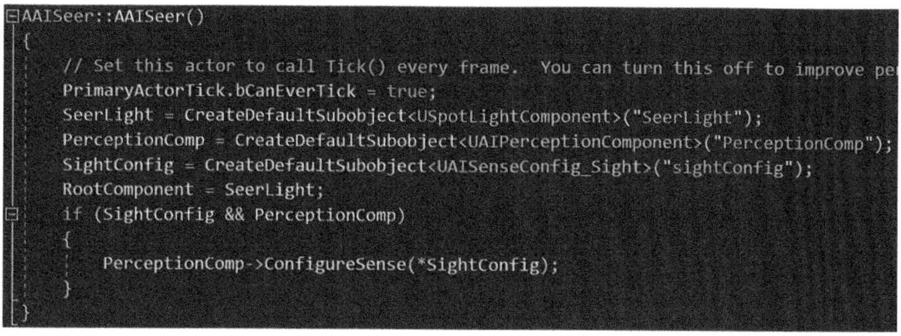

```
AAISeer::AAISeer()
{
    // Set this actor to call Tick() every frame.  You can turn this off to improve pe
    PrimaryActorTick.bCanEverTick = true;
    SeerLight = CreateDefaultSubobject<USpotLightComponent>("SeerLight");
    PerceptionComp = CreateDefaultSubobject<UAIPerceptionComponent>("PerceptionComp");
    SightConfig = CreateDefaultSubobject<UAISenseConfig_Sight>("sightConfig");
    RootComponent = SeerLight;
    if (SightConfig && PerceptionComp)
    {
        PerceptionComp->ConfigureSense(*SightConfig);
    }
}
```

FIGURE 18.8 Finalized AAISeer function.

```
    SightConfig -> SightRadius =
SeerLight -> AttenuationRadius;
    SightConfig -> LoseSightRadius =
SeerLight -> AttenuationRadius;
    SightConfig ->
PeripheralVisionAngleDegrees =
SeerLight -> OuterConeAngle;
    PerceptionComp ->
ConfigureSense(*SightConfig);
}
```

Here, we are using the if statement again, and we check if SeerLight, SighConfig, and PerceptionComp are all valid. If they are, then we move on to the code inside the curly bracket. The first three lines in the curly bracket are setting up the variables of SightConfig.

We make the SightRadius the same as the AttenuationRadius of the SeerLight. We then make the LoseSightRadius the same. The SightRadius variable defines how far the sight can reach, and the LoseSightRadius is now far the sight lose track of something after seeing it. In reality, LoseSightRadius should be slightly bigger than SightRadius, but we made them the same to simplify it. The third line makes the PeripheralVisionAngleDegrees variable of the SighConfig to the OuterConeAngle variable of the SeerLight. This PeripheralVisionAngleDegrees variable defines the peripheral vision of the sight. These three lines set the SightConfig to be the same as the reach of the SeerLight. This way, we can visualize the sight by looking at the light.

691

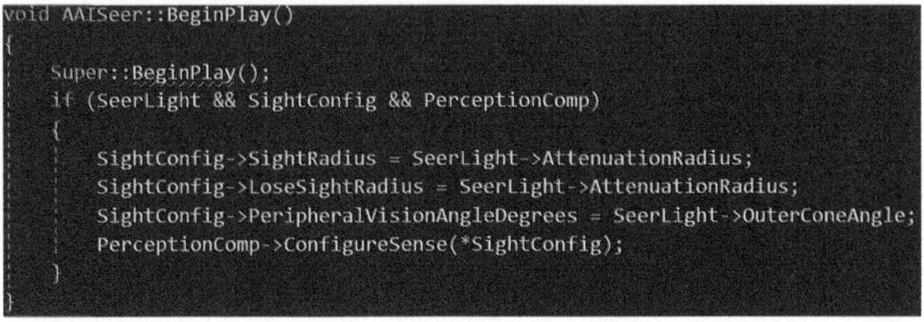

```
void AAISeer::BeginPlay()
{
    Super::BeginPlay();
    if (SeerLight && SightConfig && PerceptionComp)
    {
        SightConfig->SightRadius = SeerLight->AttenuationRadius;
        SightConfig->LoseSightRadius = SeerLight->AttenuationRadius;
        SightConfig->PeripheralVisionAngleDegrees = SeerLight->OuterConeAngle;
        PerceptionComp->ConfigureSense(*SightConfig);
    }
}
```

FIGURE 18.9 The finalized BeginPlay function.

The last line reconfigures the PercepitonComp so that the changes we've made are applied. All the attributes of the sense are reconfigured when the game starts. Figure 18.9 shows how the BeginPlay function looks like after adding our code.

Step 14: Implement SetSightRadius and SetSightPeripheralVisionDegrees. We have two functions we have created in the header file; let's implement them. At the end of AISeer.cpp, add the following code:

```
void AAISeer::SetSightRadius(float
newRadius)
{
    if (SightConfig &&
PerceptionComp && SeerLight)
    {
        SeerLight -> SetAttenuationRad
ius(newRadius);
        SightConfig -> SightRadius =
newRadius;
        SightConfig -> LoseSightRadius
= newRadius;
        PerceptionComp ->
ConfigureSense(*SightConfig);
    }
}

void AAISeer::SetSightPeripheralVisio
nDegrees(float Degree)
{
    if (SightConfig && PerceptionComp
&& SeerLight)
```

```
    {
        SeerLight ->
SetOuterConeAngle(Degree);
        SeerLight ->
SetInnerConeAngle(Degree);
        SightConfig ->
PeripheralVisionAngleDegrees =
Degree;
        PerceptionComp ->
ConfigureSense(*SightConfig);
    }
}
```

We implement both functions in here. First of all, the AAISeer:: added in front of their name is needed to indicate that they belong to AAISeer. For the first one, we did our validation check first. We then move on to set up the attenuation radius of SeerLight to newRadius by calling its function SetAttenuationRadius. This newRadius is the input parameter. When we call this function in Blueprint, we can specify this variable. The next two lines set the SightRadius and LoseSightRadius variables to newRadius as well. And then we reconfigure our PerceptionComp.

The second function is almost the same, and the difference here is that we are setting the peripheral vision.

Go back to our unreal project and hit the Compile button again. It should compile pretty fast this time.

It is very likely to get a compile failed notification if this is the first time you do C++ coding. Go back and carefully check every line and make sure you follow the code written in this book to the letter. There could be a miss-spelling, missing a parenthesis, or only have one "&" for the if statements. Don't get frustrated if you cannot find the issue right away, give it time, and you will be able to compile successfully.

If, however, you still can't make it work, in the support file, we have put both the AISeer.h and AISeer.cpp in there. You can open them with Visual Studio, copy, and paste the code from these two files to yours. One thing to avoid when copying is the THEESCAPER_API on line 13, this one is different if your project is named different; keep this one the way you have in your file (Figure 18.10).

693

FIGURE 18.10 The part to not replace when copying.

Now we have done with C++, let's keep on building our AISeer in Blueprint.

Tutorial 18.2: Create the Blueprint Version of AISeer by Inheriting from the C++ Version

Step 1: Create a BP_AISeer class and set up the light. Add a folder called Seer in the Blueprints folder. Create a new blueprint class derived from AISeer and name it BP_AISeer (you have to open the All Classes section in the Pick Parent Class window and search for AISeer to use it as the parent class). Open BP_AISeer, and you can see that the SeerLight and PerceptionComp are in the Components already; they are the components we created in C++. Select the SeerLight, go to the Details panel, and set the Light Color to a green color. We want it to look green when it does not see the player and turn red when it does. Set both the Inner Cone Angle and the Outer Cone Angle to 30, so it is a narrower light than before.

Step 2: Set the detection rules. Select the PerceptionComp in the Components panel, And go to the Details panel. Under the AI Perception section,open Sense Config and you can see that the first one in there is AI Sight Config. Expand this AI Sight config and the Sense section in it to access its settings. Expand the Detection by Affiliation section, and check on Detect Neutrals and Detect Friendlies. There is no way to define who is Enemy, Neutrals, or Friendlies without C++, so we check everything on here.

Why?

You can also see the Sight Radius, Lose Sight Radius in here, so why do we want to set them in C++? Well, the problem is not that we cannot change these in the Details panel, we can. However, you cannot change these attributes outside of the details panel. Try to set these variables in the Event Graph is impossible. We need to be able to change them with the Event Graph if we want to customize it for different purposes. Besides, with our setup, whatever we do to the light got automatically set to these values here when the game starts.

Step 3: Create a custom event to set the color of the light. Create and implement a new custom event called ChangeLightColor as shown in Figure 18.11.

This event takes a boolean input called Sensed; we set the color of SeerLight to a red color if the input is true and set it back to green if the input is false. We want to call this event when we see and lose sight of the player.

Step 4: Implement the On Target Perception Updated event. Select PerceptionComp, go to the Events section in the Detail panel, and click on the plus button labeled with On Target Perception Updated. A new event appears in the Event Graph. This On Target Perception Updated event fires whenever the PerceptionComp senses or un-senses something, the Actor input is the actor sensed or un-sensed. The Stimulus input has detailed information about the sense. Drag out from it and select Break AIStimulus to create a Break AIStimulus node, expand it, and you can see a whole lot of information there. Implement the rest of the function as shown in Figure 18.12.

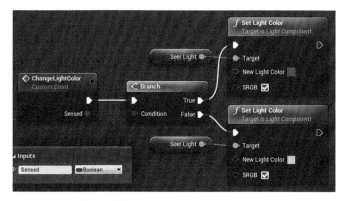

FIGURE 18.11 Implementation of ChangeLightColor.

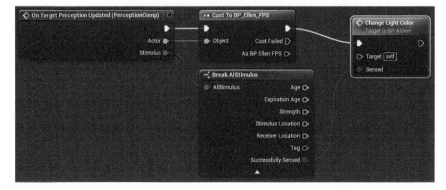

FIGURE 18.12 Implementation of On Target Perception Updated.

What we do here is to cast the Actor to BP_Ellen_FPS; this automatically filters everything else. We then use the Succesully Sensed variable of the stimulus as the input to call ChangeLightColor.

Place a BP_AISeer to the level, walk into the light, and you should see it turn red, walk out, and it turns back to green (Figure 18.13).

Step 5: *Make the light cast volumetric fog.*

Go to the World Outliner and type ExponentialHeightFog in the search bar to find the ExponentialHeightFog we positioned when we were building the level. Select it, go to the Details panel, and check on Volumetric Fog in the Volumetric Fog section. Open BP_AISeer, and select the SeerLight in the Components panel. Go to the Details panel and set the Volumetric Scattering Intensity to 500. You should now see beautiful volumetric fog cast from the light (Figure 18.14).

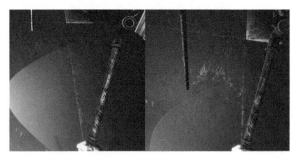

FIGURE 18.13 Test the BP_AISeer in the level.

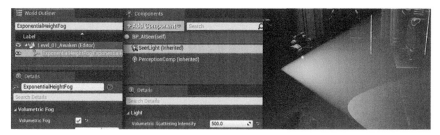

FIGURE 18.14 Enable volumetric fog for SeerLight.

Step 6: Build a scan line effect. Go to StaticMeshes/ Shared/ and look for the Sreen_Base_Mtl we have built for our screens. Drag it to the Seer folder and select Copy Here to make a copy. Go to the Seer folder and rename the copied one Seer_Light_Mtl. Open Seer_Light_Mtl; with the Seer_Light_Mtl node selected, go to the Details panel and change the Material Domain to Light Function. Remove the ScreenTexture node and the Multiply node it connects. Connect the Linear Sine output pin of the LinearSine node to the A input of the Multiply node that connects to the Emissive color. Finally, use the UGradient as the A input of the Add node instead of the VGradient. Save the material and create a material instance from it (Figure 18.15).

Step 7: Apply Seer_Light_Mtl_Inst to BP_AISeer. Open BP_AISeer and select SeerLight. Go to the Details panel, and under the Light Function section, set the Light Function Material to Seer_ Light_Mtl_Inst. The scan lines may appear too big and move too fast. Open Seer_light_Mtl_Inst and change the ScanLineSize to 0.01 and the ScanLineSpeed to 0.02 (Figure 18.16).

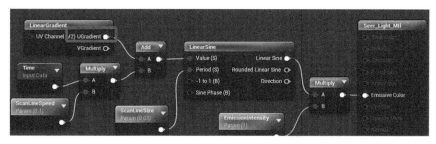

FIGURE 18.15 The graph of the Seer_Light_Mtl.

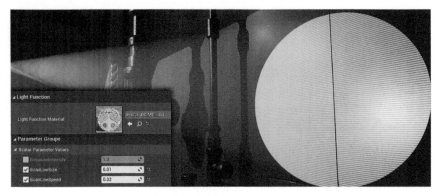

FIGURE 18.16 Set the SeerLight to use the Seer_light_Mtl_Inst.

Step 8: Create an interface for BP_AISeer. Create a new blueprint interface and name it BPI_AISeer. Open BPI_Seer, and rename the new function OnSeerTargetUpdate. Give the function an input parameter called Stimulus and set its type to AIStimulus. Give the function another input parameter called Target and set its type to BP_Ellen_FPS object reference.

Step 9: Use the interface function to inform the owner and its AI Controller. Open BP_AISeer and implement a function called InformOnwerAndOwnerAI (Figure 18.17).

This function takes the same input as the OnSeerTargetUpdate interface function we created in Step 9. What we do here is calling that OnSeerTargetUpdate interface function on both the owner and the AI Controller of the owner with its inputs.

Step 10: Call InformOnwerAndOwnerAI in the On Target Perception Updated event. Go back

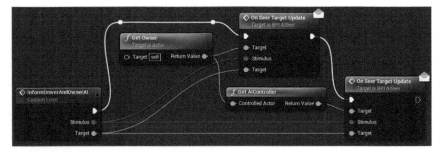

FIGURE 18.17 Implementation of InformOnwerAndOwnerAI.

698

FIGURE 18.18 Insert a call to InformOnwerAndOwnerAI in On Target Perception Updated.

*to the On Target Perception Updated event
we created earlier, and add a call to our new
InformOnwerAndOwnerAI function after Cast To
BP_Ellen_FPS. Don't forget to connect the AS BP
Ellen FPS of the Cast function to the Target and
the Stimulus output of the event to the Stimulus
input of InformOnwerAndOwnerAI (Figure 18.18).*

    *We have now created a BP_AISeer that talks
to its owner and its AI Controller whenever it sees
or loses sight of something. Let's create a security
camera and make it capture the player when the
player walks into its sight with the help of our
BP_AISeer.*

Tutorial 18.3: Create a Security Camera

*Step 1: Create a security camera class. Create a new
folder called SecurityCamera in Blueprints and
add a new blueprint class derived from Actor.
Name the new class BP_SecurityCamera and
open it. Go to StaticMeshes/security_cam and
drag all the meshes inside if it to the Components
of BP_SecurityCamera.*

*Step 2: Add rotation pivots and arrange the meshes.
Add a scene component to BP_SecurityCamera.
The scene component is a component that has
a transform, but not a visual representation,
and we can use it as a rotation pivot. Name it
CameraPitchPivot and move it down −44 units
on the Z-axis so it is at the pivot the body of the
camera should rotate around when it pitches
up and down. Select all the meshes except the
security_cam_security_cam_yaw_handle_geo
and the security_cam_security_cam_base_
geo, and drag them to CameraPitchPivot to
parent them under CameraPitchPivot. Finally,
parent CameraPitchPivot to security_cam_
security_cam_yaw_handle_geo. Rotate*

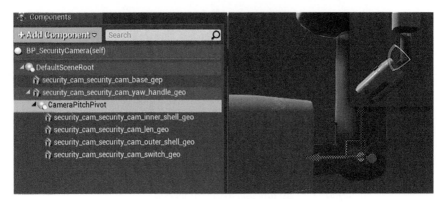

FIGURE 18.19 Add a rotation pivot for the camera to pitch and rearrange the hierarchy.

CameraPitchPivot down 60 degrees on the X-axis, and you can see that it's able to make the camera pitch down (Figure 18.19).

Step 3: Add a Light. Select CameraPitchPivot, go to Add Component, add a Spot Light component, and name it SeerRef. Rotate it 90 degrees on the Z-axis, so its X-axis (forward axis) is facing the direction of the camera. Drag it along the X-axis to position it at the lens of the camera. Set the color of the light to the same as the BP_AISeer and change its Volumetric Scattering Intensity to 500. Drag a copy of BP_SecurityCamera to the ceiling and check if we got the light positioned correctly (Figure 18.20).

Step 4: Spawn BP_AISeer and attach it to SeerRef. Add a new variable called Seer to BP_SecurityCamera. Go to Event Graph, and add the code shown in Figure 18.21 to its Event BeginPlay.

We have done very similar things in the weapon chapter. Here, we spawn a BP_AISeer at the transform of our SeerRef, store it to the Seer variable we created, and attach it to SeerRef. This way, when the game starts, a BP_AISeer got created and attached to the camera.

Step 5: Set up BP_AISeer to match SeerRef. Add the code highlighted in Figure 18.22 to the end of Event Begin Play.

After the AttachActorToComponent, we also want to match the sight of BP_AISeer to the reach of the SeerRef spotlight. We called the C++ function SetSightRadius on Seer to set its sight radius to the attenuation radius of Seer Ref. We then call the C++ function

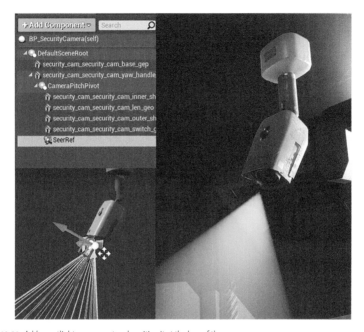

FIGURE 18.20 Add a spotlight component and position it at the lens of the camera.

FIGURE 18.21 Spawn BP_AISeer and attach it to SeerRef.

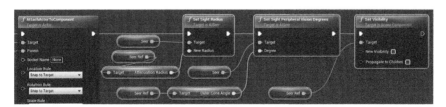

FIGURE 18.22 Set up BP_AISeer to match SeerRef.

SetSightPeripheralVisionDegrees to set its peripheral vision angle to the outer cone angle of SeerRef. Eventually, we hide SeerRef. This way, we can just edit SeerRef in the editor, and when the game starts, the BP_AISeer becomes the same.

Step 6: Create a timeline for the camera rolling. Create a new custom event called StartRollingCamera. Drag out from its execution pin and add a timeline. We had used timeline before when we were creating the sliding doors; name the timeline CameraRollingAnimationLerp. Double click to open it. Add a new float track and name it Lerp and make the length of the track 3 seconds. Add two keyframes to the track, select the first one, and set its time and value to 0. Set the time of the second key to 3 and the value to 1. This animation is changing from 0 to 1 in 3 seconds (Figure 18.23).

Step 7: Update the rotation of the security_cam_ security_cam_yaw_handle_geo with the timeline. Drag security_cam_security_cam_ yaw_handle_geo from the Components panel to the graph to create a reference for it. Drag out from the new reference and create a SetRelativeRotation for it. Right click on the NewRotation input pin and select Split Struct Pin, the NewRotation input now becomes three inputs for the X, Y, and Z of the new rotation. Call the SetRelativeRotation with the Update out execution pin of the timeline. Add two new float variables to BP_SecurityCamera: name one of them CameraLeftReach and set its value to 45 and name the other one CameraRightReach and set its value to −45. Make both new variables public. Create a Lerp node (the one named just Lerp), drag CameraLeftReach from the Variables to the A input of the Lerp node,

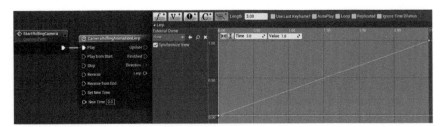

FIGURE 18.23 Add a custom event and call it with a timeline.

and drag CameraRightReach to the B input
of the Lerp node. Connect the Lerp output pin
of the timeline to the Alpha input of the Lerp
node. Connect the Return Value of the Lerp
node to the New Rotation Z (Yaw) input pin
of the SetRelativeRotation node. Finally, call
this StartRollingCamera at the end of Event
BeginPlay (Figure 18.24).

What we do here is just linear interpolates
two float values with the timeline to update the
rotation of the camera. Play the game, and you
can see that the camera rotates from its left to its
right, but it only does it once. Let's fix it by using a
Delay and a Flip Flop node.

Step 8: Make the Camera roll back and forth. Create
a Delay node with a duration value of 1.5
seconds and move the node above the timeline.
Create a Flip Flop node and call the Flip Flop with
the Completed out execution pin of the Delay
node. Connect the Finished out execution pin of
the timeline to the in execution pin of the Delay
node. Connect the A out execution pin of the Flip
Flop node to the Reverse from End in execution
pin of the timeline. Connect the B out execution
pin of Flip Flop node to the Play in execution pin
of the timeline (Figure 18.25).

When the Flip Flop is called, it fires A first;
then the next time when it's called, it fires B; after
that, it fires A again, so it's flip-flopping the out
execution pins every time it gets called.

What happens here is when the animation
is finished, the Delay node got called. After
a 1.5-second delay, the Flip Flop gets called,
and the execution goes through the A output
execution pin first. The A execution pin then calls
the Reverse from End in execution pin of the
timeline, which causes the timeline to play again
backward. The camera then rolls back because
of that. When the animation finishes again, it

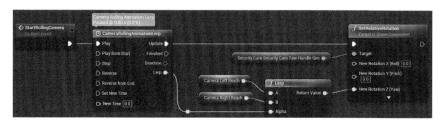

FIGURE 18.24 Update the rotation of the security_cam_security_cam_yaw_handle_geo with the timeline.

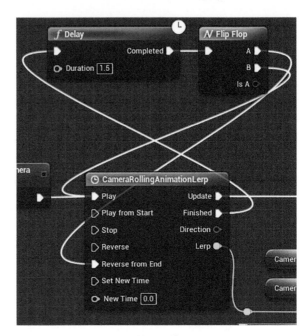

FIGURE 18.25 Make the Camera roll back and forth.

reaches to the Delay and the Flip Flop one more time. This time, the B execution pin fires and calls the Play in execution pin of the timeline. From here, the execution repeats itself.

Play the game again, and you can see the camera now rolls back and forth nicely. You can adjust the angle in whatever amount you wish for every camera you place in the level by adjusting the CameraRightReach and CameraLeftReach in the Details panel.

Step 9: Add a stop functionality. Go to the StartRollingCamera event, insert a Gate node between the Delay node and the Flip Flop node, and check off the Start Closed option. Create a custom event called StopRolling and connect it to a Sequence node. Connect Then 0 of the Sequence node to the Close in execution pin of the Gate node. Connect Then 1 of the Sequence node to the Stop in execution pin of the timeline (Figure 18.26).

The Gate node behaves like a gate. When Close is called, it closes and stops all execution from going through. When this StopRolling event

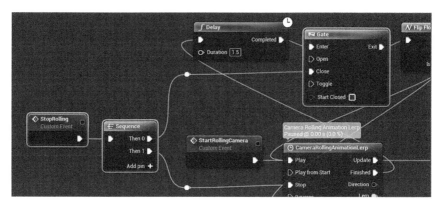

FIGURE 18.26 Add stop functionality to the camera.

is called, it closes the Gate node and stops the
timeline, which stops the camera from rolling.
Step 10: Make the camera stop when it sees the
player. Go to the Class Settings and add the
BPI_AISeer to its interfaces. In the Blueprint panel,
expand the Interfaces section. Right click the
On Seer Target Update and select Implement
function. An Event On Seer Target Update got
added to the graph, add a call StopRolling with it.

Give the game another go; the moment
you walk in the camera's sight, it stops rolling,
and the light turns red. Let's make the player
surrender to the camera when the camera sees
them.
Step 11: Create surrender animation montages. Go
to Blueprints/Characters/Ellen/Animations and
find Ellen_FPS_Grenade_Launcher_Caught,
Ellen_FPS_Gun_Caught, and Ellen_FPS_
Pipe_Caught. Create animation montages for
each one of them and make sure to check off
the Enable Auto Blend Out option for these
montages.
Step 12: Add surrender animation montages to the
weapons. Open BP_Weapon_Base, and add a
new variable called SurrenderAM. Set the type of
the variable Anim Montage object reference. Go
to BP_Gun, BP_Pipe, and BP_GrenadeLauncher,
and assign their respective caught animation
montages.
Step 13: Create a surrender functionality to BP_
Ellen_FPS. Open BP_Ellen_FPS, create a new
function called SurrenderTo, and implement it as
shown in Figure 18.27.

705

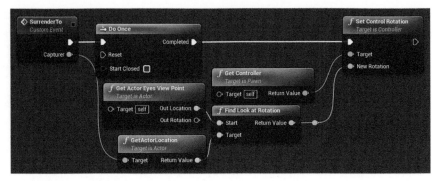

FIGURE 18.27 Implementation of the SurrenderTo event.

This event takes an actor input called Capturer. We add Do Once, so this can only happen once. We then find the look at rotation needed for the eye viewpoint (PlayerEye) to look at the Capturer input. And then, we set the controller's rotation to the rotation found.

Why?

Notice here that we did not use the PlayerEye to find the look at rotation; instead, we used the Get Actor Eyes View Point. This is because there is a possibility that the actual player is not looking through the PlayerEye camera. For the same reason, we set the rotation of the controller (the actual player) instead of PlayerEye. This part of the function makes the player look at whatever the Capturer's input is.

Step 14: Finish SurrenderTo. After the Set Control Rotation of the SurrenderTo event, add extra code to stop the movement of the character, play the surrender animation montage, and show the game over UI. Don't forget to call it at the end of the Event On Seer Target Update in BP_SecurityCamera (Figure 18.28).

Here, we set the input mode to UI only to block all player inputs. We then play the surrender montage, delay for 1.5 seconds, and then switch the UI to game over. We call SurrenderTo at the end of Event On Seer Target

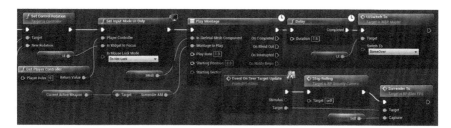

FIGURE 18.28 Finish the second part of SurrenderTo and call it when the camera sees the player.

Update of BP_SecurityCamera and use self (the camera) as the Capturer.

Play the game again and walk into the sight of the camera. The view automatically rotates to the camera, followed by the surrender animation, and the game over UI. We also want to be able to kill the camera with just one shot, so let's move on to the camera shut down sequence.

Step 15: Store the pitch rotation in Event BeginPlay. Add a new float variable called ActivePitchRotation to BP_SecurityCamera. Hold down Alt and drag ActivePitchRotation from the Variables panel to the graph to create a set node for it. Call this new Set node at the end of Event BeginPlay. Drag CameraPitchPivot from the Components panel to the graph to create a reference for it. Drag out from CameraPitchPivot, search, and create a GetRelativeRotation node. Right click on the Relative Rotation output pin and select Split Struct Pin. The output now breaks into X, Y, and Z channels. Connect the Relative Rotation X (Roll) to the Active Pitch Rotation input pin of the Set node (Figure 18.29).

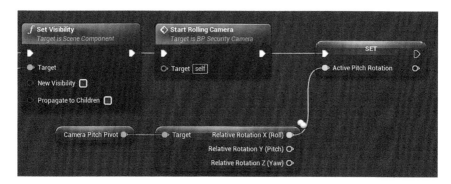

FIGURE 18.29 Store the pitch of the rotation of CameraPitchPivot to a variable.

707

Why?

You may ask why do we use X instead of Y; after all, Y is the pitch of a rotation. Well, which axis is for the actual pitch is not fixed, and it is often different under different parents. Go to the viewport and rotate the camera up and down. You can see that it is the X-axis of CameraPitchPivot that is changing.

Step 16: Create a PlayCameraDeathAnimation event. Create a new event called PlayCameraDeathAnimation and call it in Event AnyDamage (Figure 18.30).

Here, we call Stop Rolling first to stop the rolling of the camera. We then create another timeline, which is the same as the CameraRollingAnimationLerp timeline we did earlier except that its length is 2 seconds. We use this timeline to interpolate the rotation of CameraPitchPivot linearly from ActivePitchRotation to 90 (vertical). The Event AnyDamage is created by right clicking and searching.

Play the game and shoot the camera; then it should stop rolling and rotates down. However, it still captures you when you walk into its sight. Let's add a disable feature to BP_AISeer.

Step 17: Create a Disable function to BP_AISeer. Open BP_AISeer and implement a function called Disable as shown in Figure 18.31.

This function takes a Boolean input named Do Animation. We want to use it on the patrolling AI later on, and we do not want to play an animation if it's on the patrolling AI, so we added a boolean to control it. We start by dragging out the PerceptionComp and call its Set Sense Enabled function to disable the sense; make sure that you set the Sense Class to AISense Sight. If the Do Animation is true, we fire a timeline to

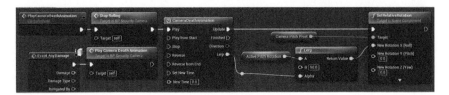

FIGURE 18.30 Implementation of PlayCameraDeathAnimation and call it In Event AnyDamage.

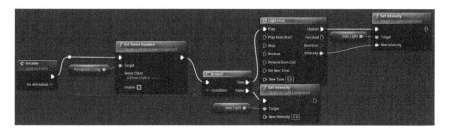

FIGURE 18.31 Implementation of Disabled.

animate the intensity of the SeerLight. If the Do
Animation is false, we just set the intensity to 0.

The timeline we did here is a bit more
interesting. We started by adding a float track
called intensity with a length of 1. We then add
two keys to it: the first key is at the beginning and
has a value of 5000, and the second key is at the
end with a value of 0, and you can hit F to frame
the whole graph. After that, we randomly add a
few more keys to the timeline and drag them up
and down dramatically to mimic a light blinking
effect (Figure 18.32).

Step 18: Call Disable at the end of Event
AnyDamage. Go back to BP_Security Camera,
find Event AnyDamage, hold down Alt, and drag
Seer to the graph. Drag out from Seer and call its
Disable event with Do Animation checked on at
the end of Event AnyDamage (Figure 18.33).

FIGURE 18.32 Creation process of the timeline.

FIGURE 18.33 Call Disable at the end of Event AnyDamage.

709

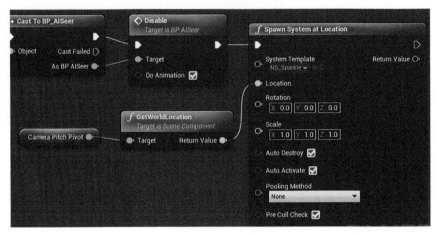

FIGURE 18.34 Add a sparkle VFX.

Step 19: Spawn VFX. At the end of Event Damage, add the code shown in Figure 18.34 to spawn an NS_Sparkle at the location of CameraPitchPivot. Alright, we have finished the security camera. Thanks to our BP_AISeer, most of the job is the animation and game over event. We are going to leverage BP_AISeer in other parts of the game as well. Let's create a monitor class that shows what the camera sees.

Tutorial 18.4: Create a BP_Monitor Class that Shows What the Camera Sees

Step 1: Add a Scene Capture Component 2D. Open BP_SecurityCamera. With SeerRef selected in the Components panel, click on Add Component and search for Scene Capture Component 2D. This Scene Capture Component 2D can capture the scene and render out a texture. It should now be parented under SeerRef, so it sees what BP_AISeer sees. Rename this new Scene Capture Component 2D to Capturer. Go to the Event Graph and find Event BeginPlay. Drag Capturer from the Components panel to the graph to create a reference node for it. Drag out from the node and add a call to its Set Component Tick Enabled function at the end of Event BeginPlay.

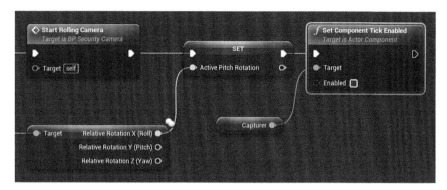

FIGURE 18.35 Call Set Component Tick Enabled on Capturer at the end of Event BeginPlay.

Make sure that the Enabled is checked off (Figure 18.35).

Rendering a scene from a Scene Capture 2D isn't cheap, it's like rendering the scene one more time! Set Component Tick Enabled can disable their tick, which prevents them from constantly rendering anything. This way, we can save much performance. We will make them tick only when the player gets close.

Step 2: Create a capture info structure. In the SecurityCamera folder, right click in the empty space and select Blueprints → Structure. Name the new structure FCaptureInfo. Double click to open it and you can see that by default, it holds a Boolean variable. Change that Boolean variable to Integer and set the name to targetElement. Click the New Variable button to add a new variable, name it SecurityCamera, and set its type to BP_SecurityCamera object reference (Figure 18.36).

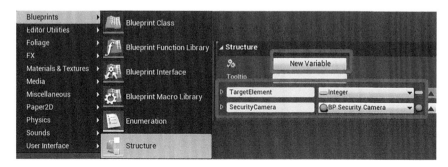

FIGURE 18.36 Create a structure to hold the material element and security camera data.

Structure

Structure is the predecessor of class. It is designed to bundle multiple variables and functions together, invented back in the C language. Blueprint ripped off its function feature, making it a pure data collection. We use structure when we want to bundle multiple variables. In our case, we want to use it to define what material element to assign the captured texture and which camera to capture from. The F added in front of its name is again a naming convention Unreal adapts. Actors start with an A, structures start with an F, and enums start with an E.

> Step 3: Create a monitor class. Create a blueprint class called BP_Monitor derived from BP_Triggerable. Open BP_Monitor, select the Trigger, and scale it up four times or so to make it easier to be triggered. Add a new static mesh component to it and set the static mesh to monitors_Monitor_02 (we can switch to anyone else when using it). Give it a new variable of the type Name, name it ScreenTextureParamaterName, and set its default value to ScreenTexture. ScreenTexture is the name of the ScreenTexture parameter we set in Screen_Base_Mtl in Chapter 4. Add another variable called CaptureInfos, set its variable type to FCaptureInfo, and make it an array. Make both variables public (Figure 18.37).
>
> Step 4: Create dynamic material instances for the mesh. Go to the Event Graph of BP_Monitor. Add the code shown in Figure 18.38 at the end of the Event BeginPlay.
>
> What we do here is to loop through the Capture Infos (which we will populate later in the editor). We break the structure so we can access its Target Element variable and create a dynamic material for the monitor mesh from

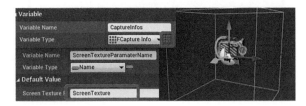

FIGURE 18.37 Set up the BP_Monitor.

FIGURE 18.38 Create dynamic material instances for the mesh.

that element. Dragged out from Array Element and select Break FCaptureInfo to create the Break FCaptureInfo node. The Create Dynamic Material Instance creates a copy of the material of the supplied Element Index. It then assigns it to the mesh supplied to the Target input. Because this is a copy of the material, changing it does not affect the original one. This way, what we do to this material only affects the supplied model.

Step 5: *Create render targets and assign them to the dynamic materials. Keep on going from the end of the code done previously, and add the code highlighted in Figure 18.39.*

In this half, we create a render target 2D, which is a dynamic texture we can assign to our screen. We set its width and height to 128×128 and set the format to RTF RGBA SRGB. This format is a little more efficient than the default settings. We get the BP_SecurityCamera from the FCaptureInfo and get the Capturer we added in Step 1. We then drag out from it and create a Set Texture Target node. We then use the Render Target 2D created as the Texture Target. The Capturer now captures what it sees to this render target 2D. Finally, we assign this render target 2D to the SceneTexture Parameter of the newly created dynamic material in the previous step.

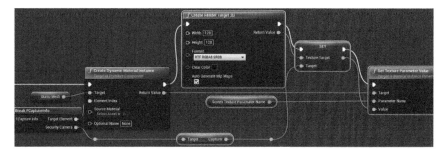

FIGURE 18.39 Create render targets and assign them to the dynamic materials.

713

FIGURE 18.40 Make capturers tick when overlayed and disable their ticking when unoverlapped.

Step 6: Make capturers tick when overlayed and stop them from ticking when unoverlapped. Because our BP_Monitor is from BP_Triggerable, we can override the Overlapped and UnOverlapped events to make the capturers tick when the player overlaps with the trigger and stop their ticking when the player leaves. Figure 18.40 shows the implementation of the Overlapped and Un Overlapped event.

Step 7: Test our BP_Monitor. Open the static mesh of the monitor and you can see that the monitor model has three monitors, each assigned with a Screen_Base_Mtl_Inst. These screen materials are on elements 1, 2, and 3. Drag a BP_Monitor to the scene, go to the Details panel, and add three elements to the CaptureInfos array by clicking the "+" sign. Set the three TargetElements to 1, 2, and 3, so they match with the material elements of the monitor.

Place three BP_SecurityCameras to the level. Put one of them in the next hallway, the other one in the storage room, and the last one to the boss room. Go back to the BP_Monitor and set the three BP_SecurityCameras to the three SecurityCamera entries of the Capture Infos variable.

Play the game now, get close to the monitor, and you can see the three captured scenes in the three monitors. You can also see them stop playing when you move far away (Figure 18.41).

FIGURE 18.41 Set up and test a BP_Monitor.

Conclusion

In this chapter, we elaborated some time with C++ to create an AI_Seer class which later on polished in Blueprint. We leverage its seeing capability to create our security camera with mostly animation setups. We practiced the component and interface programming paradigm again and will benefit from this programming pattern when we move on to the patrolling AI.

For the monitor, we have covered how to create structures to bundle data together. Structures could also be used for our weapon UI if you wish to do some refactoring.

It is exciting to have some enemies to play with finally, but it would be more fun if they can move. Let's move on to the next chapter and create our patrolling AI.

CHAPTER 19

Patrolling AI

Hello, and congratulations on coming this far. In this chapter, we are going to explore the AI system of Unreal Engine and build a patrolling AI that can make the game fun to play. As we start to make more gameplay elements, one thing to always keep in mind is the balance of the game.

We want the player to feel fun, progression, and challenged. But it does not come free as we build more and more stuff. It takes many playtests to know if something works or not, and sometimes good ideas pop up, but not really fit into the whole structure.

The game developer should always keep in mind that you are creating an experience you want the players to have. It doesn't have to be based on anything realistic. On the contrary, most of the time, you realize that it's not fun when it's too real. Instead, we want to be the director, and we direct how the player should feel when they play the game.

We will build our AI system based on that approach.

It's important to know what you want, so let's talk about what AI we are going to build. We want an AI that:

1. Patrols when it does not see the player.
2. When seeing the player or hit by the payer, move to the player and shoot the player every 2 seconds.
3. If it lost sight of the player, keep pursuing in 10 more seconds; if it still cannot see the player, go back to patrolling.
4. When touched by the player, or getting 400 units close to the player when pursuing, capture the player.
5. When dead, spawn a weapon pickup.

Here, we have made some assumptions; first of all, we assume that the AI can always reach you. However, you could be standing on a box that the AI cannot reach. But we can get away with much programming with this assumption. In this case, AI just goes back to patrolling. Second, AI just knows where you were when it got hit. Again, not true in real life, but we can get away with much programming with that assumption, and the game is still fun. Let's go ahead and start building our AI.

Tutorial 1: Create the Patrol AI Character

Step 1: Create BP_Patrol. Select the BP_Dummy_AI and rename it BP_Patrol. Create a new folder called PatrollingAI under the Characters folder and move BP_Patrol to the folder.

Step 2: Add SeerRef. Just like how we added a spotlight to the security, we can do the same here. Select the Mesh component and add a Spot

Light component. Rename the spotlight SeerRef. Under the Sockets section in the Details panel, click the magnifying glass of the Parent Socket and select head. SeerRef is now attached to the head joint. Go to the Viewport, and you can see that it's looking up. Rotate and move it, so it's in front of the eye, and the X-axis is pointing forward; the first half of Figure 19.1 shows the process.

Step 3: Spawn BP_AISeer and attach it to SeerRef. We have done this on the security camera already, and we do exactly the same thing here. At the end of Event BeginPlay, we spawn a BP_AISeer, set it to a new variable called Seer, and attach it to SeerRef. We then call SetSightRadius and SetSightPeripheralVisionDegrees on Seer to set the sight radius of Seer to the attenuation radius of SeerRef, and Seer's peripheral vision angle to the outer cone angle of the SeerRef. Don't forget to hide SeerRef. The volumetric fog is too annoying on BP_Patrol. Let's set the Volumetric Scattering Intensity to 0. The second half of Figure 19.1 shows the calling of the Set Volumetric Scattering Intensity function.

Step 4: Create a gun for BP_Patrol. Create a new gun called BP_Gun_Patrol derived from BP_Gun. In the event graph, override the Auto Reload if Clip is Empty as shown in Figure 19.2.

FIGURE 19.1 Create and set up the attachment of SeerRef and spawn it in Event BeginPlay.

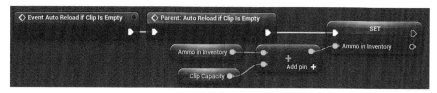

FIGURE 19.2 Create a BP_Gun_Patrol class based on BP_Gun and override Auto Reload if Clip is Empty.

719

What we do here is after reloading, give this gun more ammo, so it never runs out of ammo. That's right! We are giving the AI infinite ammo.

Step 5: Give BP_Patrol the gun. Open BP_Patrol, call AcquireNewWeapon at the end of Event BeginPlay, and set the Weapon Class to BP_Gun_Patrol. Place a BP_Patrol in the level, play the game, and we shall see it holding the gun (Figure 19.3).

Step 6: Expose the WeaponClass variable of BP_Weapon_Pickup. To spawn a weapon pick up when the AI dies, we need to be able to specify the weapon class for the BP_Weapon_Pickup. Open BP_Weapon_Pickup, select the WeaponClass variable, and check on Expose on Spawn in the Detail pane. We also want the player to be the only one who can pick up weapons. Change the Cast To BP_Character_Base at the beginning of Event Overlapped to Cast To BP_Ellen_FPS (Figure 19.4).

FIGURE 19.3 Test the AI in the level.

FIGURE 19.4 Changes made to BP_Weapon_Pickup.

720

Step 7: Make AI Spawn a weapon when dead.
Open BP_Patrol, add a new variable Loot, set its variable type to BP_Weapon_Base class reference, and make it public. At the end of Event BeginPlay, call a function named Bind Event On Destroyed. Drag out from the Event input pin of the Bind Event On Destroyed node and select Add Event → Add Custom Event. Name the new event SpawnLoot. Implement SpawnLoot as shown in Figure 19.5.

The Bind Event On Destroyed binds the event connected to the Event input to the destruction of this actor. So, when BP_Patrol is about to get destroyed, SpawnLoot is called first. In SpawnLoot, we spawn a BP_Weapon_Pick. Notice that there is a Weapon Class input. It is in there because we checked on Expose On Spawn on that variable in BP_Weapon_Pickup. What happens now is when a BP_Patrol is dead, a BP_Weapon_Pickup is created; the purple Loot variable is a new variable we added, it is of the type BP_Weapon_Base class reference. We use it as the Weapon Class to spawn the pick up.

Clean up all the weapon pickups you have in the level, place a BP_Weapon_Pickup in the start room, and set its Weapon Class to BP_Pipe in the Details panel. Drag a BP_Patrol in the next room, make it facing away from the door, and set the Loot to BP_Gun in the Details panel. Play the game, pick up the Pipe, and go knock

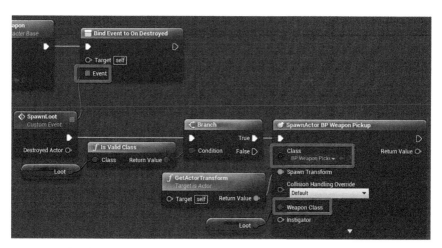

FIGURE 19.5 Make AI Spawn a weapon when dead.

721

down the BP_Patrol. A BP_Weapon_Pickup of the gun should appear and you can pick it up (Figure 19.6).

Step 8: Create a CapturePlayer and a StopAI function that make the AI capture the player and stop its AI logic (Figure 19.7).

The StopAI function gets the controller of BP_Patrol and cast it to an AI Controller. We then get its Brain Component and stop its logic. We have yet to create the AI controller and the brain of the AI. However, we can already define a function that stops them. All this falls into the Unreal Engine AI framework, and we are going to cover more later.

For the CapturePlayer function, we get the AI Controller and called its SetFocus function. The New Focus input is the player, which makes the AI look at the player. We then call our StopAI event and make the player surrender to this BP_Patrol. The Surrender To function was built earlier when we were creating the security camera.

Step 9: Call the Capture player when touched.

Select the CapsuleComponent, go to the details panel, and click on the plus button labeled

FIGURE 19.6 A gun pickup appears when the AI is dead.

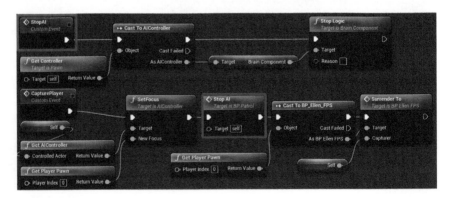

FIGURE 19.7 Implementation of StopAI and CapturePlayer.

with On Component Hit in the Events section. Implement the newly created On Component Hit (CapsuleComponent) as shown in Figure 19.8.

What we do here is check if the other actor that hits the capsule component is the player by casting and then calls CapturePlayer if it is the player. Play the game again, and approach to the BP_Patrol. The instance that you touch it, it captures you right away. The engine will complain about the brain component that does not exist. We are going to add it later.

Step 10: Disable the collision, destroy Seer, and stop the AI when BP_Patrol is dead. We have already overridden the HealthCompNotify Dead and hide the health bar there. Let's add the code highlighted in Figure 19.9 at the end of it to disable the collision of Capsule Component, Destroy Seer, and stop the AI logic.

Step 11: Add variables to store patrol points. Add a new public variable called PatrolPoints to BP_Patrol, set its variable type to Target Point object reference, and change it to an array. Add another variable of the type integer and name it CurrentPatrolPointIndex. The Target Point class is like a locator that you can place it to the level.

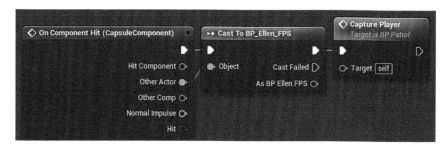

FIGURE **19.8** Implementation of On Component Hit (CapsuleComponent).

FIGURE **19.9** Disable the collision, destroy Seer, and stop the AI when BP_Patrol is dead.

You will see how it looks like when we start to place it.

Step 12: Implement a function to get the next patrol point. Create a new function called GetNextPatrolPoint, give it two outputs: the first one is named PatrolPoint and is of the type TargetPoint, and the second one is a Boolean called Found. Implement the first half of the function as shown in Figure 19.10.

In this half of the function, we check the length of PatrolPoints and see if it is bigger than 0, or in other words, has patrol points. We return an empty patrol point and false if it has no patrol point.

Step 13: Implement the second half of GetNextPatrolPoint (Figure 19.11).

This part is very similar to our GetNextWeapon function. After the True output pin of the Branch node, we increment CurrentPatrolPointIndex to get the next index. To make it cycles back, we have to do a modulo operation with the length of PatrolPoints. We then set CurrentPatrolPointIndex to the next index, get the next target point in PatrolPoints, and return it with a true value for the Found output. The difference here is that we used the index to store which one is the current one.

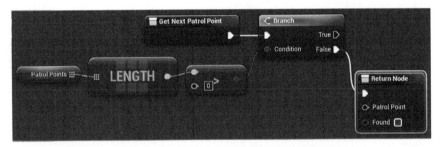

FIGURE 19.10 First half of GetNextPatrolPoint.

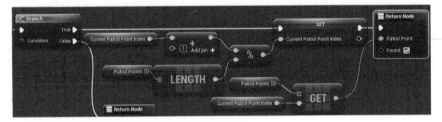

FIGURE 19.11 Implementation of the second half of GetNextPatrolPoint.

Now, we have an array we can populate and cycle through; let's move on to build the AI system and make the AI patrol.

Tutorial 2: Create AI Controller and Behavior Tree for the Patrol AI

Step 1: Create an AI Controller. Create a new blueprint class derived from AI Controller (you have to search for it in All Classes). Name the new AI Controller AIC_Patrol. Open BP_Patrol and go to its class defaults. Under the Pawn section, set the Auto Possess AI to Place in World or Spawned and set the AI Controller Class to our new AIC_Patrol. This setup makes BP_Patrol to be possessed by an AIC_Patrol when placed or spawned in the world (Figure 19.12).

Step 2: Create a blackboard and a behavior tree. Right click in the PatrollingAI folder, select Artificial Intelligence → Blackboard, and name the NewBlackBoardData to BB_Patrol. Right click again and select Artificial Intelligence → Behavior Tree, and name the NewBehaviorTree BT_Patrol.

Blackboard and Behavior Tree

People make decisions based on what they know, and AI is no different. The blackboard is the knowledge of the AI, and the behavior tree is the brain of the AI. The behavior tree decides what the AI should do based on the information populated on the blackboard. The blackboard

FIGURE 19.12 Set the BP_Patrol to be possessed by an AIC_Patrol.

725

can have information like does the AI see the player?
What is the next patrol point? And the behavior tree can
then decide if the AI should go to the next patrol point
or pursue the player based on if the AI can see the player
or not.

> Step 3: Make AIC_Patrol use BT_Patrol. Open AIC_
> Patrol and add the code shown in Figure 19.13 to
> Event BeginPlay.
> This Run Behavior Tree function makes
> the AI use the BT_Patrol as its brain (the brain
> component we saw earlier). BT_Patrol now tells
> the AIC_Patrol what to do. Because AIC_Patrol
> possesses BP_Patrol, BP_Patrol now follows the
> instructions from BT_Patrol.
> Step 4: Add a NextPatrolPoint blackboard key. Open
> BB_Patrol, click on the New Key button, and
> select Object to create a new key of the type
> Object. Blackboard keys are the knowledge the
> AI knows, and it can be an object, a location,
> a Boolean, or anything. Name the ObjectKey
> NextPatrolPoint. Go to the Blackboard Details
> panel on the right, and expand the Key Type
> option under the Key section. Set the Base class
> to Actor. This NextPatrolPoint is now of the type
> Actor and we can populate it to be the next
> patrol point we want the AI to go (Figure 19.14).
> Step 5: Create a basic behavior tree. Open BT_Patrol
> and find the ROOT node in the graph. Drag out
> from the darker gray bar at the bottom of the
> node, search for Sequence, and select Sequence
> in the search list to create a Sequence node.
> Drag out from the left side of the gray bar at the
> bottom of the sequence node, search, and create

FIGURE 19.13 Make AIC_Patrol use BT_Patrol.

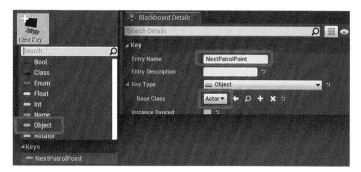

FIGURE 19.14 Add a new blackboard key called NextPatrolPoint and set its type to Actor.

a Move To node. With the Move To node selected, go to the Details panel and set the Acceptable Radius to 100. Drag out from the right side of the gray bar at the bottom of the sequence node, and search and create a Wait node. The steps and the results are shown in Figure 19.15.

Let's break it down here. The ROOT node is the starting point of the behavior tree, and all the logic starts from here. Step 1 added a sequence node, which means when the AI starts, we want the AI to do a sequence of tasks.

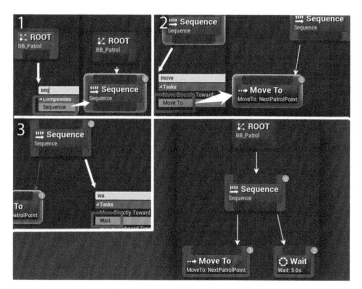

FIGURE 19.15 Steps to create basics of the behavior tree.

727

Step 2 added a Move To node under the sequence node. This Move To node is a behavior tree task that the engine provides, and it makes the AI move to something. Notice that at the bottom of the Move To node, it says MoveTo: NextPatrolPoint, and this is because NextPatrolPoint is the only key in the blackboard, so it's automatically selected as the target for the Move To task. We can change it to other blackboard keys in the Details panel. Adding a Move To node under the Sequence node means that the first task in the Sequence is Move To something. Setting the Acceptable Radius to 100 means that the AI just has to move closer than 100 units to the target.

Step 3 added a Wait node. Wait node is another built-in task that makes the AI Wait for a certain amount of time. It is currently waiting for 5 seconds. You can change the amount of time to wait in the Details panel as well.

The image at the bottom right corner of Figure 19.15 is the finished tree. The sequence node runs from left to right. In a behavior tree, things on the left always have higher priority than the right and are executed first. So, the whole AI logic here is when the behavior tree starts, do a sequence of tasks. The first task is to Move to the NextPatrolPoint, and the next task is to wait for 5 seconds. After waiting, there is nothing left in the tree; repeat from the ROOT node again. You can drag to move the tasks around to rearrange the order.

Play the game again with BT_Patrol open, and you can see the behavior tree starts to run, and the node highlighted with yellow is the current task being executed. Hit F8 to un-possess and move to the next room with regular navigation of the editor.

You can see that the AI is not moving, which makes sense because we haven't given any patrol point to it yet. Don't stop the game, and hit the Pause button in the behavior tree window to pause the game. We can then hit the Back: Over button to go back through time and see what the AI is doing previously. Click the Back Over button a few times, and then start clicking the Forward: Over to see how the AI progresses. You can see, every time it starts from Root, then to the Sequence and runs Move To, and then falls back to Root again. The Wait task is never executed.

Behavior tree tasks can fail, and what is happing here is that the Move To task fails. It fails because the NextPatrolPoint is None as shown in the green box in Figure 19.16. Whenever a task in a sequence fails, the whole Sequence fails and aborts.

The AI we are currently viewing is in the blue box of Figure 19.16, and it is an AIC_Patrol. You can view a different AI by selecting one in that dropdown list. We can pause the game any time and use the behavior tree window to debug the AI.

Step 6: Create a new behavior tree task. Stop the game and click on the New Task button in the toolbar of the behavior tree window to create a new behavior tree task. It automatically opens, and you can see a new asset called BTTaks_BlueprintBase_New got added to the Content Browser. Rename this new task FindNextPatrolPoint.

Step 7: Implement FindNextPatrolPoint. Open FindNextPatrolPoint (it should already be open if you did no close it in the previous step). Give it a new public variable called NextPatrolPointKey, and set its variable type to Blackboard Key

FIGURE 19.16 Debugging the AI behavior tree.

Selector. Override a function called Receive Execute AI and implement it as shown in Figure 19.17.

This Event Receive Execute AI is called when the task starts. The Controlled Pawn input is the pawn of the AI Controller, and the Owner Controller is the AI Controller. We cast the pawn to BP_Patrol and call its Get Next Patrol Point function to get the next patrol point from it.

We then call a function called Set Blackboard Value as Object, and this one sets the value of a blackboard key that is of the type Object. We pass the patrol point we have found to the Value input. The Key input we pass in is the new public variable NextPatrolPointKey we have created.

NextPatrolPointKey is of the type Blackboard Key Selector. Making it public allows us to select a key from the blackboard in the Details panel when this task is used in the behavior tree. Whatever we select becomes the blackboard key this Set Blackboard Value as Object function is setting.

Finally, we call Finish Execute with the Success output checked to indicate that the whole task is successful. This Finish Execute has to be called to finish the task. If you forget to call it, the task will never end, which causes the whole behavior tree to get stuck. If we don't check on the Success output, the task is considered failed by the behavior tree.

Step 8: Use FindNextPatrolPoint in the behavior tree. Open BT_Patrol, drag out from the bottom of the sequence node, and search and create a FindNextPatrolPoint task. In the Details panel, you can see the NextPatrolPointKey variable we created in the task. We have to make it public to see it here. It is now set to NextPatrolPoint, which

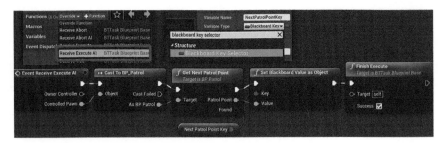

FIGURE 19.17 Add a new variable called NextPatrolPointKey and override Receive Execute AI.

means that we are setting this blackboard key to the patrol point we have found in the task. Drag the FindNextPatrolPoint task to the left, so it becomes the first to execute (Figure 19.18).

The behavior tree now finds the next patrol point first and then moves to the next patrol point.

Step 9: Set up the player for testing in the storage room. In the World outliner, search and find Player Start. Move it to the storage room. This player start is the place the player spawns when the game starts. Drag three weapon pickups in front of it, and set them to the pipe, gun, and the grenade launcher so that we can test the AI with all the weapons (Figure 19.19).

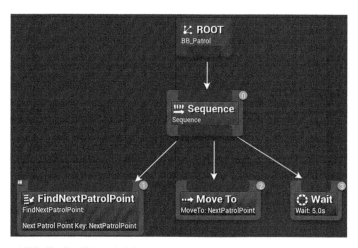

FIGURE 19.18 Add FindNextPatrolPoint to the behavior tree.

FIGURE 19.19 Set up the player for testing in the storage room.

Step 10: Add Nav Mesh Bounds Volumes. Go to the Place Actors panel on the left of the window, search for Nav Mesh Bounds Volume, and drag it to the level. Scale it up and make it encapsulate the whole room. Press the P button to make it build the navigation map. The green meshes it generates are called navmeshes, and AI can move on navmeshes through the engines built-in navigation system. The Move To task utilizes the navigation system, so we need to place navmeshes for it to work. Drag a few more copies of Nav Mesh Bounds Volume to cover the entire level. It is fine to overlap them, and press P again to toggle their visibility off (Figure 19.20).

Step 11: Fix the doors. The doors are blocking the navmeshes. To fix it, open BP_SlidingDoor and select all the meshes in the Components panel. Go to the Details panel, search for can ever affect navigation, and check it off (Figure 19.21).

Step 12: Drag a BP_Patrol to the storage room and set it up for testing. Drag a copy of BP_Patrol to

FIGURE 19.20 Add Nave Mesh Bounds Volumes.

FIGURE 19.21 Check off the can ever affect navigation for the meshes of the door.

the storage room. Go to the Place Actors panel, search for, and drag three Target Points to the level. Select the BP_Patrol you place in the room, and go to Details panel. Add three entries to the Patrol Points array under the Default section. Click on the eyedropper button and then pick the target points in the level to assign the three target points to the three entries of the Patrol Points array (Figure 19.22).

Play the game again and you can now see the AI moves to the three target points in a cycle. And wait for 5 seconds there before moving on to the next one (Figure 19.23).

Step 13: Fix the animation. Currently, the AI is using the FPS animations, which the legs do not move. We also don't have the correct attack animation in that manner. Find the animations we retargeted from Mixamo and add "Patrol_"

FIGURE 19.22 Pick the three Target points with the eyedropper.

733

FIGURE 19.23 The path AI moves.

in front of their names to make it easier to distinguish them. Figure 19.24 shows all three of them after renaming.

Create an animation montage from Patrol_Shooting. And don't forget to give it the CommitAttack animation notify. Open BP_Gun_Patrol and replace the Idle, Walk, and Attack animations to the patrol ones (Figure 19.25).

Play the game again, and this time, the AI should walk nicely.

Step 14: Add a blackboard key to store the player. Open BB_Patrol and add a new key of the type Object. Name the new key Player and change its Base Class to BP_Ellen_FPS.

Step 15: Make the AI see the player. Open AIC_Patrol, add a new variable called PlayerBlackboardKeyName, and set its type to Name. Compile it and set the default value of PlayerBlackboardKeyName to Player. This name has to be the same as the name of the new blackboard key called Player we added in Step 14 (upper- and lowercase matters). Go to class settings, and add BPI_AISeer to the Interfaces.

FIGURE 19.24 Renamed patrol animations.

Replace animations for BP_Gun_Patrol.

We made BP_AISeer inform both the owner and the AI Controller of the owner when it sees the player. To make this AI controller see the player, we just need to go ahead and implement the On Seer Target Update interface function (Figure 19.26).

Here, we break the stimulus input to know if it was successfully sensed. This Boolean is true if the BP_AISeer sees the player; it is false if the BP_AISeer lost sight of the player. If the BP_AISeer sees the player, we set the Player blackboard key of the blackboard to the Target input of the event, which should be the player in this case. The blackboard used by the AI controller is a member variable (the one in the red box), and we can access it right here. What happens now

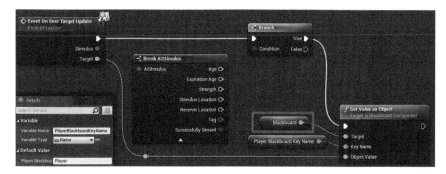

FIGURE 19.26 Implementation of On Seer Target Update.

is if the BP_AISeer attached to the BP_Patrol sees the player, it calls On Seer Target Update on AIC_Patrol. AIC_Patrol then updates that information on the blackboard and sets the value of the Player blackboard key to the player. The PlayerBlackboardKeyName we supply is how we tell the blackboard which key we want to set.

Step 16: Make the AI move to the player if it sees the player. Go to BT_Patrol, and create a Selector node (right click and search). Connect the Root node to the top of the Selector node and connect the Sequence node to the bottom of the Selector node (click and drag the darker gray bar on the nodes to make connections). Drag out from the bottom of the Selector node and create another Move To node; make sure that it is positioned on the left side of the Sequence node. With the Move To node selected, go to the Details panel, and set the Acceptable Radius to 300. Under the Blackboard section, change the Blackboard Key to Player. Play the game one more time and let the AI see you. Once it sees you, it should start following you shortly after finishing its current round of patrolling (Figure 19.27).

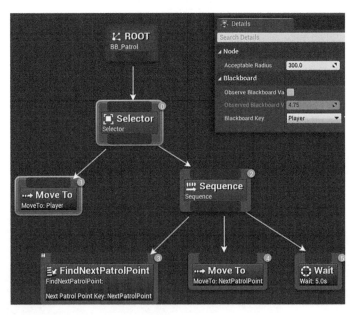

FIGURE 19.27 Adjusted behavior tree that makes the AI follow the player.

Why?

We have covered the Sequence node. It executes what's connected to the bottom of it from left to right. A sequence node fails if it encountered a failed task and aborts. A sequence only returns with success if all tasks under it had succeeded.

The Selector node also executes what's connected to the bottom of it from left to right. The difference is if a branch under it has failed, it moves on to the next one. It stops whenever a branch had succeeded, and returns to the top with success. A selector fails if all the branches fail.

Sequences and selectors fall into a bigger category called compositors because they composite other tasks together.

When the AI doesn't see the player, that Player blackboard key is None, and the Move To on the far left fails. The selector moves on to its second branch—the Sequence, and the Sequence does the patrolling. When the AI sees the player, the value of the Player blackboard key is set to the player. Next time the behavior tree loops back, the Move To on the far left will have a valid target, and the AI starts to move to the player.

The logic seems fine except that the AI does not move to the player right away if it's still doing the patrolling Sequence. Let's fix that with a blackboard decorator.

> Step 17: Abort patrolling when the player is in sight. Right click on the Sequence node and select Add Decorator → Blackboard. A decorator is something you can attach to a compositor or a task to affect its execution. The Sequence node now has a Blackboard Based Condition decorator attached to it. Select this new decorator, go to the Details panel, and set the Observer aborts to Both. Setting Observer aborts Both means if the condition becomes false, abort this node, and any lower priority takes. The condition is set in the Blackboard section. Here, we set the Key Query to Is Not Set and The Blackboard Key to Player. The condition becomes true if the Player blackboard key is not set and

becomes false if the Player blackboard key is set (Figure 19.28).

Play the game again, and this time, the instance the AI sees the player, it moves to the player. What we do here can be translated to plain English as: as long as the AI knows the player, abort patrolling and move to the player right away.

Step 18: Create a TryCapturePlayer task. In the behavior tree window, click on the New Task button on the toolbar and select BTTask_BlueprintBase. Rename the new task TryCapturePlayer. Give the task a new public float variable called AcceptableDistance and set the default value to 400. Override its Receive Execute AI function as shown in Figure 19.29.

Here, we check if the distance of the player pawn to the AI is smaller than the AcceptableDistance. If it is, we capture the player and finish with success. If the distance is not

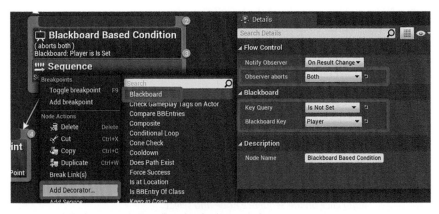

FIGURE 19.28 Add a decorator to abort patrolling when the player is in sight.

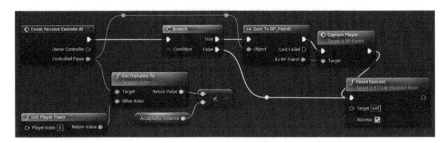

FIGURE 19.29 Implementation of the Receive Execute AI function of TryCapturePlayer.

738

smaller than the AcceptableDistance, we still
finish with success. The reason here is we just
want to try, and if the AI is too far, we still tried;
keep moving on with the behavior tree and don't
abort anything.

Step 19: Add TryCapturePlayer to the behavior tree.
Go back to BT_Patrol and modify it as shown
in Figure 19.30. If you have made any wrong
connection, you can hold down Alt and click on
any connection to break it.

Here, we inserted a sequence and added
TryCapturePlayer as the highest priority before
Move To. Play the game again, and this time, the
AI captures you when it's close enough. A little
trick we did here is we set the AcceptableDistance
to 400, that's 100 units higher than the
Move To. As long as the Move To succeed,
TryCapturePlayer should allow the AI to capture
the player. The AI is now moving too fast, which
makes the game challenging to play. Open
BP_Patrol, and select the CharacterMovement
component in the Components panel. Go to the
Details panel, search for Max Walk Speed, and
change it to 300.

Step 20: Create an Attack task. Create a new task
and name it Attack. This one is fairly simple; we

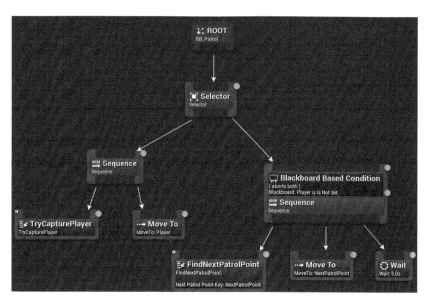

FIGURE 19.30 Add TryCapturePlayer.

739

override Event Receive Execute AI and ask the pawn to attack (Figure 19.31).

Step 21: Make the AI shoot every 2 seconds. Go back to BT_Patrol and insert a selector between the first selector and the Sequence on the left. Drag out from the bottom of the new selector and create an Attack task; make sure that the Attack task is on the right of the sequence node. Right click on the sequence node on the far left and select Add Decorator → Time Limit. With the TimeLimit node selected, go to the Details panel and set the Time Limit setting to 2.0 (Figure 19.32).

We give the TryCapturePlayer and Move To player sequence a time limit, if the AI cannot reach and capture the player after 2 seconds, the sequence fails and the selector moves on to

FIGURE 19.31 Implementation of the Receive Execute AI function of Attack.

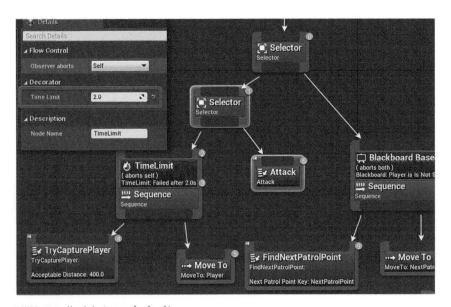

FIGURE 19.32 New behavior tree after Step 21.

*attack, and then the whole tree starts again. Play
the game again, and this time, the AI should start
to shoot you when pursuing. However, the AI
stops patrolling (Why?).*

Step 22: Make the AI go to patrolling when the player
is not seen. The reason the AI stops patrolling is
because the patrolling part is the second priority
of the selector that connects to the ROOT. As
long as the higher priority can be successful, the
selector never goes to patrolling. After adding
the Attack, the Attack task always returns with
success. To fix the logic, add a new blackboard
decorator to the second selector on the left. In
the Details panel, set the Observer aborts to
Both, Key Query to Is Set, and Blackboard Key to
Player. What this means is only to do this part if
the Player blackboard key is set. By setting this,
as long as the player is not seen, the selector goes
to patrolling (Figure 19.33).

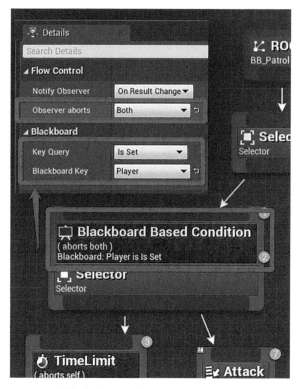

FIGURE 19.33 Make the AI go to patrolling when the player is not seen.

741

Because we have set up the weapon properly, the AI even reloads when the gun is out of ammo. However, the character is sliding during attacking and reloading. Let's fix that by improving the animation blueprint.

Step 23: Create a FullBody slot. Open AnimBP_Ellen, and go to window → Anim Slot Manager to open the Anim Slot Manager. It should appear at the bottom right corner of the window. Select DefaultGroup and click the Add Slot button. Start typing FullBody, and hit Enter to create a new slot called FullBody.

Step 24: Create a cache for full-body animations. Most of our animation montages like attacking, reloading, weapon switch, and hit should all be happening on the upper body. After all, you don't need the legs to do anything when doing these actions. The only animation montage that should be full-body is the animation montage of death.

In the AnimGraph, hold down Alt and click on the out pose pin of the IdleWalk state machine to break its connection. Move it up, drag out from its out pose pin, and create a Slot 'DefaultSlot' node. With the new Slot 'DefaultSlot' node selected, go to the Details panel and change the Slot Name to FullBody. Drag out from the out pose pin of the Slot 'FullBody' node, search for New Save cached pose, and hit Enter to create a SavedPose node. Rename this new SavedPose node to FullBody by selecting it and hit F2 (Figure 19.34).

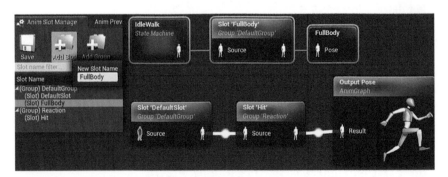

FIGURE 19.34 Create a FullBody cache for the full-body animations.

Cache Pose

The Save cached pose operation creates a cache (reference) of the animation. You can use this cache anywhere else in the AnimGraph.

> *Step 25: Create a cache for upper-body animations. In the AnimGraph, right click and search for FullBody. Select the Use cached pose 'FullBody' to create a Use cached pose 'FullBody' node, and connect it to the in pose pin of the Slot 'DefaultSlot' node. Disconnect the out pose pin of the Slot 'Hit' node, drag out from it, and create another cached pose; name the new cache UpperBody (Figure 19.35).*
> *The Use cached pose 'FullBody' node gives you the same animation that connects into the FullBody node. We then pass it through the Default slot and the Hit slot and cached it to a new cache called Upperbody. Be aware that the naming of these two caches is what we intend them to be. In this case, we want to use the IdleWalk state machine plus animation montages that use the FullBody slot to be used on the full-body of the character. We want the cached FullBody animation plus the other montages to be used only on the upper body.*
> *Step 26: Blend the FullBody and UpperBody cache. Create another Use cached pose 'FullBody' node and a Use cached pose 'UpperBody' node. Create a Layered blend per bone node (Right click and search). Connect the Use cached pose 'FullBody' node to the Base Pose input and connect the*

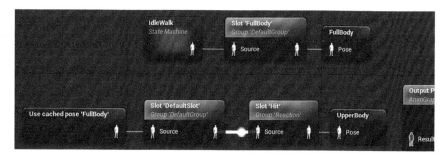

FIGURE 19.35 Create a cache for upper-body animations.

Use cached pose 'UpperBody' node to the Blend Poses 0 input. With the Layered blend per bone node selected, go to the Details panel, expand Layer Setup, and expand the 0 under it. This 0 section represents how BlendPose 0 input is blended on top of the Base Pose input.

Click on the "+" sign of the Branch Filters to give it a new entry named 0, open it, and set the Bone Name to spine_02 and the Bone Depth to 2. What this means is starting from spine_02, in the next two child bones, the pose gradually blends from Base Pose to Blend Pose 0. Any bone after two child bones under spine_02 (upper-body bones) plays the full Blend Pose 0. Any bone that has a higher hierarchy than spine_02 (lower-body bones) is going to play the Base Pose. It is here that we make the animation we intend to play on the upper body to only be played on the upper body. Let's also check on the Mesh Space Rotation Blend to avoid the offset caused by higher hierarchies. Mesh space means all bones rotation is relative to the location and rotation of the mesh, not their parent joint (local space).

Finally, connect the out pose pin to the Result in pose pin of the Out Pose node (Figure 19.36).

Step 27: Set the Death_From_The_Back_Montage to use the FullBody slot. Open Death_From_The_Back_Montage, and change its slot to DefaultGroup.FullBody. We want this one to be full-body.

Play the game one more time, and all the animation should work as expected.

Step 28: Make the healthComp notify the AI controller when damage is taken. It would be

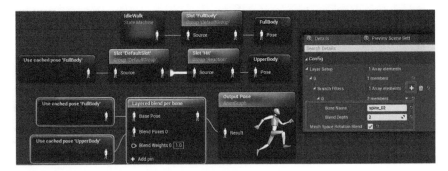

FIGURE 19.36 Blend the FullBody and UpperBody cache and use it for the final pose.

absurd if the AI stands there and take damage from you and do nothing. And currently, it is doing just that. To make it all work, we need to tell the HealthComp to notify the AI controller when the pawn took damage. Open BP_ HealthComp and find the TakeDamage event. After the HealthCompNotify_TookDamage interface call, add another HealthCompNotify_ TookDamage, and this time, we call it on the AI controller (Figure 19.37).

Step 29: *Make the AI know the player when it took damage. Open AIC_Patrol, go to its class settings, and add BPI_HealthComp as another interface. Implement the HealthCompNotify_ TookDamage interface function as shown in Figure 19.38.*

Based on our weapon setup, the damage causer would be the gun, so we need to get the owner and cast it to BP_Ellen_FPS to ensure that it was the player that causes the damage. We then set the Player blackboard key to the player.

Give the game another go, and this time, when you shoot the AI, it starts moving toward you right away.

Our AI should behave pretty well at this point. It pursues you relentlessly once it notices your existence. But let's move one extra mile to make the AI forget you after losing sight of you.

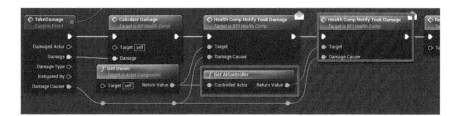

FIGURE 19.37 Make the healthComp notify the AI controller when damage is taken.

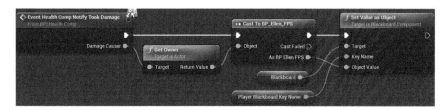

FIGURE 19.38 Implementation of HealthCompNotify_TookDamage.

Step 30: Create a Boolean to store if the player is in sight or not. Add a new Boolean variable to AIC_Patrol and name it IsPlayerInSight. Set it to the Successfully Sensed output pin of the Break AIStimulus node in Event On Seer Target update (Figure 19.39).

Step 31: Create forgetting functions that make the AI forget the player. Open AIC_Patrol and create a new custom event called StartForgettingPlayer. Drag out from its execution pin, create a branch node, and use IsPlayerInSight as the Condition input of the Branch node. Drag out from the False execution pin, search, and create a Set Timer by Event node. Set the Time input to 10 seconds.

Drag out from the Return Value of the Set Timer by Event node and select Promote to variable to add a new variable to AIC_Patrol. Go to the Variables section of the My Blueprint panel, and change the name of the new variable to ForgetPlayerTimer.

Drag out from the Event input pin of the Set Timer by Event node and select Add Event → Add Custom Event to bind it to a new event. Name the new custom event ForgetPlayer. In ForgetPlayer, we just set the value of the Player blackboard key to nothing (Figure 19.40).

Here, we used a new feature called timer, and the Set Timer by Event calls the ForgetPlayer event after 10 seconds just like a Delay node. However, it also returns a timer handle that allows us to manipulate the count down, and we can use it to cancel the timer, pause the timer, and query the progress. We also checked if the

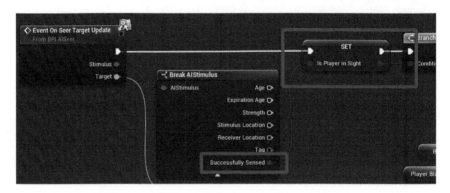

FIGURE 19.39 Create a Boolean to store if the player is in sight or not.

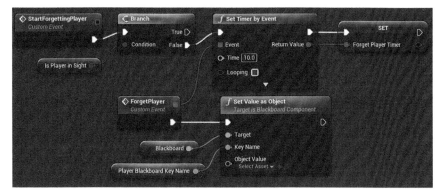

FIGURE 19.40 Create forgetting functions that make the AI forget the player.

> player is in sight because we want the weapon
> attack to trigger this event, but we never want
> the AI to forget the player when the player is
> in sight.
> Step 32: Create a CancelForgettingPlayer event that
> cancels the timer. Create a new custom event
> called CancelForgettingPlayer. In this event,
> we just get the ForgetPlayerTimer, clear, and
> invalidate it by calling the Clear and Invalidate
> Timer by Handle function. After creating the
> event, call it after the Set Timer by Event function
> in StartForgettingPlayer. This call is needed to
> ensure that the previous timer is cleared before
> adding a new one (Figure 19.41).
> Step 33: Add a call to CancelForgettingPlayer and
> StartForgettingPlayer in Event On Seer Target
> Update (Figure 19.42).

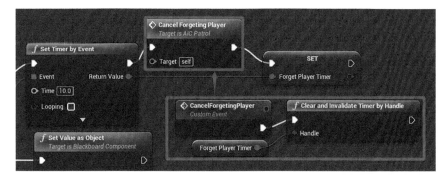

FIGURE 19.41 Implement CancelForgettingPlayer and call it after Set Timer by Event.

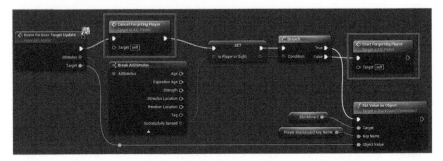

FIGURE 19.42 Add a call to CancelForgettingPlayer and StartForgettingPlayer in Event On Seer Target Update.

Here, we first cancel forgetting the player in the beginning because the perception has updated. We call StartForgettingPlayer if the Successfully Sensed is false, which means that the AI starts to forget the player at the moment it lost sight of the player.

Step 34: Add a call to CancelForgettingPlayer and StartForgettingPlayer in Event Health Comp Notify Took Damage (Figure 19.43).

We have similar logic here, and we cancel forgetting the player when the AI took damage from the player. But we start forgetting the player right away after getting hit because there is no guarantee that the AI sees the player right away after hitting by the player.

Alrighty, we have finally finished the patrolling AI. Figure 19.44 shows all the features we implemented.

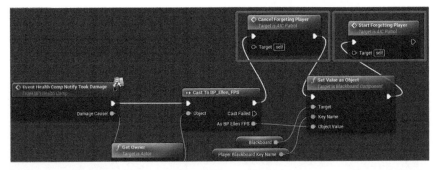

FIGURE 19.43 Add a call to Add a call to CancelForgettingPlayer and StartForgettingPlayer in Event Health Comp Notify Took Damage.

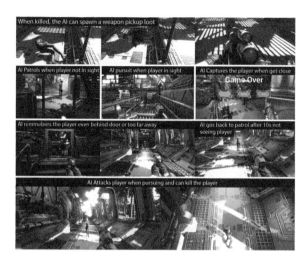

FIGURE 19.44 All the patrolling features we have implemented.

Conclusion

We have made a quite compiling AI, and you can see how the different systems we have built can tie together. Let's count these systems:

1. Character. The character is the core system that all the other systems are built around. It can attack, take damage, die, and play various animations.
2. Weapon system. Weapon system takes care of outputting damage and hold weapon-specific animations.
3. Animation system. The animation system drives character animation and helps drive weapon logic.
4. Health System. BP_HealthComp takes care of receiving damage, notify damage, and death to its owner.
5. Perception System. The perception system informs the owner and its AI what it sees.
6. AI. The AI drives the behavior of the enemy.
7. UI. UI shows the status of the game.

All these systems have their unique structure and are talking to each other to make the whole game work.

As your game becomes bigger and more complicated, it's going to get harder to keep track of everything. Making these systems simple, flexible, and elegant becomes more and more important as you progress.

Let's move on to the next chapter that we can quickly build a boss for our game.

CHAPTER 20

Boss

Welcome to the chapter of the boss! It never feels more exciting than the player finally meets the boss, and we are going to have more fun in this chapter to create our boss. We will tie our systems together and make the boss fight both fun and challenging. But before we move on to that, let's again have a list of things we want the boss to do:

1. The boss takes the form of the hero asset.
2. When the boss sees the player, it locks on the player and always facing the player.

3. The boss starts to shoot grenades toward the player every 3 seconds.
4. The boss spawn minions behind it every 8 seconds.
5. Boss minion is a child class of BP_Patrol that never forgets the player and spawn grenade launcher pickups when dead.
6. There are four health regenerations at the four corners around the boss.
7. Boss explodes when dead, kills all minions, and spawns a "you win!" sign.

Let's start assembling the boss right away!

Tutorial 20.1: Create the Boss Class

Step 1: Assemble boss visuals and create hierarchy. Create a new folder called Boss in the blueprints folder and create a new class called BP_Boss derived from the Actor class. Open BP_Boss, find all the static meshes of the hero asset in the content browser, and drag them to the Components panel of BP_Boss to add them as components, make sure their Mobility are all set to Movable. Add a new Scene component to it and name the scene component RotationPivot. In the Details panel, set the Location Z to 320 and Rotation Z to 90. This RotationPivot should now at the center of the sphere of the body and has its forward axis (X-axis) facing forward. Parent all the meshes of the spherical part of the boss to RotationPivot (Figure 20.1).

Step 2: Add SeerRef and Spawn BP_AISeer. This step is almost the same as how we set up the SeerRef and BP_AISeer on BP_Patrol. The only difference here is that we attached SeerRef to RotationPivot and moved it forward to position it at the eye (front circle) of the boss.

For the setting of the SeerRef, we set its inner and outer cone angle to 50 and the attenuation radius to 5000. These settings are set to ensure that the boss sees the player when the player enters the door. When you are done, replace the model in the boss room with BP_Boss, drag the player start and the three weapon pickups to the boss room, and test it (Figure 20.2).

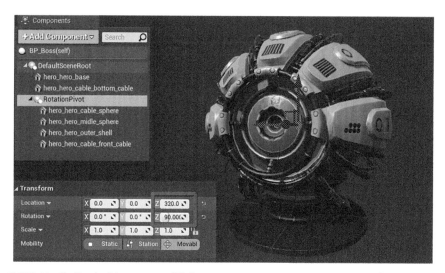

FIGURE 20.1 The hiearchy of the components of BP_Boss.

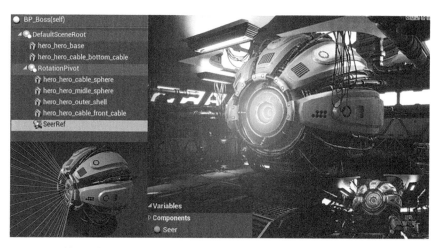

FIGURE 20.2 Add SeerRef and add spawning, matching, and attaching code to spawn a BP_AISeer.

Step 3: Make the boss know the player when the player is in sight. Add a new variable called Player and set its type to BP_Ellen_Base object reference. Add the BPI_AISeer interface to BP_Boss and implement Event On Seer Target Update as shown in Figure 20.3.

    Here, we just set the Player variable to the Target sensed by BP_AISeer.

FIGURE 20.3 Make the boss know the player when the player is in sight.

Step 4: Make the boss look at the player. Add a new float variable called RotationSpeed to BP_Boss, and set its value to 5. Create a new custom event called TryLookAtPlayer, and call it in Event Tick (Figure 20.4).

Here, we first check if the variable Player is valid. Then we find the rotation needed for RotationPivot to look at the player. We have done the same thing when doing the player surrender code.

We then called a RInterp To function. This function returns a rotation between the Current and Target input based on the Interp Speed and the Delta Time you supply. The higher the speed is and the longer the time you supply, the closer the Return value is to the Target input.

For the Delta Time, we use the Get World Delta Seconds, and this is again the time it took between the last frame and the current frame. We use Get World Delta Second because we are calling this function in Event Tick. This way, the time for the interpolation is realtime.

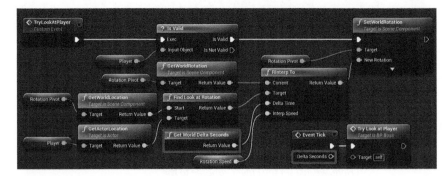

FIGURE 20.4 Implementation of TryLookAt Player.

754

FIGURE 20.5 The boss starts looking at the player.

> *Finally, we set the rotation of RotationPivot to the Return Value.*
> *Give the game another go, and this time, the boss should start looking at you right away. Notice that because there is a speed limit, the rotation of the boss has a nice lagging effect. This lag is necessary because, otherwise, the boss can always hit you (Figure 20.5).*
> Step 5: Add a health bar. Add another scene component to BP_Boss and name it HealthBarPivot. Rotate it 90 degrees to make its X-axis facing the front of the boss. With HealthBarPivot selected, add a new widget component and name it HealthBar. Go to the Details panel, and set the Widget Class to WBP_ HealthBar. Move HealthBar forward, and scale it down on the Z-axis to flatten it (Figure 20.6).

Why?

So why do we create a HealthBarPivot? Well, because we want the player always to see the health bar. To achieve that, we need to make it rotate around the center of the boss. The boss blocks it if we look from behind the boss.

> Step 6: Set the appearance of the health bar. Add the code highlighted in Figure 20.7 at the end of Event BeginPlay.

FIGURE 20.6 Add a health bar to BP_Boss.

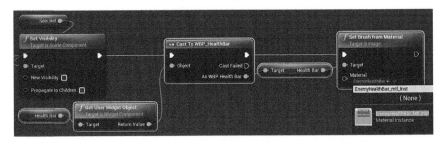

FIGURE 20.7 Set the appearance of the health bar in Event BeginPlay.

Here, we just set the material used by the health bar to EnemyHealthBar_Mlt_Inst.

Step 7: Make the health bar face the player. Implement a new custom event called RotateHealthBarToPlayer, and call it at the end of Event Tick (Figure 20.8).

Here, we first check if the variable Player is valid, and then make the HealthBarPivot rotate toward the player.

Step 8: Add BP_healthComp and update health bar. Add a BP_HealthComp to BP_Boss, and in the Details panel, set the Max Health and Current

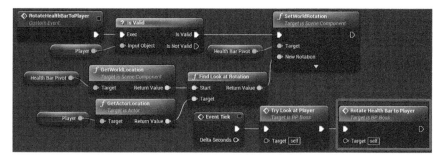

FIGURE 20.8 Implementation of RotateHealthBarToPlayer.

FIGURE 20.9 Add BP_HealthComp and BPI_HealthComp, and implement HealthCompNotify_UpdateUI.

FIGURE 20.10 Finished UI.

*Health to 1000. Add the BPI_HealthComp
in the class settings and implement the
HealthCompNotify_UpdateUI as shown in
Figure 20.9.*

*We just update the health bar the same
way we did on BP_Patrol. Play the game
again, and the health bar should update nicely
(Figure 20.10).*

*Now we have created the basics of the boss,
let's move on to make it attack.*

Tutorial 20.2: Boss Attack

*Step 1: Create a grenade spawn point. Select
RotationPivot in the Components panel, and add*

a new scene component to it. Move it forward, so it has enough distance from the boss for the grenade to spawn (Figure 20.11).

Step 2: Create a StartShootingGrenade function as shown in Figure 20.12. And call it at the end of Event On Seer Target Update.

First of all, we created two new float variables. The first one is called ShootingInterval with a default value of 3, the second one is called DirectionRandomness, and its default value is 0.1.

For the function, we start calling a Delay with the duration of ShootingInterval. This way, the boss does not start shooting right away; we then spawn a grenade at our GrenadeSpawnPoint and ignite it. We then go back to the Delay again to repeat the process.

For the Fire Direction, we first get the forward vector of the GrenadeSpawnPoint. We then add it with some random unit vector multiplied by our DirectionRandomness variable. The Random Unit Vector node returns a vector

FIGURE 20.11 Add a grenade spawn point.

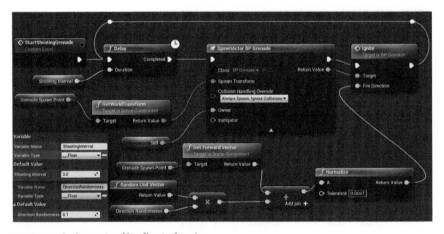

FIGURE 20.12 Implementation of StartShootingGrenade.

758

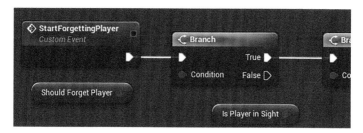

FIGURE 20.13 Add a check to ShouldForgetPlayer at the beginning of the StartForgettingPlayer function.

that has a random direction and has a length of 1 unit. We have made it smaller by multiplying it with DirectionRandomness (by using a vector * float node), so it has a lesser effect on the final fire direction. The Return Value of the Normalize node is a vector that has the same direction as the A input and has a length of one. We need to normalize it to ensure that the speed is not affected by it.

We did not show it in the figure, but please call this function at the end of Event On Seer Target Update to see the effect. Give the game another go. And the boss starts to shoot you.

Step 3: Set a Boolean to define if we want an AI to forget the player. We want the minion of the boss never to forget the player. To achieve that, we need to modify our AIC_Patrol. Open AIC_Patrol, add a Boolean variable called ShouldForgetPlayer, and set its default value to true. At the beginning of the function StartForgettingPlayer, add a Branch node with ShouldForgetPlayer to only allow the AI to forget the player when ShouldForgetPlayer is true (Figure 20.13).

Step 4: Create a BP_Boss_Minion class. Create a new class called BP_Boss_Minion derived from BP_Patrol. Open BP_Boss_Minion; in the Class Defaults, set the Loot to BP_GrenadeLauncher. Select its BP_HealthComp in the Components panel and set the Max Health to 20 and current health to 10.

Why?

First of all, the ammo is pretty limited in the game, and we set the health of the boss to 1000; we need to give the player more ammo, but that should not come free.

So, we make the boss spawn minions that pursue the player. However, when the player kills a minion, a grenade launcher pickup is spawned, which allows the player to replenish ammo.

Second, the default health of the BP_Patrol is too much to handle while fighting the boss; lowering it down helps to make the game easier. We also made the health half full. This way, there is a chance that these minions can consume the health regenerations that we will place around the boss later on.

Step 5: Set the minions not to forget the player and let them know the player when they spawn. In BP_Boss_Minion, add the code shown in Figure 20.14 to Event BeginPlay.
Here, we get the AI controller and set its ShouldForgetPlayer to false so that the AI never forgets the player. We then set the Player blackboard key to the player to let the AI know the player's existence.

Step 6: Add a sphere component to indicate the spawn parameter of the minions. Open BP_Boss, add a new Sphere Collision component, and name it MinionSpawnPerimeter. This component is intended to be used as a collider or a trigger. However, we just want to use it so we can visualize the spawn parameter of the minions. Go to the Details panel and set its Collision Presets to NoCollision. Set its Sphere Radius to 800, so its outer perimeter in the level is not blocked by anything (Figure 20.15).

Step 7: Create a function that gets a spawn transform for the minions. Create a new function called GetMinionSpawnTransform, give it an output called SpawnTransform, and set the type to Transform. Mark the function as

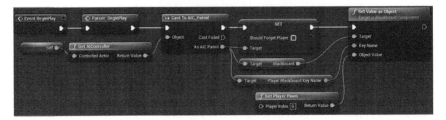

FIGURE 20.14 Set the minions not to forget the player and let them know the player when they spawn.

FIGURE 20.15 Add a sphere collision component and set its radius to a number that makes its outer perimeter rest on an empty area.

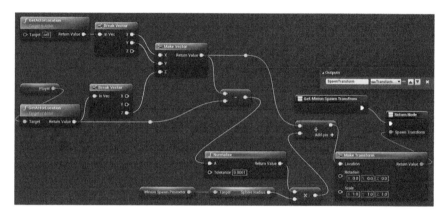

FIGURE 20.16 Implementation of GetMinionSpawnTransform.

pure, and implement the function as shown in Figure 20.16.

We have to squeeze it horizontally to make it fit into this book. Starting from the top-left corner, we get the location of the boss and the location of the player and break these two vectors using the Break Vector node. We then made a new vector that has the X, and Y from the boss, but the Z (height) from the player. This new vector then has the height of the player, but X, Y, location of the boss, we then use this new vector to subtract the location of the player. The subtraction would then be a horizontal vector pointing from the player to the boss (why?).

We then normalized the result of the subtraction to get a unit vector that again is a horizontal vector pointing from the player to the boss. This normalized vector then got scaled(multiplied) by the radius of

MinionSpawnPerimeter. We then add it with the vector that has the X, Y location of the boss, but height of the player. This resulting location would be the location on the other side of the boss (relative to the player) that is on the perimeter of MinionSpawnPerimeter and has the same height as the player.

The whole calculation throws out the height of the boss, and all vectors use the height of the player. This way, we are calculating horizontally and ensures that the spawning location is the same height as the player.

Step 8: Add a new float variable called MinionSpawnInterval, and set its default value to 8. Create an event called StartSpawnMinions and implement it as shown in Figure 20.17, and call it at the end of Event On Seer Target Update.

Just like how we did the StartShootingGrenade event, we start with a Delay with our MinionSpawnInterval. We then check if we have a valid player because the GetMinionSpawnTransform uses the player's location. We then use the GetMinionSpawnTransform function we did in the previous step to get a spawning transform, and we spawn a BP_Boss_Minion. The event then goes back to the Delay node and repeat.

Play the game again, and this time, you should see a BP_Boss_Minion got spawned behind the boss every 8 seconds (Figure 20.18).

With the boss firing grenade, and the minions pursuing you, it is pretty tough to win; let's add some BP_HealthRegens to the room.

Step 9: Add four BP_HealthRegens at the four corners of the boss (Figure 20.19).

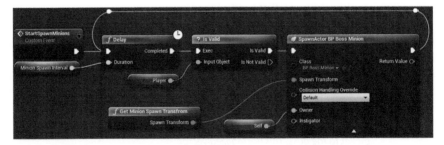

FIGURE 20.17 Implementation of StartSpawnMinions.

FIGURE 20.18 A minion spawns behind the boss every 8 seconds.

FIGURE 20.19 Add four BP_HealthRegens at the four corners of the boss.

All right, that was all the boss-attacking part; let's make the boss die when it's out of hit points.

Tutorial 20.3: Boss Death and Winning

Step 1: Enable the APEX Destruction plugin. Press the Save All button in the Content Browser to save all the work we have done. Go to Edit → Plugins to open the Plugins window. In the search bar to the top right corner, search for APEX Destruction, and there should be only one search result called APEX Destruction. Check on the Enabled option of the plugin, and click on the Restart Now button that pops up. The project restarts and loads the plugin. We want to use this APEX Destruction plugin to blow up the boss when it's dead (Figure 20.20).

Step 2: Import the combined mesh of the boss. In the support files, we have supplied a mesh called Boss_Combine, and this one has all the models of the boss merged. Import it to the hero folder

FIGURE 20.20 Enable the APEX Destruction plugin.

of the StaticMeshes folder, and assign the correct material.

Step 3: Create a Destructible mesh. Right click on the imported Boss_Combine static mesh and select Create Destructible Mesh; the plugin then creates a new asset called Boss_Combine_DM (Figure 20.21).

Step 4: Fracture the destructible mesh. Open Boss_Combine_DM, and click on the Fracture Mesh button to fracture it. The fracturing process is going to take some time because our model is a bit complicated. Unreal is going to freeze for a while as well (Figure 20.22).

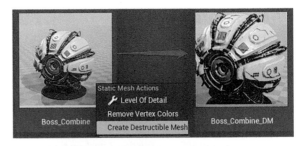

FIGURE 20.21 Create a Destructible mesh.

FIGURE 20.22 Fracture the mesh.

Step 5: Create a boss blow up actor. Create a new class derived from Actor in the Boss folder and call it BP_Boss_Blowup. Open BP_Boss_Blowup and drag the Boss_Combine_DM from the Content Browser to the Components panel of BP_Boss_Blowup to add it as a component.

Step 6: Add a "YOU WIN!" label. Add a Text Render component (click on Add Component and search). Text Render component is, well, a text. With this Text Render selected, go to the Details panel, change the Text to "YOU WIN!", set the Horizontal Alignment to Center, and set the Text Render Color to an energetic orange. Drag the TextRender up and scale it, so it's about the same size as the model (Figure 20.23).

Step 7: Implement the explosion, VFX, and rotation of the label. In the Event Graph, implement Event BeginPlay and Event Tick as shown in Figure 20.24.
In Event BeginPlay, we apply a tremendous amount of damage to the destructible mesh. The plugin works with the damage system, so we just need to apply damage to blow it up. Both the Damage Amount and Impulse Strength are set to 50,000. The GetActorBounds give us the bounding box origin and extend of this actor. We use the origin of the bounding box as the Hit Location, so the impulse starts from the center of the whole actor.

FIGURE 20.23 Add a "YOU WIN!" label.

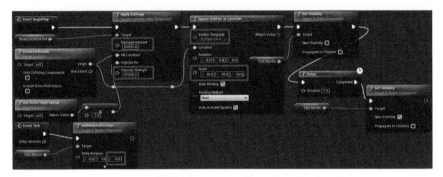

FIGURE 20.24 Implement the explosion, VFX, and rotation of the label.

The Impulse Dir is set to the reversed right vector (Y-axis) of the actor. If you look at it in the viewport, you can see that the Y-axis is pointing at the front of the mesh. We use the reversed direction (multiplied by −1) of the Y-axis as the Impulse Dir to push it backward.

We then spawned an explosion VFX. Here, we make the VFX ten times bigger to make it look like a bigger explosion. Finally, we set the visibility of the TextRender to invisible at the beginning and make it visible after 2 seconds.

In Event Tick, we simply make the Text Render rotate.

Step 8: Implement the death of the boss. Implement the HealthCompNotify_Dead event as shown in Figure 20.25.

Here, we destroy Seer first and then spawn our BP_Bose_Blowup at the transform of the boss. We then call the Get All Actors of Class to get all the actors that are of type BP_Patrol and it's child classes. We loop through all of them and tell them to die. Finally, we kill the boss.

FIGURE 20.25 Implementation of the HealthCompNotify_Dead event.

FIGURE 20.26 Boss explodes and shows the "YOU WIN!" text.

FIGURE 20.27 All features implemented for the boss.

Play the game and try to beat the boss and you see it explodes and shows the "YOU WIN!" text afterward (Figure 20.26).

It feels pretty good to finally see a "YOU WIN!" sign after a brutal fight, and this also marks the end of the tutorials for this chapter. Figure 20.27 shows all the mechanics we have implemented.

Conclusion

Surprisingly, implementing the boss does not take long. You can probably finish it in a morning, half of a morning even. For the most part, we were just assembling the various components and features we have built before. The whole point of why we carefully design and separate different parts of the game is for their ease of use and reusability. A grenade launcher is a grenade launcher, and a grenade is a grenade. If we don't logically separate them into two actors, it would be difficult to make the boss shoot the grenade. Our BP_healthComp, BP_AISeer, and WBP_HealthBar are all reusable in this manner.

Alrighty, we have finished the boss programming at this point and all other gameplay programmings as well (YEAH!!). However, there are still things to do before we finish the game. To name a few, we haven't done any audio work yet! Let's move on to that and add more VFX in the next chapter.

CHAPTER 21

Audio and VFX

Hello, and welcome to the chapter of Audio and VFX. In this chapter, we are going to explore how to use audio and add additional VFX to our game. There is a well-known joke in this industry:

No one cares about audio.

Although audio is not exactly crucial to many types of games, it is a part that cannot be ignored. Often times, audio does make a huge difference. We don't have the luxury to talk about how to record audio from scratch, but luckily, there are plenty of free assets you can find online. Just make sure that you look for royalty-free sounds.

The license can be tricky some times, although the asset is free, many authors require attribution, so you have to give them appropriate credits.

Putting audio to Unreal Engine is also a trivial task. In the support files, we have a folder called Audio; drag the folder to the root of your Content Browser to import them all. After importing, you can hover the cursor on them and hit the play button to play them.

Let's explore a few ways to add audio to the game.

Tutorial 21.1: Add Audio to the Game

Step 1: Add audio to the main menu level. Go to the Level folder and open StartMenuLevel. This one is the entry map of the game. Go back to the Audio folder, and drag the audio asset called Menu to the level (Figure 21.1).

Play the game, and you should hear the audio right away.

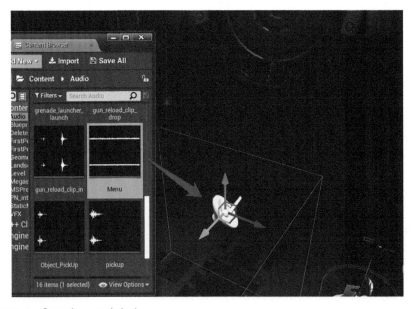

FIGURE 21.1 Drag audio asset to the level.

FIGURE 21.2 Stop playing the sound at the beginning.

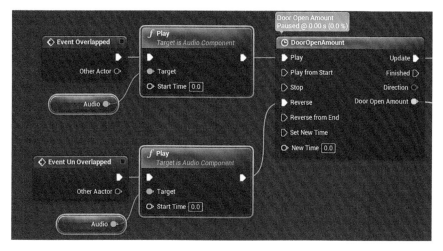

FIGURE 21.3 Make the door play the sound when starting to open or close.

Step 2: Add an audio component to the sliding door.
*Go back to Level_01_Awaken. And open BP_*
SlidingDoor. Add a new Audio component. In the
Details panel, in the Sound section, set the Sound
to door_open. Play the game, and you should
hear the door opening sound right away.

Step 3: Stop playing the sound at the beginning.
To stop the door from playing the sound right
away, add the code shown in Figure 21.2 to Event
BeginPlay.

Step 4: Make the door play the sound when starting
to open or close. Insert the code highlighted in
Figure 21.3 at the beginning of Event Overlapped
and Event UnOverlapped.

Why?

Play the game, and the sound should only play when the
door is opened. However, if you are using the project file

we provided, you can still hear the door opening sound randomly. That extra sound you hear is another door faraway and triggered by a patrolling AI. In the default settings, audio assets have no attenuation. Let's fix that in the next step.

> *Step 5: Add attenuation to the door_open audio. In the Content Browser, open door_open. Scroll down and find the Attenuation Settings. Click on the drop-down list and select Sound Attenuation under Create New Asset. In the pop-up Save Asset As window, open the Audio folder. In the Name text field, type in NaturalSoundAttenuation and hit the Save button. A new asset called NaturalSoundAttenuation appears in the Audio folder. Open it, and set its Attenuation Function to Natural Sound (Figure 21.4).*
>
> *Any other audio assets can use this new NaturalSoundAttenuation. And the ones who use NaturalSoundAttenuation is going to have a natural fall-off based on distance. We need all other audios to have natural fall-off as well. Go ahead and set the Attenuation Settings of all other audios to NaturalSoundAttenuation.*
>
> *Step 6: Create a footstep cue. To make the footstep work, we need to make it repeat. Right click on footstep and select Create Cue. A new asset called footstep_Cue got created. Audio Cue is the Blueprint for audio, open footstep_Cue, and*

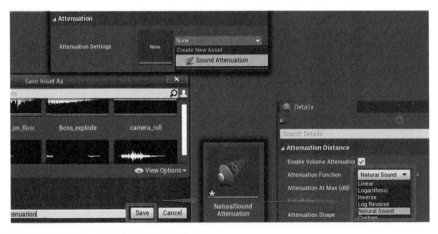

FIGURE 21.4 Add attenuation to the door_open audio.

you can see a graph in the middle with footstep connected to the Output (Figure 21.5).

Just like any other Blueprint, you can right click and search to create new nodes in the graph of a Cue, and there are plenty of nodes you can add to alter your audio.

Step 7: Make the audio repeat with a delay. Create a Delay node and a Looping node, and connect them as shown in Figure 21.6.

Select the Delay node, go the Details panel, and set the Delay Min and Delay Max to 0.1 so that the Delay node delays the audio for 0.1 seconds before the next loop. The Looping node loops what's connected to it. Select the Output node, go to the Details panel, and set the Attenuation Setting to NaturalSoundAttenuation. Press the Save button to save the change.

Step 8: Set up footsteps. Open BP_Character_Base, add an Audio component to it, and rename the component Footsteps. With Footsteps selected, go to the Details panel and set the Sound to

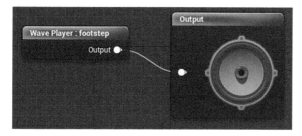

FIGURE 21.5 The graph of the newly created footstep_Cue.

FIGURE 21.6 Add a Delay and a Looping node to the Cue.

773

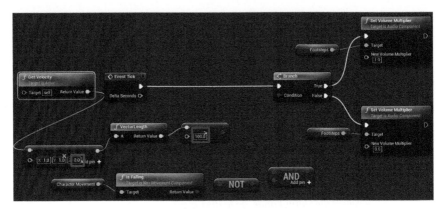

FIGURE 21.7 Add code in Event tick to control the volume of the footsteps based on the speed of the character.

footstep_Cue. Go to Event Graph and add the code highlighted in Figure 21.7 in Event Tick.

Here, we get the velocity of the character and then we multiply it with another vector that is (1, 1, 0). We do this multiplication because we only care about the horizontal velocity. We then get the length of the vector, which is the speed. We compare the speed with 100. On the bottom of the graph, we get the Character Movement component and ask if the character is falling.

If the speed is higher than 100, and not in falling (jumping in the air), we set the volume multiplier of the footstep to 1. If not, we set it back to 0. The volume multiplier we are setting is used to scale the volume of the footsteps. Our setup makes the volume of the footsteps 0 when the character is not moving, is falling, or moving slow (slower than 100 units per second).

Play the game again, both the player and the patrols should have correct footstep sounds.

Step 9: Make the camera rolling cue. Create another audio cue from camera_roll. Open it and add a Looping node, and don't forget to set its attenuation to NaturalSoundAttenuation (Figure 21.8).

Step 10: Add camera roll sound to BP_ SecurityCamera. Open BP_Camera and add an audio component to it; name the new audio component RollingAudio. Set the sound of RollingAudio to camera_roll_Cue. Add a new float variable called volume and set its default value to 0.05. Find the StartRollingCamera event

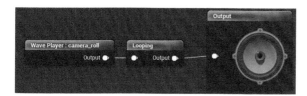

FIGURE 21.8 Create a cue from camera_roll and add a Looping node to it.

and add the code highlighted in Figure 21.9 at the end of it.

Here, we leverage the timeline to determine the volume of the camera rolling sound. However, the Lerp ranges from 0 to 1, but we want the sound to change from 0 to 1 and back to 0 again. To achieve that, we need to remap a 0–1 range to a new range that is 0–1–0.

If you have studied the sine wave, you know it is perfect for this purpose. We first remap the Lerp output value go 0–180 by multiplying it to 180. We then pass that value to a sine (Degrees) so that the output of the SINd node becomes sine (0)–sine (180), which is the first half of the sine wave.

We know that the first half of a sine wave ranges from 0 to 1 and back to 0, but we clamp it to 0–0.3 to flatten the curve. By doing the flattening, the volume in the middle stays constant. Finally, we multiply the result of the clamp with our volume to scale it as one extra adjustment.

As you can see, math is a beneficial tool in programming. But don't get too scared about it, because you are not calculating it! In the world

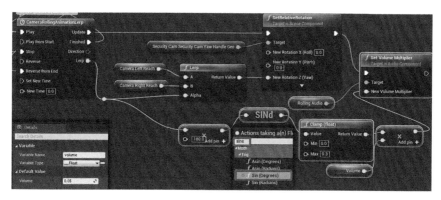

FIGURE 21.9 Code added at the end of StartRollingCamera.

FIGURE 21.10 Add the pipe_whoosh sound in the Ellen_FPS_Pipe_Attack animation as an animation notify.

of programming, math is like a religion that you either believe it or not. You just have to know what a math calculation gives you, but you do not have to understand how it works things out.

Play the game again, and you shall hear a subtle robotic arm rolling sound from the camera when it's rolling.

Step 11: Add sound to the pipe attack. Go to our animations folder, find and open Ellen_FPS_Pipe_Attack. In the timeline, find the time that the pipe starts to go down, right click, and select Add Notify → Play Sound. With the new Play Sound notify added, go to the Details panel and set the Sound to pipe_whoosh (Figure 21.10).

Give the game another go, pick up the pipe and attack, and you shall hear a "whoosh!" sound.

Tips and Tricks

If a sound is destined to happen with the animation, we add it to the animation through animation notify.

Step 12: Add the pipe hit audio. Open BP_Pipe, and find the Event Commit Attack Anim Notify. Change the Actor Class Filter to BP_Character_ Base in the SphereOverlapActors node. This setting guarantees that the pipe only hits the patrol. You could argue that the player would try to hit the boss with the pipe, but it would be strange if a pipe could hurt a giant machine like that. Add the code highlighted in Figure 21.11 to the end of the event.

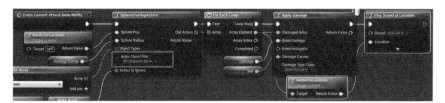

FIGURE 21.11 Add the pipe hit audio at the end of Event Commit Attack Anim Notify.

Here, we simply play the pipe_hit sound at the location of the hit actor. Play the game and hit the patrol next door with the pipe, and you should hear the hit sound.

Tips and Tricks

If a sound should only happen with a specific event, play the sound in that event.

Step 13: Add hit reaction and falling sound to the death animation. Open the Death_From_ The_Back animation. This time, we add two animation notifies. The first one is the Dead sound at the point when the character starts to struggle. The second one is the body_fall_on_ floor sound, which happens at the point that the body falls on the ground (Figure 21.12).

Step 14: Add the rest of the sounds. For the rest of the sound, they are added the same way, just make sure that you find the proper place to add it. When you need control of the sound during gameplay, you create an audio component. When you just need the sound to play once, you add it as an animation notify or play it somewhere in Blueprint. When you need more adjustment to the audio, you create a Cue. There are plenty of sounds in the support files; make sure that you take advantage of them.

Alrighty, one last thing to go before we wrap this up. We have a few more VFX assets we can add

FIGURE 21.12 Add 2 animation notifies for the sound effects of the death animation.

to the game. We only did the critical ones before so that we can see the behavior of the weapons; now let's add the additional ones real quick.

Tutorial 21.2: Add Extra VFX to the Game

Step 1: Add a gun muzzle socket. Open gun_Gun_body, and create a new socket called Muzzle. Place the new socket at the front of the gun where the bullets come out (Figure 21.13).

Step 2: Import the gun muzzle VFX asset. In the support files, there is a new asset called NS_Gun_Muzzle_Sparkle.uasset. Copy it, and paste it to the VFX folder in the Content folder of your game project. Be aware that we are not importing it through the engine. We are just copy-pasting (Figure 21.14).

Whenever you have an asset that is with the extension.uasset, you copy-paste it to the folder of your content browser to add it to your project.

Step 3: Add the muzzle effect. Open BP_Gun, and add the code highlighted in Figure 21.15 to the end of Event Commit Attack Anim Notify.

Here, we spawn NS_Gun_Muzzle_Sparkle at the location of the Muzzle socket.

Step 4: Create a grenade trail class. There is a particle effect called Projectile_back_fire in the VFX folder, open it, and you can see that it has two emitters. One of the emitters is named Flames

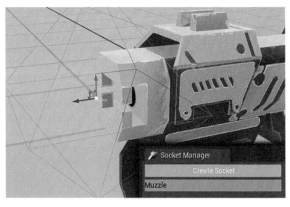

FIGURE 21.13 Add a gun muzzle socket.

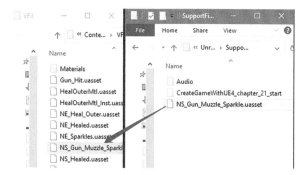

FIGURE 21.14 Copy-paste the new asset to the VFX folder of the Content folder in your game project.

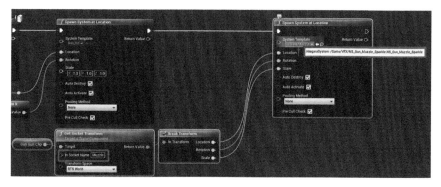

FIGURE 21.15 Add the muzzle effect to BP_Gun.

and is in charge of emitting flames. The other one is emitting smoke and named Smoke.

Create a new blueprint class derived from Actor and name it BP_Grenade_Trail. Open BP_Grenade_Trial and drag Projectile_back_fire to its components to add the VFX as a new component. Add the code shown in Figure 21.16 to its Event BeginPlay.

Here, we bind a new event called StopFireAndStartDisappearing to the On Destroyed event of the owner. This Bind Event to On Destroyed is very similar to the Bind Event to On Take Any Damage we did in BP_HealthComp. The difference here is that this StopFireAndStartDisappearing is bond to the destruction of the owner instead of

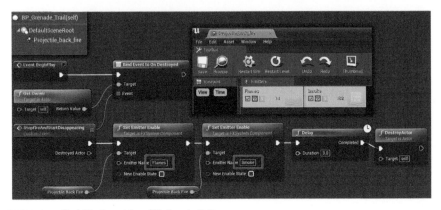

FIGURE 21.16 The full implementation of BP_Grenade_Trail.

taking damage. When the owner is destroyed, StopFireAndStartDisappearing is fired.

In StopFireAndStartDisappearing, we disabled the two emitters we have seen earlier in Projectile_back_fire, delay for 3 seconds, and then destroy self.

We did all this because we do not want the VFX to just disappear at the instance that the grenade explodes. Instead, we want the flame and the smoke to stop emitting, but keep the already existing smoke for another 3 seconds.

Step 5: Spawn and attach a BP_Grenade_Trial when the grenade ignites. Open BP_Grenade and add the code highlighted in Figure 21.17 at the end of the Ignite custom event.

Here, we simply spawn a BP_Grenade_Trial, set its owner to self, and attach it to the mesh.

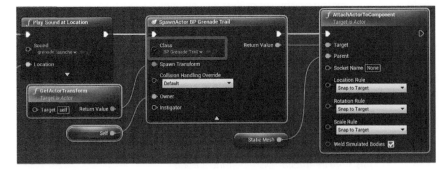

FIGURE 21.17 Code added at the end of the Ignite custom event.

Play the game again, and this time, we should see both the gun and the grenade have some cool looking trail effects (Figure 21.18).

Step 6: *Make the grenade apply impulse when hit. One more thing we want to add to the grenade is to allow the explosion push dynamic objects away. Open BP_Grenade and implement a new custom event called ApplyImpulse (Figure 21.19).*

The event task an actor as input. We get the root component of the actor and cast it to a PrimitiveComponent. PrimitiveComponent is the parent class of all components that has a shape, and components like static mesh and skeletal mesh are all child classes of it. We can then check if it is simulating physics. If it does, we add impulse to it. A critical note here is you want to check on Vel Change; this way, the velocity we supply as Impulse becomes the new velocity of the actor, so we don't have to worry about mass (Figure 21.19).

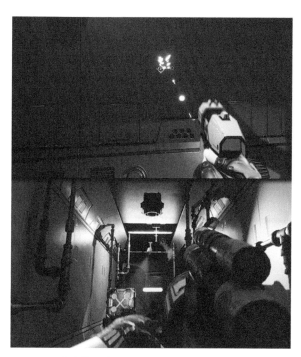

FIGURE 21.18 Trail effects of the weapons.

FIGURE 21.19 The implementation of the ApplyImpulse custom event.

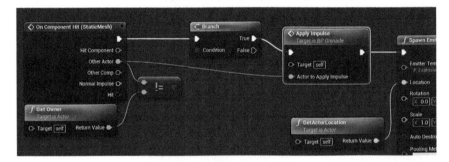

FIGURE 21.20 Call ApplyImpulse at the beginning of On Component Hit.

Step 7: Call ApplyImpulse at the beginning of On Component Hit (Figure 21.20).

Here, after making sure that the hit actor is not the owner, we call ApplyImpulse.

Step 8: Make the boxes simulate physics. Select any box you want to receive the impulse in the World Outliner, go to the Details panel, change its mobility to Movable, and check on Simulate Physics. You can search the World Outliner to get all the boxes (Figure 21.21).

Play the game, get a grenade launcher, and shoot these boxes. You should now see them getting blown away. The boss can also blow these boxes away, which makes the game more interesting to play (Figure 21.22).

After setting these boxes to be movable, it is wise to rebuild the lighting again.

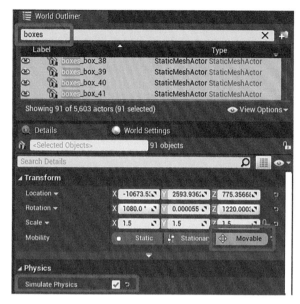

FIGURE 21.21 Make the boxes simulate physics.

FIGURE 21.22 Boxes get blown away by the grenade.

Conclusion

Alrighty, we have now finished with our audio and VFX. At this point, we can finally call our game finished. However, the game lives in the editor unless we package it, let's quickly cover that in our final chapter – packaging.

CHAPTER 22

Packaging

Welcome to this quick final chapter, where we package our game.

Packaging a game is a trivial process in Unreal Engine. We just need to make sure we set up the correct startup map, icons, splash images, and fill in the necessary information about the game.

There are two possible platforms you can try without paying for a developer license: Windows and Android; Apple iOS does require a paid developer account at the moment. However, our whole game is built based on the Windows platform; so we are not going to cover an

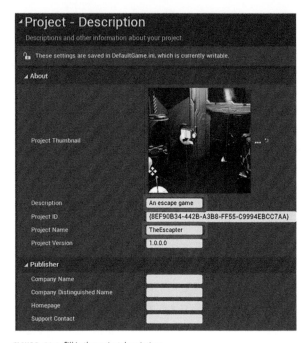

FIGURE 22.1 Fill in the project descriptions.

Android build. Most of the differences between platforms are the graphics, inputs, and necessary development kit for the targeted platform.

Just keep in mind that if you are building for Android in the future, you need the Android Software Development kit installed.

Let's move on to build our game for Windows.

Tutorial 22.1: Package the Game for Windows

Step 1: Fill in descriptions. Open Edit → Project Settings and go to the Description section. Under the About section, type in "An escape game" in the Description text field. Type in the name of your game in the Project Name text field. In our case, it is TheEscaper (Figure 22.1).

The description is whatever you want to write down to describe your game. What's in the Description text field is just information and does not change any aspect of the game. Here, we just type in An escape game.

For the Project Name, it is going to be the name of your game executable.

There are other parts you can fill in with information. Like the company name and Homepage, but they are optional.

Step 2: Set up maps and modes. Go to the Maps & Modes section. Make sure that the Default GameMode is set to GM_Ellen_FPS. Editor Startup Map is the map opened when you open the editor, and it should be the map you want to work on when you open the editor. The Game Default Map has to be the map of the Start menu, and make sure that it is set to StartMenuLevel (Figure 22.2).

Step 3: Set up packaging. For the Packaging section, all things can be left as default for the Window platform. However, the Build Configuration setting under the Project section should be set to Shipping when you do your final build (Figure 22.3).

FIGURE 22.2 Set up maps and modes.

FIGURE 22.3 Build Configuration should be set to Shipping when you do your final build.

Shipping mode excludes debugging features. Things like Print String or console commands are not going to be in the shipping build.

Step 4: Set up the Windows platform. Go to the Platforms section and click on the Windows subsection. Inside of the windows section, set the Editor Splash, Game Splash, and the Game Icon to the files we supplied in the support files. You can click on the button with "..." after them to assign a new file. When you assign the new files, a notification pops at the bottom right corner of your screen that asks if you want to import it. Click the Import button to import them (Figure 22.4).

FIGURE 22.4 Add the splash maps and the icon.

The Editor Splash is shown when you load the editor and the Game Splash is shown when you load the game. The game icon is the icon of the executable of the game.

Step 5: Build the game. Go to file → Package Project → Windows (64-bit). In the pop-up windows, find a folder to put your game, and make sure that the folder is not in your project folder. Press the Select Folder button, and the engine starts building the game (Figure 22.5).

The building is going to take a while. Make yourself a cup of tea and wait for it to finish.

Step 5: Test the game. When the building is finished, a notification should show up with an enjoyable sci-fi-ish sound. Go to the folder you specify, and

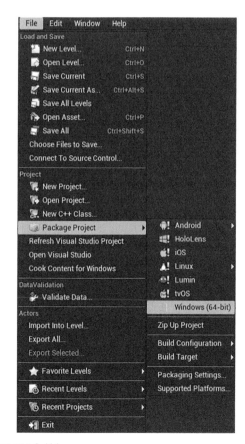

FIGURE 22.5 Build the game.

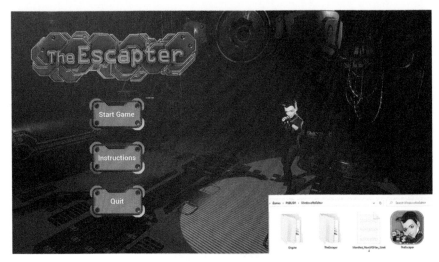

FIGURE 22.6 Test the game after building it.

open the WindowsNoEditor folder. You should see the game files built and the executable called TheEscaper. Double click TheEscaper to run the game (Figure 22.6).

Now it is time to enjoy our hard work and have some fun playing the game! More importantly, share it with your friends and family and see if they like it too!

Conclusion

Congratulations on finishing this book! You should feel proud of yourself for this great achievement. Making a game is such a time-consuming task, and doing it all by yourself requires a tremendous amount of time, patience, and dedication.

However, the journey is not over, and there is plenty of stuff we did not get a chance to cover in this book. Unreal Engine is a giant game engine that has tons of built-in features. Please keep exploring and learning new things every day.

This is also the time you can start to choose your career. You can decide to be an indie game developer that does everything or you can choose to specialize in one of the areas of game development.

If you want to be an artist, you can try to dip in a variety of different software to boost up your productivity. To name one, you should definitely learn ZBrush. It is a must-know software if you wish to make the best looking models.

There are also technical routes you can choose as an artist. We did not cover rigging on its full extent, and you can move on to study facial expression or rigging any other form of creatures. Becoming a rigger can always guarantee a decent job because 99% of the students who graduated from college don't want to do that.

On the other hand, you can also study things like procedural modeling with Houdini and procedural material creation with Substance Designer (a sister software of Substance Painter). And even shader programming that requires both an eye of an artist and the mind of a programmer.

If you want to get more serious about game programming, you should learn C++ or C#. Programming can also separate into low-level programming and high-level programming. Low-level programming creates systems that are robust and extremely efficient. C++ is, for now, the only answer to that. That is why all major game engines and 3D software are built with C++. Some programmers may argue that other programming languages like C# can be fast enough, as hardware is getting better. That might be the truth in some situations.

High-level programming builds game logic based on the systems built by low-level programming. At a high level, easier languages like C#, Blueprint, and Python are used to boost up productivity.

We want to congratulate you again on finishing this fantastic project. And we hope you can utilize the knowledge you have learned here to create your next awesome game!

Index

Note: *Italic* page numbers refer to figures.